Introduction to Ecological I

Introduction to Ecological Psychology is a highly accessible book that offers an overview of the fundamental theoretical foundations of ecological psychology. The authors, Julia J. C. Blau and Jeffrey B. Wagman, provide broad coverage of the topic, including a discussion of perception-action, development, cognition, social interaction, and application to real-world problems.

Concepts are presented in the book using a conversational writing style and everyday examples that introduce novice readers to the problems of perception and action and demonstrate the application of the ecological approach to broader philosophical questions. Blau and Wagman explain how ecological psychology is pertinent to both classic and newer issues in psychology. The authors move beyond the traditional scope of the discipline to effectively illustrate concepts of dynamics, evolution, self-organization, and physical intelligence in ecological psychology.

This book is an essential guide to the basics for students and professionals in ecological psychology, sensation and perception, cognition, and development. It is also indispensable reading for anyone interested in ecological and developmental studies.

Julia J. C. Blau is an Associate Professor of Psychology at Central Connecticut State University, New Britain, CT, USA. Her research focuses on the fractality of event perception, as well as the ecological approach to film theory and aesthetics. She is a member of the board of directors of the *International Society for Ecological Psychology*.

Jeffrey B. Wagman is a Professor of Psychology at Illinois State University, USA. His research focuses on perception of affordances and perception by touch. He is a recipient of the Illinois State University Outstanding University Researcher Award and a Japan Society for the Promotion of Science Invitation Fellowship for Research in Japan. He is an associate editor of the journal *Ecological Psychology*.

Resources for Ecological Psychology
A Series of Volumes Edited By:
Jeffrey B. Wagman & Julia J. C. Blau

[Robert E. Shaw, William M. Mace, and Michael Turvey, Series Editors Emeriti]

Perceiving Events and Objects
Edited by Gunnar Jannson, Sten Sture Bergström and William Epstein

Global Perspectives on the Ecology of Human-Machine Systems (Volume 1)
Edited by Peter A. Flach, John M. Hancock, Jeff Caird and Kim J. Vicente

Local Applications of the Ecological Approach to Human-Machine Systems (Volume 2)
Edited by John M. Hancock, Peter A. Flach, Jeff Caird and Kim J. Vicente

Dexterity and Its Development
Edited by Nicholai A. Bernstein, Mark L. Latash and Michael T. Turvey

Ecological Psychology in Context
James Gibson, Roger Barker, and the Legacy of William James's Radical Empiricism
Harry Heft

Perception as Information Detection
Reflections on Gibson's Ecological Approach to Visual Perception
Jeffrey B. Wagman and Julia J. C. Blau

A Meaning Processing Approach to Cognition
What Matters?
John Flach and Fred Voorhorst

Behavior and Culture in One Dimension
Sequences, Affordances, and the Evolution of Complexity
Dennis P. Waters

Affective Gibsonian Psychology
Rob Withagen

Introduction to Ecological Psychology
A Lawful Approach to Perceiving, Acting, and Cognizing
Julia J. C. Blau and Jeffrey B. Wagman

For more information about this series, please visit: www.routledge.com

Introduction to Ecological Psychology

A Lawful Approach to Perceiving, Acting, and Cognizing

Julia J. C. Blau and Jeffrey B. Wagman

NEW YORK AND LONDON

Cover image: Julia J. C. Blau

First published 2023
by Routledge
605 Third Avenue, New York, NY 10158

and by Routledge
4 Park Square, Milton Park, Abingdon, Oxon, OX14 4RN

Routledge is an imprint of the Taylor & Francis Group, an informa business

Library of Congress Cataloging-in-Publication Data
Names: Blau, Julia J. C., 1982– author. | Wagman, Jeffrey B., author.
Title: Introduction to ecological psychology : a lawful approach to perceiving, acting, and cognizing / Julia J. C. Blau and Jeffrey B. Wagman.
Description: 1 Edition. | New York, NY : Routledge, 2023. | Series: Resources for ecological psychology series | Includes bibliographical references and index. | Summary: "Introduction to Ecological Psychology is a highly accessible book that offers an overview of the fundamental theoretical foundations of Ecological Psychology. The authors, Julia Blau and Jeffrey Wagman, provide a broad coverage of the topic, including discussion of perception-action as well as development, cognition, social interaction, and application to real world problems"—Provided by publisher.
Identifiers: LCCN 2022012524 (print) | LCCN 2022012525 (ebook) | ISBN 9780367703271 (hardback) | ISBN 9780367703240 (paperback) | ISBN 9781003145691 (ebook)
Subjects: LCSH: Environmental psychology. | Social adjustment. | Human beings—Effect of environment on. | Human ecology.
Classification: LCC BF353 .B563 2023 (print) | LCC BF353 (ebook) | DDC 155.9—dc23/eng/20220504
LC record available at https://lccn.loc.gov/2022012524
LC ebook record available at https://lccn.loc.gov/2022012525

ISBN: 978-0-367-70327-1 (hbk)
ISBN: 978-0-367-70324-0 (pbk)
ISBN: 978-1-003-14569-1 (ebk)

DOI: 10.4324/9781003145691

Typeset in Bembo
by Apex CoVantage, LLC

Contents

Preface: Resources for Ecological Psychology

This series of volumes is dedicated to furthering the development of psychology as a branch of ecological science. In its broadest sense, ecology is a multidisciplinary approach to the study of living systems, their environments, and the reciprocity that has evolved between the two. Traditionally, ecological science emphasizes the study of the biological bases of energy transactions between animals and their physical environments across cellular, organismic, and population scales. Ecological psychology complements this traditional focus by emphasizing the study of information transactions between living systems and their environments, especially as they pertain to perceiving situations of significance to planning and execution of purposes activated in an environment.

The late James J. Gibson used the term *ecological psychology* to emphasize this animal-environment mutuality for the study of problems of perception. He believed that analyzing the environment to be perceived was just as much a part of the psychologist's task as analyzing animals themselves, and hence that the *physical* concepts applied to the environment and the *biological* and *psychological* concepts applied to organisms would have to be tailored to one another in a larger system of mutual constraint. His early interest in the applied problems of landing airplanes and driving automobiles led him to pioneer the study of perceptual guidance of action.

The work of Nikolai Bernstein in biomechanics and physiology represents a complementary approach to problems of the coordination and control of movement. His work suggests that action, too, cannot be studied without reference to the environment and that physical and biological concepts must be developed together. The coupling of Gibson's ideas with those of Bernstein forms a natural basis for looking at the traditional psychological topics of perceiving, acting, and knowing as activities of ecosystems rather than isolated animals.

The purpose of this series is to form a useful collection, a resource, for people who wish to learn about ecological psychology and for those who wish to contribute to its development. The series will include original research, collected papers, reports of conferences and symposia, theoretical monographs, technical handbooks, and works from the many disciplines relevant to ecological psychology.

Jeffrey B. Wagman and Julia J. C. Blau, Series Editors
(Robert Shaw, William M. Mace, and Michael Turvey, Series Editors Emeriti)

Acknowledgments

We thank everyone who provided support and encouragement for this project along the way. Everyone we mentioned it to seemed to think that it was a good idea. We hope that they continue to feel that way after reading the finished product.

Special thanks to John T. Capetta, who provided comments on the entire book, and Chris Pagano, who provided comments on several chapters. We are grateful to Tyler Duffrin, Stephanie Hartling, Melissa Virto, Allie Callham, and Elena Jankulovska, who provided student perspectives on many chapters. Thanks also to Raoul Bongers, Felipe Cabrera, Pablo Covarrubias, Steve Croker, Tehran Davis, Ben De Bari, Luis Favela, Claire Michaels, Ángel Jiménez, Dawn McBride, Alexandra Paxton, Larry Rosenblum, Jay Smart, Tom Stoffregen, Audrey van der Meer, and Frank Zaal, who provided comments on drafts of individual chapters. Thanks to Michaele Williams, who provided the photo for Figure 1.6, and Daniel Johnson, who provided the photos for Figure 13.5. A very special thanks to Lynda James Carroll, who took all the remaining photographs—JJCB could not ask for a more supportive and inspiring mother.

JJCB thanks Eric for the many walks and help sorting out the thorny bits, as well as being a willing model for the hand drawings and Beuchet chair illusion photographs. She also thanks Grayson for asking *so many questions*, including whether or not superheroes could exist (which led her to teach thermodynamics to a ten-year-old), and Gwendolyn for providing much-needed joy. She could not have done this without you all.

JJCB also thanks the friends responsible for helping her keep her sanity during the pandemic, without whom this book would never have been finished: A. R. Capetta and the New Journey crew.

JBW thanks Dawn for her love and support, Connor for sharing his superpowers with him, and his parents, to whom he declared at nine years old that he shouldn't have to go to school anymore because he already knew all he needed to know. This book is proof otherwise.

JBW also thanks Neko (the cat) and Willow (the dog), whose interactions inspired the examples in several of the chapters, and Deegun Kaster and his family (Dusty Kaster and Tinley McBride), who inspired the vignette in Chapter 14.

And finally, we thank the *many* ecological psychologists who have come before us. Your work has inspired and galvanized us, and we hope that we have done it justice. The careful reader will notice that most of Fred's friends and family are named after greats in the field. The exclusion of anyone was not deliberate—there were so many more names we simply could not find room for. To Claudia Carello (both authors' PhD advisor): we hope you don't mind us borrowing your name for such a purpose. We are tempted to thank you here, but after all, this book is our thanks to you.

We hope that readers enjoy reading this book as much as we enjoyed writing it.

Julia J. C. Blau and Jeffrey B. Wagman

Preface: Introduction to Ecological Psychology

James Gibson's elaboration of his ecological approach to perception culminated with his last book in 1979, but he had really been developing it over the preceding 50 years. He came to realize that bedrock assumptions embodied in prevailing approaches to psychology could not lead to a workable psychology. Those assumptions were often implicit, unacknowledged, and unquestioned. His theoretical work laid out his rationale for pursuing ecological realism, and his empirical work contributed to that rationale. Being forthright about our assumptions, wherever they take us, makes the ecological approach an important tack for contemporary cognitive science. In ecological hands, the appeal of a multidisciplinary approach resides in more than the tools it provides. The real appeal is in discovering generic principles that apply across nature's scales. Such a target de-emphasizes the human-centric and mentalistic predilections of more orthodox cognitive science.

When Claire Michaels and I began work on *Direct Perception* in the late 1970s, our goal was similar to the goal that Blau and Wagman have for this book. We strove to write an overview of the ecological approach that was accessible to undergraduates. In many respects, our timing was auspicious: Gibson's third book had just come out, Michael Turvey was beginning to articulate a theory of action that was reciprocal with Gibson's theory of perception, and large theoretical papers were being produced (especially by various permutations of Turvey, Bob Shaw, and Bill Mace) that made philosophical issues and implications explicit, often taking the evolving science outside the traditional domain of psychology. Almost unavoidably, ours was largely a book about the emerging meta-theory. Programmatic ecological research was not in great abundance at the time. Not surprisingly, much has changed in the meantime.

Introduction to Ecological Psychology: A Lawful Approach to Perceiving, Acting, and Cognizing benefits from what has transpired in the 40 years since that overview. Theoretical ideas have matured, new concepts have been uncovered, research programs have proliferated, and tools have been developed. Julia J. C. Blau and Jeffrey B. Wagman, both of whom, I am proud to say, were my PhD students at the University of Connecticut, have not only mastered these developments; they have made rich contributions to the ecological literature as clever experimenters and interesting thinkers. Even more important for the goal of this book, they are both wonderfully engaging teachers who appreciate a fundamental challenge: Helping students understand the problem is a route to understanding its solution. That appreciation is on display throughout this book. They interweave ecological theory and research to great effect, showing how principles from one domain can be leveraged in another, less-well-understood domain. In so doing, they cover ecological psychology's greatest hits as well as the territory that has shown tremendous growth in recent years. It should be exciting reading for scholars just beginning their ecological journey to see this play out in behavior by multiple kinds of perceivers (adult and child; human and nonhuman; individual and social group), across multiple settings (natural and artifactual), and in basic research on fluent behaviors as well as applied research in clinical settings. And in confronting the commonalities across all of these domains and the challenges of the multidisciplinary science needed to understand them, Blau and Wagman allow the reader to see what it really means to take a lawful approach to perceiving, acting, and cognizing.

Claudia Carello, Professor Emerita, Center for the Ecological Approach to Perception and Action, University of Connecticut

Part 1

Introduction to Theory

1 Starting the Conversation

Here is Fred (see Figure 1.1). Fred has a problem: he is hungry. Fred is standing in a field of grass, and on the other side of that field is an apple tree. The tree has ripe apples and could provide Fred with a much-needed snack. In order to enjoy that snack, Fred needs to perceive the tree and its surroundings, identify the apples as edible and ripe, coordinate his movements to approach the tree and pluck an apple, then guide the apple to his mouth.

What is remarkable about Fred's problem is that it seems unremarkable. After all, we face—and overcome—problems of this sort every day! And it's not just eating; we walk through doorways, pick up objects, and navigate through cluttered surroundings without bumping into anything. We take these everyday behaviors for granted, but they are not so simple.

Using Fred as an example, the goal of these first four chapters is to make it clear that while these are simple problems for organisms to solve, they are difficult for scientists to explain. In this chapter, we will approach the problem the way that it has been historically approached—from what we will call the *traditional* view. Then in Chapter 2, we will outline the difficulties with that perspective—in particular, how it leads to unsolvable problems. In Chapters 3 and 4, we will introduce a different approach, the ecological perspective, and explain why we think it is the most coherent approach for scientifically understanding how Fred performs this and other everyday behaviors as well as for understanding broader psychological issues.

One other note: often in this book, we intentionally set up what we know to be a false dichotomy. A false dichotomy is when you offer two choices as if they were the only possibilities when they are *not*. For example, if you ask "Which is your favorite baseball team, the Cubs or the Yankees?" Mets fans and those who are not sports enthusiasts are both left out.

Figure 1.1 Fred's dilemma, how to perceive the tree in order to get a snack?

DOI: 10.4324/9781003145691-2

In our case, we group every perspective that is not ecological into one category (which we label, for convenience, the traditional approach). It is not the case that every approach that is not ecological deserves this label, nor are all the criticisms leveled at such approaches applicable to *all* of the approaches that we put in this category. Having said that, every perspective we group into that category can be criticized on *at least* one of the points we are making, and all lead to *at least* one unsolvable problem. Our overall argument is that the ecological perspective is the *most* coherent and the *most* broadly applicable, in large part because it starts from entirely different assumptions about the nature of the problem to be explained.

The Nature of Knowledge From the Traditional Perspective(s)

Fred's apple problem (and problems like it) has been the subject of discussion by philosophers and scientists for a very long time. It is fundamentally a debate about the nature of *knowledge*. Where does knowledge come from? How can we understand our world in order to perform everyday tasks? *Do we understand our world?* This last question is where we need to begin. Can we take for granted that our perception of the world actually matches that world? If Fred sees a tree, does his understanding of that tree match the actual tree in the actual world?

Descartes (1637) attempted to answer this question by *introspection*. That is, he questioned his own beliefs and the source of those beliefs in an effort to figure out what knowledge could be trusted as certain. For example, he might start by questioning his belief that a table was in front of him. It seems an obviously true thing, but his belief in the table's existence is based on information gained from his senses. If his senses could not be trusted, then the existence of the table is in doubt because the *source* of the knowledge is in doubt.

After much thought, Descartes reasoned that the only thing he was *sure* existed was himself. His famous phrase "cogito ergo sum" (which best translates as "I am thinking; therefore, I exist") reflected this reasoning. He was not saying that the act of thinking is what made him exist[1] but rather that as he sat there doubting everything, the only thing he could be sure of was that the doubt was coming from *somewhere*. Or rather, since he was doubting, he must exist in order to have the capability to doubt. Everything else, even his own body, was open to question.

These days we know a bit more about how senses work than Descartes did, so surely we can do better, right? We know about the brain, neurons, and how sense organs operate. Without going into too much detail, the more modern take on this is that all thoughts and feelings and impressions of the world are a result of electrical impulses in our nervous system. And even with all this additional information about the inner workings of the senses, Descartes's point still holds.

Our knowledge of the world comes from (or through) our nervous system. An outside entity (say, artificial intelligence like the robots in the 1999 movie, *The Matrix*) could be imposing stimulations on our nervous system and creating an *impression* of a world where none exists. I know that I am here because I am questioning all this, but everything else could just be a trick, right? The notion that only my mind exists and the rest of the world is a trick being played on my senses (maybe by my brain itself) is called *solipsism*.

Following Descartes's logic to its conclusion, we are left with two choices: believe the world exists (realism) or believe it doesn't (solipsism). Both are possible. There is no logical proof, no evidence, no justification that will prove that one is true and the other false. Most likely, there won't ever be any such proof one way or the other.

And here we come to the crux of the matter: To make progress on understanding where knowledge comes from or how we perform everyday behaviors, we must make an *assumption*. Assumptions in science are things we hold to be true without proof. Sometimes we accept an assumption because the evidence cannot be had (as is the case here), and sometimes, because we have been—explicitly or implicitly—operating under that assumption for so long, undoing it would require massive changes to established thought. Every scientific endeavor has assumptions, and it is important to recognize them and make them thoughtfully. As we will see, some—but not all!—of these foundational assumptions separate the ecological approach from its more-traditional counterparts.

Solipsism is a dead end when it comes to Fred and his tree (or us and our various daily activities). If the world doesn't exist, there's no point in figuring out how we coordinate our activities with it, nor could we trust any answer we find. On the other hand, realism not only justifies our investigations, it is comforting to assume that our mind is not alone in a void and that our favorite coffee shop is more than a figment of our imagination. In this book, we are going to choose to believe that realism is correct. Realism is our first assumption:

Traditional Assumption 1: The world actually exists.

Once we take realism as a given, we then have to ask: how do we gain knowledge about the world? We could understand the world by referring to a collective unconscious (Jung, 1916). Our knowledge of the world could be a reflection of ideals we already know about when we're born (Plato, c. 375 BC). Or all our behaviors and knowledge could be built out of behaviors prewired in our DNA (i.e., instincts, Wundt, 1897). The list goes on.

The sciences have long followed the lead of *empiricists* such as Locke and Aristotle, who assume that all knowledge comes from *experience*. This has two principles in it: First, we begin with *no* knowledge. Locke (1690) called this the *tabula rasa*, or "blank slate". Second, knowledge can only be gained from the senses (because experience is entirely sensory). This is the next assumption of the traditional approaches.

Traditional Assumption 2: We are born with no knowledge and gain all knowledge through our senses.

If we gain all knowledge through our senses, it's worth doubting—as Descartes did—whether they are a *reliable* way to learn anything about the world. Or in other words, does our understanding of the world inside our heads correspond with the world outside our heads? There are two options: either the world's influence on our senses bears no resemblance to the world or it does. If it bears no resemblance, then we are back to the same issue we had with solipsism—there is no point in continuing! In that scenario, the world exists, but we have no ability to know it in any meaningful way. In the alternative scenario, the world does exist, and we *do* have some ability to know it in a meaningful way because our senses are a reasonably reliable way to gain knowledge about the world. Again, we cannot know which is true. This leads to the third assumption:

Traditional Assumption 3: Our senses (somehow) inform us about the world.

Note the "somehow" in that assumption! We *still* do not know how our senses are able to provide us with this information, but given how successfully animals go about their daily business in the world, it must be that the senses are at least reasonably reliable. Fred has no difficulty plucking the apple from the tree or performing any number of everyday tasks. Nevertheless, we still have a long way to go before understanding *how* Fred resolves his apple quest! All we have done so far is to lay bare some of the assumptions of (nearly every) modern theory of perception. These assumptions—the commitment to realism, the tabula rasa, and the reasonable reliability of our senses—allow us to use our senses to examine the world and ourselves. Or in other words, we can do science!

Box 1.1 The Nature of Science

Just as we did for the assumptions of reality, empiricism, and reliability of our senses, we need to be explicit and thoughtful about the assumptions we make when we choose a type of science to do. To a large extent, science is about uncovering *causes*; that is, it is about figuring out why an event happened or why it happened the way it did. In that pursuit, we can suggest a variety of options as to why something happened—these suggestions are called *hypotheses*.

Some hypotheses are better than others, and after enough experience exploring the world through science, we can start rejecting hypotheses before we ever test them because we recognize *ahead of time* that those hypotheses reflect thinking that hasn't worked out in the past. Let's work through an example. Imagine a pool table (see Figure 1.2). Fred and his best friend Claudia are playing a game of pool. Claudia uses the pool stick to strike the cue ball, the cue ball moves and strikes the eight ball, and the eight ball moves across the table and drops into the corner pocket. A scientist might look at this situation and ask: what caused the eight ball to go into the pocket?

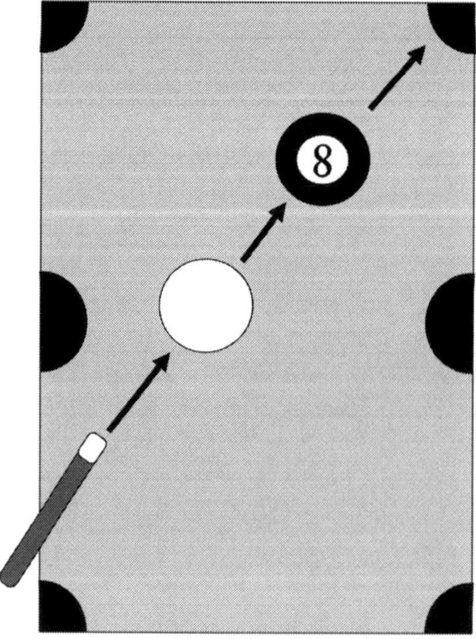

Figure 1.2 What is the cause of the eight ball moving into the pocket?

Here are some (not mutually exclusive) hypotheses for why the eight ball went into the pocket:

1. The specific materials that form the pool stick, table, cue ball, eight ball, and pocket change how they interact with each other and consequently how they enact this event (material cause).
2. The reason these objects exist is to facilitate a game in which the eight ball eventually goes into the corner pocket. That reason for being will bring about this event (final cause).
3. The person who designed the objects designed them in such a way that this event would be possible, even inevitable (formal cause).
4. The player uses the pool stick to transfer momentum to the cue ball, the cue ball transfers momentum to the eight ball, and that momentum carries it into the pocket (efficient cause).
5. God wants it this way (metaphysical cause).
6. Claudia was inspired by a Paul Newman movie and, after months of practice, managed to win a game against Fred (psychosocial cause).
7. Invisible, mind-reading gnomes read the minds of the players and the balls and scurry about the table, making certain outcomes happen according to a moral system known only to them (gnomic cause).

If you have even a passing relationship with science, you might notice that number 4 seems the most reasonable, and number 7 sounds downright silly; however, all of these (with the exception of number 7) have been used for an understanding of causality at some point. (In fact, Aristotle (c. 350 BCE) thought that we needed all of the first four in order to truly understand the "why" of this situation.) Even number 7 is not illogical, it is just impossible to disprove and thus impossible to submit to the scientific method.

The type of causality used in number four is not necessarily the most logical one, it just *feels* that way because most of modern science is based on the assumption of efficient cause, also known as *local causality*.

While science could proceed on any number of different types of causality, the traditional approaches—and most of modern science—assume *local causality*. Local causality suggests that in order for thing A to be the cause of thing B, A must be in direct contact with B.

Traditional Assumption 4: All causality must be local

Now that we have made this assumption, we can start investigating the process of perceiving and *finally* turn our attention to Fred and his apple tree. When looking for an explanation of how Fred is able to perform this incredible—and yet completely ordinary—feat, we will only allow those explanations (those hypotheses) which adhere to local causality.

Local Causality and the Problem of Action-at-a-Distance

Almost immediately, the notion of local causality runs into problems for an understanding of Fred's dilemma. Fred is clearly not touching the apple on the tree, and yet his awareness and behavior are each affected by it. He moves in the direction of the tree, reaches out to grab the apple, closes his hand around it, and until that last moment does not come into physical contact with any part of the apple or the tree. In some sense, the cause of his behavior is clearly the apple on the tree and yet he is not in direct contact with it until the very end. It seems to be in violation of the assumption of local causality! This concern, called the *action-at-a-distance problem*, must be resolved in order to continue investigating.

One possibility for resolving the action-at-a-distance problem is to propose that there is *mediated* (i.e., indirect) contact between Fred and tree. Continuing the earlier example (from Box 1.1) in local causality, the cue ball causes the eight ball to move. In mediated local causality, the pool stick causes the cue ball to move, which in turn, causes the eight ball to move. The pool stick is the ultimate cause of the eight ball's behavior, but the cue ball *mediates* the contact between the pool stick and the eight ball. Applying this to Fred's problem, we could propose that while he is not in contact with the tree, perhaps there is a third thing that goes between Fred and the tree and is in contact with both (see Figure 1.3). In fact, in order to maintain local causality, we *have* to assume something goes between them.

There are a handful of options here, but they all boil down to the same idea. There is a *copy of the world* that goes between Fred and the world, which allows him to have experience of that world despite not having direct contact with it. Or in other words, the tree gets copied (somehow), and the copy is in contact with Fred. The copy is then able to inform his behavior and influence his understanding of the world (Boring, 1950).

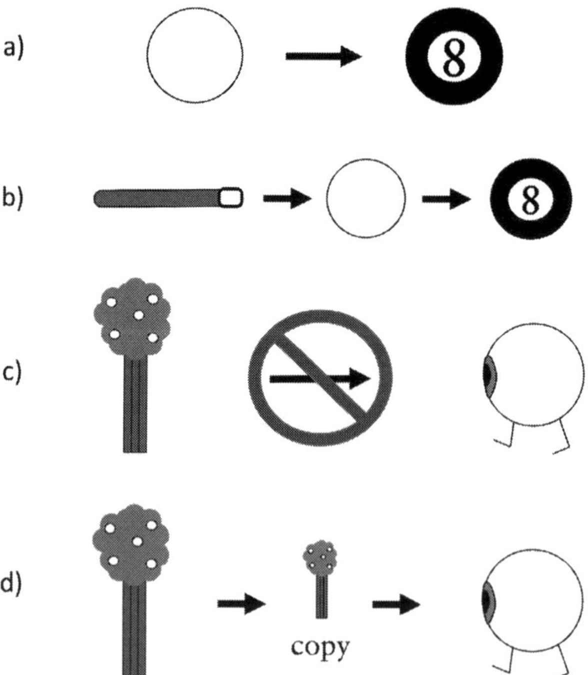

Figure 1.3 Different causal situations: (a) local causality, the cue ball causes the eight ball's movement; (b) mediated local causality, the pool stick causes the eight ball's movement, mediated by the cue ball; (c) action-at-a-distance, the tree seems to cause Fred's behavior but is not in contact with him; (d) mediated local causality, the tree causes Fred's behavior, mediated by the copy.

Traditional Assumption 5: Contact with the world is mediated by a copy.

This is where traditional approaches to perception begin. They—implicitly or explicitly—make these the five foregoing assumptions and then ask two questions: How does Fred get a copy of the world in his head? And how does that copy inform Fred about the world? Let's explore these two questions, starting with the first.

How Does a Copy Get Into the Head?

Early notions of how this was accomplished ranged from the absurd (rays of light come out of our eyes and touch the object, according to Empedocles, c. 495–435 BCE [1966]) to the merely impractical (light from the sun strikes the object and there is a chemical reaction that causes copies of the object to float through the air until they get "caught" by our eyes—the "eidolon" theory of Democritus and Leucippus, c. 400 BCE).

But the modern notion of how this is accomplished came about after two important discoveries: (1) light travels in straight lines (Alhazan, c. 1000 [1983]) and (2) we have a bunch of light-sensitive cells (called photoreceptors—of two types, *rods* and *cones*, collectively called the *retina*) on the back of our eyes. The fact that these cells are reactive to light suggests that the light is responsible for carrying the copy to the eyes, and the fact that light travels in straight lines suggests how a clear copy might be made (see Figure 1.4).

Light travels from the source (in Figure 1.4, that source is the sun, but the same would hold true if it were a candle, an LED light, or a cellphone screen) in straight lines; that light hits all

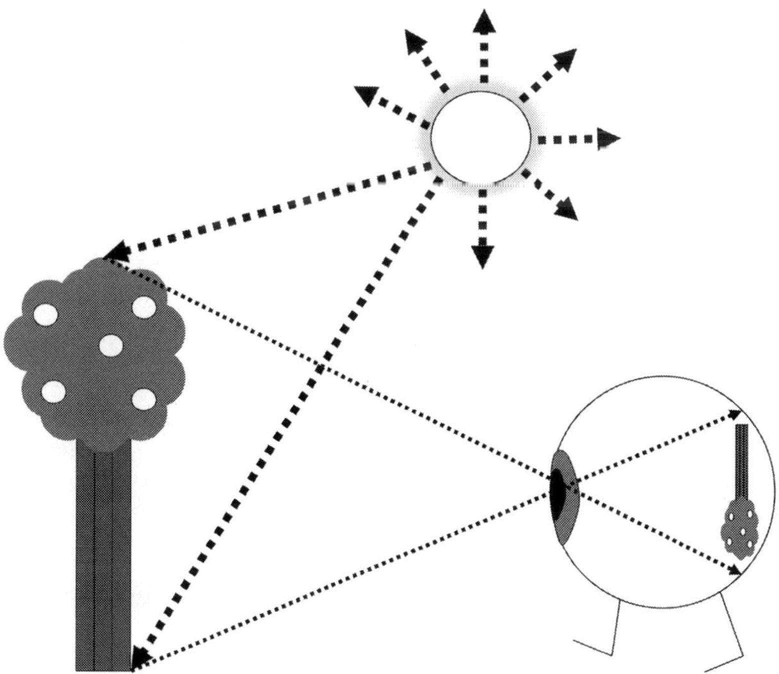

Figure 1.4 Light travels in straight lines and creates a retinal image that is upside-down, reversed, and two-dimensional.

the various substances and surfaces in the environment (here, the tree). It bounces off those objects, also in straight lines. Some of that reflected (or *ambient*) light makes its way into Fred's eye. Notice that the light from the top of the tree ends up at the bottom of Fred's eye, and the light from the bottom of the tree ends up at the top of Fred's eye. Or in other words, once the light gets to the retina, the orientation of the tree is upside-down. By the same logic, the light from the right side of the tree will end up on the left of Fred's eye, the light from the left side of the tree will end up on the right. Or in other words, the image on the retina (known as the *retinal image*) will be reversed.

Additionally, the back of the eye is like the flat but curved projector screen in a movie theater: the light reflected from the tree is projected onto this two-dimensional screen. Therefore, the image created is flat.

To sum up: the image on the retina is upside-down, reversed, and two-dimensional—but it's a copy of the world! It's a start. We have an answer to the first question—"How does a copy get into the head?" The problem, of course, is that this description of the retinal image does not match our experience. We experience the world as right side up, not reversed and three-dimensional. Moreover, on its own, this jumble of firing retinal cells does not have meaning. Spots of light on the retina (and the associated electrical activity in the brain) do not say "there is an apple here to eat". A two-dimensional image cannot convey what Fred needs to successfully approach, grasp, and eat the apple. So we are not any closer to an answer to the second question—"How does the copy inform Fred about the world?" For the moment, this copy cannot accomplish this. Somehow, Fred (or his brain) must change this stimulation (the reaction of the sensory organs—here, the retina) into his perception (his experience of the world). This is the next assumption.

Traditional Assumption 6: The copy delivered to the brain is bad and needs to be fixed.

This assumption is also known as the impoverished stimulus because it says that the incoming copy (the stimulus) is poor (impoverished) (Chomsky, 1980[2]). The second question of perception—"How does a copy inform Fred about the world?"—can only be addressed after we have attended to this concern.

Unpacking the Impoverished Stimulus

Before we go much further, it is worth asking this question: Just how challenging an issue is the impoverished stimulus for perception? Is it quickly and easily solved? Or is it more complicated? Let's examine just one of the issues in order to get an idea of the problem.

The retinal image is flat. Fred's only visual contact with the apple and the tree is a two-dimensional retinal image. Why might this cause problems for Fred? In a two-dimensional image, distance does not exist—all points are collapsed on a single surface, and therefore, distance (including between the perceiver and world) cannot be perceived. That may seem like an extraordinary statement! After all, even in (similarly two-dimensional) photographs, we are able to understand distance to a certain extent. However, the fact that distance cannot be perceived in a two-dimensional image is easily demonstrated. In the top of Figure 1.5, we see that the four points (and indeed, any one of an infinite number of points along the same line) would project to

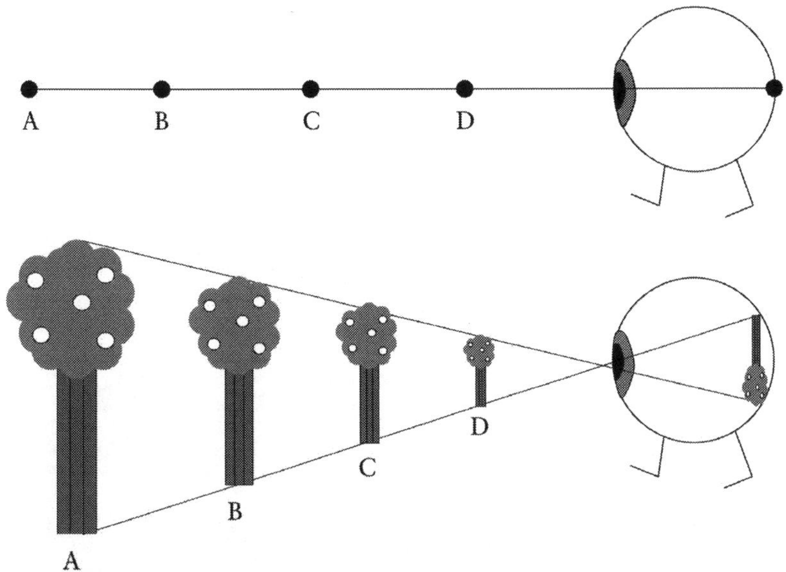

Figure 1.5 A problem of distance and size. *Top*: points A, B, C, and D all project to the exact same place on the retina. Distance is indistinguishable. *Bottom*: trees A, B, C, and D all project the exact same image on the retina. Size and distance are indistinguishable.

precisely the same point on the retina (Molyneux, 1688). If all Fred has access to is the two-dimensional retinal image, how does he know which of the points is the cause of the stimulation? Or in other words, how does he know the *distance* of the point that is the cause of the stimulation?

But wait, that's asking about perceiving disconnected floating points! That's not at all like the environment Fred normally encounters. Normally, he would encounter actual objects. What about the tree? Surely a larger—and more complex—object such as a tree would not create the same problem? Sadly, this is not the case. As you can see at the bottom of Figure 1.5, the four trees (and indeed any one of the infinite number of trees that would fit between the lines) all produce the exact same sized retinal image.

And here we also see how the image is meaningless—if the tree in the world is one of the large faraway ones (say, A or B), then it might be a real, full-size, living tree and have apples to eat. If it is one of the small close ones (say, C or D), then it is more likely a small model, a toy, or a carving and will provide no nourishment for Fred.

The inability to perceive size and distance from the perceiver is just *one* of the issues that result from the impoverished stimulus. For Fred to perceive the tree, he must also grapple with a number of other issues. For example, how does he know where the tree stops and the world around it begins? It cannot be a simple matter of contrast (see Figure 1.6). There is more contrast between the apple and the leaves surrounding it than between the leaves of the foremost tree and the leaves of the tree behind it.

Moreover, different shapes can create the same shaped retinal image depending on their orientation relative to the observer. For example, a cone, a cylinder, and a sphere all can result in a circular image on the retina (see Figure 1.7). Admittedly, that's a specialized case, but it highlights the issue: a two-dimensional retinal image is missing a lot of the information we need in order to properly understand our world. In our daily lives, we almost never mistake a sphere for a cylinder, so we must *somehow* solve this problem.

Figure 1.6 Contrast is not enough for form perception. There is more contrast *within* the tree than between the tree and its neighbors.

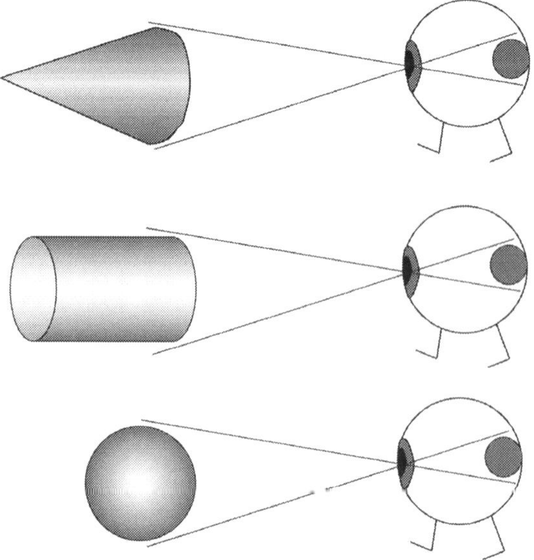

Figure 1.7 A cone, a cylinder, and a sphere could all produce a circular image on the retina.

A Systematic Approach to the Traditional Issues

While it may be possible to address each issue individually or come up with solutions that work in specific contexts (e.g., perhaps Fred knows the size of this particular apple tree, so distance is derivable from that knowledge), it is unlikely that perception is based on such ad hoc and unsystematic approaches. Knowing the size of *this* tree would not help Fred deal with the appearance of a *new* tree, and Fred cannot survive only having size knowledge *after* he has come into contact with the specific object. We need a systematic approach that will help Fred with *all* the problems of the impoverished stimulus for all the contexts in which they might be presented.

Early attempts to deal with the impoverished stimulus were varied. One answer was a sort of theoretical throwing up of hands. Some theorists suggested the problems were so intractable that the only answer was that God was intervening to fix our ability to see; in fact, at least one theorist suggested that the problems of perception were *so* difficult that they were *proof* of God's existence because such a difficult puzzle could not be solved by mere human minds (Malebranche, 1678/1997)!

A far more scientifically useful (and influential) suggestion came from Helmholtz (1910/2000). He suggested that the flat retinal image was not completely meaningless. It provided data—imperfect data—but data nonetheless. For example, the distance of the tree and its shape and form could be *inferred* from specific patterns (called cues) present in a two-dimensional image. He suggested that we learned about these cues and abstracted rules for applying them during months and years of experience perceiving the world—especially as children. Our ability to apply those rules immediately and continuously without effort or confusion was based on that experience.

To illustrate, let's look at Fred's experience with the tree. We will look at the scene from Fred's point of view (see Figure 1.8). From previous experience with exploring his world, Fred (unconsciously) knows that the farther away an object is, the higher up in the field of view the bottom of the object will be. The closer an object is, the lower down in the field of view the bottom of the object will be. That means the tree on the farthest right in Figure 1.8 is the farthest away because the bottom of it is the highest up in the image. He also knows that closer objects will block farther objects from view, so the bush is closer than the second tree from the left and so on.

According to Helmholtz's theory, Fred is not consciously aware of his interpretation. He does not have to be (or want to be). In this way, seeing is like walking—a behavior that is learned in childhood and applied situationally without conscious effort or interference (Fred's

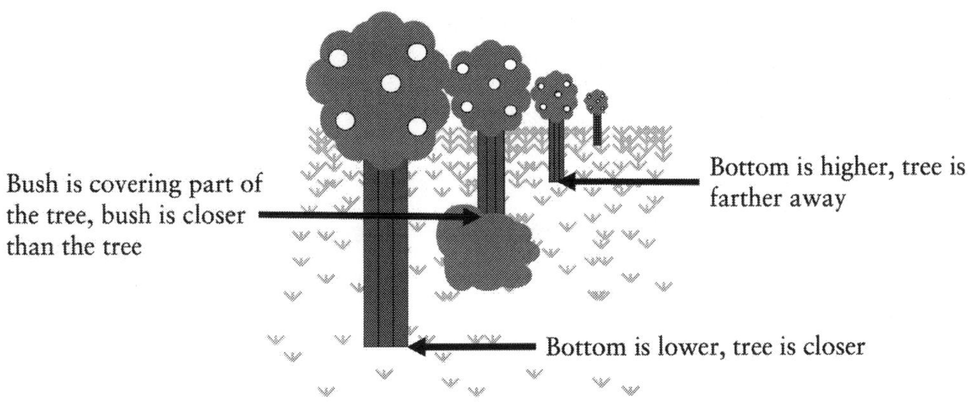

Figure 1.8 Fred's view. The size and distance of each apple tree are indicated by various cues.

stride is adjusted for uneven ground without Fred having to consciously adjust his gait). Unlike walking, however, Fred has no ability to consciously control or even be aware of this behavior. Fred's mind looks at the incoming bad stimulation, identifies the cues, identifies the relevant rules, and *unconsciously infers* what must be happening in the world in order to have created that particular stimulation in his senses. Fred's understanding of this scene can thus be illustrated like this:

> *Cue + rule + unconscious inference ⇒ understanding*

In the case of the scene, that might play out like this:

> *The bottom of the farthest right tree is highest in the image + farther-away things start higher in the image + this rule applies in this situation ⇒ the farthest right tree is the farthest away*

Or it might play out like this:

> *The bush is blocking part of the tree from view + closer objects block farther objects from view + this rule applies in this situation ⇒ the bush is closer than the tree*

In situations like Figure 1.7, where multiple circumstances in the world can cause the same pattern of stimulation on the retina, Helmholtz argued that the inference was aided by an understanding of the most likely situation. Or in other words, in the case of the ambiguous circle on the retinal image in Figure 1.7, if the rest of the field of view was a ball pit, then the sphere was the most likely shape. If the rest of the field of view was a pile of aluminum cans put aside for recycling, then the cylinder was the most likely shape. This is the so-called *principle of maximum likelihood*. Helmholtz (1910/2000) suggested that every ambiguity in the retinal image could be solved by a combination of unconscious inference and the principle of maximum likelihood. The result was a *mental representation* (a cleaned-up and interpreted copy) of the world that could be used to plan and execute behavior.

This suggestion proved so compelling that it was a very long time before anyone operated under any other supposition. The only debate was over *what* cues and *what* rules we learned during our experience. Distance, for example, could be inferred from pictorial cues like the ones mentioned previously, or we could use geometry, oculomotor cues, or binocular disparity (see Box 1.2).

Box 1.2 Depth Cues

A wide variety of cues have been proposed for the viewer to infer distance from a flat retinal image. In Figure 1.9, we present three examples. The first one is based on the geometry that emerges in the typical case in which both eyes are focused on the same object. The two eyes and the object form a triangle. The base of the triangle is the distance between the eyes. This distance never changes and is (unconsciously) known to the organism. Presumably, the angle of each eye pointing toward the object is also (again, unconsciously) known by the organism. Given these values, the organism can use trigonometry to (unconsciously) solve for the height of the triangle (the distance to the object) (see Figure 1.9a).

That's a lot of math for just one part of one object, let alone the many objects that typically fill the field of view (Malebranche, 1678/1997). So an argument was made that *absolute* distance was not as important as the *relative* distance between the organism and the many objects in the world. As long as the organism knows the distance of objects in the environment *relative to each other and to itself*, then that organism would be able to function.

Fred really only needs to know which tree is *closest*, not the exact distance to the tree. Relative distance is much easier to infer from available cues. For example, when looking at a closer object, the muscles that control the position of the eyes have to rotate both eyes inward toward the nose. In addition, the muscles in each eye have to change the shape of the lens to focus the image on the retina. When changing from fixating on a far object to a near one (or vice versa), the muscles in the eye have to rotate the eyes inward or outward (see Figure 1.9b, *left*) and change the shape of the lens inside the eye in order to keep the image clear (see Figure 1.9b, *right*). Therefore, relative distance can be inferred from our second type of cue, the movement of the eye (or *oculomotor*) muscles.

The third set of cues relies not on the organism perceiving its own body but on the organism perceiving the subtleties of the image itself. Because the eyes are in slightly different positions, even when they are both fixated on the same object, the two retinal images (one in the left eye, one in the right eye) are slightly different. The difference between the two retinal images is called *binocular disparity*. When the eyes are focused on a far object, nearer objects have greater disparity. Binocular disparity is, therefore, a cue for relative distance. This, incidentally, is how 3D movies work—through the aid of special glasses, they present a slightly different image to the left and right eyes, giving the impression of depth.

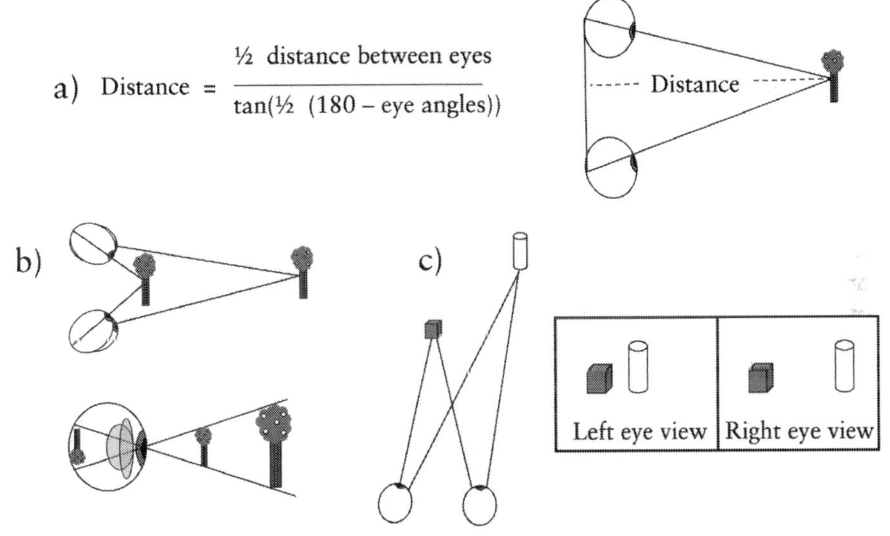

Figure 1.9 Examples of cues for absolute and relative distance: (a) geometry, (b) oculomotor cues, and (c) binocular disparity.

These are just some of the cues that have been suggested, but they are all examples of the same assumption:

Traditional Assumption 7: Unconscious inference is used to fix the bad copy—learned cues and rules are unconsciously applied to create a mental representation of the world.

One important thing to point out is the way this assumption separates the organism from the environment around them. This creates an *organism-environment dualism*—organism and environment are considered to be independent entities. Fred has no access to the world; he does not even have access to the stimulation of his sense organs (i.e., the copy of the world delivered to his brain). He only has access to his *unconscious interpretation* of this copy of that world. When proponents of the traditional approach talk of Fred's knowledge of the world, what they are really talking about is Fred's knowledge of *his representation of* that world. Because they assume that our senses are at least reasonably reliable, they further assume that the representation resembles the world, but we don't really have any way of validating whether it is or not (more on this later). Or in other words, Fred's experience is *entirely* based on the internally constructed representation, *not* the stimulation that leads to the representation.

Traditional Assumption 8: Once the copy is fixed, the representation of the world *is* your experience of the world.

These eight assumptions are the basis, the agreed-upon statutes, of what we will call the *traditional approach*. There are more modern-day versions of this same concept. For example, connectionism explains perception as a process by which the brain represents input to the visual system as patterns of activity in a network, and Bayesian modeling explains perception as a statistical process of comparing present stimulation with previous experience that echoes the *principle of maximum likelihood*. But all follow the same program and rest on the same assumptions.

Any controversy in the application of traditional approaches is generally over what type of rules should be used and how those rules should be used rather than over the assumptions themselves—those go largely unexamined. As we stated earlier on in this chapter, once you have operated under an assumption for some length of time (in this case, several centuries or more), it becomes difficult to imagine that your assumptions are, in fact, *merely* assumptions and, therefore, could be false.

Traditional Approaches Lead to (Unsolvable) Mysteries

According to the traditional approaches, this is more or less the process by which Fred sees (knows) the world (see Figure 1.10). The world exists at some distance away from Fred, and in order for Fred's behavior to be affected by anything in the world, he must make a copy of the world in his head. That copy is bad, and so it needs to be fixed in order to be useful. What's more, in order to fix it, there are a series of cues to extract, rules to apply, and likelihoods to compute. Those computations must be performed by some kind of thinking entity that is able to rationally apply all those principles. This rational entity is called a variety of things, but the most common name given to it in cognitive science is the *central executive*[3] (*depicted as little ghost Fred within bigger Fred in Figure 1.10*).

It's worth noting that the central executive is different from consciousness itself—after all, the work done by the central executive is largely *unconscious*; Fred has no awareness of that work.[4] Moreover, the central executive is entirely dependent on input from Fred's sense organs for its (and therefore Fred's) awareness of the outside world. However, there is a fundamental problem with an entity that is entirely sealed off from the world being asked to decipher (assumed bad) input from that world.

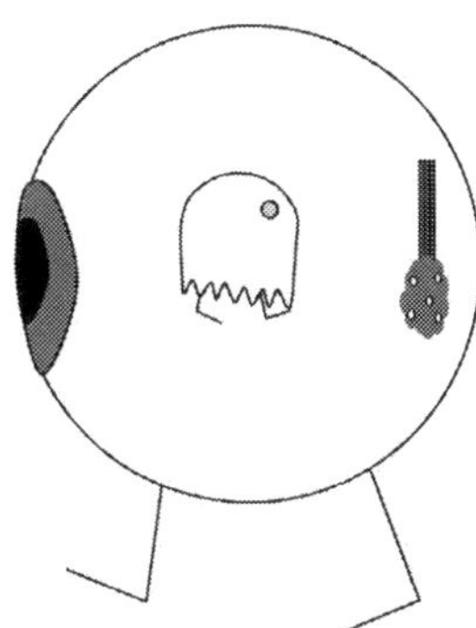

Figure 1.10 Fred's central executive has no preexisting knowledge and no access to feedback; without one or the other, he cannot "fix" the retinal image.

The Plight of the Central Executive

As an exercise, let's imagine that *we* are the central executive, being presented with stimulation on the senses (see Turvey, 2019, for more on the central executive). We start with no known information about the world. The only information we have is that which comes in through these (presumably bad) pathways. For example, in the case of vision, we as the central executive are given a pattern on the retina and are tasked with trying to figure out what caused the stimulation.

The first issue we might need to deal with is why we would assume that the stimulation came from *out there* in the world when the only data is coming from *in here* (i.e., the activity of the sense organs in the body). This is different from the concern of solipsism versus realism because we are not doubting the *existence* of the world out there but rather questioning why we would attribute the local stimulation to a distant (outside of our head) cause. This is not an issue that is unique to the visual system. All of the senses are a result of the activity in or on some sense organ. We see things because the retinal cells respond. We hear things because the cells in the inner ear (specifically in the cochlea) respond. However, we perceive the event that caused that retinal or cochlear response as being *out there* in the world. Why? This is known as the *outness problem*.

That said, the third assumption that we made was that our senses could inform us about the world, and while it's somewhat in violation of the tabula rasa, we could assume that we have at least one critical bit of information to get us started: the stimulation on our senses comes from a distant source. Our job is to figure out what that source *is*.

With the knowledge that things in the world are actually at some distance, let's take a look at the kind of incoming stimulation we have to work with: In the case of vision, the data we are given is a flat and inverted image. Why would we assume that this is *not* an accurate representation of the world? How would we know this needs fixing? The image is *always* two-dimensional, *always* inverted, so why don't we assume that the world could simply *be* flat, *be* upside-down? We have no access to the world that does not come in through the same sensory system that gave us this image in the first place. Where does the knowledge come from that this copy is *bad*? In order to begin the process of computing a representation, we'll also need to have one other critical bit of information: the world is actually three-dimensional, and the sky is up and the ground is down, so if the image says otherwise, it will need fixing.

Next, we will need to use cues, rules, and most likely scenarios in order to interpret this bad image. Essentially, we need to look at the current pattern of stimulation and compare it to previous (correctly interpreted) stimulations. We need to figure out which parts of *the current* stimulation match parts of *the remembered* stimulation so we can figure out how to construct *the current* representation based on *the previous* representation. Except, how did we get these previous representations? If all representations are generated based on comparisons to prior representations, where did previous ones come from? Or do we need still more information to get started? Perhaps we need a few early representations that could have been computed using a different sense modality like touch? Berkeley (1709) suggested that we did not need to give any special information to the central executive as long as the organism has at least one sense that does not need to be interpreted. We could then use the one unambiguous sense to inform all the others.

Berkeley made a distinction between *near* and *distance* senses. Touch, he argued, was a *near sense*—it relies on direct contact (action at *no* distance) with the world. Vision, conversely, is a *distance sense*—it is used to examine the world without being in direct contact with it (action at a distance), which is why it is subject to such concerns as the outness problem. Berkeley suggested that a near sense like touch could be used to inform ambiguous distance senses like vision because touch is *unambiguous*. Fred might, for example, notice that the apple appears different when it is held closer (and his arm is bent) than when he holds it farther away (with a straight arm). The bent arm results in a larger retinal image, the straight arm with a smaller one. In this way, over time, retinal image size is associated with felt distance.

However, this plan has (at least) three problems: If we are required to use touch to inform vision, how do we interpret the visual cues for things we have never touched or had any physical interaction with? Also, how can we compare across perceptual modalities (vision to touch and vice versa) if the stimulation from vision (spots of light on the retina) is not the same kind of thing as the stimulation from touch (patterns of pressure on the skin)? It's worse than comparing apples to oranges; it's comparing apples to the concept of justice. They are not of like kind. Last, the assumption that touch is unambiguous is debatable! After all, a light touch with a firm object will feel roughly the same as a heavier touch with a softer object (and more, see Chapter 8).

If touch cannot be used to provide information to vision, then visual stimulation will have to be interpreted on its own. Let's give ourselves (as Fred's central executive) a bit of information to get started—a representation of a previously encountered apple tree (ignoring, for the moment, where that representation came from). How can we compare the current scene to the previous one? Let's imagine what we might see. Let's say that the first time we saw an apple tree, it had a birdhouse on it, and there were six other apple trees nearby. How do we know which parts of the first stimulation were important to the formation of the accurate representation of an apple tree? If we do not know which parts were important, how do we know which parts we could safely ignore? Put it another way: If the first apple tree had a birdhouse on it and this one doesn't, is it still an apple tree? Can we still eat its apples? If the first tree was surrounded by six others, and this one only has three neighboring trees, is it also approachable? How do we know?

We would have to give ourselves *a lot* of information to get out of this one: information about birdhouses, what makes an apple tree an apple tree, and that having a birdhouse does not affect the identity of a tree, nor does the position or number of the surrounding trees. And it wouldn't just be about the birdhouse and nearby trees! What if there was a ribbon around the current tree? Or if it was a cloudy day versus a sunny one? Or if we had come to this tree from the west and the other tree from the east? Does it matter? How do we know what does and does not matter before we ever encounter the situation? And once again, when we encounter it the *first* time, how can we gain the necessary knowledge without having any ability to interpret the current situation without *past* situations that were similar?

Helmholtz attempted to get out of this puzzle by suggesting that the central executive uses the *principle of maximum likelihood* to interpret the stimulation when it is ambiguous. If we are not sure whether a birdhouse matters, we simply need to ask ourselves: of all the times we have seen an apple tree with some sort of hanging structure on it, did it affect the edibleness of the apple?

He imagined this principle as a sort of internal tally: each time you encounter the situation, add a mark next to the eventual outcome. Then when you have an uncertain situation, compare it to the tally and interpret the situation based on which outcome had the most tally marks. Modern-day Bayesian modeling of perception is just a more complex version of the same idea (Mamassian, Landy, & Maloney, 2002).

Let's return to the simpler situation earlier in the chapter in order to understand this fully: we are the central executive trying to guess what caused the circle on our retina (see Figure 1.11). Without considering context, our internal tally for this situation is that spheres are the most common source of a circle on the retina. However, if circumstances *outside* the circle are taken into consideration, we have a different tally. For example, if the circle is in the center of a bowl full of wooden balls, the sphere is still the most likely; however, if the circle is in the center of a bowl full of wooden cylinders, then a cylinder is the most common outcome.

How would we know which tally to use? When do we need to take the entire context into account, and when can we isolate certain aspects? And if the answer is to *always* take the surroundings into account, then how do we interpret *the surroundings*? After all, the only reason we knew it was a bowl of balls versus a bowl of cylinders was that we interpreted the shapes surrounding the circle on the retinal image. Where did that interpretation come from? And once again, where did the tally come from? How did we interpret all of those images in order to build up a statistical awareness of the world? How do you know what's likely if you

Figure 1.11 Since many objects could produce a circular retinal image, the central executive must use other contextual cues to figure out the correct shape.

don't *already know what's likely?* That's a lot of information we have to give ourselves just to get started!

All of this requires what Dennett (2010) called *the loan of intelligence*. The central executive needs a lot of information just to get started, and there seems to be no way to *get* any of that information, let alone all of it. Once the central executive *has* that information, it is possible to build reasonably reliable systems of cue use to detect certain patterns. These techniques have been used with some success, for example, in building robots that can move around grocery stores looking for spills and alerting the staff when they find one (e.g., Gutta & Philomin, 2004). But the robot must be programmed, must be given prerequisite information by an outside entity (the programmer). What about humans? Are we back to an all-powerful entity interpreting our senses for us? Or programming us with the prerequisite information in violation of the tabula rasa?

Another advantage the robot has over our naive central executive is the ability to get accurate feedback. Programmers can "train" these learning robots by carefully choosing the training situations and then providing feedback on repeated trials. The robot uses the feedback to update the programming: If it correctly identifies the spill, it will use that type of identification in the future. If it incorrectly identifies the spill, it will be less likely to use that type of identification in the future. For the most part, this is what is proposed to occur in connectionist accounts of perception.

This is not unlike Helmholtz's program, which runs on comparing new situations to old situations based on the eventual outcome. This program presumes that, at some point, the central executive found out what really was going on. They were able (somehow) to find out if their interpretation of the retinal image was correct. Remember: the central executive only has access to information that comes in through the (presumed bad) senses—where did this *accurate* feedback come from? How was the central executive able to access an uninterpreted (and thus trustworthy) version of the world? And if they had access to a version of the world that did not need interpretation, why are we going through all the trouble of interpreting a bad input in the first place? It seems like a waste of time.

A Plea to Start Over

The truth is, we, as the central executive, will never be able to get out of this tangle. Like asking "How do you get from California to New York?" this is a problem without enough constraints. We are being put in the somewhat unusual situation of being asked to infer cause from effect rather than inferring effect from cause (see Turvey, 2015). In a typical logical problem-solving task, a person is asked to determine what the outcome (B) would be if an event (A) occurs. For example, if you strike a wineglass with a hammer, what will happen? This situation is knowable with certainty—the glass will break.

The Helmholtzian program requires the central executive to do the less straightforward task of figuring out what the event (A) was given an outcome (B). There is a broken wineglass and a hammer present. What caused the wineglass to break? This situation is *always* uncertain. There is a most likely scenario: the hammer caused the wineglass to break. But there are other possible scenarios as well: a *different* hammer caused the wineglass to break; the wineglass was broken by a falling rock, which was then removed from the scene; the wineglass was shattered by an opera singer hitting a high C; and so on. And if the central executive had never encountered a hammer or wineglass before, what possible reason would they have for assuming the event was "hammer smashed wineglass"?

The plight of the central executive ultimately feels like bad engineering. Why design—if evolution can be considered to be designing living things—an organism that cannot perceive its world without intervention? To our knowledge, very few organisms (if any) have the higher cognitive reasoning that the Helmholtzian program requires, but *every* organism has the need to perform everyday behaviors. Food must be obtained, shelter must be acquired, mates must be located, and so on. If only those organisms with the ability to reason were able to perceive their worlds, such organisms could never have evolved because their predecessors would have died without the ability to eat, drink, and procreate!

And if the earlier, non-reasoning organisms were able to negotiate all this, does it not suggest that it is *possible* to create a perceptual system that does not require interpretation (Wagman, 2010)? If so, why would evolution go backward, as it were, and create an organism whose sensory contact with the world is ultimately not very good (and thus in need of interpretation)? Would it not make more sense that evolution had, instead, equipped every organism from the very first single-celled creature to modern-day dogs and cats (and Freds) with the ability to explore and understand their worlds? Would it not make more sense to have a program of perception that did not require such elaborate reasoning for such simple tasks?

This chapter took the eight assumptions of the traditional approach to their logical conclusion and made the argument that those eight assumptions result in an untenable situation. We cannot fix a bad copy without prior information (the loan of intelligence) or without accurate feedback. In order to untangle this, we have to start at the beginning and figure out where we went off the rails: at what point did the assumptions lead us down a path of no return? While they were presented that way, these eight statements are not really sequential; they are inextricably interwoven. Figuring out where the roots of our issues are will take revisiting each assumption with new eyes. This is the issue that will be taken up in the second chapter.

Notes

1. Descartes walks into a bar, the bartender asks if he would like a drink. Descartes says "I think not" and promptly disappears in a puff of logic.
2. Chomsky coined the phrase in reference to the acquisition of linguistics, but the idea has been applied to perception ever since.
3. Other names for the same idea are *the ghost in the machine, mind, spirit, soul, the man in the inner room*, and some theorists have derisively called it the *homunculus* (Latin for "little man").
4. It is also worth mentioning that, historically, the separation of the body from the mind was to solve another puzzle of local causality: self-action. The idea was that it was impossible, given local causality, for the body to move without something pushing it. There must be some part of the body that didn't move and instead pushed against the rest of it—Aristotle called this the unmoved mover.

2 Where We Went Wrong

The previous chapter introduced us to a series of key assumptions that guide most of the development of—and the questions in—classical perceptual theory, what we have referred to as the *traditional approach*. What we discovered, however, was that following those assumptions to their logical conclusion led to a theoretical dead end. In particular, Fred's central executive was starved for accurate, meaningful information about the outside world.

Overcoming the action at a distance problem requires that Fred's senses must first make (what turns out to be) a bad copy of the world. This bad copy is the only thing the central executive has access to, and in order to fix it, the central executive needs access to a broad range of facts about the world and how it works. In the case of visual perception, for example, the central executive needs a host of previously interpreted images and some ability to apply the statistical tallying based on those images to the *next* input, which did not (and cannot) look precisely like *the previous* input. This loan of intelligence cannot be repaid. There is no way to gift this type of information to the central executive in a way that does not violate another one of the key assumptions—the notion of the *tabula rasa*.

Additionally, there is no avenue for accurate feedback in the traditional approach. The traditional view asserts that the only access Fred's central executive has to the outside world is through the senses. But the data provided *by* the senses has been declared inadequate (it's a bad copy of the world and needs to be fixed). Therefore, there is no good mechanism by which the central executive can learn what did and did not work when interpreting bad input. Not when it's *all* bad input! There can be no *accurate feedback*.

Last, the idea that all this work would be necessary in order to do something as commonplace as seeing and approaching food in order to eat does not make good intuitive sense. *All* species of animals have to solve this problem. Is this how perception works for all of them? Even ones without sophisticated nervous systems? Only humans? If only humans, *why* only humans? No matter *what* process of fixing the input is invented, *needing* such a process at all seems remarkably inefficient. Evolution is unlikely to have equipped us with perceptual systems that need to do so much *work*. It requires a great deal of computation to achieve even the simplest of goals, like getting an apple from a tree. How would less cognitively endowed creatures like our evolutionary ancestors ever accomplish it? The logic of perception as we have explored it so far is internally inconsistent (it contradicts itself) and does not match our experience with the world (because our experience seems unmediated). Poor Fred. Perhaps it would be best to start over.

In order to start over, we need to figure out where to start over *from*. Where did we go wrong? We followed eight assumptions to the theoretical dead end. Which one(s) led us down the wrong path? For ease, here again are the eight traditional assumptions:

DOI: 10.4324/9781003145691-3

Assumption 1: The world actually exists.
Assumption 2: We are born with no knowledge and gain all knowledge through our senses.
Assumption 3: Our senses (somehow) inform us about the world.
Assumption 4: All causality must be local.
Assumption 5: Contact with the world is mediated by a copy.
Assumption 6: The copy delivered to the brain is bad and needs to be fixed.
Assumption 7: Unconscious inference is used to fix the bad copy—learned cues and rules are unconsciously applied to create a mental representation of the world.
Assumption 8: Once the copy is fixed, the representation of the world *is* your experience of the world.

Let's work our way through each, critically assessing each one. Hopefully, as we reexamine the logic at each step, we will be able to find which of these assumptions we want to keep and which will need to be adjusted or even discarded in favor of better, sounder alternatives.

Revisiting Assumption 1: The World Actually Exists

The logic here still seems sound. Certainly, the only alternative (that the world does not exist and everything is just a hallucination of some sort) is not helpful. Moreover, if the world *is* a hallucination, it would make no difference to an individual organism. Pragmatically speaking, the organism's experiences—and the scientist's investigations—would be no different if the assumption of reality *is* true or if it just *seems to be* true. Put it another way: Fred's lived experience is no different if the tree is real or if the tree he is hallucinating just *acts* as if it were real. As scientists, we are interested in the way the world works, whether it is a hallucination *or* real. In other words, if we're in a computer simulation, let's study how the computer simulation works! Therefore, there is no harm in making this assumption, and there is great comfort in doing so—which is all just a long-winded way of saying we're still going to keep this assumption as is.

Revisiting Assumption 2: We Are Born With No Knowledge and Gain All Knowledge Through Our Senses

This assumption has two parts: the *tabula rasa* and empiricism. We take no issue with empiricism—the idea that knowledge comes from experience. However, the *tabula rasa* (the blank slate), as it is typically described, has some flaws. First, it (usually) assumes that learning begins *at birth* (or at hatching in the case of an egg), but that discounts any learning that might occur during the gestational period. The time spent in the womb or the egg counts for something, right? The experience of developing a human-shaped body in a womb is fundamentally different from the experience of developing a hawk-shaped body in an egg. Before birth or after, the information that is *available* to the human is not the same as the information that is *available* to the hawk.

Second, the traditional understanding of the *tabula rasa* discounts the constraints placed on an organism because of its body and its environment. The structure and survival needs of the body constrain behavior. In our apple tree example from Chapter 1, there were embedded assumptions that were not made explicit. We began with Fred seeking a snack because needs of that kind are a given for our own behavior. We have caloric needs that drive our exploration—we seek out food when we are hungry. So does the fly. So do all organisms that are alive (Swenson, 1997).

Additionally, when he was seeking a snack, Fred had certain capabilities: he was able to walk, he had a hand that could grasp, and he was tall enough to reach the apple. All of those capabilities were with him at the outset (along with the caloric need), and they influenced his experience of the tree and the apple, *even if it's the very first time he encountered it.* Other animals would have *different* needs and *different* capabilities, and this would make their experience of the tree and the apple different from Fred's.

Box 2.1 Instincts and Constraints

It is important to distinguish inherited constraints from instincts. An instinct is a fully formed behavior that is assumed to be coded (somehow) into the DNA of the organism. It is like an unchanging computer program that is ready to run, provided the prerequisites are met. This idea is unsupportable (Wagman & Miller, 2003; Wagman, 2010). For one, DNA does not contain instructions for behaviors (Carroll, 2005; Lewontin, 2001; see Chapter 16); also, if the environment of an organism changes even minimally from one generation to the next, the "instinctual" behavior might no longer work. For example, if an owl's instinctual hunting behavior relies on the zigzag pattern that rodents make when they run away, then the owl will be unable to hunt it if a rodent suddenly starts running away in a straight line. In other words, a small change in the environment could result in a species being unable to survive in the new environment. Evolutionarily speaking, that is extraordinarily disadvantageous in a world that is constantly in flux (Van Valen, 1977).

It is the case that there are remarkable similarities in the way that organisms of a species behave across generations, but it does not follow that the behavior needs to be coded or programmed into their DNA. Instead, it could be that the shape, form, and capabilities of the body of the organism interact with the shape, form, and possibilities of the environment to produce certain behaviors. A tall person will duck under a low barrier. That does not mean that ducking needs to be coded into the DNA, but rather the constraints of the body coupled with the constraints of the environment will result in ducking behavior in order to avoid a headache.

The same *space* is not always the same *environment* (see Figure 2.1). Rather than the geometric concept of space, let's consider the *ecological concept* of niche. An ecological niche is a specific way an organism relates to the environment it inhabits, how it survives, how it finds shelter, and so on. Just as an organism's body constrains its experience and behaviors, so too does its niche. In addition to inheriting genes, organisms inherit *the environment they inhabit.* In this way, behaviors common to a species can be considered an emergent phenomenon of the varied ways in which a given species lives in its environment (Wagman & Miller, 2003)

Figure 2.1 The same *space* (say, one area of the woods) is not always the same *environment*. For the deer, the most important part of the environment is the tree and the bush, while the twig and the leaf might go unnoticed. For the worm, the tree and the bush do not provide shelter or sustenance, but the twig or leaf might.

In order to keep this assumption, we need to modify it slightly. Knowledge is gained from experience, but experience begins before birth and is shaped by the constraints of the niche and the organism (what is best described as the *animal-environment system*).

Revisiting Assumption 3: Our Senses (Somehow) Inform Us About the World

On its face, the assumption that our senses inform us about the world is good, but where the traditional approach seems to go wrong is in *how* this is accomplished. A hidden assumption is that our (or Fred's or a fly's) perceptual systems are, by and large, *passive*. Or in other words, the stimulation from the world imposes itself on our senses, and we are left trying to make sense of it. But this is not an accurate characterization of perception or behavior of organisms.

Fred does not just happen to be in the field; he is *looking for food*. What he is capable of digesting will alter what appears edible to him; for example, if Fred were a cow or a bird, different things would appear edible (see Figure 2.2, see Chapter 5). If he were looking for a place to rest, what draws his attention would change again (see Figure 2.2).

The adjustment that needs to be made to this assumption is to make the language of it *active* instead of *passive*. To wit: organisms *use* their perceptual systems to *inform themselves* about the world.

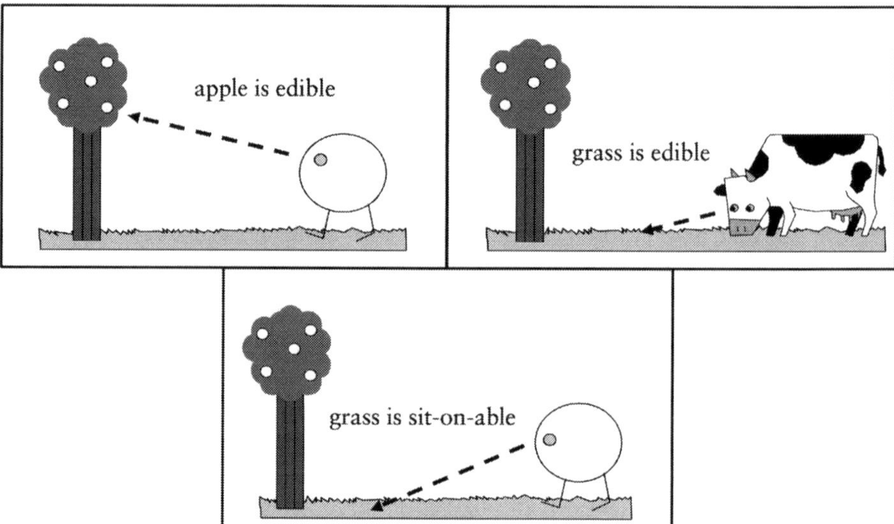

Figure 2.2 Fred can eat apples, so when he views the scene looking for food, he sees the apples (*top left*). Cows eat grass, so when the cow views the scene looking for food, she sees the grass (*top right*). When viewing the *same* scene with a different need (to rest), Fred sees the grass as a place to sit (*bottom*).

Revisiting Assumption 4: All Causality Must Be Local

The assumption of local causality was originated so long ago, it's hard to imagine questioning it, but we should. As hard as it might be to believe, causality is not limited to local processes. Let's return to the pool table from Chapter 1 (see Box 1.1). We restricted our investigations to *efficient* causality (in the case of the pool table, that was the transfer of momentum from one object to another until the ball fell in the pocket), but that kept us from understanding the many things that went into that event. Aristotle was right in his assertion that many different types of causality were needed in order to fully understand the causality of any given event. In fact, he may have been shortsighted in assuming there were only four that were necessary! (But we think we can still safely discount the invisible gnomes.)

Like all events, the event "the eight ball goes into the corner pocket" is an event that is *multicausal*. It is much easier to ask a question like "What stops the ball from going into the pocket?" than it is to ask "What caused the eight ball to go into the pocket?" because while many ongoing causes are often necessary for a successful event to occur and continue, only one cause is necessary to interrupt this process. For example, the eight ball did not go into the corner pocket because it struck another ball that was blocking its path.

What about the scenario where everything goes right? The eight ball goes into the pocket. In that case, there are impossibly many things that must have happened in order to support that event. Gravity has to exist, the felt has to be smooth enough for the balls to roll predictably, the evolution of pool as a form of entertainment has to have happened just as it did, and the player has to hit the cue ball squarely, and with just the right amount of force, Fred and Claudia have to agree to play against each other in the first place, and the table legs have to not break in the middle of the game. We could go on! And on! Causes both local and distant, obvious and nonobvious, all constrain this event.

The point is that the classical concept of causality is *linear*. Event A causes event B, which causes event C, which causes event D, and so on (see Figure 2.3, *top*). The causality goes

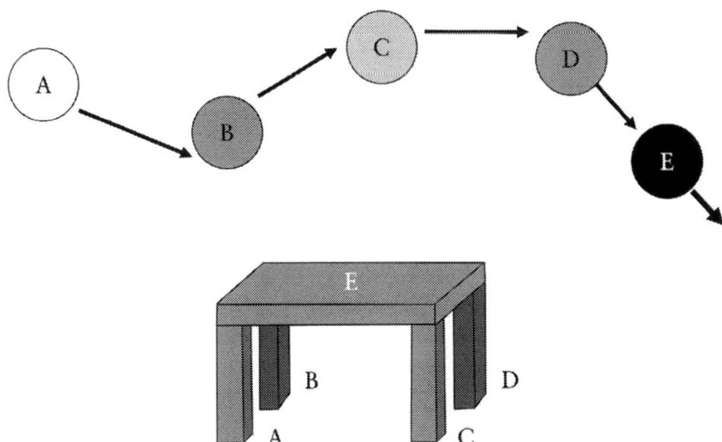

Figure 2.3 The classical view of causality is that it is like one ball hitting the next and so on in an unbroken, though not necessarily straight, line (i.e., it is *linear*). In this view, A causes B, which causes C, and so on (*top*). The ecological view embraces the idea that it is better thought of as the legs of a table. Each of the (many) events (A, B, C, D, etc.) supports the event in question, E (*bottom*).

straight from one event to the next, a single unbroken, unbranching line. This is called *linear* causality because the causal events all happen in a definite sequence, one after the other. It does *not* necessarily mean that the balls are *physically* arranged in a straight line. In Figure 2.3, for example, the balls are *not* in a straight line, but they are still in a *linear causality*.

We would like to reconceptualize causality as Bunge (1979; see also Turvey, 2013) did, as legs of a table (see Figure 2.3, *bottom*). In this view, a great many things *support* the events happening as they do. The linear version of causality makes sense in Newtonian physics and Euclidean geometry (in which the context is explicitly removed), but does this concept reasonably apply when we're talking about perception and behavior (in which context is key)? Fred is so much more complex than a ball rolling down a frictionless plane! The "legs of a table" type of causality is what we will call *nonlinear* because it is not a straight line. It is more complex (see Chapter 14).

In complex systems, like Fred and all other living systems, *nonlinear* patterns are far more common (Rosen, 1991). That means that *linear* causality is an oversimplification. An abstraction. To understand complex nonlinear systems, we need a different type of causality. That causality might be nonlocal: the game of pool was popularized in part because of *The Color of Money* (1986) and *The Hustler* (1961), neither of which directly caused the current events but without which this pool table might not exist. Our new causality might not show the usual time-order relationship: our player is trying to win a bet, so *future* earnings are the motivation for *current* behavior. Certainly, our new causality is going to be complex: even an event as simple as "the eight ball goes in the pocket" is going to have a multitude of overlapping and intersecting causes.

The concept of causality in an ecological system borrows from the language of dynamics (see Chapter 14). In brief, instead of thinking of causality as a singular unbroken line, we conceive of events as emergent from the interactions among an entire *system*. Every system has rules (gravity is one of the rules for the pool table example) that are called *constraints*. Under a given set of constraints, certain behaviors might become more likely; some might become inevitable. To understand the effect the apple tree has on Fred and his behavior, we have to look beyond the notion that it must somehow come in *contact* with Fred and instead suggest that it is one of the *constraints* that shape Fred's behavior.

Revisiting Assumption 5: Contact With the World Is Mediated by a Copy

Assumption 5, that our perceptual interactions with the world are mediated by a copy (see Figure 2.4a), was a huge part of what led us into our theoretical dead end. If perception is of—or by means of—a copy, and the copy is *bad*, then something needs to perceive (read: fix and interpret) that copy, and so we imagine an information-starved central executive. What if we could avoid all that? What if, instead of assuming that we perceive the world through an interpretation of a copy, we assume that we perceive the world *directly* (see Figure 2.4b)? In addition to simplifying the story, it puts perception on an equal footing with behavior—which would also seem to be direct (see Chapter 9). (In Figure 2.4b, the reciprocal relationship between perception and action is denoted by the two-headed arrow.)

The copy was assumed because of the need to avoid action-at-a-distance, but our commitment to look beyond local causality makes that concern moot. We can allow for Fred to know the world sufficiently to guide his behavior without needing any particular mediator (such as a copy) to preserve local causality. This will require a rethinking of the relationship between the organism and the environment, but that is doable (even preferable, see Chapters 4–5). And the benefits of removing the copy far outweigh the cost of such a reconceptualization. The assumption of a copy led to perceptual theories based on *interpreting* copies. We can instead assume that there *is no copy* and see where that leads. In other words, we are going to make the assumption of *direct perception* instead of the assumption of *indirect perception*.

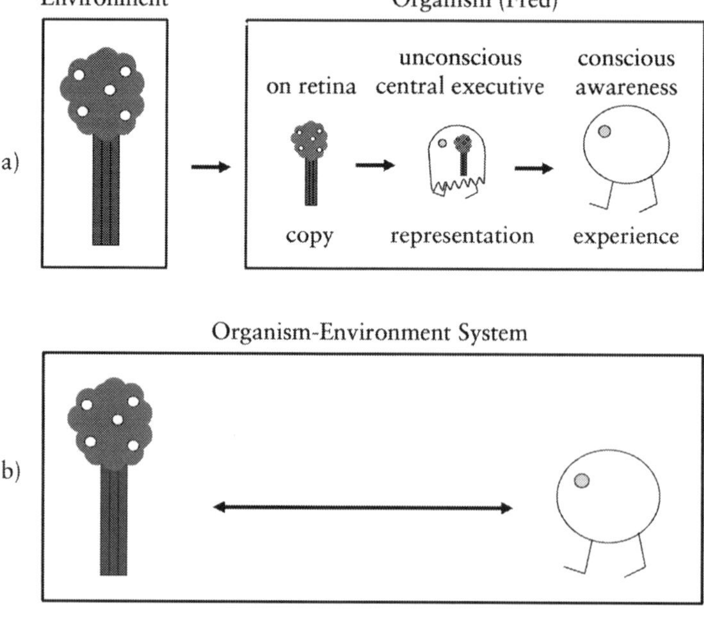

Figure 2.4 (a) Indirect perception: Organism and environment are logically separated. Perception is the central executive's interpretation (representation) of a copy of the world. (b) Direct perception: Organism and environment are part of the same system. Perception is of the world. Action is direct.

Doing away with the copy as a starting point will also help with another difficulty encountered when trying to generalize our findings to animals other than humans. More specifically, starting with a retinal image put perceptual theorists in a tangle when they considered organisms that do not have the same type of eye as Fred (see Chapters 4 and 6). Many organisms (e.g., cats, dogs, snakes, other primates) have Fred's type of eye—what is called a chambered eye, a spherical chamber (an eyeball) with a small hole in front that results in something like an actual *picture* being projected onto the back (but see Chapter 3)—but many organisms do not. The fly, for example, has a *compound eye* (see Figure 2.5). This type of eye cannot make a copy! There is no image projected on the back of the eye but rather multiple points of light being registered simultaneously. When looking at that type of eye, it is tempting to think of it as still registering a regular image, just broken up into pieces, but this is not the case. Each "tube" of the compound eye is like the opening at the front of Fred's eye: it collects light from the entire field of view. No image is formed at any point in this perceptual process. Yet the fly still sees, doesn't it? It sure moves (and avoids being swatted) like it can see just fine.

It is worth noting that the retinal image does not even *really* exist in the chambered eye. The back of the eye is *not* really a flat projection screen as it was assumed to be when the eye was first being dissected. In fact, that the back of the eye looked at all like a screen to the first scientists investigating it may have been a consequence of the way they were dissecting it! The scientists literally cut off the back of the eye and *replaced* it with a screen-like membrane. That an image was discernable on *that* was more a function of the optics of the front of the eye than a function of the anatomy or typical functioning of the retina.

In actuality, there are multiple layers of retinal cells and blood vessels that more closely resemble a "folded fishing net" (Swanson, 2015) than an opaque screen (see Carello & Turvey, 2020, for more information about the retinal image fallacy). At best, we can say that certain spatial relationships are preserved in the chambered eye, but that is not the same as starting with an image.

When faced with the evidence of (at least) two types of eyes that have very different ways of interacting with light, we have one of two choices to make: either assume that the processes by which Fred and the fly see the world are categorically different, or assume that we misunderstood how visual perception works in organisms with chambered eyes—eyes that could (but

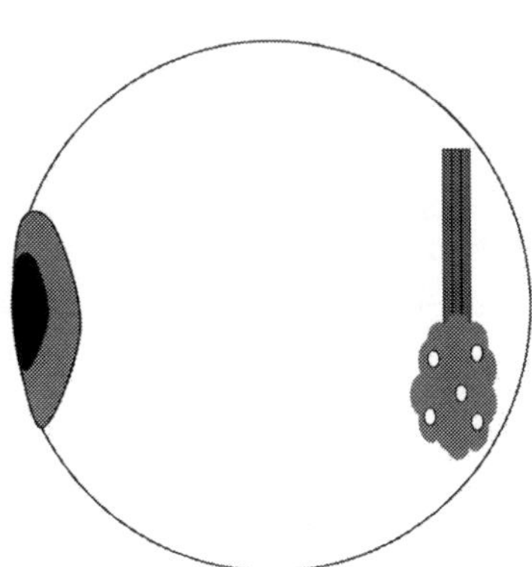

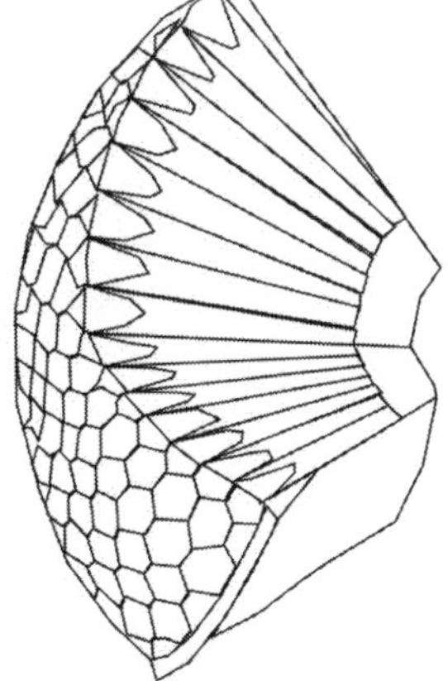

Figure 2.5 A chambered eye (*left*) is like a beach ball with a hole in the front. Light enters through that hole, and an image is produced that resembles the actual world. A compound eye (*right*) is like a collection of straws. Light enters the top of each straw and stimulates a receptor at the bottom of the straw. No image is formed.

may or may not) form an image. If Fred and the fly are going to have *similar* visual perceptual processes, then we cannot think of the retinal image as a copy of the world *as such*. Instead, it might be better to think of it as a side effect that is incidental to the perceptual process and shift our focus to what similarities exist between the fly's contact with the world and Fred's. Consequently, we reject Assumption 5 outright.

Revisiting Assumption 6: The Copy Delivered to the Brain Is Bad and Needs to Be Fixed

Whether it is considered a copy or not, we still need to address the idea that the stimulation of the senses is *bad*. The poverty of the stimulus is the bedrock on which all the traditional theories of perception are built. Without this notion, all the assumptions that come after it crumble. After all, if the stimulation reaching the sense organs and brain is *good*, then there is no need to interpret or compute anything. Having said that, the notion that the incoming stimulation is bad is compelling and has the support of Euclidean geometry. Let's examine just the notion of distance as discussed in Chapter 1: It seems pretty clear that Fred cannot know the size and distance of the tree because the light (traveling in straight lines from source to object to the retina) forms a flat image on the back of his eye. In a flat image, distance is not perceivable and so must be *computed* through the use of cues and inference.

The use of cues and inference to compute size and distance is the premise of the Beuchet chair illusion (see Figure 2.6, *left*). This arrangement is carefully constructed specifically to capitalize on the size/distance problems caused by the flat retinal image. The figure on the left seems much larger than the figure on the right because the figure on the right is actually much farther away. Traditionalists take this as evidence that the flat retinal image is interpreted via cues because the "chair" is specifically designed to make the cues contradict reality—the seat is on the floor, the legs are just posts at a much closer distance and oddly arranged, and so on—which is what leads to the confusion.

There is, however, another possibility. The Beuchet chair illusion only works if you look at the room from *one specific location*. It only works if you don't move your head, if you close one eye, if you don't sway, and if you don't shift forward or backward. It only works when the image is *static*. Honestly, it hardly works at all with your *eyes* and only *really* works in the pictures taken of it. If you move one step to the right, the entire illusion is dispelled and everything looks as it actually is (see Figure 2.6, *right*). The odd configuration of the posts and the cushion becomes clear, the relative size of the figures is easily discerned, the illusion is revealed as a conspiracy of geometry (see Runeson, 1988).

In other words, another way to look at the assumption of the poverty of the stimulus is that the stimulation is only bad if we make it so—if we remove all the information available through movement and exploration. But movement and exploration are essential features of life! As Gibson (1966) said (paraphrased), the animal that does not move is either asleep or dead (p. 10). In the traditional approach, the static retinal image is the generic case. In the ecological approach, the retinal image does not exist, and a moving animal is the generic case. In addition to the dependence on an improbably static view, the traditional approach also has a reliance on the wrong *variables*.

The Variables of Perception, Revisited

When perceptual theorists were first grappling with the notion of the retinal image, they expected it to be making an exact copy of the world. But this carries a contradiction at its core: there can be no *exact* copy of the world. Copies (however conceived) will never

Figure 2.6 The Beuchet chair illusion distorts size and distance when viewed from the "proper" location (*left*) but not when viewed from a slightly different location (*right*). These photographs of the first author (5'2") and her husband (6'2") were taken at the Museum of Illusions in New York City.

have the same inherent meaning as the world itself. Fred can eat an apple but not a copy of an apple.

The images in our eyes (however conceived) do not have mass, are not three-dimensional, and are greatly reduced in size from the object itself. The copy is not—cannot be—exact; it's not even close. If the copy is not exact, then the necessary conclusion is that the copy must be preserving *some* variables, presumably those that would be of some use to the organism. The mistake these theorists made was assuming that the variables that were relevant for the stimulation of *cells* (like those that make up the retina) would be relevant to *perception*. Investigating the stimulation of cells led them to investigate micro-level variables, such as wavelengths and amplitudes of light, instead of the macro-level variables that were actually meaningful to the organism (see Chapter 6).

The move toward micro-level variables was not accidental. These theorists were actively looking for properties that exist in the object—or more often, in the light reflected from that object—independent of any observer (see Chapter 5). They reasoned that the perceptual systems *must* use those properties for exactly that reason—objective properties would exist regardless of any changes in context that might occur. With that in mind, they looked to Euclidean geometry and Newtonian physics and found that length, width, mass, dimensionality, and shape seemed like good *objective* properties of the object and assumed the organism must be attempting to copy them.

Having made that decision, they examined the (static) retinal image and found it wanting. Size, distance, dimensionality, and shape on the retina were all ambiguous! Of course they believed the stimulation was bad! By that reckoning, it absolutely is! If the retinal image does not contain the (Euclidean, Newtonian) information that is (assumed to be) necessary, then we have no choice but to assume that it is somehow added back in.

Now we come to the first, fundamental ecological insight: properties of geometry and physics that exclude the organism and the activity of that organism are useless for perception and behavior. Instead, we need properties that include the organism and the activity of that organism. We need *relational* properties, not objective properties. The ecological program suggests that we should not be providing different answers to the same question (e.g., "How does the retinal image copy micro-level properties?"). Rather we should be asking different questions entirely. Specifically, we should be expecting the perceptual systems to be sensitive to relational variables and asking how this might be so. After all, which would be more immediately useful to Fred: the exact height and distance of the tree or the knowledge that he can walk to the tree, grasp the apple, and eat it?

Let's revisit the figure of Fred's view from Chapter 1 as he is approaching the tree (see Figure 2.7, *top*). The traditional account looked for cues to the relative distance of the objects, cues that might only be statistically related to reality. In that same scene, however, there is also a *relationship between* the observer (Fred) and the objects on the ground plane (the tree, the grass, the horizon). Specifically, because of the geometric relationship between the objects on the ground plane and Fred, the horizon will always, *always* bisect the objects at Fred's eye height (see Figure 2.7, *bottom*). The horizon (or vanishing point, as artists call it) is (practically speaking) an infinite distance away. If Fred were to look at the horizon, his line of sight would be parallel to the ground. Any object between Fred and the horizon will appear to intersect every object at Fred's eye height (Warren & Whang, 1987). This will be the case regardless of (changes in) Fred's height and regardless of (changes in) heights of the objects. Or in other words, there is no statistical inference necessary—there is an *invariant* relationship between Fred, the objects on the ground plane, and the horizon that he can reliably use to guide his snack-getting behavior. Importantly, this invariance *only* exists when you examine the scene *relationally*—that is, examine it as a relationship between Fred and his environment.

Figure 2.7 Horizon-ratio invariant. The horizon bisects the tree at Fred's eye height (*top*). This will always happen this way because of the geometry of the scene (*bottom*): The horizon is (effectively) an infinite distance away, and so the viewer's line of sight is (essentially) parallel to the ground.

The bold assertion by Gibson (1966, 1979/2015) was that the stimulation was *good*—provided we described it appropriately—at the level of the relationship between organism and environment rather than at the level of the receptor or even the organism. He further asserted that the right variables are *ecological (emerging from a relationship between organism and environment)*, not physical (existing independently of an organism). That is, he suggested that instead of looking at what variables seem useful to particular patches of the retina and then asking how those variables might be used by the central executive, we should instead look at what variables seem to be useful to the person in guiding behavior and then ask how those variables might be detected. Explaining how this might happen and what it entails is the goal of the rest of this book, so for now, we will turn to the next assumption.

Revisiting Assumption 7: Unconscious Inference Is Used to Fix the Bad Copy—Learned Cues and Rules Are Unconsciously Applied to Create a Mental Representation of the World

Assumption 7 was the logical solution to the notion that the copy was bad and needed to be fixed. The previous section discarded the notion of poverty of the stimulus, but it's worth mentioning that there are additional logical issues with using inference to "fix" a bad image. In brief, the inference is meant to be based on "priors"—that is, the central executive (however conceived) is supposed to use previous input/inferences (broadly defined) to interpret incoming information. There are two fundamental problems with this that make *any* approach of this kind impossible.

The first concern (as outlined in Chapter 1) is that no new stimulation pattern is going to perfectly match previous stimulation patterns. That is, the cues that are meant to be extracted from the previous interpretations are always going to present slightly differently in the current situation than they did in the previous situation. The lighting will be a little darker, the surrounding trees will be oriented differently, the target tree will have a birdhouse, and so on. If the new stimulation does not perfectly match the previous stimulation, then we have to ask how the central executive was able to make use of the previous information. A thoroughgoing explanation of perception needs to be applicable to every possible situation that an organism might encounter in its niche.

The second issue has to do with the internal logic of the approach. There are two assumptions here that cannot exist simultaneously: (1) we start with *no* information and (2) information is *needed* in order to interpret any input (because all input is bad). The combination of these two runs into difficulties when we try to understand how we manage to interpret the very first bad copy of the world. Either the very first interpretation had to be made with no information (in which case, it violates the notion that information is *needed*) or it had to be made with loaned information (in which case, it violates the notion that we start with *no* information).

Assumption 7 seemed like a reasonable step to take when we were initially building a theory of perception. It came directly from the previous assumption—the incoming copy is bad, perception is good, so therefore, the incoming copy must be fixed. However, this assumption can be challenged on two points: first, we have demonstrated that fixing the copy is impossible, and second, we are going to make the ecological assumption that the incoming information is *good* (and, therefore, does not *need* to be fixed).

Revisiting Assumption 8: Once the Copy Is Fixed, the Representation of the World *Is* Your Experience of the World

While it is mostly superfluous at this point to even revisit this assumption, we are going to do so for completeness' sake and to make a few final points. The notion that Fred's conscious awareness is of the fixed representation was an effort to make the theory match lived experience.

That is, Fred's (and our) experience of the world is not one that is fraught with inaccuracies and overwhelming effort. In fact, our experience is *so* effortless that it is often difficult to convince the average person that scientists and philosophers have been debating this topic for hundreds (if not thousands) of years!

The assumption of poverty of the stimulus led to the requirement of "fixing" the image; however, we do not feel ourselves interpreting the image, and we do not have conscious awareness of a bad image. The only solution at that point was to make the interpretation unconscious. Assumption 8 is a kind of curtain drawn between Fred's conscious awareness and the central executive's mad scramble for meaning and clarity. The problem, of course, is that this isolates the central executive and separates it from Fred's conscious awareness. For all the reasons that are listed in the previous chapter, that isolation keeps the central executive from being able to do the job as prescribed.

Box 2.2 The Mind-Body Problem

The division between the conscious mind and the unconscious central executive is related to the divide that is made between mind and body more generally. The idea here is that the body is a kind of machine: fully physical and operated through a series of electrical impulses delivered by the nervous system. Those electrical impulses have to be coming from *somewhere*, started by *something*—the mind is that something. In this account, the mind is purely nonphysical and completely separate from the body itself. This allows the mind to control the body without being *part* of the body. This division was made and has been reaffirmed at multiple points historically, so much so that it is a kind of hidden assumption. It's even in our language! We talk about our bodies as if they are things we *own*: "my hand," "my leg," and so on. It also matches our *experience*. We feel as though we are the thing that is in charge of our body; we even vaguely feel that our mind might occupy the space just behind our eyes.

However intuitive it might feel, the mind-body division is deeply problematic. How could a completely nonphysical thing (the mind) affect a completely physical thing (the body)? If the mind has no mass, occupies no physical space, and is completely nonphysical in every way, how could it possibly affect the body? How can it deliver the electrical impulses? And if it *can* deliver those impulses, then it *must* be physical, so how are we drawing a principled distinction between one and the other? Most importantly, this distinction seems to be unnecessary. Is it not possible that what we experience as our "minds" is a biological process? Perhaps our conscious awareness is a property of billions of neurons just doing what they do?

The division between the conscious mind and the unconscious central executive runs into theoretical problems as well—how can the two talk to each other? If the conscious mind has to remain completely oblivious to the presence of the central executive (or else it would not match our experience), then how can it use that information? Moreover, is there a need for such secrecy? It seems strange and inefficient to build an entire system out of the need to keep our conscious awareness in the dark. We submit that for these reasons, Assumption 8 needs to be discarded.

Where Are We?

Most of the research and theorizing in perceptual science has been about finding different answers to the same questions. The answers always ran into the same difficulties (it created unsolvable mysteries), and finding a coherent solution to those difficulties proved problematic at best. But the *questions* were generated by making the eight assumptions laid out in Chapter 1. This chapter has revisited and challenged those assumptions in an effort to find a way to avoid the troublesome answers. In so doing, we discovered that the assumptions—and by extension, the questions—were, by and large, flawed.

Only the first assumption can be kept as is. The second and third need slight modification to include richer information and active exploration. The rest will be discarded. Without those, the questions posed by the traditional approach are moot. If there is no copy, there need not be an interpretation of it. If the input is good, it does not need fixing.

Take a moment to appreciate the radical claim the ecological approach is making: almost all of the research that has been done was answering questions that were based on flawed assumptions. It is not possible to *modify* the approach to deal with the theoretical shortfalls; we have to *start over*. The good news is that we are not starting from *nothing*. Exploring the traditional perspective highlighted which approaches *won't* work and which variables lead to contradictory and ambiguous findings. In so doing, it has pointed the way to those variables that *will* be useful. We know, for example, that causality should be complex and dynamic instead of simple and linear; information should be organism-relevant rather than objective, and perception should be active and direct instead of passive and indirect.

Given that we have discarded so many of the assumptions of the traditional approach, we need to begin again. We need a series of assumptions, explicitly stated, that will form the foundation for the ecological approach. That is the focus of the next chapter.

3 Starting Over

Here is Fred (see Figure 3.1). Fred has a problem: he is hungry. Fred is standing in a field of grass, and on the other side of that field is an apple tree. The tree has ripe apples and could provide Fred with a much-needed snack. In Chapter 1, we looked at this as a problem to be solved primarily, if not exclusively, by Fred's *eye* and *brain*. We focused on his passive receiving of stimulation, the fixing of this stimulation, and his resulting mental experience of the world. We asked how he inferred meaning from meaningless stimulation and never really got around to asking what role this mental experience played in actually *getting* Fred his snack. Poor, hungry Fred.

We had that focus, and we asked those questions because of the assumptions that we made about organisms and knowledge and causality. Those assumptions sit at the heart of most theories of perception and have for a very long time. Chapter 2 made it clear that the assumptions were (mostly) flawed. The goal of this chapter is to establish new assumptions and present a new way to think about perception.

The first thing you might notice in Figure 3.1 is that Fred is no longer just a walking eyeball. He is *embodied*. What that means is that Fred's eyes are a *part* of him as an organism, but his eyes are in a head on top of legs. The next thing that you might notice is that Fred is now standing on the ground. Or in other words, he is *embedded* in an environment. The ecological

Figure 3.1 Fred's dilemma (revisited): how can an *embodied, embedded* organism perceive that he can get a snack?

DOI: 10.4324/9781003145691-4

perspective on perception says that we need to take an entirely different approach to how to understand perception. First, we have to stop treating organisms as if they are just eyeballs attached to brains, or just ears attached to brains, or just skin attached to brains! We also have to stop pretending that organisms are floating in a void, unaffected by their context.

Organisms are not just a collection of independent organs. Organisms are complex, embodied, perceiving-acting *systems*. We also have to acknowledge the context in which perception occurs—both in terms of what perception is *for* in the first place and in terms of the *environment* that surrounds the organism. Perception does not happen in a vacuum, and we cannot pretend that it does.

A Change in the Starting Point

The traditional approach started its investigation of visual perception at the retinal image and found that it provided ambiguous input to the brain about the world. The ecological approach challenges this strategy in several ways.

First, as we already discussed in Chapter 2, modern anatomical understanding of the chambered eye denies the existence of a flat projector-screen-like retina where a clean image is formed. The only time the chambered eye acts like a projector casting an image on a smooth screen is when the eye is dissected, the actual retina is removed, and a smooth screen is added for ease of viewing from behind the eye itself (as in the original studies by Descartes; see Carello & Turvey, 2020, for more on the historical misunderstandings of the retinal image). A more accurate characterization of the actual retina is a transparent tangled web of light-sensitive cells with no surface on which an image is produced (Bentley, 1954/1975; Swanson, 2015). Spatial relationships between points of light might be preserved in the stimulation of these cells, but that's not the same thing as an image projected onto a flat screen.

Moreover, as highlighted in Chapter 2, most animals on the planet (e.g., arthropods and insects) have compound eyes, and the compound eye *cannot* produce an image. Rather than have two different theories of visual perception (one for chambered eyes, one for compound eyes), the ecological approach seeks to unify them through an understanding of the structured light encountered by organisms. That is, we argue that the *structure* of the light is the same, *regardless* of the type of visual system. In this way, theories of visual perception should not depend on the interpretation of an image as such. And it's not just about light! Ecological perception seeks to unify theories of perception across *all* organisms and *all* types of energy, regardless of anatomy or physiology (see Chapters 4–8).

The second challenge to the traditional approach is that beginning the study of perception with the retinal image (even if it existed) ignores the fact that perception occurs *in an environment*. What happens to the light (or whatever energy form that we are talking about) *before* the animal encounters it is critical. Take Fred's situation: the light that reflects off the apple and reaches Fred originates from somewhere. In this case, that somewhere is the sun. The sun emits light. At this point, the light is unstructured. Many wavelengths of light are traveling together away from the sun. That light reaches the field in which Fred is standing and strikes all of the exposed surfaces (including Fred!). The tree, the grass, and the apple all have particular properties that affect what happens to the light when the light strikes it. The apple, for example, has a smooth surface, which means that much of the light that strikes it will be *mirror-reflected* instead of *scatter-reflected* (see Box 3.1, see Chapter 6). The skin of the apple has certain properties (depending on its ripeness)[1] that mean that it will absorb some wavelengths of light and reflect others.

By the time the light leaves the apple on its way to Fred's eye, it is radically and meaningfully altered by its contact with the apple—it is *structured* instead of unstructured (see Chapter 6). The structure of the light reflecting from the apple is not just *related to* that apple; it is *unique* to that apple. Note: the word "unique" often means "special" or "interesting" when used in everyday conversation. The true meaning of the word (and the meaning we explicitly want to use here) is "one of a kind".

In this context, that means that there is *only one* situation that could produce this distribution of light and *only one* distribution of light that could have been produced *by* this situation. Or in other words, if the properties of the apple were different (if it were rougher, were less ripe, had a worm, or were larger), then the light reflecting from it would be altered as well.

Box 3.1 An Understanding of Light

To understand the way that light is structured by its contact with the substances and surfaces of the environment, a basic understanding of light is necessary. First, light is a type of energy called *electromagnetic radiation*. The first part of this phrase, "electromagnetic", just defines what kind of energy it is—visible light is only a tiny fraction of the *electromagnetic spectrum* (which also includes x-rays and radio waves, see Figure 3.2 top left, see Chapter 15).

All that is meant by the second part of this phrase, "radiation", is that it is energy emitted or given off by a source (it might *sound* like we're talking about something that happens after an atomic blast, but that's not necessarily what the word means!). Energy *radiates* from whatever is producing it in the same way that heat radiates from a heat source. This is in contrast with other forms of energy like *kinetic* or *potential* energy, which are energies produced by movement or the possibility of movement (respectively) but are not emitted by a source.

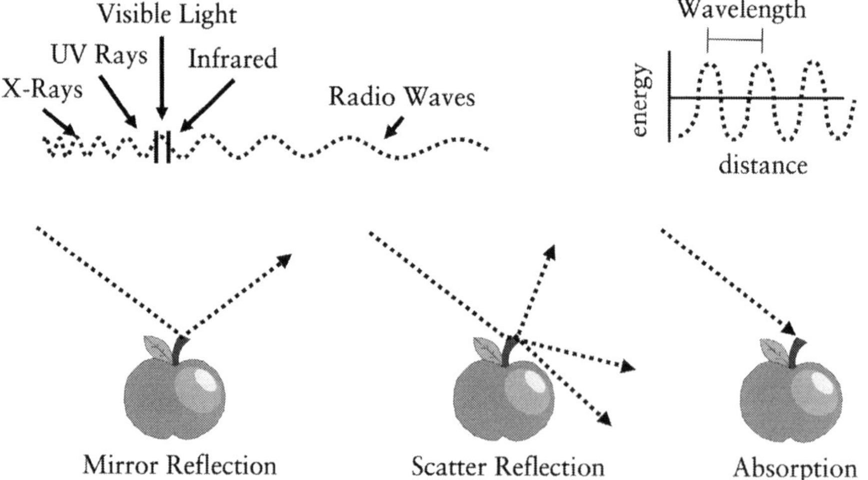

Figure 3.2 Properties of light. *Top left:* The portion of the light that stimulates the human eye is only a tiny fraction of the electromagnetic spectrum, which also includes radio waves and x-rays. *Top right:* The electromagnetic spectrum differs in terms of the wavelength of light—the distance from peak to peak. *Bottom:* The three different possibilities when light strikes an object. In *mirror reflection*, the light bounces off the object at the exact same angle it struck the object. In *scatter reflection*, the light bounces off at any other angle. In *absorption*, the light is usually converted to heat as it is soaked up by the object.

What makes one part of the electromagnetic spectrum different from another is the *wavelength* of the energy (see Figure 3.2, *top right*). Only a tiny portion of the electromagnetic spectrum is visible to humans. Within that portion, differences in wavelength are perceived as differences in *color* (but see Box 3.2 for a more nuanced take on the perception of light *as such*). What we perceive as white light is really just all the different colors of light traveling together for a while. They do not mix and are easily separated by a prism (or water—which is why rainbows are created after a storm; the sunlight passes through the rain in the air and is separated into all the different colors).

When light strikes the substances and surfaces in the world, one of three things can happen: it can be *mirror-reflected*, it can be *scatter-reflected*, or it can be *absorbed* (see Figure 3.2 bottom). Mirror reflection means that the light bounces off the object at the exact same angle that it struck the object. This is the type of reflection that happens when we look into a mirror. The light reflecting off our face goes to the mirror at roughly a 90° angle to the surface. The light bounces directly back to our eye (at roughly a 90° angle), so we are able to see our face. Scatter reflection means that the light bounces off the object at a different angle than it struck the object, like when light bounces off a rough surface like corduroy. And absorption means that the energy is taken in by the object (usually by converting to heat—which is why car seats get hot in the sun). Properties of the surface (such as smoothness and pigments deposited during ripening) determine which of these three things will happen (see Chapter 6).

The traditional concept of ambiguous input is based on—among other things—the assumption that light reflects off surfaces, then travels in a straight line, then enters the eye, and is projected as a still image onto a flat screen (the retina). For example, it's possible that a ball and the end of a cylinder could momentarily project the same geometric shape on a flat projection screen (see Figure 3.3), but why are we focused on the static geometric shape they project on a flat screen anyway? If the flat retinal image is a myth, then the flat, static retinal image is *also* a myth—and an even bigger one at that!

And even if the flat static retinal image *weren't* a myth, it is inaccurate to say that the two images would be *identical*. The light that leaves the two objects has been uniquely structured by those objects. Consequently, the variables that an animal needs to detect in order to interact with each object are entirely unambiguous (more on this later). The cylinder and the ball have radically different properties and would structure the light in radically different ways

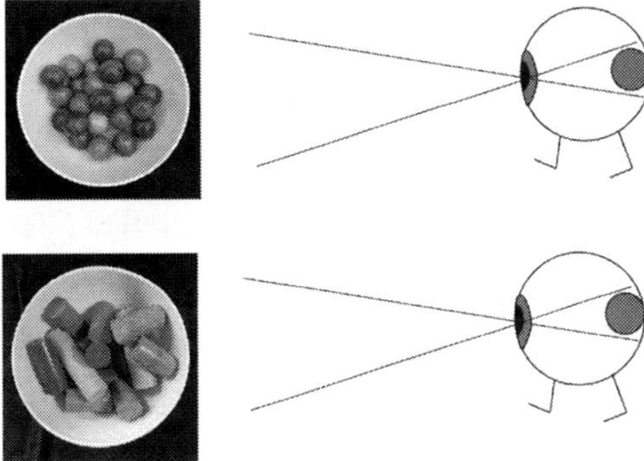

Figure 3.3 A ball and the end of cylinder will (momentarily) project a circle on the retina, but only in the static case.

(see Chapter 6 for more on ecological optics). The light that reflects off the objects is unique to each object and each context.

Meanwhile, Fred is of a particular height and is occupying a particular location in the field, and his body has certain abilities. The light that leaves the apple is reflected and scattered in every direction, but Fred occupies only one particular location (one point of observation) in the field, so he does not (and cannot) encounter *all* of the light that leaves the apple, just the light that reaches the precise place he occupies. If he were to move even a small distance to the right or left, forward or back, then he would encounter different structured reflected light. Or in other words, the light that reaches him is not just unique to the objects that it has reflected from, it is *also unique* to his location (his point of observation) in space (see Chapter 6).

By the time the light reaches Fred, it has been *uniquely* structured by its contact with the substances and surfaces in the environment. Given his location, Fred encounters a *unique* portion of the structured light. The stimulation encountered by Fred is *not* ambiguous.

A Change in the Style of Approach

Changing the starting point for studying visual perception from the retinal image to the structured light reaching an organism allows for the inclusion of a variety of factors that were excluded from a purely retina-centric approach. First, it radically expands the role of the environment in our understanding of Fred's experience.

Ecology is the study of the relationships between animals and their environments. From that, we get the name of our approach—ecological psychology. This reflects the fundamental assumption that perception cannot be understood outside of the normal circumstances of perceiving—which necessarily includes both an animal and an environment. It does us no good, the thinking goes, to discuss points of light floating in empty space (as in Molyneux's problem; see Figure 1.5) because, in real life, *this simply doesn't happen.*

Consider the effect that adding this context has on Molyneux's problem (see Figure 3.4). By adding the context—Fred's body, the ground, the fact that objects have substance and surfaces and are not a collection of dimensionless points, the fact that the objects do not float

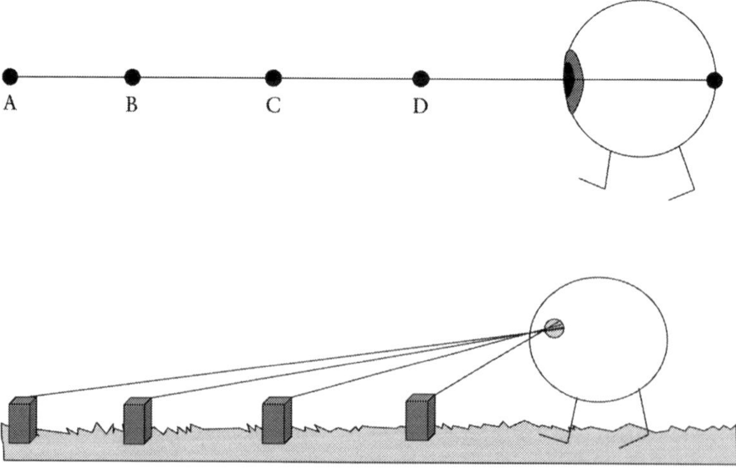

Figure 3.4 *Top*: Molyneux's problem does not have any context, and so distance is unable to be perceived or derived. *Bottom*: the ecological reformulation includes the context, and so distance is lawfully specified.

in a void but, in fact, sit on the ground due to gravity, and so on—Fred is easily able to tell which object is where.

The ecological approach requires that any explanation of perception must begin and end with the circumstances of perceiving. That Fred is seeking the apple because he is hungry is as much a part of the story as the properties of the tree (and the light reflected from it). His intentions, his body, and his behavior will change the way he explores his environment (e.g., where, when, and how he moves and looks) and will, therefore, change what information (e.g., which structured light) he encounters. Moreover, the function that perception serves cannot be an afterthought. Perceiving is *for* acting, so the story of perception should include, inextricably, the story of acting (see Chapter 9).

To truly embrace the circumstances of perceiving, there also needs to be a shift in the way we approach what properties are perceived. In classical approaches to visual perception, the variables that Fred's eye and brain were trying to copy were almost exclusively variables that were borrowed from classical mathematics and physics—in particular *Euclidean* geometry and *Newtonian* physics. They were objective facts about the world or the light independent of Fred or any other context (e.g., distance, height, angle). When the story of perception focuses on those properties, the input *is* ambiguous. The exact size or distance is not extractable from a flat retinal image.

The ecological shift is to focus on an entirely different class of properties, ones that are organism- and behavior-relevant (see Figure 3.5). While it may seem bizarre that these more complex properties are unambiguously perceivable when the less complex ones are not, this is exactly the assumption that the ecological approach makes (see Chapter 5).

In order to perceive these organism- and behavior-relevant properties, we also have to allow the organisms to engage in something the traditional approaches saw as a *problem*: movement. In the traditional approach, the movement of objects and of the perceiver in the world was something that needed to be fixed or solved (or disallowed!). Identifying any particular property of an object—shape, for example—required a static image. Then, once that property was identified on the retinal image in a static glimpse, a perceiver could compare that property to the property identified on the retinal image in the *previous* static glimpse and decide whether the object had moved since then.

This explanation runs into a number of problems, not the least of which is that the eye (and, to a lesser extent, the animal) is constantly moving. The ecological approach suggests that movement is not a problem—it is a way of exploring the world and revealing information. As far as perception goes, movement is the feature, not the bug.

Consider the concern about size perception. When Fred is viewing the tree in a static glimpse, he runs into the problem demonstrated in Figure 1.5: the tree could be of many

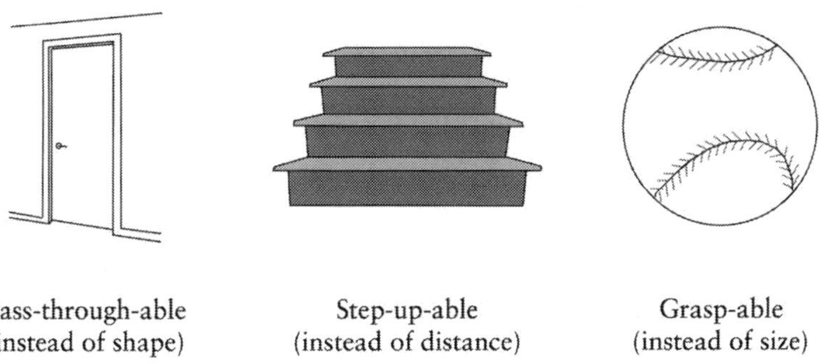

Figure 3.5 The ecological approach studies organism-relevant properties (like affordances) instead of geometry.

different sizes and distances. If perception is *not* of a series of static glimpses but *instead* an extended and continuous process that unfolds over time, then Fred's movement will *reveal information* about the tree. If he moves forward, there will be an expansion of the structured light reflecting from the tree, and he will see less of what is behind the tree as it will be obscured (or *occluded*) by that expansion (see Figure 3.6). The texture of the grass will flow outward from the point toward which Fred is moving, with some of the texture moving out of his field of view as he walks past it (see Chapter 6). This very particular pattern of changing optical structure could have only happened in one situation and one situation only. Consequently, as Fred moves, the relative size and position of the tree are unambiguously specified.

In the language of the ecological approach to perception, we would say that Fred's movement has revealed *invariants*. That is, exploration through movement is what allows Fred to differentiate between those things that change as he moves (the *exact* pattern of stimulation on the eye at any given moment) from those that *don't* (*how* that stimulation is changing as he moves *given the relationship between him and the tree*). Movement allows for a distinction between variants and *invariants*.

There is a special term in science to describe something that happens the same way regardless of circumstances or contexts—a law. The law of gravity, for example, is invariant over circumstances or context. It applies on Earth, on the moon, and in Fred's living room. It applies when Fred drops a dinner plate or when Fred trips over his roller skates. In the case of perception, a particular relationship between Fred and the tree *lawfully structures* the stimulation pattern that he encounters (see Ecological Assumption 7).

Rather than focusing on the varying size of the (probably nonexistent) retinal image of the tree, the ecological approach focuses on the invariant information generated when Fred explores his environment. The relationship between Fred and his environment (which includes his type of exploration, his body, the ways he can interact with that environment, etc.) is going to lawfully generate information for him to detect. That information, in turn, will uniquely specify the particular relationship between Fred and his environment (see Figure 3.7).

Figure 3.6 As Fred moves toward the tree (*top*), there is an expansion of the light reflecting from the tree from Fred's view (*bottom*).

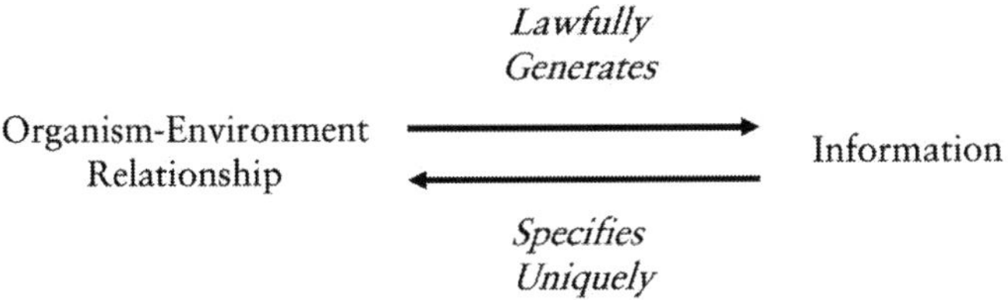

Figure 3.7 Ecological Law: the organism-environment relationship lawfully generates information which, in turn, specifies that relationship uniquely.

A great deal is left to be unpacked about the exact way the information is generated and how the environment might be specified (and that is the focus of multiple chapters in this book), but let's take a moment to appreciate the strategy. Rather than starting from the assumption that the stimulation is bad and/or ambiguous and trying to find strategies to *fix* it, James Gibson (1979/2015), the scientist who founded the ecological approach, made a bold assertion: the stimulation is *not* bad, *not* impoverished. Described appropriately, the stimulation is *good*, and the stimulation is *rich and unambiguous*.

If Gibson is right (and we think that he *is*), then many, if not all, of the problems posed by the traditional approach simply fall away. Those problems are entirely predicated on the notion that bad stimulation has to be fixed and enriched with meaning, and we have already outlined how that leads to difficulties (see Chapters 1 and 2). Even if fixing and enriching a bad input isn't an impossible task (and it feels like it *is*), it is certainly a very difficult one. Poor Fred is left unable to even identify the apple without complex statistical inference, let alone reach for it and eat it.

If, instead, we take Gibson's assertion of the unambiguous stimulation seriously, Fred's problem takes on an entirely different character. First, we would not have to worry about fixing the image: meaningful information is directly obtainable by active exploration. We would also not have to worry about explaining the abilities of an intelligent central executive because there would be *no need* for one in a system that merely *detects* information rather than *computes* it. That is, Fred would need to be a *detector* but not a *detective*.

A system that computes meaning requires a thinking entity to do the computations (or to set up computations that can be run automatically as the need arises). A system that detects information can do so without such intervention. For example, take a mercury thermometer—it does not compute or infer the temperature; the mercury expands and contracts as a direct response to a change in temperature in a lawful and reproducible way.

If the stimulation is unambiguous, then there is no need for any elaboration or representations. This allows for the perception of the world to be direct instead of indirect (see Figure 2.4). In addition to the other advantages, this is much more in keeping with Fred's lived experience: he is aware of the *world*, not of his *sensations*.

A Change in the Variables

In Chapter 1, we were explicit about the (often implicit) assumptions made in the study of perception. Those assumptions led to a choice of variables (that is, a choice of *degrees of freedom*) that ultimately *require* elaboration and interpretation because they are, themselves, inherently meaningless to the organism. Just as we were thoughtful about those assumptions, it is time to be thoughtful about the variables.

The traditional approach is built on the foundation that the retinal image is ambiguous about classic geometric and physics-based variables. As we have hinted at, a big part of why the input seemed to be impoverished was that the variables that had been chosen were relevant to mathematics or physics but perhaps not relevant to *organisms*. As (Nobel Laureate in Physics) Steven Weinberg (1983) said, "you can choose whatever degrees of freedom you like . . . but if you use the wrong ones, you'll be sorry" (p. 16).

The historical predecessor to the Helmholtzian approach to perception was the psychophysics of 19th-century German psychologists Gustav Fechner and Ernst Weber. Their research attempted to objectively describe the relationship between stimulation patterns (borrowed from classical mathematics and physics) and the sensory experience of the perceiver.

For example, they investigated *thresholds* (how much light is needed before we can sense it?) and *just noticeable differences* (how much of a *change* in light does there need to be before we notice it?), both of which focused on properties of light (e.g., wavelength or amplitude) that were meaningful to *physics* but not necessarily meaningful to their *participants*. And that's fine if we're just trying to understand the limits of our sensory physiology! But if we are trying to understand meaningful perceptual *experience*, like Fred's perception of an available snack, then using language that is *unrelated* to that experience is probably shortsighted. Nevertheless, by the time the traditional approach got its boots on, the language of perception was being conceived entirely in terms of Newtonian mechanics and Euclidean geometry.

To understand how the variables of classical physics and geometry are unrelated to experience, let's join Fred and his physicist friend, Bob, as they examine an ice cube melting on the counter. To Bob, when the block of ice melts, there is a story of conservation to be told. The water in the ice did not cease to exist—because matter can neither be created nor destroyed—but instead is just converted to a liquid state. Bob might even talk to Fred about heat energy, possibly even diffusion.

While Fred might find those lessons in physics interesting, they are not related to the experience he is having. For Fred, the ice cube is gone. His drink is not going to get the cooling he was hoping for, and now he has to clean his counter. Do you see the problem? Fred sure does—it's all over his counter! There is no way for the language of Bob's classical physics to be translated into the language of Fred's everyday experience. We need to stop using the language of physicists and mathematicians and start using the language of organisms!

A focus on the wrong variables is largely responsible for the mischaracterization of the stimulation as ambiguous. If we persist in treating *light as such* as the stimulus, we will never be able to get to our stated goal of explaining how Fred and other animals succeed in performing everyday behaviors without resorting to representations, computations, and a central executive.

Properties of light, such as wavelength and amplitude, are what the field of ecological psychology calls lower-order variables in that they are microscopic physical properties. In the Helmholtzian account, we are tasked with constructing meaning (macroscopic properties of experience) out of the lower-order variables—much the same way we could compute the area of a rectangle by measuring its length and width and multiplying. Length and width are lower-order; area is higher-order.

From the lower-order variables of wavelength and amplitude, Fred is somehow supposed to compute information about a snack. The problem is that the lower-order variables bear no resemblance to the higher-order variables that Fred actually cares about! They are not the same language. The somewhat nonobvious solution is to *ignore* the lower-order variables and focus on the higher-order ones as the *starting point*. That is, to assume that we perceive meaning *directly* by means of higher-order variables. This is a difficult concept to get one's head around when the focus has been on lower-order variables for so long. After all, how would we measure the area of a rectangle if not by measuring the length and width and then multiplying?

To appreciate the shift, a concrete example might be helpful. In 1854,[2] the Swiss mathematician Jacob Amsler invented a tool called a polar planimeter (Eggers, 2020). It is an entirely mechanical (meaning no electricity, no internal computer, just gears, wheels, and dials) tool for measuring the area of irregular shapes (see Figure 3.8). To use the planimeter, the fixed pole is kept stationary, and the index is moved around the perimeter of the figure. The measuring roller mechanically responds to the movement over the paper and the angle of the tracer arm to the pole arm, and the area of the shape is displayed on the roller. Or in other words, by virtue of its construction, the tool measures area directly, *not* by computing it out of other measurements.

The polar planimeter does not and *cannot measure length and width*. Appreciate that for a moment! This tool, which directly measures area, is *not capable* of measuring the lower-order variables that we would use to *compute* area. If we extend this metaphor to Fred and his tree, the ecological approach maintains that Fred is like the polar planimeter—capable of detecting a higher-order variable directly without relying on (indeed, *without even being able to* detect) lower-order variables (see Runeson, 1977, for a more extensive and humorous application of this metaphor).

In fact, if you were to *try* to use a polar planimeter to measure lower-order variables, you would discover quite quickly that it was terrible at doing so—much like Fred proves to be terrible at perceiving the lower-order variables used by the traditional approach.

The traditional approach is fond of pointing at illusions such as the Beuchet chair as examples of perceptual incompetence (and proof that elaboration is needed). If, instead, we consider higher-order variables as the appropriate level at which to study perception, we realize that we are *excellent* at detecting what we need in order to achieve our everyday goals (see Chapter 12 for more on so-called illusions).

So what should the language of perception be? What is the "area" equivalent in perception? The ecological approach maintains that the variables should be rooted in activity—which is what perception is *for*. When we talk about Fred and the tree, we should not be focused on the wavelength of the light or the height of the tree or the exact shape of the apple. We should instead ask: Can Fred walk across this field? Does the field *afford walking on*? Can Fred reach the apple? Does the apple *afford reaching*? Can Fred grasp the apple? Does the apple *afford grasping*? In short, we should be asking about *walk-on-able, reachable*, and *graspable*. Gibson (1979/2015) called these *affordances* and argued that they should be the primary variables of perception (see Figure 3.5).

Chapter 5 goes into detail on the concept of affordances, and Chapters 6–8 describe how those affordances are specified by information in light, vibration patterns in the air, and

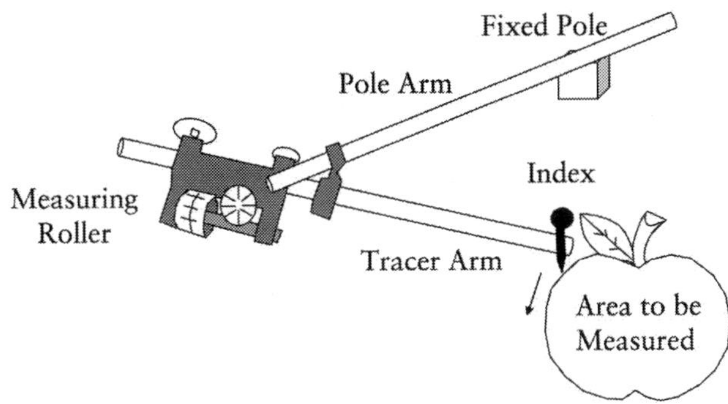

Figure 3.8 The polar planimeter: the index is used to trace around shapes and the measuring roller directly measures the area of the shape.

pressure on the skin and muscles, so we won't go into too much detail here. However, there is one more important point that needs to be made explicit regarding the variables of perception: *the medium is not the message*. Or in other words, what we perceive is *not light*; it is whether the apple can be grasped. What we perceive is *not sound*; it is the layout of surfaces. What we perceive is *not pressure on the skin or muscles*; it is the usability of a tool. Focusing on light, sound, and skin pressure distracts from the relevant information.

Right now, you are reading this book. Whether you are reading it on paper or on a screen, what you are attending to is not paper, ink, pixels, or light waves. You are reading the *content* and (we hope) gaining new information about the world of perceptual theory. Trying to understand perception by looking at light waves would be roughly equivalent to trying to understand your reading experience by looking at the chemical makeup of the ink. *The medium is not the message.*

Box 3.2 Light Is Invisible

Although it is going to seem radical to say so, particularly given the stress earlier in this chapter on the properties of light (see Box 3.1), we are now going to argue (as many ecological theorists have) that light, as such, is not visible. We never see light. We see illuminated surfaces (Gibson, 1979/2015).

Argument 1: Unstructured Light Is Not Perceived

Fred takes his friend Karen and her son Bill to the movies. Bill has the typical attention span of a four-year-old and starts looking around the theater during the film. He looks up and wonders aloud where the movie is?[3] Fred follows his gaze and realizes that Bill is referring to the fact that the projector at the rear of the theater is visible, the image on the screen opposite the projector is visible, but the space in-between appears dark. The light from the projector is streaming through that space but not visible to Bill or Fred.

What Fred and Bill are encountering is the fact that the light traveling through the air is not visible. Only the source of the light (the projector) and the light reflected off the screen (the illuminated surface) can be perceived.

Here is another example, borrowed from Carello and Turvey (2020; see also Zajonc, 1993): imagine two astronauts in space. Space is *absolutely filled* with light—there are trillions of stars in addition to our own (the sun) producing light, which travels through space until it hits an object. Or in other words, our astronauts are *swimming* in a sea of light traveling in all directions. But space appears dark. It is only when the astronauts look at each other (or at the moon, or at their spacecraft) that they are able to perceive anything. Just like Fred and Bill, they can see the source of the light (the stars) and the objects the light reflects off (the other astronaut, the moon, the spacecraft) but not the light traveling through the air.

If we were able to see light *as such*, then the light above Bill and Fred's heads in the theater (or the light the astronauts are swimming in, or the light that Fred is swimming in in the field near the apple tree) should be visible to those observers. But it is not. As Carello and Turvey (2020) put it, "with regard to the triad of *that which illuminates, that which is illuminated*, and *illumination as such* . . . they did not see *illumination as such*" (p. 60).

Argument 2: Stimulation Does Not Necessarily Lead to Perception

No one is making the argument that light is not necessary for visual perception. This is obviously false. After all, you can't see a damn thing in the dark![4] The argument being made is that light *in and of itself* is not what is *perceived*. There is a difference between the response of rod and cone cells and perception by the organism. It is entirely possible for the cells of the retina to be maximally stimulated and for the organism to see nothing.

The last time Fred went sailing, he got caught in a dense fog. It was late enough in the morning, and the sun was bright enough that it lit up the fog. Although Fred could see the deck of the boat beneath his feet, when he looked out across the water, all he could see was homogenous whiteness. He could not see the shore, the water, anything! In that case, Fred's retina was stimulated, but he was unable to perceive anything. Visual perception requires not just light but structured light (see Chapter 6). It turns out that you can't see a damn thing in the bright either[5]!

The story of Fred in the fog is an example of Metzger's (1930) *Ganzfeld* (see also Gibson & Waddell, 1952; Gibson, 1966; and Carello & Turvey, 2020). The same effect can be produced by cutting a Ping-Pong ball in half and attaching it in front of the eye—the illumination becomes uniform, and perception becomes impossible.

To put it plainly, *the medium is not the message*. Just because the rods and cones are stimulated by light does not mean that what the organism attends to is the light *as such*.

A Change in the Assumptions

Just as we were explicit about the assumptions that went into the traditional theories of perception, we need to be similarly explicit about the assumptions of the ecological approach. While some of what follows might be repetitive with and implied by the previous sections, it is worth stating each assumption plainly.

Ecological Assumption 1: The world actually exists (realism).

We spent enough time on this assumption in the past two chapters. Suffice it to say, it never does us any good to assert that the world doesn't exist, so we might as well insist that it does.

Ecological Assumption 2: All knowledge is gained from experience (empiricism).

The alternative to the idea of the *tabula rasa* is unsupportable—starting with any knowledge or gaining knowledge through anything other than experience leads to spooky circumstances and appeals to mechanisms that cannot exist (such as the transmission of situation-specific knowledge through DNA which is not what DNA does; see Chapter 16).

Moreover, as an added side benefit, if all knowledge is gained from experience, then it puts scientists in the position of being able to unpack the nature of experience (which is observable) in order to understand knowledge. Empiricism lets us do science! This isn't a good enough reason to make an assumption on its *own*, but it is a nice bonus.

The only thing that sets this assumption apart from previous incarnations is that the ecological version broadens what is meant by knowledge and by experience. Knowledge is gained from experience, but experience begins before birth and is shaped by the constraints of the ecological niche and the organism (see Chapters 2 and 10). Knowledge includes any changes in that relationship.

Ecological theorists are vigilant about disallowing accidental slips in the application of the empiricist message. When an animal performs a so-called species-typical behavior without having the (obvious) opportunity to observe or practice this behavior, we are unwilling to call it an instinct in the manner of Wundt or Lorenz (Hamlin, 1897; see Box 2.2). We look, instead, to circumstances of prenatal development, nonobvious experiences, and constraints that are similar across the species that might give rise to those behaviors (cf. Miller, 1997; Wagman & Miller, 2003; see Chapter 4).

Ecological Assumption 3: Organisms are *active*, not *passive*.

As we pointed out in Chapter 2, movement and exploration are essential features of life. Traditional theories often rely on a perfectly still organism—a fixed eye in an immobile body. In fact, huge swaths of the physiological research on the visual system relied on *paralyzing* the muscles of the eye in order to maintain that stillness (e.g., Hubel & Wiesel, 1962).

Those results were then applied without alteration or modification to understand the daily perceptual achievements of humans. But this is not remotely realistic! Organisms are always active. They are always moving. An organism that is not moving is either asleep or dead (see Figure 3.9). Assuming perfect stillness as a prerequisite for perception puts theorists in the unenviable position of explaining a situation that literally never happens and *then* having to apply that explanation to the *reality* of dynamic life. No thanks!

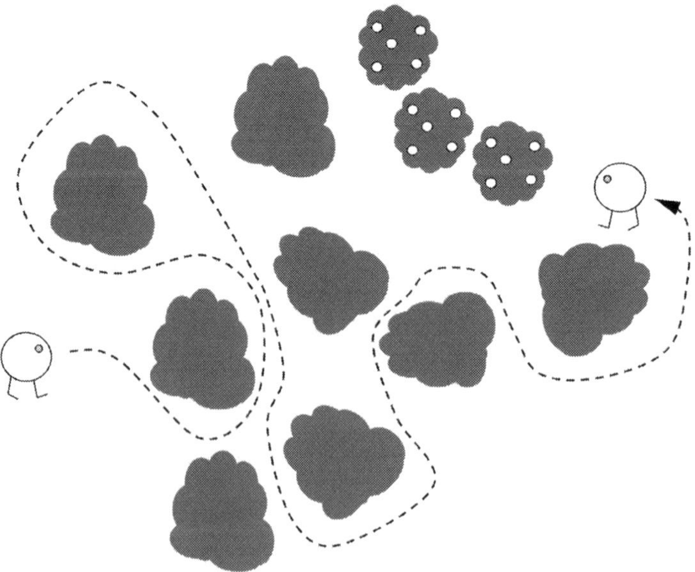

Figure 3.9 Fred's movements (top view) in search of the apple tree he knows is in this forest somewhere. Animals do not passively wait for stimulation—they *seek out* circumstances that will fulfill their needs.

The assumption of activity allows for different types of optical information that are simply not available in a static image. The Beuchet chair illusion only persists if the observer stays still—even a small movement reveals the unusual layout of objects and surfaces and the actual sizes and distances of the objects occupying the space. Movement is what allows for the distinction between variants and *invariants*. Movement is not a problem to be overcome; it is the feature, not the bug.

The assumption of activity carries with it a secondary—but no less important—implication: perception is *for action*. Fred is hungry and is trying to find food. He is exploring the environment and will eventually move in the direction of the apple and guide it to his mouth. The ecological approach stresses that the understanding of perception cannot be divorced from what perception is for.

This shift from passive receiving to active obtaining is part of the logic underpinning the shift in variables from lower-order to higher-order. It is what dictates *what type* of higher-order variables we investigate as well. It is not enough that we look for already meaningful variables, they must be ones related to the possibility of action.

Ecological Assumption 4: Causality is complex and nonlinear.

As we already covered in Chapters 1 and 2, local direct causality—while a pervasive explanation in science—is not the only possible way to look at how situations unfold (see Figure 2.3). And strict adherence to it leads to thorny problems as well as an oversimplification of the complex nature of living systems.

Local causality is what led perceptual theorists to examine light waves instead of the changing optical structure array (see Chapter 6) and affordances (see Chapter 5). It is what led to the search for an unnecessary copy of the world inside of the organism and all the issues that this entailed. It is also what led to stepwise and linear explanations of human development and behavior (see Chapter 10) that do not match up with the actual behavior of developing humans.

Embracing a different kind of causality—complex, nonlocal, nonlinear causality—will allow us to sidestep all of those issues. The problem, of course, is that this type of causality is a lot more difficult to understand! Many more factors need to be taken into account, and behavior starts to look a lot messier through that lens. In Chapter 14, we offer a way of looking at nonlinear causality that allows for the prediction of behavior even in a complex system.

Ecological Assumption 5: The animal-environment system is the fundamental unit of analysis.

In Chapter 2, we discussed two types of dualism: (1) conscious mind versus unconscious central executive and (2) mind versus body. We rejected both dualisms as unsupportable. One final dualism remains that must be discarded: the animal versus its environment. One of the outcomes of strict adherence to the notion of direct causality is that the animal (and its behavior) is somehow separate from the environment (and the cause of that behavior). We argue that the animal cannot be understood without the context of the environment and that the environment (more aptly called the *niche*) cannot be defined without the animal. They are inseparable (Turvey, 2019).

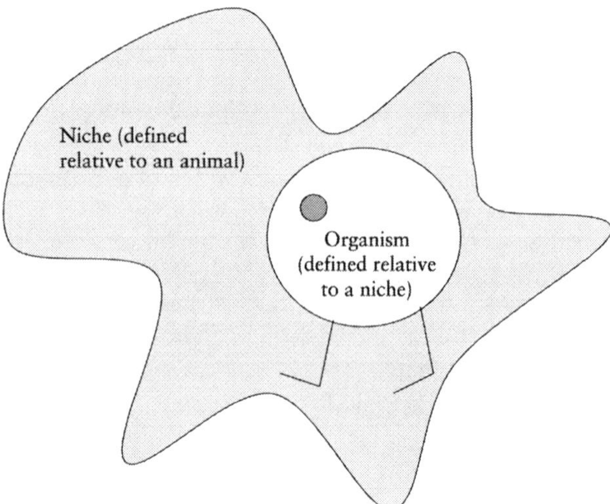

Figure 3.10 Fred cannot be logically removed from his environmental niche. The environment cannot be defined without Fred.

Look again at Figure 2.1. In order to define those parts of the environment that are relevant, you would have to decide if you were talking about the worm or the deer. In order to define what the organism was doing or what behavior it might exhibit, you would have to look at the tree or the twig. The definition of a niche includes the animal; the existence of the animal necessitates the niche (see Figure 3.10). They are part of the *same system*.

The embrace of a singular animal-environment system might be considered the most fundamental tenet of the ecological approach. The very name of the theory comes from the insistence that to divorce the animal from its environment is to destroy the lawful relationships that make perception possible. Perception *is* the reciprocity between animal and environment (Lombardo, 1987).

Ecological Assumption 6: Perception is direct (no mediation).

The separation of the animal and the environment and the insistence on local causality necessarily lead to the inclusion of a copy in the theory of perception. This has created a number of difficulties, not least of which is the invocation of an unconscious central executive in charge of understanding the representation of the world on our behalf.

But there is more to discarding the intrusion of a representation than just banishing that specter—representations remove us from the world! They sit in-between us and reality. In this system, we are never in contact with the world, just our *interpretation* of our *copy* of the world (see Figure 2.4).

In the traditional approach, this was not as much of a problem. The animal and the environment were kept logically separate, so interposing a copy was not as much of an issue. You could even make the argument that removing the organism from the environment *required* an indirect perception. However, in the ecological approach, the animal-environment system is the fundamental unit of analysis. Allowing something in-between them is in violation of that assumption.

And there's more here. No such separation exists (even in traditional accounts) between us and our actions and between our actions and the environment (Turvey, 2013). Given that perception and action are two sides of the same coin, it is paradoxical to have one (perception) mediated by a copy but not the other (behavior).

And copies cause such trouble! If there is another option, why include such interference? Why include a representation of the world when the world is its own best model?

The ecological approach explicitly bans representations. We take this as a first principle: there is no need for representations, assuming them leads to unsolvable problems, and so we will not do so. The copy was assumed as a natural consequence of local causality. We have replaced local causality with complex nonlinear causality, so the *need* for the copy has vanished. It still remains to offer an alternative.

Ecological Assumption 7: The animal-environment relationship lawfully structures information.

In order to banish the representation altogether, there must be no need for interpretation. That is, part of the problem with assuming the necessity of copy of the world was that the only copy our systems seemed to make was *bad!* It was an imperfect, ambiguous mess that needed to be fixed in order to be used. The elaborate series of computations was *necessary* in order for us to navigate our surroundings so long as the copy was lacking in the basic information needed to do so.

If the stimulation of the senses is in any way imperfect, ambiguous, or not what we need, then there *has to be* some amount of "fixing" taking place. If there is fixing, then there is a difference between the input and the awareness—a de facto representation of the world. Therefore, in order to eliminate the representation altogether, the stimulation *must be as good as it needs to be already*.

The ecological approach deals with this by insisting that the stimulation (the patterns in the energy) are *lawfully generated*. What this means is that a given relationship between animal and environment always generates a particular pattern of stimulation (what we are calling information) regardless of context or circumstance. They are invariant.

What we mean by this is illustrated in Figure 3.7. The animal-environment relationship generates information in a lawful manner. Following that logic, the information will have a unique (i.e., one-to-one) relationship with the particular relationship between animal and environment. In that case, the information is *both necessary and sufficient* to allow the animal to successfully perform a goal-directed behavior.

The traditional approach effectively stripped the copy of all meaning and then scrambled to add it back after the fact. We assert that the meaning is already in the organism-environment relationship and therefore does not need to be recovered. In this way, perception is not the processing of a stimulation, it is the detecting of information.

Unlike most assumptions, we do not take this as fact without proof. We assume that this is what we should find, but the daily work in the field is about identifying the lawful patterns in the stimulation. Chapters 6–8 detail some of the work in that direction.

Ecological Assumption 8: Variables of perception should be action-based, not physics-based.

In our search for lawful information, one of the most important moves was to change what we were examining. The classical approaches focused on *light*, but as we have discussed, light is not perceivable as such.

When the focus was on light-related variables—such as wavelength and amplitude—the discovery was that we are not particularly good at copying (and hence, perceiving) those variables. We don't always notice light if it's too dim, can't always tell the difference between that wavelength and this, and can't always sense a change in brightness. We are like the polar planimeter being asked to measure length and width—being used for a function for which we were not designed.

As long as the variables remain based in classical mathematics or physics, then there will always be ambiguity in the stimulation. Only by changing the variables of perception can the previous assumption (Ecological Assumption 7) make sense. There is no way to make lower-order variables lawful, and there is also no reason to assume that lower-order variables should be what we perceive. And there's plenty of reason to assume that higher-order variables would be a better fit.

This assumption carries with it two guiding intuitions. First, psychology, and in particular the study of perception and action, should have its own variables. Physics doesn't borrow from chemistry, and biology doesn't borrow from astronomy—if there is some overlap, that is merely because there is overlap in their phenomena of interest. Every science needs its own language and its own variables, and the science of perception is no exception. Second, the variables of interest for perceptual theorists should reflect the *purpose* of perception: action. We act to perceive; we perceive to act (Gibson, 1979/2015).

In the context of Ecological Assumption 7, Ecological Assumption 8 asserts that if we change the focus of our investigations to variables that already have meaning (see Figure 3.5), the information encountered by the organism will be lawful.

Ecological Assumption 9: There is no central executive.

Of all the mechanisms suggested by the traditional approach, the central executive is perhaps the most pervasive and insidious. The traditional approach absolutely required it, but as Chapters 1 and 2 made clear, once an unconscious central executive is part of the story, things come apart rather quickly.

The previous assumptions (most notably 6 and 7) eliminate the need for the central executive in the ecological perspective on perception. No unconscious processing is needed in a system that relies on lawfully structured stimulation patterns. Much like how the polar planimeter can measure area without computation, Fred can perceive the graspability of the apple without complex mental calculations.

But we want to go one step further: not just eliminate the *need* for the central executive, but refuse to assume its existence *at any point*. It is both *unnecessary and insufficient*. As ecological psychology has expanded beyond the study of perception (see Chapters 4, 9–17), this concept has proven to be the most difficult to eradicate. The central executive is, explicitly and implicitly, *all over* the study of psychology. We nevertheless consider it a worthy endeavor to *try* to eliminate it, for all the reasons that have been illustrated already.

These nine assumptions, taken together, form the core tenets of the ecological perspective. There are still more guiding intuitions (see Chapter 4), but the foundation of the ecological program starts here.

A Change in the Questions

Perhaps the most important insight of Gibson was that it was not enough to come up with new answers to the old questions. To get a better, more coherent story of perception, we needed to change the nature of the *questions asked.*

The assumptions of the Helmholtzian program led directly to the questions its scientists asked. They assumed a poor copy that needed to be fixed. They assumed that cues and rules for combining them were used in that fixing. And so the questions of the traditional program were as follows: What are the cues? What are the rules? How are the cues and rules combined?

Similarly, the assumptions of the ecological program will lead directly to the questions its scientists ask. We assume that the stimulation is lawful and based on the needs of the organism. And so our questions are as follows: What is perception for, and what does that imply about what the variables should be? How is information lawful? How do organisms *detect* information? How do organisms *use* information to guide behavior? How can poor Fred not only notice the apple but grasp it and guide it to his mouth?

Notes

1. A pigment called anthocyanin is deposited as part of the ripening process; this pigment is responsible for the change in color as the apple ripens.
2. Although Johann Martin Hermann invented the *first* mechanical planimeter in 1814, Amsler's invention was the first that was practical and accurate.
3. Bill's experience is based on a true story of the first author's remarkably observant four-year-old son. This story was also referenced by Carello and Turvey (2020) in their argument about the invisibility of light.
4. This is known as Liebowitz's first law, named after the influential vision scientist Herschel Leibowitz.
5. Call this Blau and Wagman's first law.

4 What Is Ecological Theory?

Let's return to the situation that began our story, but this time with some consideration of the broader context. Fred is out for a walk in the forest near his house. As he walks, he realizes that he is hungry. He remembers that there are a couple of apple trees in this forest but can't remember exactly where, so he starts wandering around, hoping to find them. Eventually, he comes into a clearing and is delighted to see one of the trees, just as he remembered it! Fred crosses the field, plucks an apple, and eats it.

The discussions of the past three chapters have not given us a comprehensive understanding of how Fred accomplishes this task, but now we at least have a sense of how we might move forward with a scientific investigation of how he does so (which is what we will do in the next section of chapters). Additionally, while seeing and doing might *feel* simple, we hope that—in attempting to understand Fred's experience—we have at least made the case that understanding it scientifically is far more complex than it feels to *perform* it.

During the past three chapters, we have, essentially, covered the historical progress from the inception of perceptual theory (when it was really sensory theory) to the ecological shift made by Gibson in the mid to late 20th century. We've come a long way! We still have a great deal of ground to cover and *so many* everyday behaviors in Fred's life to explain, but it's worth taking a step back and appreciating the overall strategy of the ecological approach.

The assumptions outlined in Chapter 3 are applicable to phenomena other than just Fred's experience with recognizing an apple. Once the work was done outlining the flaws in the traditional assumptions for the study of perception, ecological psychologists realized that the same assumptions were everywhere! The central executive shows up in theories of cognition, linear causality is championed in development, and lower-order variables invade theories of action.

It's a little bit like the time Fred deep-cleaned and reorganized his kitchen and then realized the rest of his house looked disorganized in comparison. Fred understood the situation did not call for moving to a new house (or in the case of our endeavor, the situation does not call for throwing out centuries of work in cognition, development, and action). But it might be time to rethink how the house is organized (or in our case, what this work means for the understanding of everyday behaviors). Importantly, Fred can use the same strategies and tools to clean his living room that he used in the kitchen—a top to bottom deep clean! And we can do the same in our effort to redescribe psychological processes. We can, for example, strive to eliminate the central executive, push for a more expansive understanding of causality, and turn away from lower-order variables in *all* explanations of *all* everyday (and not-so-everyday) behavior.

If we may stretch the metaphor to its breaking point, as Fred cleans the rest of his house, he might also find that there are fundamental similarities to his approach to cleaning each room—guiding intuitions for how cleaning ought to progress and a common set of tools for getting the job done. The same applies to our ecological endeavor. Our field has guiding

DOI: 10.4324/9781003145691-5

intuitions that we follow and a comparable set of tools that we use—organizational patterns that recur in various fields and subfields.

The goal of this chapter is, first, to expand on the assumptions of the ecological approach outlined in the previous chapter and the implications they have for psychological processes more diverse than the act of seeing and eating an apple; second, to outline the guiding intuitions that most ecological theorists use in applying and developing the program; and finally, to provide a brief roadmap to the rest of this book so that readers might find their way to the topics that most interest them.

Ecological Assumptions: More Than Just Apple Picking

One of the most profound and daring things Gibson did when he created the ecological approach was to stop trying to come up with better answers to the same old questions. His goal was, instead, to change the nature of the *questions themselves*. His argument (which we have outlined in the previous three chapters) was that the questions being asked were based on flawed assumptions. No matter *what* answer was posed, it would lack explanatory power. It would be like building a house on a foundation of sand. The house might stand for a while, but eventually, it would give way.

The foundational assumptions of perception that Gibson (and others) rejected are, unfortunately, foundational to a number of other areas of psychology as well. If we are going to assume, for example, that the central executive is problematic enough to be banished in theories of seeing and doing, then it must be so *always*. The theoretical problems raised by it will not disappear simply because we are discussing a different psychological process—for example, *remembering* where the apple trees are rather than seeing and picking an apple.

Although its roots are in perception (and that is where the bulk of the resulting research has been done), the ecological perspective is intended to be applied much more broadly. We see it as a way to redescribe a *number* of areas of research in the field of psychology. The approach suggests that the same sort of paradigm shift that was made for perception can, and should, be made for those areas as well. Moreover, the shifts in focus require the inclusion of areas of study under the umbrella of psychology that have not previously been so included. We are seeking a true ecological psychology (see Reed, 1996).

In order to ecologize the study of psychology, the assumptions made by ecological theorists in *perception* must be understood as needing to be applied *broadly* and *absolutely*. It does no good to allow nonlocal causality in perception only to disallow it in development. No matter the area of psychology, if someone is interested in applying the ecological perspective (and we believe that they ought to be!), there are a few principles to follow—outlined in the next sections—that will go a long way to that goal (for another take on the same notion, see Michaels & Palatinus, 2014).

It is worth pointing out that ecologizing the different areas of psychology may not always require *as complete* an overhaul as it did in the study of perception—in many cases, it may just require a slight shift in the understanding of the work that has already been done.

Banish the Central Executive

As we have mentioned, eliminating the central executive might be the most thorny and controversial move made by the ecological perspective. The notion of an internal self that organizes thoughts and produces behavior is in nearly every corner of psychology. And it's not hard to see why! After all, we do have a sense that we are sitting behind our own eyes and looking out at the world. It is a compelling notion that we inhabit our bodies like a person inhabiting a house.

Compelling as it is, however, the central executive runs into problems no matter where it arises. The central executive is mired in all of the issues we have discussed up until now: it is either weirdly intelligent (the *loan of intelligence problem*) or can't possibly learn because it can't get feedback or has no particular reason to believe that the stimulations it is receiving come from outside the body (the *outness problem*).

To all of these, we are adding one more issue: the central executive lacks explanatory power (see Figure 4.1). The same issues that plagued the notion of the central executive in perception apply in every area that seeks to *explain* (rather than just *describe*) behavior. In order to *explain* behavior, the suggested cause cannot itself require explanation. If the cause requires explanation, then all you have done is push the problem back a step.

To understand what we mean by this, let's return, once more, to the pool table from Chapter 1. Fred is playing a game against his friend Claudia. She has been beating him rather soundly and has just sunk the eight ball into the corner pocket. Let's say that we want to explain the eight ball's behavior in moving across the table and into the pocket. The closest cause is the white ball hitting and transferring its momentum to the eight ball. But in saying that the white ball is the cause, all we have done is push the question back a step—we still have to explain the white ball's behavior.

The white ball, of course, was moved by the pool stick, and the pool stick by Claudia. But what moved Claudia? If we posit the central executive as the mover of Claudia (which is what is typically done in traditional theories of action at this point, see Chapter 9), then we still have to answer this question: *what moved Claudia's central executive?* All we have done is push the question back a step. (Notice that linear causality is also inherent in this explanation. We'll need to address that as well!)

To achieve *explanation* and not merely *description*, we have to banish the central executive entirely. The ecological perspective maintains that even if we could find a way around the theoretical issues raised by the inclusion of a central executive,[1] the theoretical explanations created *without* it are more coherent and more broadly applicable.

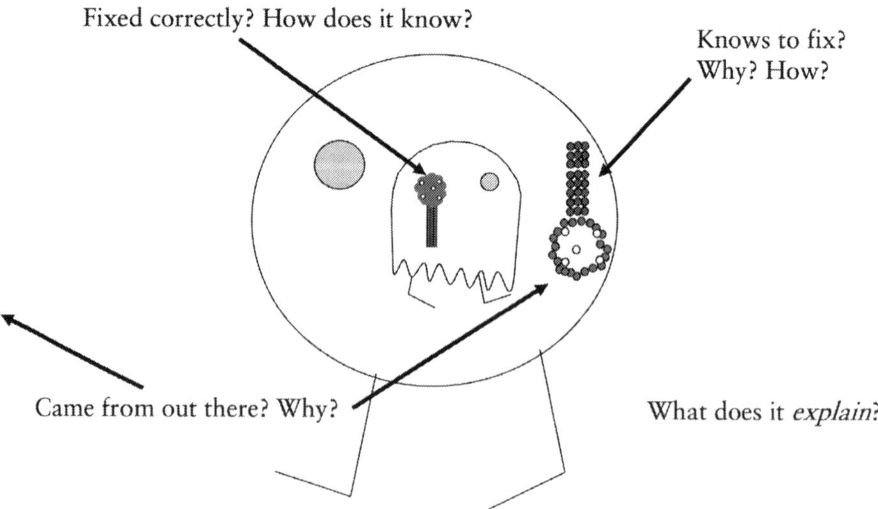

Figure 4.1 The central executive's dilemma: it must first realize the external world is what's causing the stimulation (*outness problem*), realize the stimulation is bad and needs to be fixed and know how to fix it (*loan of intelligence*), and get good feedback on how successful the fix was with no pathway other than the inadequate one. And then, it still doesn't *explain* anything.

Include the Environment as an Integral Part of the Story

One of the assumptions of the ecological perspective is that the animal-environment system must be the fundamental unit of analysis (Ecological Assumption 5). We arrived at this assumption by realizing that there was no principled way to understand the animal without understanding its environment—and there was no principled way to understand an environment without understanding the animal that inhabits it.

This realization does not become any less important when examining other aspects of behavior! Understanding the phenomenon of memory is impossible without understanding *that which is remembered*. Development cannot be understood without understanding the *nested context in which the organism is developing*.

When theories in these other areas of psychology include an understanding of the environment (and they often do!), it is usually included merely as a factor in a larger equation. For example, some theories of emotion explicitly include the environment as a component of the subjective experience of the animal (see Figure 4.2). So emotion might be understood as physical state (heartbeat, sweating, flushed face) + environment (standing on a rickety bridge over a deep chasm) = feeling (fear). If the environment were different (say, Fred is talking to Carol, his crush), then the feeling might be understood differently (attraction and nervousness).

And while the inclusion of the environment as part of the story is *good*, it would be *better* if the environment were understood as *part* of the organism-environment system from the start. Standing on a rickety bridge is only dangerous for Fred *because he cannot fly*. His particular action capabilities (or lack thereof) constrain the meaning of the event. Fred's crush on Carol is what makes that conversation exciting for him. Fred's emotions when standing on the bridge or talking to Carol are nested within the Fred-bridge or Fred-Carol system.

When we apply the ecological perspective to a given area of psychology, the environment cannot be a factor that is added in or "taken into account" in an ad hoc fashion. It has to be *part* of the system that is trying to be understood.

Figure 4.2 Fear is nested in the Fred-bridge system (because the circumstances afford danger for Fred because of his capabilities), just as nervousness is nested in the Fred-Carol system (because of his crush on her).

Choose the Appropriate Variables

The ecological perspective shifted the focus of the understanding of perceiving *away* from the lower-order variables of Newtonian physics and Euclidean geometry and *to* the macroscopic ecological variables that are relevant to organisms trying to navigate their surroundings in order to perform everyday behaviors (see Chapters 6–8). There are a number of important lessons here that we argue apply to other areas of psychology.

First, it cannot be stated strongly enough that psychology needs its own terminology. We study a different system than the physicist or the chemist or the mathematician, and it is illogical to think that we should use the same language that they do. While the physicist's explanations should be *consistent with* chemistry or mathematics, that is not the same as the explanations being *identical* in each of those fields. Physicists cannot possibly seek to explain the phenomena they study without having created an appropriate language for the variables that only make sense in the context of their science. Friction, momentum, and gravitational force are not reducible to the interactions between molecules, and no one would expect them to be.

Once we acknowledge that psychology needs its own variables, the next step is to have a guiding intuition for what the variables *should be like*. Do we follow a reductionist path, for example? Trying to reduce human behavior or experience to its tiniest elements like the chemists reduced matter to its base components? Plenty of work (the structuralism of early psychologist Edward Titchener, for example) has attempted it! But reductionism is a dead end. As the Gestaltist psychologists pointed out, the whole is different from the sum of its parts.[2]

What the Gestaltists meant by the foregoing is that even if you add the base elements of behavior together, the result is not going to be the same as what an appreciation of the whole might get you. A visual representation of this might be the pointillistic art of Seurat and Signac from the late 1800s/early 1900s. Up close, the art is composed of tiny dots of color. If all you ever measured were those dots of color, there would be no way to gain an appreciation of the meaning expressed in the painting as a whole. Only by stepping back can you see a meaningful macroscopic image (see Figure 4.3).

The ecological perspective argues that all areas of psychology can be treated in the same way. Finding the appropriate scale at which to observe a phenomenon is half the work. If the answer is still ambiguous, you are probably still standing too close. An ecological psychology is not going to run on microscopic lower-order variables.

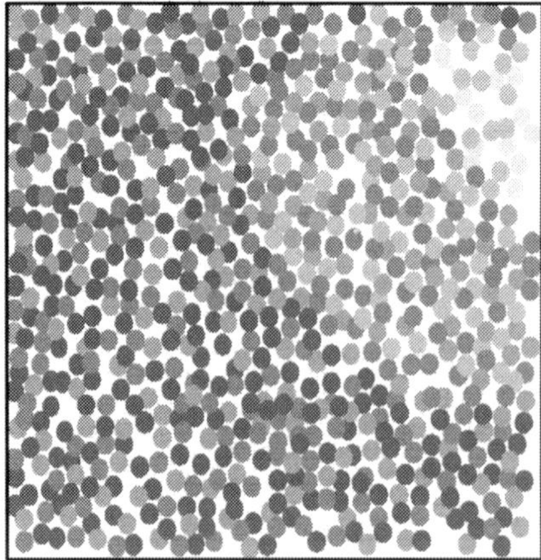

Figure 4.3 When seen too close, the dots of color in a pointillistic painting have no meaning (*left*); when viewed from a different distance, meaning is inherent (*right*).

One of the interesting effects of shifting variables in perception from lower-order physical variables to higher-order, macroscopic, ecological variables was that it also changed the character of organisms as perceivers. In the reductionistic take, we were focused on how bad we were at perceiving. In the ecological view, we are focused on how good we are at it! Rather than finding ambiguity and error in our perceptions, we found invariance and specificity. This is not an accident. Ecological perceptual scientists *purposefully* chose to focus on variables that allow for the remarkable yet everyday successes achieved by every organism.

Evolution (however conceived, see Chapter 15) is a process of survival (of individuals and ultimately of species). Regardless of the organism, they are going to be reasonably good at whatever they need to do to survive because it is impossible to imagine that they would have evolved to be *bad* at fundamental tasks of everyday life. If our goal is to understand the behavior of an organism that is subject to evolutionary pressure, then we have to assume that they are reasonably good at performing the behaviors that keep them alive. Consequently, it makes more sense to build ecological theory out of the many everyday successes rather than the rare (and often contrived) failures.

A focus on an organism's failures in artificial settings[3] can lead to interesting findings, but it is unlikely to lead to an explanation of the everyday successes in behavior in a pragmatically useful way. To do that, the ecological perspective argues, we need to focus on the goal of the behavior and the context of the behavior when it is done well (see Reed, 1996).

So to recap: we need our own variables. The variables *should not* be reductionistic, and they *should not* be based on failures. Instead, the variables *should be* macro-level and *should be* based on *successes*. In the study of perception, we argued that the appropriate variables were action-relevant because the purpose of perception *is action*. A similar argument can be made for the study of every other area of psychology: What is the purpose of the behavior? Why do we develop? Why do we remember? What is the goal of social interaction? The answer to those questions will drive the choice of appropriate variables.

Embrace Nonlocal Causality

If the central executive is the most pervasive issue, local causality is a close second. Scientists have embraced local and linear causality since the mid-16th century. There are a number of advantages to it: for one, it allows for very simple and clean explanations of complex phenomena, and it makes it easy to do science. It is possible to understand the effect of a single variable by keeping all else constant and manipulating the one thing you are examining. But it's a convenience rather than a reality. Linear causality may seem like the rule, but it is actually the exception (Turvey, 2013; see Chapter 14).

The field of statistics has known about the reality of interconnected causality for a long time. Without going into too much detail, there are ways to investigate the interactions among several variables to isolate and remove the effect of a variable you cannot control but that you know has an influence on what you are studying and to account for the variability across subjects—all in an effort to artificially isolate a single cause and a single effect from a multicausal reality.

And all of that would be fine if the scientists performing these simple, clean experiments and implementing the statistics of single causes kept in mind that the experiments and the statistics are *artificially* imposing a singular causality on a multicausal world. As Fred's Uncle Jimmy has always told him: to a person with a hammer, everything looks like a nail. Uncle Jimmy's point is that just because a problem *can* be approached with a hammer (for example, one way to remove an old toilet is to smash it to bits with a hammer) does not make the problem a nail (or the best tool a hammer).

What we are trying to get at is this: just because the tools of local causality have been used to approach the questions of psychology for generations, it does not mean that the phenomena of psychology are *best* described in terms of local, linear causality. And embracing a different causality (and its tools) may yield a clearer understanding as well as new and powerful questions.

Of course, embracing a different kind of causality means embracing a different type of experimentation, different variables, and different types of analyses. It means accepting that causality is complicated and simplifying it is *not the goal*. It also means that there are going to be times when causality is deeply nonobvious (Gottlieb, 1992, 1997, 1999, see Box 4.1).

Box 4.1 Nonobvious Causality

Developmental psychology is one clear example where implementing nonlinear causality will be helpful (see Chapter 10). Gottlieb (1992) pioneered much of the work in this area and coined the phrase "nonobvious causality" when referring to developmental events that have an effect on behavior in an unexpected and seemingly unrelated way.

As Miller (1997) pointed out, there are a number of *obvious* causes for behavior in development. For example, birds that sing regional songs must be exposed to those songs in order to sing them. However, when no obvious causes for a particular behavior could be found, that behavior was often described as innate or instinctual because there does not seem to be an obvious developmental pathway. Put another way, there does not seem to be a linear, local external cause for the behavior, so they call it instinct to avoid the problem.

Miller argued that the more innate or instinctual the behavior *seemed* to be, the more nonobvious the causality would *actually* be. He (and others: see Turvey & Fitzpatrick, 1993; Thelen, 1989; Turvey & Sheya, 2017, Wagman & Miller, 2003, etc.) collected various examples of behavior that has long been thought to be instinctual—somehow prewired, usually in DNA—that turned out to be dependent on some (albeit nonobvious) form of experience.

Some of our favorite examples include the following:

- Squirrel monkeys in the wild are afraid of snakes. It seems to be an instinctual behavior because monkeys in different areas with no contact for generations all exhibit the same fear. However, it turns out that when the monkeys are raised in captivity and are not given live spiders as part of their diet during development, they do not exhibit the same fear. If they *are* given live spiders as part of their diet, they will exhibit the same fear of snakes as their wild counterparts (Masataka, 1994).
- Baby chicks typically pick up and eat mealworms. It seems to be an instinctual behavior; however, when baby chicks are prevented from seeing their feet (either by covering them with cloth or just by painting them black), they will be far less likely to pick up or eat mealworms but instead just stare at them (Wallman, 1979).
- How birds exit the egg during hatching (they twist in a particular direction as they leave the egg) determines if they will be left- or right-footed—and experimentally altering the direction of the hatching twist changes their footedness (Casey & Martino, 2000).
- Spontaneous muscle twitching during prenatal development and during sleep alters the development of the sensorimotor system, specifically the reflex to withdraw from painful stimuli (Petersson et al., 2003), which is in turn responsible for the organization of spinal development (Schouenborg, 2008).
- Altering the temperature of the egg during days 5–8 of the incubation period of quails results in quails that fall more often, even as adults (Belnap, Currea, & Lickliter, 2019).

In addition to being entertaining, these examples demonstrate the point that a focus only on obvious—and by obvious, we mean linear and local—causality of behavior will leave many behaviors unexplainable (except by an appeal to instincts or innateness). Expanding the view and embracing other types of causality not only explains the behavior but also opens up new areas for research.

Ecological Guiding Intuitions

If the previous section outlined the steps that must be taken in order to ecologize a field, this section suggests tools for following those steps. It is not always easy to banish the central executive, and capturing nonlocal causality requires using new tools. Ecological theorists have proposed a variety of other guiding intuitions that shape the kinds of questions we ask in the field.

Not Machines but Systems

In Chapter 2, we introduced the idea of a historical division between the mind and the body (put forth by Descartes, see Box 2.2). This notion (called *dualism*) allowed Descartes to study the body independently from the soul.[4] We rejected this dualism. But Descartes's influence goes a bit further than that. Descartes additionally proposed that the body was best thought of as a *machine*.

Machines have various properties that are compelling when considering a metaphor for studying organisms. For example, in a machine, the parts are able to be studied independently of the whole. Their function *exists* independently of their context. That is, you can take a wheel off a car and understand its function without having to see it in the context of the whole car. It rolls regardless of whether it is attached to an axle. We can also replace any part with an identical part (e.g., change the tire), and the machine will continue to function as before. Moreover, the combination (by simple addition) of the parts is what defines the machine as a whole.

The advantage of this type of thinking is that it would allow scientists to, say, study the function of the heart without having to understand the context in which it beats. This has led to incredible advances in the medical field (for example, organ transplants), but that does not mean the machine metaphor is *correct*—only that it is sometimes *useful*. To paraphrase Box (1976), all models are wrong; some are useful.

To be sure, the machine metaphor *has been useful*, but the answers it gives are not always complete or fully coherent. For example, transplanting a heart is not the same as changing the tire on a car. Even when extreme care is taken to make sure the new heart is as similar to the old one as possible (matching size, blood type, antigens, etc.), it is still the case that the recipient's body might reject the organ. The machine metaphor cannot explain this. My car would never reject a new tire.

It also does not encourage nonlinear, nonlocal thinking about causality. To encourage that type of thinking, we need to change the working model to a *system* instead of a machine. A system is a collection of small, simple elements performing small, simple tasks in response to local constraints and stimuli—and from this collection, sometimes incredibly elaborate and complex (and nonobvious) behavior will emerge.

Take this example: Fred happens to have a large number of metronomes.[5] (Apparently, metronomes are the default gift once you tell people you play the cello.) He sets up a board resting on top of two soup cans on their sides (see Figure 4.4, *left*) and puts three metronomes on top. He starts them at different times and listens to the uncoordinated clicking for a few moments. Slowly at first, but then more and more, the soup cans roll from side to side, and the metronomes synchronize their behavior until all of them are beating at exactly the same time.

Fred's metronomes are a *system*. The board and soup cans are constraints on their behavior that allow the movement of one metronome to affect the others. To keep the metronomes from synchronizing, Fred flips the soup cans on their end. This prevents the cans from rolling, which means the board stays stationary (see Figure 4.4, *right*). The metronomes stay uncoordinated. Or in other words, the way to change the behavior of the metronomes *did not involve changing the metronomes.*

This example illustrates the utility of changing the metaphor we use to investigate behavior: we may uncover new ways of *changing* behavior that could not have been predicted by the machine metaphor. In this way, our first guiding intuition is the most basic: try to understand the phenomenon of interest as a *system* rather than a *machine* (see Turvey, 2019).

Self-Organization (and Flexible Assembly)

We dedicate an entire upcoming chapter (Chapter 16) to the notion of self-organization, but the basic idea is that in order to eliminate the central executive, it is necessary to provide an alternative explanation for behavior. Our argument is that behavior can be self-organized by the elements of the system operating under simple rules and in the context of constraints.

Fred was part of an orchestra when he was in high school. He was a somewhat decent cello player under the direction of Dr. Pick (a somewhat decent director). One day, Dr. Pick was sick during their regular practice time, and rather than let the opportunity for practice pass them by, the group decided to play through the songs a couple of times anyway. They accomplished

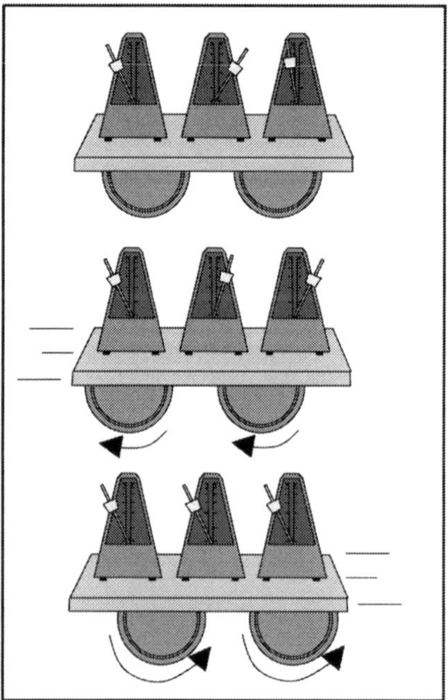

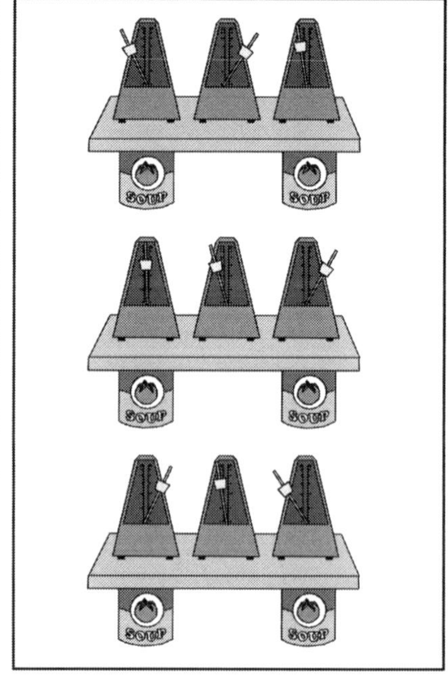

Figure 4.4 When the soup cans are on their side, the board can move back and forth, and the metronomes will synchronize (*left*). Flipping the cans up restricts the movement of the cans and the board, and the metronomes do not synchronize (*right*).

this by listening to the players on either side of them and trying to sync their playing with them. They ended up producing somewhat decent music.

Dr. Pick is like the central executive (see Figure 4.5, *top*). The director can lead the players—with specific baton movements indicating when entrances and silences are supposed to occur. However, as the day Dr. Pick was missing proves, it is possible to create music without such a leader. Care must be taken in setting up the conditions and constraints, but it *is* possible.

Let's say Claudia happened to walk by the practice room on the day Dr. Pick was missing and heard the music through the door. She could be forgiven if she thought Dr. Pick was still there. The behavior being exhibited (music) is complicated enough that it seems like it *has* to be produced by a conductor or central executive, leading the individuals in the room. With no ability to see into the room, Claudia can only guess at the organization.

What the ecological perspective suggests is that Claudia should consider the possibility that there is no conductor in the room (see Figure 4.5, *bottom*). Or in other words, scientists examining complex behavior should consider that the simple elements of the system could follow simple rules, and complex behavior is the result.

On the same day that Dr. Pick was missing, Fred was also supposed to have practice with the select orchestra String Fever. This was a smaller group of the most talented musicians from the regular orchestra and a few members of the percussion section from the band. After the success with self-organizing the regular orchestra, Fred and his group decided to do the same thing with String Fever. It was similarly successful.

Much like Fred and his friends, the elements of a system can be flexibly assembled into groups as needed. Fred can adjust his behavior and act like a part of the larger orchestra, and later the same day, he can join a different group and adjust his behavior accordingly. So, too, can the parts of a system participate in multiple different behaviors.

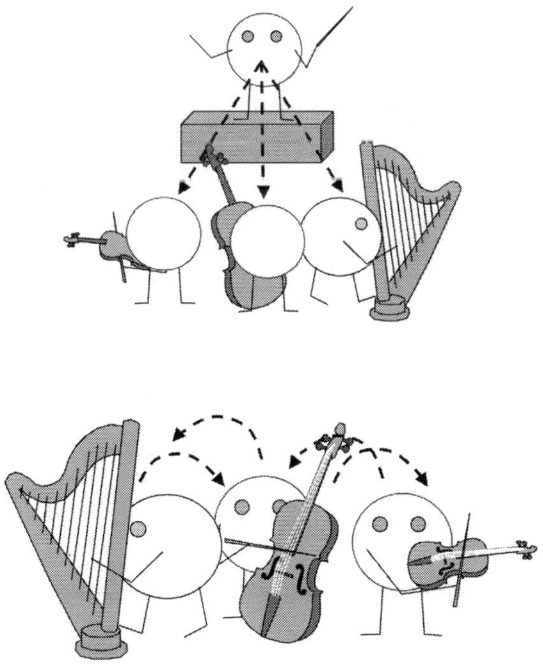

Figure 4.5 When Dr. Pick conducts the orchestra, the orchestra's behavior is dependent on him (*top*); without Dr. Pick, the orchestra self-organizes by each person coordinating with their neighbors (*bottom*).

It would also have been possible for an entirely different group of players (say, the members of the orchestra from a different high school) to perform the same task that Fred and his friends did. In the same way, the same behavior can be performed by different sets of elements within the system.

One of the consequences of considering the body as a machine is a single-function mindset when it comes to understanding parts of the body. There is a sense that if we have found a part of the brain that is involved in, say, memory, then that part of the brain cannot possibly perform any other function. Allowing for flexible, task-specific assembly results in an organism that is better able to adapt to changing circumstances (see Box 11.1).

Hume's Touchstone

In Chapter 2, we examined the fly's eye and how its structure (compound rather than chambered) suggested that theories of perception could not be based on the retinal image. After all, a compound eye does not produce an image of any kind! And it would be quite odd if a fly were capable of the intelligent unconscious inference the traditional view requires to fix that image. This example was part of a broader issue: theories of perception—and psychology more broadly—are remarkably human-centric.

Even leaving aside the sheer arrogance in assuming that the human condition is the only one that needs explaining, not examining other species leaves us open to mistakenly constructing stories of perception that *only* work for humans. Such a human-centric approach would inevitably result (as the retinal image idea did) in having to invent a new story of perception for every type of sensory machinery. Such chaos!

There is a principle called *Occam's razor*, which, put plainly, suggests that the simplest explanation is most likely to be correct.[6] Take, for example, the time that Fred's friends Claire and Jean were home and the Wi-Fi stopped working, the lights went out, and the heater stopped working. Jean suggested that the cable service was interrupted (which explained the Wi-Fi), the bulbs had broken (which explained the lights going out), and the heater was out of propane (which explained the heat turning off). Claire suggested the power was out (which explained all three). Claire was, of course, correct.

The story of Claire and Jean illustrates Occam's razor—Claire's explanation was more simple than her wife's and thus more likely to be correct. The guiding intuition we are talking about here is a specialized case of Occam's razor, known as *Hume's touchstone*:

> When any hypothesis, therefore, is advanc'd to explain a mental operation, which is common to men and beasts, we must apply the same hypothesis to both; and as every true hypothesis will abide this trial, so I may venture to affirm, no false one will ever be able to endure it.
>
> (Hume, 1739/2000, p. 118)

Or in other words, it doesn't make sense to have one explanation for humans and one explanation for animals when *both humans and animals are performing the same action.*

Hume rejected the human-animal dualism that pervades much of early research and philosophy (Reed, 1996; Turvey, 2019). Ecological psychology takes up that cause and requires that any time a phenomenon is not uniquely human (and we have yet to identify a phenomenon that unequivocally *is*), then the *explanation* of that phenomenon cannot be uniquely human either.

Theories of perception must apply equally to the fly as to Fred. Theories of development must apply equally to the chick as to Fred's niece, Eleanor. Theories of action must apply equally to Fred's horse (Sweet William) as to Claudia. Differences in sensory organs, developmental milestones, and structure of limbs cannot stand in the way of a comprehensive account.

Lawful Relations in Energy of Any Kind

Fred is in his driveway. His neighbor's son, Michael, is skateboarding a few feet away (they share a driveway, and Michael is not particularly careful about whose side he is on—the cheeky blighter). Michael is just learning to skateboard and so cannot always control his direction and speed. Fred is facing the other direction, but he hears the sound of Michael's efforts and realizes Michael is on a collision course with him. Fred turns toward him and sees precisely what he expected: a wibbly-wobbly Michael, mere inches away. He reaches out and grabs Michael's outstretched arms and helps him find his balance again.

Fred made contact with this event using (at least) three perceptual systems: hearing, sight, and touch. Every event lawfully structures multiple energy distributions simultaneously. Therefore, multiple energy distributions potentially inform every event. It is possible to be *equally informed* about Michael's behavior regardless of what anatomical components Fred uses to detect that information.

If Michael's pet ball python had been present at the scene (or any number of other animals with similar capabilities), she could have sensed the skateboarding adventure by attending to the infrared spectrum (what humans sense as heat). A mosquito might have found Fred and Michael via the gradient of carbon dioxide they are exhaling. A mole rat burrowed underneath them could have sensed their actions as vibrations. And if the whole thing had taken place in the ocean, a shark could have been aware of their movements as changes in an electrical field.

It is no accident that many organisms are sensitive to light. It is a remarkably helpful energy source that (because of its nature) is able to specify events quickly and at a distance. But light is not the only lawfully structured energy field, and the ecological perspective argues that treating the different perceptual systems of a *given* animal as requiring different explanations is just as bad as treating the perceptual systems of *different kinds* of animals as requiring different explanations. In fact, some ecological psychologists argue that the so-called five senses should be treated as a single perceptual system (Stoffregen, Mantel, & Bardy, 2017).

The ecological solution for eliminating the division between Fred's eye and the fly's eye was to turn to the lawfulness of the structure of light (see Chapter 6). We similarly suggest that the way to eliminate the division between sight and hearing and between smell and electrical sense is to turn to the lawfulness of the structure of *energy*—however conceived (see Chapters 7 and 8). Provided there is a lawful relationship between the environment and a type of energy, the ecological program of perception suggests that the job of the perceptual system is the same: to detect it.

Box 4.2 Sensory Substitution Devices

If we assume both a *tabula rasa* and that perceptual systems all work by detecting lawful information, then one logical conclusion is that perceivers should be sensitive to *any* lawful energy array—even if it is artificially generated. That is, if our self-organizing system does not know beforehand what information will be useful (see Chapter 10 for how we develop this ability over time), then it must be capable of adjusting to a wide variety of relationships—really *any* relationship that might turn out to be useful. Development is then a process of learning to rely on relationships that are lawful in order to navigate.

There is some interesting research in this direction. In Chapter 6, we discuss the ability of participants to perceive the affordances of a surface by exploring it with a handheld object (much like a blind person might use a white cane; Burton, 1992).

From the ecological perspective, participants were able to perform this task despite a lack of experience because the structure that provides information about a given affordance is analogous across energy forms (light and the physical forces acting on bodily tissues), regardless of the micro-scale differences between those energy forms.

From that perspective, perceivers ought to be able to navigate using *unusual* energy forms, provided they are lawful. Enter *sensory substitution devices*! These are devices (see Figure 4.6) that convert one type of energy pattern (usually light or sound) into another (usually vibrations). Novice participants are able to use these devices to perceive whether they would be able to walk through a doorway (Favela et al., 2018), as well as navigate among obstacles (Lobo et al., 2019).

Figure 4.6 Sensory substitution devices convert one form of energy (usually light or sound) into another (usually vibration); a participant can rapidly use the device to navigate.

Processes, Not Things

Our last guiding intuition is a reminder that organisms are dynamic. Or in other words, they change. They change *a lot*. And do so continuously. The Fred that leaves his house is not the same as the Fred that arrives at work. Any attempt to approach psychological phenomena as static will inevitably fall short or fail altogether. Therefore (as the title of our book might hint), all of them should be treated as *processes* rather than *things* (McCabe, 2014), *perceiving* rather than perception, *acting* rather than action, *remembering* rather than memory, *developing* rather than development, and so on.

Ecological Roadmap

This book has three main parts. If you have been reading in order, you are coming to the end of the first part: the introduction to ecological theory. Our goal in these chapters was to first outline the relevant problems and the previous approaches to these problems, then argue that the previous approaches have fallen short. Finally, we outlined the ecological program and argued that it provides a more coherent explanation of the things we study.

The second and third parts of this book expand on the ecological program and offer a brief review of research in the field of ecological psychology, including an expansion into fields beyond those typically considered psychology.

Part 2: Reconceptualizing Old Problems in an Ecological Way

The goal of the second part of this book is to demonstrate how the ecological approach addresses many classical (and less classical) issues of psychology. Perception is the first step, but the theory has applications beyond this as well.

Chapter 5: Affordances—What Is Perceived. Animals have options. At any given point in time, there are many available opportunities for behavior—a concept known as *affordances*. Successfully approaching, reaching for, and grasping an apple requires successfully perceiving whether, when, and how to perform many behaviors. The concept of affordances, perhaps more than any other, is fundamental to ecological psychology. Affordances are (primarily) what an animal perceives, and affordances are (primarily) what behavior is directed toward. A serious consideration of this concept requires a rethinking of the relationship between animal and environment and a fundamental recharacterization of what is perceived, how it is perceived, and why it is perceived.

Chapter 6: Ecological Optics and Visual Perception—Getting Light Into the Muscles. In more traditional perspectives, understanding how a creature sees food, approaches food, and eats food requires answering the question "How does light get into the brain?" In other words, it requires explaining how points of light become a representation in the nervous system that can provide cues about environmental properties. The question of how such cues might be used in performing goal-directed behavior (e.g., approaching or eating food) is an afterthought. The ecological perspective flips the script and places this issue at the forefront. The question posed by the ecological approach is instead the one made famous by Michael Turvey—"How does light get into the *muscles*?" In other words, the ecological approach asks how patterns of structured light encountered at a point of observation can inform surfaces and the perceiver's relationship to such surfaces. This requires a fundamental reconsideration of both light and the process of visual perception. This chapter explores both the key components and the key consequences of this reconsideration.

Chapter 7: Ecological Acoustics and Auditory Perception—Getting Sound Into the Muscles. For some creatures, approaching food requires (or can be facilitated by) *hearing* food. As in the ecological approach to seeing, the ecological approach to hearing places the issue of performing goal-directed behavior at the forefront and asks, "How does *sound* get into the muscles?" How can patterns of structured sound encountered at a point of observation inform surfaces and the perceiver's relationship to such surfaces? This chapter explores both key components and key consequences of a fundamental reconsideration of both sound and the process of auditory perception.

Chapter 8: Ecological Haptics and Perception by Touch—Muscles as the Medium. Of course, approaching food can also require (or can be facilitated by) *feeling* food. From traditional perspectives, the touch system is a bit of an anomaly. Unlike vision and hearing, touching something requires contact with the body, is not performed by a specific sense organ or body part, and is inextricably linked to doing. However, from the ecological approach, these properties make it an ideal system in which to understand how structured energy patterns (in this case, a pattern of deformation in bodily tissue that accompanies movement) can be used to guide goal-directed behaviors. Given that there is no need to explain how forces get into the muscle, the focus can instead be on how forces encountered (and generated) when moving the body can inform both the body and objects attached to it.

Chapter 9: Action and Coordination. Animals move. This is one of the fundamental characteristics of all living creatures. Perception guides movement and vice versa. Yet the ecological approach to action suffers from some of the same challenges as the ecological approach in general. Specifically, it is difficult to escape the familiar metaphors and centuries-old assumptions of the body as a machine and the brain as a (skilled) operator or programmer. Yet the sheer number of components involved in any coordinated movement combined with the speed, fluidity, and flexibility of such movement makes this unlikely. In contrast, in the ecological approach, coordinated movement emerges as a consequence of a continually unfolding collaboration among the animal's goals, generic physical principles, and the particular characteristics of the musculoskeletal system.

Chapter 10: Development of Perceiving and Acting Abilities. The abilities to see, hear, touch, and move don't come from nowhere. They develop. And this development involves more than just the typical combination of genetic inheritance and environmental experiences. Rather, it occurs within a multidirectional and multilayered developmental system. It is in this context that animals of all species (but in particular, human infants and toddlers) develop the ability to perceive and act on (continually changing) affordances for reaching, crawling, stepping, and walking, among many other behaviors. This chapter focuses on the development of these abilities and, in particular, on how what is learned allows for flexible and continual relearning during the sometimes dramatic changes in strength, flexibility, coordination, and balance over the course of development.

Chapter 11: Perceiving and Acting with Others—an Ecological Social Psychology. Animals perceive and act in the context of other animals. Importantly, the same lawful principles that underlie perceiving and acting in animal-environment systems also do so in *animal-animal*-environment systems. Therefore, the very same structure in patterned energy distributions that provides information about affordances for self also provides information about affordances for other organisms. And the very same principles that underlie coordination of the movements of an individual animal (intrapersonal coordination) also underly the coordination of the movements of two (or more) different animals with each other (interpersonal coordination). Consequently, this chapter focuses on describing perceiving and acting with others as the detecting and exploiting of lawfully structured information.

Chapter 12: Thinking, Learning, and Remembering. Animals don't just perceive and act. They think, learn, and remember. In traditional perspectives, all three of these processes are distinct from perceiving and acting. Unlike perceiving and acting, thinking, learning, and remembering are described as being entirely mental processes in that they operate on or with representations and are at some remove from both the body and the world. However, in the ecological approach, the very same lawful principles that underlie perceiving and acting in animal-environment systems also underlie thinking, knowing, and remembering in animal-environment systems. Therefore, perceiving, acting, learning, and remembering are continuous (if not identical) processes. This chapter explores the theoretical and empirical support for this claim.

Chapter 13: Applications of Ecological Psychology. The ecological approach is directed at understanding the fundamental ability of animals to perform everyday behaviors. For all animals, these behaviors include finding food, shelter, companionship, and avoiding injury. For humans, however, these behaviors can *also* include designing and operating complex machinery or computing devices, designing buildings and landscapes, and understanding and treating both physical and mental health conditions. This chapter focuses on how the ecological approach allows us to better understand (and even improve) the ability to solve these real-world problems.

Part 3: Zooming Out

The third part of this book applies the ecological approach to areas not always considered part of psychology, as well as suggests areas to which the approach might be beneficially applied.

Chapter 14: Dynamical Systems. One of the advantages of the ecological approach is that it views organisms—and other nonliving systems—as *changing* and *changeable*. This chapter explains how using a dynamical systems approach to understand systems can help address classic problems of behavior. The approach takes a macro-level view of behavior by describing it as a layout of attractors. This dynamical systems approach is then used to describe behaviors such as developmental "errors", prism adaptation, and intractable conflict.

Chapter 15: Evolution. While the Darwinian approach to evolution is able to describe the species-wide pressures that change organisms over time, it is not able to explain how life could have started in the first place. Taking a more global and systems-level view reveals that life—rather than being surprising—was inevitable. Moreover, this perspective predicted the emergence of certain organisms (such as plastic-eating bacteria) well before those organisms were discovered.

Chapter 16: Self-Organization. Explicitly rejecting the central executive of classical approaches leaves the question of how a system could be created and governed without that centralized control. The ecological approach embraces self-organization: simple rules, autonomous parts, and constraints provided by the environment can result in complex and exciting behaviors. The chapter gives examples such as the behavior of insects, the beating of the human heart, and more.

Chapter 17: Intelligent Life. There is no agreed-upon definition for life. There is no agreed-upon definition for intelligence. Most attempts at defining these concepts do so with the explicit intention of writing a definition that *includes* and *excludes* predetermined phenomena. For example, if the definition of intelligence is found to suddenly apply to plants, then it must be time to change the definition! A more sound method is to write appropriate definitions and then embrace the sudden inclusion of some things that did not previously seem to be alive or intelligent.

Notes

1. And there are efforts in this direction! The connectionist approach, for example, is the result of an effort to decentralize the central executive, as well as trying to address the problem of the loan of intelligence. Unfortunately, it still falls victim to the problem of feedback and the causal issues here described.
2. Often misquoted as "the whole is more than the sum of its parts".
3. And the study of illusions is *always* in artificial settings. The Beuchet chair does not happen without exact planning on how to remove the information we usually rely on for navigation (such as movement). And many (if not most) other illusions require a flat viewing surface (a printed page or a computer screen).
4. He was very concerned about not irritating the church—they would not allow him to study the soul scientifically (as it was the realm of God and, therefore, not subject to human science), and so he separated the body from the soul in an effort to study the body without getting in trouble.
5. A small device with a pendulum that swings mechanically and makes a "click" sound every time it passes by one part of its cycle. Musicians use it to keep time.
6. In part, this is because the likelihood of any two (independent) phenomena occurring together is less than the likelihood of them occurring separately. Believing otherwise is a reasoning error known as an conjunction fallacy.

Part 2

Reconceptualizing Old Problems in an Ecological Way

5 Affordances—What Is Perceived

Consider a playful and rambunctious dog charging a resting cat. The cat has options. She could flee by leaping over a child's video game controller and onto the coffee table. She could hide by squeezing into the narrow space between the couch and the wall. She could swat at the dog's nose. All of these are behaviors that the cat *could* (but may or may not necessarily) perform. In other words, they are all *opportunities for behavior* (see Figure 5.1). Such opportunities for behavior are known as *affordances* (Gibson, 1979/2015). This term is an invented noun form of the verb "to afford"—meaning "to provide opportunity for". The concept of affordances, perhaps more than any other, is fundamental to ecological psychology (Wagman, 2020). Accordingly, one of the central hypotheses of ecological psychology is that the primary content of animals' perceptual experiences is affordances (and not properties or lower-order variables or anything else; see Thomas, Riley, & Wagman, 2020).

Here is the crux of the matter: performing any given behavior requires perceiving affordances for that behavior. It requires perceiving *whether* the behavior is possible and, if so, *when* and *how* the behavior should be performed. Successfully jumping onto the coffee table, for example, requires that the cat perceive whether the couch is "jump-on-able", when the jump should be initiated, and how the movements of the head, legs, torso, and tail should be

Figure 5.1 A cat has options for how to respond to a playful dog. She could swat the dog's nose, hide behind the couch, or jump over the game controller and onto the table. These are all affordances—possibilities for behavior—for the cat.

DOI: 10.4324/9781003145691-7

controlled in doing so. In general, adding the suffix "-able" is often all that is required to shift from talking about a *behavior* to talking about an *affordance* for that behavior (*grasp* or *grasping* becomes *graspable*; *sit* or *sitting* on becomes *sit-on-able*).

What is so interesting (and perhaps problematic) about affordances is that, by definition, affordances are *opportunities*—things that *could* happen but have not happened yet (and may not *ever* happen). Performing any behavior means that an animal must perceive whether, when, and how that behavior *could be* performed *before* the behavior is ever attempted. This means that an animal must perceive (*not predict*) the (possible) future. This might sound supernatural and spooky, but it is not. In fact, as we will see, it is a natural and law-based process. However, it will require an explanation of perception that does not rely on the problematic assumptions that got us into this mess—in particular, local causality (see Chapter 2). Explanations of perception that rely on local causality can provide an explanation of how the past brings about the present and perhaps how the present brings about the future but not how the future brings about the present—which is exactly what happens when you perceive affordances.

When you think about it, you'll quickly see that perceiving affordances is not so spooky. Or at least, if it is spooky, it is spooky in a way that all other complex natural processes are spooky. You perceive the future *all the time*. Catching a ball requires that you put your hands where the ball *will be*, not where it was or even where it *is*. Successfully catching a ball, then, requires perceiving whether, when, and how you could get your (body and) hands to the future location of the ball (McBeath, Shaffer, & Kaiser, 1995; Michaels & Zaal, 2002; Fink, Foo, & Warren, 2009). Successfully stopping your car at a stop sign requires perceiving whether, when, and how hard you should step on the brake to bring the car to a stop at some future moment in time (Fajen, 2005a, 2005b; Fajen & Devaney, 2006; see Figure 5.2).

It is of little use for the cat to become aware that it *is not* possible for her to jump onto the coffee table only *after she has failed* in her attempt to do so. It is also of little use for her to become aware that it *is* possible for her to do so only *after she has succeeded*. It is only marginally better for the cat to become aware of either of these impending outcomes *while she is in the process of jumping*. That is not to say that successful or failed attempts to perform a behavior do not influence the ability to perceive affordances or that affordance perception is always perfectly accurate (see Chapter 12)—only that regardless of an animal's past experience, performing any behavior necessarily requires perceiving the possible (and impossible) future.

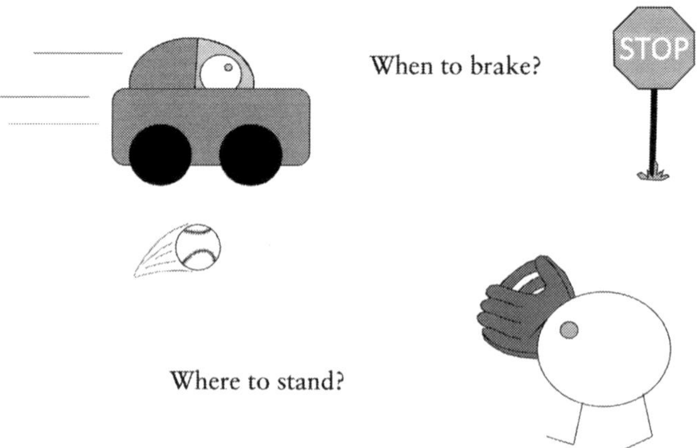

Figure 5.2 Everyday life requires perceiving the future. When should Fred start braking in order to safely stop before the stop sign? Where should Fred go in order to catch the baseball?

You can understand why there might be both confusion and controversy about the concept of affordance. Some of this has to do with misplaced spookiness. For example, perception is often defined as a process that can only provide awareness about the instantaneous present. Awareness of the past or the future, therefore, must be due to memory or imagination, respectively. Some of this also has to do with the fact that, like many concepts in the ecological approach, it runs counter to familiar metaphors and centuries-old assumptions (see Chapters 1 and 2).

One of these centuries-old assumptions is the relationship between the perceiver and what is perceived—the perceiver does the perceiving, and the environment is what is perceived. This assumption has led to a centuries-old distinction (made by Descartes, Galileo, and Locke) between *primary qualities* and *secondary qualities*. Primary qualities are properties of objects that are entirely *independent* of an observer (like size, weight, and shape). They are *objective* properties inherent in the object itself. An object's volume, for example, is what it is and does not depend on an observer in any way whatsoever. *Secondary qualities* are properties of objects that are (or seem to be) entirely *dependent* on an observer—like color, taste, and texture. They are *subjective* properties that depend on the specifics of the observer's perceptual apparatus. An object's color, for example, will look different to someone who is color blind (or someone wearing sunglasses or even a bee or dog) than to someone who is not.

The separation of perceiver from that which is perceived forces the concept of affordance to be either a primary quality (i.e., an objective environmental property) or a secondary quality (i.e., as a subjective perceptual experience) but does not allow it to be both. However, in the ecological approach, the perceiver and the environment are not separate. Therefore, the distinction between primary and secondary qualities does not hold. Affordances are *neither* strictly a property of the animal *nor* a property of the environment. At the same time, they depend on *both* the animal and the environment. In this way, affordances are a bit like friction. Friction is created only when two surfaces come into contact. Friction is not a property (or an experience) of either surface. Rather, *it emerges from a relationship between them*. In the same way, affordances are neither in the animal nor in the environment but *emerge only in the relationship between the two* (See Figure 5.3).

Researchers within the field of ecological psychology have been developing and refining the concept of affordances for the past several decades (Chemero, 2003; Heras-Escribano, 2019;

Figure 5.3 Affordances are *neither* strictly a property of the animal *nor* strictly a property of the environment. *Left:* The affordance "hide-behind-able" exists for the cat but not for the dog. *Top right:* The affordance "hide-behind-able" cannot exist without the organism. *Bottom right:* The affordance "hide-behind-able" cannot exist without the environment.

Stoffregen, 2003; Turvey, 1992). Consequently, there are many (often competing) definitions of affordances. However, for our purposes, we can define affordances as *opportunities for behavior* that emerge from the relationship between animal and environment. Affordances are what an animal can (or could) do in a particular circumstance, given the fit between its action capabilities and environmental properties.

Action capabilities are determined by an animal's size and shape but also by its mass, strength, dexterity, and skill; how it moves itself through the world; and how it moves things in the world. Some ecological psychologists have referred to these action capabilities as effectivities (Turvey, 1992). Naturally, different animals have different action capabilities. This means that affordances for one animal are not necessarily affordances for another animal. What is leap-on-to-able for a cat may not be for a dog. What is squeeze-into-able for a cat may not be for a dog. In fact, the cat is likely counting on such differences when she chooses how to avoid or fend off the dog. This implies that she is not only able to perceive affordances for herself but for the dog as well (see Chapter 11). Affordances can even differ for two members of the same species. What is leap-on-to-able for a healthy adult cat might not be for an ailing cat or a kitten. What is squeeze-into-able for a svelte cat might not be for a stout cat.

This is yet another way in which the concept of affordances runs counter to centuries-old assumptions. In large part (and for good reason), science is built firmly on a foundation of physics and math. But not just any physics and math—*Newtonian* mechanics and *Euclidean* geometry (see Chapter 3). To be sure, both provide invaluable frameworks for understanding the world. Moreover, their explanatory power comes from the fact that each framework is wholly *objective*. The laws of physics and geometry are true even in an animal-independent world. As we have already discussed, however, affordances are partly *subjective*. They are animal-*dependent*.

Slopes that afford standing on for a mountain goat might not for Fred or an elephant (see Figure 5.4). The very same surface affords certain behaviors for some animals but not others. The very same surface can also afford different behaviors for *the same animal* in *different contexts* or at *different points in time*. A puddle that does not afford stepping over while standing still

Figure 5.4 *Top:* Some slopes afford standing on for some animals and not for others. The steepest slope only affords standing on for the goat. Some slopes afford standing on for Fred but not for an elephant. *Bottom:* Movement (speed) changes available affordances. The puddle does not afford jumping over when Fred is standing still (or walking slowly), but it does afford so when he is running.

might afford so with a running start. And as every new parent finds out eventually, objects that do not afford reaching by a child early in infancy do so later in infancy (and toddlerhood). Therefore, Newtonian physics and Euclidean geometry may be inappropriate for understanding affordances. Affordances change even when physical and geometric properties of objects and surfaces remain constant and vice versa. Instead, affordances require an *ecological physics* and an *ecological geometry* (Nonaka, 2020; Turvey, 1992, 2004, 2013, 2019).

Another challenging aspect of affordances is that a given affordance is usually not a result of a *singular* fit between an animal and the environment. In other words, affordances are not usually the result of a fit between *one individual property* of the animal and *one individual property* of the environment. Rather, an affordance is (most likely to be) the result of a *simultaneous fit* among *multiple properties* of the animal and *multiple properties* of the environment. For a surface to afford standing on, for example, that surface must be sufficiently horizontal and flat (relative to the animal's ability to balance), sufficiently extended (relative to the animal's size), and sufficiently rigid (relative to the animal's mass), among others. If any one of these criteria does not hold, the surface does not afford standing on. Each one is necessary, but none of them alone is sufficient. The surface must have all of these criteria, or it does not have the affordance—much like a jigsaw puzzle piece must be fully interlocked with all of the surrounding pieces to fit appropriately and snugly in a given space (see Figure 5.5).

A final challenging aspect of affordances is that the concept changes how we think about (the origin of) meaning. For centuries or more, philosophers, psychologists, and other scholars have tried to understand meaning. They have found it quite challenging. What is it? Where does it come from? Why is something meaningful to one person but not to another? Is meaning in the thing itself or in the person? The common-sense description is that meaning is both *subjective* and *internal*. It is a complex mental state that needs to be created by some internal process and then "placed onto" external objects or situations by a person. However, from the

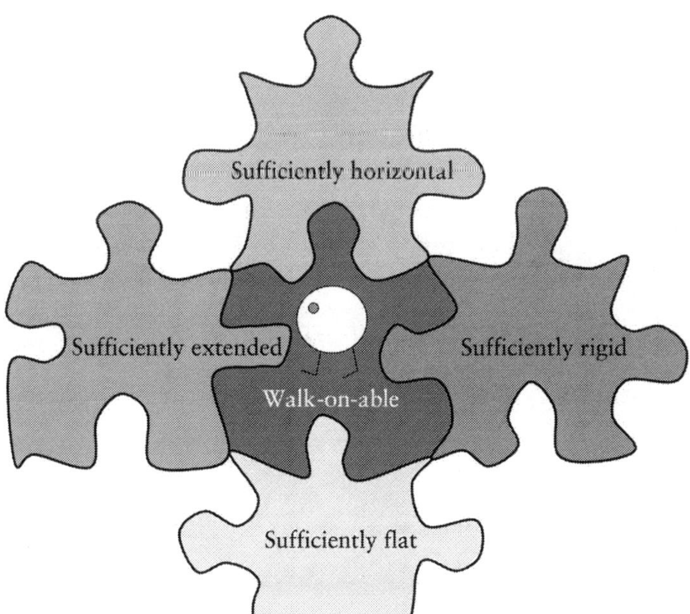

Figure 5.5 For a surface to afford walking on for Fred, several conditions must be met simultaneously—the surface must be sufficiently horizontal, extended, rigid, and flat. If any of these conditions are not met, the surface will not afford walking on.

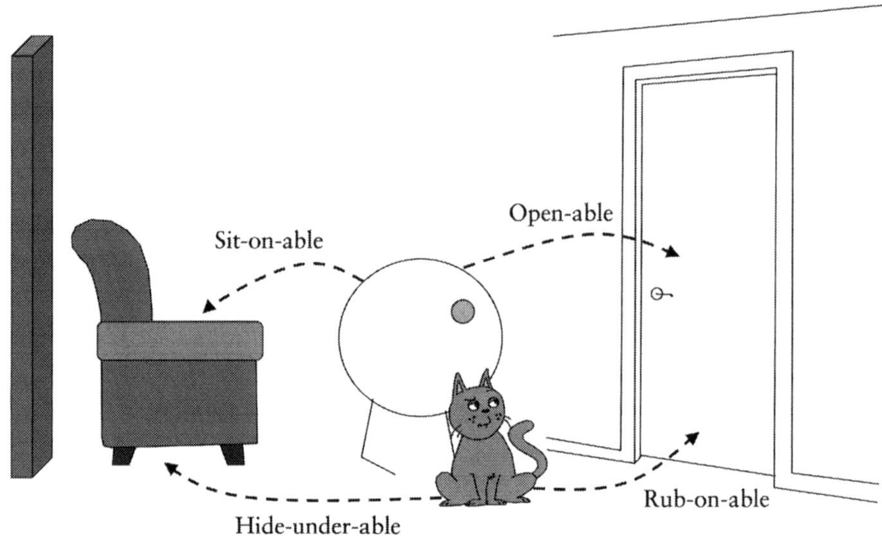

Figure 5.6 The same object can afford different things for different organisms. The couch affords hiding under for the cat but not for Fred. The door affords opening for Fred but not for the cat.

ecological perspective, meanings are *neither* subjective *nor* internal. Nor are they *objective* or *external*. Rather, meanings *emerge* from relations between animals and environments. You may notice that this is exactly how we described affordances. This is not a coincidence.

From the ecological perspective, affordances are activity-specific *meanings* of the environment (Turvey, 2013, 2019). What something affords for a given animal is what it means to that animal. If a couch affords hiding under by the cat but not by Fred, then it has this meaning for the cat but not for Fred. If a door affords opening by Fred and not by the cat, then it has this meaning for Fred and not for the cat (see Figure 5.6). So ecological psychologists claim that affordances are meaningful and that affordances can be perceived. They are not created inside the animal or represented by the animal. Therefore, ecological psychologists *also* claim that *meanings can be perceived*. They, too, are not created inside the animal or represented by the animal. This is a *huge* shift in thinking, and it has far-reaching implications (see Chapter 12).

How to Study Affordances

Gibson described the concept of affordances as early as 1966 (Gibson, 1966) and most fully developed the concept in 1979 (Gibson, 1979/2015; Wagman, 2020). However, an empirical method for studying affordances was not developed until the mid-1980s. American psychologist Bill Warren (1984) applied Gibson's definition of affordance as "a specific combination of its substance and its surfaces taken with reference to the animal" to the behavior of stair climbing. In part, climbing stairs requires that a person be able to lift their foot high enough to place it on a step so that their body weight can then be completely transferred from the trail foot to the lead (stepping) foot.

Importantly, the primary constraint on the ability to climb stairs is not an objective property of the environment—the height of the step. Rather, it is *a relationship between* the person and the environment—the height of the step *relative to that person's leg length*. At a certain ratio of step height to leg length, it would no longer be possible to perform the behavior. At values above this ratio, a person could still climb the stairs (perhaps by scrambling or crawling), just

Figure 5.7 The ratio of the height of the object to the height of the person's leg length changes possibilities for behavior with that object.

not by stepping. At higher values still, it would no longer be possible to climb the stairs by *any* means or at least without *additional* means, like a rope or rock-climbing holds (see Figure 5.7). In other words, different *modes of behavior*—climbing by different means—would be required at different values of this ratio.

Warren described the ratio between stair height and leg length at which stepping would transition from possible to impossible, and vice versa, as a *critical pi (π) value*. He then developed a biomechanical model to determine what the critical π value would be for stair climbing (under ideal circumstances). This ratio turned out to be 0.88, meaning that when the stair height is taller than 88% of a person's leg length, a person (with maximum flexibility) would no longer be able to climb that stair by stepping. This means that taller people ought to be able to step on taller step heights than shorter people, but the boundary between steps that are "step-on-able" and those that are not ought to occur at a leg-length-to-step-height ratio of 0.88 for *both groups*. Warren then hypothesized that the *perceived* critical π value for this behavior would *also* be 0.88. In other words, he hypothesized that perception of affordances for climbing stairs would be constrained by a relationship between step height and leg length because this relationship places limits on the actual biomechanical ability to climb stairs. He then conducted an experiment to test this hypothesis.

He recruited a group of taller participants (average height: 189.8 cm, approximately 6′3″) and a group of shorter participants (average height: 163.7 cm, approximately 5′4″). He showed each participant photos of an adjustable two-step stairway projected on a large screen. In each photo, the stairs were configured to one of five-step heights, ranging from 50.8 cm (20″) to 101.6 cm (40″) in 12.7 cm (5″) increments. For comparison's sake, a typical step height for a stairway in a US home is approximately 18 cm (7″). Each participant viewed each of the five sets of stairs twice in random order. For each photo, the participant reported—yes or no—whether they would be able to climb the stairs by stepping. Let's plot the percentage of "yes" responses at each step height for short and tall participants (see Figure 5.8).

You can see that, for the shortest step height (20″, approximately 50 cm), both the shorter and taller participants said "yes" on every trial. As step height increased, both groups said "yes" less often, but the curve for the taller participants is shifted to the right of the curve for the shorter participants. This means that, in general, taller participants said "yes" more often to the middle three-step heights than the shorter participants. Eventually, at the tallest step height—over 1 m (3′)—all participants said "no" on every trial.

Warren then determined the perceptual boundary for each group of participants—the step height at which each group switches their answer from "yes" to "no" or vice versa. This is the

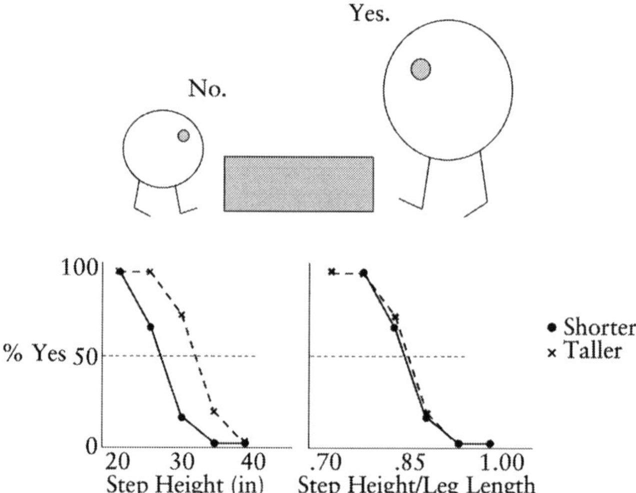

Figure 5.8 Using objective properties like step height results in different curves for different people. Using a *relational* property like step height/leg length reveals a single curve.

boundary between steps that are perceived to be "step-on-able" and those that are not. One way to figure this out is to determine the step height at which each group says "yes" 50% of the time (notice where the horizontal line in the middle of each graph intersects each curve). At step heights shorter than this, participants in that group are more likely to say "yes" than "no". At step heights taller than this, participants in that group are more likely to say "no" than "yes". The perceptual boundary can then be derived by tracing down from each intersection point to the corresponding value on the horizontal axis.

The perceptual boundary occurred at a step height of 67 cm (approximately 26″) for the shorter participants and 81 cm (approximately 32″) for the taller participants. This is not particularly surprising. But look what happens when we plot the data differently. Let's divide the five-step heights by the average leg length (step height/leg length) of each group of participants and plot the percentage of "yes" responses at each ratio. What does the graph look like now? The curves for the shorter and taller participants overlap almost completely! You can see that, for the smallest ratios of step height to leg length, both groups of participants said "yes" on every trial. As this ratio increased, both groups of participants say "yes" less often, and at the largest ratios, both groups said "no" on every trial. The overlap of the curves shows that shorter people and taller people perceive whether the stairs are "step-on-able" *in analogous ways*—both groups do so relative to their leg length.

Warren (1984) then determined the perceptual boundary (this time in terms of step-height-to-leg-length ratio) for each group of participants. And he was right—the perceived critical π value was 0.88 for each group! This is important for at least two reasons. First, it confirms that perception of affordances for stepping on is body-scaled—in particular, it depends on the relationship between step height and leg length—and not step height alone. Second, the perceived critical π value was *identical* to the critical π predicted by the biomechanical model (0.88). This means that perceivers are sensitive to the biomechanical limits on their ability to climb stairs.

While many researchers (both inside and outside of ecological psychology) are aware of this first experiment, fewer know about the *second* and *third* experiments that Warren published along with it in his 1984 paper. In many ways, these two experiments are more ingenious and more important than the first one. What makes them so is an explicit recognition that affordances are determined by that animal's *action capabilities*, not just its geometrical, physical, or even biomechanical properties. Rather, affordances for stair climbing are determined not only by the ability of the person to lift their foot high enough to place it on a step *but also* by the ability to *transfer the mass of their body* from their foot on the lower step to their foot on the higher step. This requires generating muscular forces and *doing work*. The second experiment was aimed at determining the *optimal π value*—the ratio of step-height-to-leg-length at which such work would be *the least effortful*. The third experiment attempted to determine the *perceived optimal* π value. It investigated whether participants would be able to see (ahead of time) which set of stairs would require *the least work*. Would they be able to see which set of stairs *afford climbing most efficiently*?

Again, Warren recruited a group of taller and shorter participants who all performed a brief (five minute) stair climbing task on an adjustable stair mill (sort of a fancy stair stepper exercise machine). On different days, they performed this task with the stairs adjusted to heights ranging from 12.7 cm (approximately 5″) to 25.4 cm (approximately 10″) in 2.54 cm (1″) increments. Oxygen consumption was measured by a mouthpiece and valve apparatus—like the ones used to evaluate the performance of endurance athletes—to determine how much energy the participants were using when climbing stairs with steps of each height. Warren found that *minimum energy use* (i.e., minimum work) occurred at shorter step heights for shorter participants than for taller participants, *but at the same ratio of step-height-to-leg-length for each group*—an optimal π value of 0.26. This means that stairs were easiest (least effortful or most energetically efficient) to climb when step heights were approximately 25% of the climber's leg length—a little lower than mid-calf on most people.

In the third experiment, Warren attempted to determine whether the *perceived* optimal π value for this behavior was *also* (approximately) 0.25. Again, he recruited a group of taller participants and a group of shorter participants. He showed each participant photos of pairs of adjustable two-step stairways on a large screen using the same range of step heights as in the second experiment. Each participant reported which set of stairs "would be more comfortable . . . to climb to the top". All combinations of all pairs of stairs were presented multiple times. Following this task, he showed each participant photos of each individual set of stairs one at a time on a large screen. Each participant then rated how *comfortable* it would be to climb that set of stairs on a scale of 1–7.

Warren found that taller participants most frequently chose (and most highly rated) stairs with a step height of approximately 23 cm (9″), and shorter participants most frequently chose and most highly rated stairs with a step height of approximately 18 cm (7″). Again, this is not particularly surprising. But when he divided the five step heights by the average leg length (step height/leg length) of each group of participants, he found that the most frequently chosen and the most highly rated ratio (for both groups of participants) was 0.25! The perceived optimal π value was (nearly) identical to the optimal π value. This means that participants could not only see *whether* a given set of stairs is climbable (Experiment 1) but also *how effortful* (or efficient) it would be to climb them (Experiment 3). In other words, perception of whether steps can be climbed (by stepping) is *action-scaled*. It is scaled to the ability to do work.

How Are Affordances Perceived?

As we have seen, the ecological approach requires a fundamental rethinking of what the relevant stimulation variables are and how the process of perception relies on those variables. In traditional approaches, it is taken for granted that the stimulation patterns are variables that have been useful in Newtonian mechanics and Euclidean geometry (e.g., light described as particles traveling in a straight line) and that the animal passively receives this stimulation (e.g., these particles enter the eye and strike the retina). Unfortunately, such variables are (hopelessly) *ambiguously* related to environmental properties and require extensive processing to convey any meaning whatsoever to the animal. For example, the image on the retina is ambiguous about size and depth, and perceiving these properties requires the unconscious learning of cues and application of rules (see Chapters 1 and 2).

In the ecological approach, researchers instead seek stimulation variables that are *unambiguously (i.e., lawfully) related to relationships between animal and environment*. Finding these variables requires developing an *ecological physics* and an *ecological geometry* (see Chapters 6–8). Moreover, these variables are *patterns in structured energy* that are *actively detected* by an animal in the course of performing everyday behaviors. The lawfulness (the lack of ambiguity) means that these variables *don't need to be processed*. They need only be *detected* to provide *information about* affordances (Wagman, 2020). These complex patterns can provide information about affordances because substance and surface properties *lawfully structure* energy patterns, such as reflected light.

More detail on this concept will be provided in Chapters 6–8, but for now, consider that animals are constantly immersed in an ocean of energy—patterns of light, vibrations and chemicals in the air, and pressure on the skin, connective tissue, and muscles. This ocean of energy completely surrounds each animal, but it does not do so in a uniform way. Instead, the distribution of these energy patterns lawfully depends on the *identity* and *location* of the energy sources, as well as the location, orientation, and other properties of nearby surfaces and substances. For example, just as the distribution of odor molecules *close* to an odor source is different from the distribution *far* from that odor source, the distribution of light energy *close* to a light source is different from the distribution *far* from that light source. At the same time, the distribution of light energy *under* a table is different from the distribution *above* the table—even if those locations are equidistant from the light source.

At any given moment, a given animal finds itself at a particular location (a *point of observation*) in this ocean of energy, at which it encounters a *particular pattern* of structured energy. Naturally, the point observation will differ for different animals due to their different heights, shapes, modes of walking, and so on. It will be different for Fred, or a cat, or an elephant—even if all three animals each stand at the same (geographic) location—hopefully, for Fred and the cat, not at the same time! And the point of observation for a given animal at a given moment may be different from the point of observation for that same animal in the *next* moment as it changes posture or otherwise moves through the world.

Nonetheless, at every point of observation, a given animal encounters *a unique distribution* of energy patterns. Therefore, the pattern of structured light energy encountered by Fred is different from that encountered by a cat or an elephant. The pattern of structured light energy encountered by Fred standing at *this* location is different from the one encountered Fred standing at *that* location. The pattern of structured light energy encountered by Fred while *standing still* is different from the ones he encounters while *moving* (see Chapter 6).

So where does this leave us? Here is a summary of the moves made by ecological psychology so far: substance and surface properties *lawfully structure* energy patterns such as reflected light, and the structured energy is unique at each point of observation—the points of observation that an animal occupies and how these points of observation change over time are each determined by an animal's size, shape, mass, strength, dexterity, and skill; how it moves through the world; and how it moves things in the world. Therefore, the structured energy patterns encountered at a given point of observation (and how these patterns change over time as the points of observation change over time) inform its *possible relationships to the surrounding substances and surfaces*—they are information about *affordances* (see Chapters 3–4 and 6–8)!

What Affordances Are Perceived?

Perceiving is no different from any other natural, lawful process. A lawful process is one in which the same principles apply across all conditions. In other words, the same phenomena ought to occur, and the same explanations of those phenomena ought to apply across conditions. Gravity works the same way regardless of whether we are talking about the Earth orbiting the sun or Fred tripping over his untied shoelaces. These situations are not identical, of course, but with respect to the lawfulness of gravity, they are *analogous*. In particular, the forces encountered by Fred are analogous to those encountered by planet Earth.

The lawfulness of *perception* means that the same principles apply across all conditions as well. These conditions include the particular energy form structured by the relationship between animal and environment. Perception ought to work the same way regardless of whether we are talking about patterns of light, patterns of vibrations or chemicals in the air, or patterns of pressure on the skin, connective tissue, and muscles. These situations are not identical, of course, but with respect to the lawfulness of perception, they are *analogous*.

The structured energy patterns encountered by a given animal at a given point of observation ought to be analogous across different energy forms. In other words, a given relationship between animal and environment will lawfully structure multiple energy forms *simultaneously*. Consequently, *the very same affordance ought to be perceivable by means of multiple perceptual modalities*—vision, hearing, and touch, among others.

There will be more on this in Chapters 6–8, but for now, consider (once again) Fred and the tree. Standing at some distance from the tree and facing the tree, Fred encounters the structured light reflecting off the apple he intends to grasp, the other apples on the tree, the branches and trunk of the tree, the grass, and other nearby objects. As he moves toward the tree—and in particular, toward the particular apple on the tree—he will progressively encounter more and more of the structured light reflecting from the apple he intends to grasp and less and less of the structured light reflecting from the other surfaces (see Figure 5.9). This is information about his movement toward the apple, and how quickly this occurs *is information about when he will arrive* at the apple (see Chapter 6). Now, imagine that there is a bird—chirping quite loudly—perched near the apple that Fred wants. As he approaches the apple (this time with his eyes closed), he will encounter more and more of the structured sound produced by the chirping bird and reflected off the other surfaces and less and less produced by any other sound source (see Figure 5.9). This is *also* information about his movement toward the apple, and again, how quickly this occurs *is information about* when he will arrive at the apple (see Chapter 7). The lawfully changing pattern of structured energy is important; the details of the energy form itself are not.

Figure 5.9 *Left:* As he moves toward the tree (*top*), Fred encounters more of the structured light reflecting from the apple and less of the structured light reflecting off the other surfaces (*bottom*). *Right:* As Fred approaches the bird (this time with his eyes closed, *top*), he encounters more of the structured sound produced by the bird and less of the structured sound produced by other sources (*bottom*).

Equally importantly, the lawfulness of perception means that the same principles apply regardless of the (complexity of) the nervous system and brain of the perceiving animal. As described previously, the lawfully generated patterns in structured energy provide information about affordances. Such patterns do not need to be processed. They need only be detected. Therefore, so long as the animal is capable of detecting the structure in a given energy array[1] that provides information about a particular affordance, it can perceive that affordance, and the details of its nervous system and brain are (potentially) irrelevant. *This makes ecological psychology a psychology for all animals—not just humans* (Covarrubias, Cabrera, & Jiménez, 2017; Turvey, 2013; Wagman et al., 2019).

With this in mind, let's return to the cat's options in dealing with the playful and rambunctious dog. Recall that these options included fleeing by leaping over the child's video game controller and onto the coffee table, hiding by squeezing into the narrow space between the couch and the wall, and swatting the dog's nose. Choosing from among these options requires perceiving affordances for getting across or over, passing or squeezing through, and reaching. Let's consider each of these in turn.

Perceiving Affordances for Getting Across

If a gap or puddle is not too wide or the obstacle is not too tall relative to an animal's leg length, then that animal can step over it. Therefore, perception of affordances for stepping over an obstacle, gap, or puddle—like perception of affordances for stair climbing—ought to be constrained, in part, by leg length. Burton (1992) investigated this, basing his methodology on Warren's (1984) stair-climbing experiments. The participants stood at one edge of a platform and viewed a second platform that was placed at a number of different distances. The participants reported whether they would be able to cross each gap between the platforms by stepping. As expected, the results showed that, for the most part, visual perception of affordances for stepping across the gap was body scaled—it depended on the fit between leg length and gap width (see Figure 5.10)

Figure 5.10 Affordances for crossing over a gap can be perceived when the surfaces are explored visually (*top*) or when they are explored haptically (*bottom*).

What is perhaps more impressive is that in another condition, participants completed the same task, but instead of *looking* at the gaps, they were blindfolded and *explored* the gap with a hand-held wooden rod (see Figure 5.10). Using a hand-held rod in this manner is relatively common among visually impaired people, but it is very rare among sighted people. Nonetheless, the participants—who were all sighted and had no experience using a hand-held rod in this way—were still (highly) capable of performing this task. As you might expect, participants were *more cautious* in reporting that they could step over the gaps when they explored those gaps with a hand-held object than when they looked at those gaps. However, participants perceived affordances for stepping over the gaps *in analogous ways in each condition*. In both conditions, perception of this affordance was body-scaled.

We'll return to a discussion of perception of affordances by using a hand-held object as a perceptual tool in Chapter 8. In the meantime, though, it is important to point out that the fact that a given relationship between animal and environment lawfully (analogously) structures multiple energy distributions simultaneously is what allows for the analogous ability to perceive affordances by different perceptual modalities. In this case, the way in which a "step-over-able" gap structures the light encountered at a given point of observation occupied by the perceiver is analogous—but not identical—to how it structures the vibrations encountered at the grasp position (i.e., the point of observation) on the hand-held rod.[2]

Of course, there is more than one way to get over an obstacle or across a gap. If the gap is not too wide—or the obstacle is not too tall—relative to an animal's arms and legs, then the animal can *crawl* over it. If the gap is wide enough—or the obstacle is tall enough—relative to an animal's arms and legs that stepping over is not possible, then they might need to *leap* over it. If there are suspended objects—such as a rope or handholds—of appropriate sizes and spacings relative to the shapes and sizes of the animal's appendages, then they can *swing* over it. Again, different modes of behavior—different means of getting over or across an obstacle or gap—are possible depending on the specifics of the relationship between animal and environment.

And studies have shown that people can perceive affordances for each of these different means of getting over or across an obstacle or gap (Cole et al., 2013)! Given that leaping and arm-swinging require launching (part of) the body from place to place, people are initially not quite as good at perceiving affordances for these behaviors as for stepping and crawling. But the ability to perceive affordances for such behaviors improves after practice performing these behaviors (see Day, Wagman, & Smith, 2015).

And humans, of course, are not the only animals that can cross gaps. Nor are they the only animals that make appropriate choices about how to do so depending on the simultaneous fit among multiple properties of the animal and multiple properties of the environment. For example, toads *crawl* across a gap when it is wide but shallow, *leap* across a gap that is narrow but deep, and *refuse* to cross a gap that is both wide and deep (Lock & Collet, 1979). Tree snakes make these choices based on their ability to support their body weight as they stretch across the gap—they crawl when the gap is narrow, launch themselves when the gap is large, and even use their tail to hold on to the initial perch as they move across the gap (Jayne & Riley, 2007). Again, the lawful structuring of energy distributions allows for analogous abilities to perceive affordances by animals possessing very different brains, nervous systems, and body constructions.

Perceiving Affordance for Fitting Through (or Into)

If the space between two objects is wide enough relative to an animal's body size, how it moves through the world, and its ability to compress its body, then it can fit into (and through) the space between these objects. Therefore, perception of affordances for passing between obstacles ought to be constrained by these factors. Initial research focused on the primary *geometric* constraint on affordances for walking through an opening—shoulder width. Such research found that the perceptual boundary (the perceived critical π value) between openings that afford walking through—without turning the body—occurred at a larger opening width for people with wide shoulders than for people with narrow shoulders but at the same ratio of opening-width-to-shoulder-width for both groups (approximately 1.16; see Warren & Whang, 1987). This value was not much different from the critical π value at which participants actually begin to turn their bodies when walking through openings (approximately 1.3).

Other experiments have shown that just as it is possible to use perceptual modalities other than vision to perceive whether a gap can be stepped across, it is possible to do so to perceive whether an opening affords passing through. People can *hear* whether an opening affords passing through by listening to sounds being projected *through* that opening (Gordon & Rosenblum, 2004) or by listening to sound being produced by the objects that *form* the opening (Russell, 1999; Riehm et al., 2019).

People can also *feel* whether an opening affords passing through through by exploring that opening with a hand-held rod or with an enactive torch—a hand-held flashlight-sized device that emits infrared light and converts distance information into vibrations (Favela et al., 2018; see Chapter 5, Box 4.2). Here again, the lawful structuring of energy distributions allows for the analogous ability to perceive affordances across these very different means.

More recent research has focused on *dynamic*—rather than geometric—constraints on affordances for walking (or squeezing) through openings—in particular, how the body moves and how the body can be compressed. As a person walks, they sway from side to side and bob up and down. Consequently, a person's body takes up more space while moving than while standing still. Accordingly, researchers found that the *size of the body in motion* (i.e., standing height + vertical bob or standing width + horizontal sway) more closely constrains perception of affordances for fitting through an opening than does static body size alone (Franchak, Adolph, & Celano, 2012; van der Meer, 1997). Researchers have also found that people can also perceive affordances for *squeezing or wriggling* through a very narrow space. Again, given the complexity of squeezing or wriggling the body, people are initially not quite as good at perceiving affordances for this behavior as for other means of passing through an opening. However, the ability to perceive affordances for this behavior improves after practice performing this behavior (Franchak, van der Zalm, & Adolph, 2010).

Body size, how an animal moves through the world, and the ability to compress the body are all affected when an object is carried by or attached to the body. Think about something as mundane as carrying groceries or as unusual as wearing a suit of armor or other (more modern) protective equipment or even operating a wheelchair. In these cases, affordances for fitting through—or any other behavior—are determined by a relationship between the *animal-plus-object* and the environment. We'll return to this concept in Chapter 8, but for now, it will suffice to point out that, in general, people can perceive how affordances for passing (or squeezing) through openings change when carrying hand-held objects (Higuchi et al., 2006; Wagman & Taylor, 2005), when using (and learning to use) a wheelchair (Higuchi et al., 2004; Stoffregen et al., 2009), when wearing protective athletic equipment (Higuchi et al., 2011), and during body growth over the course of pregnancy (Franchak & Adolph, 2014) (see Figure 5.11).

Other animals, too, choose whether, when, and how to fit through openings based on *dynamic constraints* such as the changing shape of their body in motion or when objects are attached to their body. When frogs sit on their hind legs, they are compact, almost round. When frogs jump, however, their body flattens out, and their limbs are splayed out from their body. Consequently, when given the choice between jumping through a *horizontally oriented* rectangular opening and a *vertically oriented* rectangular opening, they tend to choose the horizontally oriented one—even when the openings are identical in size and merely rotated

Figure 5.11 Fred is able to perceive changes in affordances for fitting through when he's wearing a suit of armor, football pads, or using a wheelchair.

90° relative to one another (Ingle, 1973). Given that the jump is initiated *when sitting*, the frogs seem to be making this choice based on *impending* changes to the shape of their body—based on an impending future!

Hermit crabs wear shells on their body for protection. As they grow, they need to change shells multiple times throughout their lifetime. The particular size and shape of each shell affect their ability to pass through narrow openings and move down narrow paths. Researchers have shown that hermit crabs make choices about how to move through narrow winding paths based on the relationship between the width of the path and the size of the shell they currently occupy. More impressively, they change *how* they do so when an artificial extension is glued to their shell—they take tighter turns around corners when the size of their shell is artificially extended than when it is not (Sonoda et al., 2012; see Sonoda et al., 2013). Crabs are making these choices based on the dynamically changing relationship between the animal-plus-object and the environment.

Box 5.1 Perceiving Affordances Does Not Require Perceiving Geometric Properties

The ecological approach makes radical claims about what affordances are and how they are perceived. Namely, affordances are activity-specific meanings for a given animal. And a given affordance is perceived by detecting the structured energy pattern at a given point of observation that provides information about that affordance. That is, affordances are perceived. And they are perceived *directly*. Perceiving an affordance requires detecting information about that affordance. Full stop. Perceiving affordances does not require perceiving properties of the animal (e.g., leg length) and properties of the environment (e.g., step height) and then performing a mental calculation comparing these two values (e.g., step height $< 0.88 \times$ leg length = affords stepping on).

Research has shown that this is the case. For example, researchers asked perceivers to report how high they could *jump and reach*. They also asked perceivers to report how high they could *stand and reach* and how high they could *jump*. They found that perceived maximum jump-and-reach height was not the same as perceived maximum stand-and-reach height plus perceived maximum jump height (Thomas, Hawkins, & Nalepka, 2017). Other research has shown that improvements in the ability to perceive properties of the animal or properties of the environment that comprise a given affordance do not necessarily transfer to improvements in the ability to perceive that affordance and vice versa (Mark, 1987; Yasuda, Wagman, & Higuchi, 2014).

These results are consistent with the proposal that perceiving affordances for a given behavior does not require independently perceiving the properties of the animal or the environment that comprise that affordance (Thomas et al., 2020). Rather, such results suggest that a given affordance is perceived *in and of itself*, regardless of how complex that affordance may be (Wagman & Stoffregen, 2020). This is not to say that isolated properties of the animal or environment cannot be perceived. They can. But they are not the primary content of animals' perceptual experiences. Affordances are. And perceiving affordances does not necessarily require perceiving isolated properties of the animal or environment.

Perceiving Affordances for Reaching

If an object is close enough to an animal relative to that animal's arm length and body posture, then they can reach that object with an outstretched arm. Accordingly, the perceptual boundary between objects that afford reaching in this manner and those that do not occurs at a farther horizontal distance for longer-armed people than for shorter-armed people but at the same ratio of object-distance-to-arm-length for both groups (Carello et al., 1989). And at this point, it should not surprise you that people can also *hear* whether an object can be reached by listening to sounds produced by that object (Rosenblum, Wuestefeld, & Anderson, 1996).

Importantly, though, reaching with an outstretched arm becomes uncomfortable when the object is at the limits of a person's reaching ability. At that point, most people typically change *how* they are reaching for the object, perhaps by leaning forward or taking a step toward the object (i.e., they change the mode of performing this behavior). To this end, studies have shown that people choose to transition from reaching with an extended arm to reaching by leaning not at the absolute limits of their ability to reach with an outstretched arm but when it becomes more comfortable to do so (Mark et al., 1997). The researchers referred to this as the *preferred reaching boundary*, a concept similar to Warren's optimal π value.

Other animals, too, choose whether, when, and how to reach an object based on geometry, body posture, and comfort. Wagman, Langley, and Farmer-Dougan (2017) investigated how dogs of different sizes—ranging from beagle to golden retriever—chose to reach for a treat at different heights. In particular, they were interested in the height at which dogs transitioned from reaching for the treat with the head only to reaching by rearing (i.e., standing on their hind legs). They found that this transition occurred at taller heights for taller dogs than for shorter dogs but at the same ratio of treat-height-to-shoulder-height for both groups (see also Wagman, Langley, & Farmer-Dougan, 2018).

Demonstrating that perception is body-scaled usually requires comparing perception of a given affordance by different groups of people (or groups of animals of a given species) who differ in body size. In a clever twist on this procedure, Cabrera, Sanabria, Jiménez, and Covarrubias (2013) compared perception of a given affordance by animals of entirely different *species* that differ in body size. They compared perception of affordances for lever pressing by rats and by hamsters. It may not seem so, but rats are typically heavier and larger than hamsters. The animals were placed individually in operant conditioning chambers (small plexiglass boxes) with levers of different heights that they could press. The lever that was pressed *most often* was a taller height for rats than for hamsters but was *the same ratio* of lever-height-to-maximum-reaching-height for both species. Importantly, though, this ratio was less than 1.0. This suggests that animals of both species chose to press levers most often at heights that were *shorter* than their maximum reaching ability. Like people, rats and hamsters demonstrated a preferred reaching boundary based on comfort and not on their maximum reaching ability (see also Jiménez, Sanabria, & Cabrera, 2017; Jiménez et al., 2019).

Notes

1. An array is a patterned distribution that can vary in multiple ways simultaneously.
2. Note that the proposal that the relationship between animal and environment simultaneously and analogously structures multiple energy arrays is very different from the proposal that a less ambiguous sense must be used to disambiguate a more ambiguous sense (see Chapter 1).

6 Ecological Optics and Visual Perception—Getting Light Into the Muscles

In Chapter 5, we explored how it is that affordances are perceived. This required a rethinking of both *what* the relevant stimulation variables for perception are in general and *how* those variables are used in the perceptual process. In this chapter, we will apply this rethinking to the variables of relevance for *visual perception* in particular and how those variables are used in this process. This requires developing an *ecological optics*—an understanding of light not at the micro scale of photons and receptor cells but at the macro scale of (the relationship between) animals and their environments.

As a reminder, in the traditional approaches, both the description of the relevant properties to be perceived and the stimulation variables by which such properties are perceived have been imported from Newtonian mechanics and Euclidean geometry. With respect to visual perception, the relevant properties to be perceived are height, width, depth, shape, motion, and color, among others. The relevant stimulation variable by which these properties are perceived is light described as photons traveling in a straight line from light source to object and then from object to retina. Described this way, the animal (or really, the *sense organ* of that animal) *passively receives* the relevant stimulation—the light "strikes" or "falls on" the retina). Given that the mosaic of light on the retina—the retinal image—is *ambiguously related* to environmental properties such as the ones listed earlier, the stimulation delivered to the brain must be "fixed" for it to inform the perceiver about the world (see Chapter 1). Consequently, the fundamental question to be answered in the traditional approaches to visual perception is—how does light get into and then get fixed by the brain?

In contrast, in the ecological approach, both the description of the relevant properties to be perceived and the stimulation variables relevant to perceiving such properties are developed in-house in the context of an *ecological physics* and an *ecological geometry*. The relevant properties to be perceived are not really *properties* at all—they are *relationships* between animal and environment. And the relevant stimulation variable(s) are those that are *lawfully structured* by this relationship and that are *actively detected* by a behaving animal. In the case of visual perception, this is the pattern of structured reflected light that surrounds an animal—the ambient optic array (see the next section; Gibson, 1979/2015; Mace, 2020). This optical structure is *unambiguously* related to the properties of those surfaces and the properties of the underlying substances. Moreover, the optical structure at *a particular point of observation*—a location where an animal could be—is information about the animal's (potential) relationship to those substances and surfaces. It is information about affordances. Consequently, the fundamental question in the ecological approach to visual perception is—how does light get into and used by the muscles? (Turvey, 1977, 2019). This is yet another instance of the ecological approach asking entirely new questions rather than providing new answers to the same old questions (see Chapter 4).

DOI: 10.4324/9781003145691-8

Ecological Optics—a Description of Light for Seeing (and Doing)

Most animals that live aboveground, like Fred, are constantly immersed in an ocean of light. Just like the ocean of water that surrounds sea creatures, the ocean of light that surrounds land creatures is *not* uniform. On the contrary, this ocean of light is both different in different *locations* and different in different *directions* at a particular location. However, the light does not start out this way. The ocean of light *is uniform* when it is initially produced by a light source. It only *becomes* structured once it *reflects off* surrounding surfaces (see Figure 6.1). This is the key to ecological optics (Gibson, 1979/2015; Mace, 2020; Turvey, 2019).

Imagine that Fred is standing in a sparsely furnished room. In the center of the room is a light source. It could be an artificial light source like a bright round LED bulb or a sun-like object floating there. Whatever it is, if it is a light source, it *radiates* light. More importantly, the light that it radiates is *pure and unstructured*. It is completely uniform.[1] If Fred faces the light source and stares directly at it, he would see *nothing but brightness*. Moreover, the light source radiates this pure and unstructured energy equally in all directions simultaneously. The light radiating 1 m to the left of the light source is exactly the same in every way as the light radiating 1m to the right of the light source. In fact, if Fred were to walk around it in a perfect circle while staring directly at it, it would look no different to him anywhere along that path. He would see nothing but pure unadulterated brightness all the way around.

Now imagine that Fred faces *away* from the light source and *toward* one of the walls in the room. The light Fred encounters now is no longer coming *directly* from the light source. Instead, it is coming only *indirectly* from the light source by *reflecting off* the wall (and the other surfaces) in the room. This might seem obvious, but it is really important to make it explicit—the light reflecting off the wall allows Fred to see the wall. In fact, everyday visual perception occurs by means of *reflected* (i.e., ambient) light, not radiant (i.e., radiated) light.[2] *Radiant light reveals brightness (if anything at all). Reflected light reveals surfaces* (and underlying substances). This is a key point because what happens to the light when it strikes a surface is that it becomes differentiated and structured—as opposed to remaining uniform and unstructured.

When light radiating from a light source strikes a surface, some of that light is absorbed, and some of that light is reflected. This is a natural and law-based process. *How much* light is reflected by that surface and *how much* light is absorbed by that surface depends on the various properties of that surface. More light will be reflected if the surface is *wet* than if it is *dry*, for example. In addition, *how* the light is reflected will *also* depend on the various properties of

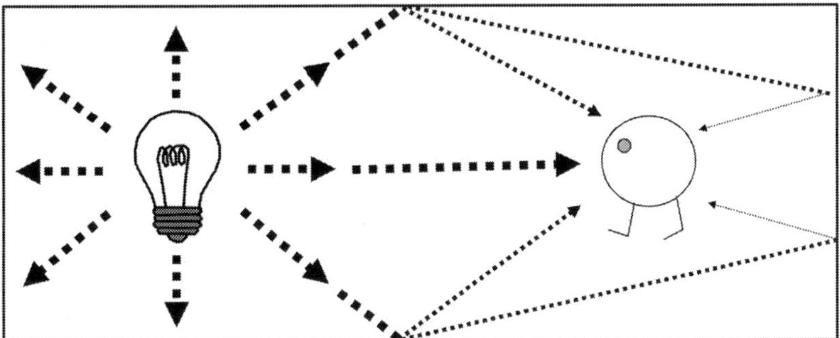

Figure 6.1 Radiant light (emanating from the lightbulb is uniform and unstructured. Ambient light at a point of observation (encountered by Fred) is differentiated and structured.

that surface. Light will be scattered *more* if a surface is *textured* than if it is *smooth*. So reflected light will have different intensities in different directions depending on the surface(s) that it strikes. *These differences give reflected light structure.* And this *optical structure* is lawfully related to the surface that it strikes (see Figure 6.2).

But wait, there's more! Light doesn't just reflect off a given surface and stop. It reflects off that surface and *then* reflects off other surfaces. Light reflecting off the wall and *then* on Fred's checkerboard patterned floor will be different from the light reflecting *only* off the wall or *only* off the floor. It will be structured by both the wall and the floor. And this, too, is a natural and law-based process. The light radiating from the light source reflects from surface to surface, reverberating in the room until the light source stops radiating light. The continuous radiation and reflection of light *fill the room with structured light* in a way that is similar to how the continuous shaking of a half-empty bottle of water fills the bottle with water. So long as the light source continues to radiate light, there will be a steady state of structured light in every part of the room.

Let's go back to Fred facing the wall in the sparsely furnished room. The pattern of structured light that he encounters will consist of light reflected from many surfaces. Most of the light that he encounters will be light that reflects directly from the wall, and some of the light that he encounters will be light that reflects indirectly from the wall and then the floor or vice versa. Now imagine that Fred looks down at the floor. The pattern of structured light he encounters will be different than it was. Now most of the light that he encounters will be light that directly reflects from the *floor*, and some of the light that he encounters will be light that indirectly reflects from the floor and then the wall, or vice versa (see Figure 6.3).

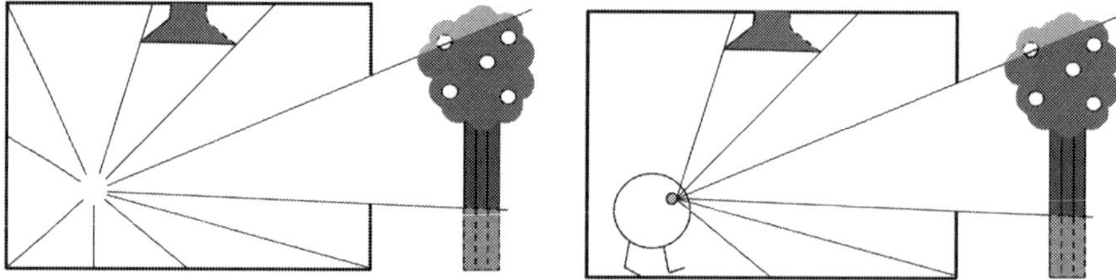

Figure 6.2 The optical structure at a point of observation is lawfully related to the surfaces that it strikes (*left*). When an animal occupies that point of observation, the optical structure at that point of observation provides information about those surfaces (*right*).

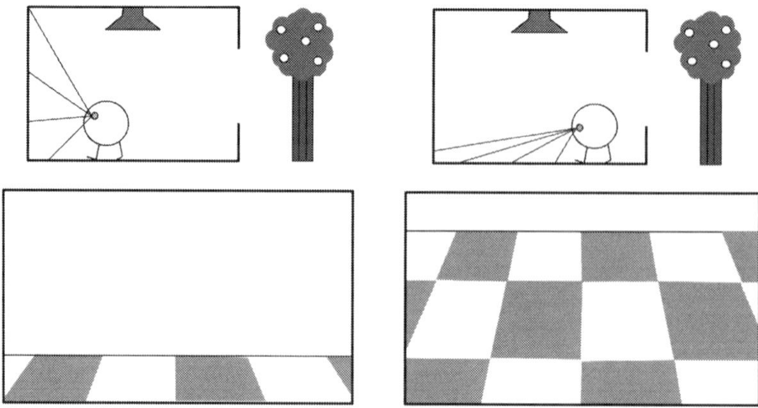

Figure 6.3 Fred's actions (*top*) and his view (*bottom*). The pattern of structured light that Fred encounters will be different when he looks at the wall (*left*) than when he looks at the floor (*right*).

Now imagine Fred looks to his left. The pattern of light he encounters will be different still. We have arrived at a fundamental tenet of ecological optics—at any given point in that room, there will be differences in structured light in different directions. The structured light at a particular point of observation will be different in different directions because of differences in how the reflected light reached that location from those directions.

But wait, there's *still* more! Imagine that Fred takes a step to his right or left and repeats the procedure—looks straight ahead, then down at the floor, then to his left. Each time, there will be differences in each direction, but these differences will not be exactly the same as those at his previous location. This is another fundamental tenet of ecological optics—the pattern of structured light at each and every point in the room (at each and every point that Fred could be) *is unique* (meaning entirely distinctive). In other words, at every point of observation, Fred would encounter *a unique distribution* of structured light—a unique set of differences in different directions. The totality of structured light at each and every possible location in the room is called the *ambient* (meaning *surrounding*) *optic* (meaning *light*) *array* (meaning *distribution*).

In the ecological approach to visual perception, the *ambient optic array*—the surrounding light distribution—is the relevant stimulation pattern for visual perception. Notice there is no mention of rods and cones or a retina, let alone a retinal image. And there is no mention of a copy, getting that copy into the animal's head, or "fixing" that copy. That is because the ambient optic array *surrounds* an animal. It is *encountered* by the animal. It or a copy of it does not (and cannot!) enter the eye or the brain. Therefore, no fixing of a copy is needed (or even possible!). The animal just has to be sensitive to differences in light intensities in different directions that comprise the optic array. This requires a *visual system*, but it does not require a particular *type* of visual system—more on this later.

Information About Surfaces

Now imagine that Fred has purchased a few pieces of furniture to make the room slightly less sparse. Imagine that he is sitting in his favorite chair a short distance from a table. On the opposite wall of the room is a window, through which (part of) a tree is visible (see Figure 6.4). Recall that the structure in reflected light is lawfully related to the surfaces that it strikes. How much light is reflected and how that light is reflected will depend on the various properties of those surfaces.

Therefore, the structured light at Fred's point of observation provides *information about* surface layout. In particular, it provides information about those surfaces, how those surfaces are oriented, and how those surfaces are situated among other surfaces. A *bumpy* surface—like a tree trunk—will structure light differently than a *smooth* surface—like a hardwood floor. A *vertical* surface—like a wall—will structure light differently than a *horizontal* surface—like the

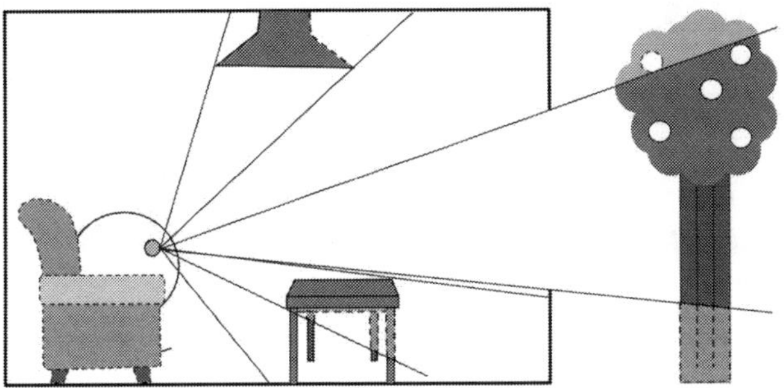

Figure 6.4 The structured light at Fred's point of observation is information about the layout of surfaces.

top of the table. A *continuous* surface—like a large wall—will structure light differently than *two surfaces separated by a gap*—like the portions of the wall separated by a window.

Moreover, a surface *nearer* to his point of observation—like the wall that he is facing—will structure light differently than a surface *farther* from the point of observation—like the tree outside. In addition, something very particular happens if the nearer surface is *partly between* the point of observation and the farther surface—as is the case with the wall and the tree. In that case, the structured light reflecting from part of the farther surface will be blocked by part of the nearer surface and will not reach the point of observation, although it may reach some other point of observation (see Figure 6.4). In more technical language, part of the near surface occludes part of the far surface and the structured light reflecting from it (Gibson, 1979/2015; Heft, 2020). Therefore, differences in the structured light reflecting from the nearer surface and from the farther surface—in particular along the outer edge(s) of the nearer surface (called the occluding edge)—provide information about the separation of these surfaces with respect to one another.

So let's recap. In the ecological approach to visual perception, the relevant stimulation is not the unstructured light produced by a light source passively received by the eye. Rather, it is structured light reflected from surfaces actively encountered by a behaving animal. An animal is surrounded by an ocean of structured light—the ambient optic array. Moreover, the structured light encountered by a given animal at its point of observation is information about the surrounding surfaces.

Depth Perception Reconsidered

Armed with these facts of ecological optics, we are now in a position to reconsider depth perception. Recall that how depth is perceived across space is one of the fundamental problems of visual perception (see Chapter 1). From the ecological perspective, this is a problem without a solution. Both depth and space are abstract, geometrical concepts that only exist *in the absence* of objects. They describe the properties of the container in which objects exist—not the objects themselves. Objects exist *in* depth and *in* space. They do not *have* depth or *have* space. A *hole* might have depth, and a *room* might have space. But in either case, these words refer to the absence of objects in those containers. So the question of how depth and space are perceived is really about how the absence of objects is perceived (Carello & Turvey, 2020). A problem without a solution indeed!

This is a great example of how unsolvable problems arise when concepts imported from Newtonian physics and Euclidean geometry are—explicitly or implicitly—used to understand the problem of how animals perceive and act successfully. The world of Euclidean geometry is completely abstract and imaginary. But the world of animals and environments is concrete and real. When we instead apply concepts from *ecological geometry* and *ecological physics*, the problem of how depth is perceived across space becomes reconfigured as how *distances* are perceived across *surfaces*—or more generally, *how surface layout* is perceived.

Imagine that Fred is looking at a surface such as the one in Figure 6.5. Minimal differences in the structured light (the optical texture) that Fred encounters in different directions—as he looks up and down the surface perhaps—provide information that the surface is oriented vertically (see Figure 6.5a). It is a wall or a door or the side of truck, perhaps. *Systematic* differences in the structured light (the optical texture) that Fred encounters reflecting from different parts of surface are information that the surface is not oriented vertically (see Figure 6.5b). It is a hill or a ramp, perhaps. The specifics of these systematic differences—in particular, how quickly the optical texture changes across different parts of that surface—are information about how *steeply sloped* this surface is. The more quickly the optical texture changes across different parts of that surface, the more horizontal the surface is—it is a floor or grass field, perhaps (see Figure 6.5c).

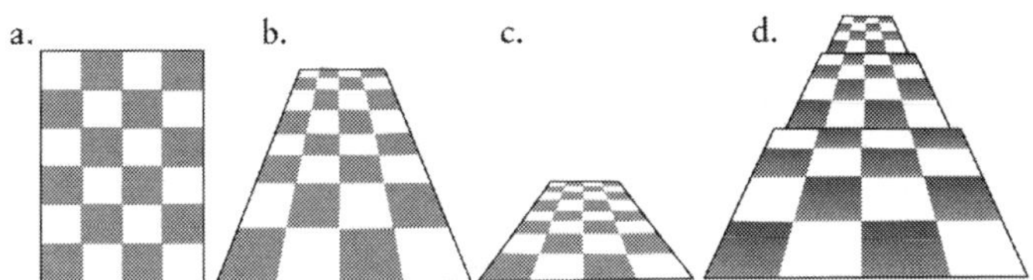

Figure 6.5 Optical structure differs based on the surface: (a) a vertical surface creates minimal differences in differences in the optical structure; (b) and (c) a slanted surface creates systematic differences in optical structure depending on how slanted that surface is; d) drop-offs between surfaces create dramatic differences in optical structure.

When this pattern of *systematic* differences reflecting from different parts of a surface is interrupted by an occluding edge, this is information that there are two separate surfaces. When there are dramatic differences in the optical texture of the occluding surface and of the occluded surface, this is information about a drop off between these two surfaces (see Figure 6.5d)

Box 6.1 The Visual Cliff

The facts of ecological optics described in this chapter and the reconsideration of depth perception that follows from them invite a reconsideration of some of the most classic studies in visual perception research. These include studies using one of the most famous pieces of laboratory equipment in all of visual perception research—the visual cliff (Adolph, Kaplan, & Kretch, 2021; E. Gibson & Walk, 1960; see Figure 6.6, and Chapter 10). In studies using a visual cliff, a baby is placed in the center of a clear plexiglass table. One half of the table—the "shallow" side—has a checkerboard pattern right under the plexiglass, and the other half—the "deep" side—has the checkerboard pattern on the floor. Both sides are in actuality safe for the baby to crawl on, but the question is whether the "deep" side *looks unsafe* to the baby. Does the baby avoid the "deep" side of the table? If so, when does the baby start to do so, and why?

Figure 6.6 In the visual cliff paradigm, a baby is placed on the "shallow" side of the cliff, and a caregiver encourages the baby to crawl to the "deep" side of the cliff. The tabletop is plexiglass, so both sides are safe to crawl on.

Results have shown that, in general, younger babies crawl right "over" the cliff and onto the "deep" side of the table. Older babies avoid doing so. Historically, these results have been interpreted in terms of the age at which babies or other animals develop depth perception abilities or a fear of heights. However, such explanations have not stood up to scrutiny. In the past several decades, it has become clear that what determines whether the babies crawl over the visual cliff is not age but crawling experience. And what develops is not depth perception or fear of heights but the ability to perceive surface layout (see Chapter 10). Surfaces can be crawled upon. Depth cannot. The infants are learning to perceive what is and is not safe to crawl upon and what each of these kinds of surfaces looks like. Crawling experience enables babies to learn about what different patterns of optical texture mean for where and how they can crawl. Inexperienced crawlers have not learned what patterns of optical texture are information about a drop-off between surfaces, and so they crawl right over the cliff. Experienced crawlers have learned this, and so they avoid doing so (see Adolph & Hoch, 2019; Adolph, Kretch, & LoBue, 2014).

Information About *Relationships Between* Animals and Surfaces

Imagine now that Fred stands up and turns around to face *away* from the table and tree. The optical structure that he encounters now is different than it was. In particular, he no longer encounters the structured light directly reflecting off these surfaces. Looking at a blank wall is pretty boring, so he turns around to face the table and tree (through the window) again. Again, he encounters structured light reflecting off these surfaces but not the structured light directly reflecting from the wall. This is a mundane but important point. Fred, like every other animal with front-facing eyes, only has access to the structured light *in front* of him and not the structured light *behind* him—at least not at this particular moment. In this way, the structured light that an animal encounters is information about *its orientation* to surrounding surfaces.

Now imagine that Fred tires of standing (and turning!) and sits down again. The optical structure that he encounters at this point of observation is different than it was when he was standing (see Figure 6.7). When sitting, he encounters *more* of the structured light reflecting from the floor in front of the table, *less* of the structured light reflecting from the surface of the table, and *none* of the structured light reflecting from the floor behind the table (due to the table now occluding this surface). If Fred were to stand on a step stool instead of sitting in a chair, there would be *different changes* in the structured light he encounters. Remember that the pattern of structured light at each and every point in the room—at each and every point that Fred could be—is unique (meaning distinctive). In this way, the structured light that an animal encounters is information about its relationship to surrounding surfaces.

So the structured light at a point not only provides information about surface layout; it *also* provides information about the *surface layout in relation to the animal.* The structured light encountered by a *taller* animal is different from that encountered by a *shorter* animal. The structured light encountered by a *standing* animal is different from that encountered by a *sitting* animal. This means that the structured light encountered by a given animal at a given point of observation provides information about its body size and location *relative* to surrounding surfaces. It is body-scaled! This is a critical point. This allows for the possibility that perceiving affordances such as *getting across or over, passing or squeezing through*, and *reaching* (see Chapter 5) may (merely) be a matter of detecting the structured light at a given point of observation. This does not make perception of affordances a simple process (to do or to study), but it does

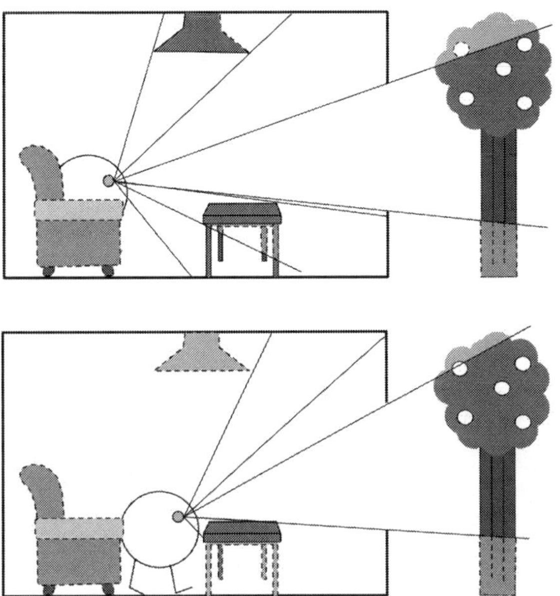

Figure 6.7 When Fred changes his point of observation, he encounters different patterns of structured light. These patterns are information about his *relationship to* the layout of surfaces that the light strikes.

mean that the focus shifts to understanding how it is that such patterns are *detected*—rather than how copies are *fixed*. Consequently, changing a person's (perceived) point of observation changes the affordances that the person perceives. For example, if a person's point of observation is raised with respect to a particular surface layout (e.g., by standing on blocks attached to their shoes or by lowering the floor in front of them), they will—initially, anyway—perceive affordances as if they were taller (Mark, 1987; Warren & Whang, 1987)!

We're not done quite yet, though. The description that we have provided so far—more or less—assumes stationary objects and a stationary animal. But animals are almost never stationary. Or if they are stationary, they are not so for very long. On the contrary, animals move—a lot. For example, in just the last few moments, Fred has already looked to his right, looked down, stepped to his right, turned around, and sat down in his favorite chair. Now, imagine that Fred *walks toward the window*—that's where the tree (and the apple) is, after all. As Fred walks toward the window, he will encounter a *changing pattern* of structured light. There will be continual changes in the structured light he encounters as he moves along this path. For example, he will progressively encounter *more and more* of the structured light reflecting from the tree through the window and *less and less* of the structured light reflecting off the other surfaces in the room—like the wall, the floor, or the table. This changing pattern is called *optic flow*. The word "flow" here is important. The pattern emerges not by stitching together snapshots but rather by experiencing a continuously unfolding optical event. And the specifics of the optic flow pattern inform *how* the animal is moving, *where* it is going, and *when* it will get there (see subsequent sections).

The optic flow pattern encountered by a *crawling* animal will be different than that encountered by a *walking* animal. The optic flow pattern encountered by a *more massive* walking animal—like an elephant or a sumo wrestler—will be different than that encountered by a less massive walking animal—like a poodle or a marathon runner. The optic flow pattern encountered by a *walking* animal will be different than that encountered by a *running* animal. And the optic flow pattern encountered by a *galloping* animal will be different than that encountered by a *bounding* animal. So the changing pattern of structured light encountered by an animal not only depends on its size and shape but also by its mass, strength, dexterity, and skill; how it moves through the world; and how it moves things in the world. Therefore, the optic flow pattern encountered by an animal is not just body-scaled—it is also *action-scaled*.

So let's recap (again). In the ecological approach to visual perception, the seemingly unsolvable problem of how (empty) space is perceived is replaced with the solvable (but still challenging) problem of how surface layout is perceived. The structured light encountered by an animal at its point of observation provides information not only about the layout of the surrounding surfaces but also about *its relationship to* this layout—the affordances of those surfaces for the animal!

Perception of Movement Reconsidered

Armed with these facts of ecological optics, we are now in a position to reconsider another fundamental problem of visual perception—the perception of motion. As in perception of depth, most traditional explanations of perception of motion are based on the mosaic of light striking the retina—the retinal image. In particular, motion of objects in the world creates a sequence of stimulation across different locations on the retinal surface. However, given the ambiguity inherent in the retinal image, this stimulation must be "fixed" by the brain for it to inform the perceiver about movement in the world. For example, given that the "image" on the retina is pixelated, how is movement of an object in the world perceived as smooth rather than as a sequence of still images? And how does the brain tell the difference between the pattern of stimulation on the retina created by a moving object from right to left and the eye (or head) moving from left to right? As you might expect, from the ecological perspective, perception of motion is yet another problem without a solution. The fundamental issue is this—motion, like depth and space, is *an abstract concept*. Objects *move*, but they don't have motion—motion is not a property to be possessed by an object. Moreover, motion does not exist in the absence of a moving object. Moving objects, of course, *can* be seen. But motion itself cannot. In particular, the movement of objects and surfaces relative to the perceiver and the movement of the perceiver relative to surfaces can each be seen. Let's discuss these in turn.

Movement of Surfaces Relative to the Perceiver

Imagine that the apple that Fred wants falls from the branch of the tree and lands in front of the trunk of the tree. The falling apple will create a changing pattern of optical structure in a particular location—*a localized optic flow pattern*. In particular, at some point during its descent, it will begin to *occlude* the trunk's surface and the structured light reflecting from it. However, it will do so in a very particular pattern. As it moves toward the ground, the bottom edge of the apple will progressively occlude (the structured light reflecting from) lower and lower portions of the trunk until it comes to rest on the ground. As it falls in front of the trunk, the bottom of the apple is an occluding edge, and the trunk is the occluded surface (see Figure 6.8). At the same time, the upper edge of the apple will progressively reveal (the structured light reflecting from) portions of the trunk that had just been occluded by the apple. This pattern of progressive deletion of optical texture at an occluding edge with the progressive revealing of optical texture at the opposite (trailing) edge is information about one surface moving in front of another surface. In this case, it is information about the apple falling in front of the trunk.

Now, imagine that the apple that Fred wants falls from the branch of the tree, bounces on the ground, and lands behind the trunk of the tree. At some point, after it bounces, it—and

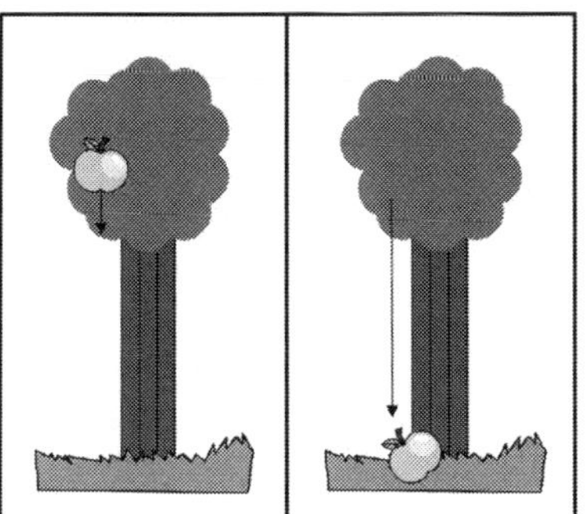

Figure 6.8 When an apple falls in front of a tree (*left*), the bottom of the apple progressively occludes the tree, and the top edge of the apple progressively reveals the tree. When an apple falls and bounces behind a tree (*right*), the edge of the apple is progressively occluded by the edge of the tree.

Figure 6.9 Different optical patterns (*bottom*) are created by different situations (*top*): (a) Claudia has an apple that Fred wants; (b) when Claudia throws the apple to Fred, the optical texture of the apple expands, and there is occlusion at the outer edge of the apple; (c) when Fred walks toward Claudia, the optical texture of everything in Fred's field of view expands, and there is occlusion at the edges of his field of view.

the structured light reflecting from it—will be occluded by the trunk's surface. Again, this will occur in a particular pattern. In this case, the edge of the trunk will progressively occlude more and more of the (structured light reflecting from the) apple until the apple comes to rest on the ground partly behind the tree. Here, the outer edge of the trunk is an occluding edge, and the apple is the occluded surface. However, unlike the case where the apple falls in front of the trunk, there will be no progressive revealing of (structured light reflecting from) the trunk or the apple. This pattern of progressive deletion of optical texture at an occluding edge *without* the progressive revealing of optical texture at the opposite (trailing) edge is information about one surface moving *behind* another surface. In this case, the apple falling *behind* the trunk.

Now imagine that Claudia picks the apple for Fred and tosses it to him (see Figure 6.9a-b). Her aim is particularly good, and so the apple is heading right for Fred's nose. As the tossed apple approaches Fred, it will progressively occlude all of the (structured light reflecting from the) surrounding surfaces. In this case, *the entire outer contour* of the apple is an occluding edge.

In addition, as more and more structured light reflecting from the surrounding surfaces is occluded, more and more structured light reflecting from the apple is revealed. That is, *the optical texture of the apple will (appear to) expand*. Moreover, this expansion will be *symmetric*. The optical texture will expand at the same rate in every direction, and the center of this expansion pattern will be the center of the apple. This pattern of *deletion* of optical texture at an object's outer edges plus *symmetric expansion* of that object's optical texture is information about that object moving *directly toward the perceiver*. In this case, it is information about the apple moving directly toward Fred's nose (see Figure 6.9b).

Fred, of course, does not want the apple to hit him in the nose—or anywhere else, for that matter. He wants to catch it and then eat it. To do so, he needs to know *when* the apple will get to him. This seems like the kind of thing that Fred would need to guess or maybe even calculate based on speed and distance—especially given the ambiguity inherent in the retinal image. But it turns out that the time until the apple arrives is (potentially) available to be detected in the optic array—no calculations needed! More specifically, it is available in *how quickly* the optical texture of the apple expands as it approaches (how quickly it occludes the background relative to how much it currently occludes the background) (e.g., Lee, 1976, 2009). This relative rate of expansion is a variable called tau (τ), and it is information about *time to arrival*—assuming that current conditions continue. The variable τ reveals that there is potential for optical variables to provide information about when and where an object will arrive so that the animal can behave accordingly before the object gets there. For example, the optical texture of the apple will expand slowly at first and then expand more and more rapidly as the object gets closer. The bottom line, though, is that movements of objects relative to an animal—in front of other surfaces, behind other surfaces, toward an animal—lawfully generate local patterns of change in the optic array.

But what if Claudia's aim is not so good and the apple will miss to Fred's right? In this case, the right edge of the apple will progressively occlude the (structured light reflecting from the) surrounding surfaces. And the left edge of the apple will progressively reveal (the structured light reflecting from) the surrounding surface that had just been occluded by that edge of the apple. At the same time, there will be an expansion of the optical texture of the apple, but this expansion will be *asymmetric*, and the center of the expansion pattern will be toward the right of the apple. The optical texture will expand more quickly on the right side of the apple than on the left side. This pattern of progressive deletion of optical texture at an occluding edge and progressive *revealing* of optical texture at the opposite (trailing) edge *plus* the *asymmetric expansion* of optical texture is information about that surface moving *indirectly* toward the perceiver. How Fred can use optical information to move into position to catch an object under these circumstances will be discussed in an upcoming section.

Movement of Perceiver Relative to Surfaces of Objects

Now imagine that Fred doesn't trust his ability to catch the apple, so instead of waiting for Claudia to throw it to him, he walks toward her (see Figure 6.9c). As he approaches her and the apple, he will encounter a *changing pattern* of optical structure. In particular, more and more of the structured light reflected from Claudia will be revealed and will appear to expand symmetrically, and more and more of the background will be occluded. However, unlike the situation in which the apple moves toward Fred, when Fred approaches Claudia, occlusion will also occur at the edges of Fred's field of view. Remember that Fred only has access to the structured light in front of him and not the structured light behind him. As he moves forward, he will see more and more of the structured light in front of him and less and less of the structured light behind him. In other words, when Fred moves through the world, the *entire outer contour* of his field of view is an occluding edge (see Figure 6.9c). This pattern of *deletion* of structured light at the outer edges of the field of vision accompanied by *global expansion* of the optical texture—and specifically the symmetric expansion of the optical texture of a given surface—is information about the animal moving *directly toward that surface*. In this case, it is information about Fred moving toward Claudia. This pattern is not a *localized* optic flow but a *global* optic flow. And the specifics of the global optic flow pattern are informative about how the animal is moving, where it is moving, and when it will get there.

If Fred decides that he is not getting to Claudia and the apple fast enough and breaks into a run, the *rate* of global optic flow will increase. If he slows down again, the rate of optic flow will decrease. The rate of global optic flow is information about his movement speed. In particular, *how quickly* the optical texture of the apple expands (τ) is (again) information about *time to arrival* (assuming that current conditions continue). If Fred sees a bee buzzing around the apple—he *hates* bees—and stops, the global optic flow will decrease to zero. If he then decides to backpedal away from the bee, the optic flow will *reverse*. This time, there will be a progressive revealing of structured light at the outer contours of his field of vision accompanied by a global contracting of optical texture—specifically, a symmetric contracting of the optical texture of the apple. This pattern is information about Fred moving directly away from the apple and the bee.

Two Simple Rules for Outfielders and Dogs

What if Claudia is feeling ornery and has a strong throwing arm and decides to throw the apple over Fred's head? He would need to run and catch it. This is the challenge faced by athletes in sports such as baseball, softball, cricket, soccer (what most of the world calls football), and football (what most of the world calls American football), to name a few. Athletes in these sports often need to get themselves to the place where the ball is going to land before it gets there so that they can make the appropriate play (e.g., catch it, deflect it, kick it). How do they—and how would Fred—do this? One possibility is for the athlete (and Fred) to (perhaps unconsciously) use the variables of Euclidean geometry and Newtonian physics. Doing this would require—likely unconsciously—calculating where the object is going to land, when it will land there, what path along the ground Fred should take to get there, when Fred should start moving along that path, and how fast he should do so. Although it seems unlikely given what we have already discussed in previous chapters, it is *possible* that people such as the athletes mentioned previously are doing exactly this and that the ability to do so quickly and unconsciously is one of the skills that develop with athletic experience.

But what if information about how to get into position to catch an object is available to be detected in the optic array? A number of studies have shown that this is, in fact, the case. Rather than calculating anything—implicitly or explicitly—a person may only need to—implicitly or explicitly—follow two simple rules based on such information:

Rule 1: Move so that the ball appears to be traveling a straight-line path.
Rule 2: Stop running when the ball is (and stays) directly overhead.

Think about what the trajectory of a thrown, kicked, or batted ball looks like. Imagine standing to the side of two people having a catch where they each throw the ball high in the air to each other. What will the path of the ball look like to you? The path will look like an upside-down U—something like this: ∩ (see Figure 6.10a). You will see the ball go up from the person throwing the ball, reach a peak at the top of the curve, and then down to the person catching it. Note that the ball *will not* appear to be traveling in a straight line, and you *are not* in a position to catch it. Now imagine standing directly *between* the two people who are having a catch (by throwing the ball over your head to each other), facing one of them, and looking up.

What will the path of the ball look like now? You are now *under* the curved path of the ball, so it will not look like this ∩ anymore. Instead, you will see the ball travel a straight-line path.

So following Rule 1 will put you in the path of the moving ball. However, in your current position between the two people having a catch, you are *still* not in position to catch the ball. But you *are* aligned with the path of the ball. You will see the ball travel a straight-line path *and keep going over your head.* Now imagine backing up way too far to a spot behind where the ball will land. You will now see the ball stop moving along the straight-line path *before* it is over your head as it begins to descend in front of you. Now imagine moving forward until you are *exactly* where the ball will land. What will the path of the ball look like now? You will see the ball travel a straight-line path *until it is directly over your head.* At this point, the ball will appear to stop moving along this path (because it is now falling straight down directly to where you are standing). You will then see the optical texture of the ball expand symmetrically, occluding what is behind it (see Figure 6.9b). Following Rule 2 will put you *in the location along the ball's path* where it will land when it lands there. It will put you in the right place at the right time (Turvey, 2019)

Researchers investigated this by attaching a small video camera to a person's shoulder (this was in the mid-1990s before GoPros and other more convenient options were available). They then launched balls toward the person from a distance of 50 m (about 164 feet) and used the video from the camera to analyze what the person saw when they were moving into position to catch the ball. They found that people got to the right place at the right time by synchronizing

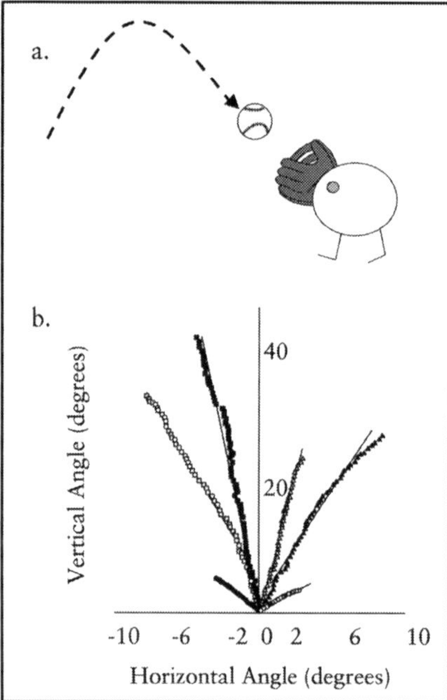

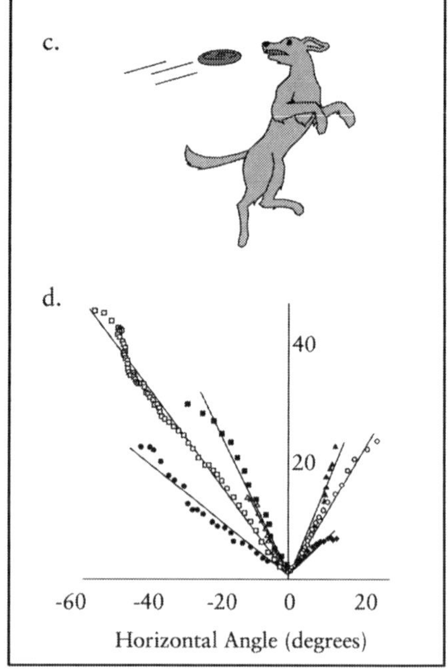

Figure 6.10 (a) When a baseball outfielder catches a fly ball, they run so that the ball appears to travel in a straight line (even if it is not actually doing so). (b) The apparent trajectory of the ball from the person's perspective on several different trials (*left*). (b) When dogs catch Frisbees, they do the exact same thing (even though the Frisbee curves in flight). (c) The apparent trajectory of the Frisbee from the dog's perspective in several different trials. Note the similarity between the graphs in b and d.

their movements with the changing optical structure available at their point of observation in the optic array (see McBeath et al., 1995; Michaels & Zaal, 2002; Fink et al., 2009).

In particular, they moved so that the ball appeared to be traveling in a straight line (see Figure 6.10b). What is critical about this is that the relevant information for getting into position to catch a ball *is not on the retina*. It is not *in the brain*. It does not need to be "fixed" or calculated or modeled. It does not require a particular kind of visual system. It only requires that the visual system be sufficiently sensitive to detect such changing optical structure. In other words, it has the potential to provide a general explanation for the visual control of pursuit, interception, and catching behaviors by a wide variety of animal species.

To test this hypothesis, researchers investigated how two dogs—a springer spaniel named Romeo and a border collie named Lilly—caught Frisbees (Figure 6.10c). Similar to the human outfielders, the dogs were fitted with head-mounted micro video cameras (this was in 2004, the year GoPros were invented, but before they were widely available). The researchers then threw the Frisbees from a distance of 10–20 m (about 32–65 feet) so that the dogs had to run to catch them. As in the study of outfielders, they used the video to analyze what the dogs saw when they were moving into position to catch the Frisbee. They found that the dogs that used an analogous strategy to get to the right place at the right time (see Figure 6.10d). Just like the humans, the dogs did so by synchronizing their movements with the changing optical structure available at their point of observation in the optic array (Shaffer et al., 2004).

Box 6.2 The Birds and the Bees

What makes the variables of ecological optics so powerful is that they are available to be detected by any animal that has a visual system with appropriate sensitivity (satisfying Hume's touchstone, see Chapter 4). They have the potential to provide *a general explanation* for the visual control of behavior by all animal species. For the most part, the sophistication of the visual system and/or brain do not matter. The fact that dogs seem to catch Frisbees by using the same optical patterns as humans use to catch balls is evidence of this. Two other examples of animals using optical patterns to perform complex behaviors are birds and bees.

Gannets are seabirds that hunt by diving from the air, plunging into the water, and pursuing fish. They can dive from heights of 30 m (nearly 100 feet) and reach speeds of 100 km/h (over 60 mph). The problem for the gannets is this: they have to keep their wings extended for as long as possible during their descent so that they can steer toward their moving prey. However, they also have to retract their wings *before* entering the water so that they make a streamlined entry—and don't injure themselves—or worse!. How do they know *when* to retract their wings? They don't start their dives from the same height every time, so they can't simply time when to do so. Besides, they would need to know the height, velocity, and acceleration of a particular dive and then and use these variables to *compute* time—all while hurtling toward the water at highway speeds!

Researchers analyzed videos of gannets diving from different heights and found evidence that the birds were choosing when to retract their wings based on the optical expansion of a particular patch of water. In other words, they were using τ, which provides information about time to arrival (Lee & Reddish, 1981; see Lee, 2009). Similar strategies are used by insects attempting to land on (or avoid) a surface and may even be used to program wheeled, hovering, or flying robots to do the same (Serres & Ruffier, 2017).

You may already know that bees communicate the location of nectar sources to other members of their hive by dancing. For a particular species of bee (*Apis mellifera ligusta*), a round dance is used when the nectar source is near, and a waggle dance is used when the nectar source is far. But how does a bee know how far it has flown so that it can communicate this information in its dance? One possibility is that they estimate distance based on the amount of energy used flying from the source to the hive. The more energy used, the greater distance they must have flown. Another possibility is that they use (the rate of) *global optic flow*. Researchers measured the duration of the waggle portion of the dance performed by bees who had flown through two different tunnels to a nectar source. The tunnels were the same length (6 m), and the nectar source was the same distance away from the hive (35 m). The only difference between them was what the tunnels *looked like on the inside*. One—the line tunnel—had a single black line running down the length of the tunnel. The other tunnel—the ring tunnel—had black rings every few centimeters. The bees that flew down the line tunnel were more likely to perform the round dance, indicating that the nectar was *near*, and the bees that flew down the ring tunnel were more likely to perform the waggle dance, indicating that the nectar was *far*—even though the distance flown was identical. Why? Flying through the ring tunnel generated *more optic flow* than did flying through the line tunnel—which produced little to no optic flow—suggesting that the bees had used (the rate of) optic flow and not the energy used to determine the distance flown (Srinivasan et al., 2000; Esch et al., 2001; see Chiovaro & Paxton, 2020).

The Promise of Getting Light Into the Muscles

At the beginning of the chapter, we proposed that the fundamental question of the ecological approach to visual perception is how does light get into and used by the muscles? (Turvey, 1977, 2019). To this end, we have talked about how the optical structure at a point of observation changes when surfaces move relative to a perceiver—*local optic flow*, including occlusion—and when a perceiver moves relative to surfaces—*global optic flow*. We have also discussed how the optical structure at a point of observation provides information about what movements a person or dog would need to make to perform a given behavior like catching a ball.

However, the movements that the person or dog would need to make may not be ones that they are capable of making. The optical structure at a point of observation must provide information not only about how to perform a given behavior but also about that animal's ability to do so. The optical information must provide information about the perceiver's ability to *do the required work*—it must be action-scaled. This has been the focus of recent research on affordance-based control of visually guided action (Fajen, 2007, 2013; Fajen & Matthis, 2011). For example, Fajen (2005a) found that the changes in optic flow that occurred when applying the brakes in a simulated driving task enabled drivers to make adjustments in their braking behavior so that they were able to stop the car safely. The changing optical structure that occurred while accelerating and decelerating during the driving task allowed them to (quickly) learn how to use the brake so that the deceleration required to bring the car to a stop did not exceed their maximum deceleration ability—how quickly they could bring the car to a complete stop. This was the case even when the strength of the brake increased or decreased—such as occurs when driving a friend's car or a rental car (Fajen, 2005a).

Along similar lines, researchers found that participants who performed a simulated chasing task in a virtual reality environment were able to use optic flow patterns to determine whether to continue to pursue the target or abandon the chase. That is, the changing optical structure informed the participants about whether the acceleration required to catch the target (before it escaped) exceeded their maximum acceleration ability (Steinmetz et al., 2020).

Notes

1. The light radiating from a fire is a little bit of an exception because as the fire burns, the light that is produced is structured by the substances that are burning, the airflow, and so on.
2. Exceptions, of course, include ever-present LED screens (like TVs, computers, tablets, and phones). LED screens *do* radiate light, and you are able to see what is on the screen but only because of how the (depicted) text or objects on that screen change the properties of that radiated light. In this way, looking at text on an LED screen is like looking at a high-tech silhouette of an object in the real world.

7 Ecological Acoustics and Auditory Perception—Getting Sound Into the Muscles

In Chapter 6, we discussed an ecologically inspired rethinking of variables of relevance to visual perception of surfaces and relationships between animals and those surfaces. This required developing an ecological optics—an understanding of light at the macro scale of (the relationship between) animals and their environments. In this chapter, we will take an analogous approach to auditory perception. And analogously, this will require developing an *ecological acoustics*—an understanding of *sound* at the macro scale of (the relationship between) animals and their environments. The energy form differs, of course, but the overall approach to ecological acoustics will be very similar to that of ecological optics.

This is not just a matter of convenience. *It is a matter of necessity*. This is because, from the ecological perspective, perception is a lawful process. Specifically, properties of surfaces and relationships between animals and those surfaces lawfully structure energy patterns. In most cases, however, such properties and relationships lawfully structure *multiple energy patterns simultaneously*.

Energy is energy regardless of form, and all energy forms abide by the laws of physics. Thus, the same lawful processes apply across energy forms. A given property of a surface or a given relationship between an animal and that surface ought to structure energy form A (e.g., light) and energy form B (e.g., sound) in analogous ways. The structure in energy form A ought to be analogous to the structure in energy form B, *but it won't be identical*. It can't be. Light is different from sound and has different properties. Therefore, the specifics of the pattern will be different, but there will be an analogous structure—an analogous patterning of the energy form—in each case.

Regardless of the differences at the micro scale, in each case, the structure in different energy forms at the macro scale (have the potential to) carry *the same information about* surfaces and relationships between animals and those surfaces. Remember—the medium is not the message (see Chapter 4). In principle, the structure in any given energy form can provide information about affordances—so long as the relevant animal-environment relationship structures that particular energy form and so long as the animal is capable of detecting that structure. Analogously, the fundamental question in the ecological approach to auditory perception is this—how does sound get into and used by the muscles?

Ecological Acoustics—a Description of Sound for Listening (and Doing)

Imagine that Fred is standing in his sparsely furnished room daydreaming about obtaining more furniture when he hears the familiar buzzing sound of a bee. Fred *hates* bees. He can't see the bee, but nonetheless, he knows that it *is* a bee, that it is nearby, that it is on *this* side of the window pane rather than on *that* side of the window pane, and that it is—to his horror—getting closer. How does he know these things? Applying the lessons from ecological optics, we

DOI: 10.4324/9781003145691-9

can propose that Fred knows all of these things (and more) based on the structured sound that he encounters at a point of observation (i.e., at a listening point).

Animals, like Fred, are not only immersed in an ocean of light; they are also immersed in an *ocean of sound* (see Figure 7.1). To some extent, the ocean of sound surrounding every animal is easier to imagine than the ocean of light surrounding every animal. And just like the ocean of light, the ocean of sound is not uniform. This ocean of sound also differs in different locations and in different directions (at a particular location). However, unlike the ocean of light, the ocean of sound does not start out unstructured. Instead, it is structured by the (vibrations created by the) interacting materials that generate the sound. And it *becomes* differently structured when those vibrations *reflect off* surrounding surfaces (see Figure 7.1). This is the key to ecological acoustics (Carello, Wagman, & Turvey, 2005).

Although it may seem strange, sound is caused by colliding materials. These collisions can be subtle and gentle, like when the wings of the bee rapidly collide with the surrounding air molecules. And they can be violent and forceful, like when the hooves of a herd of stampeding buffalo collide with the dry prairie bed. But in both cases, the sounds are produced by collisions. The interaction between the materials (i.e., the collisions) creates vibrations in the air that are lawfully structured by the nature of the materials, how they are interacting, and where they are interacting, among other factors (Carello et al., 2005; Gaver, 1993a, 1993b; Gibson, 1966). And this *acoustic structure* is lawfully related to the properties of the sound-producing object(s).

As we discussed in the last chapter, the light that Fred encounters comes both directly from a light source and indirectly from surfaces that reflect that light. The same thing is true of the vibration patterns that Fred encounters. Some of the vibration patterns encountered by Fred at his current listening point come directly from the bee. But some of the vibration patterns come indirectly from the bee by reflecting off nearby surfaces in the room (e.g., the walls, the window, the table). In fact, everyday auditory perception typically occurs by means of both vibration patterns that are generated by a sound source and vibration patterns that are reflected from surrounding surfaces[1] (Carello et al., 2005; Gaver, 1993a, 1993b).

And just like light reflecting off surfaces, sounds reflecting off surfaces are lawfully structured by those surfaces. When a vibration pattern comes into contact with a surface, some of that vibration pattern is absorbed by the surface, and some of it is reflected by that surface. This is a natural and law-based process as well. *How much* of the vibration pattern is reflected and *how much* is absorbed depends on the properties of that surface. For example, more of the vibration pattern will be reflected by a *metallic* surface than by a *plush* surface. In addition, how

Figure 7.1 Sounds generated by a sound source are structured by the interacting materials that create the sound. They are then differently structured by reflecting surfaces. Ambient sound provides information about both the sound source and the surrounding surfaces.

Figure 7.2 The acoustic structure converging at Fred's point of observation is information about the layout of surfaces.

the vibrations are reflected will *also* depend on various properties of that surface. Sound will be scattered *more* if a surface is *textured* than if it is *smooth*. So just like reflected light will have different intensities in different directions depending on the surface(s) that it strikes, reflected sound will have different intensities in different directions depending on the surface(s) that it strikes. These differences give reflected sound *structure*. And this *acoustic structure* is lawfully related to the surface(s) that it strikes.

Like reflected light, sounds reflect from surface to surface, reverberating in the room until the interacting materials creating the vibrations in the air cease to interact. This *fills the room (at least temporarily) with a steady state of structured sound*. And now we have reached a fundamental tenet of ecological acoustics—at any given point in the room, there will be differences in structured sound in different directions. The structured sound converging at a particular location (at a particular listening point where an animal could be) will be different in different directions because of both the specifics of the interacting materials that created that sound and how the reflected sound reaches that location from those directions (see Figure 7.2).

Moreover, the structured sound converging at a given location in the room will be different than the structured sound converging at any other location in that room. This is yet another fundamental tenet of ecological acoustics—the pattern of structured sound converging at each and every point in the room—at each and every point that Fred could be—is unique (meaning entirely distinctive). In other words, at every listening point, Fred would encounter a unique distribution of structured sound—a unique set of differences in different directions (see Figure 7.2).

The totality of structured sound at each and every possible location in the room is the *ambient acoustic array* (the acoustic equivalent of the ambient optic array). In the ecological approach to auditory perception, the ambient acoustic array is the relevant stimulation pattern for auditory perception. And the ambient sound converging at a given listening point provides information about surfaces, their relationships to one another, and the listener's current relationship to these surfaces. Let's consider these in turn.

Information About Surfaces

Imagine that Fred has finally bought more furniture for his room and is now setting the table for dinner. He is carrying various plates, bowls, glasses, and silverware on a tray to the table when a bee appears outside his window (as an unnecessary reminder—he *hates* bees). This startles him so much that one of the items falls from the tray. He does not know which one because he continues to stare down the bee. He hears the object strike the ground. From the sound alone, however, he can tell quite a bit about the object, where it went, and what happened to it. For one thing, he knows that it is a ceramic object—a plate or bowl as opposed to silverware or glassware. For another, he knows that it is flat, circular, and large—a dinner plate as opposed to a salad plate or a soup bowl. For another, he knows that it ended up on the floor by his feet and not under the table. And finally, he knows that it bounced and did not shatter—whew! Each of these interactions among surfaces lawfully structures the ambient acoustic array.

Hearing Objects

Fred's ability is fairly typical of everyday experience, though it might not seem so. In some ways, *hearing* properties of surfaces and relationships between surfaces and animals may seem to be an even bigger challenge than *seeing* such properties and relationships. In fact, strictly based on the complex Euclidean geometry, it should be difficult—if not impossible—to perceive geometric properties of objects based on sound alone. This is because for two-dimensional objects—which, strictly speaking, have no thickness and thus only exist in the abstract—there is an ambiguous relationship between frequency and shape[2] (Kac, 1966; Gordon & Webb, 1996).

A series of experiments conducted at the turn of the 21st century, however, demonstrated not only that people can do this, but that they can do it quite well (Kunkler-Peck & Turvey, 2000). Researchers built a rectangular wooden frame and used a fishing line to suspend thin, flat plates of different sizes, shapes, and materials within that frame—one plate at a time. A pendulum bob was attached by string to the top of the frame and was used to strike each object (see Figure 7.3, *left*). The movement of the pendulum bob was restricted so that it was released from the same location—and therefore struck each plate with the same amount of force—each time. Participants were on the other side of a screen and could not see either the plate or the pendulum, but they could hear the sound produced when the pendulum bob struck the plate.

The researchers conducted numerous experiments, but two in particular are relevant for our purposes. In the first one, the plates were made of three different materials—wood, plexiglass, and steel—and were three different shapes—circle, square, and triangle. The materials were the same thickness, and the shapes of all plates had the same surface area. Of course, the steel

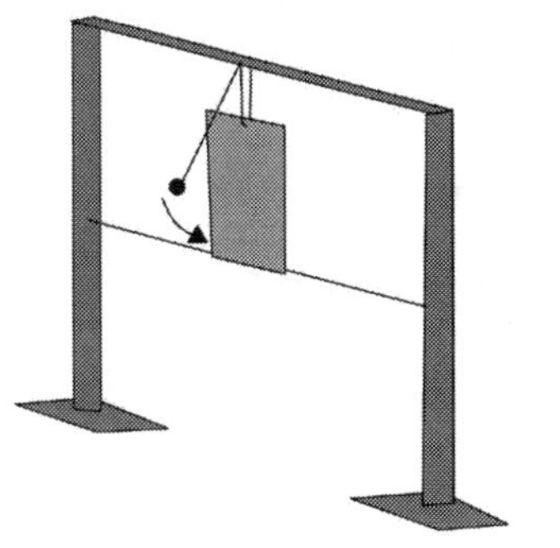

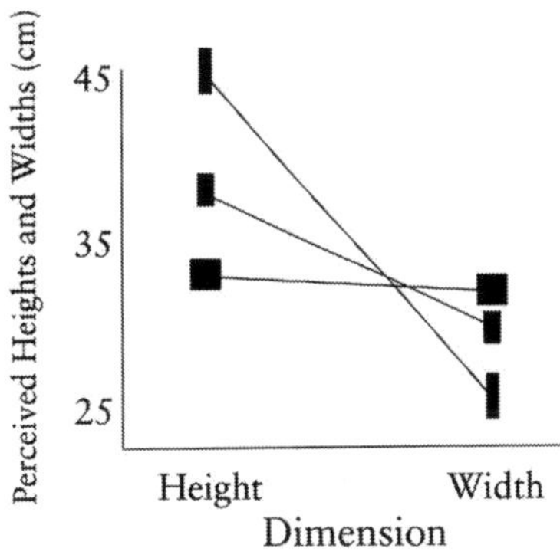

Figure 7.3 *Left*: The apparatus used by Kunkler-Peck and Turvey (2000). A pendulum bob was struck against suspended plates of different shapes and materials. Participants were able to hear both properties at a level above chance. *Right*: In another experiment, a pendulum bob was struck against metal rectangles of different dimensions. Participants could hear whether the rectangle was taller than it was wide, as tall as it was wide, or wider than it was tall.

plates weighed more than the wood plates, which weighed more than the plexiglass plates, but all shapes of a given material weighed the same (e.g., the wood triangle weighed the same as the wood square and the wood circle). On a given trial, one of the nine plates was suspended from the frame, and the pendulum bob was released to strike the plate three separate times. The participant's job was to listen to the sound produced when the pendulum bob struck the plate and identify both the material and the shape of the plate by pointing to one of nine example objects.

Participants were pretty good at this task. As you might expect, they correctly identified the material in 99.4% of the trials—there was only one misidentification across all trials for all participants. And they correctly identified the shape in 56% of the trials. This doesn't sound—no pun intended!—so impressive until you consider that chance performance on shape perception would have been 33%. In other words, their reports of object shape were not perfectly accurate, but they were not random either. As strange as it might be to consider, triangles sounded (more or less) like triangles, squares sounded (more or less) like squares, and circles sounded (more or less) like circles.

This is all well and good, but participants in this experiment were essentially completing a multiple-choice test. They knew ahead of time that there were only three options for material and three options for shape. Maybe this made the task too easy? What if all of the plates were the *same* shape but had different sizes—rectangles of different heights and widths? And what if participants were not told how many different plates there were or how big or small they could be? And what if participants had to report an *exact size*—height *and* width—of each plate? This is precisely what happened in a different experiment. The plates were metal rectangles of three different sizes—one was over three times as tall as it was wide, one was about one and a half times as tall as it was wide, and one was perfectly square (remember that all squares are rectangles but not all rectangles are squares). All of the plates were the same thickness, had the same surface area, and weighed the same amount.

On a given trial, one of the plates was suspended from the frame, and the pendulum bob was released to strike the plate three separate times (see Figure 7.3, *left*). On one set of trials, the participant's job was to listen to the sound of the pendulum bob striking the plate and then to adjust two movable markers on a horizontal track so that the distance between them was the same as the *width* of the struck plate. In another set of trials, the participant adjusted the distance between two movable markers on a vertical track so that the distance between them was the same as the *height* of the struck plate.

So how did participants do? Participants performed this task remarkably well. Even though participants underestimated the overall sizes of each rectangle, they reported the relative heights and widths of the rectangles appropriately. As the rectangles got taller and thinner, they were perceived to be taller and thinner. In addition, both the perceived heights and the perceived widths were in the approximate range of the actual heights and actual widths (see Figure 7.3, *right*). This is all the more impressive when you consider that participants had no advance knowledge of how many plates there were or how big (or small) they could be. Rather, they were able to *hear* the approximate relative dimensions of each object when it was struck with the pendulum. What was the structure in the acoustic array that could have provided information about the relative dimensions of the rectangle?

The researchers proposed that such information was provided in the vibrational dynamics of the plates—how the material properties and shape of the plates influenced how they vibrate along each of their axes when struck (Kunkler-Peck & Turvey, 2000). In other words, the researchers proposed that for real plates made of real materials in a real environment—not two-dimensional objects that exist only in the abstract—there was an *unambiguous* relationship between sound and shape.

One potential objection to the research that we just described on hearing the shape of a struck plate is how controlled the collision of the pendulum bob was with each plate.

Remember that each plate was suspended in a wooden frame so that its position was relatively stable, and the pendulum bob struck each plate at the same location and with the same amount of force each time. Everyday auditory perception is much messier—and much less predictable—than this. When Fred dropped his dinner plate, it likely tumbled unpredictably from the tray, striking the ground awkwardly, clattering and rolling until it came to a rest. Can participants still hear the geometric properties of objects under these conditions? Yes. Yes, they can.

In particular, people can hear how long a wooden rod is based on the sound it makes when it is dropped to the floor. Like perception of height and width of a struck plate, perception of rod length was underestimated. Nonetheless, as the actual length of the rod increased, so did the perceived length of the rod (Carello, Anderson, & Kunkler-Peck, 1998). What was the information about length in this scenario? The researchers proposed that, again, such information was provided in the vibrational dynamics of the rods—how the rod's material properties and shape influence how it vibrates along each of its axes. An object's mass determines its inertia—its resistance to being moved. And inertia is one of the factors that influence the pattern of vibration when one object collides with another object. But when a rod collides with the ground, it doesn't just land with a thud—it *clatters and rolls*. How much it clatters and how much it rolls is determined by its *rotational inertia*—its resistance to rotation in different directions (see Chapter 8). And it turned out that the rotational inertia did a better job at predicting perceived length than many acoustical variables—such as signal duration, amplitude, and frequency (Carello et al., 1998).

An object's resistance to rotation in different directions *also* influences the patterning of muscular forces required to manipulate that object in different directions when it is held in hand. In fact, as we will see in the next chapter, the rotational dynamics of an object *also* provide information about the properties and affordances of unseen hand-held objects. This is an example of structure in different energy forms—in this case, vibrations in the air when an object strikes a surface and deformations of bodily tissue when a person lifts or otherwise manipulates an object (see Chapter 8)—carrying the same information about a given object property—in this case, length (Wagman & Abney, 2012).

Hearing Occluding Objects

And what about hearing whether the plate landed on the floor by Fred's feet and not under the table? Think about this for a minute. So far, we have been discussing cases where a person hears the properties of a sound-producing object itself: What shape is it? What material is it? However, this particular task—hearing whether the plate rolled under the table—seems to require hearing a *silent* object (see Rosenblum, 2011). It requires hearing where the object is relative to the table when the table makes no sound at all! Ponder this for a moment, but then remember that everyday auditory perception occurs by means of both sounds *generated by* a sound source and sounds *reflected from* surrounding surfaces. These reflecting surfaces typically don't make any sound at all, but they do change *how* that sound is structured when it is encountered by the listener. In this case, the table is one of those surrounding surfaces.

Accordingly, people can hear whether or not a surface sits *between* them and a sound-producing object. Moreover, they can hear whether the surface mostly or only partly blocks the sound-producing object (Russell & Brown, 2020). In this experiment, a wooden board was placed completely in front of, mostly in front of, halfway in front of, only a little in front of, or not at all in front of a loudspeaker (see Figure 7.4). On a given trial, the board was positioned at one of these five locations relative to the speaker. A sound was played through the speaker, and a blindfolded participant was asked to report—yes or no—whether the board was blocking the speaker in any way whatsoever. In general, participants performed this task

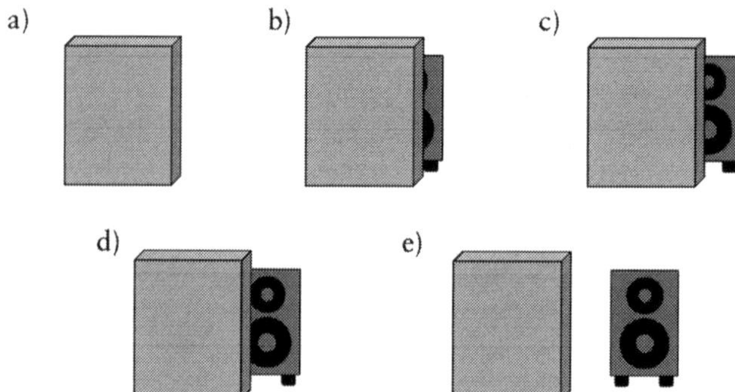

Figure 7.4 In the experiment by Russell and Brown (2020), participants could hear the extent to which a surface (a wooden board) blocked a sound source (a speaker). In their experiment, the surface was (a) completely in front of the sound source, (b) mostly in front of the sound source, (c) and (d) partly in front of the sound source, or (e) not at all in front of the sound source.

quite well. When the board was *completely* in front of the speaker, the participants correctly said "yes" approximately 90% of the time, and when the board was not in front of the speaker, the participants correctly said "no" approximately 85% of the time. Moreover, participants were more likely to say "yes" when the board was *mostly* in front of the speaker than when it was only *partly* in front of the speaker (Russell & Brown, 2020).

Amazingly, not only can people hear whether there is a surface between them and a sound-producing object, they can hear *what shape that surface is* (Rosenblum & Robart, 2007). In this experiment, foam shapes—a square, a circle, and a triangle—were positioned on a stand in front of loudspeakers. Each of the shapes had the same surface area. On a given trial, one of the shapes was placed on the support, and blindfolded participants stood with their ears next to the shape while a sound—in this case, white noise or static—was played through the speakers for ten seconds. Their task was to listen to the sound and determine which of the three shapes was positioned on the stand. On average, participants correctly identified the shape in 43.2% of the trials. Specifically, they correctly identified the square 38.9% of the time, the circle 42.2% of the time, and the triangle 49.2% of the time. Again, this doesn't sound—again, no pun intended!—so impressive until you consider that chance performance would have been 33%. Like the experiment in which participants listened to shapes that were struck by a pendulum bob, reports of object shape were not perfectly accurate, but they were not random either. As strange as it might be to consider, silent triangles sounded (more or less) like triangles, silent squares sounded (more or less) like squares, and silent circles sounded (more or less) like circles!

Hearing What Happened—Bouncing Versus Breaking

And what about hearing whether the plate bounced or broke? The study demonstrating this ability may very well have been the first one on ecological acoustics (Warren & Verbrugge, 1984; see Carello et al., 2005). In the first experiment in this study, researchers recorded the sound that three different glass objects each made when they fell to the ground from a shorter height—resulting in the object bouncing—and from a taller height—resulting in the object breaking. They then played these recordings to people and asked them whether they thought that the object bounced or broke—or whether they were unsure. Participants were almost 100% accurate despite not having any information about what kind of object was dropped, the height from which each object was dropped, and the surface on which each object was dropped, among many other factors.

The next two experiments in the study were geared toward understanding *how* participants were able to do this. In other words, the experiments were geared toward discovering what information about bouncing or breaking is available in the acoustic array. The researchers used a description of bouncing and breaking events at the macro scale as a guide in this investigation. In particular, when an object bounces, there will be an initial impact with the ground that sets the *entire object* into vibration depending on its size, shape, and composition—a lot like the struck metal plates that we discussed earlier. The object will then fall back to the ground and bounce again. As the object loses energy, each successive impact will occur more and more rapidly until the object stops moving altogether. How quickly these successive bounces occur will *also* depend on the object's size, shape, and composition. In other words, when an object bounces, it generates a singular repeating pulse of energy that decreases over time—a single "damped" energy pulse (see Figure 7.5, left)

When an object *breaks*, however, there will be an initial impact that breaks the object into pieces and sets *each individual piece* into vibration. This means that each piece will vibrate (slightly) differently because each one is a (slightly) different size and shape. Then each piece will fall to the ground and bounce again. As each piece loses energy, each successive impact will occur more and more rapidly until each piece stops moving altogether. However, the timing of the successive impacts will differ for each piece because each piece will differ in size and shape. In other words, when an object breaks, it generates *multiple* repeating pulses of energy that decrease over time, but these pulses will be *out of sync* with each other—*asynchronous* damped pulses of energy (see Figure 7.5, *right*).

To test this, the researchers collected the four largest pieces of a broken glass bottle. They dropped each piece to the floor—one at a time—and recorded the (bouncing) sound that each piece made when it fell to the ground. They then digitally manipulated these recordings—a big deal in the early 1980s—in an attempt to create an *artificial breaking sound* and an *artificial bouncing sound*. To create an artificial bouncing sound, the researchers adjusted the timing of the impacts to be the same across all four pieces. In other words, the researchers took four out-of-sync pulses of energy and artificially put them in sync. (Figure 7.6, *left*). To create an *artificial breaking sound*, they adjusted the timing of the impacts to be *different* across all four pieces. In other words, they ensured that the pulses of energy were out of sync. (Figure 7.6, *right*). When participants listened to these sounds, they identified the artificial breaking sound as a breaking object over 85% of the time, and they identified the artificial bouncing sound as a bouncing object over 90% of the time.

Figure 7.5 *Left*: a bouncing object produces a single damped pulse of energy. *Right*: a breaking object produces several asynchronous damped pulses of energy.

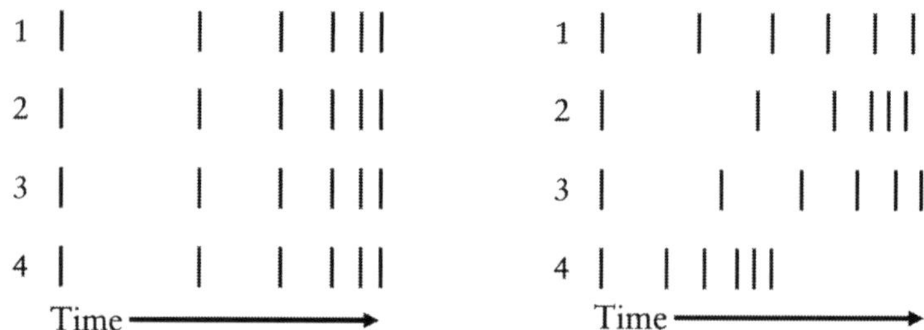

Figure 7.6 The timing of four separate acoustic energy pulses used by Warren and Verbrugge (1984). When the pulses were artificially put in sync (*left*), participants heard a bouncing object. When the pulses were artificially put out of sync (*right*), participants heard a breaking sound.

Information About Relationships Between Animals and Surfaces

Meanwhile, Fred is still engaged in his stare-down with the pesky (but perhaps friendly) bee. Fred, like the cat from Chapter 5 faced with the playful and rambunctious dog, has options for what to do. For example, he could swat at the bee or try to run past it to get to the door. Failing that, he could try to escape through an open window—let's hope it doesn't come to that! However, Fred is so startled after the plate-dropping fiasco that he closes his eyes tight. He can't bear to look at the bee. What can he *hear* about his options for dealing with the bee? If he chooses to swat at it, can he *hear* whether it is within swatting distance? If he chooses to flee, can he *hear* whether he could fit between the bee and any other objects in the room? And if he must escape through the window, can he *hear* whether he would be able to fit based on the sounds coming *through* the window? The answer to each of these questions is "yes."

Hearing What Is Reachable

We briefly discussed the first two of these abilities in Chapter 5. We can provide a little more detail here. The study investigating hearing whether an object was within reach (Rosenblum, Wuestefeld, et al., 1996) was based on studies on visual perception of affordances (in particular on experiments investigating the visual perception of whether an object was within reach; Carello et al., 1989). Consequently, the researchers recruited a group of taller participants and a group of shorter participants under the (relatively safe) assumption that taller people have longer arms than shorter people. Each participant was seated and blindfolded. A rattle consisting of paper clips in a small box was attached to a pole on a movable cart. The cart was placed at a particular distance from the listener, and the rattle was shaken. The participant's job was to report—yes or no—whether they would be able to reach the object (see Figure 7.7).

The researchers were interested in two different types of reaches. When the object was placed within a range of *near* distances, the yes-or-no answer referred to whether the listeners could reach the object with their arm only (without bending forward at the waist). When the object was placed within a range of *far* distances, the yes-or-no answer referred to whether the listeners could reach the object with their arm if they were to bend forward at the waist. In both cases, participants with long arms said "yes" more often than participants with short arms. Moreover, the perceptual boundary between objects that were perceived to be reachable occurred at a larger distance for participants with long arms than for participants with short arms but at the same ratio—the same perceived critical π value—of object distance to arm length or object distance to arm-plus-torso length for each group. In short, participants

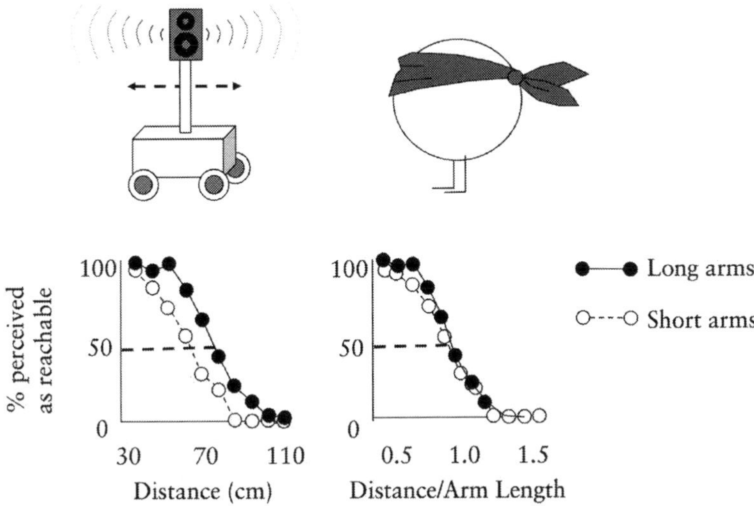

Figure 7.7 *Top*: In a study by Rosenblum, Wuestefeld et al. (1996), blindfolded participants listened to a sound-producing object at different distances and reported whether they would be able to reach that object. The boundary between objects that were perceived to be reachable and those that were not occurred at farther distances for people with long arms than those with short arms (*bottom, left*) but at the same ratio of object-distance-to-arm-length for both groups (*bottom, right*). Note the similarity between this graph and the one in Figure 5.8 showing results from an experiment on visual perception of affordances for climbing stairs.

could *hear* whether an object was within reach for two different styles of reaching, and such perception was body-scaled (see Figure 7.7).

Hearing What Is Pass-Through-Able

Listening to the sound of the bee, Fred determines that it is not within his reach, at least not at this moment. So he considers running to the door—yes, with his eyes closed. Doing so, however, would require that he pass between the bee and the wall. Does he have enough space to do this, or would he run smack into the bee? Unsurprisingly, the researchers who investigated whether people can hear if they can fit between a sound-producing object and a wall did not use a bee sound. Instead, they used a duck sound (yes, really[3]; Russell, 1999).

Participants were brought into a room and stood with their shoulder against a wall of the room and closed their eyes. A speaker was placed a few feet in front of them at different horizontal distances from the wall. A duck call—consisting of eight distinct "notes" and lasting for approximately three seconds—was played over the speaker at each of these distances. Participants reported—yes or no—whether they would be able to pass through the space between the sound source and the wall without turning their shoulders (see Figure 7.8).

The perceptual boundary—the perceived critical π value—between openings that afford walking through—without turning the body—occurred at a ratio of opening-width-to-shoulder-width of 1.11, which is quite comparable to the value obtained for visually perceiving whether an opening could be walked through (1.16, Warren & Whang, 1987, see also Riehm et al., 2019). More recently, researchers have investigated whether people can hear if they can *roller skate* between two sound-producing objects (yes, really; O'Neill & Russell, 2017). In this case, the perceptual boundary occurred at a ratio of opening-width-to-shoulder-width of

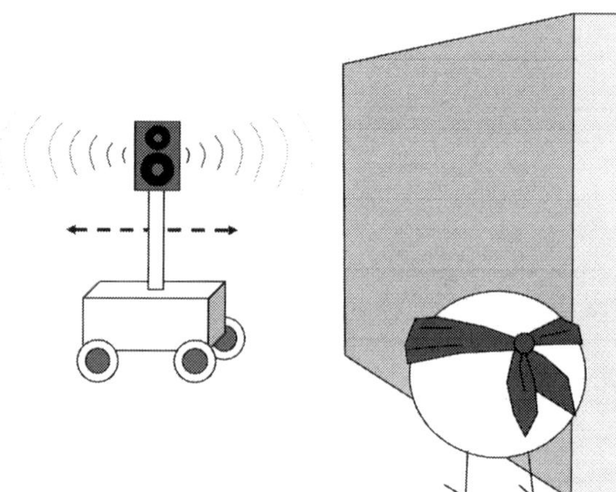

Figure 7.8 Blindfolded participants can hear whether they would be able to walk between a wall and a sound-producing object (a speaker).

1.69, which was no different from the perceptual boundary for visually perceiving whether they can roller skate between two obstacles, which was 1.72. If only Fred had not left his roller skates at Claudia's house!

Based on the structured sound that he encounters at his listening point in the acoustic array, Fred realizes that it would not be possible for him to pass between the bee and the wall. So he considers his last option—escaping through the open window (thankfully, Fred's dining room is on the ground floor). Is the window open enough for him to fit through? He can't bear to open his eyes, so again, he must rely on the sounds that he hears. Like the table, the window itself does not make any sounds. But unlike the table, some of the sounds being produced outside will *pass through* the window opening. How much of the sound from the outside passes through the window will depend on how much the window is open.

An experiment investigating whether people can hear if they can pass through an opening based on the sound passing through that opening was conducted by Gordon and Rosenblum (2004). In the first experiment, blindfolded participants stood on one side of two sliding panels on a horizontal track. When the panels were slid together, they formed a wall; when they slid apart, they formed an opening—like a doorway. On the other side of the panels were six loud-speakers that played crowd noise, recorded from a large lecture hall just before class started.[4]

The panels were adjusted to form an opening of a particular size, and the crowd noise was played. The participants' job was to say—yes or no—whether they would be able to walk straight through the opening without turning their shoulders. The perceptual boundary (the perceived critical π value) for openings that affords walking through occurred at the same ratio of opening-width-to-shoulder-width for participants with narrow shoulders and participants with wide shoulders (on average 1.06, again comparable to the experiments on visual and auditory perception of affordances for passing through).

In the second experiment, the panels were adjusted to form an opening large enough to walk through, and a third panel was placed behind this opening that could be raised or lowered (like a window through which the participant could flee a bee!). This panel was adjusted to a particular height, and the sound was played through the loudspeakers. The participant's job was to say—yes or no—whether they would be able to walk straight through the opening without ducking. The perceptual boundary (the perceived critical π value) between openings that afford walking under occurred at the same ratio of opening-height-to-standing-height for both groups—on average 1.00.

Hearing Time to Contact

Unfortunately, based on the structured sound he encounters, Fred realizes that he cannot fit through the window. Drat! Now there is no escape. It is only a matter of time before the bee reaches him. *But how much time?* Fred squeezes his eyes closed and prepares to be stung. If Fred were to keep his eyes open, he would be able to see when the bee would arrive based on τ. That is, he'd be able to see how quickly the optical texture of the bee expands as it approaches—how quickly it occludes the background relative to how much it currently occludes the background (see Chapter 6). Can he also *hear* when the bee will arrive based on an acoustic equivalent of τ? Based on our claims that the structure in one energy form ought to be analogous to the structure in another energy form, then yes.

As a sound source approaches, the acoustical structure created by the object will expand as it approaches and will occlude background sounds. This will be experienced as the sound getting louder and louder, and clearer and clearer, and progressively drowning out any other sounds. And just as in the case where the person can *see* the approaching object, how *quickly* this structure expands as it approaches is information about its time to arrival. In this case, the buzzing sound will get louder and clearer slowly at first and then more and more rapidly as the bee gets closer (Guski, 1992; Neuhoff, 2018; Rosenblum, 2011).

Accordingly, research has shown that both blind people and blindfolded sighted people can use acoustical τ (or related variables) to determine when an approaching vehicle or person will arrive or pass by their current location[5] (Rosenblum, Carello, & Pastore, 1987; Rosenblum, Wuestefeld, & Saldaña, 1993; Schiff & Oldak, 1990), and bats can use acoustic τ (or related variables) to avoid obstacles while flying (Lee et al., 1992). Fred hears the acoustic structure generated by the bee get louder and clearer slowly at first and then more and more rapidly (see Figure 7.9). The bee is very, very close. It lands on his nose, but it doesn't sting him. The bee *is* friendly.

Figure 7.9 As the bee approaches Fred, the acoustic structure produced by its vibrating wings will get progressively louder and progressively occlude background sounds. How quickly this occurs is information about time to arrival. Note the similarity between this figure and the one in Figure 6.9 showing optical time to arrival.

Fred is so relieved that he decides to pour himself a drink. He exhales in relief and again closes his eyes. He puts the glass on the table and starts pouring (with his eyes still closed). But when should he stop? He doesn't want to overflow the glass—what a mess that would make!—but he wants enough to quench his thirst. Does acoustical τ provide information about the time to arrival of the liquid to the top of the glass? Cabe and Pittenger (2000) investigated this in a series of experiments. In one of the experiments, participants were blindfolded and seated in front of a spigot. On a table below the spigot was a cylindrical plastic container—the size of a medium water glass. In one condition, the participants were asked to turn the spigot on, listen to the sound of the container filling, and then turn the spigot off when the glass was *just full to the brim* without allowing it to overflow. In a different condition, participants were asked to do the same thing, except they were to turn the spigot off when the water was at a preferred drinking level—which would presumably be lower than all the way to the brim. In the full-to-the-brim condition, the participants filled the glass to 88% to the top on average, and in the preferred-drinking-level condition, the participants filled the glass to 70% to the top on average. Allowing participants to both see and hold the container as the water poured into it improved both accuracy and consistency of performance. Nonetheless, participants did not need to do either one to successfully perform the task. They could differentiate the two levels of fullness *just by listening*.

A follow-up study investigated whether participants were, in fact, using acoustical τ to perceive the time to arrival of the water to the top of the container. The researchers derived an acoustic variable that was analogous to optical τ—how quickly the vibrations of the column of water and air in the glass change as the container fills. They investigated whether participants (could) use this variable to perceive when the water would reach the top of the container. Blindfolded participants listened to water flowing from a spigot into a cylindrical plastic container—this time, the size of a tall water glass—at three different fill rates. The researchers wanted to ensure that participants were not simply waiting for the water to overflow the container to make their response.[6] So they only filled the glass partway (1/4, 1/2, or 3/4 full) and then turned the spigot off. The participant's job was to indicate when the container *would have been* completely filled had the water continued to pour in from the spigot. The researchers found that perceived time to fill tracked actual time to fill quite well. In fact, the results paralleled those investigating visual perception of time to contact—like the one on diving gannets (see Chapter 6). After ruling out an alternative explanation based merely on time spent listening, the researchers concluded that the participants used acoustic τ to perceive time to fill.[7]

Box 7.1 Echolocation

From the ecological perspective, perception is an active process. In the case of auditory perception, for example, listeners move around and turn their heads to help orient to a sound source or cup their hand over their ear to better hear a sound source. These behaviors help the listener to explore the acoustic array by changing what structure they encounter or how much of that structure they encounter. You turn your head when you want to change what you are hearing. You cup your hand over your ear when you want to change how much you are hearing. However, such behaviors don't (necessarily) *alter* the structure of the acoustic array. Certainly, neither of these behaviors creates *new* structure in the acoustic array—they only help to reveal *existing* structure in the acoustic array.

However, auditory perception can be active in a way that *does create new* structure in the acoustic array. Echolocation is a process by which listeners use reflected acoustic structure (i.e., echoes) to perceive surface layout. But sometimes, there may not be enough existing reflected acoustic structure to provide the necessary information about surface layout. In these cases, listeners can (and do) purposefully create their own acoustic structure by making sounds (e.g., words or tongue clicks, claps, or taps of a cane) and then listening to how the reflected sound is structured by surrounding surfaces—much like bats (Griffin, 1958; Lee et al., 1992). In this way, the listener purposefully performs behaviors (making the sounds) that create new structure in the acoustic array so that they can perceive surrounding surfaces more effectively (see Figure 7.10). Accordingly, echolocation can be considered a basic form of perception and action (Stoffregen & Pittenger, 1995).

Often, people who echolocate both move their bodies and heads while they are producing sounds and even adjust the properties of the sounds that they make to further explore the reflecting surface (Thaler & Goodale, 2016). Some blind individuals are able to use echolocation to perform everyday activities, such as locating obstacles and doorways, and others are even able to perform not-so-everyday-activities, such as hiking, mountain biking, skateboarding, and playing sports (Kolarik et al., 2014; Rosenblum, 2011).

Importantly, even people *without* visual impairment can learn to echolocate, with practice. In one study, after a brief familiarization task, sighted—but blindfolded—participants were asked to make a sound of their choice (e.g., a repeated word or a mouth click) to locate a wall placed at four different distances from them. Then the wall was removed, and they were asked to walk to where *the wall had been*. In general, participants were able to perform the task. They tended to walk farther when the wall had been farther away, though they overshot the target at the nearest distance and undershot it at the farthest two distances. Participants were slightly better at the task when they echolocated the surface while moving when they did so while stationary (Rosenblum, Gordon, & Jarquin, 2010).

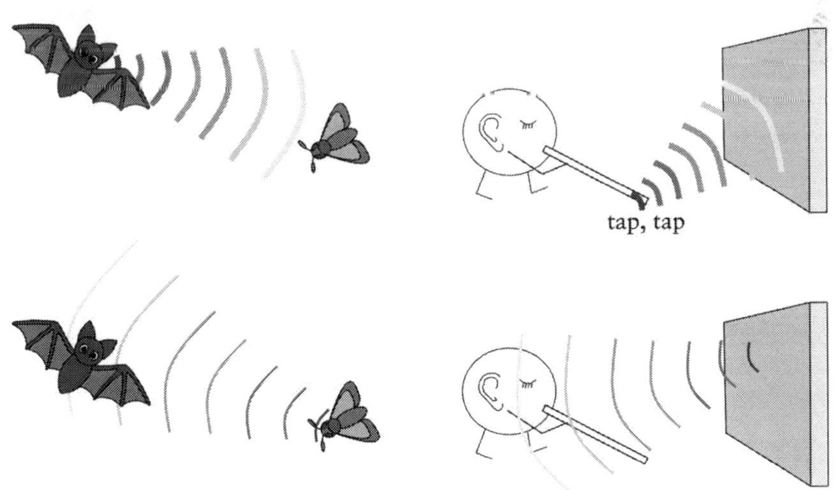

Figure 7.10 Bats echolocate—they produce sounds and use the reflected sounds to hear whether, when, and how to perform behaviors (*left*). People can do the same thing by making vocalizations (such as clicks or by tapping with a tool such as a long cane) and listening to the reflected sound (*right*).

Speech Perception

Fred wants to share the news that he has overcome his fear of bees, so he stops by Claudia's house. He says, "Claudia, guess what? I made friends with a bee!" Claudia not only *hears* the sounds that Fred makes, but she perceives the *meaning* of what Fred has said. How? Before we answer this, consider that Claudia likely would have perceived the meaning of what Fred said even if his voice were higher or lower pitched, even if he spoke more quickly or more slowly, even if he yelled or whispered, and even if he spoke with an accent. And she understood him despite the fact that, like most people, Fred does not articulate every sound of every word perfectly, and the sounds that he does produce "blur" together to form words and sentences. In short, the acoustic signal itself varies greatly depending on the context, but for the most part, speech is perceived independent of that context.

From the ecological perspective, Claudia's ability to understand what Fred says begins with what Fred *does* while speaking. What Fred does when speaking is coordinate the movements of his vocal tract, including but not limited to his lips, teeth, mouth, tongue, and throat. This coordination brings about collisions of the various parts of Fred's vocal tract (see Figure 7.11). These collisions create vibrations in the air that are lawfully structured by the nature of these parts, how they are interacting, and where they are interacting, among other factors. And this structure in the acoustic array is lawfully related to how these sounds were produced by the movements of Fred's vocal tract. In other words, the *sound itself* is not what is perceived. The *movements of the vocal tract* are what is perceived by means of the sound (Carello et al., 2005; Fowler, 2018, 1986). In principle, this is no different from perceiving whether an object bounced or broke by means of sound or when an object will arrive by means of sound. In all these cases, structure in the acoustic array provides information about an event, not the sound itself. To repeat, the medium is not the message.

To the extent that the movements of the vocal tract lawfully structure multiple energy patterns simultaneously, structure in any one of these patterns ought to carry the same

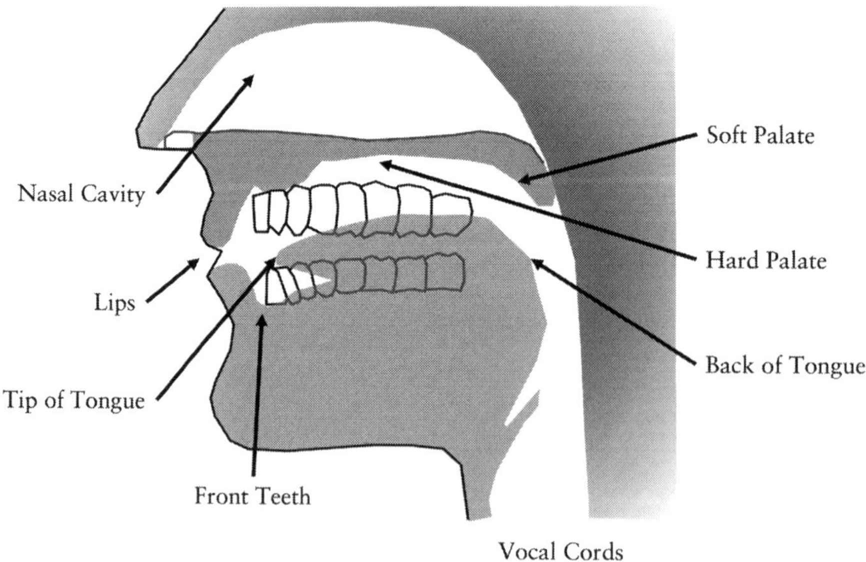

Figure 7.11 Vocalizations are produced by coordinated movements of the vocal tract, including the lips, teeth, mouth, tongue, and throat. The structure in the acoustic array is lawfully related to how those sounds were produced in the vocal tract.

information about such movements. The movements of the vocal tract *also* structure the optic array. Consequently, these movements can be *seen*. Research showed that even people without hearing impairment read lips during everyday speech perception (though perhaps not as well as someone who is hearing impaired, Rosenblum, 2005). Along these lines, *watching* someone speak helps the listener in understanding what the speaker is saying—especially in noisy environments and even when only parts of the speaker's face are visible (see Bernstein, Auer, & Takayanagi, 2004; Rosenblum, Johnson, & Saldaña, 1996).

Perhaps more impressively, the movements of the vocal tract *also* structure the bodily tissue of the speaker, especially their face, lips, and throat. Consequently, these movements can be *felt* by someone who places their hands on the speaker's face. And research has shown that *feeling* someone speaking also aids in understanding what they are saying (Reed et al., 1985).

Notes

1. If you have ever been in a room specifically designed to reduce reflected sounds (like the rooms in which some hearing tests take place), you know that things sound quite odd without (much) reflected sound.
2. More technically put, it is possible for two 2D mathematical objects called manifolds to have different geometries but the same fundamental modes of vibration.
3. They used this sound because it is a naturally occurring sound with complex acoustic structure (as opposed to a computer generated tone, for example).
4. Crowd noise is also a naturally occurring sound with complex acoustic structure. And crowd noise would likely be a familiar sound to students.
5. While the prevalence of hybrid and electric cars is great for the environment, it is not so great for blind pedestrians (or inattentive sighted pedestrians). This is because these cars are *so much quieter* than gas powered cars. Consequently, blind pedestrians may have a harder time hearing whether hybrid or electric cars are approaching and, if so, how quickly the car might reach them (Robart & Rosenblum, 2009).
6. After all, this was a study about hearing when the glass would *become* full, not hearing when it *had already* become full.
7. People can even perceive whether a *hot or cold* liquid is being poured into a container just by listening (Velasco, Jones, King, & Spence, 2013).

8 Ecological Haptics and Perception by Touch—Muscles as the Medium

In Chapters 6 and 7, we developed an *ecological optics* and an *ecological acoustics*—an understanding of both light and sound at the macro scale of (the relationship between) animals and their environments. In both of these cases, the medium—the structured light or sound—*surrounds* the animal. That is, the animal is *embedded within* the medium. In this chapter, we will develop an *ecological haptics*[1]—an understanding of patterns of *physical forces* on bodily tissue at the macro scale of (the relationship between) animals and their environments. In the case of touch, the *medium* is embedded within *the animal*. This might seem like it makes perception by touch an exception or a special sense, but it is not—the medium is not the message.

Remember that understanding perception as a lawful process requires uncovering how properties of surfaces and relationships between animals and those surfaces unambiguously structure energy patterns. In the case of perception by touch, the energy patterns of relevance are the physical forces on the skin, muscles, tendons, and other bodily tissues when a person moves their body or manipulates an object. Moving the body or manipulating an object requires *doing work*. It requires applying muscular forces. And the required muscular forces continually change (i.e., they are "dynamic") depending on what that person is doing. This is why perception of properties of the body itself or of objects manipulated by the body is called *effortful* or *dynamic touch* (J. Gibson, 1966; see Carello & Turvey, 2015, 2017).

Even though we are dealing with a different form of energy (physical forces instead of light or sound), the conceptual moves that we will make in understanding perception by touch will be similar to those that we made in understanding perception by vision and by hearing. This is because the structure in the energy pattern ought to be analogous across energy forms (see Chapter 5–7). In fact, we will see that patterns of structured physical forces on bodily tissues have the potential to carry *the same information about* surfaces and relationships between animals and those surfaces as patterns of structured light or sound.

The fundamental question to be answered in the ecological approach to perception by touch is not about how such physical forces get into and are used by the muscles. After all, this is what muscles do. They already work in the medium of forces. Rather, the question is about the best way to *describe* such physical forces such that they can serve the purpose of guiding goal-directed behavior (see Chapter 5).

Ecological Haptics—a Description of Physical Forces for Feeling and Doing

Fred has *finally* gotten some more furniture—and gotten over his fear of bees. One dark evening, he is sitting down on his couch to binge watch some episodes of his favorite show—*Crafting with Masato*—when the power goes out. Drat. He fumbles his way to the junk drawer in his kitchen—everyone has one, right?—to dig out a small LED flashlight and a set of candles. In the complete darkness, he pulls an object out of the drawer, holds it firmly in

DOI: 10.4324/9781003145691-10

one hand by what seems to be a handle of some kind, and moves it around with his wrist. Immediately, though, he *knows* that it is not the flashlight or the candles. He knows that it is *much longer* than either one of them and *quite a bit wider* as well. He also knows that it is *mostly flat*, perhaps *circular*, and that it is *pointing straight up* toward the ceiling. And he also knows that it is *heavier* than either a flashlight or a candle as well. He's not sure exactly what it is, but he does know that he could use it to *hit another object*—a ball maybe?—but probably not to *poke or push another object*. Aha! It's his old tennis racket! How did *that* get in there?

Think about this for a moment. When Fred holds the unseen object, which turned out to be a tennis racket, he is touching only a small part of the object—whatever portion of the grip that happens to be in his hand. Yet he knows things about the *entire* object. How can he know the length, width, shape, heaviness, orientation, and "hit-with-able-ness" of the *whole* object when he touches only a part of that object? Ponder this for a moment, but then realize that this is really no different from *visually* perceiving properties (and affordances) of objects. You can never see the *entire object* all at once. At any given moment, you will only be able to see *part* of the object given your *current point of observation*. Yet you can perceive many properties and affordances of that entire object. Why? Because at that single point of observation, you are encountering a pattern of structured light in the optic array that provides information about that object (see Chapter 6). Perceiving properties and affordances of a hand-held object from a single grasp position is no different. Fred knows all of these things and more about the object based on the structured forces that he encounters at a point of observation (in this case, his grasp position on the object) (see Figure 8.1).

Remember that in the ecological approach, the relevant stimulation patterns for perception can be found in structured ambient energy arrays—the ambient *optic* array in the case of vision and the ambient *acoustic* array in the case of audition. Regardless of the form of energy, differences in structured energy in different directions at a point of observation provide information about surfaces, their relationships to one another, and the person's current relationship to these surfaces. What is the equivalent energy array for perception by (effortful or dynamic) touch?

Animals are not only immersed in an ocean of light and an ocean of sound. They are also immersed in an *ocean of forces*. And like all of the other oceans of energy surrounding an animal, the ocean of forces is *not uniform*. On the contrary, it is an *array*. It is both different in different *locations* on the body and different in different *directions* at a given location on the body. This is especially so when a person holds and manipulates an object but also when they do not. Gravity is the primary physical force acting on animals. At a minimum, moving the body, a limb, or a hand-held object requires overcoming—and often cooperating with—gravity (see Chapter 9). This requires generating different forces at different bodily locations in different

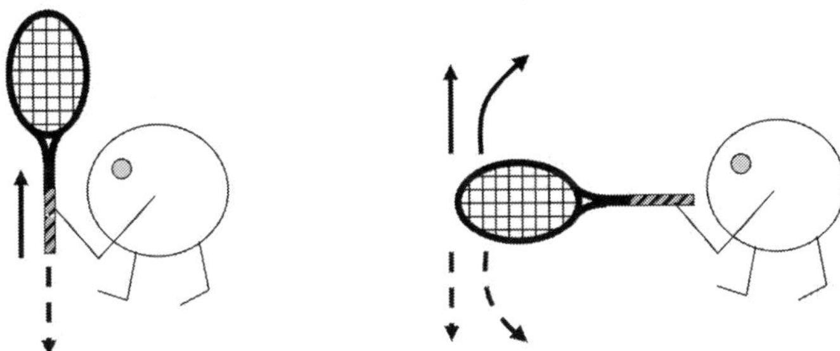

Figure 8.1 When Fred holds the racket still and vertically (*left*), he only has to apply forces (solid lines) to keep it from falling straight down. When he holds the racket still and horizontally (*right*), he has to apply *additional* forces to keep it from rotating.

directions. This is the key to ecological haptics (Carello & Wagman, 2009; Carello & Turvey, 2017).

Let's consider Fred's tennis racket. When Fred bought his tennis racket, the friendly saleswoman at the sporting goods store told him that it weighed 330 g (about 2/3 of a pound). But what does this *mean* exactly? This means that if Fred were to put it on a scale, the scale would read 330 g. If he were to put it on one tray of an old-fashioned balance scale and he were to put some other thing that weighed 330 g on the other tray (say, a large potato), the two trays would be even. The mass of an object indicates how much force is required to overcome the pull of gravity to support the object. Fred picks up his new tennis racket and holds it completely still and completely vertically (see Figure 8.1, *left*). To hold it still like this, he must produce muscular forces—the *effort* in *effortful touch*—that are proportional to the racket's *mass*. This will keep it from falling straight down to the ground. However, this is a bit of a special case. Both in tennis and in life more generally, we don't tend to hold objects completely still in exactly this way.

Fred tries holding the racket more like he would if he were about to hit a forehand shot. Now, he holds it completely still and completely horizontally (see Figure 8.1, *right*). When he does this, though, he has to work a little bit harder to hold the racket in this position. Why? When he is holding the racket vertically, he has to apply muscular forces in a *straight line*—in this case, straight up—and these forces must be proportional to the racket's mass. However, when he is holding the racket horizontally, he not only has to keep it from falling straight down to the ground, he also has to keep the head of the racket from *rotating toward* the ground. To do so, Fred has to apply *rotational force*.

Now, it's not just the *mass* of the racket that matters. It's how that mass is *distributed*. In particular, what matters is how far the *center of mass*—the point about which the mass of the object is distributed evenly—is from his hand. In the case of a tennis racket, the center of mass is more or less halfway up the length of the racket—approximately where the handle and the head meet. So to hold the racket like this—completely still and completely horizontally—he has to produce a force that is proportional to a *combination* of mass and distance between the center of mass and his hand—specifically mass × distance to the center of mass. This is why Fred has to work harder (and differently) to hold the racket still horizontally than to hold it still vertically. But even this is a special case! Both in tennis and in life, we don't tend to hold objects still *at all*. Instead, we move them about this way and that.

Fred tries moving his tennis racket around this way and that as he would in the context of an actual match. Now, he has to work *even harder*—or at least he has to *change* how much he is working more often—than when he held it still either vertically or horizontally. Why? When he holds the tennis racket still, either horizontally or vertically, the amount of force he has to apply never changes. It is *static*. However, when he moves it around, the forces that he has to apply are constantly changing—the *dynamic* in *dynamic touch!* To move the racket in a given direction, it is not sufficient to merely apply muscular forces that *support* the racket and *keep it from rotating*. He has to *make it* rotate. When he *moves* it in a given direction, he has to apply muscular forces to increase its velocity from zero to some other value. He has to *accelerate* it. In doing so, he has to overcome its inertia—its resistance to being moved. Specifically, he has to overcome its *rotational inertia*—its resistance to being rotated about an axis (see Figure 8.2).

When Fred *moves* the head of the racket toward his imaginary opponent—maybe as he practices his forehand shot—he has to produce a rotational force in a particular direction about a particular axis—in this case, the axis running vertically through his wrist and perpendicular to the handle of the racket. The force is still proportional to a combination of mass and the distance between the center of mass and his hand, but in this case, this distance plays an even larger role—specifically, mass × the distance to the center of mass squared. Notice that the exponent makes the distance to the center of mass more influential.

Now, Fred has gotten the racket to move toward his opponent. At the end of his swing, though, he will need to *decelerate* the racket so that it stops moving in this direction and *then* apply the muscular forces required to *accelerate* it in the *opposite* direction so that he is in position to take the next forehand shot.[2] This is why Fred has to work *harder*. He has to *continually change* how much he is working to move the object back and forth compared to when he holds it still.

But we're still not quite where we need to be yet. Recall that both the optic and the acoustic arrays consist of differences in different directions at a particular point of observation. We need to describe the stimulation for perception by effortful or dynamic touch in an analogous way. Fred can move the tennis racket in *lots* of different ways. He could move the head of the racket up and down (rotate it toward and away from the ground), he could move the head toward or away from his imagined opponent, or he could twist it—like a doorknob—so that it is parallel or perpendicular to an imagined net. Each of these movements requires applying a *different rotational force* about a *different axis* running through his wrist. So the differences in different directions refer to differences in *resistances to rotations* in different directions. And the point of observation refers to his *grasp position* on the object. Where an object is grasped doesn't affect the mass of that object (it can't) but *does* affect the distance between the center of mass and the rotation point. And this will affect the rotational forces required to move that object in different directions. If you've ever wondered why an object like a baseball, softball, or cricket bat feels so much heavier when held on the handle than when held at the barrel (or blade), that's why!

At every grasp location on the tennis racket, Fred encounters a unique set of differences—in this case, a unique set of resistances to rotations—in different directions. The set of resistances to rotations in different directions at a given grasp location can be described as an *inertial array*—analogous to an optic array or an acoustic array. The set of resistances to rotation in different directions can be described by something called an *inertia tensor (I)* (see Figure 8.2). Admittedly, a tensor is a somewhat complex mathematical concept. Simply put, though, it is a *multidimensional array*—a quantity that varies in multiple ways *simultaneously*. If a quantity only varies in one way (like speed), then you only need one value to describe it—called a scalar. If a quantity varies in two ways (like speed *and* direction), then you need *two* scalars—together called a vector. If a quantity varies in multiple ways simultaneously, like simultaneous differences in speed in different directions—or simultaneously stretching an elastic sheet in multiple directions at the same time—then you need a more complex value, called a tensor[3] (see Figure 8.2).

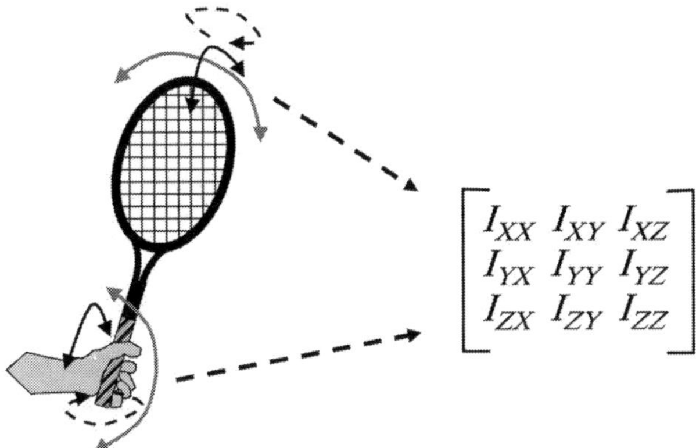

Figure 8.2 The inertia tensor is a 3 × 3 matrix that describes the inertial array—differences in resistance to rotation in different directions at a given grasp position on an object. Note that the matrix is symmetric about the diagonal. The values along the diagonal (I_{XX}, I_{YY}, and I_{ZZ}) are moments of inertia. The values off the diagonal (I_{XY}, I_{XZ}, and I_{YZ}) are the products of inertia.

Imagine that you are pushing a shopping cart with one bad wheel (annoying, right?). When you push the cart forward with a particular amount of force, it is liable to wobble off in a different direction (off to the side!) with a different amount of force (slower!). A tensor describes this transformation. In the case of wielded objects, we are using the tensor to describe the simultaneous differences in resistance to rotation in different directions about a rotation point. When you are holding an object and apply a particular amount of force in a particular direction, it is liable to move with a different amount of force in a different direction, depending on its mass distribution. A tensor *also* describes this transformation. A tensor transforms one vector—a given force in a given direction—into another vector—a *different force* in a *different direction*.

We can depict the inertia tensor as a 3 × 3 matrix of values (see Figure 8.2). Keep in mind that the matrix is symmetric along the diagonal going from the top left to the bottom right—I_{xy}, I_{yz}, and I_{xz}—are redundant with I_{zx}, I_{zy}, and I_{zx}, so it is not quite as complex as it seems.

Each of the values along the diagonal that runs from the top left to the bottom right (I_{xx}, I_{yy}, and I_{zz}) (more or less) describe the resistances to rotational acceleration about the three major axes of the object. Consider Fred and his racket: I_{xx}—*the major principal moment of inertia*—describes the resistance to rotating up and down (toward and away from the ground). I_{yy} describes the resistance to rotating it toward and away from his imaginary opponent. I_{zz}—*the minor principal moment of inertia*—describes the resistance to rotating it (twisting it like a doorknob) so that it is parallel or perpendicular to an imagined net (see Figure 8.2). We'll get to the other (so-called off-diagonal) values—I_{xy}, I_{xz}, and I_{yz} in a bit.

But we haven't even gotten to the coolest part yet! When Fred plays a tennis match, he swings the racket with all kinds of different motions—forehand shots, backhand shots, overheads, slices, and serves. He moves the racket in all sorts of directions, with all sorts of speeds, using all sorts of forces, creating all sorts of patterns of deformation of the skin and muscles of his hand, forearm, and shoulder. In other words, throughout the match, lots and lots of things are changing with respect to Fred and the racket. However, two things will not change, they are *invariant*, with respect to Fred and the racket—the inertia tensor at a particular grasp position and Fred's perception of the properties and affordances of the racket. This means that it is likely—perhaps even certain—that the inertia tensor is the description of physical forces on bodily tissues at the macro scale that can serve to guide goal-directed behavior. In other words, it is likely—perhaps even certain—that this stimulation pattern is the one that is lawfully structured by the relationship between animal and environment and is actively detected by a behaving animal. To the extent that this is the case, then the inertia tensor ought to provide *information about* the body and objects manipulated by the body.

Information About Surfaces

Feeling Length (Affordances for Reaching)

Recall that one of the things that Fred knows about the unseen tennis racket is that it is relatively long—longer than a small LED flashlight or a candle anyway. How does he know this? One of the first studies conducted on effortful or dynamic touch investigated exactly this (Solomon & Turvey, 1988). In the first experiment in this study, participants sat in a chair, put their right hand through a curtain, and placed their forearm onto a support surface. An experimenter placed a rod into their hand so that the participant was holding it firmly at the very bottom—just like Fred, or anyone else, would hold a tennis racket (see Figure 8.3, *left*). The participant's job was to wield the rod with movements of their wrist only and to try to get an impression of how long the rod was. Then they were to adjust the distance of a visible movable marker with their left hand so that the distance between them and the marker was the same as the length of the rod—so that the marker would be *just reachable* with the other end of the rod. Rods were all made of the same material (in this case, aluminum) and were the same diameter. They were cut to seven different lengths—ranging from approximately 30 cm to 125 cm. Each rod was wielded six times. Overall, participants performed this task quite well. Perceived rod length very closely tracked actual rod length but was slightly underestimated—especially for longer rods (see Figure 8.3, *right*).

The next three experiments established that this same pattern held when the rods were heavier—made of steel instead of aluminum, held across the body rather than alongside the body, and wielded—up and down—at a particular tempo. In other words, these four experiments established that perceived length remained constant regardless of changes in how the rod was wielded. These results suggest that perception of length must depend on a variable that *also* remains constant despite these changes. The researchers proposed that this variable was a particular component of *I*.

Specifically, they hypothesized that perceived length would depend on the major principal moment of inertia (I_{xx}, in Figure 8.2) *and not actual length*. It might seem strange to predict that perceived length does not depend on actual length—after all, isn't that what Experiment 1 showed? Not exactly. Experiment 1 found that people can perceive the length of a wielded rod and that—for the most part—perceived length tracks actual length. However, length is a *geometric property*, and as we mentioned previously, the touch system works with *forces*. Besides, the person only ever touches a small portion of the rod—the part of the rod that is actually in their hand—yet they can perceive the *entire length* of the rod. There must be something else

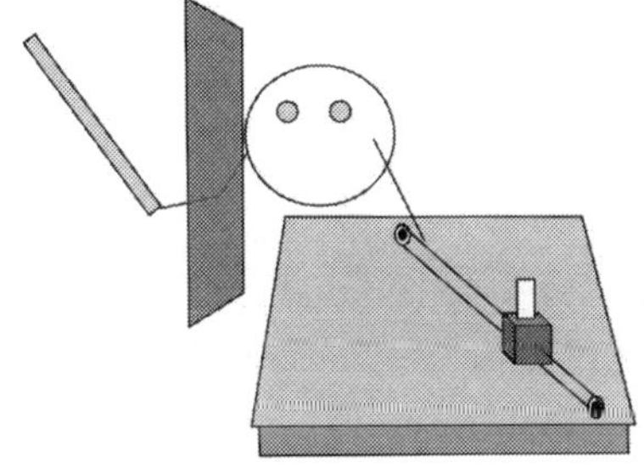

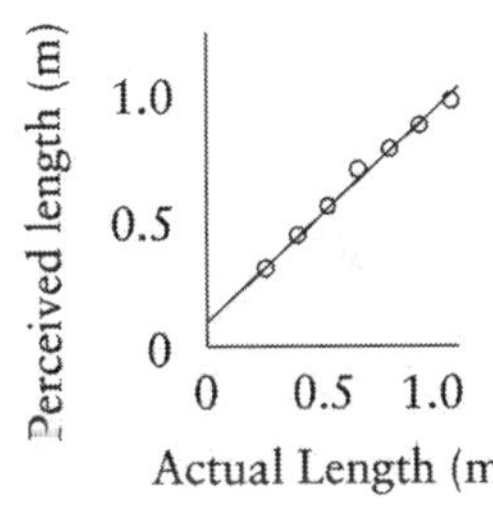

Figure 8.3 *Left*: in a typical experiment on perception of length by effortful touch, a person wields a rod with one hand out of sight and adjusts the distance of a visible marker with the other hand so that the marker would be just reachable with the tip of the rod. *Right*: perceived length isn't perfect, but it very closely tracks actual length.

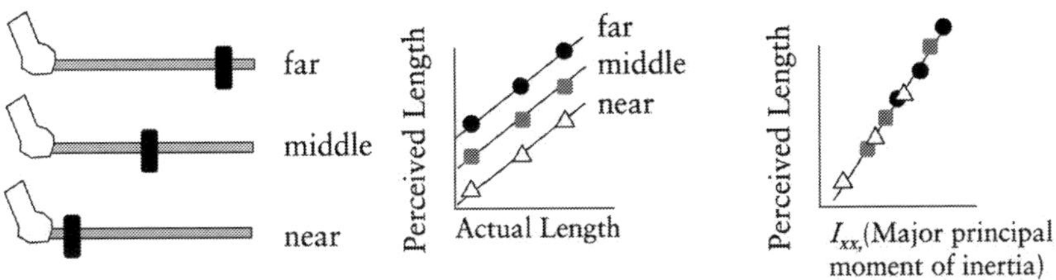

Figure 8.4 *Left*: Experimental conditions. The length of the rod is the same, but the position of the weight is either far from the hand, in the middle, or close to the hand. *Middle*: Perceived length when graphed by actual length and weight placement. *Right*: Perceived length when graphed by the moment of inertia (an organism-relevant variable).

going on. The researchers were proposing that I_{xx} was this something else. Specifically, they were proposing that I_{xx} was the information about object length (or really, about how far the person could reach with the object).

The researchers ran additional experiments to investigate this. In one of these, the researchers created objects, each consisting of an aluminum rod with a cube-shaped weight attached at a particular location along the length of that rod. Rods were one of three different lengths—approximately 60 cm, 75 cm, and 90 cm. Weights were placed at one of three different locations along the length of the rod—25%, 50%, or 75% along its length (see Figure 8.4, *left*). What is so clever about this design is that by adding weights to the rods, the researchers were able to create sets of objects that had the *same* length and the *same* mass but *different values* of I_{xx}. In particular, the added weight changes the location of the center of mass of the object and therefore changes the distance between the center of mass and the rotation point in the wrist. And this changes I_{xx}. Specifically, I_{xx} increases as the weight is placed farther along the length of the rod—and farther away from the wrist. So if perceived length depended on I_{xx} and not actual length, then rods would feel longer as the weight was moved farther along the length of the rod—even for objects that were the same length! And this is exactly what they found (see Figure 8.4, *middle*). And as they expected, perceived length increased as I_{xx} increased (see Figure 8.4, *right*).

But they weren't done quite yet. They ran a few more experiments to make the case even stronger. In one of these experiments, they used unweighted rods of three different lengths. This time, however, they varied the *grasp location* along the length of the rod—at 25%, 50%, or 75% along its length (see Figure 8.5, *left*). Doing this *also* allowed them to create sets of objects that had the *same* length and the *same* mass but *different* values of I_{xx}. Changing the grasp position on the rod changes the distance between the center of mass and the rotation point in the wrist. And this changes I_{xx} but in a different way than adding weights. The center of mass of a uniform rod is halfway along its length. When a person grasps the rod at the midpoint (50% along its length), this should minimize the distance between the center of mass and the rotation point in the wrist—and therefore minimize I_{xx}. If perceived length depended on I_{xx} and not actual length, then rods would feel *shorter* when grasped at 50% than when grasped at either 25% or 75% of the length of the rod—even for objects that were the same length! And this is exactly what they found (see Figure 8.5, *middle*). And as they expected, perceived length increased as I_{xx} increased (see Figure 8.5, *right*).

Feeling Shape

Recall that Fred also knows that the unseen tennis racket is *relatively wide*—wider than a flashlight or a candle anyway, *mostly flat*, and perhaps *circular*. How does he know these things? If *I* really *is* the appropriate description of forces on bodily tissues at the macro scale, then

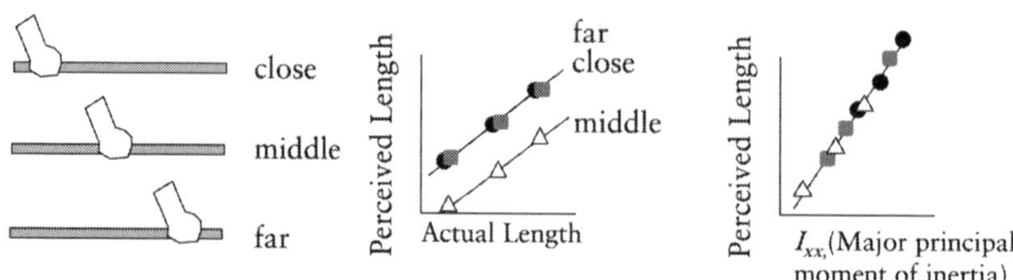

Figure 8.5 *Left*: Experimental conditions. The length of the rod is the same, but the position of the hand is either at the close end, the middle, or the far end. *Middle*: Perceived length when graphed by actual length and hand placement. *Right*: Perceived length when graphed by the moment of inertia—an organism-relevant variable.

perception of these and all other properties of wielded objects ought to depend on components of I as well. Researchers conducted a series of experiments to investigate this. They hypothesized that perceived object *height* would depend on I_{xx}—and not necessarily on actual height—because I_{xx} describes the resistance to rotating the object toward and away from the ground. They also hypothesized that perceived object *width* would depend on I_{zz}—and necessarily on actual length—because I_{zz} describes the resistance to twisting the object, like a doorknob.

Researchers conducted two studies to investigate this hypothesis. In the first one, they used three-dimensional rectangular wooden blocks (i.e., shapes known as parallelepipeds) mounted on handles (Turvey et al., 1998). The procedure was similar to the experiments investigating perception of length. Participants sat in a chair and put their right hand through a curtain and their forearm onto a support surface. An experimenter placed the handle of the object into their hand so that the participant was holding it firmly at the very bottom. The participant's job was to wield the object with movements of their wrist only and to try to get an impression of the height and the width of the block on the end of the handle. The participant adjusted the distance between two visible movable markers on a vertical track to indicate the perceived height of the block, and they adjusted the distance between two movable markers on a horizontal track to indicate the perceived width of the block. The first experiment found that, in general, when the blocks were tall and thin, they were perceived to be tall and thin, and when they were short and wide, they were perceived to be short and wide. Consequently, perceived height increased with I_{xx} and perceived width increased with I_{zz}.

The second experiment used so-called tensor objects (Amazeen & Turvey, 1996). These are objects consisting of a number of metal rods. One rod (or stem) was held in the hand, and the other rods were fitted into a movable joint that could be attached anywhere along the length of the stem—to form "branches" in an X pattern (see Figure 8.6). Small weights could also be attached anywhere along the length of each branch. What is so valuable about using such odd-looking branched objects is that by positioning the joint—and the connected

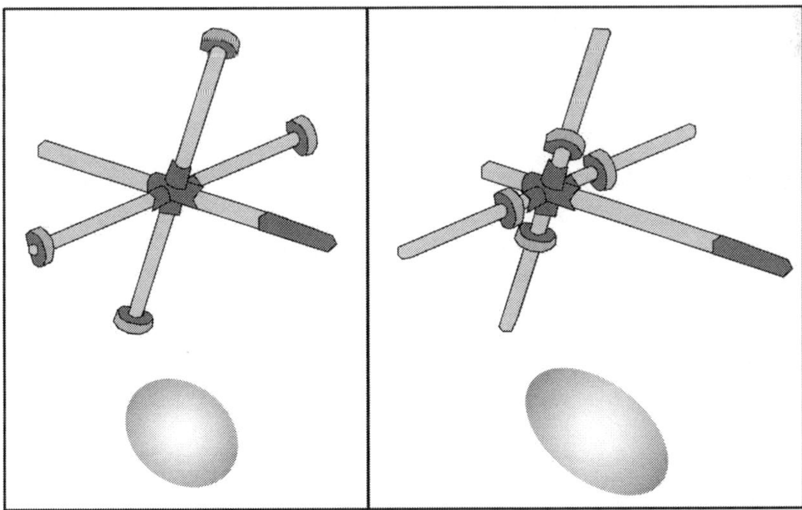

Figure 8.6 Tensor objects developed by Amazeen and Turvey (1996) allow researchers to systematically vary the mass distribution of an object—and hence, the inertial ellipsoid of that object. The two objects depicted here (*top*) have different inertial ellipsoids (*bottom*) even though the objects themselves are the same length, width, and mass. Given the differences in inertial ellipsoids, the object on the left will feel shorter and wider than the object on the right.

branches—along the stem and by carefully positioning the weights toward or away from the stem, the researchers could create objects that were the same length, width, and mass but that had different values of I_{xx} and I_{zz}.

These two values can be thought of as forming the axes of an ellipsoid of inertia (an ellipsoid is a three-dimensional ellipse, see Figure 8.6). The length of the ellipsoid depends on the value of I_{xx}, and the width of the ellipsoid depends on the value of I_{zz}. The ellipsoid is what the object "looks like" to the haptic system. The *size* of the ellipsoid indicates the overall amount of force that is required to move the object. The *shape* of the ellipsoid indicates the relative amount of force required to move the object in different directions. Specifically, the length of the ellipsoid indicates how hard or easy it is to rotate the end of the object toward and away from the ground, and the width of the ellipsoid indicates how hard or easy it is to twist it like a doorknob.

Sliding the joint of the tensor object toward or away from the grasp location will decrease or increase I_{xx} respectively—changing the height of the inertial ellipsoid—without changing the mass or geometric height of the object itself. Sliding the attached masses on the cross-pieces toward or away from the stem will decrease or increase I_{zz}, respectively—changing the width of the inertial ellipsoid—without changing mass or geometric width (compare Figure 8.6 *left* and *right*). The results showed that as I_{xx} increased (as the length of the ellipsoid changed), participants perceived the objects to be taller, and as I_{zz} increased (as the width of the ellipsoid changed), participants perceived the objects to be wider—even though the actual heights, widths, and masses of the objects were unchanged (see also Wagman et al., 2001).

In a different study, researchers investigated whether people could perceive the shape of a larger variety of three-dimensional objects mounted on handles—a hemisphere, a cylinder, a rectangle (i.e., a parallelepiped), a cone, and a pyramid (see Figure 8.7, left; Burton, Turvey, & Solomon, 1990). They created sets of objects of three different sizes—small, medium, and large. They hypothesized that perceived object shape would depend on the *ratio* of the major principal moment of inertia to the minor principal moment of inertia (i.e., I_{xx}:I_{zz}). This ratio reflects how the mass of the object is distributed about these axes—the shape of the inertial ellipsoid—in a way that does not depend on the absolute size of the object. That is, the ratio for a hemisphere ought to be different from that of a cone, but the ratio for a *large* hemisphere ought to be very similar if not identical to that of a *small* hemisphere.

The procedure was similar to the other experiments, except that sample objects of each of the five shapes were on a table in front of and visible to the participant. The participant's job was to wield the object in their hand with movements of their wrist only and identify the shape of the objects by pointing to one of five visible sample objects on the table (see Figure 8.7).

Figure 8.7 Experiments on perception of object shape (*left*) and object orientation (*middle* and *right*) by effortful touch.

They found that participants correctly identified the shape of the object 38% of the time. As in the experiments on hearing shape from Chapter 7, this doesn't seem so impressive until you consider that chance performance would have been 20%. As in those experiments, reports of object shape were not perfectly accurate, but they were not random either. Pyramids attached to handles felt (more or less) like pyramids attached to handles, cylinders attached to handles felt (more or less) like cylinders attached to handles, and so on. Performance in this task is even more impressive when you take a closer look at the trials where participants *incorrectly* identified the shapes. It turned out that there was a *pattern* to how participants were misidentifying the shapes. Participants were more likely to confuse shapes that had similar ratios of I_{xx}:I_{zz}—and similar inertial ellipsoid shapes, such as a cone and a pyramid. They were less likely to confuse shapes that had very different ratios of I_{xx}:I_{zz}—and different inertial ellipsoid shapes, such as a cone and a hemisphere. In other words, people could correctly identify shapes to the extent that the ratios of I_{xx}:I_{zz}—the shape of the inertial ellipsoid—uniquely identified that shape.

Feeling Orientation

When Fred grabbed what turned out to be his tennis racket, he could perceive many different properties of the as-of-yet unidentified object itself—including its length, width, and shape. In addition, however, he could also perceive relationships between himself and the racket—he could tell how the object was oriented relative to his hand—it was pointing straight up—and where he was holding—at the bottom. Does I provide information about these relationships? Yes. Yes, it does.

And this is where the *other values* of I (I_{xy}, I_{xz}, and I_{yz}) of the 3 × 3 matrix come into play (see Figure 8.2). As described previously, the terms along the (top left to bottom right) diagonal of the matrix (I_{xx}, I_{yy}, and I_{zz}) are the *moments of inertia*. Each of these values describes how much the object resists rotation about each of the main axes. In particular, I_{xx} and I_{yy} describe the resistance to rotating the object toward and away from the ground and from side to side, respectively. I_{zz} describes the resistance to twisting the object like a doorknob).

The off-diagonal terms—in the upper-right and lower-left corners of the matrix (I_{xy}, I_{xz}, and I_{yz})—are the *products of inertia*. These terms each quantify *asymmetries* in the mass distribution. These asymmetries describe how much the mass distribution of the object tilts away from these main axes. In other words, they describe how the *mass* of the object is distributed relative to the *geometry* of the object.

Collectively, the products of inertia describe the *orientation of the mass distribution*—the orientation of the inertial ellipsoid—in particular, how much it is tilted off the main axes and in what direction(s). Objects in Fred's junk drawer that are bent or tilted relative to the hand—like his boomerang or his hockey stick—will exhibit a more tilted mass distribution than objects that are not—like his jousting lance (yes, he has a jousting lance) or his conducting baton. Consequently, the products of inertia ought to provide information about how such objects are oriented with respect to the hand.

In experiments investigating this hypothesis, participants wielded unseen L-shaped objects—consisting of a long stem and a single branch at a 90° angle (see Figure 8.7, *middle*). The researcher handed the object to the participant so that they were holding it firmly at the bottom of the stem and so that the branch was pointing at one of eight different angles—0° to 315° in 45° increments, where 0° was straight up. The participant's job was to report the angle (the pointing direction) of the branch by rotating a visible pointer with their left hand. Perceived angle tracked actual angle very closely. Given that orientation itself is a geometric property, and the touch system works with forces, the researchers proposed that the products of inertia—the orientation of the inertial ellipsoid—must be providing information about orientation (Turvey et al., 1992).

To conclusively demonstrate that this is the case, researchers conducted a follow-up study in which participants wielded objects with two branches—forming a V (see Figure 8.7, right). Unbeknownst to the participant, a small weight was placed on one of the branches. This shifted the orientation of the mass distribution without changing the actual orientation of the object. Perceived orientation of the V was shifted in the direction of the branch with the added weight (Pagano & Turvey, 1992). In other words, perceived orientation of a hand-held object depended on the orientation of the mass distribution of that object—the orientation of the inertial ellipsoid—and *not* the actual orientation of that object.

Feeling Orientation (of the Body Itself)

These studies provide a law-based explanation for how a person perceives the orientation of a hand-held object. Does this same explanation apply to how a person perceives the *orientation of their own limbs*? How does a person know where their limbs are and how they are oriented—especially in cases where they cannot see them? This ability is known as proprioception, and at first glance, it seems like a job for the central executive. After all, the central executive ought to know the size, shape, and orientation of the body itself. In fact, at least some traditional explanations of proprioception rely on a type of internal representation of body space called a body schema. In most descriptions, the body schema is a brain-based mapping or model of the body's spatial properties that must be referenced in the course of performing everyday behavior and must be updated when there are long-term or short-term changes in the body—such as growth or use of a hand-held object (see Holmes, Spence, Giard, & Wallace, 2004).

From the ecological perspective, however, perception of properties of the objects held by the limbs and perception of properties of the limbs themselves ought to occur by the same (lawful) processes. Does *I*—in particular, the orientation of the inertial ellipsoid—also provide information about the position of the limbs of the body? Yes. Yes, it does. Clever experiments by Pagano and Turvey (1995) investigated this hypothesis. Participants held a cross-shaped object so that the two branches extended horizontally from their fist. This created a kind of pointing tool that included both their arm and the object (see Figure 8.8, *left*).

Participants held the pointing tool under a screen and were asked to point to a location below one of three visible targets above the screen (see Figure 8.8, *right*). Unbeknownst to the participant, weights were attached to one or both of the branches. When the weights were placed *asymmetrically*—either on the right or the left branch, the orientation of the mass distribution of the arm and tool was shifted in the direction of the weight and away from the actual pointing direction of the arm—without changing the angle of the arm at the shoulder. When the pointing tool was weighted on the left branch, participants tended to point slightly to the right of each target. When the pointing tool was weighted on the right branch,

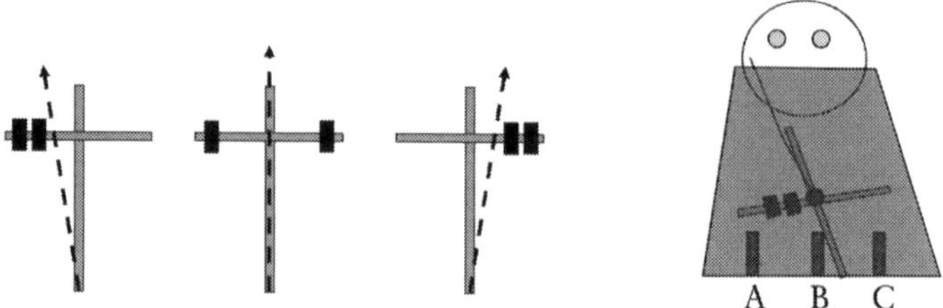

Figure 8.8 *Left*: The cross-shaped objects used by Pagano and Turvey (1995) to investigate perception of limb orientation. The participant grasps the object where the branches intersect. *Right*: The participant then points to a target with the unseen tool. Participants tended to point with the mass distribution of the tool + arm and not their anatomical arm.

participants tended to point slightly to the left of each target (see Figure 8.8, *right*). When it was weighted on both sides equally, participants pointed accurately. This pattern showed that participants were pointing with the mass distribution of the pointing tool and arm rather than with the arm itself. These and other experiments have shown that perceived orientation of the limbs depended on the orientation of the mass distribution of the limb—the orientation of the inertial ellipsoid—and not the actual orientation of that limb (Garrett et al., 1998; van de Langenberg, Kingma, & Beek, 2007; see Pagano & Turvey, 1998).

Box 8.1 Tensegrity Structures and Perception by Touch

When Fred was little, he had a somewhat unusual favorite toy—a gift from Uncle Jimmy! The toy was a three-dimensional shape made of small wooden rods held together with elastic strings. The odd thing about the construction of this toy was that the wooden rods didn't touch each other at all. Instead, the wooden rods were held in place by the tension provided by the elastic strings (see Figure 8.9). This toy was very different from most other toys that Fred played with—like his Legos. When Fred would build something using Legos, whatever he built would be supported entirely by hard and inflexible components—the Legos themselves. However, this toy was supported entirely by soft and flexible components—the elastic strings. In addition, the things that Fred built with his Legos were not springy at all—just ask any parent who has stepped on Legos left strewn on the floor!

However, this toy *was* a spring! When Fred pressed on it, it *compressed* (see Figure 8.9, *right*). And no matter where or how he pressed on it, the *entire structure* changed shape and rebalanced itself—kind of like a balloon does when you poke it or press on it. This certainly didn't happen with his Legos. If he pressed on a Lego structure in a particular place, that part might break off, or the whole structure might collapse! Fred's favorite childhood toy is an example of a *tensegrity*[4] *structure*—a structure in which inflexible components are flexibly held together by elastic tension.

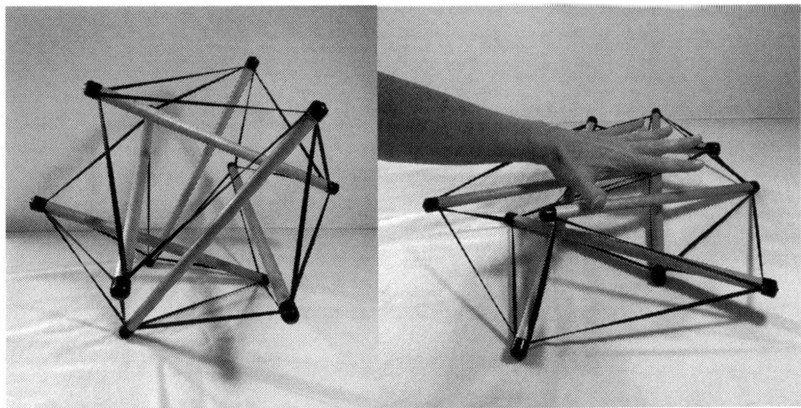

Figure 8.9 A tensegrity structure consists of hard and inflexible components supported by soft and flexible components. It changes shape when compressed but does not collapse. Recently, researchers have suggested that the musculoskeletal system can be understood as a bio-tensegrity structure.

Recently, researchers have suggested that the musculoskeletal system is a *biotensegrity structure* (Turvey & Fonseca, 2014; Scarr, 2014). Considered this way, the bones are analogous to the wooden rods, and the muscles and other connective tissue are analogous to the elastic bands. This proposal reflects the fact that, unlike the other perceptual modalities, there is no specific organ for touch comparable to the eye, the ear, the nose, or the mouth. The touch system includes the *entire body*—the skin, muscles, tendons, ligaments, and other connective tissue. And all of these bodily tissues are connected—the touch system is *a continuous system*.

If the musculoskeletal system is organized this way, it would mean that when a person moves a particular part of their body or manipulates an object, *the entire body* is involved (at least to some degree; see Chapter 9). It would also mean that the particular body part being moved or manipulating an object is less important than the overall patterning of forces that occurs when this happens. In other words, it would be consistent with the ecological proposal that the stimulation of relevance to perception by touch is the macro-scale pattern of *physical forces* on the bodily tissue and not the micro-scale activity of receptor cells (Mangalam, Wagman, & Newell, 2018; Wagman & Hajnal, 2014a, 2014b, 2016).

Information About *Relationships Between* Animals and Surfaces

Feeling Affordances for Moving

Fred knows about more than just the shape, size, and orientation of the unseen tennis racket. He also knows that it is relatively heavy—*heavier* than either a small LED flashlight or a candle anyway. How does he know this? Perception of heaviness has been a topic of investigation in psychology since the 1800s (Weber, 1834). And since that time, researchers have known that the mass of the object plays at least some role in how heavy it feels. For example, Fred's jousting lance will feel heavier than his conducting baton. But it also is the case that under the right circumstances, two objects of the *same mass*—say, Fred's tennis racket and the large potato—can feel *differently* heavy. And two objects of *different masses*—say, the LED flashlight and the conducting baton—can feel *equally heavy*. Something else must be going on here. In traditional explanations, this something else is representation and computation.[5] In ecological explanations, this something else is I.

Recall that I describes the forces required to move an object in different directions. Ecological psychologists have hypothesized that it is these forces—which depend partly, but not completely, on mass—that determine how heavy an object feels. Researchers investigated this hypothesis using the tensor objects that we described earlier (see Figure 8.6). Remember that the value of such objects is that researchers can create objects that differ in I—or specific components of I—but that do not differ in other properties, such as mass.

A series of studies in the late 20th and early 21st centuries established that perception of heaviness of unseen objects is lawfully related to I (Amazeen & Turvey, 1996; Shockley, Grocki, Carello, & Turvey, 2001; Turvey, Shockley, & Carello, 1999). In particular, objects feel heavier to the degree that I_{xx}, I_{yy}, and I_{zz} increase and become more unequal—as changes in the *size and shape* of the inertial ellipsoid require *more overall force* to move the object and more *diverse forces* to move the object in different directions.

Think about it this way: If I_{xx}, I_{yy}, and I_{zz} are relatively small and relatively equal, moving the object will require very little force, and moving it in different directions will require producing approximately the same amount of force in any given direction. The object will be *easy* to control, and consequently, it will feel *light*. If I_{xx}, I_{yy}, and I_{zz} are relatively large and relatively unequal, moving the object will require a lot of force, and moving it in different directions will require producing different amounts of force in each direction. The object will be *hard* to control, and consequently, it will feel *heavy*. In fact, research has shown that when people report how heavy an object is, they are really reporting how *movable* that object is (Shockley, Carello, & Turvey, 2004). Or in other words, they are perceiving affordances for moving the object.

This is why two objects of the same mass (e.g., Fred's tennis racket and the potato) can feel unequally heavy. In these cases, the respective combinations of mass and mass distribution—*especially* the size and shape of the inertial ellipsoid—of each object make one object more difficult to control than the other even though they have the *same* mass. This is also why two objects of different masses (e.g., Fred's LED flashlight and conducting baton) can feel equally heavy. In these cases, it is because the respective combinations of mass and mass distribution of each object—again, *especially* the size and shape of the inertial ellipsoid—make the two objects equally difficult (or in this case, equally easy) to control even though they have *different* masses (Shockley et al., 2004).

Box 8.2 Perceiving by Means of an Object Attached to the Body

In Chapter 5, we briefly discussed a study in which blindfolded participants were able to perceive affordances of a surface when they explored gaps in that surface with a hand-held object (Burton, 1992). What is perhaps most impressive about this is that the participants were blindfolded (sighted) people who had no experience whatsoever in such a task. From the ecological perspective, participants were able to perform this task despite this lack of experience because the structure that provides information about a given affordance is analogous across energy forms—light and the physical forces acting on bodily tissues—regardless of the micro-scale differences between those energy forms (see Chapter 4).

Even within the touch system itself, though, there are micro-scale differences across different body parts. For example, some body parts are more powerful, more sensitive, or more dexterous than others. However, given the lawful structuring of the physical forces acting on the body, these micro-scale differences ought not to matter in perception of a given affordance.

In fact, studies have shown that blindfolded participants can perceive whether an inclined surface affords standing on when they explore that surface with an object held in their preferred hand, their non-preferred hand, or both hands (Wagman & Hajnal, 2014a). They can even do so when they explore that surface with an object attached to their preferred foot or non-preferred foot or even with an object attached to their head (Wagman & Hajnal, 2014b, 2016)! These abilities are analogous to the abilities of nonhuman animals to perceive affordances by means of body parts that are not directly connected to the nervous system like claws, whiskers, antennae, horns, and quills (Blaesing & Cruse, 2004; see Burton, 1993).

Feeling Affordances for Tool Use

Without knowing what the unseen object was, Fred knew that he could use it to hit another object but probably not to poke or push another object. In other words, he was able to perceive *affordances* of the unseen hand-held object. Recall that in the ecological approach, the primary content of animals' perceptual experiences is affordances (and not properties, see Chapter 5).

So ecological psychologists would say that when Fred perceived other properties of the object—length, shape, orientation—he was really perceiving affordances—for reaching with, for example. And we have just seen that perception of heaviness is best described as perception of movableness. So *I* provides information about how an object can be moved, in general. But using an object as a tool requires moving it *in a particular way* with *a particular intention*. Hammering movements are different from poking movements, for example. Does *I* provide information about the affordances of an unseen object for specific goal-directed behaviors?

This hypothesis was investigated by Wagman and Carello (2001). They started with the assumption that hammering and poking are relatively distinct tasks with relatively distinct movements and goals. Hammering requires forceful up and down movements, whereas poking requires relatively precise back and forth movements—compare the movements required to use a rubber mallet and a pool cue, for example. The experiments they conducted were similar to many of the ones described previously. Participants wielded unseen objects of different lengths with weights attached at various locations along those lengths. But this time, the participants rated how well they would be able to use each object for hammering or poking on a scale of 1–7.

Objects were rated as better *hammers* as the values of *I* changed the size and shape of the inertial ellipsoid such that more force was required to move the object—and thus, more force could be *delivered with* that object to a struck surface. Objects were rated as better *pokers* as the values of *I* changed the size, shape, and *orientation* of the inertial ellipsoid such that the object tip could be more easily controlled.

But what if a person perceives that a given object is not particularly suited for the tool use task they are about to perform. Fred remembers when he was a little boy using his dad's tennis racket. It was much too big for him, and it was difficult for him to hit the ball with it. One—albeit impractical—option would have been for Fred to (somehow) assemble an entirely different tennis racket. Practicality aside, let's say a person does choose to assemble a hand-held implement. Does *I* provide information about how to do so? Yes. Yes, it does. Wagman, Caputo, and Stoffregen (2016) gave participants a set of wooden rods of different lengths and a set of weights that could be attached to those rods (see Figure 8.10, *left*).

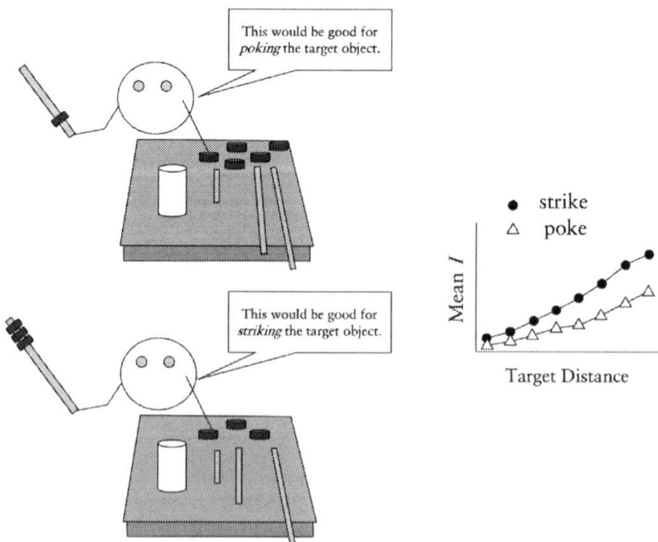

Figure 8.10 *Left*: The tool assembly task used by Wagman et al. (2016). Participants assembled tools by choosing a rod of a particular length and attaching weights to that rod. *Right*: Participants assembled tools with different values of *I* depending on the tool use task and the distance of the target object.

In one condition, participants assembled tools that could be used to *strike* a target object placed at different distances from them. In another condition, they assembled tools that could be used to *poke* a target object placed at different distances from them. Participants assembled tools with different mass distributions depending on both the tool use task and the distance of the target object. In particular, they assembled tools with larger values of I—larger values I_{xx}—(1) when the tools were to be used as striking implements than when they were to be used as poking implements and (2) when the target object was farther away than when it was closer.

Of course, most people can't simply just assemble an entirely new tool on the spot. More than likely, they are stuck with the one they have—at least for the time being. But they still can make that object more appropriate for the particular task. Remember that I depends on the resistance to rotation in different directions relative to a rotation point—relative to where the object is grasped. One option for changing I is to change the object. Another option for doing so is to change the rotation point by changing the grasp location on the object. Does I provide information about how to do so? Yes, again. In the experiment investigating this, the objects were hollowed-out wooden rods that were internally weighted in different locations (Wagman & Carello, 2003) (see Figure 8.11).

Participants were handed a given object and were asked to grasp that object in a location that would best enable them to perform a striking task that emphasized power over precision or vice versa. In the power striking task, participants chose grasp locations so that I_{xx}, I_{yy}, and I_{zz} were large and unequal (see Figure 8.11, *left*). This changed the size and the shape of the inertial ellipsoid such that a large amount of force could be delivered by a particular part of the object. In the precision-striking task, participants chose grasp locations so that I_{xx}, I_{yy}, and I_{zz} were small and relatively equal (see Figure 8.11, *right*). This changed the size and the shape of the ellipsoid such that the tip of the object could be easily controlled.

Striking an object requires more than just selecting an appropriate striking implement, however. It also requires bringing the striking implement (say, Fred's tennis racket) into contact with the object—say, a tennis ball—at the *right location* on that striking implement. Fred remembers the friendly and knowledgeable saleswoman at the sporting goods store telling

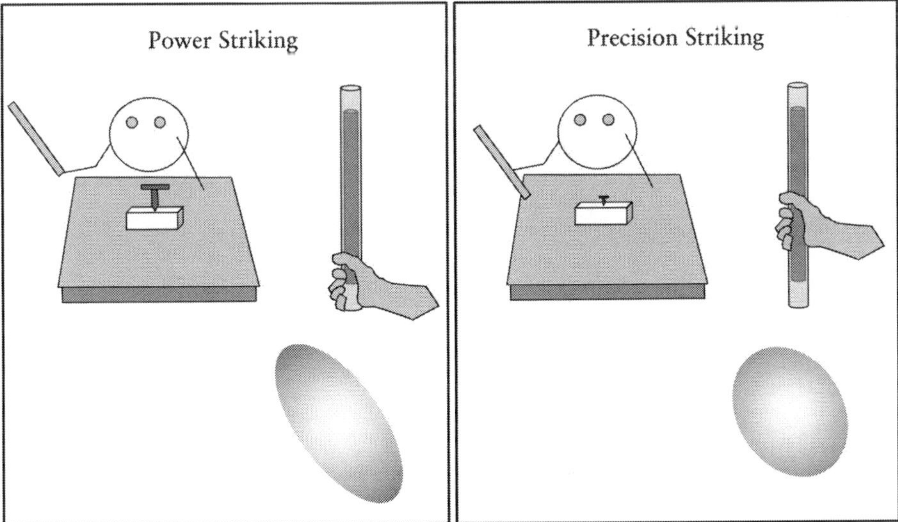

Figure 8.11 In the experiments by Wagman and Carello (2003), participants grasped internally weighted rods in different locations—and thus created differently shaped inertial ellipsoids—in a power striking task (*left*) and in a precision-striking task (*right*).

him that every tennis racket head has a sweet spot at which energy is maximally transferred from the racket to the ball—and thus minimally transferred to the hand. In order to bring the sweet spot on the racket into contact with the ball, he'll need to be able to perceive where the sweet spot is. Experiments have demonstrated that *I* provides information about the location of the sweet spot on a striking implement (Carello et al., 1999; Wagman & Carello, 2001; Wagman & Taylor, 2004).

Notes

1. The word "haptic" comes from the Greek word *haptikos*, which means "able to touch or grasp".
2. This is somewhat analogous to putting a car in drive, stepping on the accelerator, stepping on the brake, putting the car in reverse, and stepping on the accelerator again.
3. In fact, the word "tensor" comes from the Latin word *tender*, which means "to stretch".
4. "Tensegrity" is a combination of the words "tension" and "integrity".
5. Perceived heaviness is sometimes proposed to be a combination of independent sensations of properties such as mass, size, and density or a comparison of the expected to actual muscle activity required to lift the object (see Buckingham, 2014).

9 Action and Coordination

In Chapter 5, we argued that perception is primarily of affordances—opportunities for behavior. Fred's cat can perceive *what possibilities exist* for avoiding the rambunctious dog. It could flee. It could leap. It could hide. In that chapter, we made the case that affordances exist neither in the micro-scale properties of the animal nor in the micro-scale properties of the environment. Rather, affordances emerge in the macro-scale *relationship between* animal and environment. This required a rethinking of the variables of relevance to perception. The next three chapters (6–8) outlined this rethinking with respect to seeing, hearing, and feeling. In particular, we provided a description of the macro-level stimulation variables that are lawfully structured by the relationship between animal and environment. These variables were to be found in structured energy arrays, and we described such variables in such a way that they could "get into the muscle". We then described the results of experiments showing that these variables inform whether, when, and how to perform goal-directed behavior.

From the ecological perspective, the purpose of perceiving is to guide *doing*—performing coordinated goal-directed actions.[1] Getting light, sound, or forces into the muscle is only *part* of the story. Avoiding the rambunctious dog means turning a possibility (or multiple possibilities) into a reality. It means *actually* fleeing, *actually* leaping, or *actually* jumping. How goal-directed actions like these are performed is the focus of this chapter. In this chapter, we take an analogous approach to action as we did (and do) to perception. Specifically, we *also* describe the performance of goal-directed behaviors as a lawful process that occurs at the macro scale of the relationship between animal and environment. This will require a rethinking of both *what* the relevant variables are for movement and *how* those variables are controlled and coordinated in performing such movements. Describing perception and action as analogous processes occurring at the same level of analysis is an important step in developing an ecological science of perception and action—and eventually cognition (see Chapter 12).

Traditional Approaches to Movement

Just as there are traditional approaches to perception, there are traditional approaches to action (for an overview of some of these, see Rosenbaum, 2017; Schmidt et al., 2020). Importantly, our goal in the next few paragraphs is not to evaluate or even completely describe these approaches but rather—in very broad strokes—to show how they are incompatible with the ecological approach that we have been developing so far.

In some versions of these traditional approaches to action, the nervous system is—more or less—*exclusively* responsible for movements of the body. In these versions, the brain—as a central executive—issues *specific and explicit* motor commands to particular muscles, and these commands are, more or less, followed exactly as issued. In this case, the central executive is like an army general who not only develops the battle plans but also issues specific orders to each individual soldier or a group of soldiers. Movement plans could originate, for example,

DOI: 10.4324/9781003145691-11

in the frontal lobe—the part of the brain that seems most especially involved with planning and thinking. And these plans would likely take into account remembered consequences of previous movement patterns (see Figure 9.1).

The *commands themselves*, however, likely originate in the motor cortex—the part of the brain that seems especially involved with moving individual body parts. They are sent from the motor cortex through the spinal cord to the relevant body part(s). There they affect the moment-to-moment activity of the micro-scale components of that body part (e.g., individual muscles or joints). Let's say that Fred wants to wave to Claudia from the other side of his kitchen. Doing so may be a matter of Fred's brain (1) figuring out that this requires (a) the muscles of his shoulder to raise his upper arm by a certain amount, (b) the muscles of the upper arm to raise his forearm by a certain amount, and (c) the muscles of his forearm and wrist to move his hand back and forth by a certain amount, and then (2) issuing the appropriate sequence of commands to make these exact movements happen. Consequently, in these explanations of action, the central executive is seemingly in charge of both *planning* and *executing* every detail of a given movement.

In other versions of these traditional approaches to action, the nervous system is primarily—though perhaps not exclusively—responsible for movements of the body. Instead, in these versions, the body itself plays a key secondary role. The brain is still in the role of central executive and still issues motor commands, but these commands are *neither specific nor explicit*. Instead, they are *abstract or generalized*. Here, the central executive acts like an army general who *develops the battle plans* but then leaves it to lower-ranking officers to get the job done however they can. These plans are followed to the extent that they can be reconciled with the limbs that are being moved, how those limbs are currently positioned, and the specifics of the planned movement, among other factors.

Rather than affecting the moment-to-moment activity of individual muscles or joints, the commands are in the form of *programs* that affect the sequential activity across groupings of

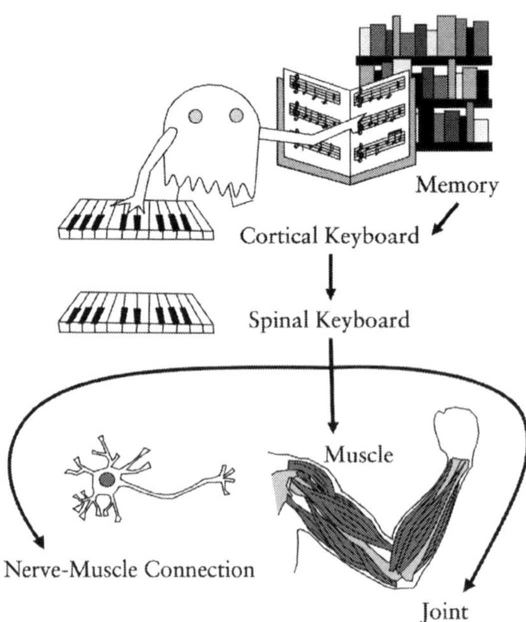

Figure 9.1 In traditional explanations of movement, the central executive plans (and sometimes executes) movements by issuing commands that get delivered to different levels of the motor system. (Adapted from Turvey, Fitch, & Tuller, 1982.)

muscles or joints. Performing a given movement is a matter of the brain figuring out what *general movement patterns*—what abstract or generalized movement programs—are required and then tasking the lower levels of the nervous system with altering those movements to fit the specific circumstances. Let's say that Fred wants to wave to Claudia from the other side of a crowded theater (i.e., requiring a larger movement in order to be seen). Rather than explicitly planning and executing every detail of this movement pattern, Fred's brain might only be responsible for identifying what *general pattern* is required—the waving pattern described previously. The brain leaves it up to the lower levels of the nervous system to execute this general plan under *these specific circumstances*—making these movements *twice as large as before*. Consequently, in these explanations of action, the central executive is in charge of *planning* but not necessarily executing every detail of a given movement (see Figure 9.1).

These two versions of traditional approaches to action differ in the type and amount of knowledge required of the central executive (i.e., in the type and amount of the loan of intelligence required), but crucially, both still ultimately require a loan of intelligence (Turvey & Fonseca, 2009). In the first version, the central executive is charged not only with making the *decisions* required to develop an appropriate plan but also with *controlling* the individual muscles or joints in executing that plan. As you might expect, being a general *and* a platoon commander requires an inordinate amount of intelligent behavior—for example decision-making, planning, monitoring, managing, and implementing.

In the second version, the central executive is still charged with making appropriate decisions, but not necessarily with controlling individual muscles or joints—a task that is merely passed along to lower levels of the nervous system. But while being a general—and *only* a general—saves the central executive from the burden of implementing, it still requires all of the other intelligent behaviors. And the burden of implementing is merely shifted to the platoon commanders, who may require their *own* loan of intelligence.

In addition, both approaches assume *linear causality*—remember that this was one of the assumptions that started the whole mess in Chapters 1 and 2. That is, in both cases, moving the body requires that plans or programs be sent in a one-way fashion from a higher level of a hierarchy (e.g., the brain) to a lower level of a hierarchy (e.g., the muscles). Moreover, this *linear neural process* is complemented with a *linear mechanical process*. These commands set into motion a one-way stereotyped sequential process in which one part of a muscle or group of muscles moves one part of the body, and then another muscle or group of muscles moves a different part of the body, and so on—kind of like the billiard balls in Chapters 1 and 2.

This focus on linear causality leads to a focus on micro-scale units (muscles, joints, etc.) and, consequently, a necessary insertion of representation and computation (e.g., commands or programs sent from a central executive) to account for the intelligent control of these many micro-scale units. These features make any and all traditional approaches to action incompatible with an ecological approach (for an overview, see Turvey & Fonseca, 2009; Wagman, 2010). Instead, the ecological approach seeks a lawful explanation of goal-directed action at the macro scale of the relationship between animal and environment without the need for mediating processes or loans of intelligence. In the rest of this chapter, we outline just such an approach.

The Degrees of Freedom Problem

After a befuddling phone call with the electrical company, Fred's power is now back on. Hooray! Ever since he found his old tennis racket in his junk drawer, Fred has been practicing his forehand swing—first in the dark and now in the light. As he swings the racket back and forth, he begins to think about *how* he is doing so. He imagines himself as sort of a realistic Fred marionette puppet with wooden appendages that rotate about joints. What would the puppeteer of the Fred marionette—called a marionettist—need to do to control Fred's upper arm, lower arm, hand, and ultimately, the racket?

Fred thinks about what is involved in moving all the parts of his arm (see Figure 9.2). His shoulder is a ball-and-socket joint. Fred can move his upper arm in three different ways. He can move it up and down relative to his body, he can move it side to side relative to his body, and he can rotate it relative to his body. In other words, his shoulder joint has three *degrees of freedom*. Three values—how much up and down, how much side to side, and how much rotation—must be known to determine the position of the upper arm relative to his body. The elbow joint is a hinge joint. Fred can rotate his forearm toward or away from his upper arm, and that's it. His elbow joint only has *one* degree of freedom—only *one* coordinate must be known to determine the rotation of his forearm relative to the upper arm. The radioulnar joint in his forearm is a pivot joint. Fred can twist his forearm relative to his upper arm, and that's it. This joint also only has one degree of freedom—again, only one coordinate must be known to determine how "twisted" the forearm is relative to the upper arm. The wrist is a little more complicated. It is a gliding joint. Fred can move his hand up and down and side to side relative to his forearm. So the wrist has *two* degrees of freedom. *Two* coordinates must be known to determine the position of the hand relative to the forearm.

If you are keeping track—and even if you are not—this means that if Fred's puppeteer ("the marionettist") wanted to control the exact position of Fred's arm and hand using movements about these four joints, they would need to maintain control of *seven degrees of freedom*. They would need to explicitly control the values of seven different variables *simultaneously*. This sounds hard to Fred, but maybe if the marionettist were really skilled, it might work—maybe. But then he remembers that this level of skill would be necessary just to control *one* limb—and a limb made of wood at that! Fred's body is much more than just his arm (see Figure 9.3, *left*).

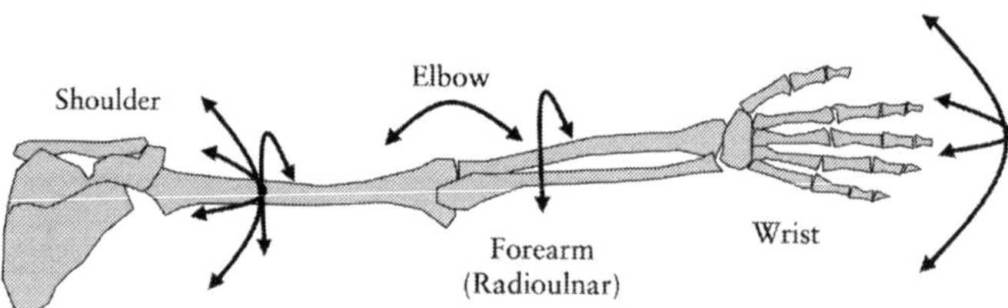

Figure 9.2 Controlling the arm requires controlling seven degrees of freedom—three at the shoulder, one at the elbow, one at the forearm, and two at the wrist.

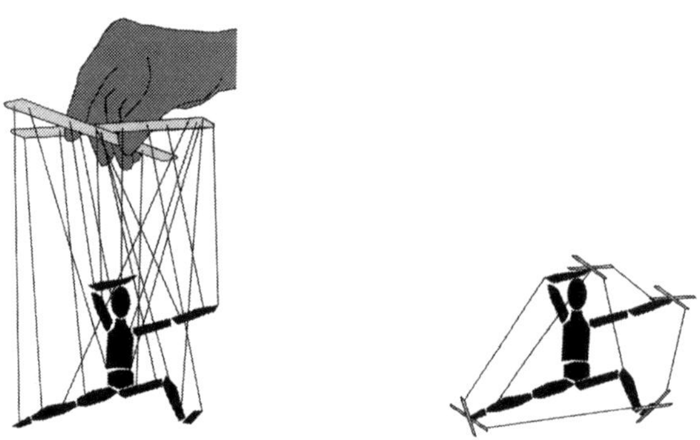

Figure 9.3 When anatomical components are considered independently, there are far too many degrees of freedom to be controlled (*left*). The concept of synergies—functional groupings of anatomical components that work together to exploit information about affordances—reduces the number of degrees of freedom to a manageable number (*right*). (Adapted from Turvey, 1990.)

He has two arms, two legs, a torso, and a head, all of which would need to be controlled—250 to 350 joints in all—depending on how you count! And of course, Fred's arm is not made of wood. Neither is the rest of his body. *He's a real boy!* And real boys are made of bodily tissue like muscles, tendons, ligaments, and skin. This makes things much, much more complicated.

Fred thinks about what it would take to control the entire arm of a more realistic Fred marionette that includes muscles. There are at least ten muscles that work to control the shoulder joint, six that work to control the elbow joint, four that work to control the radioulnar joint, and six that work to control the wrist joint. This is a total of *26 degrees* of freedom—that's 26 variables that would need to be controlled *simultaneously*—creating an unfathomably large total of 4.03×10^{26} possible combinations! And that's *just his arm*. None of this includes any of the many other movements that Fred would need to make with the rest of his body—600+ muscles in all—that *support* the behavior of moving his arm—more on those later.

It would seem that controlling individual anatomical units (e.g., joints or muscles) creates far too many degrees of freedom to be controlled without a *huge* loan of intelligence—in particular, the ability to make an inordinate number of decisions and control an inordinate number of degrees of freedom (see Figure 9.3, *left*). This is a nonstarter for an ecological approach to movement (Turvey et al., 1982).

The Degrees of Freedom Solution

In large part, the ecological approach to the control of goal-directed movement has its roots in the work of Russian neurophysiologist Nikolai Bernstein.[2] Bernstein (1967; Latash & Turvey, 1996) realized that goal-directed movements could *only* be performed if the very many degrees of freedom to be controlled were somehow reduced to a manageable number. Consequently, the degrees of freedom problem described previously is often described as the Bernstein problem.

One of Bernstein's greatest insights was that it is not necessary for a person to provide *each and every one* of the forces required to perform a given goal-directed movement. In fact, it turns out that a person has to provide far fewer forces than might seem necessary. This is because the performance of any goal-directed behavior occurs in a context. Specifically, movements take place *in* a world and *with* a body, both of which abide by the laws of physics. This means that at least some of the forces required to perform a goal-directed behavior are provided *for free* (see Chapter 13). How so? Some forces are provided by the *world itself*—gravity, for example. When Fred takes a step, he needs to provide the muscular forces required to *raise* his foot off the ground—and push his body forward—but he does not need to provide the muscular forces required to bring his foot *back to the ground*. Instead, he just needs to *let the foot fall forward*. Gravity will do the work for him. Walking is merely controlled falling! (Alexander, 1992). It is this fact that has made developing a walking robot so challenging. In fact, there were robots that could play chess *decades* before there were robots that could walk.

Other forces are so-called *reactive forces* provided by the fact that the body parts are connected (perhaps as a tensegrity structure; see Chapter 8). Moving any particular body part will move, or at least affect, the other parts. When Fred takes a step, he does not need to explicitly control the position of his hips, torso, shoulders, arms, and head. Once his front foot falls to the ground and his body weight shifts forward, these other body parts will come along for the ride. The *connectivity of his body* will do the work for him.

This does not mean that goal-directed movement is any easier—to perform or to explain. It just means that it is a *different kind of problem*. For one thing, performing a coordinated goal-directed movement requires *capitalizing on* and *cooperating with* the forces that are given for free to bring about the intended movement. It requires applying just the right forces at just the right times—not providing all of the forces all of the time. Moving in a coordinated way requires transforming the forces that are given for free into the forces that are needed (Bernstein, 1967). It is more like sculpting—transforming what is already there into what you want—than it is like building—constructing what you want from nothing or from separate raw materials.

Fred remembers when he was just learning to dribble a basketball. His first attempts were a disaster because he either slapped the ball too gently and too infrequently that it lost energy and just rolled away. Or he shoved it too hard and too quickly so that it bounced wildly. As he got better, he realized that all he needed to do was to tap the ball with just enough force to *guide* it to the ground so that it would bounce back to his hand. The fact that many of the degrees of freedom in dribbling a ball are controlled for free—by gravity and the elastic properties of the ball, among other factors—reduces the number of degrees of freedom that he needed to actively control.

Learning which degrees of freedom need to be explicitly controlled and which do not is part of learning how to perform a coordinated goal-directed behavior. Consequently, performing a coordinated goal-directed behavior is as much—or more—about "freezing out" or "clamping down" on unnecessary degrees of freedom as it is about engaging or controlling the necessary ones. For a person just learning a skill, the task of controlling exactly the right degrees of freedom at exactly the right times is often so overwhelming that they often resort to clamping down on almost every available degree of freedom—save one or two. This makes the task easier overall, but it makes the performance much less skillful.

When Fred was first learning to dribble a basketball, both his posture and the movements of his dribbling arm and hand were *stiff* or *rigid* because he was clamping down on too many degrees of freedom. He was *fighting* the reactive forces (and necessarily so at this stage of skill development) rather than attempting to cooperate with them. As he got better, his posture became looser—but not too loose—and the movements of his arm and hand became more fluid—but not too fluid—because he was able to free up more and more of the right degrees of freedom. This allowed him to dribble the ball more and more dexterously.

The Concept of Synergies

So far, we have seen that from the ecological perspective, anatomical units are not the right level of analysis for understanding the performance of goal-directed behavior. Focusing on the moment-by-moment control of individual anatomical units—muscles or even joints—requires too many decisions and creates a far-too-large degrees of freedom problem. So what *is* the appropriate level of analysis from an ecological perspective?

In the context of *perceiving* affordances for goal-directed behaviors, the fundamental unit is the *perceptual system*—a grouping of potentially independent anatomical components that work together as a functional unit in detecting information about a given affordance (J. Gibson, 1966). Recall that it ought to be possible to perceive the very same affordance by different perceptual modalities or by different configurations of the same perceptual modality (see Chapters 5–8). Given the symmetry between perception and action in the ecological approach, there ought to be an analogous or symmetric fundamental unit for *performing* goal-directed behaviors.

Fortunately, Bernstein provides us with exactly this. For Bernstein, *a synergy* is a grouping of potentially independent anatomical components that work together as a functional unit in *exploiting* information about affordances for a given behavior—that is, in performing a given behavior (see Figure 9.3, *right*). More specifically, they are a grouping of muscles spanning several joints that are constrained to act as a functional unit—they are a "choir of muscles" that "harmonize" (Profeta & Turvey, 2018). Analogously, the very same function(s) can be achieved by different anatomical components or different configurations of the same anatomical components.

Swinging Hammers and Tugging Jaws

A synergy is a functional relationship among independent anatomical parts. The key feature of this relationship is that it brings about an intended outcome. The purpose of synergy is not to produce a *movement* but rather to achieve a *goal*. One of the best examples of this is from research conducted by Bernstein himself in the 1920s and '30s. He recorded the movement patterns produced by the hammer strokes of expert blacksmiths with a high-speed film camera equipped with a motion analysis system called a kimocyclograph (Bernstein, 1967). We might expect that for expert blacksmiths, the movements of the shoulder, arm, and hand would be *identical* on every strike. That is, we might expect that part of what makes an expert an expert is the ability to perform the *exact same movement* again and again.

But this is not what he found. Instead, he found that the movements of the shoulder, arm, and hand *differed* from strike to strike. However, what did not differ (as much) from strike to strike was the *trajectory of the hammer head*. In fact, he found that when there was *more* variability in the position of the joints, there was *less* variability in the trajectory of the hammer. The synergy created among the muscles of the shoulder, upper and lower arm, and hand produced a different pattern of muscle contractions and limb movements on every swing but a consistent pattern of hammer movements (see Figure 9.4). The movements showed micro-level variability but macro-level consistency. This is exactly what a well-formed synergy does.

So performing a skilled movement again and again is not about performing a *specific movement pattern* again and again. It is about using slightly different movement patterns across slightly different contexts to *achieve a given outcome* again and again. No two instances of a given behavior are exactly the same. They *can't be*. The context will always differ. An expert has learned how to achieve the same outcome despite (or perhaps partly because of) these differences in context. Bernstein (1967) called this "repetition without repetition". And this concept has important implications for how people should practice a skill in order to master it. *Learning a skill* may very well require the person to repeatedly practice performing the specific set of behaviors required to achieve a goal in a given context. However, *mastering a skill* may require the person to repeatedly practice achieving the goal using different sets of behaviors across different contexts (see Ranganathan, Lee, & Newell, 2020, see Chapter 13).

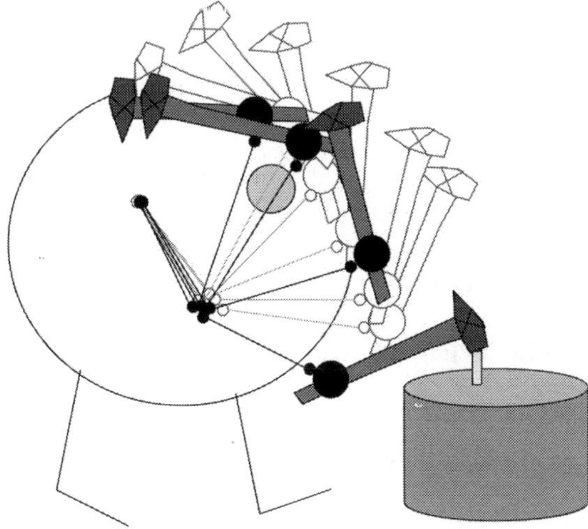

Figure 9.4 When hammering, the trajectory of the limbs varies from movement to movement, but the trajectory of the hammer head—and especially the final position of the hammer head—remains relatively constant. Here the upswing of the hammer is shown in white and the downswing is shown in gray.

Given that the purpose of any synergy is to achieve a particular goal, the components of a given synergy can change from moment to moment, depending on how the context changes. One of the best examples of this comes from speech production (i.e., the act of speaking). In general, speech production is remarkably complicated. Even producing a single syllable (like "pa") can involve up to 70 different muscles (see Abbs & Connor, 1989; Turvey, 2007). Given that normal speech produces four to five syllables per second, speaking involves continual, rapid, and precise coordination of many, many components. It is like a complex ballet performed with the lips, teeth, mouth, tongue, larynx, and more. What would happen if one of the dancers in this ballet (i.e., one of the components of the speech production system) is bumped just slightly as she attempts to perform a *grand jeté* (i.e., as she attempts to produce a particular syllable)? This was the question posed by Kelso, Tuller, Vatikiotis, and Fowler (1984). Specifically, they investigated what happened when someone's jaw was tugged just slightly as they were producing a given syllable. Would they still be able to produce the intended sound? If so, *how* would they do so?

In this experiment, a participant was fitted with a custom orthodontic device, and the movements of his lips, jaw, and tongue were recorded while he repeated a particular syllable—either "bab" (rhymes with "lab") or "baz" (rhymes with "has") (see Figure 7.11). During some of these repetitions, his jaw was unexpectedly tugged down with the orthodontic device just slightly as he was forming the final syllable (the second "b" in "bab" or the "z" in "baz"). The researchers were interested in what the *other parts of the vocal tract* did when this disturbance occurred *the very first time* for each syllable.

When the participant's jaw was tugged while he was making the final "b" in "bab", the upper and lower lips but not the tongue quickly compensated to preserve the intended sound ("b"). What is interesting about this is that the anatomical components) doing the compensating—the lips—were different from the one being disturbed—the jaw. This highlights that the purpose of a synergy is to achieve a particular *goal* and not use a particular set of *anatomical components*. But it gets even more interesting! When the participant's jaw was tugged while making the "z" in "baz", the tongue—but *not* the upper and lower lips—quickly compensated to preserve the intended sound ("z"). What is so interesting here is that the anatomical component doing the compensating differed when *different sounds* were being produced—the lips when making the "b" sound and the tongue when making the "z" sound. In short, the synergy formed was *functional and flexible*, not *anatomical or stereotypic* (Kelso, 1995). A synergy is self-correcting and goal-preserving. The components of a synergy relate among themselves—they are self-organizing! We will return to this topic in Chapter 16).

Synergies in Postural Control

Fred is exhausted from thinking about all the work that the marionettist would need to do to control his arm. So he decides to rest by not doing anything at all. He *just stands there*—as still as possible. Much to his dismay, after a while, he begins to notice that just standing there requires *doing work*. When Fred held his tennis racket so that it pointed straight up, he had to apply forces proportional to the racket's mass so that it did not fall straight down to the ground. He has to do the same thing in order to stand straight up. He has to apply muscular forces with his upper and lower legs, hips, torso, and lower and upper back to keep his body from falling straight down to the floor. If he stops doing this, he will collapse to the ground in a heap. If walking is controlled falling, standing is (in part, anyway) the *prevention* of falling!

Standing requires that Fred keep his center of mass positioned over a roughly rectangular patch of ground that outlines his feet—known as his base of support. If his center of mass moves too far outside of the boundary of this shape (if he is leaning too far in one direction or the other), he will fall over or he will have to take a step to catch himself. This is why it is harder to stand with your feet touching each other (smaller base of support) than with your feet roughly shoulder-width apart (larger base of support). Fred's center of mass is located roughly in the middle of his torso—roughly at his belly button. Standing up places his center of mass at some distance from the ground. This necessarily makes standing a somewhat unstable behavior. Standing is really a *balancing* task. Not only does he have to keep his center of mass over his base of support, he also has to keep his base of support *under* his center of mass.

His task in standing upright is less like *holding* the tennis racket upright with his fist than it is like *balancing* it placed upright on his open palm. But it is actually even more challenging than this. Unlike the tennis racket, Fred is made of many interconnected jointed parts, each of which is controlled by multiple muscles—remember the degrees of freedom problem? Fred is a multisegmented, unstable system, and balancing such a system is not easy (see Bardy et al., 2002). It requires the continual application and adjustment of muscular forces to keep the center of mass aligned with the base of support and vice versa. This causes the body to continuously sway back and forth and side to side just a little bit—millimeters in each direction. Standing still isn't really standing still at all! Fred notices this—especially when he closes his eyes or attempts to stand on one foot—or both at the same time. The continual application and adjustment of muscular forces to maintain upright posture is performed by flexibly organized synergies spanning multiple body parts. And these synergies support the everyday behaviors involved in doing and perceiving.

Postural Synergies Are Built With Perceptual Information

Before postural synergies can help Fred play tennis or joust or roller skate, they need to keep him standing upright. Recall from Chapter 6 that global optic flow provides information about how a person is moving and how they need to control their movements to achieve a goal. Postural sway is movement. It's just subtle movement. So optic flow from postural sway will be subtle. But can it provide information about how postural sway must be controlled for a person to stay upright? Yes. Yes, it can. Maybe this is why it is easier for Fred to stand on one foot with his eyes open than with his eyes closed.

In the 1970s, researchers developed an apparatus called the moving (or gliding) room to investigate the influence of optic flow on postural sway (Lishman & Lee, 1973). In the moving room, a participant stands inside a small enclosure—consisting of three walls and a ceiling—inside of a larger room. Importantly, though, the walls of the smaller enclosure don't touch the floor of the room (see Figure 9.5, *left*). Instead, they are suspended just above the floor

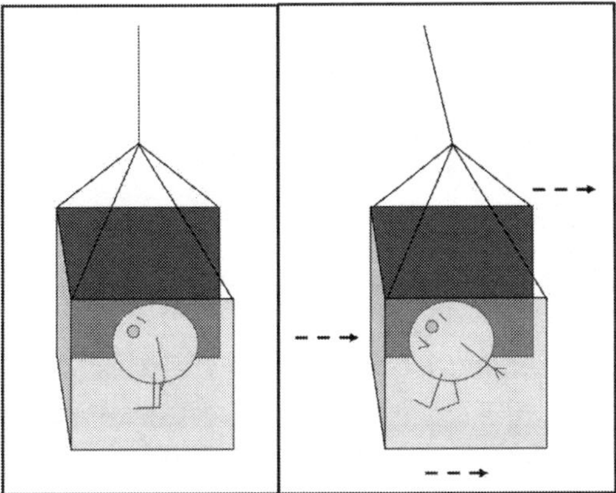

Figure 9.5 In the moving room paradigm, the walls of a room can be slid toward or away from a person. This will cause them to sway (if the room is moved back and forth a small distance) or to lose their balance (if the room is moved a large distance).

and are connected to pulleys so that the entire enclosure can be moved back and forth—while the floor and the person standing on it both remain perfectly stationary—hence the *moving* or *gliding* room. In the 21st century, these effects can be studied with both moving rooms and virtual reality headsets, but in the 1970s, the latter technology did not exist.

Moving the room creates patterns of global optic flow—and these patterns are sufficient to influence posture. Imagine that Fred is facing the back wall of the moving room, and the room is moved toward him approximately 50 cm. This creates a pattern of global optical expansion and—except in very unusual circumstances like a moving room—provides information that he is moving toward the wall—having seemingly lost his balance! Most likely, he will lean or step back to steady himself (see Figure 9.5, *right*). If the room is moved *away* from him, there will be a pattern of global optic contraction, and he may lean or step *forward* to steady himself. In either case, he might even fall over—especially if he is standing in an unusual or challenging posture—like on one foot or with his heels touching and his toes pointed out. This is exactly what happens to people in the moving room (Lee & Aronson, 1974; see Shaw & Kinsella-Shaw, 2020; Smart, Hassebrook, & Teaford, 2020).

But wait, there's more! What if the room is moved so subtly back and forth that the person does not lose their balance? In such a case, the subtle patterns of optic flow brought about by subtle movements of the room still influence postural sway. When the room is moved back and forth 5 mm instead of 50 cm, people don't lose their balance or step in one direction or the other. Instead, their postural sway movements forward and backward *synchronize with the movements of the room* (Lee & Lishman, 1975). The optic flow pattern generated by the moving room guides the formation of the synergy controlling posture. The same thing can happen in walking (Bruggeman, Zosh, & Warren, 2007). And in most cases, participants do not ever become aware that this is happening!

Box 9.1 Motion Sickness as a Movement Disorder

Fred's last jousting tournament required that he take a long boat ride on choppy seas. It was not pleasant. Fred was dizzy and nauseated the entire ride and very nearly lost his lunch over the rail and into the sea. Fred had motion sickness. But *why*? Most theories of motion sickness claim that it has something to do with the brain getting conflicting information about whether and how the body is moving. For example, on his ill-fated boat ride, the central executive does not plan for Fred to move up and down with the motion of the water and the boat. Certainly, the central executive has not issued motor commands that would bring about this movement pattern. So when Fred's eyes and other sensory systems report back to his brain that he is moving in this way, the central executive gets very confused—so much so that Fred feels sick. In these theories, motion sickness is a result of the brain (and central executive) getting confused about what exactly the body is doing because of a conflict between expected and experienced movement patterns.

But this may not be what motion sickness is. Rather than being the result of a confused central executive, motion sickness may be the result of *unstable posture* (Stoffregen, 2011). That is, motion sickness occurs when postural sway and other coordinated movements that are used to stabilize upright posture are ineffective in a specific context—like on a boat in rough seas. Some of the evidence supporting this view is that motion sickness is more likely to occur when people *stand* than when they *sit* and more likely to occur when they stand with their *feet closer together* than with *their feet farther apart* (see Stoffregen, 2011). Both of these behaviors would be expected to stabilize posture but *not* necessarily help the confused central executive figure out what the body is doing.

In addition, it is possible to predict who will experience symptoms of motion sickness based on subtle movement patterns in their postural sway—*even before that person is exposed to a situation in which they might get motion sickness* (Curry et al., 2020; Koslucher, Haaland, & Stoffregen, 2016)! More recently, these effects have been investigated in the context of head-mounted virtual reality displays that can also cause symptoms of motion sickness. Such studies have shown that women are more susceptible to symptoms of motion sickness from such devices than men and that symptoms of motion sickness can be predicted by subtle differences in body sway between men and women (Munafo, Diedrick, & Stoffregen, 2017).

In this theory, motion sickness is a *movement disorder*, not a *perceptual disorder*. Therefore, preventing or reducing the symptoms of motion sickness requires learning new movement patterns that help stabilize the body in an unusual context. This seems to be exactly what happens in people who have just begun a sea voyage. Researchers found rapid changes in postural activity among novice mariners just beginning a sea voyage—in particular, within the first few hours of the trip, novice mariners adopted a wider stance on the boat than they did on land, a behavior that was associated with lower instances of seasickness. (Stoffregen et al., 2013). No wonder this process is called getting your sea legs (and not getting your sea brain!).

Postural Synergies Provide Support for Doing

Avoiding falling, of course, is not the only purpose of maintaining stable posture. In fact, stable posture itself is almost never the end game. Rather, the end game is to provide support for other behaviors—what are called suprapostural behaviors.[3] These suprapostural behaviors include most of the everyday behaviors that Fred (or anyone else) performs—reaching and grasping apples, talking with Claudia, cooking, working on a novel, playing tennis, avoiding—or maybe, interacting with—bees. Performing any of these behaviors requires that Fred maintain a stable posture. He learned this the hard way when he tried to cook while wearing roller skates.

Performing suprapostural behaviors requires maintaining stable upright posture. But performing suprapostural behaviors also can *disturb* or at least affect stable upright posture. Think about what happens when Fred tries to swing his tennis racket. When Fred is standing still—perhaps with his arms at his sides, his center of mass is positioned squarely over his base of support. When he raises his arm and tennis racket at the shoulder joint so that the racket points straight in front of him, the center of mass of his body shifts ever so slightly forward—closer to and perhaps even over the boundary of the base of support. If Fred were a wooden marionette, this might cause him to tip over. But he is a real boy. And for real boys, movements and posture are *cooperative*, not competitive. In fact, when a person raises their arm so that it points in front of them—like Fred did with his racket—the muscle activity in their arm is *preceded by* muscle activity in their legs and back that serves to preemptively stabilize posture *in preparation for* the arm movement (Belen'kii, Gurfinkel, & Pal'tsev, 1967; see Moreno, Stepp, & Turvey, 2011). Stable posture and the behaviors that are supported by stable posture are mutually constrained by synergies (see Fitch, Tuller, & Turvey, 1982; see Haddad et al., 2013).

Like the synergies created for swinging hammers and producing speech, postural synergies are organized to achieve a particular suprapostural goal, not to create a particular movement pattern or use particular anatomical components. In a study investigating this (Balasubramaniam, Riley, & Turvey, 2000), participants held a laser pointer in one hand and stood directly facing a small square target. Their task was to stand with their arms at their sides against their thighs, aim the laser beam at the target, and keep it on the target by merely standing still. In performing this task, postural sway serves the dual purposes of maintaining upright posture *and* maintaining the position of the laser beam on the target. Too much postural sway will move the beam off the target. But in this task, side-to-side sway is more problematic than front-to-back sway—which would really only serve to move the beam closer to or farther away from the target without changing its position *on* the target.

So performing this task well means minimizing side-to-side sway—but not necessarily front-to-back sway. And this is exactly what they found—overall, participants showed less side-to-side sway than front-to-back sway. But they went further. As the task became more difficult with a smaller or farther target, side-to-side sway *decreased*, but front-to-back sway *increased*. These results showed that postural synergies were organized to achieve the goal by minimizing sway in directions that would affect task performance but allowing—and even increasing—sway in directions that would *not* affect task performance. And all of this happened even though the participants were instructed to stand still!

But the researchers made one more key manipulation. In a second experiment, the task of the participant was the same, except that instead of standing *facing* the target, they turned 90° so that they were *looking at the target sideways* (over their shoulder) and aiming the laser pointer to the side. What is important here is that although *the goal* remains the same (keep the beam in the target merely by standing still), performing the task requires a *different pattern of postural sway*—minimizing *front-to-back sway* but not necessarily *side-to-side sway*. And they found that the pattern of results *reversed*. Overall, participants showed less *front-to-back sway* than *side-to-side sway*. And as the task became more difficult, *front-to-back sway* decreased but *side-to-side sway* increased. These results showed that the postural synergies were organized

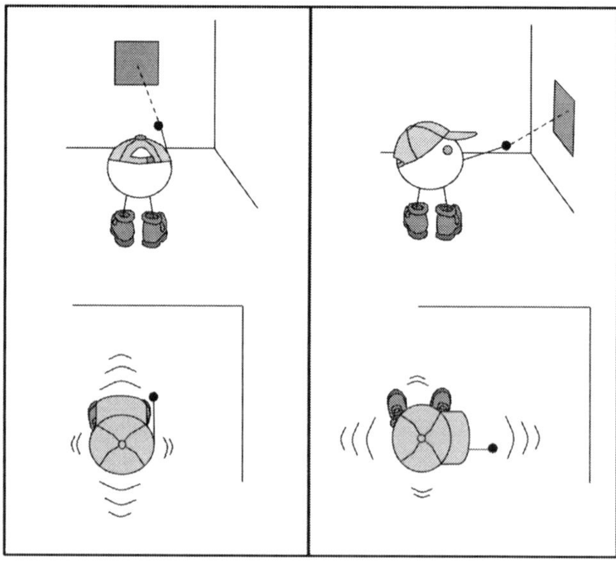

Figure 9.6 When Fred points a laser at a target directly in front of him (*left*), his body sway forward and backward increases and his body sway from side to side decreases. When Fred points a laser at a target to his right (*right*), his body sway from side to side increases and his body sway forward and backward decreases.

to achieve the *goal* and not to maintain a particular pattern of movement or use of particular muscles. So much for merely standing still! Impressively, an analogous pattern of results occurred when a similar experiment was conducted on a ship at sea where the task of merely maintaining upright posture is much more challenging than on dry land (Chen & Stoffregen, 2012).

Postural Synergies Provide Support for Perceiving

Stable posture not only keeps a person upright and provides support for *doing*—reaching, eating, and jousting, it also provides support for *perceiving*—looking, listening, and feeling. Stoffregen, Pagulayan, Bardy, and Hettinger (2000) investigated how posture supports visual perception. They asked participants to perform two different visual tasks for 30 seconds—"inspect" a blank piece of paper or "search" a piece of paper with printed text and count how many times a given letter occurred.

The researchers recorded the moment-to-moment postural movements that each participant made in each condition. They reasoned that searching—looking *for* something—is a more difficult visual task than merely inspecting—looking *at* something—and that postural sway would be modified accordingly. In particular, they thought that postural sway would be reduced in the search task relative to the inspection task. This is exactly what they found. Postural synergies were organized to improve the performance of a suprapostural perceptual task (see Saeedpour-Parizi et al., 2020).

Postural sway can also aid in perception of the properties of an object by effortful touch (see Chapter 8). In a study investigating this, participants wore a harness-like apparatus on their shoulders. A wooden rod was placed into this harness. It was either weighted on one end or the other or not at all.[4] On a given trial, the participant's task was to remain as still as possible and try to determine either how long the entire rod was or how long the portion of the rod extending to their left was. The researchers expected that there would be differences in postural sway related to differences in how focused attention needed to be in these two tasks. In particular, they expected that there would be smaller fluctuations in postural sway when attention had to be more focused—on the length of a portion of the rod—than when it could be less focused—on the length of the entire rod. This is exactly what they found (Palatinus et al., 2014, see also Mangalam et al., 2020)

Keep in mind that as far as a central executive is concerned, suprapostural tasks—reaching, pointing at a target, searching, wielding—would presumably *add* to the burden of controlling the body (Stoffregen, 2016). Any given suprapostural task would be yet another thing that the central executive has to worry about. Doing two things at the same time ought to be more difficult than doing just one of those things, right? Therefore, suprapostural tasks might be expected to *interfere* with the ability to maintain stable posture or vice versa (see Woollacott & Shumway-Cook, 2002). Consider the study by Balasubramaniam et al. (2000), where participants were asked to keep a laser beam on a target by merely standing still. If a central executive were in charge of performing this task, they might try to make the aiming task as easy as possible. They might do this by *decreasing* or even *eliminating* postural sway *in all directions* so that the laser beam moved as little as possible.

In other words, the central executive would treat all variability in postural sway as "bad" variability with respect to the aiming task. Of course, that is not what happened. The results showed that when postural sway *decreased* in a direction that would interfere with the aiming task, it *increased* in a direction that would not interfere with the aiming task. *The overall amount of postural sway was more or less unchanged.* In other words, suprapostural tasks and postural movements are *cooperative*, not competitive. Suprapostural tasks and postural movements don't interfere with one another. Rather, they *support* each other in ways that improve the ability to achieve the suprapostural behavioral or perceptual goal. It eliminates (or reduces) "bad" variability and *harnesses* "good" variability (Latash, 2012).

Synergies in Everyday Behaviors

Locomotion—Getting From Place to Place

Once stable posture has been achieved, the person can perform other everyday behaviors like getting from place to place, moving the hands, and manipulating objects. For many animals, getting from place to place requires coordinating the movements of two or more limbs. One way that these limbs could be coordinated is to move in the same direction at the same speed at the same time. When Fred takes a two-footed bunny hop, for example, his legs and feet move up and down together. The technical term for this is that they are completely in-phase. A synergy spanning his two legs is responsible for coordinating the independent muscles of his torso, hips, legs, and feet *so that the two legs act as a single limb* by maintaining this in-phase relationship on each hop. However, if you have ever tried to bunny hop any more than a few meters—like in a sack race, you know that this is not a very efficient way of getting from place to place—for humans, anyway.

Another way that two or more limbs could be coordinated is to move in the same direction at the same speed but at *different* times. When Fred takes a few walking steps, for example, his right foot swings up and forward while his left foot remains on the ground (and stationary). After his right foot lands on the ground, his left foot swings up and forward while his right foot remains on the ground and stationary. As Fred walks, one leg and foot is *one-half cycle* behind the other leg and foot. They are completely out of phase—or anti-phase. And when Fred is walking, one foot is always on the ground at all times. Remember, walking is controlled falling. Here again, a synergy is responsible for coordinating the independent muscles of the torso, hips, legs, and feet to act as *a single functional unit* by maintaining this anti-phase relationship on each step.

But something very interesting happens when Fred tries to walk faster. At some point, as he increases his walking speed, he *can't help but break into a jog or a run*. What is so interesting about this is that jogging or running is *a completely different behavior* than walking. When he jogs or runs, his legs are moving faster, and they have more or less the same out-of-phase relationship as they do when walking. However, he is now *propelling himself forward* rather than merely letting himself fall. And there is a point in the step cycle *where both feet are off the ground at the same time*. If walking is controlled falling, jogging or running is controlled leaping. *Running is not just fast walking*—it is an entirely different coordination pattern and requires an entirely different synergy to control it.

The point here is that at some particular speed, there is a relatively dramatic transition between walking and running. This concept will be discussed in more detail in Chapters 14 and 16, but this is known as a phase transition—an abrupt change from one stable state (in this case, walking) to another—in this case, jogging or running.[5] What is so interesting about phase transitions is that they are often *nonlinear*. This means that slow and continuous changes to a system can bring about fast and discontinuous reorganization. Slowly and continuously increasing the speed of a treadmill will bring about a fast and discontinuous shift from walking to running. This is not all that different from other more familiar phase transitions, such as the change in water from solid to liquid to gas (and vice versa) with continuous changes in temperature and pressure (Camazine et al., 2001; Kelso, 1995; Wagman, 2010). Solids, liquids, and gases have very different properties. They are completely different organizations of the same chemical substance. Ice is not just cold water, and water is not just cold steam. Fred is willing to stand on ice but not water. And he is willing to breathe steam, but not water.

For a four-legged animal like Fred's horse, Sweet William, the required coordination and the resulting phase transitions are even more complicated (see Figure 9.6). When walking, his front legs and his back legs each exhibit the same out-of-phase pattern as Fred's legs. However, the coordinated movement of his front legs is slightly offset from that of his back legs, creating a sequence of four beats—like this: clop, clop, clop, clop (see Figure 9.6, *left*). When he increases speed, he can't help but break into a *trot*. When he trots, the movements of his front and back legs on opposite sides (*right front* leg and *left back* leg and vice versa) are coordinated with each other approximately in-phase so that they are on the ground at approximately the same time.[6] This creates a sequence of two beats—like this: ba-bum, ba-bum, ba-bum, ba-bum (see Figure 9.6, *middle*).

When he increases speed even more, he can't help but break into a *gallop*. Here, his two front legs are coordinated with each other approximately in-phase so that they move forward and backward together as a unit. His two back legs are also coordinated this way. However, the movement of his back legs as a unit is also coordinated with the movement of his front legs (as a unit) approximately anti-phase. As his front legs are moving forward, his back legs are moving back. And there is a point in the step cycle *where all four hooves are off the ground at the same time* (Muybridge, 1957). However, the coordinated movement of each of his two front legs or each his two back legs is slightly offset from the other. This means that one of the front or back limbs usually lands slightly before the other—creating a sequence of three beats (ba-da-ba, ba-da-ba, ba-da-ba, ba-da-ba, see Figure 9.6, *right*).

Bimanual Tasks—Coordinating the Two Hands

The ecological approach seeks a lawful explanation of goal-directed action at the macro scale of the relationship between animal and environment. The lawfulness means that these same principles ought to apply, and the same phenomena ought to occur when coordinating any two or more body parts. And many of the activities of daily life—reaching and grasping apples, cooking, working on a novel, playing tennis, jousting—require coordinating the movements of the arms and hands.

The last time Fred saw Uncle Jimmy, he challenged Fred to simultaneously pat his head with one hand in an up and down motion and rub his belly with the other hand in a circular motion. Fred gladly accepted the challenge, but he had a harder time than he thought getting his two hands to do two *different things at the same time*. Sometimes he ended up alternating between the two different behaviors—rub, pat, rub, pat. Other times, he ended up performing the same behavior with both hands—rubbing or patting *both* his belly and his head. Why is this so challenging?

Figure 9.7 Many four-legged animals, like Sweet William the horse, have (at least) three distinct stable gait patterns. As Sweet William increases in locomotion speed, there is a nonlinear phase transition from walking to trotting and from trotting to galloping. (Adapted from Tuller, Turvey, & Fitch, 1982.)

As we discussed in the previous section, two basic patterns of coordinating two or more limbs are moving them in the *same direction* at the same speed at the same time—completely in-phase—and moving them in *opposite directions* at the same speed at the same time—completely anti-phase. Other patterns are possible, of course, but these two are the *most basic* and the *most stable*. Rubbing your head and patting your belly is neither completely in-phase nor completely anti-phase. The two hands are not moving in the same direction, but they are not really moving in opposite directions either. Performing both behaviors at the same time requires a pattern that is somewhere between completely in-phase and completely anti-phase. As a result, it is unstable—certainly less stable than alternating between the two behaviors or performing one behavior with both hands. As we have seen in the coordination of the legs for walking, unstable states do not typically last very long, and there are often abrupt (nonlinear) changes from one stable state to another. That is exactly what is happening in this case.

Here is another example. Make a (naked) hand puppet with your left hand using your four fingers as the upper jaw and your thumb as the lower jaw—name this one Fred. Now do the same thing with your right hand—name this one Claudia. Now make the puppets face each other and "talk" to each other in sequence. Open Fred's mouth. Next, as you are closing Fred's mouth, open Claudia's mouth. Then as you are closing Claudia's mouth, open Fred's mouth. If you are doing this right, Fred and Claudia will be coordinated completely out of phase. As Fred is opening his mouth, Claudia will be closing his mouth, and vice versa. Now go faster. Faster still. Even faster. At some point, as you keep increasing speed, it should be very difficult to maintain the completely anti-phase pattern for this particular behavior. In fact, you may feel yourself *moving toward an in-phase pattern* where Fred and Claudia talk at exactly the same time. You may even actually *switch* to an in-phase pattern without meaning to do so.

Now do it the other way around. Open and close Fred and Claudia's mouths *at the same time*. Now go faster. Faster still. Even faster. As you increase speed, it probably won't be difficult to maintain the completely in-phase pattern for this behavior—at least compared to maintaining the anti-phase pattern. And you probably won't feel yourself moving toward or even switching to an anti-phase pattern. It turns out that although anti-phase and in-phase are both relatively stable, in-phase is more stable than anti-phase.[7]

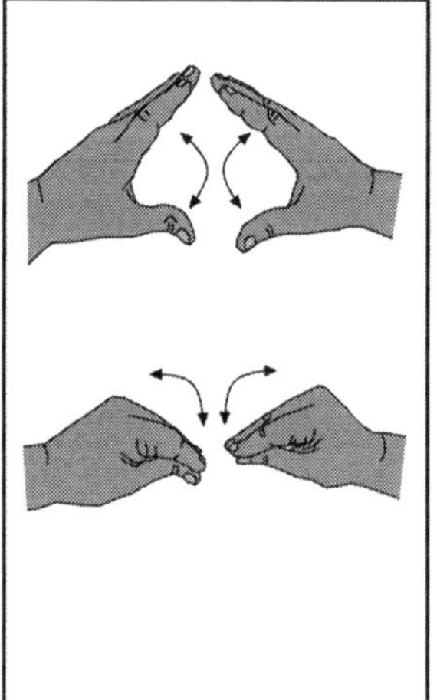
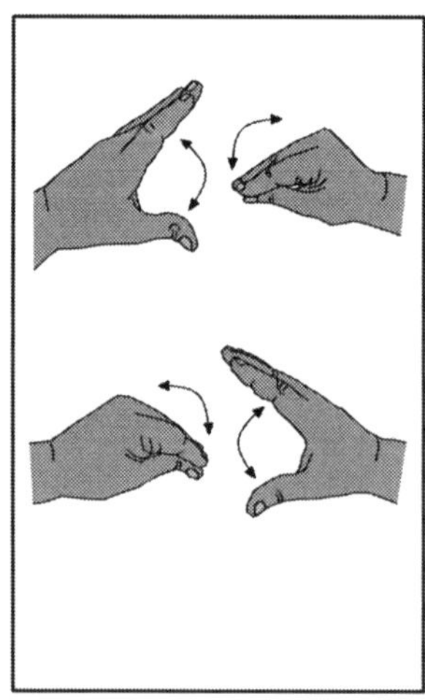
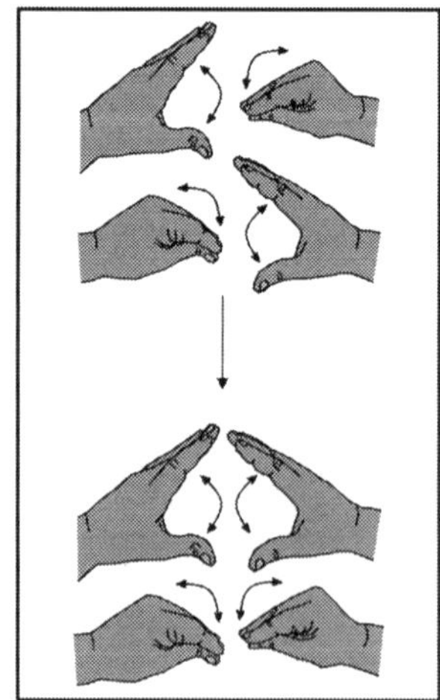

Figure 9.8 In phase movements (*left*) are more stable than anti-phase movements (*middle*), so when a person performs an anti-phase movement faster and faster, it will eventually convert to an in-phase movement (*right*).

In the mid-1980s, researchers developed a mathematical model that described this switching from anti-phase to in-phase but not vice versa (e.g., Haken, Kelso, & Bunz, 1985; see Keslo, 1995; see Chapter 14). The model has been revised several times since then. It is not really necessary for us to go into all of the gory details here. What is important is that this model makes specific predictions about how easy or difficult it will be to maintain a given coordination pattern between two limbs (i.e., what stable coordination pattern will eventually emerge between those limbs) based on how fast the movements are, how stable the pattern is, and how much the two limbs being coordinated differ in physical properties such as length or mass. These predictions have been confirmed over decades of experiments.

In such experiments, participants are asked to swing two pendulums with particular physical properties in a particular coordination pattern—in-phase, anti-phase, or somewhere in between (Kugler & Turvey, 1987). The results have confirmed the predictions of the model. In general, stable coordination patterns emerge when the stability of the movement pattern can overcome differences in the physical properties of each pendulum. In addition, they have also confirmed new predictions about learning a new coordination pattern, how handedness influences coordination, and how attention affects coordination (see Amazeen, Amazeen, & Turvey, 1998). As we will see in Chapter 11, the very same principles that apply to how a person coordinates the movements of one limb with the movements of another limb also apply to how two people coordinate the movements of their limbs with each other.

Notes

1. The term "action" is sometimes preferred over the term "behavior" given that it implies that movements are functional and not merely mechanical (Reed, 1982, 1996). However, given that we are focusing exclusively on goal-directed behaviors, we will use these terms more or less interchangeably.
2. Bernstein did most of his work in the first few decades of the 20th century in the former Soviet Union. Consequently, his work was not widely available until English translations of his books were published decades later.
3. The term "supra-" is a prefix that means "above." It is in contrast to "sub-", a prefix that means "below".
4. As in other experiments on effortful touch, this was to change the inertial properties of the rod without changing the geometric properties of the rod.
5. This is presumably why race-walking looks and feels kind of awkward and is so much work! The racewalker is forcing themselves to remain at an inefficient and unstable walking pattern at speeds that would ordinarily force a transition to running.
6. This is not so different from Fred's right arm being coordinated with his left leg (and vice versa) when he walks.
7. How stable an in-phase or anti-phase pattern is depends on the particular behavior. Thumb twiddling, for example, is easier to maintain in an anti-phase pattern than in an in-phase pattern.

10 Development of Perceiving and Acting Abilities

In the last five chapters, we described the abilities of animals to perceive and act with respect to affordances. By detecting and exploiting lawfully structured energy patterns, animals are able to perceive whether, when, and how to perform goal-directed behaviors. Fred's cat can not only perceive what possibilities exist for avoiding the rambunctious dog, but it can also perform the behaviors required to turn these possibilities into a reality. But where do these abilities come from?

In our ecological reformulation of how animals perceive and act, we abandoned some longstanding assumptions about these processes. However, we did not entirely abandon the assumption that all knowledge comes through experience (see Chapter 2). Fred's cat was not born with the ability to perceive affordances for avoiding rambunctious dogs or the ability to perform the behaviors necessary to do so—or even with the knowledge that it was probably a good idea!. However, it *was* born with *some* perceiving and acting abilities. And these existing abilities changed over time—they *developed*—into its present-day perceiving and acting abilities. Likewise, Fred—then known as li'l Freddie—was born with *some* perceiving and acting abilities that developed into his present-day perceiving and acting abilities.

Throughout the book, our description of perceiving and acting as *processes* (and not things) was very much intentional (see E. Gibson, 2003).[1] By definition, processes are *dynamic*—they continuously change over time. In other words, perceiving and acting are *activities* that occur over seconds, minutes, or even hours. Moreover, all processes, including perceiving and acting, occur *in a context*. Development of any kind occurs in the context of the *relationship between* animal and environment. And this relationship is *also* dynamic. It too continuously changes over time—over the course of seconds, minutes, or hours but also over the course of weeks, months, or even years.

Fred's Uncle Jimmy used to tell him, "A person never puts their foot in the same stream twice because both the person and the stream will be different the next time.[2]" In other words, everything continuously changes. Some things just change more slowly than others (McCabe, 2014). The processes of perceiving and acting are no different. They undergo continuous change across multiple time scales over the course of an animal's lifespan—they *develop*. This development is the focus of this chapter.

Traditional Approaches to Development

Just as there are traditional approaches to perceiving and acting, there are traditional approaches to *the development of* perceiving and acting. And for the most part, these approaches attribute the development of perceiving and acting to the development of cognitive abilities (for an overview of some of these approaches, see Bjorklund & Casey, 2017, Croker, 2012; Shultz, 2003). As in the previous chapter, our goal here is merely to show in very broad strokes how such approaches are incompatible with the ecological approach that we have been developing so far.

DOI: 10.4324/9781003145691-12

Figure 10.1 Traditionally, the development of motor skills (*top*) and cognitive abilities (*bottom*) are described as orderly and age-related progressions from less sophisticated to more sophisticated

As you might expect, more traditional approaches to development are built on many of the explicit and implicit assumptions about how we know the world that were considered and ultimately rejected in Chapter 2 and elsewhere. Three of these assumptions are (1) that all causality is *local and linear*, (2) that the phenomena of interest occur entirely *within* the animal, and (3) that the stimulation patterns reaching the animal are either *meaningless*—at worst—or *ambiguous*—at best.

The assumption that causality is *local and linear* has led to explanations of development that follow a predictable sequence of steps or stages from less sophisticated states of development to more sophisticated states of development (see Figure 10.1). It has also led to attempts to discover straightforward causal connections between past experiences (e.g., falling) and future development of complex behaviors (e.g., avoiding dangerous drop-offs). The assumption that the phenomena of interest occur entirely *within the animal* has led to explanations of development that focus on internal processes that are mostly devoid of context (i.e., the *animal* develops, the environment does not). And the assumption that *stimulation is meaningless or ambiguous* has led to explanations of development that focus primarily on the increasing sophistication of the cognitive processes required to make sense of the world.

Consequently, the general focus of such theories of development has been on when, how, or why a child exhibits a specific set of behaviors or cognitive abilities in a relatively stereotyped sequence over time. In particular, researchers have investigated the orderly and age-related progression of the acquisition of motor skills (e.g., developmental milestones such as rolling over, sitting, crawling; McGraw, 1935, 1945) or the orderly and achievement-related increases in sophistication of the ability to perceive, think, remember, or reason about the world (see Figure 10.1; Piaget, 1954, 1952).

An Ecological Approach to Development

As you might expect, an ecological approach to development is built on very different assumptions—namely, that causality is often *nonlocal and nonlinear*, that the phenomena of interest occur in the *relationship between* animal and environment (i.e., in the animal-environment system), and that the stimulation patterns encountered by the animal are *lawfully related* to the relationship between animal and environment (Dent-Read & Zukow-Goldring, 1997; E. Gibson & Pick, 2000).

The assumption that causality is often *nonlocal and nonlinear* has led to explanations of development in which behaviors emerge in a developmental cascade—in many cases, from a combination of subtle or otherwise nonobvious influences (see Figure 10.2; Gottlieb, 1999; Turvey & Sheya, 2017; see Box 4.1). It has also led to explanations in which a given developmental outcome (e.g., a particular perceiving or acting ability) can be reached by *multiple possible* developmental pathways. The assumption that the phenomena of interest occur in the *relationship between* animal and environment has led to explanations in which development occurs within an animal-environment system—the context changing along with the animal (see Figure 10.2). And the assumption that stimulation patterns are *lawfully related* to the relationship between animal and environment has led to explanations that focus on the increasing ability to detect and exploit informative stimulation patterns.

Consequently, the focus in the ecological approach to development is on when, how, and why a child *learns to flexibly modify behaviors* to achieve a given goal in a given circumstance in the context of rapidly changing perceiving and acting abilities (see Figure 10.3; E. Gibson & Pick, 2000; Adolph, 2019). In particular, researchers have investigated development as a process in which changes in an animal's body, brain, and skill set influence the ability to perceive and act on affordances, which subsequently changes the affordances that are available to that animal (Adolph, 2019; Campos et al., 2000).

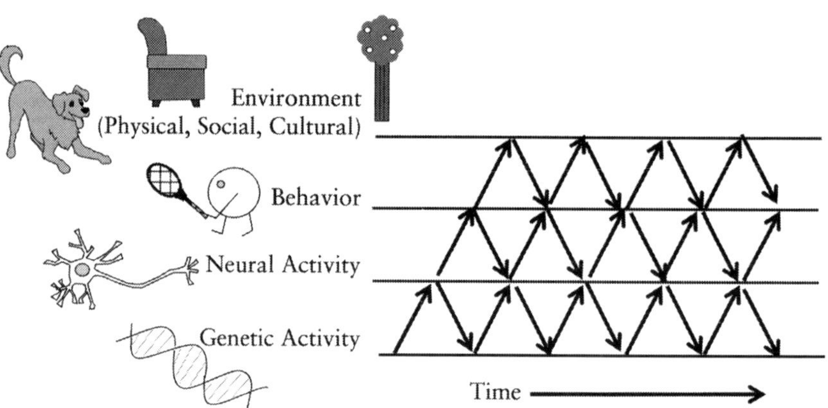

Figure 10.2 In the ecological approach, development is an ongoing process occurring across levels of the animal-environment system. All levels *contribute* to development, but no particular level has *causal control* over development (see Gottlieb, 1999).

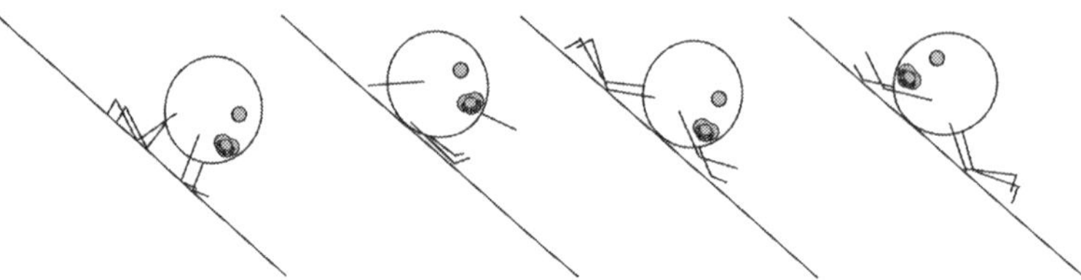

Figure 10.3 In the ecological approach to development, the focus is on how animals learn to flexibly perform behaviors to achieve goals. For example, an infant can (attempt to) descend a slope in many different postures, depending on circumstances.

To be sure, perceiving and acting abilities change throughout a person's lifespan. Fred had different perceiving and acting abilities when he was an infant—li'l crawlin' Freddie!—than he does now, and he has different perceiving and acting abilities now than he will when he is an older adult—old man Fred. In this chapter, however, we will focus mostly, though not entirely, on the development of perceiving and acting abilities that occurs during the first few years of life because this is when the most dramatic changes in such abilities take place. In particular, in the first two or so years of an infant's life, body weight quadruples and height doubles. Strength, balance, and coordination improve dramatically. And typically developing infants and toddlers will learn to roll over, sit, crawl, stand, walk, and so on. It is an exhausting and exhilarating time for parents and caregivers. And probably for the children themselves too.

Perceiving Affordances by Crawlers and Walkers

Fred is visiting with his infant niece, Eleanor. After a vigorous round of peekaboo, they both lay down on the floor to rest. Fred closes his eyes. After what feels like just a few seconds, he opens his eyes again, ready to begin the next round. He is *determined* to win this time. He turns toward Eleanor with his game face on—except she isn't where he left her! Wait, she can crawl now? Uh-oh. His mind boggles. Where could she be? He imagines all of the trouble that she could get into. He imagines all of the trouble that *he* could get into. What if she gets into his junk drawer? What if she is poised at the top of his basement stairs? Would she know that this is not a safe place for her to be? Would she perceive that these stairs *don't* afford crawling down for her? Would he ever be allowed to visit with Eleanor again?

The dramatic changes in action capabilities over the first few years of life bring about dramatic changes in available affordances (E. Gibson & Pick, 2000). We have already discussed a groundbreaking study that investigated the development of perception of affordances using an apparatus known as the visual cliff (Chapter 6, Box 6.1; E. Gibson & Walk, 1960). Remember that in these studies, a baby is placed in the center of a clear plexiglass table. The "shallow" side of the table has a checkerboard pattern right up under the plexiglass. The "deep" side of the table has the checkerboard pattern on the floor. This makes it look like there is a steep drop-off on the deep side of the table even though both sides are perfectly safe for the baby to crawl on.

The study found that older infants who had more experience crawling—avoided the "deep" side of the cliff, whereas younger infants—who had less experience crawling—did not. These results are typically interpreted in terms of the development of depth perception. Interpreted in this context, the results suggest that older infants are better at using depth cues than are younger infants. However, the results are perhaps better interpreted in terms of the development of perception of surface layout (see Box 12.1). Interpreted in this context, the results instead suggest that infants with more crawling experience are better able to perceive what a steep drop-off does or does not afford than are infants with less experience crawling.

Many, many studies have followed up on this research since it was initially reported in the 1960s (e.g., Dahl et al., 2013; Witherington et al., 2005; see Rodkey, 2015). But the visual cliff has at least one important limitation. The cliff is not really a cliff. It might *look* dangerous, but *it feels safe* because *it is safe*. Crawling is *always* possible on *either side* of the cliff. And once the baby figures that out, the game is over. The baby will happily crawl on both sides of the cliff regardless of whether it looks safe or not. So how do you investigate perception of affordances by infants in a way that doesn't give the game away before—or shortly after—it starts?

Learning Is of Specific Affordances, Not of General Facts

The best way to investigate perception of affordances by babies is to put them in situations where a given behavior—crawling, for example—is sometimes possible and sometimes not, and then see whether or not the baby attempts to perform that behavior—with appropriate safety precautions in place, of course. And this is what ecologically minded developmental researchers have done. Many of these studies used, more or less, the same basic methodology of the studies on perception of affordances that we described in Chapter 5. In particular, researchers placed babies on the edge of *real drop-offs* or *real gaps*, at the top of *real slopes*, at one end of *real bridges*, and at the edges of *real pools of water*(!). They varied how deep the drop-offs were, how large the gaps were, how steep the slopes were, how narrow the bridges were, and how far away desired objects were, among other factors. And they watched which drop-offs or slopes the babies attempted to descend and which gaps the babies attempted to reach, crawl, and walk across (see Figure 10.4; Adolph & Hoch, 2019; Burnay & Cordovil, 2016). And they caught the babies when they fell. Which they did. A lot.

Overall, these studies showed an interesting pattern of results. Consider babies who have just learned to crawl, who are placed at the top of a real slope, and who are encouraged by caregivers and researchers to crawl down that slope (see Figure 10.4, *right*). You might guess that since these babies have just learned to crawl, they would not be very good at telling the difference between slopes that they could safely crawl down and those that they could not. And you would be right. Many new crawlers attempted to crawl down slopes that were *way* too steep and had to be quickly rescued by alert and agile researchers. You might also expect that as the babies became more and more experienced with crawling over weeks and weeks, they would *become better* at determining which slopes afforded safely crawling down and which did not. And again, you would be right. You are on a roll! Experienced crawlers generally chose to crawl down safe slopes and refused to crawl down risky ones—and they were accurate to within 2° of their actual crawling abilities!

But what do you think happened when these *very same babies* returned to the lab a few months later after they had just learned how to walk? You might think that since these babies have *already learned to tell the difference* between slopes that afford safely *crawling* down and which do not, they would also be pretty good at telling the difference between slopes that afford safely *walking* down and those that do not. But this time, you would be wrong. Many of these same babies quite happily attempted to walk down slopes that were *way too steep* and had to be even more quickly rescued by alert and agile researchers. After weeks of walking experience, however, they became better at determining which slopes afforded safely walking down and which did not.

An analogous pattern occurred in tasks in which babies attempted to reach across a gap or climb down from a drop-off before and after learning how to crawl or walk (see Adolph & Hoch, 2019; Adolph, 2019). In all of these cases, the babies seemingly had to *start over from zero* after learning a new motor skill. And learning was no faster the second time around. In other words, what they learned about perceiving affordances for crawling did not seem to help in any way whatsoever when they were learning to perceive affordances for walking.

Figure 10.4 Studies on the development of perceiving-acting skills, such as reaching across a gap, walking across a narrow bridge, and crawling or walking down a slope, have shown that infants learn specific affordances, not general facts about the world.

This does not make sense from more traditional perspectives. Previous experience should always *help* the central executive—even a baby central executive—in making future decisions. Learning about what is safe and unsafe in situation A should help decision-making in situation B, at least a little bit, right? But it *does* make sense from an ecological perspective. The relationship between the animal and the environment is *completely different* in crawling than in walking. Different limbs are involved, different coordination patterns are required, and different stabilities and bases of support are created. And crawling and walking bring about very different points of observation in the optic array and create different patterns of optic flow—more on these points later (Adolph & Hoch, 2019). In other words, the *information about* affordances for crawling is entirely different from *the information about* affordances for walking. Consequently, the baby needs to (re)learn to perceive affordances in each case.

Box 10.1 Are Babies Afraid of Heights?

Why do older infants with more experience crawling avoid the "deep" side of the visual cliff? A seemingly obvious answer is that they are wary of falling over the edge. In other words, experience crawling—and presumably experience falling!—leads to fear of heights. And this fear is what leads to avoidance behavior.

But this obvious answer doesn't really hold up to scrutiny (Adolph et al., 2014). For one thing, infants who do crawl on the "deep" side of a visual cliff or over an actual drop-off don't generally look or act very afraid (Saarni et al., 2006). In fact, some even seem to be having fun! For another thing, infants tend to linger on the edge of real drop-offs (even steep ones), reaching, touching, rocking back and forth, and looking over the edge—much to the chagrin of many caregivers (Kretch & Adolph, 2013).

However, perhaps the strongest evidence against this is the research that we described earlier showing that knowing what is and is not safe to *crawl* down does not help at all in learning what is and is not safe to *walk* down. If babies learn to fear heights, they ought to avoid the steep drops the second time around. But they don't.

In addition, walking infants treat the same drop-off or slope differently *depending on the context* (e.g., whether or not they are wearing a weighted vest or whether or not they are wearing slippery soled shoes; see Adolph et al., 2014). If babies learn to fear heights, they ought to treat steep drop-offs or slopes the same way *regardless of context*. It seems that rather than leading to a fear of heights, crawling and walking and falling leads to learning how to perceive affordances!

Perceiving Affordances Across the Lifespan

While it is the case that the most dramatic changes in perceiving and acting abilities occur during the first few years of life, such abilities *change throughout the lifespan*—especially as younger adults become older adults. It is a fact of life that most older adults don't see or hear as well as they did when they were younger and are not as strong or flexible as they were either. Such changes, of course, influence the fit between action capabilities and environmental properties—and perhaps the ability to perceive that fit.

Perceiving Affordances for Stepping On

In Chapter 5, we described a study investigating perception of affordances for stair climbing that was a paradigmatic example of studies investigating perception of affordances (Warren,

1984). To remind you, this study found that the boundary between stair heights that were perceived to afford climbing and those that were not occurred at a taller stair height for tall than for short participants. However, this boundary occurred at the *same ratio* of stair height to leg length—approximately 0.88—for both groups. In other words, perception of affordances for stepping on was body-scaled.

Like participants in many, if not most, psychological studies, the participants in this study were younger (college-age) adults. Given the changes in action capabilities—especially strength and flexibility—that occur in later adulthood, you might expect that older adults would be less able to climb stairs, especially tall stairs, than younger adults. But would perception of affordances for stair climbing by older adults reflect such changes in stair climbing ability?

A study conducted a few years later explicitly investigated this hypothesis (Konczak, Meeuwsen, & Cress, 1992). It compared perception of affordances for stair climbing by younger adults (in their early to mid-20s) and older adults (in their late 60s to early 70s). They found that, as expected, younger adults were able to climb taller stairs than older adults. Perhaps more interestingly, they found that this pattern also showed up in the perceptual boundary on affordances for stair climbing for each group. The boundary between stair heights that were perceived to afford climbing and those that were not occurred at *a shorter stair height* and *a smaller ratio of stair height to leg length* for older adults than for younger adults. The ratio was approximately 0.90 for the younger adults and was approximately 0.70 for the older adults. The older adults were indeed sensitive to their reduced ability to climb (taller) stairs compared to the younger adults. In fact, younger adults tended to *overestimate* the maximum stair height that they would be able to climb, but older adults did not.

Perceiving Affordances for Fitting Through

More recent research has investigated the lifespan development of perception of affordances for passing or reaching through narrow openings. In one of these studies (Franchak & Adolph, 2012), researchers and caregivers coaxed 18-month-old infants to walk through a narrow opening in two different conditions (see Figure 10.5, *top*). In one condition, the *doorway* condition,

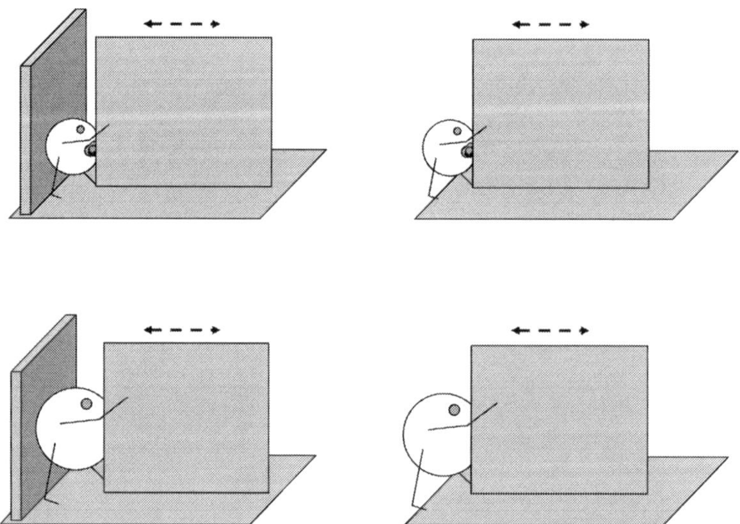

Figure 10.5 Both infants (*top*) and older adults (*bottom*) are more willing to attempt to pass through smaller openings when the penalty is getting stuck than when the penalty is falling.

the opening was between a sliding door and a wall. In this case, if the infant attempted to walk through openings that were too narrow, they would get *stuck*. In another condition, the *ledge* condition, the opening was between a sliding door and a (small) drop-off. In this case, if the infant attempted to walk through openings that were too narrow, they would *fall*.

So what did they find? In the *doorway* condition, infants repeatedly tried to squeeze through openings that were too small and got stuck. This might suggest that infants cannot tell the difference between openings that afford fitting through and those that do not. However, in the *ledge* condition, infants generally attempted to walk through only those openings that they could fit through and refused to walk through those that they could not. This suggests that, for the most part, infants *can indeed* tell the difference between openings that afford fitting through and those that do not. It's just that getting stuck is not enough of a penalty to discourage them from trying!

A follow-up study compared younger and older adults performing these same tasks (see Figure 10.5, *bottom*; Comalli et al., 2013). The results showed more or less the same pattern as with the infants. In particular, both younger and older adults were more willing to attempt to pass through smaller openings when the penalty was getting stuck than when it was falling. In addition, the boundary between openings that were perceived to afford passing through and those that did not occurred at a larger opening for older than for younger adults. And this difference was due to differences in *action capabilities* (e.g., balance and coordination) between these two groups, not differences in *perceptual capabilities*.

Development of Visual Perception of Surface Layout

Fred begins to—calmly at first—search for Eleanor. She could be anywhere. But given that she's more likely to be somewhere down low than somewhere up high, Fred gets down on his hands and knees and crawls around to look for her. In Chapter 6, we argued that the information for visual perception is in the ambient optic array (the structured reflected light) at a given point of observation (see Figures 6.2–6.4). Fred has changed his point of observation in the optic array so that it is more like that of a crawling baby. Immediately, he notices that things look very different from down here.

Changes in Action Capabilities Change What Is Seen

An adult's point of observation in the optic array changes over the short term—over seconds and minutes as they go about their daily business of standing up, sitting down, turning around, and moving from here to there (see Figure 6.7). A child's point of observation changes over the short term too, but it also changes over the long term—over weeks, months, and years as they grow and develop new ways to move around in the world. As we have mentioned, typically developing babies will learn to roll over, sit, crawl, stand, walk, and so on. These different postures place the baby at very different points of observation in the optic array. Consequently, babies in these different postures *see the world differently*.

A baby who cannot yet roll over has, more or less, access only to the structured light available at this particular point of observation in this particular location. A baby who *can* roll over has access to the structured light available at *different* points of observation in this particular location. A baby who can crawl or walk has access to the structured light at *different points of observation* in *different locations*. And crawling or walking, of course, creates a pattern of *global optic flow* that provides information about *where and how* that baby is moving. The optic flow pattern encountered by a *crawling* baby will be different from that encountered by a *walking* toddler (see Figure 10.6). The optic flow pattern encountered by an unsteady new walker will be different from that of a steady, experienced walker. And of course, as a child *grows taller*,

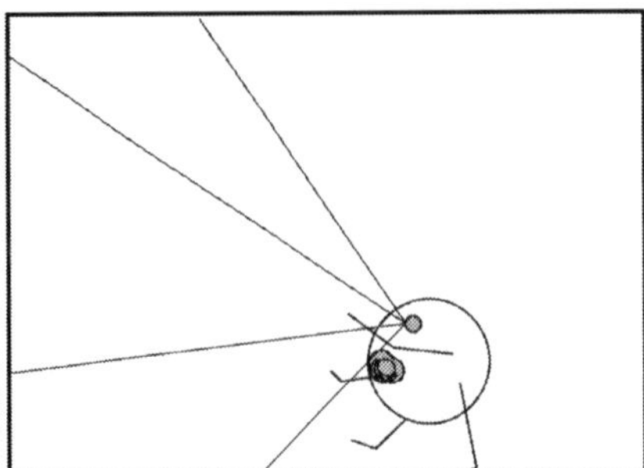

Figure 10.6 Infants look in very different directions when walking and when crawling. Consequently, they encounter very different aspects of the optic array and see very different things.

they encounter structured light at higher and higher points of observation and see more and more of some parts of the world and less and less of other parts of the world.

Where Babies Look and What They See

Fred notices that things look very different while crawling on his hands and knees, at a point of observation relatively close to the floor, than they did when he was standing, at a point of observation relatively far from the floor. In particular, while crawling, Fred encounters *more* of the structured light reflecting from the floor, *less* of the structured light reflecting from the walls, and *none* of the reflected light coming from surfaces that he crawls under—like his table. In addition, he notices that he *can't help but look mostly at the floor* while crawling. It takes a lot of effort to lift his head high enough to look up (or even just straight ahead). He can't really see very far away either.

Is this what the world looks like to Eleanor? Is this what the world looked like to li'l Freddie? Where do infants look, what do they see, and how does this change when they learn new postures and ways of moving around in the world? And how does this compare with what adults see and where they look? Answering these questions requires using small mobile head-mounted eye-tracking devices to record what infants and adults see when they perform everyday behaviors. And this is exactly what some ecologically minded developmental researchers have done (see Franchak, 2020). So what did they find?

Well, as Fred realized, infants spend much more time looking at the floor when crawling than when walking. In fact, one-quarter of the time, crawling infants see *nothing but* the floor (Franchak et al., 2011; Kretch, Franchak, & Adolph, 2014)! And when crawling infants *do* look up from the floor, they see less of the room than walking infants do. Crawling infants see more of the ground directly in front of them but less of what is farther away and higher up (see Figure 10.6).

Walking infants, on the other hand, mostly look straight ahead. Consequently, they are better able to see other things in the room, such as objects and other people—especially the *faces* of those other people. This might explain why walking infants show more interest in retrieving faraway objects and showing those objects to caregivers, while crawling infants show more interest in nearby objects (Franchak, Kretch, & Adolph, 2018; Karasik, Tamis-LeMonda, & Adolph, 2011; Yu & Smith, 2013). Given that posture and skills dramatically influence what babies can see, the developmental milestones that caregivers celebrate (rolling over, sitting, crawling, standing, and walking) are also visual perception milestones!

Do Babies Know What Movement Looks Like?

In Chapter 6, we described what Fred would see if the apple that he was planning to pick and eventually eat fell from the branch. In particular, there would be *localized optic flow*—in particular, deletion (or occlusion) of optical texture that may or may not be paired with revealing of optical texture. If the apple landed *in front* of the tree, there would be progressive *deleting* of the optical texture of the tree at the bottom edge of the apple and progressive *revealing* of the optical texture reflecting from the tree at the upper edge of the apple. If it landed on the ground and then bounced *behind* the trunk, there would be a progressive *deleting* of optical texture of the apple at the edge of the trunk.

Given the lawful relationship between object movements and patterns of local optic flow, these patterns were informative to Fred about where and how the apple was moving. But would these patterns be just as informative to li'l Freddie? Not immediately. Babies are not born knowing what different patterns of occlusion mean. Why would they be? The womb is a pretty dark place. There are no optical patterns *at all* in there. Outside of the womb, however, there is an ambient optic array and lawful relationships between object movements and patterns of occlusion. But babies still need to *experience* this lawful relationship by observing objects moving around in order to learn what these different patterns of changing optical texture mean. And this experience takes time.

At a few months of age, babies show that they are beginning to understand what different patterns of occlusion mean (Baillargeon, 1993; see E. Gibson & Pick, 2000). In particular, when babies who are a few months old watch a toy temporarily move behind a screen, they tend to look *where they expect the toy to reappear*—at the far end of the screen—rather than where it disappeared—at the near end of the screen (see Figure 10.7). At about a year of age, they tend to *put their hands* where they expect the toy to reappear as well (van der Meer, van der Weel, & Lee, 1994; van der Meer et al., 1995; see van der Meer & van der Weel, 2020).

We also described what Fred would see if Claudia were to toss the apple directly at his nose. In this case, there would be a different kind of local optic flow—*deletion* of optical texture at the apple's outer edges object plus *symmetric expansion* of optical texture of the apple. Again, given the lawful relationship between object movements and patterns of local optic flow, this pattern was informative to Fred about where and how the apple was moving. The pattern was also informative to Fred about *when* the apple would reach him. Remember that how quickly the optical texture of the object expands relative to the background is a variable called tau (τ) and is information about *time to arrival*—assuming that current conditions continue. But would these patterns be just as informative to li'l Freddie? Would li'l Freddie be sensitive to τ? If you said "not immediately", you are on another roll!

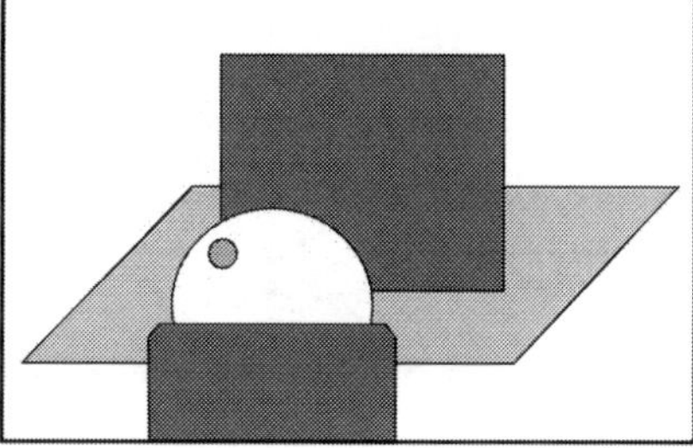

Figure 10.7 At just a few months old, babies begin to understand what different patterns of occlusion mean. When a toy disappears behind a screen, they look for it where they expect it to reappear (rather than where it disappeared).

Infants may or may not be coordinated enough to move out of the way of an object heading directly toward them—let alone *catch* the object. But this doesn't mean that they can't do *anything* to prepare for the impending collision. One thing they *can* do is close their eyes. Defensive blinking is something that just about all animals do when a collision is just about to occur—think about what you would do if a ball was about to hit you in the nose. But how do infants know *when* to close their eyes? Do they use τ?

Research has shown that when an object appears to be on a collision course with them, younger infants—closer to five months old—seem to blink based on distance more so than on time, leading them to blink too late when an object is moving quickly. However, older infants—closer to seven months old—seem to blink based on τ, enabling them to blink appropriately regardless of how fast the object is moving (Kayed & van der Meer, 2000, 2007; Kayed, Farstad, & van der Meer, 2008). When babies who are about a year-old attempt to catch a toy that disappears behind a screen, they use τ to get their hands to the right location (where they expect the toy to reappear at the far end of the screen) at the right time (van der Meer et al., 1994, 1995; see van der Meer & van der Weel, 2020).

Do Babies Know What Their Own Movement Looks Like?

In Chapter 6, we also described Fred's visual experience when he walked toward the apple in the tree. His movements lawfully created a *global optic flow* pattern. In particular, moving *toward* the apple lawfully created a global *expansion* pattern centered on the apple itself. And moving *away* from the apple created a global *contraction* pattern—again centered on the apple itself. These patterns were informative to Fred about where and how he was moving (and when he would get there). But would these patterns be just as informative to li'l Freddie? If you said "not immediately", then you are, once again, spot on! To know what different patterns of global optic flow means li'l Freddie would need to experience the lawful relationship between his movements and these patterns. And the best way to do this is by moving himself around.

Younger infants with less crawling experience are generally unable to tell the difference between a global expansion pattern (information that they are moving forward), a global contraction pattern (information that they are moving backward), and random motion (not information about any kind of movement). Older infants with weeks of crawling experience *are* able to tell the difference among these patterns (Agyei et al., 2015; Vilhelmsen, van der Weel, & van der Meer, 2015; Vilhelmsen et al., 2019). And this ability, of course, is likely related to why inexperienced and experienced crawling infants behave so differently on the visual cliff (Campos et al., 2000; Dahl et al., 2013).

Development of Auditory Perception of Surface Layout

Fred is getting a little more desperate in his search for Eleanor. He can't see her—especially while crawling around on all fours. He can't *hear* her either. But maybe *she* can hear *him*. In Chapter 7, we argued that the information for auditory perception is to be found in the ambient acoustic array—the structured sound—converging at a given listening point (see Figure 7.2). Fred attempts to structure the acoustic array by calling for Eleanor: "Elllll-anor! Elllll-anor! Elllll-anor! Where are you?" But will this do any good? Even if she can hear him, will she know where he is based on the sound that she hears? More importantly, will she know *how to get to him* based on this sound?

Hearing How to Move

Researchers investigated the first question with newborn infants between three and six weeks of age—babies who are much younger than adventurous Eleanor! In this study, tiny speakers

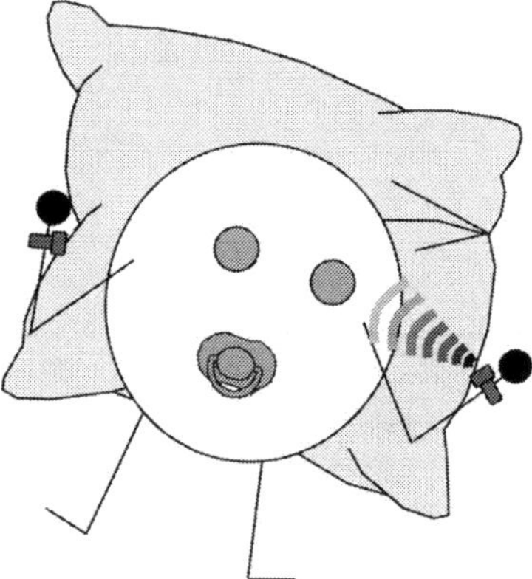

Figure 10.8 Studies have shown that very young infants with small speakers attached to their wrists learn to move their arms in a coordinated way to hear the sound better.

were attached to each of the baby's wrists (van der Meer & van der Weel, 2011). The baby's mother was in another room and spoke or sang to the baby into a microphone. Her voice was played (in real time) through one of the wrist speakers (see Figure 10.8).

The researchers were interested in what the baby did with their arms. When the mother's voice was played through a speaker on a particular wrist, did the baby move that wrist closer to them? And when the mother's voice was played through the other speaker on the other wrist, did the baby move that wrist closer to them instead? Yes and yes. When the mother's voice was played through a given speaker, the baby was more likely to move the wrist with that speaker toward them than away from them. When no sound was played, they were just as likely to move their wrist toward them as they were to move it away from them. So newborn babies can use sound to control the movements of their arms. They know what to do so that they can hear something better. This is good news for Fred—especially given that Eleanor is a few months older than the babies in this study.

The question that is more relevant for Fred is whether Eleanor will know *how to get to him* based on the sounds that she hears when he calls for her. Researchers investigated this question with babies who were closer to Eleanor's age—between six and nine months old (van der Meer, Ramstad, & van der Weel, 2008). The baby was placed on a circular mat in a prone position (i.e., on their bellies). On a given trial, mother and baby were positioned so that the mother was at one of ten different locations behind the baby on the outside of the circle—ranging from directly to the baby's right to directly behind the baby to directly to the baby's left. Once the mother and the baby were positioned, the mother called for the baby in whatever way seemed natural to her—perhaps by calling "Elllll-anor!"

The researchers were interested in whether and how the babies turned themselves toward their mother. Did the babies turn toward the mother at all? If so, did they take *the shortest way around*? Or did they just turn at random until they ended up facing her? They found that *almost 90% of the time*, the baby chose the shortest route to their mother. And they turned more quickly when they had to turn farther. Not surprisingly, infants had slightly more difficulty when the mother was directly behind them than she was directly to the right or to the left. In short, the results showed that six- to nine-month-old infants could hear how—and how quickly—to take the shortest route to their mother. This is good news for Fred.

Development of Perception by Dynamic Touch

Like the babies in the studies that we discussed previously, Eleanor hears Fred call and takes the shortest route to his location. She surprises him immensely when she reappears. Fred is so relieved that she didn't get into any trouble during her adventure. And he is equally relieved that *he* won't get into any trouble either—so long as Eleanor can keep a secret.

It's official—Eleanor is the undisputed peekaboo champion! Fred celebrates Eleanor's victory by feeding her lunch. He places her in a high chair and opens a jar of baby food—sweet potatoes, her favorite! After feeding her a few spoonfuls, she playfully grabs the spoon from his hand. This gets Fred thinking. When he was rummaging through his junk drawer in the dark, he was able to tell a great deal about whatever object he happened to find (e.g., tennis racket, jousting lance) just by holding it firmly and moving it around with his wrist. Does Eleanor have the same ability? In Chapter 8, we argued that the information for perception by effortful or dynamic touch is the resistance to rotation in different directions—the rotational inertia—at a rotation point, usually in the wrist. Is Eleanor sensitive to this information?

Feeling Length (Affordances for Reaching)

The ability to perceive properties of surfaces and objects by touch develops quite early. Infants touch all kinds of things—much to the dismay of many parents and other caregivers. When they become mobile, babies probe, poke, and press surfaces—like a visual cliff or a waterbed—to determine whether that surface will support their weight (e.g., E. Gibson et al., 1987). And when their hands are free, they grasp, shake, rub, and squeeze objects.

For a number of reasons, there have not been systematic investigations of perception by effortful or dynamic touch in children until they are about preschool-age. One study investigated the ability of three- to five-year-old children to perceive the length of wielded objects (Fitzpatrick & Flynn, 2010). It was set up a lot like the studies using adult participants described in Chapter 6. In this case, the children wielded occluded rods and completed several different tasks that required them to compare or report the perceived lengths of those rods.

In one task, each child wielded pairs of rods that differed in length and reported which rod in each pair felt longer. Overall, children chose the longer rod over 80% of the time, but older children were no better at the task than younger children. In another task, each child wielded pairs of rods of the same length but with different rotational inertias—with weights attached at different locations. Again, they reported which rod in each pair felt longer. Overall, children chose the rod with the larger rotational inertia almost 70% of the time, and this time, older children—who did so about 75% of the time—were more likely to do so than younger children—who did so about 60% of the time.

In a third task, each child wielded multiple rods of different lengths and different rotational inertias and reported how long each rod felt by positioning a visible marker along a growth chart. Much like adults, children perceived longer rods to be longer than shorter rods and rods with larger rotational inertias to be longer than rods with smaller rotational inertias. Older children were more sensitive to changes in rotational inertia than younger children. Even the oldest children, however, were not as sensitive to rotational inertia as adults.

Overall, the results of the study show that preschool-age children can perceive the length of a wielded object and that they are sensitive to rotational inertia. However, the results also suggest that, like sensitivity to other informative stimulation variables—like optic flow patterns, sensitivity to rotational inertia is not a given. Rather, it *develops*. In this case, children seem to become increasingly sensitive to the relationship between rotational inertia and length throughout early childhood and into early adulthood.

Figure 10.9 When children use a hand-held object to displace a toy from a table with a rod, they choose a stopping distance and arm posture based on the length of the rod.

A related study investigated how children used a hand-held object as a reaching tool (Bongers, Smitsman, & Michaels, 2003). In the task in this experiment, two- to four-year-old children held a rod in one hand with the tip pointing up while walking toward a small table with a toy duck on it (see Figure 10.9). Their task was to come to a complete stop at some point before they got to the table, lower the rod, and then use the rod to slide the duck off the table and into a container of water. The researchers were interested in, among other things, where each child chose to stop walking before performing the task. Was this distance related to properties of the rod such as length, mass, or rotational inertia?

In the first experiment, the researchers varied both the length and the mass of the rods that the children used to complete the task. In the second experiment, the researchers varied length, mass, and rotational inertia. Overall, the results of both experiments showed that children chose a stopping distance based on length but not mass or rotational inertia. In addition, children leaned forward more and extended their arms more when completing the task with shorter rods than with longer rods. And older children chose to stop farther from the table than younger children and were generally more successful in performing the task.

Like the study on perception of length described previously, the results of this study suggest that preschool-age children can perceive length-related affordances of a wielded object, but they are less sensitive to the relationship between rotational inertia and such affordances than adults are. Again, such sensitivity *develops*—children seem to become increasingly sensitive to this relationship throughout early childhood and into early adulthood.

Box 10.2 What Can Babies Teach Soccer-Playing Robots?

Needless to say, infants walk very differently than adults do. Partly, this is because infant walking is *much more variable* than adult walking—both in terms of bodily movements and in terms of walking paths. Infants have a hard time making the same leg movements from step to step; they stop and start; they take short paths, long paths, and everything in between. They take twirling roundabout routes from place to place, not unlike the bees that used to worry Fred so much. And they fall down. A lot. It could be that infants are just bad at walking. And to some extent, this is absolutely true.

But maybe there is a *benefit* to all of this variability. In fact, infant walking shows many of the same characteristics of a concept that we discussed in Chapter 9—repetition without repetition. In that chapter, we argued that whereas learning a skill may require repeatedly practicing the *same movement pattern over and over in the same context*, mastering a skill may require repeatedly practicing *different movements over and over in different contexts*. Is this what is happening in learning to walk? Is it possible that all of this variability is *a good thing* when learning how to walk?

One way that researchers have tried to answer this question is by studying the performance of virtual soccer-playing robots—yes, really (Ossmy et al., 2018). The researchers programmed the robots so that five teams of robots had equivalent skills in every aspect of a virtual soccer match (e.g., shooting, passing, dribbling, cooperating with teammates) except one. The teams differed *only in how they were trained to move around on the virtual field*. One team was trained to move based on the (highly variable) walking patterns recorded from 90 infants during 20 minutes of free play. The other teams of robots were trained to move around based on much-less-variable walking patterns (e.g., lines, circles, or squares) or were not trained in any particular way. Which team do you think did best in a 4,000-game virtual tournament? If you said "The team trained on infant walking paths", you are *still* on a roll. That team had 2,888 wins, only 75 losses, and 1,037 ties. This study suggests that variability in infant walking serves the role of repetition without repetition. It is the feature, not the bug (Ossmy et al., 2018).

Development of Action

Of course, like adults, babies not only perceive, they *move*. Fred figured this one out the hard way! In some ways, the movement challenges faced by babies are no different from those faced by adults. They must learn to control a very large number of degrees of freedom by creating synergies—functional relations among independent anatomical parts (see Chapter 9). And they must learn which forces need to be explicitly generated, which do not need to (or should not) be explicitly generated, and which can be exploited because they are provided for free.

But in other ways, the challenges faced by babies are very, very different from those faced by adults. Applying the right forces at the right times requires the ability to produce *sufficient* forces in the first place. And this is something that babies just can't do—at least not at first. To a large extent, babies are prisoners of gravity for the first few months of their lives (Adolph & Franchak, 2017).

Overcoming gravity is critical in establishing stable—and eventually upright—posture. And stable posture is an obvious prerequisite for many of the things that typically developing babies eventually do, such as sitting, crawling, standing, walking, and running. But it is also a less obvious prerequisite for many other things that typically developing babies eventually do, such as looking, reaching, grasping, manipulating, eating, and interacting with others.

As in adults, postural synergies are built with perceptual information. And also as in adults, optic flow can provide information about how postural sway must be controlled for a person to stay upright. Recall that when adults are in a moving room, and the room moves toward or away from them, they will lean or step in the direction that the room is moving to steady themselves. If the room moves back and forth very subtly, they will unknowingly synchronize their postural sway movements with the movements of the room (see Chapter 9). Given their years of experience balancing on two feet, children older than three years old will more or less behave the same way. However, children younger than this are not so fortunate. They will often stagger or fall over—and are quite displeased about the whole mess (E. Gibson & Pick, 2000; Bertenthal & Bai, 1989; Uchiyama et al., 2008)!

Once stable posture is achieved, the baby can try to move from place to place. And they often succeed. They belly-crawl, inchworm-crawl, hands-and-knees-crawl, and hands-and-feet-crawl, among other variations. Hands-and-knees crawling and hands-and-feet crawling are more challenging than other kinds of crawling because babies must raise their center of mass off the ground and keep it positioned over the base of support. Even though the base of support is both larger and more symmetrical when crawling than when standing, this is still a significant challenge. And crawling requires the coordination of front and back limbs in a pattern that is not terribly different from the trotting gait exhibited by horses like Sweet William and other four-legged animals (Patrick, Noah, & Yang, 2009, see Chapter 9).

Standing raises the center of mass even farther from the ground and requires the baby to keep the center of mass balanced over a much smaller and less symmetrical base of support between the feet. And walking requires the ability to keep the center of mass (temporarily) balanced over an even smaller base of support (a single foot) in the process of stepping. Remember, standing is the prevention of falling, and walking is controlled falling!

As we might expect, walking is unsteady and rigid at first, with a wide stance and short, quick steps. This is likely because babies who are just learning to walk are clamping down on almost all available degrees of freedom and are necessarily fighting (rather than cooperating with) the reactive forces that their movement produces. However, walking skill improves quickly over the next few months and continues to improve slowly over the next few years (Adolph, Vereijken, & Shrout, 2003; Bril & Brenière, 1993; Bril, Dupuy, Dietrich, & Corbetta, 2015). But this improvement does not happen on its own. It requires lots and lots of practice. And lots and lots of falling. On average, in just one hour of free play, new walkers take over 2,300 steps, travel over 700 m, and fall 17 times (Adolph et al., 2012)! This works out to 14,000 steps, over 4.5 km, and over 100 falls in a six-hour day. Being a new walker (and a caregiver of a new walker) sure is exhausting!

Notes

1. Occasionally, we may refer to perception and action (as nouns), but our definition of these as processes rather than things is implied in these instances.
2. The original quote is credited to Heraclitus—an ancient Greek philosopher.

11 Perceiving and Acting With Others—an Ecological Social Psychology

In Chapter 5, we argued that animals primarily perceive affordances—opportunities for behavior. Fred's cat, for example, can perceive *what possibilities exist* for avoiding a rambunctious charging dog. She could flee. She could leap. She could hide. In that context, we presented a foundational argument of ecological psychology—that perceiving affordances for a given behavior means actively detecting patterns in lawfully structured energy arrays at a given point of observation. Such patterns provide *information about* the animal's *possible relationships to the surrounding substances and surfaces*—whether, when, and how to move to perform that behavior. In short, perceiving affordances is a process of detecting lawfully structured information.

In Chapters 6–8, we explored the information for seeing, hearing, and feeling affordances. The lawfulness underlying the perceptual process guaranteed that the same principles apply and that the same phenomena occur when perceiving a given affordance in different circumstances—regardless of the energy form being structured and regardless of the perceptual machinery used to detect such structure.

In Chapter 9, we argued that perceiving affordances is only useful to the extent that it enables an animal to perform coordinated goal-directed behaviors. Avoiding the rambunctious dog means *actually* fleeing, *actually* leaping, or *actually* jumping. Moreover, we made the argument that performing a given behavior requires exploiting *the very same lawfully structured energy patterns* that provide information about affordances for that behavior. Perceiving affordances is the detection of information that "gets into the muscle", and performing behaviors is the utilization of this information to establish and control synergies. In Chapter 10, we described how these processes develop over time—especially in early childhood.

So far, so good, right? Well, sort of. Wait, what? *Sort of?* Yes, sort of. So what's missing? Here's a hint: our discussion of affordances began with the behaviors of *two* animals, not just one. Fred's cat wasn't just perceiving affordances for fleeing, leaping, or hiding for the heck of it (though she *could* do this). Instead, she was perceiving affordances for fleeing, leaping, or hiding *to avoid the rambunctious dog*. And successfully avoiding the dog likely requires not only perceiving affordances for herself *but for the dog as well*—perhaps that *she* can fit under the couch, but the dog cannot (see Figure 11.1).

But wait, there's more! Successfully avoiding the dog *also* likely requires coordinating her behavior *with the dog's behavior*. If the dog goes *right*, maybe she ought to go *left*. If the dog moves *toward* her, maybe she ought to *back up*. Or maybe she ought to *move toward the dog* if she intends to swat the dog's nose rather than flee. In this chapter, we will present evidence that the lawfulness underlying the processes of perceiving and acting guarantees the same phenomena will occur, and the same explanations of those phenomena ought to apply when an animal perceives affordances and coordinates behavior for itself as when it does so for or with other animals.

DOI: 10.4324/9781003145691-13

Figure 11.1 In order to successfully avoid the rambunctious dog, Fred's cat must be able to perceive affordances both for herself (what behaviors *she* can perform) and for the dog (what behaviors *the dog* can perform).

Traditional Approaches to Perceiving and Acting With Others

Just as there are traditional approaches to perception and action, there are traditional approaches to social interaction (for an overview of some of these; see Bargh, 2017; Iacoboni, 2009; Loehr, Sebanz, & Knoblich, 2013). As in previous chapters, our goal in the next few paragraphs is not to evaluate or even completely describe these approaches but rather—in very broad strokes—to show how they are incompatible with the ecological approach that we have been developing so far.

It should be no surprise that many of these approaches borrow key concepts from traditional approaches to perception and action. If perceiving properties of *things in the world* requires interpreting representations (see Chapter 1), then so too should perceiving properties and behaviors of other animals, including other people. And if coordinating *one's own behavior* requires generating and deploying motor programs (see Chapter 9), then so too should coordinating one's behavior with that of other animals—again, including other people.

The traditional approaches to social interaction that have been developed since the turn of the 21st century are based, in large part, on the discovery of so-called mirror neurons in monkey brains (see Cook et al., 2014; Rizzolatti & Fabbri-Destro, 2010). These cells were called mirror neurons because they showed increased activity (1) when a monkey *performed* a particular goal-directed behavior—such as reaching for an object and (2) when that monkey *observed someone else* performing that same goal-directed behavior—such as watching someone else reaching for an object. In other words, *observing* a particular behavior and *performing that same behavior* activate the very *same brain circuits* in the *very same way* (see Figure 11.2). Since the discovery of mirror neurons in monkey brains in the early 1990s, researchers have found neurons that seem to do similar things in similar places in the human brain (Rizzolatti & Sinigaglia, 2008; Kilner, Paulignan, & Blakemore, 2003; Kilner et al., 2009).

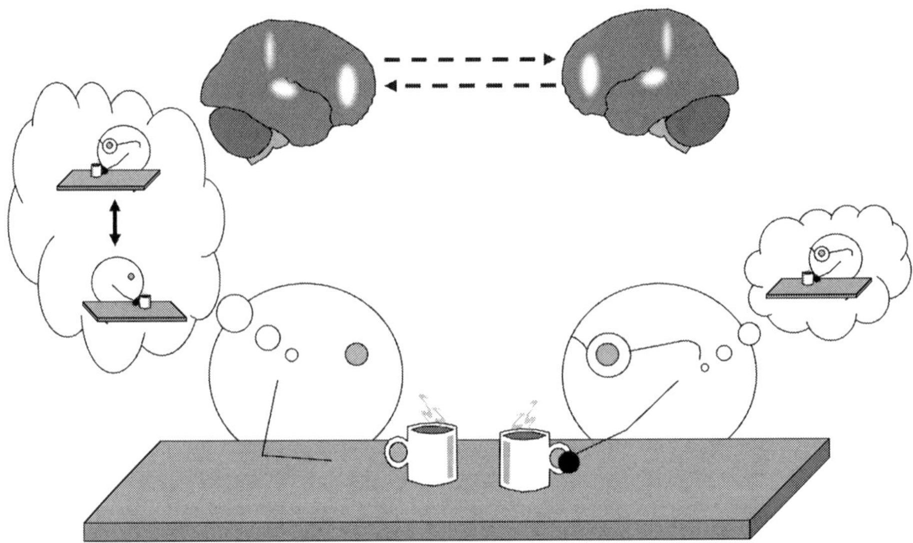

Figure 11.2 So-called mirror neurons show increased activity both when a person *performs* a particular goal-directed behavior and when that person *observes* someone else performing that same goal-directed behavior.

The discovery of mirror neurons was a big deal for traditional approaches because it seemed to provide a *neurological basis*—a locally causal mechanism!—for how animals and people can perceive the actions of others (see Iacoboni, 2009). Critically, *the very same brain circuits* seem to be involved in both *performing and perceiving* a given behavior. Consequently, if Fred watches Claudia reach for a cup of tea, doing so *automatically* generates a pattern of activity in Fred's brain, just like the one that would be generated if *Fred* were to perform that very same behavior. In other words, if Fred watches Claudia reach for a cup of tea, it activates a neural simulation *of him* reaching for a cup of tea.

The key implication is that Fred is able to successfully *perceive* what Claudia does because watching her perform a given behavior automatically stimulates *the exact same brain cells* in his mirror neuron system that would be stimulated if *he* were to perform that same behavior. All Fred, or his central executive, has to do is figure out what behavior this particular pattern of brain activity in Fred's mirror neuron system—this particular neural simulation—refers to. And *voila*! He knows exactly what particular behavior Claudia is performing. Fred perceives *Claudia's* behaviors in the same way and by the same brain mechanisms that he perceives *his own* behaviors!

This explanation applies not only to how an animal *perceives* the behaviors of other animals but also to how it *performs behaviors* in the context of other animals. Again, when Fred observes Claudia reaching for a cup of tea, it automatically generates a neural simulation in Fred's brain of him performing that same behavior. Therefore, it should be relatively easy—even automatic—for Fred to *imitate* Claudia's reaching movement (Iacoboni, 2009). Fred, or his central executive, just has to allow the neural simulation to generate the associated set of motor commands that would be generated if Fred were performing the behavior on his own (see Chapter 9). It may even be *more work* for Fred to *stop himself from imitating* Claudia because he would need *to actively prevent* (inhibit) the neural simulation from generating these motor commands. Proponents of mirror neuron explanations might say that this is the reason for the awkward dance that occurs when you and someone else are trying to get out of each other's way but only end up getting *more in* each other's way.

The fact that perceiving another person perform a given behavior generates a neural simulation (i.e., activates a representation) *in the exact same brain cells* as performing that behavior is also key in explaining how a person *coordinates their behavior with*, rather than merely imitates, others. When Fred observes Claudia reaching for the cup of tea, *the exact same brain cells* are stimulated in Fred's brain and in Claudia's *at the exact same time*. It is as if, at that particular moment, Fred and Claudia are experiencing a shared representation of this particular behavior—even though only one of them is performing the behavior. In such explanations, "sharing" this representation may enable each of them to generate and execute *related but independent* motor programs (see Chapter 9), allowing them to coordinate their behavior with each other, even if they don't necessarily plan to do so (Sebanz, Bekkering, & Knoblich, 2006).

An Ecological Approach to Social Interaction

As you might expect, the ecological approach to perceiving and acting with others is quite different from the traditional approach based on mirror neurons that we just described.

Perceiving with Others

As we discussed in Chapter 5 and elsewhere, in the ecological approach, perceiving affordances requires detecting information about affordances by means of perceptual systems. As a reminder, a perceptual system is a grouping of potentially independent anatomical components that work together as a functional unit in detecting information about affordances for a given behavior (see Chapters 6–8). The lawfulness underlying the perceptual process means that the same phenomena ought to occur, and the same explanations of those phenomena ought to apply across conditions. These conditions include the various *means by which* an animal can perceive an affordance for a given behavior.

Fred's dog, for example, has a certain shape, mass, strength, dexterity, skill, and way of moving through the world. These properties both determine what affordances are available to Fred's dog and lawfully structure the various energy patterns that Fred's dog encounters. And Fred's dog can detect these energy patterns in different ways. It can perceive the affordances of a surface by looking at it, by probing it with an outstretched paw, or even by sniffing it, and in each of these cases, the relevant perceptual system spans a set of potentially independent anatomical components. And these perceptual systems can span the body and an external object. For example, if Fred were to perform the same task by probing the surface with a hand-held rod, the relevant perceptual system would span Fred and the rod.

But these conditions also include the social contexts in which the animal perceives a given affordance—in particular, whether that animal perceives affordances for themselves or for another animal. The very same properties of a given animal that lawfully structure the various energy patterns that the animal itself encounters *also lawfully structure the energy patterns that other animals encounter*. In other words, the very same properties of *Fred's dog* (its shape, mass, strength, dexterity, skill, and way of moving through the world) also lawfully structure the various energy patterns encountered by other animals—including, say, *Fred's cat*. These patterns inform *Fred's cat* about *affordances for Fred's dog*. In other words, structure in patterned energy distributions provides information both about affordances for the self *and* about affordances for others (Marsh et al., 2006; Marsh, Johnston, Richardson, & Schmidt, 2009; Richardson, Marsh, & Schmidt, 2010; see Jones & Garcia, 2021).

Acting With Others

As we discussed in Chapter 9, in the ecological approach, performing coordinated behavior is a lawful process of establishing and controlling synergies. Synergies are analogous to perceptual systems. They are groupings of potentially independent anatomical components that work together as a functional unit in *exploiting* information about affordances for a given behavior. Here again, the lawfulness of the underlying process means that the same principles apply across conditions. These conditions include, for example, the various means by which a person can perform a given behavior.

Fred's dog can get from place to place by walking, trotting, or galloping. Each of these means requires a unique synergy—a unique coordination pattern among a unique set of potentially independent anatomical components. And these synergies can span the body and an external object. For example, when Fred's grandfather gets from place to place by using a cane, the relevant synergy is a functional unit spanning his grandfather and the cane.

But these conditions also include the social context in which the animal performs a given behavior—in particular, whether that animal is coordinating its behavior with another animal or with a group of animals. In the case of coordinating behavior with another animal or a group, the relevant synergy is a functional unit that spans the individual animals. Two or more animals perceiving and acting together create *social (or interpersonal) synergy* (Marsh et al., 2006; Riley et al., 2011) (see Figure 11.3). In other words, the very same lawful processes that occur when an animal coordinates the movements of its own limbs (intrapersonal coordination) also occur when two or more animals coordinate their movements with each other (interpersonal coordination).

In short, the same lawful principles that underlie perceiving and acting in animal-environment systems also do so in *animal-animal*-environment systems (Marsh et al., 2006, 2009; Richardson et al., 2010). And in neither case are simulations or representations—shared or otherwise—required (see Box 11.1).

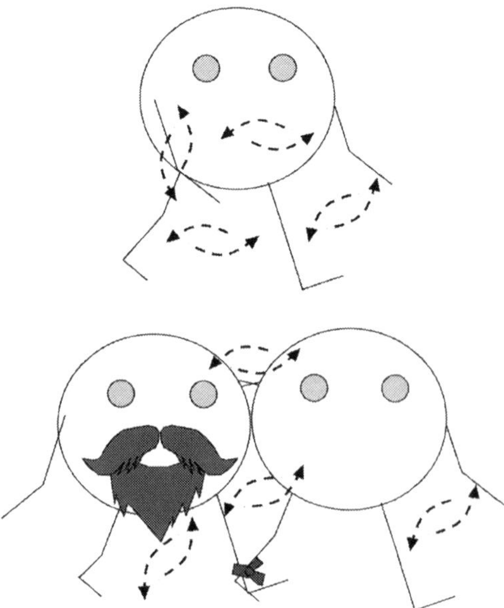

Figure 11.3 When one person performs a behavior by themselves (such as walking), they establish a synergy that spans the individual muscles and joints (*top*). When two (or more) people perform a behavior together (such as in a three-legged race), they establish a synergy that spans the individual people (*bottom*).

Box 11.1 The Ecological Take on Mirror Neurons

As we described previously, there has been much excitement in the psychological community over the discovery of mirror neurons. They have been used as a means to understand not just perceiving and acting with others but also language, empathy, and even disorders, such as autism. But not all are convinced. No one is arguing that mirror neurons don't exist. They do. The question is, though, what exactly they do and to what extent they play a role in the wide range of phenomena that they have been proposed to explain (see Hickok, 2014).

From the ecological approach, the larger question is about the role of the brain and the nervous system in perceiving and acting (and cognizing). As we have discussed, from the ecological approach, the lawfulness underlying perception and behavior means that the brain and nervous system play more peripheral roles in such processes. And as we will see, organisms with minimal nervous systems (or even no nervous systems—like plants!) nonetheless show impressive perception-action abilities (see Chapter 17).

This does not mean that the brain and nervous system do not play *any role whatsoever* in perception-action—trust us, we are happier to have a nervous system than not—only that these components do not play the central locally-causal representational or computational roles that are typically assumed of them. So then, from the ecological approach, what are we to make of the brain and nervous system in general and of mirror neurons in particular?

What the ecological approach needs is a description of the brain and nervous system that is neither computational nor representational and that respects the animal-environment system as the fundamental unit of analysis. One such description relies on the concept of resonance. This term is typically used in the context of sounds or vibrations—when one object that is vibrating at a particular frequency causes a nearby object to vibrate at the same frequency. For example, resonance is how a powerful singer can break a wineglass just by singing a loud, sustained note that matches the natural, or resonant, frequency of the glass.

In an ecological approach to the brain and nervous system, resonance—or something like it—also happens *within the brain and nervous system* during the active detection of information in structured energy arrays (Raja, 2018; Raja & Anderson, 2019). That is, the nervous system and brain *resonate to*—rather than fix, represent, or compute—the information detected by an actively behaving animal. It is as if the animal-environment system is the singer and the nervous system is the wineglass—though hopefully one that doesn't break! Note that this more or less *reverses* the typical sequence of events in which activity in the brain and nervous system control what the animal does. In this way of thinking, the activity of the *animal*—within an animal-environment system—controls what the *brain and nervous system* do (see van Orden, Hollis, & Wallot, 2012)!

Moreover, resonating does not require fixing, representing, or computing. And given that the information being detected is lawfully related to the relationship between animal and environment, the animal-environment system remains the fundamental unit of analysis. We're off to a great start, but what kind of a description of the nervous system might support resonance?

One possibility is *neural reuse theory* (Anderson, 2014). This theory proposes that the main function of the brain is the control of action. And the brain controls particular actions by establishing something akin to brain synergies—collections of potentially independent networks of neurons working together as a temporary, functional unit to achieve a goal.

In neural reuse theory, the particular components of the brain are less important than the functional relationships established among those components (see Chapters 4 and 9).

If this is the case, then mirror neurons might still be *involved* in the process of interacting with others. However, it is more likely this involvement is a *consequence* of detecting information that specifies affordances for the self and for others than it is a (local) cause of either process. In addition, while it is somewhat straightforward to provide an explanation for how mirror neurons play a role in the ability to *imitate* the behavior of another person, it is less clear how they might play a role in *coordinating behavior* with another person—especially when doing so requires rapidly and flexibly performing behaviors that complement, compensate for, or react to the behaviors of others (Hickok, 2014; Riley et al., 2011). In these cases, it seems more likely that two or more perception-action systems are *resonating to the same information* than being causally directed by overlapping neuroanatomical activity.

Perceiving Affordances for Others

Fred has invited Claudia over for dinner. They are setting the table together when Fred realizes that the fancy salad bowls (the ones that his mother gave him that he rarely has an opportunity to use) are on the very top shelf of his kitchen cupboard. Drat. He looks way, way up at the bowls. He is pretty certain that he would *not* be able to reach the bowls merely by reaching up with an outstretched arm (short arms are *something else* that his mother gave him). He wonders if he *might* be able to reach the bowls by jumping *and then* reaching. Then again, maybe he ought to go get a step stool. But his step stool is stored in the dark, creepy part of the basement. There are *spiders* down there. He doesn't want to have to go to get it unless he really, really needs to.

Fred decides that it is too much of a bother and too creepy to go down into the basement to get the step stool. Besides, he's feeling limber today. He decides to try to jump and reach for the bowls. He bends his knees and looks up at the bowls. Ready? On three . . . One . . . two . . . Just then, Claudia enters the kitchen. She is amused at Fred's predicament and a bit skeptical of Fred's jumping ability. She is fairly certain that Fred will be *unable* to reach the bowls even by jumping and then reaching. She suggests that he go get the step stool instead. Fred is not convinced. He decides to go for it. He bends his knees and jumps. Calamity ensues. He gets his fingertips on the bowls, but that's it. His elbow clips the shelf below the bowls on the way down. Fred is uninjured but is buried in an avalanche of snacks, cereal, and paper products.

Fred is incredulous. How did Claudia know that he would be unable to reach the bowls by jumping and then reaching? She has never seen Fred try to jump to reach anything on this shelf before. In fact, she has never really seen him jump like this *at all* before. Claudia smirks. She explains that while she has never seen him jump like this before, she has seen him do *other* things—like walk around and pick things up off the floor. And she reminds him, somewhat slyly, that she played competitive basketball for many years. Could these experiences (i.e., watching Fred do other things and playing basketball) have somehow played a role in Claudia's ability to perceive whether Fred could jump to reach the bowls?

Perceiving How High Another Person Can Jump and Reach

Can Watching Walking Inform Jumping Ability?

Obviously, different people have different abilities to jump. These abilities are determined by their size and shape but also by their mass, strength, dexterity, skill, and how they move through the world. In Chapter 6, we described how it is that *exactly these properties* lawfully structure the changing optical pattern that a person encounters at a point of observation as they move through the world. In other words, we described how the optical pattern encountered by a person like Fred at a point of observation that he occupies is *action-scaled* with respect to his own action capabilities. It provides *information about affordances*—such as whether he would be able to jump and reach an object.

But can optical patterns *also* provide information to one person about affordances for another person—like how high *the other person* can jump and reach? From the ecological perspective, the answer is "yes". As described previously, although affordances for the self and affordances for another person are not identical, they are *analogous*. Consequently, they ought to *analogously structure* patterned energy distributions at many different points of observation.

As a person moves through the world, they not only *encounter* action-scaled optical patterns at their own point of observation, they also *generate* such patterns that are available to be encountered by other people *at other* points of observation. A person's size and shape, mass, strength, dexterity, skill, and how they move through the world not only lawfully structure the optical patterns that *they* encounter; such properties also lawfully structure the optical patterns that *other people* encounter. In other words, it is likely that the optical pattern *encountered by Claudia* at a point of observation that *she occupies* is *action-scaled* with respect to *Fred's* action capabilities. This optical pattern would provide her with information about affordances for Fred—such as whether he would be able to jump and reach an object.

Researchers investigated this possibility by bringing participants into the laboratory in pairs. Each person reported the maximum standing reach height and maximum jumping reach height for themselves and for the other person (see Figure 11.4). Not surprisingly, people were better at perceiving maximum standing reach height than maximum jumping reach height and were better at perceiving their own abilities than those of the other person. Nonetheless, they were pretty accurate—to within 8% of actual reaching ability—in all cases (Ramenzoni et al., 2008).

Figure 11.4 People can accurately perceive maximum standing reach height and maximum jumping reach height both for themselves (*top*) and for another person (*bottom*).

To try to determine what the information about another person's maximum jumping reach height might be, the researchers investigated what experiences might improve a person's ability to perceive another person's maximum jumping reach height. They reasoned that if a particular experience improves the ability to perceive affordances for another person, then some aspect of that experience is likely providing information about affordances for that person. So in a follow-up experiment, each participant (the perceiver) reported the perceived maximum jumping reach height of another person (the actor) on three separate occasions.

First, the perceiver watched the actor walk around the laboratory and then reported the actor's maximum jumping reach height. Second, the perceiver watched as ankle weights were attached to the actor's legs and then reported the actor's maximum jumping reach height—assuming that the weights would be worn while the actor jumped. Third, the perceiver watched the actor walk around the laboratory while the actor was still wearing the ankle weights and then reported the actor's maximum jumping reach height—again, assuming that the weights would be worn while the actor jumped.

So what happened? You might expect that perceived maximum jumping reach height *would decrease* from the first report (when the actor was not wearing ankle weights) to the second report (when the actor was wearing ankle weights). After all, the weights would make it harder for the actor to jump as high, and the participant would probably know this. And you would be right—go you!

While the perceivers knew that the weights would decrease the maximum jumping reach height of the actor, they tended to *overestimate* how much the weights would do so. So what happened after the perceivers watched the actor *walk around* while wearing the ankle weights? Well, perceived maximum jumping reach heights increased—just slightly—which better reflected how much the weights actually decreased the actor's maximum jumping reach height. The authors hypothesized that the optical patterns that the participant encountered when watching the actor walk around while wearing the weights provided information about the actor's ability to jump and reach while wearing the weights. And that this information served to fine-tune the participants' perception of the actor's maximum jumping reach height.

This is a perfectly reasonable explanation. But the researchers had a problem. Before making the second report of the actor's maximum jumping reach height, the participant *was aware that the actor had put on ankle weights*. Maybe this knowledge affected their subsequent reports in ways that had nothing to do with action-scaled optical patterns. Maybe they, or their central executive, just recomputed perceived maximum jumping reach height based on this information. So in a follow-up experiment, the researchers engaged in a bit of trickery in the name of science—which is the *best* kind of trickery.

In one condition, the perceiver watched the actor walk around the laboratory (without ankle weights) and then reported the actor's maximum jumping reach height. In another condition—out of view of the participant—ankle weights were attached to the actor's legs and were hidden under the actor's pant legs. Sneaky! Then the perceiver watched the actor walk around the laboratory while the actor was wearing the hidden ankle weights, and the perceiver again reported the actor's maximum jumping reach height.

And what was the result of all of this trickery and sneakiness? It turned out that perceived maximum jumping reach height *was lower* in the (hidden) ankle-weight condition than in the no-ankle-weight condition—just like the previous experiment when the weights were not hidden. Given that the participants *were unaware* that the actor was wearing the weights in one case but not the other, the most likely explanation is that the optical patterns that the participant encountered *when watching the actor walk* provided information about the actor's different abilities to jump and reach in each condition (Ramenzoni et al., 2008).

What About Watching Squatting or Twisting?

The previous study suggested that watching another person walk provides information about that person's ability to jump and reach. Admittedly, this is a little strange. After all, walking is not the same as jumping and reaching. Consequently, this doesn't really make sense from a more traditional perspective. Why (and how) would watching a person perform one behavior help a central executive to figure out how well the person can perform another behavior—especially when the central executive is being deceived by sneaky researchers!

However, this makes much more sense from an ecological perspective. Walking and jumping do have *something* in common—both require producing dynamic vertical forces with the legs. So maybe watching someone *walk* provides information about their ability to *jump and reach* because it provides information about their general ability to produce dynamic vertical forces with the legs. If this is the case, then watching someone perform a behavior that *does not* require producing dynamic vertical forces with the legs—like twisting from side to side—*should not* provide information about that person's ability to jump and reach.

This was the hypothesis investigated by Ramenzoni, Davis, Riley, and Shockley (2010). In this experiment, one set of participants reported the perceived maximum jumping reach height of another person—the actor—before and after watching them *squat down and pick up an object.* Another set of participants reported the perceived maximum jumping reach height of the actor before and after watching them *twist in place from side to side.* And the results supported the hypothesis. Perceived maximum jumping reach height improved—that is, they more closely matched the actor's actual maximum jumping reach height—after watching the actor squat and lift. However, perceived maximum jumping reach height *did not change* after watching the actor twist in place from side to side. In other words, participants learned about the actor's ability to jump and reach by watching them squat (a behavior that also requires producing vertical forces with the legs) but not by watching them twist (a behavior that does not).

What Do Basketball Players Know About Affordances for Others?

So to some extent, the research described in the preceding paragraphs explains how Claudia knew that Fred would be unable to jump and reach the bowl even though she had never seen him perform this exact behavior before. Watching a person perform one behavior (e.g., walking or squatting) may provide information about that person's ability to perform other behaviors (e.g., jump and reach) that have certain similarities in how they are performed—in this case, the production of dynamic vertical forces.

But how might have her experience playing basketball helped her? And would this experience help her perceive whether Fred could perform *other* behaviors like reaching without jumping? One thing that basketball players do during the course of practice and games is jump and reach—to shoot the ball, to block a shot, to rebound. A lot. But this also means that they *watch other people* jump and reach. A lot.

Presumably, all of this experience watching other people jump and reach ought to lead to an enhanced ability of basketball players to perceive affordances for jumping and reaching for other people. And not just *those exact people*, but other people as well. This seems likely because the optical patterns that provide information about a given affordance ought to be invariant across these contexts.

But will this experience lead to an enhanced ability of basketball players to perceive *any and all* affordances for other people? Even affordances for behaviors that are irrelevant to or less commonly observed in playing basketball, such as sitting or reaching while standing? This seems unlikely because the optical patterns that provide information about affordances for jumping and reaching are unlikely to be invariant across behaviors.

In other words, given their sport-specific experience, basketball players ought to be better than non-basketball players at perceiving another person's maximum jumping reach height. But they ought to be no better than non-basketball players at perceiving another person's maximum sitting height or their maximum standing reach height.

To test these hypotheses, researchers brought both basketball players and non-basketball players into the laboratory (Weast, Shockley, & Riley, 2011; Weast Walton, Chandler, Shockley, & Riley, 2014). All participants reported perceived maximum jumping reach height, perceived maximum sitting height, and perceived maximum standing reach for another person—the actor. Not surprisingly, the basketball players were more accurate than the non-basketball players at perceiving how high the actor could jump and reach. However, they were no more accurate at perceiving how high the actor could sit or how high the actor could stand and reach. And related studies found that basketball players were more sensitive than non-basketball players to subtle patterns in walking movements that provided information about the walker's ability to jump and reach (Weast et al., 2019).

And this explains how Claudia's basketball experience may have helped. Experience watching a group of people jump and reach improved her ability to detect the optical information about Fed's jumping and reaching ability. But this experience likely would not have helped her if she was perceiving how high Fred could sit or how high Fred could reach while standing.

Perceiving (and Acting On) Affordances *for Us*

Fred and Claudia are finished with dinner. As they are cleaning up, Fred asks Claudia if she would mind helping him to move some of his many jousting lances from one side of his garage to the other. He needs the room for when his horse, Sweet William, comes to visit. Fred has learned his lesson from the salad bowl fiasco and realizes that he will need Claudia's help to move at least some of the lances. Some of them are pretty long and unwieldy! But he doesn't want to waste any more of Claudia's time. She has already helped him clean up an avalanche of snacks, cereal, and paper products. As a result, he only wants her to help him move the larger lances *that he would be unable to move on his own*. After that, he'll move the rest of the smaller lances by himself. But which lances will he need help with?

Perceiving What We (and I) Can Grasp

In Chapter 5, we discussed a number of studies showing that perception of whether, when, and how a given behavior can be performed depends on the fit between action capabilities and environmental properties. At a particular critical ratio of action capabilities to environmental properties—at a particular *critical π value*—a person would no longer be able to perform a given behavior in a particular way and would need to transition to a different way of performing that behavior. People are generally quite good at perceiving when they would need to make these transitions. For example, people can perceive when they would need to transition from an arm-only reach to a leaning—arm-plus-torso—reach (Carello et al., 1989) and when they would need to transition from a one-hand to a two-hand grasp on an object (Cesari & Newell, 1999, 2000).

But can a person perceive when they would need to transition from performing a given behavior by themselves *to doing so with another person*? Does this transition *also* reflect the fit between action capabilities and environmental properties? Is perception of *interpersonal affordances* (i.e., affordances for more than one person) action-scaled? And if so, is this action scaling analogous or even identical to the action scaling that occurs when perceiving *intrapersonal affordances* (i.e., affordances for one person)?

Researchers investigated these questions in a series of studies using a plank-moving task similar to one that Fred and Claudia are about to perform with the jousting lances (Richardson,

Marsh, & Baron, 2007a; see also Isenhower et al., 2010). In one experiment, individual participants looked at (many) wooden planks of different lengths that were placed on a shelf—one plank at a time. For each plank, their task was to report how they would choose to grasp and lift that plank to move it off the shelf—if they were *only* allowed to touch the *very ends* of each plank.

The participant had three options for what they could say. Option 1 was to say that they would choose to grasp the plank with *one hand*—by placing a thumb on one end of the plank and some number of fingers of that same hand on the other end of plank. Option 2 was to say that they would choose to grasp the plank with *two hands*—by placing some number of fingers of one hand on one end of the plank and some number of fingers of the other hand on the other end of the plank. Option 3 was to say that they would choose to grasp the plank *together with another person*—with the participant grasping one end and the other person grasping the other end.

You would probably guess that the perceptual boundary between planks that they would choose to grasp (by themselves) with one hand and with two hands occurred at a smaller plank length (approximately 17 cm) than the perceptual boundary between planks that they would choose to grasp with two hands and with another person (approximately 163 cm). And you would be right. What you might not guess is that these values corresponded to (identical) ratios of plank length to maximum grasping width[1]—identical perceived *critical* π *values*—of 0.98 in each case! In other words, perception of when a person would need to transition from a one-hand grasp to a two-hand grasp and from a two-hand grasp to a two-person grasp occurred at the same ratio of action capabilities to environmental properties in each case.

This experiment provided some albeit preliminary answers to questions posed previously. Yes, a person can perceive when they would need to transition from performing a behavior—in this case, grasping an object—by themselves to doing so with another person. Yes, perception of this interpersonal affordance is action-scaled. And yes, this action scaling is analogous or even identical to the action scaling that occurs when perceiving a comparable intrapersonal affordance—when they would need to transition from grasping an object with one hand or two hands. In short, this experiment provides support for the claim that perception of interpersonal affordances is *continuous with* perception of intrapersonal affordances—that perception of interpersonal affordances exhibits the same phenomena and has the same explanations as perception of intrapersonal affordances.

Grasping What We (and I) Can Grasp

But these researchers were not finished yet. In the experiment that we just discussed, people merely *said* what they *would* do. They did not actually attempt to move any of the planks from one location to another with or without another person. So the experimenters conducted another experiment that required another set of participants to do just this. In this experiment, participants performed the task in pairs. A slightly longer set of planks and a different setup were used—this time with a fancy conveyer belt that sent the planks one at a time to the pair of participants! When each plank reached the pair of participants, their task was to move the plank from the table to another location by only touching the very ends of each plank. They could choose to move each plank by grasping the plank on their own with *two hands*—with one hand on each end of the plank—or by grasping the plank *together with the other participant*—with one participant holding each end of the plank.

The transition between moving the plank on their own with two hands and moving the plank together with the other person occurred at a ratio of plank length to maximum grasping width—a *critical* π *value*—of about 0.85. This value is smaller than the crticial π value in the perception task (0.98). But remember that when an individual person performs a task on their own, they shift how they are performing the task based on comfort and not necessarily on the absolute limits of their action capabilities (see Chapter 5). The same thing seems to be happening in this case when two people are performing a task together. Nonetheless, the choice of whether to perform a behavior—in this case, grasping a large object—alone or together with another person was action-scaled.

Fitting Where We (and I) Can Fit

The experiments described previously show that people can perceive when they would need to transition from performing a behavior by themselves *to doing so with another person* and that this transition reflects the fit between action capabilities and environmental properties. In other words, they showed that a person can perceive when their action capabilities would need to be supplemented with those of another person. But consider a situation where a person has *no choice but* to supplement their action capabilities with those of another person.

Last year, Fred and his friend Reed entered a three-legged race at a neighborhood picnic. In running the race, Fred had no choice but to supplement his action capabilities with Reed's (and vice versa) (see Figure 11.3). In a situation like this, can Fred (or Reed) perceive affordances for the two of them as a unit? If so, does perception of such affordances reflect an action capability or geometric property that spans both of them? And are affordances for the pair of them merely an additive combination of the affordances for each of them as individuals (do affordances for Fred + Reed = affordances for Fred + affordances for Reed)? Or are the affordances for the pair of them something very different from this—an *emergent property* (see Chapter 16)?

Researchers investigated these questions by investigating when, whether, and how people choose to pass through a doorway together (Davis, Riley, Shockley, & Cummins-Sebree, 2010; see Chang, Wade, & Stoffregen, 2009). In one of these studies, adult participants attempted to walk through doorways of different widths both alone and side-by-side with another person. The researchers were interested in the doorway width at which the participants began to turn their shoulders when walking through doorways in each condition. As you might expect, they found that this critical doorway width was larger when participants were walking side-by-side with another person (approximately 105 cm) than when doing so alone (approximately 57 cm).

But what the researchers were really interested in was whether the critical doorway width for the pair was merely the sum of the critical doorway widths for each individual person. They found that it was not. When walking through the doorway alone, participants began to turn their bodies when the doorway was 1.22 times that individual person's shoulder width. This is comparable to previous research and suggests that individual participants are allowing for space for side-to-side body sway as they pass through the aperture (Franchak et al., 2012; Warren & Whang, 1987).

If affordances for walking through the doorway side-by-side with another person were merely the *sum* of affordances for each individual person, then we would expect that the two people would start to turn their shoulders when the door width was 1.22 times the *combined* shoulder width. However, when performing this task together, participants began to turn their bodies when the doorway was about *1.13 times* the combined shoulder width of both people. That is, when walking through the doorway with another person, the pair allowed for *less space* for side-to-side body sway as they passed through the doorway than when walking through the doorway alone. This suggests that, like perceiving affordances for the self, perceiving affordances for another person is not an additive process (see Chapter 5, Box 5.1). Instead, the results suggest that—at least in the context of performing this task—participants were willing to share their personal space with the other person. When walking through the doorway, the space between them was shared interpersonal space. And just like sharing a snack with someone means that each person gets less snack than they would have if they were eating alone, sharing interpersonal space means that each person gets *less personal space* than if they were performing the task alone.[2]

This experiment provided some albeit preliminary answers to the questions posed previously. Yes, a member of a pair can perceive affordances for the pair—in this case, whether they could fit through a doorway together. Yes, perception of this affordance reflects an action capability or geometric property that spans the individual members of that pair or group. And no, affordances for the pair are not merely an additive combination of affordances for the individuals. Instead, they are an *emergent property* (see Chapter 16).

Fitting Between Other People

Walking through a doorway together with another person requires sharing personal space with that person. Personal space is like a social bubble that surrounds an individual. Most people feel uncomfortable or awkward when someone gets into that bubble or when they get into someone else's. But the size of that bubble is not fixed. Context changes the size of personal space (e.g., smaller with friends or romantic partners, larger with strangers). And the shape of that bubble is not symmetric. It typically extends out farther in front of a person than behind that person (Tanaka, 1973). So what if instead of passing through a narrow space *with* another person as in the experiment described previously, a person passes through the narrow space *between* two other people? Would this change how that person passes through this space? And would it matter which way those people who form the edges of the space are facing?

Researchers investigated these questions by asking participants to walk between two box-shaped frames placed at different distances from each other (Tomono, Makino, Furuyama, & Mishima, 2019, see Figure 11.5). In some conditions, the frames were empty. *No problem!* But in other conditions, *other people* stood inside those frames. *OK, this could get awkward.* And the people in the frames stood in six different configurations: both facing forward (*toward* the approaching participant—*awkward!*), both facing backward (*away* from the approaching participant—*not so awkward*), both facing each other (*really awkward!*), both facing away from each other (*not so awkward*), both facing to the participant's left (*somewhat awkward*), or both facing to the participant's right (*also somewhat awkward—but in the other direction*). So what happened?

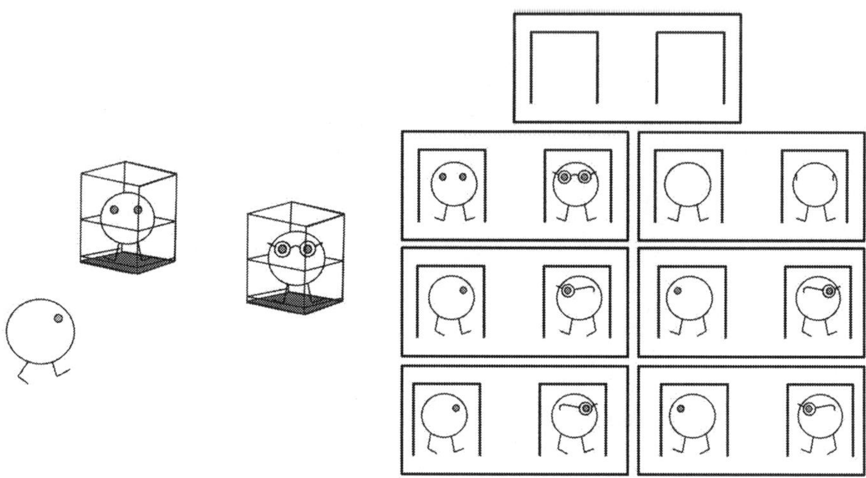

Figure 11.5 In an experiment by Tomono and colleagues (2019), participants were asked to walk between two box-shaped frames (*left*). In one condition, the frames were empty (*right, top*). In the other conditions, two people stood in the frames in one of six configurations (*right*).

Well, a number of things—all of which were fascinating (and some of which were awkward). First, when walking between two empty frames, participants began to turn their bodies when the space between the frames was about *1.4 times* their own shoulder width. This is very close to the value that we have seen several times so far. But when walking between two people who were facing each other, participants began to turn their bodies when the space between the people was *1.7 times* their shoulder width! And not only that, they rotated their bodies *more* when walking between people who were facing each other than when walking between two empty frames. This makes sense, right? Empty frames have no personal space that needs to be avoided. Other people do. And given that personal space extends farther in front than behind a person, more care needs to be taken to avoid the personal space of two people who are facing each other than two people facing away from each other.

Second, when only one person was facing toward the center and the other person was facing away from the center, participants tended to both *walk away from and turn their bodies away* from the person facing the center. That is, they tended to walk toward the right and turn their bodies to the right—clockwise—when they were passing between people who were both facing to the right. Conversely, they tended to walk toward the left and turn their bodies to the left—counterclockwise—when they were passing between two people who were both facing to the left. This *also* makes sense. Moving away and turning away from someone who is facing you—and toward someone who is not—minimizes the degree to which your personal space overlaps with someone else's.

Imagine that you are sitting in the window seat of an airplane with strangers in the middle and aisle seats. Think about how you would get to the lavatory without asking your seatmates to get up. You would turn to face *away* from them and then do a side-to-side shuffle. Less sharing of personal space (well, a little less anyway) and less uncomfortable or awkward (much less, actually) than the alternative!

Third, participants started turning their shoulders *sooner*—at a farther distance away—when the two people were facing forward—toward them as they approached—than when they were facing backward—away from them as they approached. This makes sense too. You will encounter someone's personal space sooner if they are facing you than if they are not. So avoiding that personal space means turning sooner when they are facing you than when they are not.

Coordinating Behavior with Others

Rocking Out

Claudia has finished helping Fred move the larger jousting lances in his garage. They are chatting about the evening's events while walking to Claudia's car. Fred's attention drifts from the conversation because he notices that they are walking completely in sync with each other. As Claudia lifts her right foot off the ground, so does Fred. And when she places her right foot down, so does Fred. The same thing with her left foot and his left foot. Right, left, right, left. Stride for stride, in sync. Fred is certainly not trying to do this. And he's pretty sure that Claudia isn't either. Nonetheless, right now, it is like they are their own two-person precision marching band.

Fred thinks that this is quite odd, but then he realizes that the movements of the *different parts of his own body* are in sync as well. As his left leg swings forward, so does his right arm. And as his right leg swings forward, so does his left arm. Just then, he has a grand epiphany. He begins to wonder whether the coordination he observes between his movements and Claudia's movements (*interpersonal* coordination) and the coordination he observes between the parts of his own body (*intrapersonal* coordination; see Chapter 9) are, in fact, *the very same phenomena with the very same explanation*. But just as he is having this thought, he trips over a skateboard that the neighbor's kid, Michael, left in his driveway—*the cheeky blighter!* That's the third time this week! For Fred, grand epiphanies are best left for sitting.

Toward the end of Chapter 9, we discussed studies investigating intrapersonal coordination. In these studies, participants were asked to swing two pendulums in a particular coordination pattern—in-phase (in the same direction at the same time), anti-phase (in opposite directions at the same time), or somewhere in between. The results of these studies showed that (1) in-phase and anti-phase are the easiest patterns to maintain, with in-phase being easier and more stable, especially at higher movement speeds, than anti-phase; (2) differences in the physical properties of the pendulums (length or mass) can shift people away from these two stable coordination patterns; and (3) people often *unintentionally switch* from anti-phase to in-phase, especially at higher movement speeds. Do the same phenomena occur in *interpersonal* coordination?

Researchers have investigated Fred's epiphany and these exact hypotheses in many different studies (e.g., Schmidt & Turvey, 1994; Schmidt, Carello, & Turvey, 1990; Schmidt, Nie, Franco, & Richardson, 2014; see Shockley, Richardson, & Dale, 2009). In one of these studies (Richardson et al., 2007b), participants sat next to each other in rocking chairs. In one of the experiments, participants were explicitly instructed to coordinate their rocking movements with each other in-phase (so that they rocked in the same direction at the same time) or anti-phase (so that they rocked in opposite directions at the same time).

The researchers found that people could maintain both of these patterns but that in-phase was easier and more stable than anti-phase. They also found that these stable patterns were shifted just slightly away from these two patterns when weights were added to one or the other chair—making it more difficult to rock them exactly in sync or exactly out of sync. Both these results are consistent with those from experiments investigating *intrapersonal* coordination.

In a follow-up experiment, participants sat next to each other in rocking chairs, just like in the first experiment. However, unlike in the first experiment, *each participant in the pair was instructed to rock at whatever tempo felt most comfortable to them*. And participants did this in one of three conditions—while looking at the other person's rocking chair, while looking straight ahead, or while looking away from the other person's rocking chair (see Figure 11.6).

The researchers found that when people looked *away* from the other person's rocking chair, the rocking movements were not coordinated in any way. In other words, each participant

Figure 11.6 When two people sitting next to one another in rocking chairs are asked to rock at their own tempo, they tend to rock in-phase (together in sync) when they look at the other person's chair (but not when they look away from the other person's chair).

was successfully able to abide by the instructions to rock at their own preferred tempo. The two rocking chairs were just as likely to be in-phase or anti-phase or anywhere in between.

However, when the participants looked at each other's rocking chairs, their rocking movements became *unintentionally coordinated* with those of the other person (see Figure 11.6). And they were more likely to *rock together in-phase* than anti-phase or anywhere in between. In other words, despite the instruction to rock at their own preferred tempos, they *couldn't help but rock in sync* with the other person. This is exactly what happened when Fred and Claudia were walking to Claudia's car!

Box 11.2 Perceiving and Acting with Others in Individual and Team Sports

Social or interpersonal synergies are especially useful in explaining coordination of behavior that requires rapidly and flexibly complementing, compensating for, or reacting to the behaviors of others. There may be no better example of this than in competitive sports. As we have described, athletes are particularly sensitive to sport-specific affordances for themselves and for other people (Weast et al., 2011, 2014). Success in an individual or team sport may depend on how well attuned a given competitor or team is to sport-specific affordances for themselves and for their opponents—in the context of both the overall goal and the particular situation (see Silva et al., 2013).

For example, in an individual combat sport such as kendo, competitors must move relatively close to their opponent to strike—with bamboo swords—but must move relatively far from their opponent to avoid being struck. In other words, kendo competitors are likely to exhibit *two different* preferred interpersonal distances—one that is *relatively close* for performing offensive maneuvers and one that is *relatively*

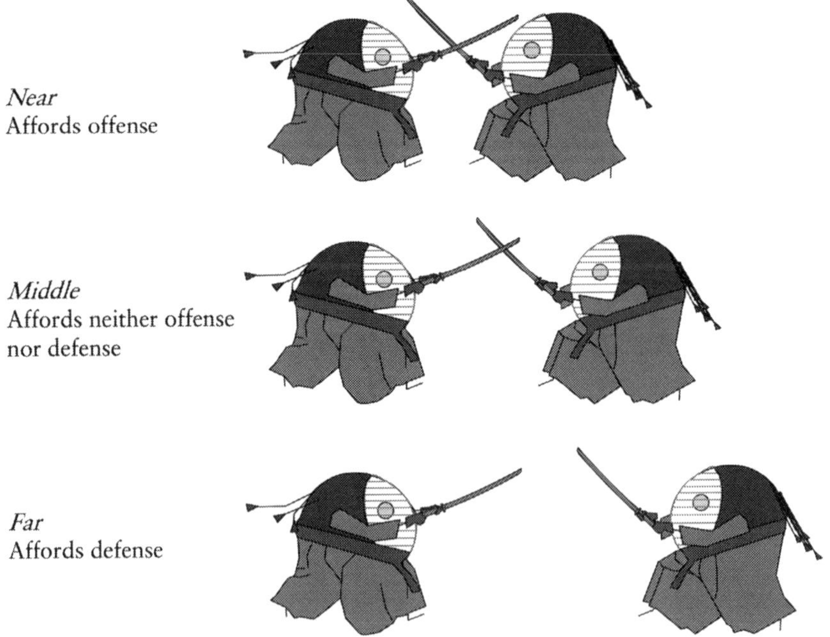

Figure 11.7 Kendo competitors exhibit two preferred interpersonal distances—a close interpersonal distance that affords offense (*top*) and a far interpersonal distance that affords defense (*bottom*). They tend to avoid a middle interpersonal distance that affords neither (*middle*).

far for performing defensive maneuvers—and generally avoid the interpersonal space *in between* these two preferred distances. And a given competitor's choices about whether to step toward or away from an opponent ought to be based on perceived affordances for striking that opponent.

Researchers investigated these hypotheses by analyzing the movement patterns of competitors in real kendo matches *and then* conducting an experiment on perception of affordances for striking using the very same pairs of competitors (Okumura, Kijima, & Yamamoto, 2017, see Figure 11.9). The analysis of competitor movement during the kendo matches showed that competitors did, in fact, exhibit two preferred interpersonal distances—one approximately 1 m from the opponent and one approximately 2.75 m from the opponent—and tended to avoid interpersonal distances between these values. More-experienced competitors spent more time at the *far* interpersonal distance, and less-experienced competitors spent more time at the *near* interpersonal distance—likely because the experienced competitors could move into striking position faster than the less-experienced competitors (see Okumura et al., 2012). And movements of a competitor toward or away from an opponent in the competition setting were related to perceived affordances for striking exhibited in the experimental setting!

In a team sport such as rugby, players must make choices about whether to attempt to advance the ball by running or by passing it to a teammate. Such choices likely require perceiving affordances for quickly fitting through spaces between defenders both for themselves and for their teammates. Moreover, this is likely to be a rugby-specific skill that ought to improve with rugby experience. To investigate these hypotheses, researchers conducted an experiment using a virtual reality (VR) rugby task—with both rugby players and non-rugby players as participants.

In this task, the participant and two virtual teammates were opposed by three virtual defenders (Passos et al., 2012). The experimenters varied whether each virtual defender was moving *directly* toward or *at a slight angle toward* the participant or one of the virtual teammates. In other words, they varied whether the participant or any of the virtual teammates (or no one) had an open running lane. They found that the participants chose whether to run with the ball or to make a short or long pass to one of the virtual teammates based on perceived affordances for advancing the ball (see Correia et al., 2012). And experienced rugby players did this more successfully than less-experienced rugby players or non-rugby players.

Of course, there are many other examples of perceiving and acting with others in the context of individual and team sports, including soccer (what most of the world calls football), team handball, hockey, volleyball, and tennis, among others (see Caldeira et al., 2020; Passos, Araújo, & Volossovitch, 2016; Pereira et al., 2018).

Horsing Around

Fred and Reed are back this year to defend their title in the three-legged race that they won at last year's neighborhood picnic. The secret to winning a three-legged race is to walk as much like a three-legged animal as possible. The more you walk like two two-legged animals with one of your legs tied to one of the other person's legs, the less you move together and the more you fall behind the other racers. Ideally, you would want to do this without thinking too much about it—maybe even unintentionally, like the coordination of the people in the rocking chairs. But can this really happen? Since there aren't any three-legged animals, let's ask a slightly different question. Can two people who are connected together in some way coordinate their walking movements so that they walk more like a single four-legged animal—such as Fred's horse, Sweet William?

This hypothesis was investigated by Harrison and Richardson (2009). In this study, pairs of participants walked around a 35 m path in a number of different conditions. In one condition, each person did so on their own—one person walked around the track, and then the other person did so. In another condition, the two people walked around the track together—with one person following the other at a distance of 0.75 m. In yet another condition, the two people performed the same following task, but this time, they were connected to each other—with each person strapped to one end of a 0.75 cm foam block (see Figure 11.8)! In all conditions, participants were instructed to maintain their own comfortable walking pace—much like the participants in the rocking chair study were instructed to maintain their own comfortable rocking tempo.

The researchers were interested in whether and how the leg movements of the two people would be coordinated in each condition. They were especially interested in if, in either or both of the latter two conditions, the two people would coordinate their walking movements so that they walked a little more like a single four-legged animal—and a little less like two two-legged animals.

As you might expect, when the two people walked around the track on their own—one and then the other—the leg movements of the two people were not coordinated at all. Why would they be? Each person performed the walking task independently while the other person was standing still.

But something different happened when they performed the following task. In the condition where one person followed the other but they were not physically connected, the leg movements of the two people became *unintentionally coordinated*, at least some of the time.

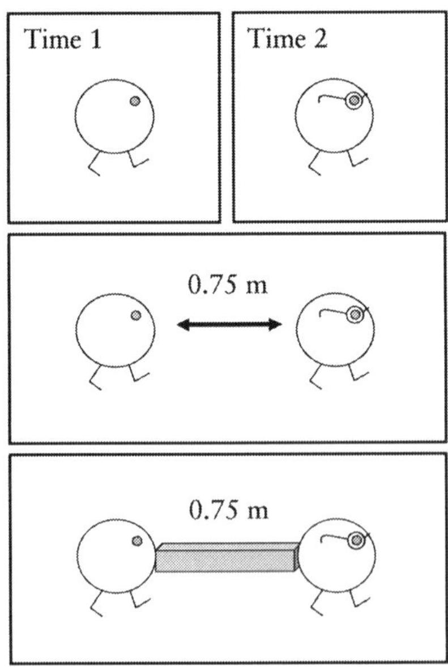

Figure 11.8 Harrison and Richardson (2009) asked pairs of participants to walk around a track in three different conditions—one at a time (*top*), one following behind the other at a distance of 0.75 m (*middle*), and one following behind *and connected to* the other by a 0.75 m foam block (*bottom*).

And when they were coordinated, they were coordinated in a particular way. In particular, the two people walked more or less in sync with one another. Their right feet moved forward together, and then their left feet moved forward together—just like Fred and Claudia! In this case, if we were to describe the two people as a single four-legged animal, we would say that they exhibited a four-legged gait called a *pace*. It is a common gait in animals such as camels, giraffes, elephants, bears, and some breeds of horses.

In conditions where the participants performed the following task and were physically connected to each other, they sometimes exhibited this particular coordination pattern. But other times, they became unintentionally coordinated in a different way such that the step cycle of each person was one-half of a cycle apart. When the *right foot* of one person moved forward, the *left foot* of the other person moved forward, and vice versa. In this case, if we were to describe the two people as a single four-legged animal, we would say that they exhibited a four-legged gait called a *trot* (see Chapter 9). It is a common gait in many kinds of four-legged animals, such as dogs, cats, and of course, Fred's horse—Sweet William.

The results of this experiment show that two people's walking movements can become unintentionally coordinated so that they walk more like a single four-legged animal—and less like two two-legged animals. This bodes well for Fred and Reed's chances to repeat as three-legged race champions!

The results of these and other experiments suggest that interpersonal coordination is *continuous with* intrapersonal coordination—that interpersonal coordination exhibits the same phenomena and has the same explanations as intrapersonal coordination. What is so critical about the results of these studies is that what seems to be driving the coordination in each case is not that each person is getting information from shared or overlapping nervous systems but rather that they each have the ability to detect lawfully structured—optical and mechanical—energy patterns. It was only when one or both of them could see or feel each other performing the task that the unintentional coordination occurred.

The detection of lawfully structured information enables the formation and control of synergies—collections of independent anatomical components that work together as a functional unit to achieve a goal (see Chapter 9). In the case of an individual animal performing a given behavior, the relevant synergy is a functional unit spanning several independent body parts. When two or more animals perform a behavior together, *the relevant synergy is a functional unit that spans two or more independent animals—a social or interpersonal synergy* (Marsh et al., 2006; Riley et al., 2011).

Notes

1. This ratio was determined by taking into account how much the tips of the fingers would wrap around the plank when performing a one-handed or two-handed grasp.
2. The proprietor of a pub frequented by the authors would often respond to requests to split a beer with "Good idea! Let's split two". Unlike the sharing of interpersonal space described here, this kind of sharing does *not* result in each person getting less than they would have if they were not sharing.

12 Thinking, Learning, and Remembering

In Chapter 5, we argued that all animals primarily perceive affordances—opportunities for behavior—and that perceiving affordances for a given behavior means actively detecting patterns in lawfully structured energy arrays at a given point of observation. In Chapters 6–8, we described the information for perceiving affordances by seeing, hearing, and feeling. Importantly, the lawfulness underlying the perceptual process guarantees that the same or analogous patterns provide information about a given affordance in each of these cases. That is, even though different perceptual machinery may be sensitive to different kinds of stimulation, the perceptual systems are each in the business of detecting *information*—which, as a reminder, is *independent of* a particular kind of stimulation. Therefore, perceiving by means of one perceptual system *is continuous with* perceiving by means of any other perceptual system—just like the surface of a Möbius strip[1] is one continuous surface (see Figure 12.1, *top left*).

In Chapter 9, we argued that *performing a given behavior* requires *exploiting* the very same lawfully structured energy patterns that provide information about affordances for that behavior. Light, sound, and physical forces don't so much get *into the head* as they get into and get used by the muscles. That is, *doing* is continuous with perceiving (see Figure 12.1, top right). And in Chapter 11, we argued that perceiving and acting with others requires detecting and exploiting the same or analogous lawfully structured energy patterns as when doing so alone. The very

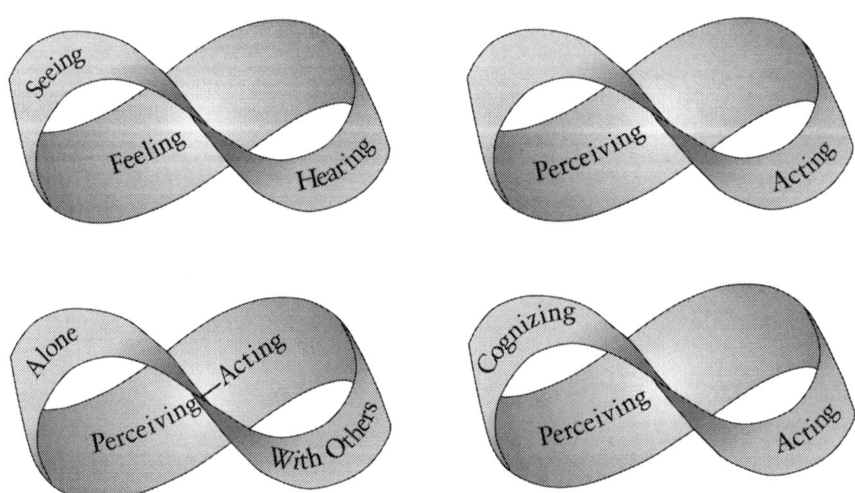

Figure 12.1 In the ecological approach to perception, perceiving is continuous across perceptual systems (*top left*), perceiving is continuous with acting (*top right*), perceiving and acting are continuous across social contexts (*bottom left*), and perceiving and acting are continuous with cognizing (*bottom right*).

DOI: 10.4324/9781003145691-14

same lawful relations that underlie perceiving and acting in animal-environment systems also do so in *animal-animal*-environment systems. That is, perceiving and acting with others *is continuous with* doing so alone (see Figure 12.1, *bottom left*).

We are now well equipped to use the ecological approach to explain how a hungry creature sees or smells an apple on a tree from across a field, approaches it by walking (or running or crawling or flying), and reaches out to grasp and eat it, all while coordinating its behavior with that of other creatures. And we can do so without appealing to a central executive, without mediating entities such as copies or representations, without loans of intelligence required to make unconscious inferences or control an inordinate number of degrees of freedoms, and without leading to unsolvable mysteries (see Chapters 1–4).

This is all well and good—*great, in fact!*—but it is not the end of the story. It can't be. A true *ecological psychology* has to be about more than just apple picking! It has to apply to the full range of phenomena that occur in animal-environment systems. Explaining how it is that animals skillfully perceive and act alone or with others falls squarely into the wheelhouse of the ecological approach. It is its purpose, its *raison d'etre*, if you will. It is how it makes a living. And it makes a *really good* living. But the ecological approach must also apply to problems that may seem, at first glance, to fall far outside of its wheelhouse. That is, it must apply to problems that seem to require—*demand, even*—all of the entities and processes that the ecological approach denies.

In this chapter, we will apply the ecological approach to exactly these problems—in particular, knowing, learning, and remembering. However, we will argue that the same lawful principles that underlie perceiving and acting in animal-environment systems also underlie *cognizing* in animal-environment systems. In other words, we will argue that these and all other aspects of cognizing are, in fact, *continuous with* perceiving and acting (see Figure 12.1, *bottom right*).

Traditional Approaches to Cognition

Just as there are traditional approaches to perception and action, there are traditional approaches to cognition (for a more detailed overview of some of these, see Goldstein, 2018; McBride & Cutting, 2019). As in previous chapters, our goal in the next few paragraphs is not to evaluate or even completely describe these approaches but rather, in very broad strokes, to show how they are generally incompatible with the ecological approach that we have been developing so far.

Traditional approaches to understanding how we know anything about the world almost always include the related assumptions that contact with the world is mediated by a copy, that this copy is bad and needs to be fixed, that the fixed copy is in the form of a mental representation, and that this fixed representation is what is experienced by the perceiver (see Chapter 1). In other words, knowing anything about the world requires being in the representation business at all points in the supply chain—including production, manipulation, distribution, storage, and use. Thinking is the *possessing and manipulating* of such representations, learning is the *modification or enrichment* of such representations, and remembering is the *storing and accessing* of such representations. Consequently, cognition is typically defined as a collection of *mental processes or actions*, including (but not limited to) thinking, learning, and remembering.

In the traditional view, perception is the *input* to cognitive processes. It provides the raw material for the formation of representations. Yet at the same time, what is perceived is *influenced by* the modifying, enriching, storing, accessing, possessing, and maintaining of these representations. After all, the fixed representation forms the basis of perceptual experience! And movement is the *output* of cognitive processes. That is, moving the body is also a *consequence of* the modifying, enriching, storing, accessing, possessing, and maintaining of these

Figure 12.2 In traditional approaches, cognition is described as a mental process of manipulating representations, requiring a central executive to perform these manipulations.

representations (see Chapter 9). After all, motor commands are *also* representations—coded instructions about how and when to move specific body parts.

But perception and movement require at least some honest-to-goodness contact with the body and the world outside of it. These processes involve *energy* on the front end and *forces* on the back end. Therefore, perception and behavior can be, at best—or worst, depending on your perspective—only *partly* mental process. However, the manipulating of representations occurring in processes such as thinking, learning, and remembering does not necessarily require any direct contact with the body or the outside world. Therefore, cognition can be, or perhaps *must be*, a *completely mental process*, one that is entirely walled off, or at least is at some distance removed, from both body and environment (Fodor, 1980). And this is exactly how most traditional approaches choose to study it (Goldstein, 2018; McBride & Cutting, 2019, see Figure 12.2)

In short, in the traditional approach, cognition is described as a set of mental processes or actions that operate on or with representations and that are somehow removed from both the body and the world. This would seem to require—*demand, even!*—the activity of a central executive and all that this entails (see Figure 12.2, Chapter 1). From traditional approaches, then, all cognition—including thinking, learning, and remembering—would seem to necessarily fall squarely *outside* of the wheelhouse of the ecological approach.

An Ecological Approach to *Cognizing*

As you might expect, the ecological approach to cognizing is quite different from the traditional approach sketched previously. There are at least two fundamental differences. First, whereas the traditional approach defines cognition as a set of mental processes or actions, the ecological approach does not. In the ecological approach, cognition—like perceiving and acting—is an *ongoing relationship* between an animal and an environment (hence, *cognizing* instead of *cognition*). And as in perceiving and acting, the relevant functional units of cognizing can and do span the brain, the person, and the environment. That is, cognition is distributed not just across different parts of the brain or across the brain and the body *but across the animal and a structured environment* (Chemero, 2009; Favela et al., 2021).

Second, the traditional approach typically builds a theory of perception on a foundation of cognition in which perception is in the service of cognition and in which both processes rely on the processing of representations. In contrast, the ecological approach puts these processes on equal footing. In this view, cognizing is *continuous with perceiving and acting*—both of these processes rely on the detection and exploitation of lawfully structured stimulation patterns (see Figure 12.1, *bottom right*). In short, the same lawful principles that underlie perceiving and acting in animal-environment systems underlie cognizing in animal-environment systems. And in neither case are representations or a central executive or any of the associate baggage required!

Box 12.1 Are Illusions Illusory?

From the traditional approach, perception is a cognitive process because it requires interpreting or processing copies to produce mental representations. And the *outcome or result* of this process is perceptual experience (see Chapter 1). Almost all of the time, this process occurs without a hitch, and subjective experience matches objective reality. More specifically, subjective experience of geometric or physical properties, such as length, orientation, or brightness, matches objective reality as measured by an artificial measuring device, such as a meter stick, a protractor, or a photometer. For example, a short horizontal dark line is perceived as a short horizontal dark line. And certainly, two *identical* short horizontal dark lines are perceived as being identical. Likewise, two *identical* small dark circles are perceived as being identical (see Figure 12.3, *top*).

In some situations, however, there seem to be "hiccups" or "glitches" in the processing or interpreting of copies (i.e., in the creation, manipulation, distribution, and use of mental representations). In these cases, subjective perceptual experience of a particular geometric or physical property *does not* match objective reality as measured by an artificial measuring device. These hiccups or glitches result in *perceptual illusions* (Gregory,

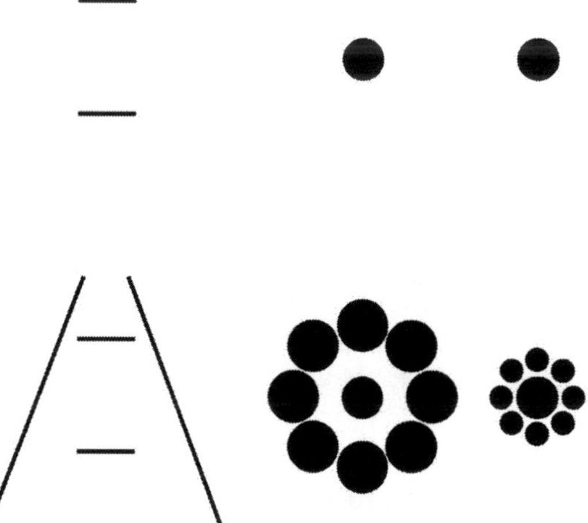

Figure 12.3 In traditional approaches, perception is the result or output of a cognitive process. This output almost always matches objective reality (*top*). When it does not (due to a glitch in this process), the result is a perceptual illusion (*bottom*).

2009; Shapiro & Todorović, 2017). For example, in the bottom figure on the left, the two short horizontal lines are identical in length, but the top line *looks* longer. And in the bottom figure on the right, the two inner circles are identical in diameter, but the one on the right *looks* bigger (see Figure 12.3, *bottom*).

From the traditional perspective, the primary interest in perceptual illusions is that they provide a window into how processing or interpretations of copies is supposed to work under normal circumstances. Kind of like how a glitchy video game controller might provide a window into how its various electronic components are supposed to work in a properly functioning controller.

From the ecological approach, however, illusions are not what they seem be. They can't be. From this approach, perceiving is a *process*—not an outcome. More specifically, it is a lawful process of actively detecting information about affordances by means of perceptual systems (see Gibson, 1979/2015). The primary content of perceptual experience is affordances—not geometric or physical properties (see Chapter 5). And perceptual systems are very much *unlike* artificial measuring devices (see Chapters 6–8)—they don't measure the same properties, and they don't work in the same way. Think about it—why would the visual system have evolved to measure properties such as the lengths of lines or the diameters of circles and do so in arbitrary units such as centimeters? It wouldn't have.

And now, for the mind-blowing part—given that perception is a lawful process (and not an outcome)—*the accuracy of perceiving can never be evaluated.* Just like any other lawful process, perceiving is neither correct nor incorrect. Consider an infant Eleanor who refuses to crawl on the deep side of the visual cliff (see Chapter 9) or a grown-up Fred who inadvertently walks into a sliding glass door. In neither case is perception illusory. In both cases, affordances were perceived (or were not perceived), but only because the information about those affordances was detected (or not, or was not detectable at all).

Consequently, the ecological approach argues that a theory of perception should be developed from the countless everyday successes of perception rather than the rare (and artificial) so-called failures of perception. For us, illusions are interesting not because they fool perceivers but because they challenge researchers to better understand the lawful process of detecting information about affordances.

Thinking, Learning, and Remembering in the Animal-Environment System

Fred and his friend Benoît (pronounced "Ben-wah") are hanging out playing their favorite video game, *Homunculus: The Infinite Regress*. Fred is playing a masterful game. His thumbs and index fingers are playing a symphony on the game controller, and he is scoring points all over the place. In fact, he is on track to set a new high score and knock Benoît right off the top spot on the leaderboard! As he plays, Fred feels *connected to* the game controller in his hands—it is like they are fused. But not in an uncomfortable, clunky sort of way. The controller feels *like a part of him*, much like a white cane or a prosthetic limb or a tennis racket might feel to a person who uses any of these objects on a daily basis. In fact, it sort of feels like the controller *is not even there at all*, like he's controlling the movements of the main character, the Mighty Sverker, *directly*. Fred is part of a smoothly operating Fred-controller-Sverker system (see Figure 12.4), and at the moment, this system is kicking Homunculus butt!

Slowly but surely, Benoît is getting jealous of Fred's performance in the game and is becoming nervous that he will lose his treasured spot atop the leaderboard. He hatches a plan. But

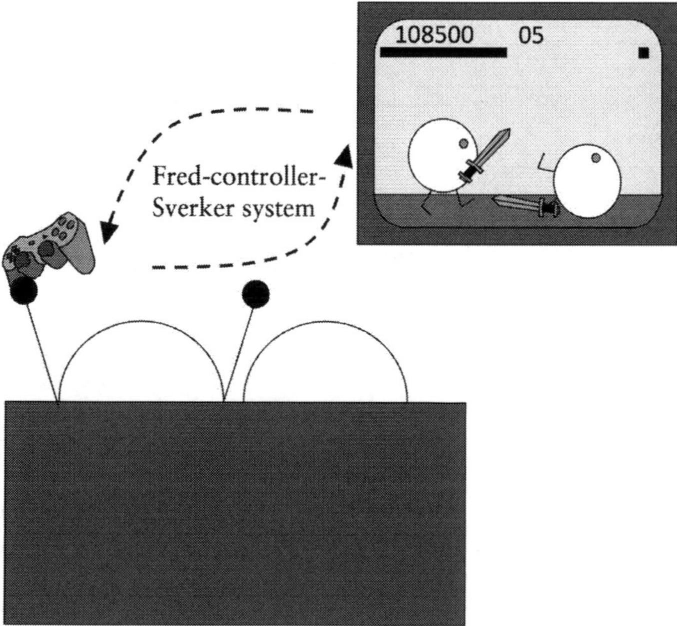

Figure 12.4 External objects (such as a video game controller) can become part of a person-tool-environment system, especially when the person is capable of skillfully using those objects.

the plan requires that Fred stop playing and put the game controller down for just a moment. *But how?* He's got it! He tells Fred that he's not sure, but he thinks that Carol—*Fred's crush! (gulp!)*—is standing right outside. It works! Fred puts down the game controller and runs to the window to look, and when he does, Benoît switches it for the glitchy controller that Fred has been meaning to get fixed. *Sneaky*.

Fred is initially disappointed that Carol is not there, but he quickly regains his composure and turns his attention back to the game—after all, he's got a high score to beat! But . . . something . . . is . . . wrong. His thumbs and index fingers are still flying all over the controller, but the Mighty Sverker is not responding as Fred expects. Instead, the Mighty Sverker is hopping around the screen but in ways that are only *sort of* related to what Fred is doing with the controller. Movements of the joystick don't immediately result in Sverker charging toward the Homunculus, and button presses don't immediately result in flying kicks or sword strikes. *How frustrating*! Suddenly, Fred no longer feels connected to the controller. In fact, he is *very* aware that he is holding a piece of molded plastic. It feels so weird to him now. It's as if a part of his body has gone limp. Fred is no longer part of a smoothly operating Fred-controller-Sverker system, and now the Homunculus is taking full advantage. Ugh.

Benoît sees how frustrated Fred has become—and how bad the Mighty Sverker is faring—and starts to feel bad about his ruse. So he hatches another plan. This time, he convinces Fred that closing his eyes, putting the controller down, and collecting himself might help him to play better. Fred closes his eyes, puts the controller on the couch, and Benoît deftly swaps it for the one that Fred was using initially. Fred opens his eyes and begins to play again. Now the feeling is back! Once again, he feels *connected to* the game controller. Once again, Fred is part of a smoothly operating Fred-controller-Sverker system, and slowly but surely, the Mighty Sverker is mounting a comeback. Hooray!

Thinking

Thinking is generally depicted as quiet, passive contemplation. On the contrary, however, in the ecological approach to perceiving, acting, and cognizing, thinking is an *active and dynamic process*. It has a *trajectory* (Kelso, 1995; Spivey, 2008). Like perceiving and acting, it is a continually unfolding *activity*. But not just any kind of activity. It is a *whole-body* activity that occurs in the context of other processes (e.g., developing, perceiving, moving) and within a structured animal-environment system. That is, like perceiving and acting, thinking is an *embodied* (it occurs in a body) and *embedded* (it occurs in a structured environment) process (see Chapter 3).

Explicitly describing thinking as an embodied and embedded process allows for thinking to be described *in the same way* as perceiving and acting (see Figure 12.1). For example, in previous chapters, we have described perceiving and acting each as processes that require coordinating independent components into a functional unit—a perceptual system and a synergy, respectively (see Chapters 6–9). *Thinking can be described in exactly the same way.* And just as in perceiving and acting, the functional units of thinking are *flexibly assembled* and can span the brain, the body, and external objects (Chemero, 2009; Dotov, Nie, & Chemero, 2010; Favela et al., 2021).

It may sound strange to claim that thinking can occur outside of the brain—and even stranger to claim that it can occur *outside of the body*—but really, it isn't so strange at all. When you count on your fingers, do a long division problem with pencil and paper, or use a GPS app to get to your destination, where exactly is the thinking occurring? The ecological approach argues that, in each case, the thinking is occurring at the level of the animal-environment system.

And in thinking—just as in perceiving and acting—the components influence the activity of the system as a whole and vice versa. For example, using pencil and paper to solve a long division problem *reduces* the amount of information that the person needs to remember at any given step, which *makes it easier* to solve the problem. The pen and the paper are like a thinking accelerator! None of the parts involved could—or could easily—do the thinking required to solve the problem on their own. But when used with the brain and the body, the pencil and paper *amplify* the person's problem-solving ability because they change *what the brain can do*. Consequently, the behavior of the system as a whole is *different from* the sum of its parts.

And it is this coordination *across levels of the system* (i.e., across micro and macro levels) that brings about self-organization in complex natural systems (see Chapters 3, 14, and 16). As we will see, there is evidence of exactly this kind of self-organization in thinking (Anderson, Richardson, & Chemero, 2012; van Orden, Holden, & Turvey, 2003).

The Structure of Thinking

So how would we investigate the *trajectory of thinking*? Well, for one thing, we would need participants to engage in the activity of thinking long enough to produce a trajectory that can be analyzed. In a study conducted by Van Orden et al. (2003), participants had a pretty easy—if somewhat repetitive—job. They had to look at a computer screen and, as quickly as possible, read aloud the four- or five-letter words that appeared.[2] Then they did this again. And again. Until they had read about 1,100 words. At that point, they might have felt like saying other four-letter words!

You would probably expect that participants were pretty good at this task—and maybe a little bored. And they were—both. On average, participants made a mistake in reading the word only about 2% of the time. But the researchers weren't necessarily interested in accuracy. *Wait. What? Why did they read 1,100 words aloud then?* Because the researchers were interested in *how long* it took the participant to begin reading the word on a given trial, usually a second or two at most and, *more importantly*, how this *response time* changed from trial to trial—and over groups of many trials—over the course of the 1,100 trials.

Response times didn't vary all that much over the 1,100 trials, but they did vary a little—0.5 s here, 0.25 s there, and so on. And the researchers used these changes to investigate the trajectory of thinking. Ordinarily, when researchers do experiments, this variability across trials is treated as background noise or error that *gets in the way* of the actual data—the signal. Consequently, *it is either ignored or corrected before the data are analyzed*. But for these researchers, *the noise was the signal*. The researchers were convinced—and for good reason—that this background noise would reveal the underlying dynamics of thinking. In other words, they suspected that this background noise is the "hum" that occurs when a perceiving-acting-cognizing engine is running smoothly (see Gilden, 2001). And they were most interested in whether thinking would exhibit the same kind of coordination across time scales—across the micro and macro levels—that is observed in other complex natural systems (see Box 12.2).

Box 12.2 The Random Racer, the Brown Bomber, and the Pink Punk

Fred bought his younger cousin, Guy, a motorized toy car—the *Random Racer*. When Guy placed the *Random Racer* on the floor and pressed the go button, the car turned a particular amount—say, 90° to the left—and then moved a particular distance in that direction—say, 10 cm. On the very next run, it turned in a completely *different direction*—say, 45° to the right—and moved a completely *different distance*—say, 100 cm. And then it did that—turned in a completely different direction, moved a completely different distance—again. And again. And again.

It turned out that *how much* the *Random Racer* turned and *how far it moved* was—as the name implies—*completely random on every single run*. Where the *Random Racer* ended up on a given run was *completely independent from*—*was completely uncorrelated with*—where it ended up on the previous run. Consequently, the car went *all over the place* but *nowhere in particular*—much to Fred's chagrin.

In fact, if you were to graph the movements that the *Random Racer* made over many, many runs, it would look like a mess. It would be complete randomness (see Figure 12.5, *top*). Technically, this kind of pattern—the absence of *any particular pattern*, really—is called *white noise*. A system that exhibits white noise is a completely random system.

Fred and Guy—but mostly Fred—were dissatisfied with how random the movements of the *Random Racer* were—after all, it didn't end up going anywhere in particular! So they exchanged it for a different motorized toy car called the *Brown Bomber*. The saleswoman assured them that the movements of the *Brown Bomber were not completely random*. Initially, Fred was skeptical. When Guy placed the *Brown Bomber* on the floor and pressed the go button, the car did exactly what the *Random Racer* did. It turned a particular amount—say, 90° to the left—and then moved a particular distance in that direction—say, 10 cm. *But wait!* On the very next run, the Brown Bomber turned in a completely different direction—say, 45° to the right—but *moved the same exact distance*—10 cm—that it did on the previous run. Then it did the same thing—turned in a completely different direction but moved 10 cm—again. And again. And again.

It turned out that how much the *Brown Bomber* turned changed on every run, but the distance that it moved in that direction always stayed the same. Unlike the Random Racer, where the *Brown Bomber* ended up on a given run was *completely correlated with*

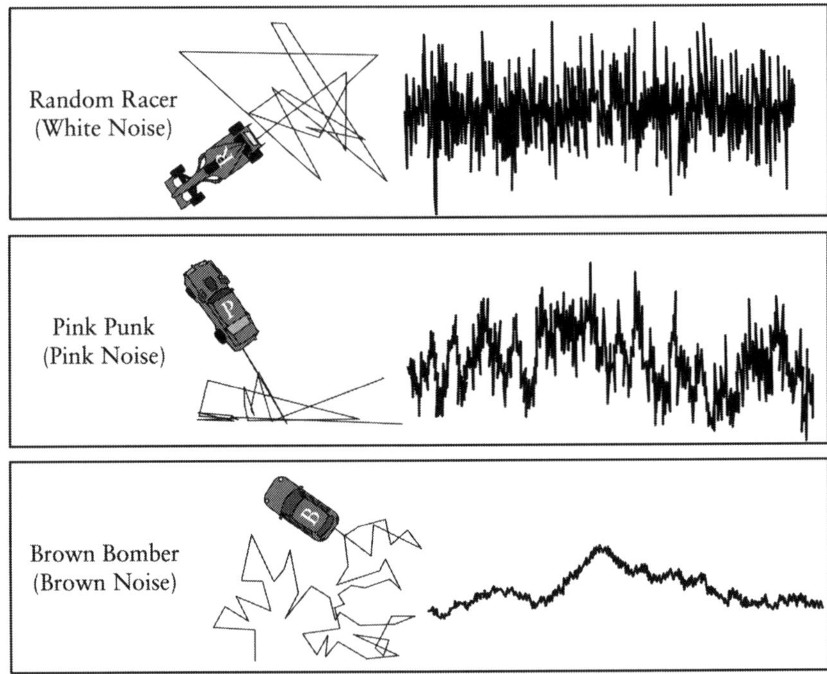

Figure 12.5 The Random Racer's movements are completely random—they exhibit white noise (*top*). The Brown Bomber's movements are completely correlated—they exhibit brown noise (*bottom*). The Pink Punk's movements are neither completely random nor completely correlated—they exhibit pink noise (*middle*).

where it ended up on the previous run—after all, the distance it moved in a given direction never changed! As a result, over many runs, the *Brown Bomber* eventually moved in a particular direction and then eventually moved in a different direction—it just took its sweet time getting from place to place. If you were to graph the movements that the *Brown Bomber* made over many, many runs, it wouldn't look so much like a mess (see Figure 12.5, *bottom*). There would be slow and steady drifts from one location to another over time. Technically, this kind of pattern is called *brown noise*. A system that exhibits brown noise is *not* a completely random system.

Fred was much happier with the *Brown Bomber* than he was with the *Random Racer*. So he went back to the saleswoman to see if she could recommend *another* toy racecar for Guy—which was, of course, really for Fred. She recommended—and Fred decided to buy—one called the *Pink Punk*. The saleswoman told him that the *Pink Punk* was particularly special. Fred was very curious to see why. When he—not Guy, mind you—placed the *Pink Punk* on the floor and pressed the go button, the car turned a particular amount—say, 90° to the left—and then moved a short distance in that direction—say, 10 cm—just like the other two cars. But wait! On the very next run, the *Pink Punk* turned in *a completely different direction*—say, 45° to the right—and moved *a different but still short distance*—say, 20 cm. Then it did the same thing—turned in a completely different direction and then moved a different but still short distance again. *But wait again!* On the next set of runs, it did something different. It turned a different amount on every run, just like before, but now, instead of moving *different short distances* on consecutive runs, it moved different *long distances on consecutive runs* (say 100 cm, followed by 90 cm, followed by 150 cm).

It turned out that how much the *Pink Punk* turned changed on every run, but the distance that it moved in that direction *depended on how much it moved on the previous run.* Long distances were more likely to be followed by long distances, and short distances were more likely to be followed by short distances. The movements of the *Pink Punk* were somewhere *in between* those of *Random Racer* and the *Brown Bomber.* In other words, where the *Pink Punk* ended up on a given run was *correlated with* where it ended up on the previous run—but not completely so. It didn't randomly move all over the place, nor did it slowly drift from one location to another. Instead, it seemed to *linger* or *explore.* It traveled to one place, hung out there or in the vicinity for a bit before moving on, and then did the same thing again.

If you were to graph the movements of the *Pink Punk,* it would look like more of a mess than the *Brown Bomber* but less of a mess than the *Random Racer* (see Figure 12.5, *middle*). There would be both randomness *and* steady drifts over both the short term and the long term. Technically, this kind of pattern is called *pink noise—yes, pink!* A system that exhibits pink noise is *not* a completely random system but also *not* a completely correlated system. It *has* flexible structure. This flexibility is one of the features that make pink noise—and the *Pink Punk*—so special. The other thing that makes pink noise so special is that the movements exhibit something called *self-similarity*—the larger patterns over many, many runs look similar to the smaller patterns over just a few runs. This is the kind of coordination across time scales—across the micro and macro levels—that brings about the self-organization of complex natural systems, including heartbeats, earthquakes, and thunderstorms (Kello & Van Orden, 2009; Newman, 2005; see Chapters 3, 14 and 16)!

If the trial-to-trial variability in reaction time for reading words aloud really is just meaningless noise, then this variability should have *no particular pattern,* like the Random Racer (see Box 12.2). However, when the researchers analyzed how the reaction times changed over the course of the 1,100 trials of the experiment, they found that these changes exhibited pink noise, like the Pink Punk. The changes in reaction time were not completely random but not completely correlated, like the Brown Bomber, either. A system that is in between these two extremes is *poised* and *flexible.* It is stable but also able to transition between stable states when necessary—from one cognitive "gait" to another. And the reaction times exhibited self-similarity—the changes over many, many trials were similar to the changes over just a few trials. The researchers proposed that pink noise is a hallmark of a self-organizing and smooth-operating cognitive system (see Gilden, 2001).

Thinking with the Body

So there is evidence for self-organization in word naming. To be sure, word naming involves thinking, but in an automatic under the radar kind of way—especially for common four- or five-letter words. What about a task that involves more challenging *on purpose* thinking? Like maybe working on the solution to a logic problem? Sometimes, in such circumstances, a person suddenly realizes what the solution is—what is often called an "aha" moment. In other words, they suddenly shift from a state of not knowing to a state of knowing. If thinking really is *continuous with* perceiving and acting, then this transition ought to be just like other sorts of nonlinear phase transitions in the course of perceiving and acting—like those observed in gait transitions from walk to run and vice versa—or walk to trot to run in horses like Sweet William (see Chapter 9).

When animals transition from one gait to another, their gait becomes momentarily *less stable* just before it becomes *more stable*. Think about walking on a treadmill that is slowly speeding up. At some point, you will find yourself in an awkward race-walking gait just before gait stabilizes and you settle into a comfortable and stable run. Researchers (Stephen, Dixon, & Isenhower, 2009) hypothesized that a similar pattern would *also* occur in thinking—just before a person discovers the solution to a problem. To investigate this, they asked participants to solve a "gear systems" problem (see Figure 12.6).

Participants looked at a drawing of several interlocking gears. One of the gears—the driving gear—had an arrow on it indicating whether it would turn to the right—clockwise—or to the left—counterclockwise. The participant's job was to use this information to figure out which way a different gear in the system—the target gear—would turn.

Participants tend to follow a particular pattern when solving sets of gear-systems problems. Initially, they tend to trace the path of turning directions of each gear with their finger, starting with the driving gear and moving all the way to the target gear—what the researchers called force tracing. After participants have solved a number of problems this way, however, they realize that the direction of neighboring gears alternate. *A-ha!* When that happens, they usually stop *tracing* as much and start *classifying alternating gears* (e.g., "right vs. left" or "clockwise vs. counterclockwise") until they get to the target gear. *Easy-peasy!*

Stephen et al. (2009), recorded participants' hand movements with a motion capture camera while they solved 36 gear systems problems. So what did they find? As expected, they found that *all* of the participants initially used the *force tracing method*—almost all used their finger, but some even used their heads or just their eyes! And at some point over the course the 36 trials, over 2/3 of the participants discovered the *alternation* method—many within the first ten trials or so. The researchers then analyzed the finger movements made by the participants in the course of solving each gear systems problem. They found that the discovery of the alternation method by a given participant was predicted by a *decrease in the stability* of finger movement *followed by an increase in the stability* of finger movement in the trials that immediately preceded

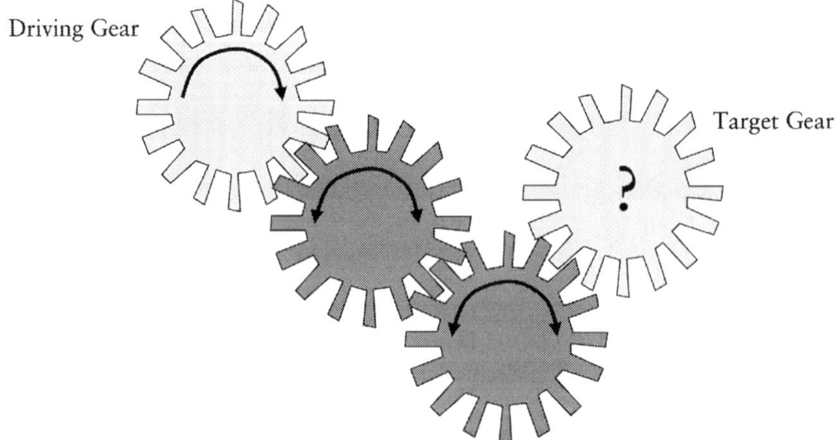

Figure 12.6 In a "gear systems" problem, the task of the participant is to determine the turning direction of the target gear given the turning direction of the driving gear.

the discovery. In other words, the "aha" moment looked like a lot like other kinds of nonlinear phase transitions from one stable state to another—such as gait transition. *Aha!*

Thinking with External Objects

So there is evidence that the body is used in thinking. Big deal. The brain is connected to the body by the nervous system, so this is not all that much of a surprise. But surely thinking can only occur *within the boundary of the skin*, right? It would be weird if thinking were spread out across the brain, the body, and an inanimate object, wouldn't it? But this is exactly the claim that the ecological approach makes. Just as the *functional units of perception and action* are flexibly assembled across the brain, the body, and external objects, so too are the *functional units of thinking*. But how would you ever demonstrate this?

As we have described previously, pink noise is thought to be a hallmark of a self-organizing and smooth-operating cognitive system. Maybe it is *also* the hallmark of a smoothly operating *extended cognitive system* that includes an external object. Researchers (Dotov et al., 2010) hypothesized that this would be the case. More importantly, they hypothesized that the pink noise *would disappear* when the system was disrupted so that it was no longer operating smoothly. And that it would *reappear* when the disruption was removed, and the system was operating smoothly again. *Genius!*

They asked participants to perform a video game herding task (see Figure 12.7, *left*). Participants used a computer mouse to move a pointer dot on a computer screen (a virtual herding dog) to keep another continually moving dot (a virtual sheep) within a prescribed area on the screen (a virtual herding pen). Participants performed this task for a total of 60 seconds. Easy-peasy. *Except* that about 30 seconds into the task, the mouse "glitched" for three seconds such that the pointer dot (the herding dog) "jumped around" and became hard to control. *Annoying, right?* After the three seconds were up, the glitch stopped just as suddenly as it began, and the pointer dot again responded normally, as it did before, until the trial ended. Well, *that* was weird. Sounds a lot like what happened to Fred when he was playing *Homunculus: The Infinite Regress*.

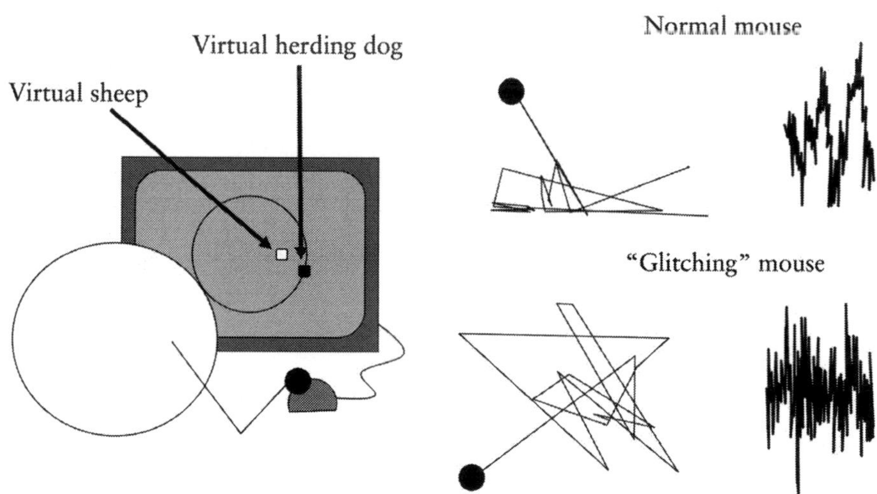

Figure 12.7 The video game herding task used by Dotov et al. (2010) (*left*). When the mouse was working normally, the mouse movements exhibited pink noise (*right, top*). When the mouse "glitched", the mouse movements were more random (*right, bottom*).

The researchers recorded the mouse movements that the participants made while they were performing this task. And they found that when the mouse was operating normally (i.e., before *and* after the glitch), these movements exhibited pink noise (see Figure 12.7, *top right*). That is, when the mouse was operating normally, mouse movements exhibited *self-similarity*—patterns over fractions of a second at the micro scale were similar to patterns occurring over several seconds at the macro scale. There was coordination across time scales! *During the glitch*, however, the mouse movements did not exhibit pink noise. In fact, during the glitch, the mouse movements were more like random noise (see Figure 12.7, *bottom right*). They looked more like white noise—there was much less coordination across time sales.

So what does this mean? This means that when the participants were able to perform the task smoothly, they flexibly assembled an *extended cognitive system* that included the brain, body, and mouse. These components were so seamlessly coupled that they were indistinguishable. The brain-hand-mouse system was a self-organizing and smooth-operating cognitive system! When the participant could not perform the task smoothly (i.e., when the mouse glitched), the cognitive system no longer included the mouse. The mouse once again became just another external object. Self-organization of the brain-hand-mouse system failed.

Learning

In the ecological approach, the primary challenge facing any animal is the successful performance of everyday goal-directed behaviors. Therefore, it should be no surprise that from this approach, learning is more about the fine-tuning of perceiving and acting abilities than it is about the accumulating of facts about the world (Gibson & Pick, 2000; Higueras-Herbada et al., 2019). Moreover, this fine-tuning is the result of the refinement of the ability to detect and exploit information about affordances rather than the *modification or enrichment* of representations.

Education of Intention

One of the ways in which perceiving and acting abilities can be fine-tuned is in the selection of which action(s) to perform—and hence, the selection of which *affordances to perceive*—in a given circumstance. Animals have options, after all. Should Fred's cat attempt to flee the rambunctious dog? Swat the dog? Something else? And once Fred's cat makes this choice, it must then actively explore the available energy arrays (i.e., by looking, listening, sniffing) in a way that reveals a stimulation pattern that might provide information about that affordance. Learning what behaviors to perform, what affordances to perceive, and how to explore to uncover possible information about those affordances is called the *education of intention* (Jacobs & Michaels, 2007).

Education of Attention

Another way in which perceiving and acting abilities can be fine-tuned is in subtle adjustments of which specific components of a given structured energy array are detected and exploited when intending to perceive a given affordance. Ideally, over the course of learning, the animal will progress toward detecting stimulation patterns that provide more useful information about an intended affordance and away from detecting patterns that provide less useful information about that affordance. For example, over the course of repeated attempts to swat the dog, Fred's cat might progress toward detecting patterns in the optic array that provide information about the dog's time to arrival (e.g., τ; see Chapter 6) and away from patterns that provide less useful information (e.g., about the dog's distance or speed). Learning which (components of) patterns in a given structured energy array provide information about a given affordance has been called the *education of attention* (Gibson, 1966; see Jacobs & Michaels, 2007).

Both of these concepts—the education of intention and the education of attention—are illustrated very nicely in a study by Arzamarski et al. (2010). These researchers asked participants to wield three-dimensional rectangular wooden blocks mounted on handles. As in other studies on effortful or dynamic touch (see Chapter 8), the participant sat in a chair and put their right forearm and hand through a curtain and onto a support surface. An experimenter placed the object into the participant's hand so that they were holding it firmly at the very bottom of the handle. The participant wielded the object with movements of their wrist and tried to perceive either the length or the width of the block (see Figure 12.8, *left*).

Participants completed five sets of trials. One group of participants attempted to perceive the *length* of each block in the first four sets of trials—with feedback provided on each trial in the second and third sets. Then they attempted to perceive the *width* of each block in the fifth set of trials—with no feedback. The other group of participants did the opposite. They attempted to perceive the *width* of each block in the first four sets of trials—with feedback provided on each trial in the second and third sets. Then they attempted to perceive the *length* of each block in the fifth set of trials—with no feedback. The movements of the hand wielding the object were recorded with a motion capture device.

The researchers hypothesized that all participants would show changes in the *education of attention* over the first four blocks of trials—when they attempted to perceive the same property again and again, with feedback. Specifically, participants would show relatively subtle shifts in *how* they were using particular components of the inertia tensor (*I*, see Chapter 8) to perceive that particular property.

They also hypothesized that participants would show changes in the *education of intention* in the fifth block of trials—when they intended to perceive the new property, without feedback. That is, participants would show relatively dramatic shifts in *which components* of *I* they were using to perceive the new property. And they hypothesized that these changes would be accompanied by changes in *how exploratory wielding movements* were used to detect information about the new property.

The results more or less supported all of these hypotheses. In the first four blocks of trials, participants made relatively subtle shifts in *how* they were using components of *I* to perceive length or width. Participants who were attempting to perceive *length* made incremental shifts toward using I_{xx}, which describes the resistance to rotating the object toward and away from

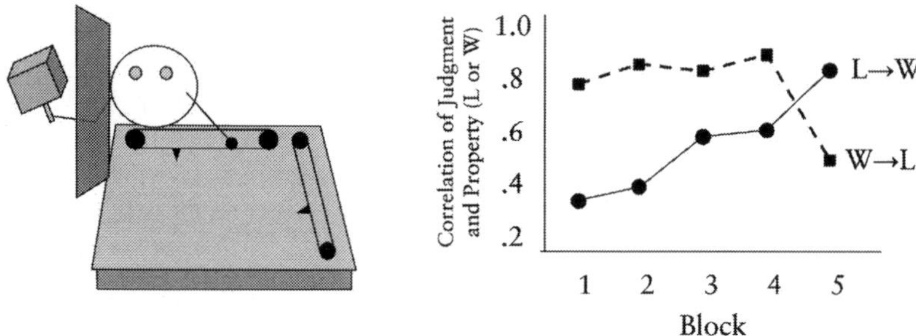

Figure 12.8 The wielding task used by Arzamarski et al. (2010) (*left*). When participants attempted to perceive a given property (either height or width of the block) and were provided with feedback, they showed relatively subtle shifts in how they were using the informative component of *I* (see Chapter 8). When participants then attempted to perceive *the other property* and were not provided with feedback, they showed relatively dramatic shifts in which component of *I* they were using.

the ground—like shaking someone's hand (see Chapter 8). For these participants, reports of perceived length became increasingly correlated with I_{xx} over the first four blocks of trials. Participants who were attempting to perceive *width* made incremental shifts toward using I_{zz}, which describes the resistance to twisting the object—like turning a doorknob (see Chapter 8). For these participants, reports of perceived length became increasingly correlated with I_{zz} over the first four blocks of trials (see Figure 12.8, *right*; see also Chapter 8, Figure 8.2 and 8.6). Then, in the fifth block of trials, when participants intended to perceive a different property, they more or less jumped from one component of I to the other. Participants who had been moving closer and closer to I_{xx} when perceiving length suddenly shifted to using I_{zz} to perceive width and vice versa (see Figure 12.8, *right*). And these changes in intention were accompanied by changes in *how* participants wielded the objects to reveal information about the intended property (Arzamarski et al., 2010).

Calibration

The education of intention and the education of attention often—but not always—result in changes in *how an animal uses* a given stimulation pattern to perceive a given affordance. But detecting the *appropriate stimulation pattern*—and specifically the appropriate *component* of that stimulation pattern—is one thing. Using that component properly is another. Learning *how to use* the information about a given affordance to appropriately perceive a given property or perform a given behavior is called *calibration* (see Jacobs & Michaels, 2007). In other words, calibration is about the mapping between (1) the information about a given property and (2) perceiving and acting.

Many studies have shown that perception of a given property becomes increasingly calibrated to that property—more and more closely matches that property—with practice, especially when that practice includes feedback. For example, in the study described previously, perceived length more closely matched actual length after participants were provided with feedback (see Figure 12.8, *right*). To some extent, this is not terribly surprising. What is perhaps more surprising are the circumstances under which calibration transfers—and does not transfer—from one context to another. These circumstances may inform what it is exactly that participants are learning when calibration occurs.

For example, in a study on calibration in visual perception, participants wore a virtual reality headset and walked toward a (virtual) target that appeared at some (virtual) distance in front of them (Bruggeman & Warren, 2010; see Bruggeman et al., 2007). Except as they walked straight toward the target, it looked to them—through the magic of VR—like they were drifting off at a slight angle from the target—say, off to their right. It was enough of a (virtual) drift that, fairly quickly, they made a correction in their walking path—by walking a little bit in the other direction, say, to the left—but not enough that they noticed that they were doing this. In other words, they were becoming *calibrated* to a new relationship between optic flow direction and walking direction.

And now comes the cool part. The participants were again asked to walk toward the target, but this time the virtual drift was turned off. This time, they initially walked at a slight angle *in the other direction*—say, to the left—and then had to make a correction by walking a little bit in the other direction—to the right. Makes sense, right? They had learned that they needed to walk slightly to the left to go straight. But now, with the virtual drift turned off, they were off target because this caused them to drift to the left of the target.

Now for the *even cooler* part. The participants were then asked to *throw a ball* and *kick a ball* toward the (virtual) target. If they had become calibrated to some general fact about the (virtual) world (e.g., straight = slightly to the left), then they would throw and kick the ball slightly to the left as well. But they did not. What they learned about walking *did not transfer to* throwing or kicking. Why? Because what they had become calibrated to was not a fact about the world *but a specific relationship between optic flow direction and walking*. Walking to a target requires becoming calibrated to this relationship. Throwing or kicking a target requires becoming calibrated to a different relationship between optic flow patterns and outcomes.[3]

Remembering

In the traditional approach, perception begins when an ambiguous energy pattern stimulates sense organs and ends with an unconscious inference about what the source of the stimulation is. The upshot is that perception only occurs—and can only occur—when the energy pattern stimulates sense organs. When this stimulation stops, contact with this particular part of the world no longer occurs by perceiving. Instead, such contact can only occur by remembering, which, as discussed previously, necessarily involves the storing and accessing of mental representations.

However, in the ecological approach, the energy patterns of relevance to perception are not ambiguous, and more to the point, perception does not begin with the stimulation of sense organs and does not end with any kind of inference. In fact, it does not begin or end *at all*. Instead, perceiving is a continuous process of detecting information about the relationship between animal and environment. And this process does not—and cannot—happen instantaneously. It can only occur as an animal *engages in activities*—in particular, looking, listening, feeling, smelling, and tasting. These activities unfolding over time reveal information about affordances. For example, patterns in the optic array that inform affordances of surfaces (e.g., τ) can only be detected only as the animal or an object moves. And patterns in the inertial array that provide information about the affordances of parts of the body or objects attached to the body (e.g., I) can only be detected when the animal moves that body part.

The point is that these activities, and hence perceiving, necessarily *occur over time*. Consequently, there is no sharp dividing line when perceiving stops and other processes—like remembering—begin. When in the process of taking a walk, does *seeing* stop and *remembering* what you have seen begin? You might think that it is in the moment that you pass by a particular object such that it is no longer in your field of view. However, from the ecological approach, occlusion at the edges of the field of view is *part of the process of seeing*—it provides information about where and how you are moving and where and how you *have been* moving (see Chapter 6).

Consequently, from the ecological perspective, there really is no sharp distinction between perceiving and remembering. Instead, perceiving is an ongoing process of detecting information that results in awareness of affordances. And remembering is merely the persistence of this awareness over time (Wagman et al., 2013; Wagman, Thomas, & McBride, 2018). In other words, rather than being a process that is completely separate from perceiving and acting, remembering is *continuous with* perceiving and acting (see Figure 12.1, *bottom right*).

Remembering Affordances

Researchers (Wagman et al., 2013) investigated the continuity of perceiving and remembering in the context of perceiving and remembering affordances for reaching in tasks much like the one that Fred faced in Chapter 11. To remind you, he was deciding whether or not to use a step stool to help him reach the fancy salad bowls on the very top shelf of the kitchen cupboard. The step stool was not present—it was in the spooky part of the basement with the spiders—but Fred was still aware of how much it would increase his maximum reaching height. In other words, he was faced with the task of remembering how the step stool would change affordances for reaching. This is exactly the kind of task that these researchers were interested in.

In this study, participants viewed both a stick and a step stool from across the laboratory (the stick was slightly taller than the step stool—remember that for later) and were asked to name three possible uses for each object. Why would the researchers want them to do this? The idea was for the participants to become *familiar with* each object without necessarily knowing that they were going to need to remember anything particular about either object later on. *Sneaky!* Then both objects were removed from view. The participants were then asked how high they would be able to reach (1) if they were to reach with the stick and (2) if they were to reach while standing on the step stool. In other words, they were asked to *remember affordances* for reaching with each object. Then both the stick and the step stool were brought back into view, and the participants were asked the same questions. That is, they were asked to *perceive affordances* for reaching with each object.

The researchers then compared remembered affordances for reaching with each object with the perceived affordances for reaching with each object. The results showed that participants both perceived and remembered that they would be able to reach higher with the stick than with the step stool—because the stick was longer than the step stool.

Both perceived and remembered affordances for reaching with a particular object reflected how that object would change the person's reaching ability. Remembered affordances scaled to action capabilities *in the same way* as perceived affordances. In other words, *both perceived and remembered affordances were action-scaled!* These results, together with the results of studies along similar lines (Boschker, Bakker, & Michaels, 2002; Thomas & Riley, 2015; Wagman et al., 2018), suggest that remembering is a process that is continuous with perceiving and, more generally, that cognizing is *continuous with* perceiving and acting (see Figure 12.1, *bottom right*).

Notes

1. A Möbius strip is one-sided continuous surface with no boundaries. You can make one by taking a strip of paper, twisting it halfway and then connecting the ends. If you trace a line all the way around it, you will return to where you started after covering both sides without ever crossing an edge.
2. Word naming is widely used to investigate thinking because it is assumed to require a process of mapping one mental representation (spelling) onto another (pronunciation) (see Chapter 7).
3. Before virtual reality technology was widely available, similar experiments were conducted in which participants walked on a treadmill that was being towed by a tractor (Rieser, Pick, Ashmead, & Garing, 1995). When the tractor (and treadmill) stopped, participants were asked to walk to a target or turn in place.

13 Applications of Ecological Psychology

In the first 12 chapters of this book, we have presented the motivation for and a description of the ecological approach to perceiving, acting, and cognizing. We hope that this has made clear that (we think that) the ecological approach is the best way to understand perceiving, acting, and cognizing—in part because the ecological approach does not lead to unsolvable theoretical problems (see Chapters 1–4). But avoiding *theoretical problems* is one thing. Avoiding or solving *real-world problems* is another. Can the ecological approach be used to do this? If not, its value as a general theory of perceiving, acting, and cognizing would surely come into question. After all, a theory is only as good as the practical problems it can help to solve!

In other words, it must be possible to bring the ecological approach out of the laboratory and into people's homes, workplaces, schools, and everywhere else people go. It must be possible to use the ecological approach to make people's lives easier, safer, and (maybe even) more enjoyable. It must be possible to use the ecological approach to better understand how and why perceiving, acting, and cognizing abilities differ for people with certain disabilities or mental health conditions. And it must also be possible to use the ecological approach to help prevent or rehabilitate injuries or movement disorders.

Given its focus on explaining the successful performance of everyday behavior, the ecological approach was developed with such real-world problems in mind (e.g., landing an airplane on a runway; see Gibson, 1979/2015; Reed, 1988). And this focus has been implicit (if not explicit) in the research conducted by ecological psychologists in the subsequent decades. In this chapter, we focus on the explicit application of the ecological approach to understanding and solving real-world problems. These problems range from the mundane (using doorknobs, sitting less, driving safely) to the profound (performing surgery, understanding autism spectrum disorder, using prosthetic limbs).

We will argue that the lawfulness underlying the processes of perceiving, acting, and cognizing guarantee that the same explanations apply when those processes occur in a simplified laboratory setting and when they occur in a complex real-world setting. In other words, the fact that the ecological approach provides a law-based theoretical framework for understanding perceiving, acting, and cognizing means that it provides a law-based theoretical framework for avoiding or solving real-world perceiving, acting, and cognizing problems as well (Vaz et al., 2017; Flach & Voorhorst, 2019; Pagano, Day, & Hartman, 2021).

Traditional Approaches to Solving Real-World Problems

As you might expect, traditional approaches to solving perception, action, and cognition problems in the real world are firmly rooted in traditional approaches to understanding perception, action, and cognition in general (see Chapters 1–2). To review, in such approaches, the sense organs are sensitive to basic physical and geometric variables (e.g., light described as photons traveling in a straight line from a light source to the retina). But—and it's a *big* but—these

DOI: 10.4324/9781003145691-15

variables are ambiguously related to environmental properties. So perceiving anything in the real world requires processing or fixing the mental representations that (1) form the basis of perceptual experience *and* (2) provide the raw material for the mental acts of cognition. In particular, thinking, learning, and remembering require—respectively—possessing and manipulating representations, modifying or enriching representations, and storing and accessing representations. Finally, performing behaviors in the real world requires quickly issuing motor commands or programs to the various components of the movement system.

Consequently, using the traditional approach to make people's lives easier, safer, and maybe even more enjoyable essentially requires changing how people create, manipulate, distribute, and use mental representations (e.g., Evans, 2017; Norman, 2013). Let's consider a specific real-world problem. Let's say that you are a traffic engineer. In your town, there is a curvy section of road that is particularly dangerous because drivers don't slow down (enough) before entering the curve. How do you solve this real-world perception, action, and cognition problem and get drivers to slow down?

If your approach to this real-world problem is based on a traditional approach to perception, action, and cognition, then your solution would most likely include providing the driver with stimulation in the form of lights, words, or symbols that can, after sufficient processing and manipulating, generate the conscious thought: *I ought to slow down now*. This thought can then be used by the driver's brain to generate the motor commands required to step on the brake. Maybe a sign that flashes the driver's current speed along with the speed limit will do the trick? Or maybe a bright yellow sign with a curvy black arrow? Or maybe a *different* yellow sign that simply says "Dangerous Curve Ahead"? Or one that says "Slow"? Maybe *all of them*? The point is that each of these solutions serves to generate a mental representation of some kind serving as *instructions* for what the driver should do and that hopefully encourages them to do it (see Figure 13.1).

Figure 13.1 From a traditional (representation-based) perspective, solving real-world problems requires providing instructions in the form of words, numbers, or symbols.

Ecological Approaches to Solving Real-World Problems

As you might expect, the ecological approach to solving perceiving, acting, and cognizing problems in the real world is quite different (Flach & Voorhorst, 2019; Pagano et al., 2021; Vicente, 2004). In the ecological approach, perceiving, acting, and cognizing are ongoing *relationships* between an animal and the environment that require *detecting and exploiting* lawfully structured energy patterns that provide information about affordances. So then, how would you solve the real-world traffic problem described previously if your approach is based on the ecological perspective?

In short, you would want to provide the driver with *information about affordances*. Specifically, you would want to provide them with information about how they are moving, where they are moving, and when they will get there. Most especially, you would want to provide information about their current movement speed that *compels them* to slow down without any conscious thought on their part whatsoever.

In Chapter 6, we introduced the concept of global optic flow. The rate of global optic flow is information about movement speed. The faster the global rate of optic flow, the faster the perceived movement speed. So if you want drivers to slow down, then one way to do it is to *manipulate the rate of global optic flow* so that drivers perceive that they are accelerating, even though their actual speed is not changing.

One way to do this is to paint lines across the road that become more and more frequent as the driver approaches the curve (see Figure 13.2). If the driver maintains their current speed, the rate of global optic flow will *increase*, leading them to perceive that they are somehow accelerating without intending to do so. Consequently, they will be very likely to slow down.[1] No representations. Just lawfully structured energy patterns. And most importantly, safer driving.

This is exactly what the city of Chicago did to get drivers to slow down on a particularly dangerous curvy stretch of Lake Shore Drive in 2006 (Jancer, 2018; Thaler & Sunstein, 2006). And it worked! Traffic engineers found a 36% drop in crashes at this curve in the first six months after the lines were painted.

Figure 13.2 From an ecological perspective, solving real-world problems requires providing information about affordances. Here, the spacing of the lines increases the rate of global optic flow as drivers approach the curve, compelling them to slow down.

Designing Affordances and Generating Information About Affordances

Ever since Fred and Claudia moved his jousting lances (in Chapter 11), Fred's shoulder has been hurting him. Not bad enough that he can't joust, mind you. Just bad enough that he wants to have it checked out by his orthopedist, Dr. Chris. He drives over to the new medical center building where Dr. Chris's office is located. As he approaches the front door, he notices the door handle. It looks *exactly* like it should be grasped and pulled (see Figure 13.3). What a relief—the front door on the old medical office building was so confusing. It looked like a *push*, but it was really a *pull*—or was it the other way around? Either way, he would always do the wrong one on the way in—and then do the wrong one *again* on the way out.[2] How frustrating! It was so bad they even had to put up a sign, one on each side of the door. And even then, the sign only helped *a little*. Life is so much easier when affordances—of door handles and everything else—are obvious!

As Fred enters the waiting room, he sees that it has no chairs—*none at all*. This isn't so bad for Fred, actually. He has a hard time fitting into chairs that are not specifically designed for spherical bodies. Instead, Dr. Chris's waiting room has weird furniture consisting only of angled support surfaces—in most cases, the larger angled support surfaces have smaller angled support surfaces attached to them. Weird.

Fred has never seen this type of furniture before, but he *is immediately aware* that the larger angled surfaces are for leaning against, and the smaller attached angled surfaces are for holding

Figure 13.3 Objects that are designed with affordances in mind (e.g., a door handle that clearly affords either pushing or pulling but not both) are likely to be easy, safe, and even enjoyable to use.

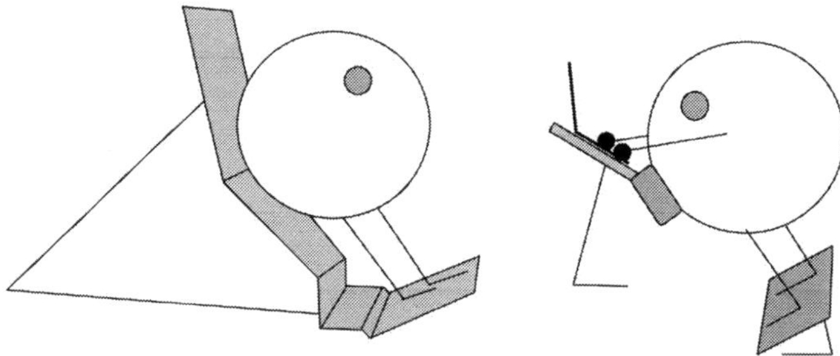

Figure 13.4 The furniture in Dr. Chris's waiting room is designed to afford supported standing rather than sitting (based on the work of Rietveld, 2016).

reading material, laptops, or tablets (see Figure 13.4). So he leans in and leans on. After a while, he realizes that his legs are *doing work* and are getting a little tired. So he switches to a slightly different angled support surface and leans on it instead. Just then, he is called in to see Dr. Chris.

Dr. Chris proceeds to examine Fred's shoulder. Dr. Chris determines that Fred has merely *strained* his shoulder and will just need to rest it for a few weeks. He is especially relieved that he does not need to have surgery. Fred wonders, though, how in the world anyone could perform surgery in such a compact space like the shoulder joint without disassembling and reassembling the whole thing. Dr. Chris explains that many shoulder surgeries are performed by inserting a thin fiber-optic camera and specialized surgical tools through one or more very small incisions—called arthroscopic surgery. The surgeons can *see* how they are using the tools to manipulate bodily tissue tools by watching the video screen, but they can also *feel* how they are doing this as well.

Given the very small incisions, procedures like this greatly reduce the risk of infection to the patient and decrease recovery time but can *increase* the risk of accidentally tearing healthy tissue if the surgeons stretch or push on it too much too quickly. Dr. Chris reassures Fred that the surgeons in this particular medical group are very skilled in performing these procedures. They even hone their skills by practicing on a state-of-the-art surgical simulator that makes it *feel as if* they are actually pressing on bodily tissue with surgical tools. This helps the surgeons learn how much they can press on the tissue without tearing it. Fred is even more fascinated. He wonders how such a device might work. He wants to hear more about it during his follow-up appointment in a few weeks.

As Fred is gathering his belongings, Dr. Chris tells him about a patient who came in earlier that day. Fred is luckier than this particular patient—a middle-aged woman who was walking down an unfamiliar curved staircase. The entire staircase was carpeted, except for the very bottom step—which was *exactly* the same color and texture of the hardwood as the floor itself. It was not clear at all that there was a drop-off between the last step and the floor. *Uh-oh.* Fred is able to guess what happened next. The woman thought that she was stepping on the *floor* when she was actually stepping on the *bottom step* of the staircase—a so-called "bottom of flight" illusion (Johnson, 2012). Her foot slid off the bottom step and impacted the floor, resulting in an injury called a Lisfranc fracture—one requiring surgery. Life can be frustrating or even dangerous when affordances—of steps and everything else—are ambiguous or hidden.

As Fred leaves Dr. Chris's office, he reaches the exit door of the medical building. Fred wonders if the woman's accident could have been prevented if the stairs were more like the door. Maybe the stairs could be designed so that it was perfectly clear which behaviors were possible and safe to perform and which were not—maybe a difference in surface texture between the step and the floor (see Chapter 6). Fred thinks about this a little more, then pushes on the door, leaves the building, and goes on with the rest of his day.

Designing With Affordances in Mind

As you might expect, one way to bring the ecological approach out of the laboratory and into people's homes, workplaces, and schools is through the concept of affordances. People interact with dozens of different objects (e.g., coffee mugs, stairs, doors, cell phones) within dozens of different

Figure 13.5 Using objects or products that are not designed with affordances in mind (e.g., a surface that does not clearly afford stepping down from, falling off, or slipping on) can be difficult, frustrating, and even dangerous. Reprinted from *Work, 41*, Stair Safety. Bottom Flight Illusion, Copyright (2012), with permission from IOS Press. The publication is available from IOS Press through http://dx.doi.org/10.3233/WOR-2012-0607-3358.

spaces and places (e.g., kitchens, classrooms, offices, grocery stores, waiting rooms) throughout the course of their day. Making those interactions easier, safer, and perhaps more enjoyable requires that those objects, spaces, and places are designed with affordances in mind (Zaff, 1995).

As we have discussed in Chapter 5, in the ecological approach, affordances are the primary content of perceptual experience. Moreover, perceiving an affordance does not require independently perceiving the properties of the animal or the environment that comprise that affordance. Affordances are perceived *in and of themselves*. And if affordances can be perceived, then they can be *designed*. If it is possible for something to *look* sit-on-able, then it ought to be possible to *design something* so that it looks sit-on-able. Conversely, it ought to be possible to design something so that it *does not* look sit-on-able.

In other words, objects, places, and spaces can be designed so that certain behaviors are allowed or even encouraged and other behaviors are discouraged or even disallowed entirely (Rietveld & Kiverstein, 2014; Vicente, 2004). At a minimum, designing with affordances in mind can make interactions with objects, places, and spaces smoother and less frustrating—think about Fred's experience with the doors on the medical office building. Perhaps more importantly, designing with affordances in mind can make situations less dangerous—think about the unfortunate woman's fall on the stairs or the speeding drivers on Lake Shore Drive in Chicago.

Encouraging Healthier Behavior—the End of Sitting?

You may (or may not) be surprised to hear that the strange, angled surfaces that Fred saw and leaned on in Dr. Chris's waiting room and office actually exist. They were developed and built by Dutch philosopher Erik Rietveld and his colleagues at the Rietveld Architecture-Art-Affordances studio (Rietveld, 2016). But *why*? Rietveld and his colleagues were trying to solve a real-world problem by designing with affordances in mind.

The problem is sitting. People sit too much. And sitting too much is unhealthy (e.g., Biswas et al., 2015). Both people and designers seem to know this. This is one of the reasons that both wearable fitness trackers (that often remind the wearer to move) and standing desks are popular. But if people know that sitting too much is unhealthy, why do they still sit so much? Rietveld and his colleagues argue that people sit so much because the places where people go—schools, offices, cars, theaters, waiting rooms—*are designed to afford sitting*. Not only this but the *activities* that occur in each of these places are *structured around sitting* (Rietveld, 2016). You sit in the context of learning, working, driving, watching, and waiting. It would be weird not to, right?

He and his colleagues reasoned that encouraging people to sit less in the context of these activities requires designing entirely new affordances in these contexts. What if these spaces and places were designed to encourage a healthier behavior—*supported standing*—instead of sitting? They chose supported standing because it is comfortable, unlike using a standing desk, but not too comfortable, unlike sitting on a sofa. It encourages changing positions and locations every so often, which encourages people to move without being pestered to do so by a wearable fitness tracker.

They started with reimagining an office space without chairs or desks. They spent quite a bit of time tinkering with different combinations of angled surfaces to find ones that fit best and felt best within the context of the activities people engage in when in an office. Some combinations of surfaces allowed for the support of a laptop, a book, or a cup of coffee. Others did not. Some allowed for leaning; others, for standing. In other words, they studied the fit between the person and the environment when embedded in this context.

Based on this, they developed a large-scale (13.5 m × 21.9 m) art installation called *The End of Sitting*—a reimagined office space consisting of a *landscape of affordances* for working from different supported standing positions (Rietveld, 2016; Rietveld & Kiverstein, 2014). The landscape looks quite a lot like a wide rock formation consisting of surfaces and crevices of

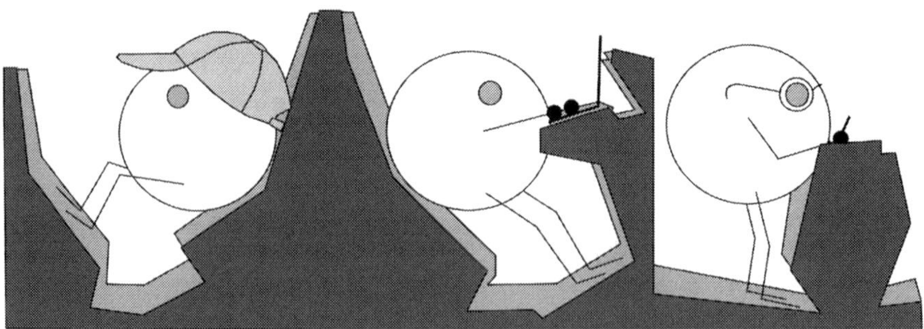

Figure 13.6 In *The End of Sitting*, surfaces and crevices of different sizes and shapes afford working from various supported standing postures. Participants using such a space to work tend to sit less (or not at all) and tend to move more.

different heights, widths, and angles relative to each other (see Figure 13.6). The positioning of the surfaces and the crevices affords many different behaviors—standing, leaning, squatting, lying, and even spanning across a crevice.

The End of Sitting is provocative, interesting, and engrossing. In other words, it is very effective as a work of art. But it is also effective as an alternative workspace? Does it afford working productively without sitting? Does it encourage changing working postures? Withagen and Caljouw (2016) investigated these questions. In their study, groups of participants worked together on preparing two different presentations. For one presentation, they worked in a traditional office with tables and chairs, and for the other, they worked in *The End of Sitting* workspace. In each location, they were given 35–40 minutes to work on the presentation.

The researchers found no differences in how the participants divided their time across the two main components of the task in each location. In both locations, they spent about 60% of their time reading and about 40% of their time on computer work. However, they found large differences in *the postures from which* the participants chose to complete these tasks. In the traditional office, *all but one* of the participants spent 100% of the time working while sitting in a chair. And this one participant spent less than two minutes in a non-sitting posture!

Alternatively, in *The End of Sitting* workspace, participants spent approximately 60% of the time standing, approximately 20% of the time leaning, and the remaining 20% of the time squatting or lying down. Not only did they work from postures other than sitting, but they also *switched from one posture to another* while working. Forty-four percent of participants worked in *two* different postures, 17% worked in *three* different postures, and 22% worked in *four* different postures! In total, *83% of participants worked from more than one posture.* And participants chose the height of their work surface based on their own standing height—the taller the person, the taller the chosen work surface. Body-scaled office work!

Finally, there was no difference in how well participants felt that they could concentrate in each space or in how satisfied they were with the presentations completed in each workspace. However, they reported that working in *The End of Sitting* workspace better supported their overall well-being than working in the traditional office space. And it made them feel more energized—even though it made their legs feel more tired!

Ecological Interface Design

Fred comes home from his appointment with Dr. Chris and decides to spend the afternoon playing with his remote-control drone—another great gift from Uncle Jimmy! There is a camera on the drone and a small monitor on the remote control so he can control the drone by watching the view from the camera on the monitor. This is especially handy if the drone is out of view (which happens often). As he has gotten better at flying it, he has found that his awareness has shifted from what his fingers and thumbs are doing and what he is seeing on the monitor to what the *drone itself* is doing. It occurs to him that this probably is something like what the surgeons in Dr. Chris's medical group experience once they have become well practiced at performing arthroscopic surgery.

In most everyday settings, information about affordances is available in the lawfully structured energy encountered at a point of observation. But in the case of flying a drone that is out of view or performing arthroscopic surgery, information about affordances is available only by means of an *interface*—in these cases, artificially designed visual displays and hand-held devices. It might seem that direct perception would be impossible under such circumstances. After all, the person's ability to perceive and act *is mediated by* an artificially designed device. But not so fast!

Whether perception is direct has nothing to do with whether perception is mediated by something *physical*—such as a tool or a display. Rather, it has to do with whether the perception is mediated by something *mental*, like a representation or an inference. Perception is direct if the person can detect and exploit the lawfully structured stimulation patterns that provide information about the fit between animal and environment. If the interface supports or possibly even enhances this ability, perception is (still) direct. Designing displays or devices that support direct perception is the focus of ecological interface design (EID) (Vicente & Rasmussen, 1990).

EID has been applied in the context of complex work environments in which people need to monitor and control many different components of a system in real time—such as in operating rooms, power plants, and airplane cockpits. EID is best understood in contrast to a more traditional approach to interface design in which the strategy is to (1) provide the user with lots (and lots) of data and (2) train that user on how to appropriately create, manipulate, distribute, and use mental representations so that they can make the right decisions at the right times. Memorize! Calculate! Problem-solve! Don't crash! Don't tear healthy tissue!

For example, a traditionally designed interface in an airplane cockpit might have lots of different dials and gauges that provide the pilots with data about heading, orientation (yaw, pitch, and roll), altitude, distance to a target, ground speed, wind speed, wind direction, and so on (see Figure 13.7). It would be up to the pilots to use this information to determine how to

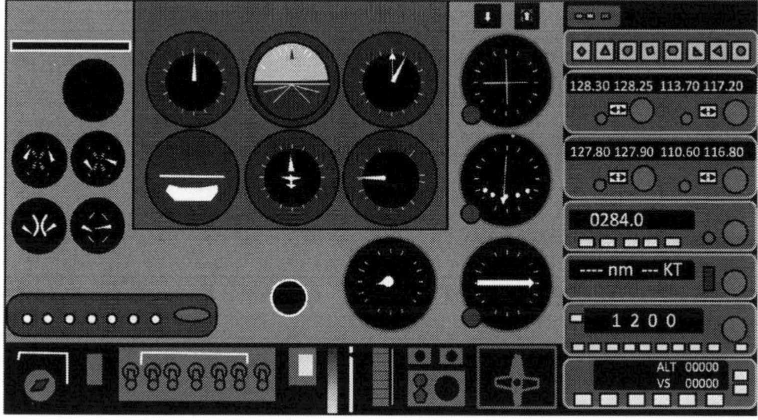

Figure 13.7 A traditionally designed interface such as in an airplane cockpit provides the user with lots of data and requires skill in thinking, remembering, and calculating.

manipulate the yoke, throttle, and flaps (among other components) to control the airplane in flight or during a landing. The problem is that is there is . . . just . . . so . . . much . . . data. It is difficult to know what matters and what doesn't, and it is far too easy to make a *big* mistake.[3]

In EID, however, the interface is designed so that it displays only those meaningful higher-order *relationships* among the data points that are relevant to performing a particular task. Metaphorically speaking, this kind of interface does the job of the polar planimeter discussed in Chapter 3 (see Figure 3.8). Rather than displaying a large number of lower-order variables, it displays a small number of higher-order variables—invariants—that can much more easily be used to perform the tasks at hand.

Moreover, the higher-order variables of relevance are presented not in the form of data but instead in the form of an *interactive and dynamic graphical display* that updates in real time as the person performs the task. In other words, the interface provides artificial but still lawful information about whether, when, and how to perform the task. Using an interface like this is more like playing a video game than it is like doing a complex math problem.

For example, rather than displaying data about heading, orientation, altitude, distance to runway, ground speed, wind speed, and wind direction, an interface in an airplane cockpit designed using EID might display invariants like optic flow or time to contact (see Figure 13.8; Bennett & Flach, 2011; for other examples of EID, see Vicente, 2004; Flach & Voorhorst, 2019). Moreover, manipulating the yoke, throttle, and flaps (among other components) will update the display in real time, providing information about whether, when, and how to control the airplane in flight or during a landing. For example, the interface depicted in Figure 13.8 uses an optic flow analogy. In this display, the depression flow lines and the splay flow lines are texture elements on a simulated ground surface. Keeping the plane moving at a constant speed at a constant altitude means manipulating the controls so as to (1) keep the depression flow lines flowing toward the pilot at a constant rate and (2) prevent the splay lines from expanding (or spreading out) (see Figure 13.8; Bennett & Flach, 2011).

As you might expect, learning to use an interface designed using EID still takes training, but of a very different kind than when using a traditional interface. Instead of focusing on improving the ability to form, modify, or use mental representations, training focuses on becoming attuned to (1) which patterns—which higher-order variables—provide information about whether, when, and how to perform the required behaviors and (2) how to explore to uncover these patterns. In short, the training focuses on the *education of intention* and the *education of attention* (see Chapter 9). Ideally, when the user is well practiced in using the interface, they will feel like Fred did when flying his drone. That is, their awareness will be shifted away

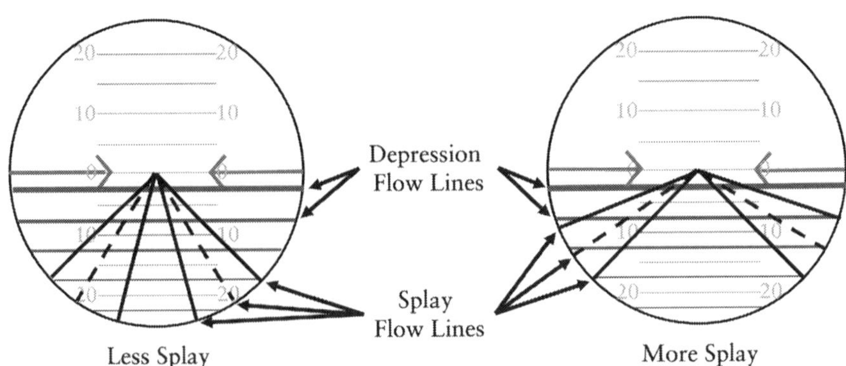

Figure 13.8 An ecologically designed interface (e.g., in an airplane cockpit) provides the user with information about affordances and requires skill in detecting and exploiting such information.

from (how exactly they are controlling) what is being displayed on the monitor and toward the task being performed.

EID Applied to Laparoscopic[4] Surgery

Fred is just about finished flying his drone for the day, and he is trying to bring it in for a safe landing. As he does so, Fred thinks back to the surgical simulator that Dr. Chris mentioned. Dr. Chris said that the simulator makes it feel as if the user is pressing on internal bodily tissue with surgical tools and that this helps them learn how much they can press on such tissue without tearing it.

As he lands the drone, Fred can see a patch of ground on the monitor of the remote control. As he lowers the drone, the patch appears to expand slowly at first and then more and more quickly just before the drone touches down. As Fred has practiced landing the drone, he has learned to control the speed of the descent based on how quickly this patch ground appears to expand. If it expands too quickly, he'll likely crash the drone. *Hmmm . . .* Fred wonders if what the surgeons *feel* as they press on bodily tissue is in any way like what he just *saw* as he landed the drone.

When Fred goes back to see Dr. Chris for his follow-up appointment, he is very excited to hear more about the surgical simulator. Dr. Chris goes one step further and invites Fred *to try it out.* It looks like a large, curved pair of scissors that passes through a surface of some kind and attaches to a bunch of mechanical and electronic parts (see Figure 13.9). Dr. Chris instructs Fred to push down on the grip like he is pressing the tool into someone's body. Fred pushes. *The device pushes back!* He pushes a little harder. *The device pushes back a little harder!* It really does feel like he is pushing into something stretchy but not too stretchy. And something that could tear if he pushes too hard. How does it work?

In Chapter 6, we introduced a variable called τ. In the context of visual perception, it is the relative rate of expansion of the optical texture of an object. How quickly this texture expands is information about the object's time to arrival, like what Fred saw when he landed his drone. But the lawfulness underlying the perceptual process guarantees that the same—or

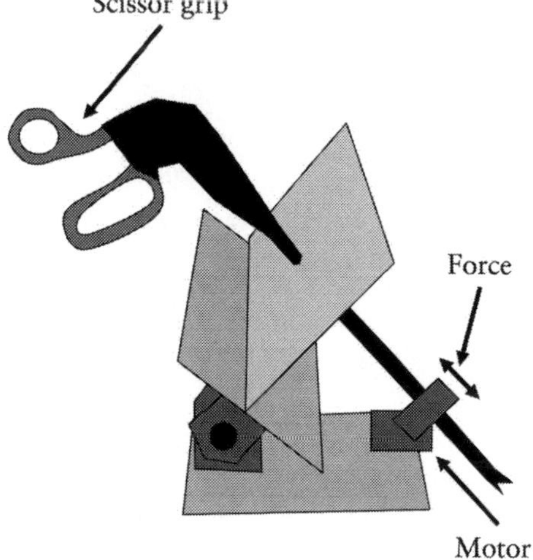

Figure 13.9 The laparoscopic surgery simulator used by Pagano and colleagues. Pushing down on the scissor grip causes the motor to push back. This provides information about how far the tool can be pushed before tearing the virtual tissue.

analogous—patterns provide information about a given affordance *regardless* of the particular energy form. The researchers took advantage of this lawfulness in designing and programming the surgical simulator.

They reasoned that while surgeons in a laparoscopic surgery task don't need to know about *time to arrival* per se, they *do* need to know about *distance to break*—how far they can push on bodily tissue until it tears. Specifically, they need to know *when to stop pushing*. When surgeons push on bodily tissue with a laparoscopic tool, the tissue resists being deformed. As they push harder, it resists more and more. So the amount of force they need to apply increases. Think about pushing into an inflated balloon. It is relatively easy to do so at first. But then as you push it more and more, it gets harder and harder because the balloon resists being pushed more and more. Then, eventually, the balloon bursts—especially if you push it too much too quickly. In both cases, how quickly the resistance increases with more and more pushing is information about the distance to break. This is a haptic τ.

The surgical simulator consists of a laparoscopic tool attached to a motor. When the tool is pushed down, the motor pushes back in a way that simulates how different kinds of artificial materials will increasingly resist being deformed and eventually tear. Importantly, different simulated materials will tear with different amounts of force, but τ will inform distance to break in each case!

The researchers investigated whether novice participants—with no surgical experience whatsoever—could perceive distance to break of various simulated tissues. The task of the participant was to push on the tool as far as possible without tearing the tissue. After only about 10–15 minutes of training with the simulator, these participants became quite good at the task—coming within just a few millimeters of the breaking point of each simulated tissue (Altenhoff et al., 2017; Hartman et al., 2016; Pagano & Day, 2019). The researchers also ran experienced laparoscopic surgeons through the same procedure. As you might expect—and hope!—the surgeons were better at the task than the novice participants. But the surgeons *also* improved after the same 10–15 minutes of training (Long et al., 2016). These results suggest that interfaces of all kinds can be designed with affordances in mind and that both novices and experts can benefit from training that focuses on the detection and exploitation of information about those affordances (see Box 4.2 and Box 8.2).

Understanding a Diversity of Perceiving-Acting-Cognizing Abilities

On his way out of the medical center building, Fred holds the door open for a little boy who has braces on his legs and is using a long cane to feel his way toward the door. Despite his obvious challenges, the boy is as cheerful as can be. Fred stops to chat with the boy and his parents. He learns that the boy's name is Deegun and that he has Loeys-Dietz syndrome—a connective tissue disorder that, among other things, affects the muscles and joints of the neck, back, and legs, as well as the muscles of the eyes. Naturally, this affects his ability to get around (and even look around). After the chat, Deegun and his family go on their way to see Dr. Chris. Fred stops to think about the challenges that Deegun faces in performing the activities of daily life and is inspired.

Not everyone has the same perceiving-acting-cognizing abilities. This should be clear, given that we dedicated an entire chapter to development (Chapter 10) and parts of another chapter to learning (Chapter 12). Still, it is worth stating explicitly. Perceiving-acting-cognizing abilities not only vary *within* a person over time; they also vary *from person to person*. Person-to-person differences can be quite subtle when we consider only those people without particular disabilities or mental health conditions. They are much less so when we consider all people—people with and without such disabilities and mental health conditions. Recently, researchers have used the principles, methods, and tools of the ecological approach to better understand the perceiving-acting-cognizing abilities of people with disabilities or mental health conditions.

To be sure, researchers have investigated a variety of differences in a variety of disabilities and conditions, including attention-deficit/hyperactivity disorder (e.g., Avelar et al., 2019; Nikolas et al., 2016), body image and eating disorders (e.g., Keizer et al., 2013), developmental coordination disorder (e.g., Wade & Kazeck, 2018), intellectual disabilities (e.g., Mauerberg-deCastro, Moraes, & Campbell, 2012), vision or hearing impairments (e.g., Burton & Cyr, 2004; Schellingerhout, Smitsman, & Cox, 2005; Schellingerhout, Bongers, Van Grinsven, Smitsman, & Van Galen, 2001), stroke and paralysis (Silva, Harrison, Kinsella-Shaw, Turvey, & Carello, 2009; Nonaka, 2013), and upper and lower limb disabilities (e.g., van Dijk, van der Sluis, van Dijk, & Bongers, 2016a, 2016b). In the next two sections, we will focus on perceiving-acting-cognizing differences in people with particular mental health conditions (i.e., depression, obsessive-compulsive disorder, and schizophrenia) and in people with autism spectrum disorder (ASD) (but see Box 13.1).

Box 13.1 Why Do Stroke Patients Collide with Obstacles?

Stroke is a potentially debilitating condition in which disruption of blood flow to parts of the brain causes varying degrees of brain damage. Strokes can result in paralysis or partial paralysis (called paresis) of upper or lower limbs on a particular side of the body. As you might expect, this can lead to difficulties in performing many of the activities of daily life, such as walking around or between obstacles. Consequently, stroke patients are at increased risk of falling or colliding with objects in their path—especially in situations where there are increased demands on balance.

A particularly challenging task, even for people who have not had a stroke, is walking through a narrow space between two obstacles (such as a doorway; see Chapter 5, Figure 10.5, and Figure 11.5). This not only requires coordinating the muscles and joints of the upper and lower legs into a stable walking gait but also rotating parts of the body, reducing body sway in some directions but not others, and maintaining the position of the center of mass with respect to a smaller base of support (Chapter 9)—all without changing walking direction.

Researchers were interested in how the performance of this task might differ among (1) healthy people (with no history of stroke or falling), (2) stroke patients who have a history of falling since suffering the stroke, and (3) stroke patients who do not have a history of falling since suffering the stroke (Muroi, Hiroi, et al., 2017). They asked these three groups of people to walk through doorways of different widths.

Predictably, they found that stroke patients with a history of falling made more accidental contact with the sides of the doorway than did healthy people—especially when passing through narrow apertures. In fact, *more than half* of stroke patients with a history of falling and *none* of the stroke patients without a history of falling made *multiple accidental contacts* with the sides of the doorway. But—and here is the key question both for understanding the phenomenon and possibly even preventing collisions or falls—*why*?

One possibility is that patients with a history of falling simply misperceived affordances for passing through the doorway and therefore attempted to pass through doorways that were just too narrow. Good guess, but no. It turned out that there were no differences in perceived *critical π values* across the three groups. In fact, the perceived *critical* π value was a ratio of doorway-width-to-shoulder-width of approximately 1.0 for each group.

Another possibility is that stroke patients with a history of falling were not adjusting their waking behavior appropriately—especially when approaching narrow doorways. *Bingo!* It turned out that when approaching narrow apertures, stroke patients both with and without a history of falling took longer to pass through the doorway and took more steps along the way than did healthy people. And stroke patients with a history of falling rotated their shoulders *less* than the other two groups did as they moved through the doorway itself.

In other words, for stroke patients with a history of falling, it wasn't an issue of misperception or an issue of taking sufficient time. Rather it was an issue of making *effective adjustments in their movements*—in particular, shoulder rotations. Ideally, studies like this can provide a starting point for interventions designed to prevent (or reduce) collisions or falls by stroke patients (see Muroi, Ohtera, et al., 2019; see "An Ecological Approach to Rehabilitation" below).

Mental Health Conditions

Mental health conditions are a wide range of disorders and illnesses that affect mood, thinking, and behavior. These conditions vary in how common they are and how severely they disrupt a person's ability to go about daily life. Granted, it may be challenging to see how such conditions could be understood at all from the ecological approach.[5] After all, the word "mental" is right there in the name. While the ecological approach does not deny that mental life exists per se, it denies that mental entities or processes mediate perception-action-cognition. Still, this has not stopped some ecologically minded researchers from applying the core concepts and tools of the ecological approach to better understand the effects of mental health conditions such as depression, obsessive-compulsive disorder, and schizophrenia.

Depression and Obsessive-Compulsive Disorder

As you might expect, perhaps the easiest way to understand mental health conditions from an ecological approach is through the lens of affordances. As a (probably unnecessary) reminder, affordances are what an animal can (or could) do in a particular situation, given the fit between action capabilities and environmental properties. Given that an animal has many action capabilities and the environment has many properties, there are *always multiple affordances available to any given animal in any given situation* (see Chapter 5). Which of these affordances are noticed or attended to, however, depends on the animal's goals in that particular situation.

The set of affordances available to a particular person in a particular situation can be depicted as a dynamic "field" of affordances, with each individual affordance depicted as a column in that field (see Figure 13.10; see de Haan et al., 2013). The "width" of the field corresponds to the number of affordances available to that person in that situation. For example, in a party setting, in which sitting alone, conversing with others, drinking, dancing, and leaving are all afforded, the field would be five affordances wide. The "depth" of the field refers to the affordances that *could become* available later if certain behaviors are performed now or in the near future. For example, in a party setting, drinking now may allow for dancing later. The height of each column corresponds to the *relevance* of that affordance to the person, given that person's goals. If a person is hungry, the column representing affordances for eating will be quite tall, for example. And the color of each column refers to the affective state (the feelings) associated with that affordance. For example, if a person *really likes* dancing, affordances for dancing may be associated with positive affect even if the person has no intention of dancing at this particular moment.

For a neurotypical person (a person without a psychological disorder), the field of affordances varies along all four dimensions (see Figures 13.10 and 13.11, *left*). The person can perceive many affordances. Some are available now, and others could become available later. Some are more relevant than others, and some are more positive than others. Moreover, the person can easily shift to perceiving a different affordance if their goal or the context changes.

For people with certain psychological disorders, however, the field of affordances may be quite different. Depression is a psychological disorder in which a person feels extreme sadness, pessimism, and hopelessness, often accompanied by changes in daily behaviors, such as eating, sleeping, and socializing (APA, n.d.). For people with depression, it may be that the field of affordances is narrower and does not vary in *any* dimension (see Figure 13.11, *middle*). The person may feel as if very few affordances are available, all are equally unattractive, and ones that are available now are no different from ones that might become available later.

Obsessive-compulsive disorder (OCD) is a psychological disorder in which a person experiences intrusive thoughts (obsessions: e.g., "there are germs everywhere"), which typically are accompanied by unwanted behaviors (compulsions: e.g., elaborate cleaning rituals). For a person with OCD, it may be that the field of affordances varies along all four

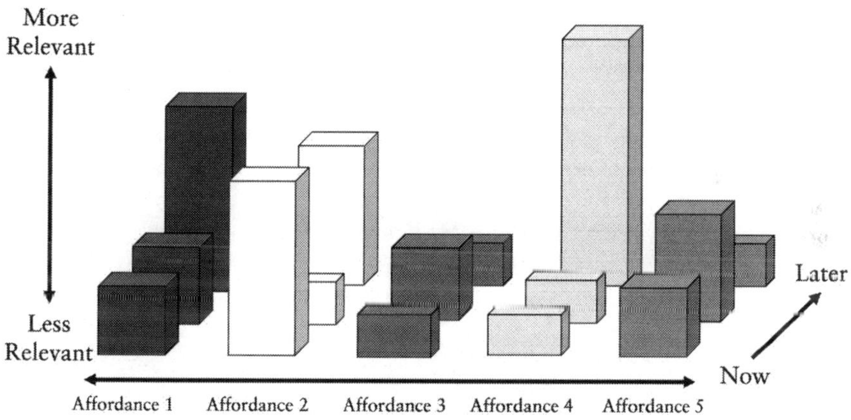

Figure 13.10 The set of affordances available to a particular person in a particular situation can be depicted as a dynamic "field" of affordances (de Haan et al., 2013).

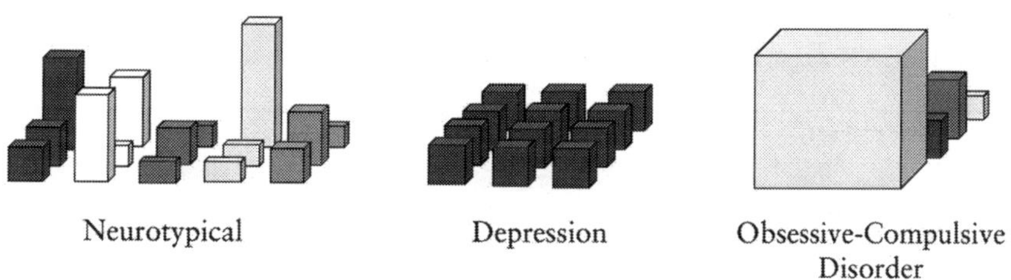

Figure 13.11 The field of affordances likely differs between a neurotypical person (*left*) and someone with depression (*middle*) or obsessive-compulsive disorder (*right*) (de Haan et al., 2013).

dimensions. However, it may also be that the affordance for performing the compulsive behavior is so relevant and so urgent that it obscures all other available affordances (see Figure 13.11, right). Other affordances *might* become available later, but *only after* the compulsive behavior is performed.

Schizophrenia

Schizophrenia is an often-debilitating psychological disorder in which people exhibit detachment from reality in some form or another (sometimes in the form of delusions or hallucinations). In some sense, schizophrenia is a disorder of the sense of self. People with schizophrenia sometimes feel as if they are "disembodied" or are a spectator of their own perceptions, thoughts, and actions (Parnas & Henriksen, 2018).

Researchers hypothesized that this distorted sense of self (this feeling of disembodiment) would impair perception of affordances because perceiving affordances means perceiving a *relationship between* the self and environmental properties (Kim & Kim, 2017). Researchers conducted several experiments in which they showed people with and without schizophrenia pictures of about two dozen common objects (e.g., a sponge, an envelope, a plastic ruler, a plush bunny doll), all of which had multiple affordances.[6]

In the first experiment, both groups of participants were shown each picture one at a time and asked—yes or no—*whether the object afforded a given behavior* (e.g., does this object afford cutting with?). In general, participants with schizophrenia took longer to respond and were less accurate than people without schizophrenia. In a follow-up experiment, the researchers repeated the procedure with two new groups of participants with and without schizophrenia. But this time, the participants were asked *whether the object had a particular physical or geometric property* (e.g., is this object pink?). So what did they find? As in the previous experiment, people with schizophrenia took longer to respond. But this time, there were *no differences in accuracy* between people with and without schizophrenia. In other words, as the researchers hypothesized, people with schizophrenia were impaired when asked to perceive affordances—which requires perceiving the self in relation to the environment—but not when asked to perceive physical or geometric properties—which requires perceiving *only* the environment.

Autism Spectrum Disorder

Autism spectrum disorder (ASD) is a complex developmental condition that, among other things, adversely affects a person's ability to successfully interact with and communicate with other people.[7] Many of the skills impaired in people with ASD are ones that seem to come naturally or intuitively to most typically developing people (e.g., making eye contact or showing empathy).

As we discussed in Chapter 11, successfully interacting and communicating with another person requires *synchronizing* or *coordinating* behavior with that person. It requires creating a *social or interpersonal synergy* (e.g., Riley et al., 2011). In some cases, these social synergies are created very much intentionally (like a rugby team working to advance the ball down the field). Other times they are created *unintentionally*—like two people walking in stride while engaged in conversation.

Researchers reasoned that people with ASD may be less able to detect and exploit information about social affordances—what they called the "rhythms of the world." They may, therefore, be less able to establish social synergies. They may be less likely to be "pulled into the natural orbit of another person's rhythm" than their typically developing peers (Marsh et al., 2013). For multiple reasons (both theoretical and practical), the researchers were specifically interested in the ability to establish *unintentional* social synergies.

Figure 13.12 Children with ASD are less likely to rock in sync with a caregiver than their typically developing peers.

In Chapter 11, we discussed a study in which people who sat next to one another in rocking chairs unintentionally coordinated their rocking behavior with each other (Richardson, Marsh, Isenhower, et al., 2007b). Researchers adapted this task for children—both with and without ASD—and a caregiver. The child and the caregiver sat next to each other in rocking chairs that were appropriately sized and weighted so that the chairs naturally rocked at the same frequency. The caregiver read the child a brief (approximately 30 s) story while rocking back and forth to a metronome that only the caregiver could hear (see Figure 13.12).

The researchers hypothesized that children with ASD would be less likely to rock in sync with the caregiver than their typically developing peers. And this is exactly what they found. Children with and without ASD spent more or less the same amount of time rocking back and forth during the story. However, children without ASD spent more of this time rocking *in phase with* (in sync with) their caregiver than children with ASD. The researchers concluded that difficulty perceiving and acting with respect to the rhythms of the world and of other people is an important prerequisite for social connection and that impairments in this ability may play a role in ASD.

An Ecological Approach to Rehabilitation

As we have discussed, people with certain disabilities or mental health conditions may struggle with at least some of the activities of daily life. In the best-case scenario, a person's ability to perform some or all of these activities can be improved through rehabilitative interventions. If we can use the ecological approach to better understand why and how these struggles occur, can we also use the ecological approach to develop more effective rehabilitation techniques? Yes. Yes, we can. Again, if we could not, the value of the ecological approach as a general theory of perceiving, acting, and cognizing would come into question.

In large part, traditional theories of rehabilitation are based on traditional theories of movement (Chapter 9). As a reminder, in these approaches, movements are a consequence of the brain issuing a sequence of commands or programs to lower-level components of the movement system (e.g., muscles). Rather than being *specific or explicit*—affecting the moment-to-moment activity of individual muscles or joints, these programs are thought to be *abstract or generalized*—affecting the sequential activity across groupings of muscles or joints. Consequently, the focus of traditional rehabilitation interventions is on helping the brain of the patient to relearn the context-independent programs that were impaired or impeded by the injury or disease. This is accomplished by the therapist leading the patient through a lengthy regimen of performing repetitive, isolated movements (see Figure 13.13, left). Anyone who has ever undergone a physical therapy regimen knows exactly what this is like.

Fred remembers when Great Aunt Blandine had a stroke, which impaired her use of her right arm. He dutifully took her to her rehabilitation sessions three days a week for four weeks. Her rehabilitation regimen mostly focused on strengthening the movements of her affected arm and avoiding so-called learned disuse. During each session, she had to repeatedly pull on a resistance band in different directions in different orientations—about 180 times over the course of the half-hour session. That's over *2,000 pulls* over the 12 sessions! And after all that, Great Aunt Blandine wasn't really convinced that it improved her ability to perform everyday activities like reaching and grasping the television remote control or her favorite coffee mug—the one with a photo of baby Fred on it.

From a traditional approach, whether the movements being practiced are relevant to a specific activity of daily life is less important than the *generality of* such movements. The idea is that if the practiced movements are *general enough*, and if they are practiced *often enough*, then learning ought to *transfer to other contexts*—including the activities of daily life. However, these traditional regimens often have only limited success in improving a patient's ability to perform these activities (Muroi, Ohtera, et al., 2019; van Dijk, van der Sluis, & Bongers, 2017). Why?

As you might expect, an ecological approach to rehabilitation practice (Vaz et al., 2017; van Dijk et al., 2017; see Goldfield, 2018) is very different and is based on many of the principles that have been discussed in previous chapters (and some that will be discussed in more detail in Chapter 14). First and foremost, whereas the traditional approach focuses on the *person* or even just particular *body parts* of that person, the ecological approach focuses on *the person-environment system*. This means that rather than emphasizing isolated *movements*, the ecological approach focuses on performing *perception-action tasks*—perceiving and behaving with respect to affordances. The goal, then, of an ecological approach to rehabilitation is not the relearning of a set of brain commands or programs but the *improvement of the person-environment fit—in particular, the person-environment fit in the context of the activities of daily life*. Hence, from this approach, whether the movements being practiced are relevant to a specific activity of daily life is critical (see Figure 13.13, right).

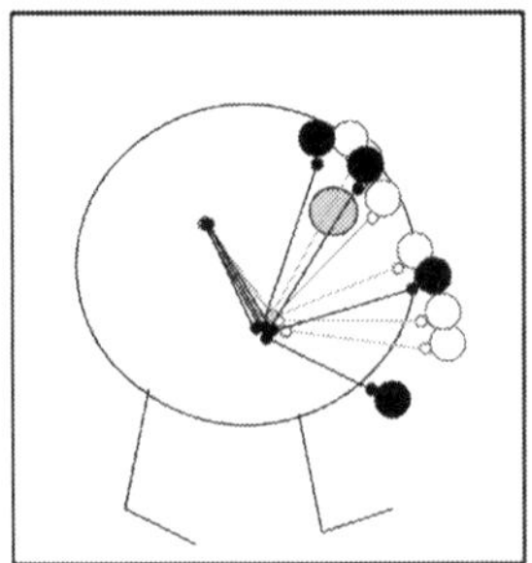

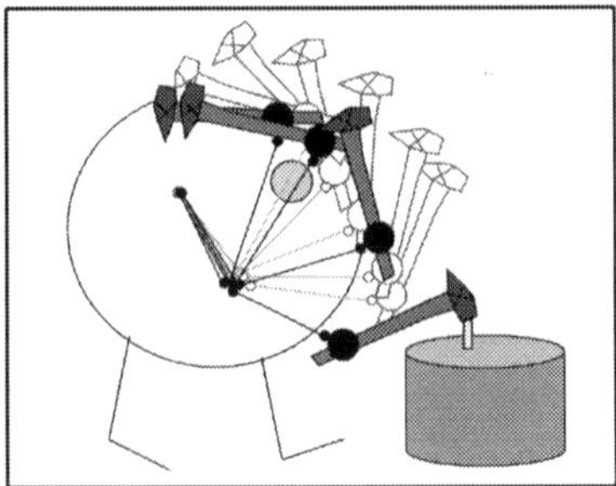

Figure 13.13 Whereas the traditional approach to rehabilitation focuses on the repetitive performance of isolated movements (*left*), the ecological approach to rehabilitation focuses on the variable performance of activities or perception-action tasks (*right*).

Second, whereas the traditional approach focuses on the isolated movements of anatomical units with prescribed roles, the ecological approach focuses on the performance of activities with *functional units* with *flexible roles* (i.e., synergies). Rather than emphasizing the *one way* in which a *movement pattern* ought to be performed, the ecological approach emphasizes the *multiple ways* in which *a movement goal* might be achieved. Ideally, practice ought to consist of performing multiple movement patterns across multiples contexts to consistently achieve a given outcome—repetition without repetition (see Chapter 9).

In Great Aunt Blandine's case, a more ecologically oriented rehabilitation regimen would have instead focused on immediately improving her abilities to perform activities of daily life. During a given rehabilitation session, she might have repeatedly reached to grasp objects of different sizes, shapes, and weights located at different distances, at different heights, and in different directions. She still would have the need to go to several sessions per week over several weeks, and she still would have performed *lots* of reaches. *But these would have been goal-directed reaches*, and the end result might have been different. Research has shown that these kinds of rehabilitation regimens—ones that focus on *activity* rather than movements—help people like Great Aunt Blandine more effectively and more efficiently perform everyday behaviors like reaching for and grasping everyday objects (Thielman, Dean, & Gentile, 2004; see van Dijk et al., 2017).

Training Prosthetic Use

Fortunately for people who have lost an arm or a hand due to injury or disease, there have been amazing advances in the technology of prosthetic arms and hands. In particular, myoelectric[8] arm or hand prostheses are powered by an electric motor but are *controlled* by subtle muscular activity at or near the amputation site. Electrodes are attached to these muscles, and the electrical signals generated by those muscles are amplified and fed into the electronic and mechanical components of the prosthesis. A user might open or close a myoelectric hand by contracting or relaxing specific muscles in their forearm or upper arm, for example. It is truly a marvel of modern engineering! Skilled users of such prostheses can perform many of the activities of daily life, such as grasping and drinking from a cup, holding heavy or delicate objects, and reading from a tablet or smartphone.

The question, of course, is how to help *new users* of such devices become *skilled users* of such devices. One approach is to start by teaching the person to control the electrical activity of the muscles at or near the amputation site *in the absence* of the prosthetic device. And one clever way to do this is to gamify the learning process by feeding the electrical signals produced by these muscles directly into the electronics of a fun video game—though probably not *Homunculus: Infinite Regress*. By playing the "myogame", the person learns to control these muscles. The hope is that any learning that occurs in this context will transfer to contexts when the person actually uses these muscles to control the myoelectric prosthetic limb in the activities of daily life.

But is this hope realistic? From an ecological approach, the worry is that the isolated muscle movements required to play the game are so different from the movements required in the context of performing the activities of daily life that there will be little, if any, transfer of learning.[9] To investigate this, researchers trained a group of able-bodied participants to play a version of a video game called *Breakout*[10] over four days using only the electrical activity of their forearm muscles (see Figure 13.14, top; van Dijk et al., 2016a). Over the course of several training sessions, their ability to play the myogame improved. However, their ability to control the grasping movements of a myoelectric prosthetic arm using the same forearm muscles did not (see Figure 13.14, *top*).

The authors proposed that to be successful as training devices, myogames must be purposely designed with *very specific perception-action tasks*—very specific person-environment

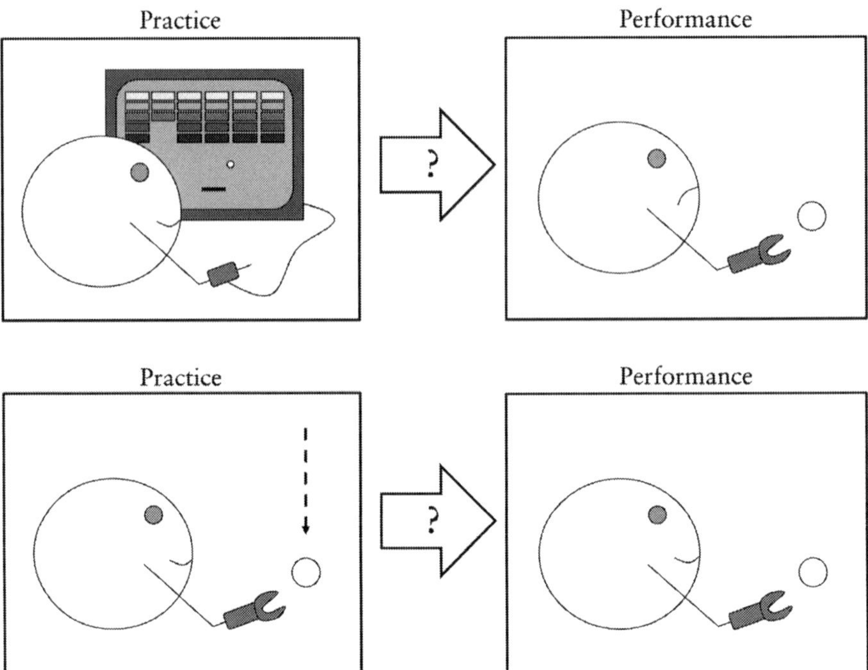

Figure 13.14 Participants trained to play a video "myogame" did not necessarily improve in their ability to control a prosthetic limb (*top*). However, people trained on an "adaptive catching" myogame did improve in their ability to control a prosthetic limb (*bottom*).

relationships—in mind. To make their point, in a later study, they trained another group of able-bodied participants to play an "adaptive catching" myogame by controlling the movement of a virtual grabber using the electrical activity of their forearm muscles (van Dijk et al., 2016b). In this game, the task was to catch virtual falling objects of different sizes, shapes, and fragilities (see Figure 13.14, bottom). Catching the object required appropriately flexing and relaxing the muscles of the forearm with respect to these three properties as the virtual object fell. Participants were given feedback in the context of the game play about the fit between grabber width and object size and about whether the fragile virtual objects would have broken.

Over the course of several training sessions, their ability to play the myogame improved. And unlike in the other study, their ability to control the grasping movements of a myoelectric prosthetic arm using the same forearm muscles *also* improved (see Figure 13.14, bottom)! This study and others like it highlight the value of the ecological approach to rehabilitation and its focus on improving the person-environment fit in the context of the activities of daily life (Vaz et al., 2017; van Dijk et al., 2017).

The lawfulness underlying the ecological approach to perceiving, acting, and cognizing makes it possible to bring this approach out of the laboratory and into people's homes, workplaces, schools, and everywhere else people go. In particular, it makes it possible to use the ecological approach (1) to make people's lives easier, safer, and perhaps more enjoyable; (2) to better understand how and why perceiving, acting, and cognizing abilities differ for people with certain disabilities or mental health conditions; and (3) to help prevent or rehabilitate injuries or movement disorders.

Notes

1 This is very much like what happens in a moving room that moves toward the perceiver (see Chapter 9). The perceiver will sway or step backward without planning to do so or thinking about it at all.
2 These kinds of ambiguously operated doors are called Norman doors after the cognitive psychologist Don Norman. If you look for them, you will start seeing them *everywhere*.
3 The challenge is analogous to the degrees of freedom problem faced by the central executive attempting to control the movements of the Fred marionette in Chapter 9.
4 An arthroscope is used to perform surgery on joints (like the shoulder or the knee). A laparoscope is used to perform surgery on organs in the abdomen (such as the stomach or the liver).
5 Though mental health conditions, like all other complex systems, have multiple interacting causes (see Chapters 4 and 14)
6 This task was adapted from one developed by Ye, Cardwell, and Mark (2009).
7 As you might expect, there are explanations of ASD rooted in the (mal)functioning of mirror neurons (see Box 11.1)
8 "Myo" is derived from the Greek "mys" which means "muscle".
9 Recall that learning does not transfer across tasks if the animal-environment relationship differs across those tasks (see Chapter 10 and Chapter 12)
10 A Ping-Pong-like game in which players slide a virtual paddle back and forth to bounce a virtual ball to destroy virtual rows of bricks.

Part 3

Zooming Out

14 Dynamical Systems

The first four chapters of this book set up the ecological perspective, and the next nine chapters expanded on how it might be applied to classic problems of psychology—mostly perceiving, acting, and cognizing (hence the title of the book!) but also other areas (such as development and social interactions) that one might find in any introduction to psychology textbook. The final four chapters of this book are different. In these, we are going to introduce topics that you would likely *not* find in a typical introductory text but are nevertheless fundamental to a thoroughgoing ecological psychology.

In the first four chapters of this book, we discarded the notion of linear causality as too simplistic and limiting for complex systems. At the same time, we embraced the notion of a more complex *nonlinear, multicausal, nonlocal*—often nonobvious—causality (see Chapter 4). This change removed the barrier to direct perception by eliminating the need for mediating representations, which was the basis for the ecological perspective as outlined in Chapters 5–13. What we *haven't* done yet is explore how this more complex version of causality has been used in scientific exploration. After all, it is difficult to imagine a scientific methodology that *doesn't* rely on linear causality.

The typical scientific methodology is rooted in an assumption of linearity: it requires keeping everything constant except one factor, which is manipulated. The scientist then observes a given phenomenon to see if manipulating that factor makes a difference. Any changes in the observed phenomenon are then directly attributed to the manipulated factor. This methodology works well in a linear system—that is, one where *only* linear causality is present. In a linear system, the manipulated factor (the cause) will have a proportional relationship to the measured outcome (the effect). Or in other words, if the experimenter changes X, Y will change by a proportional amount.

Moreover, in a linear system, causes are additive. If there are multiple factors affecting a phenomenon, each can be studied in isolation, and then any of their interactions on that phenomenon can be studied for a complete picture of the entire system. In this view, complexity[1] is a function of the number of and interactions among the factors that affect a particular outcome (Vallacher, Read, & Nowak, 2002).

This methodology is simple and easy to use, but it relies on assumptions that apply to very few real-world scenarios (Carello & Moreno, 2005). In the real world, linear relationships are vanishingly rare. Even ones that might seem linear in a restricted case often reveal themselves to be nonlinear when the range is expanded. (For example, the relationship between wealth and happiness is *curvilinear.* People who have moderate wealth are happier than people with little wealth, but people with lots of wealth are often less happy than people with moderate wealth.)

Nonlinear relationships are far more common in the real world. In this type of relationship, the relationship between cause and effect might be a lot less straightforward. For example, changing variable X may have no impact on variable Y below a certain threshold and cause a dramatic change in Y *above* that threshold. One example of this is the phase transition as water

DOI: 10.4324/9781003145691-17

freezes—it doesn't slowly become thicker until it solidifies; it goes from liquid to solid all of a sudden. Or X might only have an effect on Y when a third variable, Z, was present years ago—even if Z is *no longer present*.

Nonlinear systems are, by their very nature, deeply interconnected. The behavior of the system is not an eventual *outcome* predicted by a series of variables. Rather, the behavior *emerges* out of the low-level interactions in ways that are not obviously predictable from studying the factors themselves. This is how you end up with the nonobvious causality discussed in Chapter 4. Or in other words, in a nonlinear system, complexity is unrelated to the number of factors but instead is about the way those factors interact and change over time. The whole is different from the sum of its parts!

So linear methods are not the best way to investigate systems we assume to be multicausal—these systems embody an entirely different set of assumptions about the world. We cannot simultaneously manipulate everything that affects Fred as he stands contemplating his apple tree, or tries to make a shot in his billiards game, or jumps and reaches a bowl that is stored on the top shelf—let alone everything that is happening when he sees his crush and wonders how to ask her out. And isolating the individual effect of the color of the bowl or even the height of the bowl (probably) won't help us predict Fred's complex behavior.

Just as causality is multifaceted, *behavior* is multifaceted as well. Changing the circumstances might not cause Fred to jump *higher* but instead cause him to try an *entirely different behavior*—like getting the stepstool from the spider-infested basement.

On a similar note, we have frequently stressed in this book that organism-environment systems *cannot* be understood as static. By definition, systems are not static. Rather, systems are in a constant state of *change* (which is why we call them *dynamic*). And so any science that artificially freezes a system and attempts to explain a given behavior via linear causality is explaining an unnatural—and here we mean "not occurring in nature"—phenomenon using a methodology that excludes most of the story!

This, then, is the charge of this chapter: explain how we can scientifically investigate *dynamic* systems while embracing *nonlinear* and *complex* causality.

The Sheet Game

One afternoon, Fred's friend Gunnar asked Fred to help him with a puzzle his philosophy teacher, Professor Kelso, had given to him. He brought over a tennis ball and a top sheet from his bed; in the center of the sheet, he had marked an X (see Figure 14.1). Professor Kelso gave Gunnar the following instructions:

> Your job is to lift the sheet in the air with a partner and place the ball somewhere on the sheet. As a team, your goal is to get the ball to the target (the X in the center of the sheet) in the shortest amount of time. Once the ball is on the sheet, you cannot touch the ball. The sheet and ball must stay suspended in the air at all points in time (so you can't put the sheet on the ground and then just drop the ball on the target). Also, the ball has to stay on the target for at least three seconds in order for it to count.

At first, Fred and Gunnar struggled with this task. They held the sheet tight between them and tried tilting it this way and that to get the ball to roll over the X. It was incredibly difficult! They sometimes could move the ball *across* the target but getting it to stay there was starting to feel like an impossible task.

Then Fred had an idea: what if, instead of holding the sheet taut, they took a step toward each other, creating a kind of basin in the sheet? As long as they positioned the X at the bottom of that basin, the ball would roll right to it! Gunnar and Fred each stepped forward,

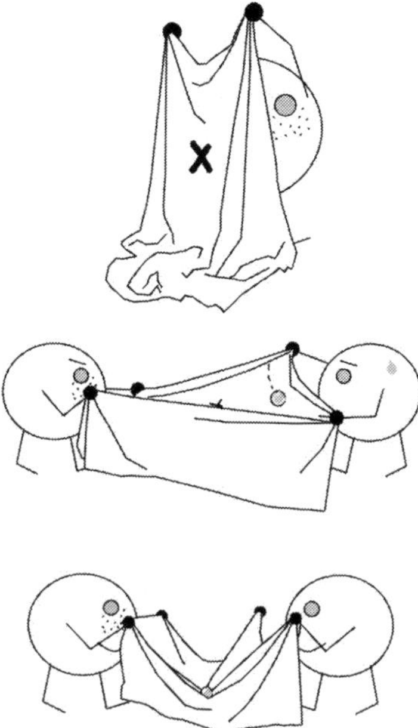

Figure 14.1 *Top:* Gunnar with the top sheet marked with a target (X) for the ball. *Middle:* Fred and Gunnar try to force the ball onto the target and have difficulty. *Bottom:* Fred and Gunnar create a basin (an attractor) with the target at the bottom, and the ball falls directly to it.

repositioned the sheet, and dropped the ball in, and *every time* it rolled straight to the target and stayed there. Fred even realized that he could drop the ball *anywhere* on the sheet, and it would *still* roll to the target each time.

Attractor Layouts

Professor Kelso's game illustrates the idea of the *dynamical systems* perspective for understanding perceiving, acting, and cognizing. The basic idea is to imagine that the set of all of a person's possible behaviors can be likened to different locations on the sheet, and the ball is their *current* behavior. The ball rolling from one area of the sheet to another would indicate a change in behaviors, such as a change in coordination of limbs—there are a lot of possibilities!

For our purposes, let's start with talking about the coordination of limbs, or of *fingers*, anyway. You can try this yourself at home! Put your hands above a table, with your index fingers extended (see Figure 14.2). You can tap the table with both fingers at the same time (in-phase) or tap with the left while the right is extended in the air, and vice versa (anti-phase). But that's not all! You can tap with your right finger just a bit ahead of your left or tap twice with your left finger while simultaneously tapping only once with your right.

Imagine that all those possible coordination patterns were represented by a location on the sheet. For simplicity, let's confine ourselves to just those situations where each finger is tapping only once. There's still plenty of variability in that situation because the right- and left-hand taps can be coordinated in a bunch of different ways. In Figure 14.3, the different coordination patterns are represented by different positions on the horizontal axis. In Chapter 9 (see Figure 9.8), we described a similar situation and made the case that the in-phase coordination pattern was more stable than the anti-phase coordination pattern. In Figure 14.3, the "sheet"

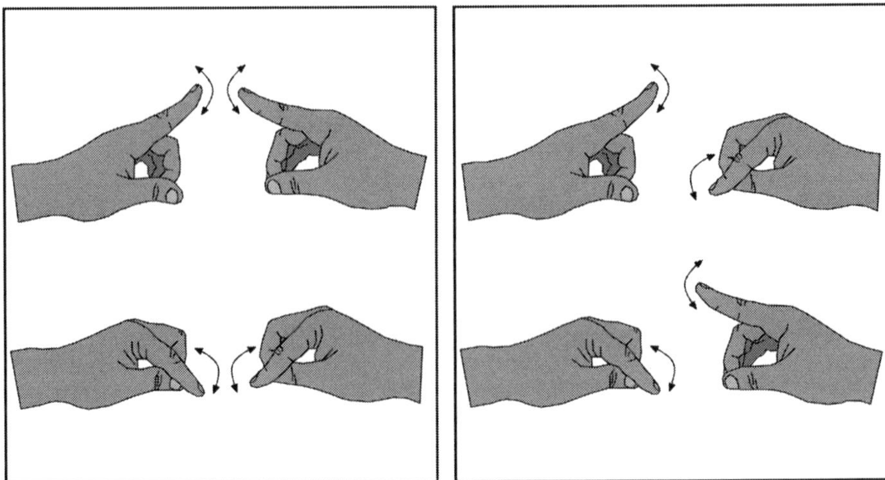

Figure 14.2 Left: in-phase coordination. *Right:* anti-phase coordination.

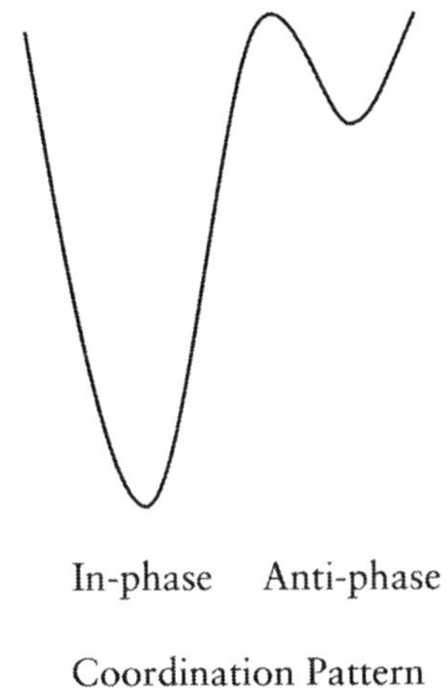

Figure 14.3 The Haken-Kelso-Bunz attractor layout. There is a deep attractor at the in-phase coordination and a shallow attractor at the anti-phase attractor.

(more properly called the *attractor layout* or *attractor landscape*) has a deep basin (an *attractor,* see Box 14.1) at the in-phase position. There is also a less deep attractor at the anti-phase position—it's a relatively stable coordination pattern when compared to, say, the right finger leading the left by a quarter of a cycle.

In any given attractor layout, the deepest attractor is the most *stable*—meaning that the system will be the most able to maintain that behavior. Moreover, the deepest attractor is also usually the most efficient for the current conditions—meaning that the system will be using the least amount of energy in order to exhibit that behavior. For example, at slower movement speeds, it takes less energy for four-legged animals like Sweet William to *trot.* At higher movement speeds, it takes less energy for them to *gallop* (see Chapter 9).

Now imagine we are playing the same game that Fred and Gunnar were: we drop a ball into this layout; where will it go? Most of the time, it will fall into the deeper (more stable) attractor basin at the in-phase coordination. It will also fall into the less deep (and less stable) anti-phase attractor sometimes. All other coordination patterns will be unlikely. In real-life terms, this means that maintaining in-phase and anti-phase are going to be easier than any other coordination pattern—say, the left finger leading the right by a quarter cycle. *And* if the person starts at one of these less-stable coordination patterns, they will likely "fall" into the nearest, more stable pattern after a while.

The curve in Figure 14.3 is described by an equation[2] (called the Haken-Kelso-Bunz [HKB] equation; Haken et al., 1985; see Chapter 9). It is one of the first—and most prominent—applications of the dynamical systems approach in psychology. And it doesn't just describe the coordination of tapping fingers! It has been expanded to interpersonal coordination (Schmidt & Richardson, 2008) and a variety of other coordinated systems (such as rowers [Cuijpers et al., 2019] and people in rocking chairs [Richardson, Marsh, Isenhower et al., 2007b]; see Chapter 11).

Box 14.1 Different Types of Attractors

The bottom of the basin in Fred and Gunnar's sheet—and the bottom of the basin in the HKB layout—are called attractors. They are called that because they attract nearby behaviors the way a magnet attracts iron. If a person is exhibiting behavior that is near an attractor (say, the left hand and the right hand are tapping together, but the left hand is just slightly ahead of the right hand, a behavior that is close to in-phase), they will be attracted to the more stable pattern (in-phase) and will move in that direction, just like the ball rolling to the bottom of the sheet.

What we are describing here and throughout this chapter is what's called a *fixed point* attractor because the attractor stays more or less in one point, and the system tends to move in that direction (though see more about changing layouts in the next section). There are, however, at least two other types of attractors (see Figure 14.4b and c).

Periodic Attractors: If a system never approaches a single point and instead visits a series of states in order repeatedly, it is considered to have a periodic attractor. The pendulum in a grandfather clock, for example, has a periodic attractor. There are other types of periodic attractors that are less regular than the clock, like the life cycle of leaves on a deciduous tree—which do not always grow, turn red, and fall on *exactly* the same days, but *nearly so*. If a system only *kind of* returns to the same spaces in a cycle then it is considered *quasi-periodic*.

Chaotic Attractors: These types of attractors are more complex but, importantly, are *not* random. In a chaotic attractor, there is a rule-governed process (sometimes a simple one!) that gives you the position of the system at n + 1 (where n is the current state and n + 1 is the future state), although you may not be able to guess from n + 1 where the process will be at n + 20 without going through each step along the way. Chaotic attractors are very sensitive to initial conditions. In Figure 14.4c, we show the same attractor with two different starting points: they have wildly different paths through the space but exhibit the same overall pattern. The overall pattern of a chaotic attractor is complex and fractal. While it may appear to do so, the system will never revisit the exact same space.

Repellers: A repeller is the opposite of an attractor—it is a state that the system actively tries to avoid—the way someone might avoid their ex by not attending a party they know their ex will be attending. These can exist in layouts that have fixed-point attractors (they are the high bumps the ball has to roll away from), periodic attractors (they are the spaces outside or inside of the cycle), and chaotic attractors (they act as the boundaries for the chaotic attractor's basin, see Figure 14.4d).

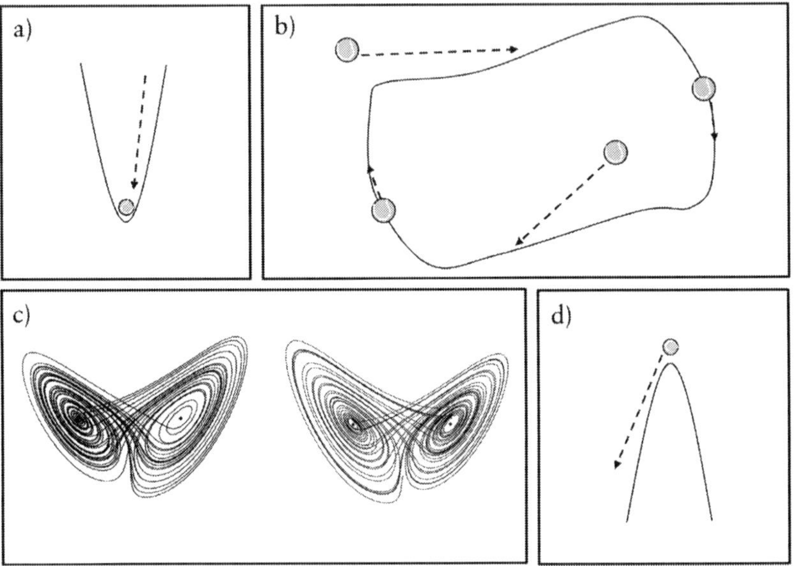

Figure 14.4 Different types of attractors and the way a system might behave near that attractor: (a) fixed point attractor, (b) periodic attractor, (c) chaotic attractor (Wernecke, 2018), and (d) repeller.

Changing Layouts

One of the most important aspects of the dynamical systems approach is that it is *not* intended to describe static behavior. Change is represented in the approach in a variety of ways. We have already talked about the transition from a less-stable pattern to a more stable one, but there's more! For one, the *layout itself* does not remain static. The layout can change over time and with experience (e.g., development or learning, see Chapters 10 and 13) or changes in circumstances. In this way, we can represent the dynamic nature of living (and some nonliving!) systems. They grow and change and learn and adapt and forget and do it all while successfully navigating their surroundings. Rather than trying to ignore that or sidelining it as a secondary problem, the dynamical systems approach *embraces* the evolving nature of systems and builds everything around it. There are three basic ways a layout can change: death of an attractor, birth of an attractor, and movement of existing attractors.

Death of an Attractor

Let's start with the model we already know: the HKB equation modeling finger tapping (and other kinds of coordination involving two things). In the main case, there are two attractors:

in-phase and anti-phase. The anti-phase attractor is only *relatively* stable—meaning it's more stable than the surrounding coordination, but it's not the most stable coordination available.

Try this at home (or wherever you are): start with your fingers tapping in an anti-phase pattern (tap with the left while the right is extended in the air and vice versa) at a relatively slower pace. Now speed up. And speed up again. Go faster and faster! If you are anything like the participants in the HKB study, eventually your fingers will suddenly shift to an in-phase pattern. And if you then slow down, you will not spontaneously return to the anti-phase coordination (remember the Fred and Claudia hand puppets from Chapter 9).

According to Haken et al. (1985), you have experienced the death of an attractor (albeit a *temporary* death, see Figure 14.5). At slower speeds, the anti-phase pattern is stable enough to stay in the attractor basin. As the pace increases, however, the layout *changes*—the anti-phase attractor becomes far less stable until even a minor fluctuation will result in the ball rolling down to the in-phase attractor. When the pace slows, the original layout returns, but the ball is still firmly at the bottom of the deeper basin.

There are other examples of an attractor getting less stable or even disappearing, both on an individual level like forgetting (think all the things you learned for exams and then promptly forgot) or breaking a habit (think quitting biting your nails) and on a societal level like discontinuing use of disappearing technology (think butter churns or phonebooths) or behaviors that are no longer as useful (think horseback riding).

Birth of an Attractor

Just as we can *forget* something we once knew, we can also *learn* something new. As part of the ecological version of the tabula rasa, we assume that there are some attractors that are already

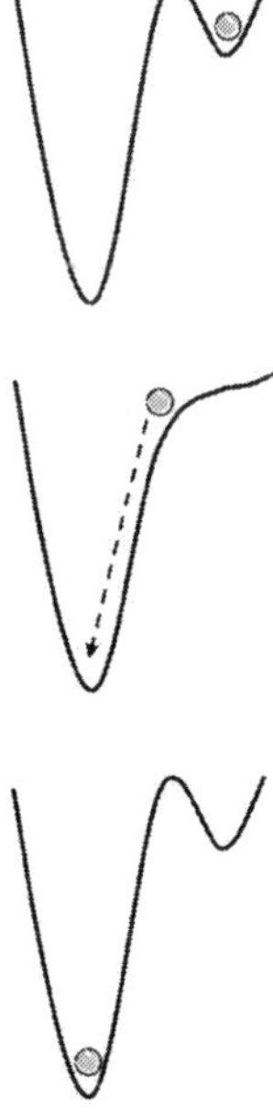

Figure 14.5 *Top*: coordinating at anti-phase is reasonably easy at slower speeds. *Middle*: increasing the speed changes the layout, making the anti-phase attractor less stable. The participant's behavior (represented by the ball) falls into the in-phase attractor. *Bottom*: returning to slow speeds does not spontaneously return the participant to the anti-phase attractor because the in-phase attractor is more stable.

present by virtue of the constraints of our environment as well as the physical properties of our bodies. But the ecological notion of empiricism (see Chapter 2) *also* assumes that experience changes us. In that view, we have to assume that some of the attractor layouts described by these models are *created* over time and experience. Studying this experimentally proves somewhat difficult. After all, participants already *have* the finger-wagging layouts when they enter the lab. To investigate the learning of a new attractor, Beek and Santvoord (1992) had participants learn a new skill: juggling. They had participants come in over a two-week period for ten half-hour sessions to train with an experienced juggler. While some of the participants learned faster and some learned slower, all were able to find a stable juggling pattern. In the case of juggling, the coordination of interest is the amount of time spent with the ball in the hand relative to the total time required for an entire cycle of the hand's movement. In Figure 14.6, the path of the hand is indicated by the dotted line. The expert juggling three balls carried the ball for about 70% of that cycle.

In this study, the newly minted jugglers explored that attractor landscape. In the language of dynamical systems, exploring an attractor landscape means trying out a bunch of coordination patterns—say, only holding on to the ball for 60% of the cycle, or for as much as 80% of the cycle—to discover the ones that are the *most* stable. In this study, over time, the participants became more and more likely to return to the stable pattern (70%) and remain there even when something happened—like a ball slipping from their hand a bit and delaying the cycle briefly. This was taken as evidence of the creation of a juggling attractor. While the participants in that study did not *quite* reach the stability of the professional juggler, their behavior closely mimicked his.

Attractors can form for a variety of reasons, and the organism actively practicing a given behavior is only one of them. Attractors can also form because of societal pressures (think social norms), interactions between political leaders (think sustained conflicts between nations), the physical orientation of the furniture in a room (think how you walk across your living room after you move the sofa), or any number of other things, large and small.

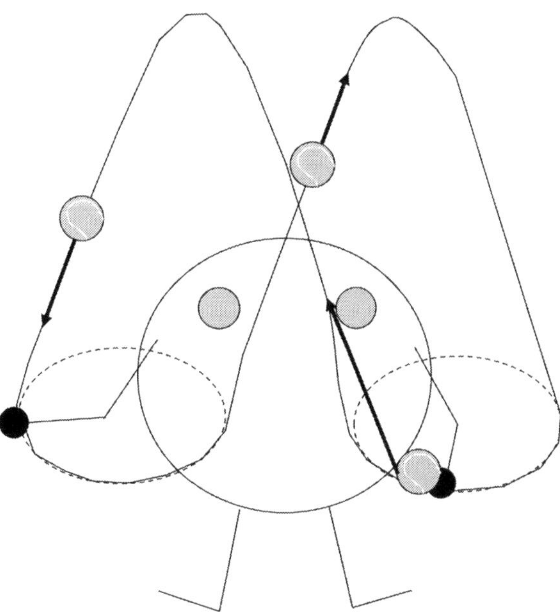

Figure 14.6 Cascade juggling is stable when the amount of time the ball spends in the hand is about 70% of the entire cycle (hand cycle represented by dotted lines, path of the balls represented by solid lines).

Movement of Existing Attractors

The dynamical systems approach is also good at describing the phenomenon of *adaptation*. Adaptation is different from learning. Learning[3] is about developing a new skill. Adaptation is about changing an old skill to reflect a new context. In terms of our attractor layout, adaptation is the movement of an existing attractor to a new location.

Let's take, for example, the act of underhand throwing a bean bag at a target. This is a skill that many adults can (more or less) accomplish. They may not hit the target each time, but the misses are unsystematic—meaning they'll miss to the left just as often as they will miss to the right. An experimenter can mess with this system by using special glasses that have a prism on the front. The light entering these glasses is shifted (technically *refracted*) in a particular direction. The experimenter can give our reasonably accomplished participant these prism glasses to wear, and the person's experience will be that the field of view (including the target) has shifted in a particular direction. For our purposes, let's say the glasses shifted the perception of the target, so it now appears a few feet to the right of where it actually is.

When the person tries to underhand throw to the target in these circumstances, they will, at first, miss dramatically to the right. And then, as with most things, they will adapt! It is not one-trial learning, but over several trials, they will gradually get back to their baseline accuracy, missing just as often to the left as to the right. Once they have comfortably adapted to the prism glasses, the experimenter then has them take the glasses off. Once again, they miss dramatically at first! But this time, they miss to the *left*. This is called an *aftereffect*. Over repeated trials, the aftereffect diminishes, and the person returns to baseline (see Figure 14.7, left side and middle of each box).

From a dynamical systems perspective, the changes in throwing accuracy reflect the movement of an attractor (Frank, Blau, & Turvey, 2009; see Figure 14.7, right side of each box).

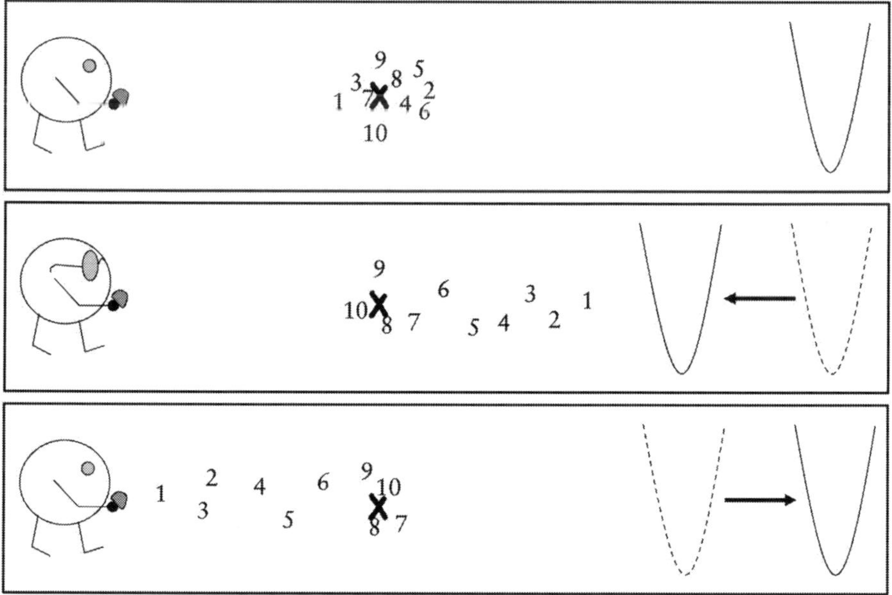

Figure 14.7 *Top*: baseline throwing. *Middle*: during training with the glasses. *Bottom*: after the glasses are removed. On the left side of each box is whether the participant is wearing the prism glasses; in the middle of each box is the throwing pattern; on the right side of each box are the corresponding changes in the attractor layout.

Our reasonably accomplished adult has performed underhanded throwing enough times in their life to develop a stable throwing behavior. When the glasses introduce a new context, the person has to change their behavior to account for it (see Chapter 9 for a discussion of calibration). Removing the glasses reestablishes the normal orientation of the field of view, but their throwing attractor has been shifted, causing them to miss in the opposite direction. Eventually, the attractor returns to its initial location.

If the changes in their throwing accuracy were due to the birth of a new attractor (rather than the shifting of an existing attractor), we would expect a different pattern of behavior—unsystematic but larger error, on the first throws with the glasses on, eventually becoming smaller and (still) unsystematic error, as the attractor deepened. In that scenario, the removal of the glasses should cause *no* difficulty in returning to throwing at the target (no aftereffect). This is not what occurs.

The ability to *shift* attractor location is a crucial part of our ability to adapt to changing bodily conditions (think pregnancy or height during puberty or even just putting on high heels; see Figure 5.11), but it can also describe changes in collective behaviors as well (think changing social norms or how languages shift over time).

Nonlinear Solutions to Linear Problems

The mechanistic hypothesis asserts that if you know all the starting conditions and all the things that can affect something, then you ought to be able to perfectly predict the behavior of that thing. If you're not able to predict the outcome, then you have missed some factor. And when you apply linear methods to linear systems, that works fine. But as we have pointed out, *most* complex systems are nonlinear.

One of the characteristics of nonlinear systems is that they behave in ways that aren't always predictable from the simple addition of lower-level factors. Attempting to understand nonlinear systems using linear methods has led to a variety of difficulties and unexplainable phenomena. However, when approached from a nonlinear perspective, such systems *are* lawful and sometimes even predictable. We are going to discuss three such issues here. Keep in mind that this is not an exhaustive list—it just provides a couple of examples.

Noise

Noise is typically seen as a *problem* in linear science. It's something that is accounted for, removed, and averaged over. Noise is imagined as the static heard on the radio when you're having trouble finding the station or that interferes with the signal when you get too far away from the source. It's not interesting; it's in the *way*. It's an error. In the dynamical systems view, however, noise is part of the system—an *integral* part (see Chapter 12 and Box 12.2 for a discussion of noise in thinking). Noise allows us to flexibly respond to situations and find new ways of doing things.

Let's return to Fred and Gunnar playing the sheet game. They are holding onto the sheet edges, and they start shaking the sheet causing the ball to bounce around a bit on the sheet. They could shake it a little (even just standing there will cause it to move a bit as their bodies are never really still), or they could shake it a lot. This movement is like noise. Noise is always present in any complex system. Like an animal that doesn't move, a system without noise is likely inert—or dead. Even in its most basic form (the HKB equation, for example), the system does not rest on one fixed coordination—there is always noise pushing our ball around. In real terms, even in-phase coordination is not perfect.

Let's say Fred and Gunnar had set their sheet up to look like the HKB layout—with two unequal basins. They start by dropping the ball in the shallower anti-phase attractor basin, and then they start shaking the sheet. The increased bouncing of the ball might be enough to get the ball to pop out of the anti-phase attractor and into the in-phase attractor. The reverse is a *lot* less likely. Even if Fred and Gunnar shake the sheet pretty hard, the ball probably won't bounce around high enough to get out of the in-phase attractor and then into the anti-phase attractor. Or in other words, noise makes it more likely for the system to find the deepest attractor—the most stable (and efficient) form of our behavior.

In Chapter 12, we talked about experiments involving gear systems. Recall that the task of the participant was to look at an interlocking gear system and determine which way the target gear would turn given the direction of the driving gear (see Figure 12.6). In this paradigm, participants typically start by force tracing—using their fingers or eyes to follow the path of each subsequent gear—a stable but not completely efficient strategy. Eventually, most participants discover the alternating strategy—realizing that gear direction alternates from gear to gear—a far more efficient strategy. They also exhibit more fluctuations just before transitioning between one (less stable) mode to the other (more stable) mode. Stephen et al. (2009) reasoned that the *noise* might be what *prompted* the discovery. Or in other words, rather than just being a side effect of the transition, the noise *generated* the transition. It bumped them just enough that they landed in a new (more stable) attractor. Just like Fred and Gunnar shaking the sheet might prompt the ball to fall into the deeper basin.

To test this, the researchers created a gear system that would jump around the screen while the participant was trying to complete the game. That is, they introduced additional *noise* to the participant-gear system. And it went exactly as predicted! The more noise that was introduced to the system (the more the gears hopped around the screen), the more likely it was that the participant discovered the alternation method.

This is what people are (informally) attempting when they do something differently for a while to shake things up. They are perturbing the system in the hopes of escaping a local (less efficient/stable) attractor state and finding a global (more efficient/stable) attractor state.

In short, noise is what keeps us from getting stuck in one particular attractor; it allows for *flexibility*. Noise is *also* what allows us to flexibly respond to *perturbations*—any unexpected bumps along the way in performing an intended behavior (think tripping over an untied shoelace). Having noise—especially pink noise (see Chapter 12)—as an inherent part of the system means that we are well practiced at falling back into a particular attractor when the system is disturbed in any way. Adding a bit of extra noise via a perturbation is something we can handle!

Equifinality

According to the mechanistic hypothesis, outcomes are dictated by starting conditions plus factors encountered along the way. The corollary to that is that if two systems start in very different locations, they should end up in very different locations. Except that's not always how it goes! *Equifinality* (meaning "equal ends") is when two systems start in very different positions but end up in roughly the same place (see Figure 14.8, *left*).

For example, for humans at least,[4] language is an almost-universal outcome of development. The two authors of this book grew up in very different locations at different times and still ended up with roughly the same understanding of the words and rules of English. While it's true that we both had English-speaking homes primarily on the East Coast of the US, the words spoken, the conversations had, and the usage of the language itself were all quite different (e.g., "grinders" vs. "hoagies"). And yet we are able to use our mutual understanding of the language to have conversations and even write a book together!

And it's more than that! The use of language as a *tool* seems to be an inevitable outcome for humans that desire to communicate. If you put a group of people together that *don't* have a common language, they will *create* one! Under experimental conditions (see Galantucci, 2005), participants with no access to the usual modes of communication (i.e., no audio, visual, or textual communication is possible) *created* a system of communication out of small marks on a screen. In a more naturalistic setting (see Goldin-Meadow, 2005), deaf children who had *no* linguistic input (that is, they were not taught to sign, and they could not hear the spoken language in their homes) *created a signed language* when they got together. This language even has many of the same linguistic features as other, more established languages.

The dynamical systems approach suggests that, rather than being surprising, equifinality is perfectly understandable when examined using an attractor layout model. The system simply has one strong attractor (see Figure 14.8, *right*). No matter the starting point or path through the layout, the person's behavior will always end up at the bottom of the basin. In the case of language acquisition, there are contextual factors that are common to all humans living in social contexts (the need to communicate, repeated interactions, etc.; see Lightfoot, 1991) that make finding that attractor an inevitability.

Pluripotentiality

Just as two systems with different starting conditions can end up in the *same* final location, two systems with the *same* starting conditions can end up in very *different* final positions (see Figure 14.9, *left*, and Figure 14.4c). Think of the identical twins (or even just siblings) who end up with very different personalities and lives. Or think of the squirrel monkeys (see Chapter 4)

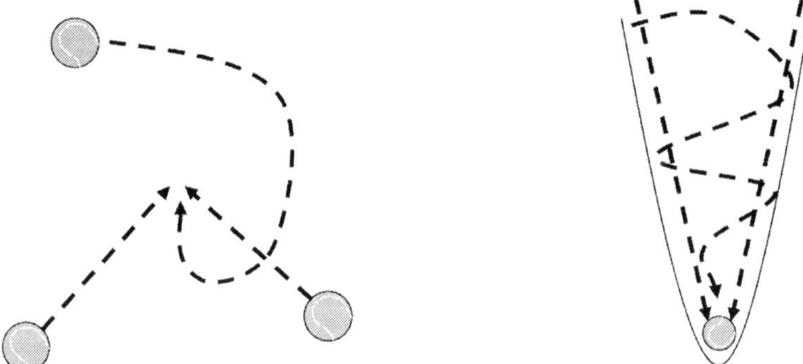

Figure 14.8 *Left*: multiple pathways end up at the same location. *Right*: this behavior is explained as one (deep) attractor, pulling everything in regardless of starting point or path.

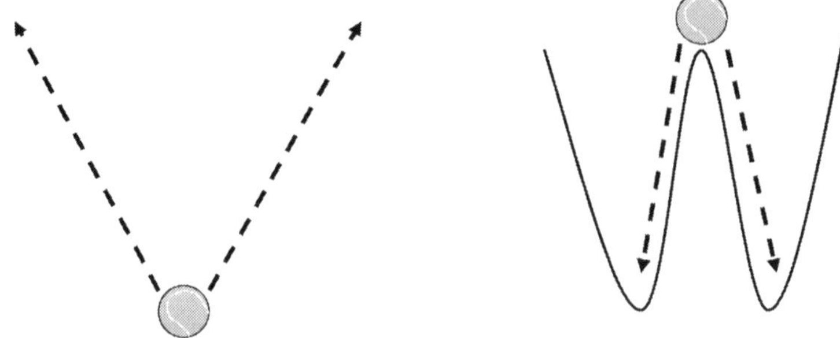

Figure 14.9 *Left*: the same starting condition can result in radically different ending conditions. *Right*: this behavior is explained as multiple nearby attractors combined with (generative) noise.

who grow up afraid of snakes if they eat live spiders but do *not* fear snakes if they don't—tiny changes in development can result in huge (nonlinear) changes in the outcome.

The dynamical systems perspective explains this type of progression as one where there are *two* (or quite possibly more) attractor states and the initial condition is balanced between them (see Figure 14.9, *right*). Small changes—such as the always-present noise—will cause the ball to tip into one attractor or the other. (This balance point can also be thought of as a repeller—see Box 14.1.)

Changing the Focus from the Static Outcome to the Dynamic Process

Up until now, this chapter has focused largely on outcomes (as in, where does the ball end up by the end of the trial? are the fingers in-phase or anti-phase?). However, the focus of the approach is often more about the ongoing changes in behavior over time—the journey rather than the destination. As we have already mentioned, the static case is both uninteresting and unrealistic.

The daily work in the dynamical systems approach is in, well, *dynamics*. It's in investigating the way a system moves and inferring both the layout and the constraints that might form that layout.

Discovering Layouts: Phase Space Reconstruction and Recurrence Quantification Analysis

When first investigating a system, we do not always know what the attractor layout of that system might look like. After all, one of the characteristics of a nonlinear system is that it is not always predictable, even with careful analysis of the smaller pieces. Behavior is an *emergent* phenomenon, not the sum of the parts. In the case of the HKB equation, the attractors were easily observable: in-phase and anti-phase are macro-level behaviors that can be consciously manipulated and easily seen (see Box 14.2 for more on the methods of measurement).

Box 14.2 Measurement Tools

In order to perform any of the nonlinear methodologies mentioned in this chapter, the first step is to measure the system. However, the usual methods for measuring human behaviors might not be appropriate for these types of investigations. For one, in those methodologies, the system is usually only measured *at one particular moment in time.* Given the over-time nature of these phenomena (and methodologies), that just isn't going to cut it. Instead, it's necessary to find a measurement that can be taken (usually, we say the system is being "sampled") frequently, if not continuously.

There are a *lot* of ways to do this! Often, research of this kind is focused on moment-to-moment fluctuations in the relative coordination of limbs, so a lot of the methodologies are based on identifying those fluctuations. For example, goniometers are small devices that stretch across a joint and continuously measure the angle of that joint. And motion tracking can be used to measure the position of the limbs. Researchers have even hacked commercially available gaming technology like Nintendo Wii (since the remotes are essentially motion trackers) and Microsoft Kinect.

Beyond just the coordination of limbs, however, any technology that measures the movement of the body can be useful in this field. A common methodology is eye tracking (cameras are pointed both at the eyes and at the scene so the researchers can track what the participants are looking at). Body sway is measured through force plates that the participant stands on (it measures the center of pressure and can track how that moves over time, see Chapter 9). Google Glass comes equipped with an accelerometer and a gyroscope that can also be used to measure body sway even while seated. Even tracking the movement of a computer mouse while a participant makes a response can be informative.

What's great is that these methodologies can be used on *anything* that can be measured over time. The analysis can be performed on both continuous and categorical data. For example, one set of researchers used these techniques on language use during monologues versus conversations (Müller-Frommeyer, Kauffeld, & Paxton, 2020).

So what do we do in the case where a system's attractors are not so immediately observable? The goal is to figure out what "locations" in the "sheet" the system returns to frequently. The problem is that it's not always immediately apparent what the sheet is (that is, what the variable of interest might be), let alone the frequently visited locations. For example, think about the juggling study mentioned previously. The coordination variable of interest turned out to be the ratio of the amount of time the ball spent in the hand versus the overall cycle time of the hand. But it could have been a lot of other things! It could have been the height of the ball versus the width of the hand space or the exact time per cycle or any number of other things. In that case, the researchers had a reason (careful analysis of the physics of juggling) to suspect that this ratio was important, but what about cases where they *don't* know that?

In these cases, you can use *phase space reconstruction*. To use this technique, you can measure *any part* of the moving system and use those measurements to recreate the sheet and figure out how the system travels through that space. The actual math involved is a little complicated for this text, but the short version is that, since the whole system is interconnected, measuring any one part will give you information about the rest. From that, you can figure out where the "good stuff" is happening. This is not possible in a (simple) linear system, but it *is* possible in a nonlinear (complex) system because of the interconnectedness of the pieces.

In other situations, you might know what the "sheet" is but not be sure where the basins of attraction are. For that, there's a technique called *recurrence quantification analysis* (RQA; see Carello & Moreno, 2005, for more). Again, without going into the gory details, this analysis looks at the behavior of the system (which can be measured in a variety of ways; see Box 14.2) and figures out what behaviors recur and how frequently. From this, the attractor layout can be inferred.

Using these techniques in combination allows you to reconstruct the space and discover the layout, all from careful observations of the system. Once the layout is modeled, it becomes possible to make *new, testable predictions* about the behavior of the system. Knowing the attractors means you know what behaviors the system is going to return to; knowing the relative strength of those attractors means you know what behaviors are going to be more likely; knowing the amount of noise a system exhibits means you know how likely it is that it will switch from one kind of behavior to another. So while the behaviors of a nonlinear system may not be predictable from the lower-level interactions, they *are* predictable from a dynamical systems analysis.

Nonstationary Systems: When an Average Just Won't Do

As we introduced at the outset of this chapter, linear methods involve manipulating a single factor and then measuring how the behavior of the system changes in response to those manipulations. We've been mostly talking about why altering a single factor is inadequate, but we also need to talk about how the measurements themselves are inadequate as well. Typically, the linear techniques will *average* the measurements of a given behavior. But taking an average assumes a stationary system—or at least assumes that whatever is interesting about this system can be approximated by a stationary value.

But what if the system is not stationary? What if the interesting part is in the fluctuations? What if knowing the way that the system shifts over time is more informative than knowing the average state? For example, take a person who sometimes *loves* their job and sometimes *hates* their job and nothing in-between: their average job satisfaction will be somewhere in the neutral zone. But that person never actually has a neutral feeling about their job! Instead, investigating the temporal variation of the feelings might reveal why they visit the loving state versus the hating state.

RQA is *excellent* for these types of systems. Its purpose is to watch the trajectory over time; from that, we can infer things about the system. Previously, we talked about the case where we didn't know what the attractor states are, but even when we *do* (as in the example of our fictional employee in a love/hate relationship with their job), watching the trajectory through those states can tell us about the depth of those attractors, how noisy the system is, and how likely they are to, and how often they, switch from one state to another.

Experimental Examples

The goal of this chapter was to present a new, nonlinear, scientific methodology. So far, we've outlined how that might be done, but we think it would be helpful to give real-world examples of the dynamical systems method in action. We (obviously) cannot present all of the research in this area, but we picked a few informative (and diverse) examples.

A-Not-B Error

Fred's niece, Eleanor, participates in a study. The researchers sit her in front of two containers (one is called A, the other one B; see Figure 14.10, *top*). They then wave her favorite toy (a stuffed llama named Esther) and make sure they have her attention before they "hide" it in container A and put the cover on the container (she watches them put it in there, it's not the sneakiest of hiding). She pulls the cover off container A, grabs Esther, and hugs her with delight! The researchers perform this same sequence of events over and over until Eleanor is *very good* at finding Esther in the A container. Then they try something new: they have her watch as they hide Esther in the B container. They (gently) hold Eleanor's arms so she can't reach right away, but when they let go a few seconds later, she pulls the cover off the A container instead of the B container. She has made what is called the A-not-B error.

Some developmental psychologists (following the work of Piaget, see Chapter 10) *love* this task. They interpret it as a lack of *object permanence*—the knowledge that an object still exists even after it goes out of sight. As evidence, they point to the fact that older children (like Bill, who went to the movies in Chapter 3) aren't fooled by this; they pull the lid off the B container. But last week, Fred's chef friend Claes helped him rearrange his kitchen. Ever since then, Fred keeps opening the wrong drawer looking for his can opener. This is, essentially, the A-not-B error with Claes as the experimenter, Fred as the participant, and the can opener as the toy llama. Fred has no difficulty with object permanence; he just has the *habit* of reaching into a particular drawer.

Developmental psychologists with a more dynamical systems approach looked at this phenomenon and reimagined it as a shifting attractor layout (Thelen et al., 2001). They suggested there were three constraints acting on the layout: (1) the history of the training, (2) the distinctiveness of the toy/container, and (3) the immediate signal from the experimenter. The combination of these factors predicts which attractor will "win" and thus which container Eleanor will reach for. In Figure 14.10 (during training trials), the A attractor "wins". In Figure 14.11 (the first trial where the toy is hidden at B), the A attractor *still* wins.

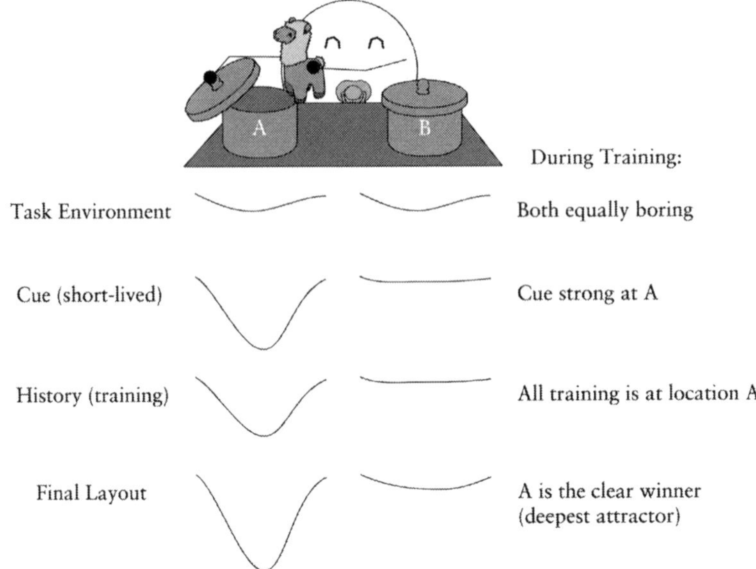

Figure 14.10 *Top*: Eleanor participates in a study where her toy is hidden in one of two locations; in this case, it was hidden at the A location. *Bottom*: The dynamical systems account for the A-not-B error; several factors contribute to the overall attractor landscape. During training, A will "win" and Eleanor will open the A container.

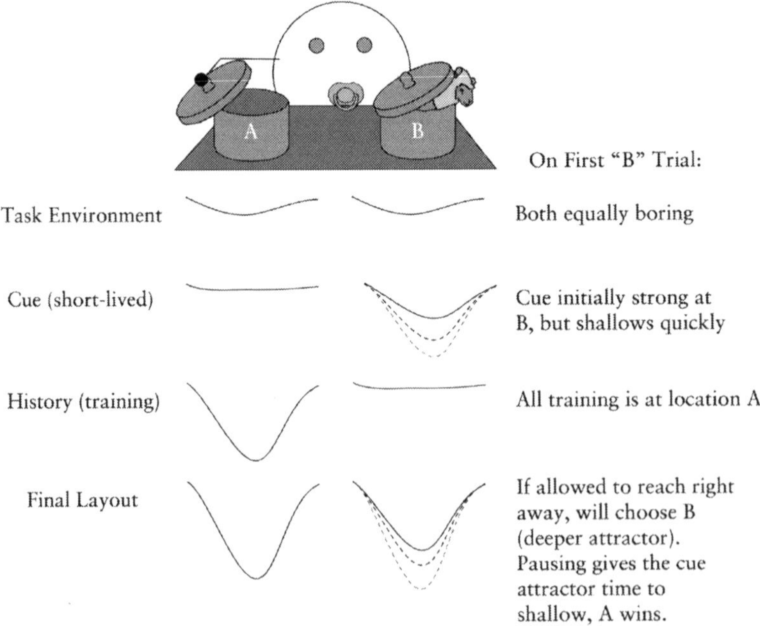

Figure 14.11 *Top:* Eleanor participates in a study where her toy is hidden in one of two locations; in this case, it was hidden at the B location (after several trials where it was hidden at the A location). *Bottom:* The dynamical systems account for the A-not-B error; several factors contribute to the overall attractor landscape. During the first B trial, A will "win" (and Eleanor will open the A container) if there is a long enough pause to allow the cue attractor to shallow.

Moreover, the new dynamical systems account of the A-not-B error explains many variations of the paradigm that cannot be accounted for with the notion of object permanence alone. For example, lack of object permanence cannot explain why just waving the target lid (without actually hiding a toy) will generate the same error or why having a more exciting toy or a more distinctive lid will keep the child from making the error. And here is the crux of the matter: the dynamical systems model accounts for more of the behavior than the previous explanations. It also predicts novel behavior that is then empirically testable.

Reading Comprehension

Assuming that you are a student (of life, if not of a particular educational system), you know that the ability to gain information from reading a text is a vital skill. Typically, reading comprehension is measured as an *outcome*. That is, a person is given a text to read, then given a series of questions about the text and their ability to answer those questions correctly is the indication of how well they read the text. Or in other words, comprehension is taken as an outcome of the factors of quality of text plus the reader's skill.

However (and this should come as no surprise to our readers at this point!), there's much more going on here. The *process* of comprehension is just as important as the outcome. Researchers (Allen et al., 2017) developed a cunning method of looking at the process of comprehending via RQA. They had participants read texts (on heart disease and red blood cells) and write explanations of what they read as they went. They then performed RQA on the text generated by those explanations.

In terms of recurrence (how often the written explanations return to the same areas of the "sheet"—here, semantic content), those who had higher comprehension scores had significantly higher recurrence than those that had lower comprehension scores. Or in other words, the better readers explored the semantic landscape and found those attractors that helped guide their understanding. The less-apt readers explored the space but were unable to find areas of recurring content.

What's *great* about understanding reading comprehension as a process of finding attractors (rather than just an outcome) is that it suggests a way to *help*. It suggests that the skill that needs improving is the ability to find the attractors—the recurring themes across a text.

Intractable Conflict

Basic conflict—when two or more groups have differing needs—is not necessarily bad. Much like noise in a dynamical system, it can be an agent of positive change. *Intractable* conflict, on the other hand, is different. This is when two (or more) groups cannot seem to get past those differing needs. Given the high cost of conflict (emotional cost in relationships, for example, or loss of life in a large-scale conflict like a war), it seems as though resolving conflict would be such a highly desirable outcome that even a partial compromise would be preferred to continued hostilities. But time and time again, we see interpersonal relationships devolve into (seemingly) unresolvable conflict.

It is possible to think of relationships (whether global or personal) as an attractor layout (Vallacher et al., 2010). In situations in which intractable conflicts exist, the layout might look an awful lot like the HKB system (see Figure 14.12), where there is a deeper attractor at conflict and a shallower attractor at peace. For a system with this underlying dynamic that is currently in the peace attractor, very small perturbations (like the assassination of the Archduke of Hungary, for example, or forgetting to put the milk away in the fridge for the umpteenth time) might be enough to start an all-out war (i.e., a jump from the peace attractor to the war attractor). And just like the transitions in the HKB model, those shifts will be abrupt.

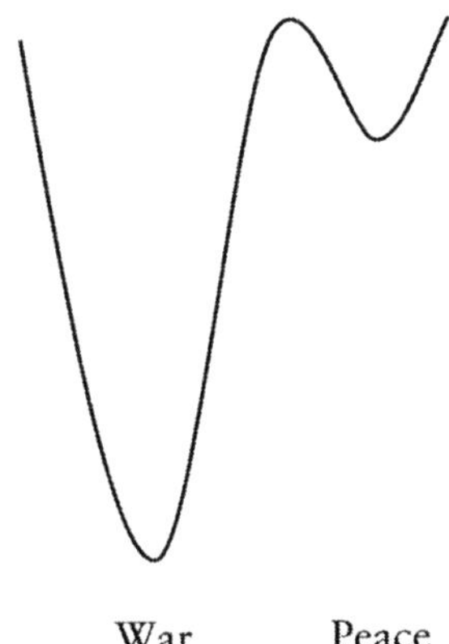

Figure 14.12 The attractor layout of a relationship in intractable conflict. There is a deep (stable) attractor at "conflict" and a shallow (less stable) attractor at "peace".

These systems will also exhibit another characteristic of dynamical systems: hysteresis, or a "memory" within the system. Because of the nature of attractors, a system's *current state*, whatever that state might be, will be shaped by its earlier trajectories. In our examples, the same event—like increasing funding to the air force, for example, or your partner cracking a joke—would be seen as positive and healthy when you are in the peace attractor or negative and provoking when you are in the war attractor.

The advantage of this theory of intractable conflict over other (usually static, linear) theories is that it accounts for several things not accounted for in those theories. For example, conflict persisting far past the point of being healthy or productive or why a seemingly peaceful area might suddenly erupt into violence.

Vallacher et al. (2010) also suggest that there is a way to *resolve* conflict in this account. Specifically, while direct attempts to change the conflict attractor will not work (and are, indeed, more likely to entrench both sides, known as the *backfire effect*), *destabilizing* the attractor layout might be more effective. Think about the finger tapping in the HKB paradigm: increasing the speed made the anti-phase attractor disappear. Speed, in that system, is called a *control parameter*. Changing a control parameter will change the layout. If you could discover a control parameter for a particular relationship (perhaps global political context or the family's finances in our examples), then provide a more stable arrangement while the system is destabilized, it might be possible to create new, lasting patterns of behavior.

Nonlinear Methods Are Just Better

This chapter first made the argument that linear static methodologies are not a good way to investigate nonlinear dynamic systems. We then described a number[5] of nonlinear methods and gave examples of how well they captured nonlinear systems. We also made the assertion that *most* systems are nonlinear, and so these methodologies are *necessary* for capturing most phenomena.

But what if we're wrong? What if a system is actually linear? Or stationary? That's the great thing! Nonlinear analyses will *still work*. Let's say that the system *is* linear and stationary. RQA will pick up that the system does not move. It will clearly indicate a system that has found a point and is staying there. The methods responsible for picking up the constraints that form the attractor will still pick them up even if there is a simple linear relationship between the constraints and the (in this case, stationary) outcome.

The reverse is not the case. Linear methods will dramatically miss the important and exciting parts of nonlinear systems (see Carello & Moreno, 2005), providing inaccurate and potentially misleading pictures of the system. So given a choice between linear methodologies (which can accurately capture linear systems but not nonlinear ones) and nonlinear methodologies (which can accurately capture both), we think the choice is clear.

Notes

1. Scientists who study dynamical systems often refer to this type of system as *complicated* rather than *complex* in order to delineate between the two types more clearly.
2. For those that are curious, it is $\dot{\varphi} = -a\sin\varphi - 2b\sin 2\varphi$, where φ is the relative phase between the fingers.
3. There are as many definitions for learning as there are people that study learning. This definition is an incomplete placeholder and is no better than any of the rest.
4. Though there is plenty of evidence that other species develop language as well (see Von Frisch, 2014, for more on the language of bees, for example).
5. Though not nearly all, we recommend the reader check out the edited volume *Tutorials in Contemporary Nonlinear Methods* (Riley & Van Orden, 2005) for more on this.

15 Evolution

One lazy summer afternoon, Fred was hanging out with his friend Harry who was a *huge* comic book fan. We're talking about the kind of fan with an encyclopedic knowledge of even the most obscure comics, the kind of fan that—once you get them talking about it—can't seem to talk about anything else. Fred doesn't mind this; he finds the whole world fascinating, particularly the stories about mutants with different powers from just a random quirk of genetics. There was something intriguing about the possibility of human evolution just spontaneously producing some kind of superpower.

Harry told him about Betty the Bomb, whose skin produced nitroglycerin-like sweat that she could throw at her enemies—*boom!* Peter the Protector, who could create a force field around him that could stop anything moving quickly toward him (like bullets) but was vulnerable to slower things (like gas). Len the Linguist, who could instantly understand (and speak) any language. Pat the Portal, who could open a portal to *anywhere*. Richard the Ripper, who grew shards of bones out of his arms and could rip them off and throw them at people like knives (that one sounded *painful*). Even Goldfield the Glowworm, who could, well, glow (apparently it came in very handy sometimes).

For days after this conversation, Fred couldn't get it out of his mind. He kept thinking about the plausibility of it all—I mean, sure, opening portals was probably nonsense, but it felt like glowing *could be possible*. After all, there *are* animals who can glow. (And not just glowworms! The angler fish can create a glowing lure that draws the attention of prey so the angler fish can eat them.) And the force field sort of sounded like something he read about called a non-Newtonian fluid.[1] Even the nitroglycerin sweat sounded like something that *could* happen, right? Was there any reason these *couldn't* happen? Fred's Uncle Jimmy suggested he go talk to Grandpa Tom, reminding Fred that Grandpa Tom is an evolutionary biologist.

Grandpa Tom was more than happy to talk about evolution with Fred but cautioned him that it was a complicated subject with a lot of possible answers to the superhero question.

Darwin and Neo-Darwinism

When considering the question of whether a particular change in a species is probable (or even possible), we are considering questions of *evolution*. Evolution is the development and diversification of species over time. Those changes can happen relatively slowly (like the emergence of land animals in a world dominated by sea animals) or quickly (like the emergence of darker-colored moths in a post–Industrial Revolution world in which surfaces became darkened due to soot).

When thinking of evolution, the first name that comes to mind is Charles Darwin. He wasn't the first[2] or the only person to write about evolution, but he *was* the first person to write a comprehensive account that gained widespread popularity. He lacked only the knowledge of genetics that would complete his account. Years after his death, the work of Gregor Mendel

DOI: 10.4324/9781003145691-18

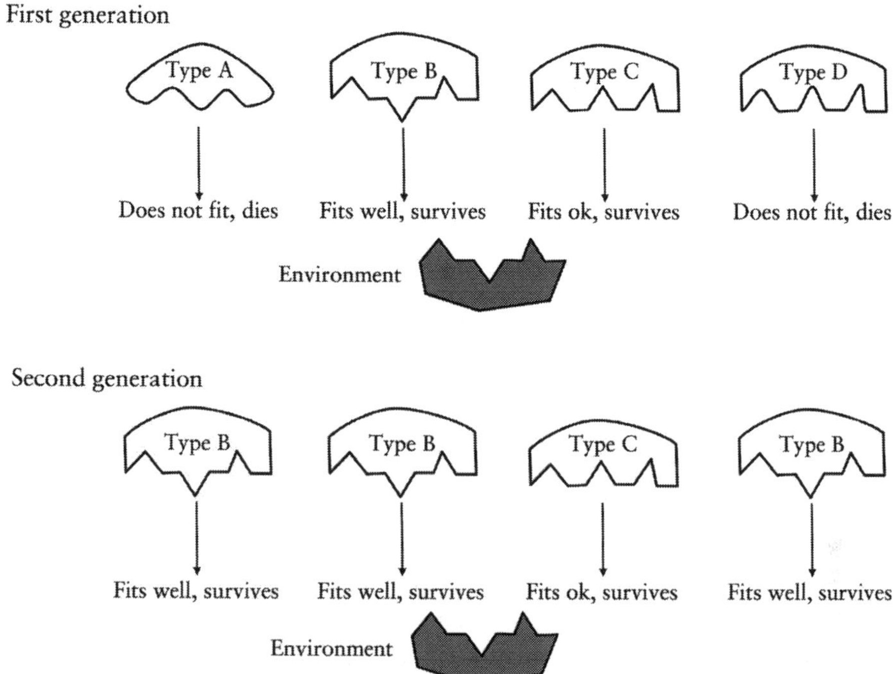

Figure 15.1 In neo-Darwinian evolution, the environment presents problems (here represented by the dark-gray shape), and organisms have variability (represented by the white shapes). Those organisms that are better fit to the environment (Type B and, to a certain extent, Type C) will survive and pass their traits on to the next generation (note the second generation has more Type B organisms than the first generation).

(a biologist, among other things, who explored the genetic variation and trait inheritance in pea plants) was combined with Darwin's ideas, and this combined work was called neo-Darwinism. While deeply controversial at first, neo-Darwinism—colloquially referred to as Darwinian evolution—is now part of mainstream scientific thought.

As Grandpa Tom explained to Fred, Darwin's model of evolution is summed up as "survival of the fittest". This is a bit short on details, however! And the devil really is in the details. In broad strokes, neo-Darwinism works like this (see Figure 15.1):

A) The world (read: environment) has certain problems that need to be solved by a particular species. These might be problems of harsh environments (blistering hot, freezing cold, subject to earthquakes or sudden violent storms, etc.), predators, lack of edible nutrients, or any number of other threats to an organism's continued survival.
B) Individual members of a species have natural variations. Some individual members are bigger, smaller, faster, or have longer beaks. These variations are heritable—taller members of the species will tend to have taller offspring, those with denser bones with have offspring with denser bones, and so on.
C) A variation that allows a given member of a species to solve a given problem makes it more likely that this member will survive—maybe having longer limbs means you can reach higher leaves, or having darker skin means you have greater protection from the sun, or a sharper beak means you can break open tougher nuts.

D) Members of a species are in competition with each other (and with other species) for limited resources, and the better fit organisms will win. In this way, the members of a species that fit their environment better will survive in greater numbers and reproduce in greater numbers. Those who are less fit will be more likely to die and less likely to reproduce, and as a consequence their variations will become less common. Over time, a species as a whole will eventually be better fit for the environment.
E) Different groups of the same species can diverge from each other if they end up in different habitats with different problems to solve. They might eventually become different enough to be considered different species.
F) Members of a species will go extinct if they can't solve the problems of the environment.

And so what about Fred's superheroes? Could neo-Darwinian evolution allow for Betty the Bomb to make nitroglycerin sweat? Or for Goldfield the Glowworm to glow? What if the environment had a problem that only glowing would solve, would that make glowing skin more likely? As Grandpa Tom cautioned Fred, the neo-Darwinian program doesn't really allow for that kind of situation-specific change. The variations within a species are *random*, so even if the environment presented a problem that only glowing would solve, it would not make glowing more likely to appear in the first place. Once it *appears* in one or more members of a species, it might be more likely to *continue* based on those circumstances, but that doesn't change the likelihood of it happening. Moreover, the program *only* allows for evolutionary pressures that affect *procreation*. Or in other words, if having the ability to immediately understand any language doesn't affect whether an animal will reproduce, then it cannot be selected for. This is also why, for example, something like Alzheimer's—which primarily affects people *after* they are past the age of procreation—will be unlikely to disappear due to evolution.

And of course, it's all a bit more complicated than that. To understand this, though, we have to understand what is meant by "natural variations" and "heritable". And to understand *that*, we have to understand DNA (see Box 15.1).

Box 15.1 DNA

The discovery of deoxyribonucleic acid (DNA) was a *very* big deal—it seemed to fulfill the promise of Gregor Mendel's idea that there was *something* that transmitted information from one generation (of pea plants or any other organism) to the next. Something that dictated whether the plant produced green or yellow peas, whether a person has freckles or not, whether a dog's tail was curly or straight.

Every organism has a set of DNA strands that collectively make up that organism's *genes*. In sexual reproduction (how, for example, humans, other mammals, and birds reproduce), at least two parents produce offspring that are a mix of both parents' DNA. It is not always an even split between the two parents, and each of the offspring only gets a subset of each parent's DNA. Siblings—unless they are identical twins—have completely different subsets, and so they will exhibit different traits from each other—one might be taller; one might have darker hair. In asexual reproduction (how, for example, bacteria, single-celled organisms, and some fish reproduce), one parent produces theoretically genetically identical offspring.

The most well-known description of DNA is as a kind of blueprint—that is, the DNA contains a specific plan for every part of the body, and it feeds information to the body on how to function. The mechanics of this are a little complicated, but it's worth understanding the basic process. DNA is made up of two strands (made of sugar phosphates and bases) wound around each other in a shape known as the *double helix*[3] (see Figure 15.2). The two sides are held together via base pairs made of the four base chemicals: adenine always bonds with thymine, and cytosine always bonds with guanine. If you think of the DNA as a kind of twisted ladder, the base chemicals are the rungs of that ladder.

DNA "talks" to the body by pulling apart one section of the strand—so you end up with one side of the ladder split through the rungs. Then an enzyme called RNA polymerase creates the other half-ladder, which is called messenger ribonucleic acid (mRNA). The mRNA, in turn, creates protein strands, which might do any number of things[4] (build cell walls, cause muscle contraction, transport molecules across the cell membrane, etc.). In short, DNA → mRNA → proteins → bodily functions (see Figure 15.2).

If this is an entirely feed-forward mechanism, meaning influence is only in one direction, then it is reasonable to consider DNA a kind of blueprint from which the entire body and all its subsequent behaviors are made. So you have a specific gene that tells your body how tall to grow, another that changes the density of your bones. *But it turns out that this is not really how any of this works.* It should come as no surprise to the reader of this book that causality in this system is actually complex and multidirectional rather than simple and linear. In fact, there are documented cases for each of the arrows of causality in Figure 15.2 bottom diagram (Gottlieb, 2000; Lewontin, 2001).

In other words, a person's height might be affected by the environment, and that might, in turn, affect the DNA of the person in a way that might get handed down to their offspring.[5] Bone density might be affected by the actions of the person

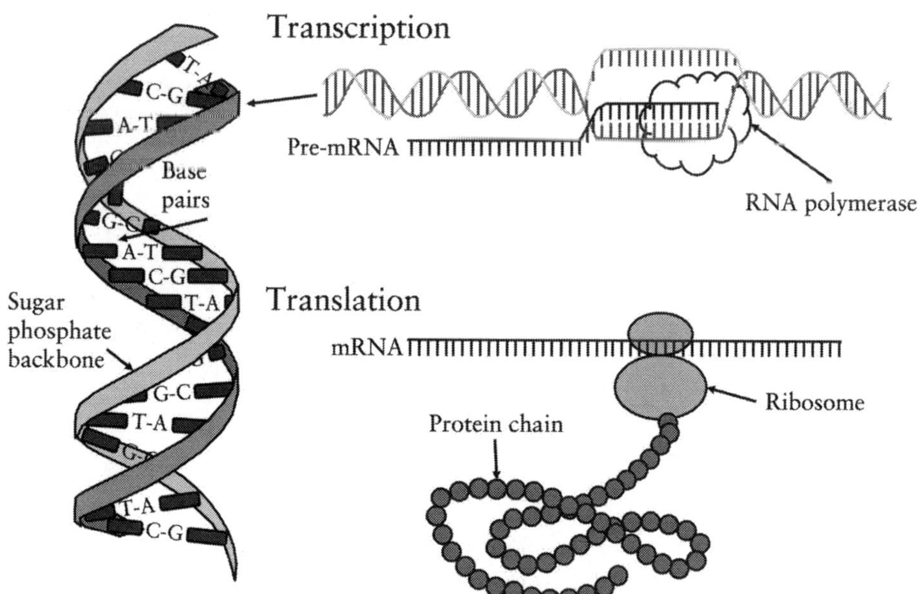

Figure 15.2 DNA has a double-helix structure (it looks like a twisted ladder). To affect the body, DNA (using RNA polymerase) creates mRNA (a process called *transcription*); The ribosome works on the mRNA to create protein chains (a process called *translation*).

Fully feedforward, DNA as "blueprint":

DNA ⟶ mRNA ⟶ Protein chains ⟶ Body/behavior

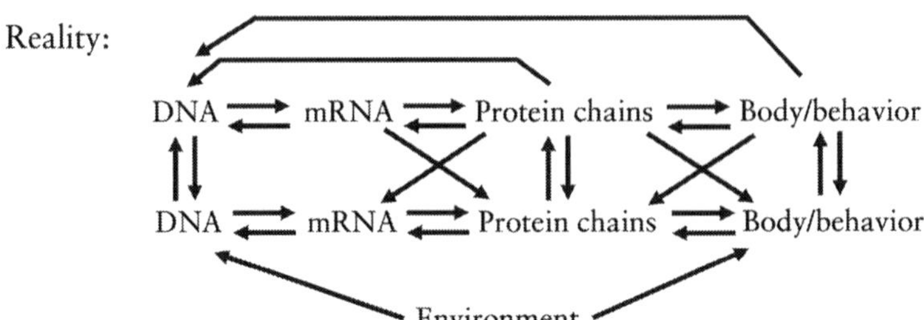

Figure 15.3 Instead of an exclusively feed forward system (top), the function of DNA is as one part of a complex web of causality (bottom).

(like exercise or diet), and change the way the muscles interact with mRNA. It is anything *but* straightforward and simple. There is an entire branch of science, called *epigenetics*, that studies the complex question of how genes express themselves in development.

The important takeaway here is that DNA is *not magic*. It is not a blueprint or a set of instructions that the body blindly follows without reference to context. Ascribing all differences between species and between members of a species to specific changes in DNA is both shortsighted and in direct contradiction to the evidence (see Chapter 16 for more on the role of DNA in development).

Genetic Variation and Inheritance

In the steps listed at the beginning of this section, part B of Darwin's program assumes that natural variation exists and is heritable. But neither variation nor inheritance is as simple as Mendel's pea plants make it seem. As discussed in Chapter 10 (see Figure 10.2) and in Box 15.1 (see Figure 15.3), the relationship between the DNA one inherits and the organism one becomes is *not* straightforward and linear. Even identical twins (who start with *identical* DNA) do not end up the same as adults. Depending on their life experiences, they might be of different heights, weights, hair colors, and so on. Their actions and environment shape what the DNA does and can even alter the structure of the DNA itself in a way that changes how it gets passed on to the next generation (Gottlieb, 2000).

And inheritance is not as straightforward as merely passing unaltered DNA on to the next generation. Even in the simplest of cases, there is more complexity in inheritance than Darwin's program would predict. For example, a single-celled organism called *Paramecium* reproduces (asexually) by doubling all the internal structures (including the DNA) and then pulling apart into two organisms. The paramecium has rows of tiny hairs on its outside (see Figure 15.4) that help it move around (to find food).

A scientist by the name of Sonneborn performed surgery on an individual paramecium (see Goodwin, 1994). He removed a few rows of the tiny hairs and reattached them in the reverse pattern, creating what he called a melon stripe. After the surgery, the paramecium

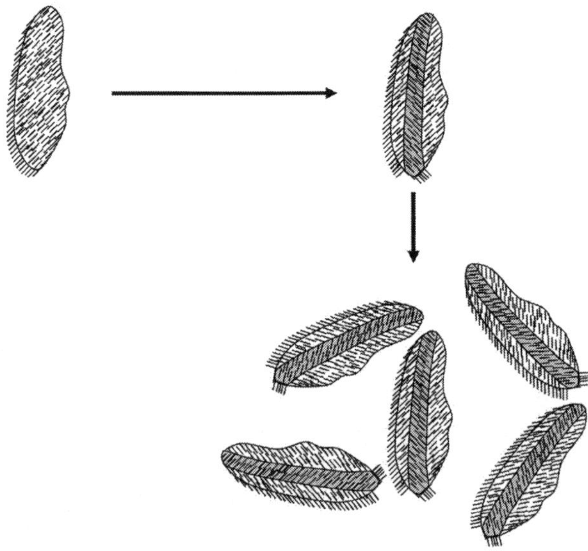

Figure 15.4 Sonneborn surgically altered the single-celled paramecium so that it had one stripe of hair cells going in a different direction; later, the offspring of the altered paramecium inherited the alteration.

once again began to reproduce. And all of its subsequent offspring had the same melon stripe! Sonneborn did not change (could not change) its DNA, but the acquired structure was still passed on.

And there's more! Pea plants (and paramecia) exhibit what is called *homozygosity*, which is to say that if you plant a pea, you will get a pea plant that looks very much like the one you got the pea *from*. The offspring are very like the parents. A single trait is easily passed on to the offspring.

Other species (apples, for example) exhibit *heterozygosity*. In these species, the offspring are very *unlike* the parents. If you take the seed from a Gala apple and plant it, you will *not* get a Gala apple tree. In fact, you could plant an entire *orchard* of trees from Gala apples, and it's likely that none of the apples produced will even be edible, let alone as delicious as the Gala.[6] The advantage of this for the species of apple tree is that it shows *extreme diversity*, which makes it more likely to survive (and thrive!) in new or changing environments.[7]

What is interesting about the case of the apple tree is that its extreme heterozygosity does not really follow Darwin's notion of species becoming *more fit* to their environments over time. If the tree were following Darwin's plan and becoming more fit to the environment, then a single trait (thickness of the branches, sweetness of the fruit, dispersal of the leaf pattern, etc.) would be selected for and passed down to the next generation. Instead, the apple tree shows extreme diversity *every single generation*. Interestingly, rather than making it more difficult for the tree species to survive, the extreme diversity ensures that the species *as a whole* is more likely to survive (because it can meet any environmental challenge)—even if an individual tree is *less* likely to survive.

Survival of What?

The extreme diversity of the apple tree brings up another question. What, exactly, does it mean to get more *fit* over time in the Darwinian program? The accepted definition is about the prevalence of different genes in a *population*, but all of the pressure (as described by Darwin) is on *individuals*. It is not the entire herd that needs to be fast, it is the *individual* members of the herd that need to be fast enough to outrun the predator and live to reproduce.[8]

One of the most common examples given for the issue of individual versus species-wide survival is the paradox of altruism, specifically the kind that leads to someone risking their own life to save others. Altruism increases the chances that the species as a *whole* will survive but decreases the chances that the *altruistic individual* will do so and pass on its particular set of genes. Although it's hard to imagine that there is a gene that codes for altruistic intent—remember, DNA is not magic!

Another example is cooperative breeding. These are situations where the breeding pair raises their young with helpers—members of the same species (but not always the same *family*) that help keep the offspring alive into adulthood (Riehl, 2013). There does not appear to be any direct genetic benefit to the helpers in this case. The typical workaround to explain behavior of this kind is that the helpers increase the chances of survival for their (helped) family members. The helper then preserves DNA that is *related* to theirs, which is almost as good as preserving one's own DNA. Alternatively, it could be that helping *now* increases their chances of being able to mate *later* with members of the cooperative breeding group. But both of those explanations feel like an attempt to make the observed data fit the theory rather than the other way around.

Although, it's also worth mentioning that not everything is (or can be) *directly* selected for in evolution. Or in other words, there might be some aspects of a species that exist not because survival directly pressured them to exist but rather because they came as a kind of gift-with-purchase of another useful trait. It can be fun to come up with reasons why this or that trait might be adaptive in the neo-Darwinian sense, but it's entirely possible that the trait in question came about in an *incidental* way.

Take, for example, the redness of human blood (and that of many other animals). Blood is red because the hemoglobin in the blood—which is what transports oxygen from the lungs to the rest of the body—happens to be red.[9] Having red blood did not make us more fit to survive, but having blood that transports oxygen *did*. There are, however, other ways to transport oxygen in the blood. Octopuses have blue blood because their blood transports oxygen using hemocyanin (which is blue). In either case, the trait that is selected for is having blood that transports oxygen around the body; the color is a gift-with-purchase.

At this point, Fred was starting to feel a little less confident that his superheroes were plausible in a neo-Darwinian sense. Even though humans are (like apples) heterozygotic, it didn't seem that random variation might be enough to get us nitroglycerin sweat! It was hard to imagine that glowing would come as a gift-with-purchase of something else useful. But just when he was about to give up, Grandpa Tom (now in full lecture mode) started talking about the ways in which the neo-Darwinian program didn't *quite* get everything right. Fred perked up; if the neo-Darwinian program was *wrong*, maybe his superheroes were possible after all!

Role of the Environment

One of the biggest difficulties with the neo-Darwinian program is the way that the environment is described and the role it plays in the program as a whole. The neo-Darwinian program treats the environment as something that exists, unchanging, independent of the organism.[10] Look again at Figure 15.1; the environment is represented as a shape. That shape does not require the existence of an organism to define it and does not change once it comes into contact with the organism. Both of these properties are unsupportable.

The ecological program does not allow for a separation between animal and environment (see Chapters 3–5, 9, and 12)—so from our standpoint, this is problematic on the face of it. But it's worth unpacking *why* it's problematic (other than violating one of the ecological assumptions). The neo-Darwinian program defines evolution as a species changing to better fit the environment. But organisms don't interact with the *whole* environment (humans never lay eggs, for example; birds never dive to the bottom of the ocean); they interact with a *subset* of the environment (called a niche).

If species are evolving to get more fit to a niche, then in order for new species to evolve, there must exist niches that are currently unoccupied (that is, niches without an organism in them), and that's not possible. A niche implies a specific fit between organism and environment. A niche implies an animal, and an animal implies a niche. No two species have *exactly* the same niche, even if they are competing over the same resources and live in the same geographic area.

Moreover, a niche *cannot* be defined without an organism. If you think of the niche as a subset of the whole environment, then defining a niche is deciding on what subset of that environment should be included. But there are uncountably many ways to break up the environment! We could suggest a niche for an egg-laying creature that lives in trees and feeds off geothermal vents on the ocean's floor. We could suggest a niche for a creature that has warm blood, lives in the curtains of human houses, and eats houseplants. And so on. And on. And on. Anything can be a niche! If anything can be a niche, we cannot decide *in advance* what a species might be trying to get *fit* to. In this sense, evolution loses explanatory or predictive power.

Also, the idea of an unchanging environment is patently false! The environment changes (often rapidly) based on any number of factors. The climate might shift, an invasive species might change the entire balance of available resources, or an opportunistic bacteria might kill off entire crops, which changes the landscape.

And—and this is important—organisms affect their environments! Humans are the most obvious example of this, but there are plenty of other examples of species making dramatic changes to their environment, often (though not always) on purpose (a process called *niche construction*, see Laland, Odling-Smee, & Feldman, 2000; Withagen & van Wermeskerken, 2010). The beaver purposefully dams water to change the flow, termites build skyscrapers and plant crops, and grazing deer will eat their favorite grasses and deposit the seeds in their excrement, making the grass more likely to grow in that area.

Other Concerns

Darwin's description of evolution is like an asymptote in math (see Figure 15.5)—species get closer and closer to the existing environment, each generation being just slightly more fit than the last. In this view, it is theoretically possible that a species could evolve enough that it would reach perfect fitness with the environment (that is, it would be completely *adapted*), and it would stop changing. But that does not match the existing data!

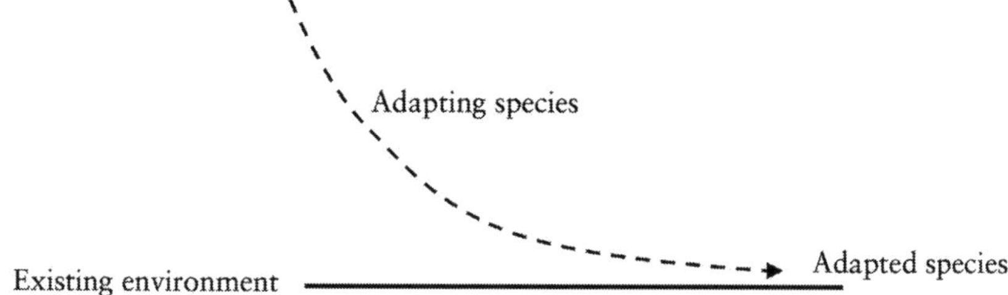

Figure 15.5 Darwin's evolution is like an asymptote; the species gets more and more fit to the environment, eventually becoming adapted.

If this were the case, then the longer a species had managed to survive, the better it should be at *continuing to survive* because it had been through the process of adaptation and come out fitter on the other side. Or in other words, we would expect that the longer a given species had been around, the less likely it would be to go extinct. However, extinction rates appear to be roughly similar for all species—*independent* of the length of time a species has been in existence (Lewontin, 1978).

However, the *biggest* concern with the neo-Darwinian program is that it has *no way* to account for the origins of life. Even if we ignore the other concerns, this one would keep the program from being completely comprehensive. Darwin's model of evolution *presupposes* existing life with existing variations. This does not mean that the theory does not have scientific or pragmatic value! As we said in Chapter 4 (paraphrasing Box, 1976), all models are wrong; some are useful. To be sure, Darwin's theory has been very useful. It can explain most of the observed evolutionary phenomena, which accounts for its acceptance by both scientists and the general public, but even Darwin acknowledged this particular shortcoming. As Grandpa Tom put it, it's not that the insights from the neo-Darwinian approach are *wrong*; it's that they're *incomplete*.

The Red Queen Hypothesis

One attempt to complete the neo-Darwinian program included an explicit role for the ever-changing nature of the environment. The neo-Darwinian program doesn't expressly forbid a changing environment; it just doesn't *assume* it or make extended space for it. Instead, the focus is entirely on the changing organism.

From the ecological perspective, it's not logical to focus on *either* the organism *or* the environment to the exclusion of the other (or even to assign them unequal roles). The organism cannot be understood without the ecological niche, and the ecological niche is defined by the (possible) actions of the organism. By definition, the niche and the organism already fit each other—they are reciprocal and interdependent.

So what to do? If organisms are perfectly fit to their environment, then according to Darwin, there would be no changes in a species over time. *But there are obviously changes.* To reconcile this, Van Valen (1973) suggested that the environment is in a constant state of change *ahead of* the organism. Or in other words, an organism's evolution is always a generation behind, adapted to the circumstances that applied to the *previous* generation, and the organism has to constantly change just to keep up with the changes in the environment (see Figure 15.6). This,

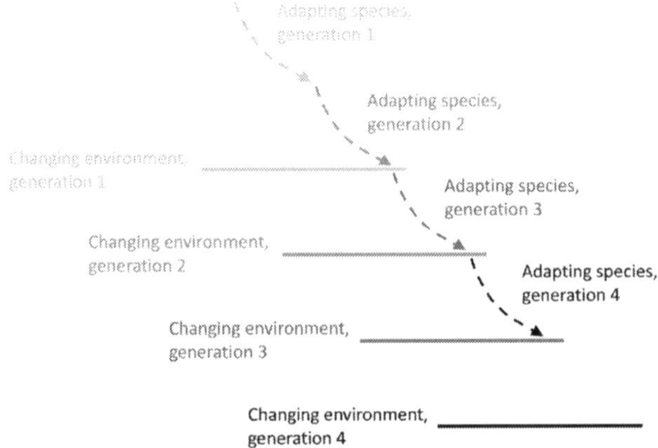

Figure 15.6 According to the Red Queen hypothesis, the environment is in a constant state of change, so the organisms have to continuously change just to keep up.

by the way, is why he called it the Red Queen hypothesis—it comes from *Through the Looking Glass* by Lewis Carroll. In it, the Red Queen forces Alice and other denizens of Wonderland to run a race where they have to keep running and running just to stay in place.

The Red Queen hypothesis avoids the empty niche problem—here, the organisms are in a niche (defined by their interactions with the environment). The niche is just continuously changing. It explains why extinction rates might be independent of the time a species has been around—if the niche is always changing and the organism is constantly having to change to keep up with it, then no species is in a privileged place in terms of being good at surviving in the *next* generation.

In this view, niches are gradually but continuously changing, and species are gradually but continuously running along behind. Since every *new* niche is very similar to the *old* niche, each *new* generation of a species can be very similar to the *last* generation and keep surviving. Now, let's say, for (a hypothetical) example, that the world changed in such a way that humans had to glow in order to survive (absurd, we know, but go with us here). Humans are just not going to make it. There's no part of our DNA that has glowing as one of the accessible variabilities. We have genes that make us shorter or taller, have different skin color (or have patterns on the skin, like freckles), stronger or weaker, better or worse at absorbing iron—but none that could, in one of their variations, produce *glowing* skin. Van Valen (1973) suggests that such changes in the environment are extinction events—when a niche changes in such a way that the existing genetic variation is inadequate, then that's the ballgame.

While it goes a long way to helping complete the neo-Darwinian program, the Red Queen hypothesis *still* separates the animal and the environment. And this is a non-starter for ecologically minded theories of evolution. Moreover, it doesn't explain discontinuities in evolution. If a species is "keeping up" more or less with its environment, why would a new species emerge? Why would warm-blooded creatures evolve when cold-blooded ones are doing fine? Why would birds evolve when the land-dwellers are making it work? Why bother making something that *eats* the plants when plants are happily photosynthesizing? It can explain why a brand-new species might survive once it gets here, but not why it might happen in the *first place*. And again, in a similar way, it still does not have an answer for the beginning of life.

Fred is feeling like there might be *no* complete answer to the questions of evolution, and he's pretty well convinced that his superheroes just aren't possible. He's also starting to wonder if maybe this whole evolution thing isn't as well understood as his biology teacher in high school led him to believe! Grandpa Tom reminded Fred that while neo-Darwinism is the most widespread version of selectionism, it is certainly not the *only* one. He suggested that if Fred (or our reader!) were curious, he could check out the work of Stephen Jay Gould, Conway Morris, or Susan Oyama (whose work embraces the full complexity of epigenetics). Their programs each address concerns raised in this chapter and go a long way to explaining many of the issues raised.

But Fred is still somewhat unsatisfied. He is still troubled by the question of the *beginning* of life on Earth. Regardless of the *method* of selection (or subsequent development), *any* selectionist account still assumes that life already exists. Was the beginning of life just a completely miraculous event—unlikely to ever happen again somewhere else? Grandpa Tom suggested Fred might want to consider the problem from an *entirely different* perspective, one far less embraced by mainstream evolutionary biology: thermodynamics.

Thermodynamics

First, don't panic. Thermodynamics is a scary word for an admittedly complex topic, but we promise, it's going to be worth the effort! Briefly, thermodynamics is the study of energy—what energy is, how it moves and changes, and what it does over time. As it turns out, an understanding of *this* might help us understand what the selectionist theories aren't great at (i.e., why there might be discontinuous shifts in species evolution and why there might be *so many different kinds* of life) and what they simply cannot explain (i.e., why and how life started in the first place).

The First Law of Thermodynamics

Unlike in some other areas of science, thermodynamics has *laws*. What this means is that they are principles that *cannot* be violated. It's not a matter of personal opinion; there *are no exceptions*. Everything *must* conform to them.

The first law of thermodynamics has two parts: first, all energy is the same (whether it's currently in the form of heat, mechanical energy, electromagnetic energy, etc.). Second, energy can neither be created nor destroyed. It can be *converted* (which is what happens when light energy is absorbed by a surface and is converted into heat) or moved from one place to another (which is what happens when electricity runs through a wire from the power plant to your house), but it cannot be *lost* or *gained*.

If you're looking at a particular system and it seems as if that system has lost or gained energy, then you need to expand the size of your view—that energy is actually going to or coming from somewhere. And therefore, you *must* expand the scope of your system to include that somewhere else as *part of your system*. Our thermodynamic view on evolution (or anything else, really) is going to have to have a very wide-angle lens. We cannot focus on just one species; we're going to have to expand the view to include the entire Earth *and* the sun *and* a little of space besides.

The second important thing for us to pay attention to here is that the energy in a given system might take different forms—heat, food, trapped energy in the form of fossil fuels, etc. All of the different forms are going to matter because tracking the *conversions* from one form of energy to another is going to explain some of the things that neo-Darwinism and the Red Queen hypothesis could not.

The Second Law of Thermodynamics

To understand the second law, we first have to understand the different types of distributions of energy. Imagine energy is like grains of sand, and the universe is like the top of your dining room table. You could spread the sand evenly across the entire table. This is what is called thermodynamic equilibrium. No one part of the table has any more sand than any other part (see Figure 15.7, *top*).

You could also clump the sand into piles—maybe a big pile over here and a smaller pile over there (see Figure 15.7, *bottom*). The clumpy distribution is more like the current state of our universe. There are massive deposits of energy (like the sun) and smaller deposits of energy (like you!). And there are some places with no energy at all.

Clumpy energy (properly known as *potential energy*) can do mechanical work—as the energy moves from a clump (like Fred) to another location (like when he moves a rake), it causes a physical change in the world (the leaves are moved from one location to another). Energy that is evenly distributed cannot do work because it can't move from a clump to a not-clump. *Entropy* is the measure of how much energy in a system is unavailable for mechanical work.[11] In the example where the sand is evenly distributed across the table, the table is in a state of *maximum entropy* because *none* of the energy is available for mechanical work.

Another way of talking about the same kind of entropy[12] is that it's a measure of the *disorder* in the system. By definition, clumpy energy is considered ordered, and spread-out energy is considered disordered. The more disorder you have, the more entropy you have.

Figure 15.7 Two types of energy distributions imagined as sand (energy) on a table (in the system). Fully spread-out sand is like thermodynamic equilibrium; clumped-up sand represents energy that is still ready to do work. At equilibrium, entropy is at maximum; in clumps, entropy is lower.

The second law of thermodynamics says that the state of highly clumpy energy (low entropy) is not a stable distribution; the system will always move to a state of more evenly distributed energy (high entropy). If you define right now as Time 1 and some time in the future as Time 2, then the amount of entropy at Time 2 *has to be higher* than the amount of entropy at Time 1.[13]

Energy Sinks and Negentropy

We're almost to the point of being able to use these concepts to explain evolution! But there are two more concepts that will help in that endeavor. First, an *energy sink* is a structure (broadly defined) that can trap energy and store it for some amount of time. It is possible to *create* an energy sink on purpose, and we usually do this for one of two reasons—either to use the energy later or to get the energy out of the way. An example of the first kind is a battery. An example of the second kind is a structure in computers that absorbs heat energy to keep the processor from overheating (which allows it to run more efficiently).

Energy sinks also exist in nature. For example, plants are an energy sink—they trap energy from the sun, and that energy is used when the plant is eaten by another organism. Another example is fossil fuels. A very long time ago, plants[14] lived and died. At the time, there were no bacteria or bugs to eat the dead plants (they hadn't evolved yet), so they did not decay. Instead, they got covered over by years of dirt and stone accumulation. With lots of pressure and lots of time, those plants turned into oil. That layer of plant material trapped an impressive amount of energy from the sun, energy we now use to power just about every technology on the planet.

Our last useful concept is *negentropy*. Recall that, according to the second law of thermodynamics, entropy has to be increasing over time. Or in other words, the system has to be getting more *disordered* over time (the sand has to be getting more spread out). But (and it's an important but) evolution appears to be creating *more* order—after all, life started as single-celled organisms and progressed to multicellular organisms with complex metabolic systems.

Anything that is getting more ordered—for example, if the sand were to spontaneously clump together again—is said to be *negentropic* (negentropy is the noun form). Negentropy is a problem because it is seemingly in violation of the second law of thermodynamics. So anything that appears to be negentropic needs further investigation. Evolution appears to be negentropic (in fact, some early scholars argued against evolution on these grounds), but as we will see, that is not the case.

Is Evolution Negentropic?

According to the second law of thermodynamics, clumpy energy is not sustainable, and any system that exhibits clumpy energy is going to move toward a less clumpy state as soon as it can. Or in other words, the system is going to *dissipate* the energy as quickly as possible. Here, to dissipate means to spread out. This does not have to be an intentional thing. A ball does not have to *intend* to roll down a hill, it will just do so. And in this way, its energy will dissipate.

A single-celled organism is not going to dissipate much energy; it can only eat so much and turn that energy into movement, hunting more energy to eat, and procreating. Multicellular organisms (especially ones with relatively sophisticated perceiving-acting-cognizing abilities), on the other hand, dissipate energy at a *much* faster rate (see Swenson & Turvey, 1991). Even if they confine themselves to the same activities of moving, eating, and mating, their efforts in this respect require an order of magnitude more energy than the single-celled organism. They will consume more food and dissipate more energy as a multicellular unit than they would if each cell in their body was a cell on its own.

Or in other words, evolution has moved living organisms from a state of increasing entropy very slowly (as single-celled organisms) to increasing entropy much more quickly (as multicellular organisms). Evolution is not negentropic. It appears to be so only when you consider the system to be an isolated organism. When you consider the system to be the *whole planet*, evolution is doing an excellent job of increasing entropy production over time.

Of course, just because evolution does not *violate* the second law of thermodynamics, it does not immediately follow that evolution is *driven* by the second law of thermodynamics. To show this, we must demonstrate that this theory does a better job explaining the observed data *and* can explain things that all the selectionist theories cannot.

Thermodynamic Explanation of Evolution

The first thing a thermodynamic view on evolution does is shift the focus from the *current state* of the *organism* to the *end state* of the *whole system*. That is, rather than wondering how a particular organism came by a particular trait, it assumes a particular *endpoint of the whole system* and asks how different evolutionary shifts lead to that end.

Thermodynamic equilibrium (maximum entropy, energy evenly spread out) is the inevitable end of the universe (a long, long time from now, don't worry!). There is no other option. From this view, all of the activity in evolution has to be in service of achieving that end state by dissipating energy and increasing entropy. Understanding evolution in this way is akin to looking at the graph in Figure 15.8 and asking what is the fastest path from the current state to maximum entropy. Note the differences from Figure 15.5—instead of a single species getting closer to an environment, this tracks the production of entropy of the *whole Earth* as it moves toward a clearly defined endpoint.

Importantly, this view of evolution does not (cannot) focus on just one organism or one species. The progression has to be of the system as a *whole*. Remember, in thermodynamics, the system is defined as the entire set of things that are exchanging energy (the whole dining room table from the sand example). You cannot focus on one particular pile of sand and understand

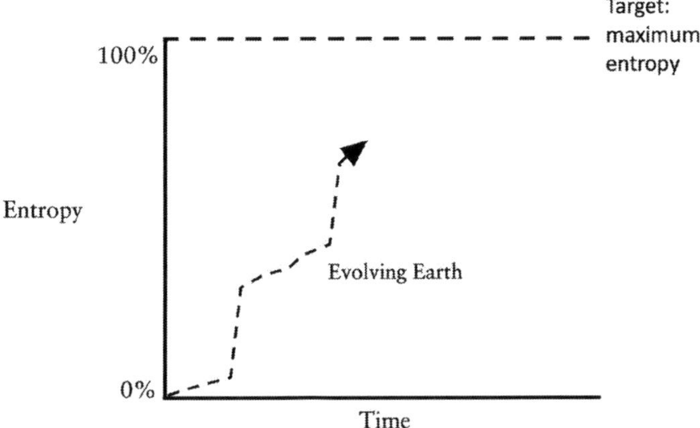

Figure 15.8 Evolution from a thermodynamic perspective. The endpoint is a given, and the slope can only be positive. Note the discontinuous jumps in entropy—these are places where a new species evolved to more efficiently dissipate energy.

its behavior; you *have* to view the entire system (the entire table) to understand the flow of energy. Local decreases in entropy lead to global *increases* in entropy *every time*.

And so, the pressures of evolution are not about pressures to survive and procreate (at least not directly). Instead, they are pressures of dissipating more energy more quickly. Survival is a necessary part of that (a dead organism no longer dissipates energy[15]), as is procreation (one of the fastest ways an organism can increase entropy is to create *more* organisms, which will *also* dissipate energy), but neither of those is the main driving force of evolution.

So far, the two theories (neo-Darwinism and thermodynamics) do not make different predictions. Since survival and procreation are *in service of* energy dissipation, both would result in species striving to do both. Where thermodynamics triumphs is in explaining some of the phenomena that Darwinian evolution *can't*.

Discontinuities of Evolution and the Variety of Life

Neither the Red Queen hypothesis nor neo-Darwinism can fully explain what we have called discontinuities of evolution.[16] These are scenarios where a new type of life spontaneously emerges even when the previous type of life was doing just fine surviving—land mammals appearing when aquatic life is thriving, for example. From the thermodynamic perspective, however, it is perfectly sensible.

To understand this, we have to imagine the system as a *whole*. The sun is an absolutely enormous source of energy (it's a *huge* pile of sand). Everything the various structures and life-forms on Earth are doing ultimately dissipates that energy. Energy that is being dissipated by one source (like plants) sometimes ends up in an energy sink (like oxygen in the air—the plants create it as a by-product of using photons to process water; see Box 15.2). Energy sinks, particularly widespread ones, are going to create a pathway for evolution. *Something* is going to evolve to make use of that energy sink—it *has to do so* in order to satisfy the second law of thermodynamics.

Discontinuities of evolution can occur when there is an energy sink that has trapped so much energy over time that, in order for the system continue to efficiently dissipate energy, something has to start dissipating the energy trapped in that sink. Land animals evolved even though aquatic life was thriving because there was a *lot of energy* available on the land (and in the air—from the plants!).

And from that perspective, the extreme variety of life is also perfectly understandable (see Colinvaux, 1979). After all, every new form of life offers *itself* as an energy sink for something else. And sometimes, a form of life creates (as in the case of plants creating an oxygen-rich atmosphere) energy sinks elsewhere. Each new energy sink is a new opportunity for (possibly multiple) species to evolve.[17]

The fascinating thing about this is that it allows for something remarkable—the ability to predict the evolution of a new species. If we are aware of an available and currently untapped energy sink, then we would predict that something would evolve to dissipate it. Humans, for example, have trapped a great deal of energy in plastic. Plastic is nonbiodegradable. When we say something is nonbiodegradable, we are saying there are no species that are around (yet) to eat it.

We would predict that, particularly given how widespread plastic is, eventually something would evolve to eat it. And that's exactly what happened! Enter the plastic-eating wax worms (Yang et al., 2014), the plastic-eating fungus (Russell et al., 2011), and the plastic-eating microorganisms (Iram, Riaz, & Iqbal, 2019). Now, these species aren't consuming nearly enough plastic to solve our garbage problems or anything, but according to the thermodynamic approach, the *existence* of these species was an inevitability.

The Beginning of Life

Perhaps the most valuable contribution of the thermodynamic approach is that it provides insight into why (and how) life began in the first place. In fact, according to this approach, life beginning was a far more probable event than life *not* beginning. Under these conditions, life was *inevitable*. To explain why, it helps to have an illustrative example: the Rayleigh-Bénard convection cell (Bénard, 1900; Rayleigh, 1916).

Grandpa Tom takes Fred over to his stove and pulls out a frying pan (Fred is a little concerned that Grandpa Tom might have forgotten what they were talking about and is just getting lunch ready, but then he resumes his explanation). He pours cooking oil in a very thin layer into the pan. Before the burners are turned on, he explains, the oil is the same everywhere in the pan. The molecules of the oil are moving around randomly and bumping into each other, but no one place is any different from any other. Right now, the pan is the same temperature as the air (see Figure 15.9, *top*).

But wait! He turns on the stove, and the pan starts to heat up. There is now a difference in temperature between the pan and the air (we'll call that ΔT). As long as ΔT stays below a certain threshold, the oil in the pan can dissipate the energy without doing anything fancy. The heat energy gets converted into movement energy of the oil molecules. That movement pushes the (hotter) oil molecules to the top of the oil layer, where it releases the energy to the air (cooling the oil molecules), and then they can sink to the bottom and repeat (see Figure 15.9, *middle*).

However, once ΔT reaches a certain threshold, there is simply too much incoming energy to dissipate with the movement of single molecules working on their own. What happens next is quite amazing but is nothing more than the second law of thermodynamics at work—*order spontaneously emerges*. The oil molecules abruptly start working in *a coordinated pattern* called convection cells (see Figure 15.9, *bottom*), and there is a discontinuous and dramatic increase in the dissipation of heat energy with the emergence of the cells.

While it is just one example, there are many others like it (see Chapter 16). Presented with a large energy sink in need of dissipation, previously random elements of a system will spontaneously coordinate in order to dissipate the energy faster. It is not a stretch to imagine that life began in just this way—the sun providing a massive energy differential and cells spontaneously forming to dissipate the energy.

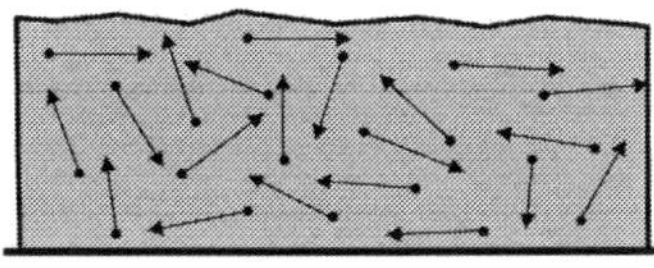

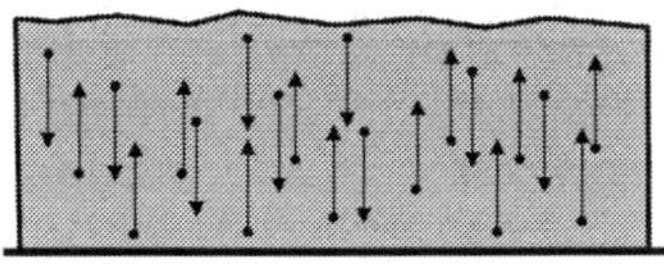

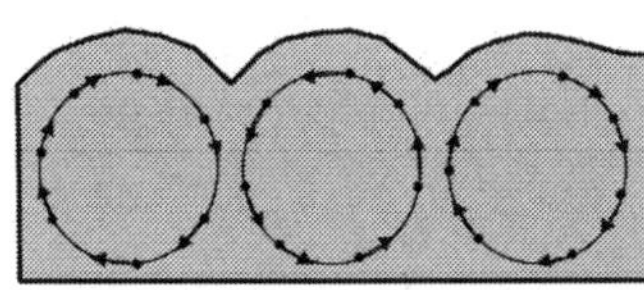

Figure 15.9 When there is no difference between the pan and the air, the oil molecules move randomly (*top*), but when the pan is heated (*middle*), the molecules start to move in order to dissipate the energy. Once the difference in temperature between the pan and the air reaches a critical threshold, convection cells are spontaneously formed to dissipate the energy faster (*bottom*).

Box 15.2 Visible Light Spectrum

As we pointed out in Chapter 3, visible light is a small part of the electromagnetic energy that is emitted by the sun. It's worth investigating *why* that is the portion of the light spectrum that we are sensitive to. It is not just that it reliably bounces off matter (unlike, say, x-rays, which go *through* some kinds of matter) because there are parts of the spectrum that we cannot see that also do that. So why just this portion?

First, not all of the energy that is emitted by the sun reliably makes its way to the surface of the Earth. Consider Figure 15.10. Many wavelengths of electromagnetic energy are absorbed by the water vapor, carbon dioxide, and ozone in the atmosphere. It turns out that the largest window of light that reliably makes its way to Earth is in the 400- to 700-nanometer range—the visible light spectrum!

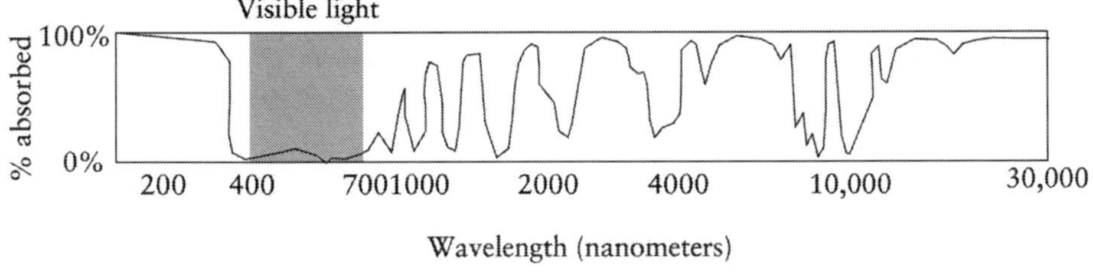

Figure 15.10 Different wavelengths of light are absorbed in different amounts by the water, water vapor, carbon dioxide, oxygen, and ozone present on Earth and in its atmosphere. The visible light spectrum (400–700 nanometers) is largely not absorbed by any of those elements.

But there's more to it than this! The light that was available *also* dictated how perceptual systems *began in the first place*. Life on Earth started as something akin to fermenting bacteria, called prokaryotes, who survived by breaking down organic compounds (like carbohydrates) in the absence of oxygen (because there wasn't any yet!). As part of this process, they created carbon dioxide as a by-product (an energy sink).

The next type of life emerged to take advantage of that energy sink—photosynthesizing bacteria called protocyanobacteria. They figured out how to use two photons (light energy from the sun) to break apart one water molecule. In this way, they took advantage of the virtually infinite source of energy from the sun *and* the virtually infinite source of energy from the water. They used the now readily available carbon dioxide to store the energy in the cell for later use. As a by-product of this process, they released tons of oxygen (another energy sink!).

And here's where the light spectrum comes in: wavelengths of light higher than 700 nanometers are too weak to power the photosynthesis reaction. Wavelengths of light below 400 nanometers chemically destroy the proteins and DNA in organic life-forms (what we might think of as radiation poisoning).

And so these protocyanobacteria largely lived in one depth of the early oceans—deep enough to protect themselves from the harmful end of the radiation spectrum, high enough to soak up the 400- to 700-nanometer wavelength light rays and photosynthesize to their heart's content. One of the *next* life-forms to emerge ate the protocyanobacteria (you might think of them as the first predators). To catch their prey, they evolved to be able to sense this exact light range (the current visible light spectrum) in order to find the correct depth in order to hunt and eat the protocyanobacteria. This is the historical beginnings of the visual system (Swenson & Turvey, 1991).

Fred's hopes for a mutant superhero revolution might be well and thoroughly dashed, but he is still excited by all he learned. Evolution turned out to be a *lot* more complicated (and interesting) than he had expected! Grandpa Tom's last point was that the thermodynamic approach and the neo-Darwinian approach were (on a theoretical level, if not a practical one) incompatible. Thermodynamics essentially requires that the entire planet is a system that is evolving over time, and neo-Darwinism does not allow for that type of evolution (Dawkins, 1982). Neo-Darwinism requires multiple members of the same species exhibiting variability. There are not multiple, varying Earths competing for resources. There is just one Earth. Happily, the insights gained from years of study on the neo-Darwinian approach can (largely with little alteration) be applied to the thermodynamic approach; the latter just offers a more comprehensive framework by which to understand those insights.

Notes

1 We encourage the reader to try this for themselves: mix one part water to two parts cornstarch. It will act like a solid if you hit it, but act like a liquid if you stir it slowly. *Excellent* use of an afternoon.

2 Jean-Baptiste Lamarck published his theory of evolution nearly 50 years earlier in 1809. And Darwin was nearly "scooped" by a contemporary, Alfred Wallace, but the two communicated via letters and eventually held a joint conference in 1858 to share their work. *On the Origin of Species*, Darwin's seminal work, was published a year later in 1859.

3 The first person to image DNA was Rosalind Franklin. Later, James Watson and Francis Crick used her work (without crediting her) to figure out the structure.

4 Including masquerade as the "spike protein" that allows the deadly COVID-19 virus to attack cells. The mRNA vaccines introduced during the COVID-19 pandemic essentially used the body's natural protein

production to create proteins that did just that. The immune system can then learn the shape of that protein and be more efficient in its response to an actual COVID-19 infection.

5 Interestingly, this notion of an organism's behavior and/or experiences affecting the traits passed on to the organism's offspring was more or less what Lamarck proposed in 1809—an idea that was abandoned when Darwin's account was published.

6 To get another Gala apple tree, you have to take a cutting from the already existing tree and graft it on to an existing root system. In this way, all Gala apple trees are *clones* of the first Gala apple tree. Same goes for Red Delicious, Granny Smith, and so on.

7 This is why John Chapman (known as Johnny Appleseed) was able to grow apple trees all over the United States and Canada, even though there are wildly different climates from one area to the next.

8 As the saying goes, you don't need to be fast enough to outrun the bear, you just need to be faster than the people you are camping with.

9 It's high in iron, which is red when its oxidized (think of rust).

10 It's worth mentioning that this was not true for Darwin *himself.* In fact, he referenced Charles Lyell's *Principles of Geology* which describes the changes in geography as due to small changes in the Earth's crust over time. Darwin reasoned that if the Earth was changing over time, then in order to survive, organisms would need to do so as well! However, neo-Darwinism often treats the environment as static or at least *more* static than organisms.

11 There are a lot of different definitions of entropy. This one is an incomplete definition and is no better than any of the rest.

12 There *are* other kinds. We're not going to talk about them here.

13 In fact, this is how some people *define* time—it is the dimension over which entropy increases. Move in the direction of entropy increase; you are moving forward in time. Move in the direction of entropy decrease; you are moving backward in time. This isn't an important point for our purposes, but we thought it was interesting.

14 Oil is not made from dead dinosaurs, no matter what anyone tells you.

15 You might wonder why we die at all—after all, if death stops entropy production, then pressures to *increase* entropy production should predict organisms that live forever! The answer, of course, is entropy itself. The body will tend toward disorder (and eventual death) just as surely as the entire system is. That said, the second law predicts that organisms will seek to extend their own life as long as possible and that is on the whole what we see.

16 Other selectionist accounts do a better job, see Stephen Jay Gould's work, for example.

17 One could argue that these energy sinks are not entirely dissimilar to the problems in the environment as presented in the selectionist accounts. And that's true! The difference here is that it is explicit about the types of problems that will impact evolution—which allows for prediction.

16 Self-Organization

Ever since his conversation with Grandpa Tom, Fred has been thinking about the Rayleigh-Bénard convection cells (see Chapter 15) that were used as an example of the kind of conditions that could have supported the sudden emergence of life. He found it fascinating that organization would spontaneously emerge when the conditions were *just right*. Fred started talking about it with his friend Claudia, and she mentioned that she had heard of other things like this. That these so-called *self-organized systems* were actually quite common, and he might be able to find more examples if he looked in the right places and talked to the right people.

The notion of self-organization is fundamental to the ecological perspective. The alternative to *self*-organization is *other*-organization, and that raises the specter of the central executive or magical DNA or even some deity with an eye for creative design. The ecological perspective has a commitment to disallowing all of these as explanations for behavior (and for good reason!). There's a similar commitment to disallowing intelligence as a starting condition of the system (that is, we won't take the *loan of intelligence*, see Chapters 1–4). These commitments leave us in the position of having to explain intelligent behavior *without* taking such a loan—it sounds impossible, but it's not.

From the ecological perspective, the solution to this is in natural laws, such as the laws of thermodynamics (see Chapter 15, and Turvey & Carello, 2012). Using natural laws, even the extraordinarily complex behavior of systems can be explained without having to rely on spooky mechanisms or ghostly central executives.

What Is Self-Organization?

In Chapter 4, we joined Fred during an orchestra practice when his director, Dr. Pick, was missing. The members of the orchestra were able to create music without Dr. Pick's direction just by coordinating with their neighbors. And in Chapter 15, Fred's Grandpa Tom showed him a demonstration of Rayleigh-Bénard convection cells by heating oil in a pan. Once the temperature of the oil reached a critical difference from the air above the oil (ΔT), large-scale organization of the oil molecules spontaneously emerged. These are both *examples* of self-organization, but we'll need a *definition* in order to fully explore the concept. The definition has multiple parts (see Camazine et al., 2001).

Not Other-Organized

First, and not to be redundant, self-organized systems need to be *self-organized*. That is, they cannot be led by some external influence (like Dr. Pick, the director); they can't be following some kind of blueprint or plan; they can't be part of a rigid hierarchy.[1] Instead, they have to be composed of individual units, each of which exerts an influence on other local elements (the players in the orchestra were listening to their neighbors; the oil molecules moved each

DOI: 10.4324/9781003145691-19

other via friction). Importantly, no unit can have direct, nonlocal influence (a player cannot be directly influencing another player on the other side of the room; an oil molecule cannot be directly influencing another oil molecule on the other side of the pan). The behavior of a player on *this* side of the room might *eventually* affect the player on *that* side of the room (by affecting, in turn, the behavior of every player in-between them), but that influence is not a direct one.

Just because there is no blueprint does not mean there are no *rules*. This difference is the same as the difference between designating the specific locations along the wall in a room where there should be power outlets versus saying "there should be power outlets every 12 feet". In the first case, there is only one set of acceptable outcomes. In the second, there are an infinite number of possible outcomes, and the solution will *emerge* out of the building process.

It's also possible for a system to be *partially* self-organized (Juarrero, 2013). Imagine a business where the manager tells a group of workers what the desired outcome is (putting all of the merchandise on the shelves, for example, or digging a 50-foot-long trench) but does not designate who should do what. If the workers manage to perform the task just by watching each other and taking over parts of the job that need doing (and assuming none of the workers gets bossy and starts handing out jobs), you might consider this a partially self-organized behavior.

To be clear, we are not suggesting that other-organized systems do not exist! Rather, we are suggesting that *self-organized* systems make up the bulk of biological systems, a number of social systems, and all other natural systems (like those that generate earthquakes). Additionally, we are suggesting that there are a wide variety of phenomena that have been seen as being built via reference to some template (such as the influence that DNA has on development) that are *actually* self-organized. Moreover, viewing them as such can provide new, clearer insights.

Components Are Minimally Intelligent

When we say that the components of a self-organized system are minimally intelligent, we are not saying they are dumb (at least, not always). In the example of the workers digging a ditch, the workers could be *brilliant!* What we mean is that they are not acting any more intelligently than necessary. Or in other words, we are trying to avoid (some of) the problems caused by the *loan of intelligence* that we discussed in the first few chapters. We do not want to ascribe any more intelligence to the components than is *absolutely necessary*. And in a self-organized system, usually very little intelligence is necessary. We are saying that regardless of their inherent intelligence, the components of the system are only following relatively simple rules—just like the outfielders and dogs in Chapter 6.

Rules Are Local

This is related to (possibly even redundant with) the insistence that there can be no nonlocal influence. The simple rules the components are following must be able to be followed *locally*. What this means is that the rules must be able to be followed using only local information. What counts as "local" is relative—the size of the "local" area of an oil molecule is vastly smaller than the size of the "local" area relative to Fred and his cello.

One corollary to this is that there must be constant interaction (read: mutual communication and/or influence) among the individual components. That interaction can take *many* forms—the oil molecules are interacting via friction, the diggers are interacting via watching each other, the orchestra members are interacting via listening to *and* watching each other. In each case, there is a local exchange of influence. If you remove the source of interaction, the complex behaviors stop. Think of the metronomes in Chapter 4. As long as the metronomes were on a surface that could freely move and transmit vibrations back and forth, the metronomes could interact via these vibrations, and they would synchronize their movements. When Fred put the metronomes on a surface that could not transmit vibrations back and forth, it removed their ability to influence each other, and the metronomes did not synchronize (see Figure 4.4).

Patterns Emerge

The next requirement is that self-organized systems must have emergent patterns. Here the definition of pattern is a nonrandom configuration that is not able to be comprehended at the scale of the individual parts (see Figure 4.3). The convection cell cannot be seen by viewing a single oil molecule, the song of the orchestra cannot be heard by listening to just the cello, and the size and shape of the trench cannot be revealed just by watching the actions of one digger. In each case (as in all self-organized systems), the organization can only really be comprehended by looking at a larger scale.

Additionally, these patterns are usually not immediately predictable from an understanding of the smaller pieces. The simple local rules discussed previously do not (cannot) have relevance to the larger pattern that appears (the friction that guides the oil molecules does not bear any resemblance to the eventual convection cells).

Putting these pieces together: A self-organized system is one in which small, minimally intelligent pieces follow local, simple rules by constantly interacting with each other. And from this, (sometimes very complex) patterns spontaneously emerge.

Characteristics of Self-Organized Systems

While self-organized systems come in all shapes and sizes, there are certain characteristics that self-organized systems share. They are not part of the *definition* of such systems, but rather they are behaviors and features that seem to be a consequence of *being* a self-organized system.

Self-Organized Systems Are Dynamic

This characteristic should come as no surprise to the readers of this book. One of the running themes has been that static (unchanging) systems are—if not impossible—vanishingly rare (McCabe, 2014). Certainly, a static system would be exceedingly dull! Moreover (as we argued in Chapter 14), the insights gained from investigating (interesting, common) dynamic systems often transfer to (boring, less common) static systems. But it does not often go the other way around. This has led some theorists to suggest that self-organized dynamic systems are more general than static systems (Rosen, 1991). They are the rule, not the exception!

Leaving aside the idea that dynamic systems are vastly more prevalent and so self-organized systems are more likely to *be* dynamic just by playing the odds, it is also a near-requirement of self-organizing systems that they are constantly undergoing change. Self-organized systems require continuous interactions among the parts—Fred watches his neighbor musician and changes his playing. His neighbor, in turn, watches Fred and changes her playing. This constant interaction will result in a dynamic (ever-changing) system.

What is interesting about a self-organized system being dynamic is that it allows for a system that can respond to *perturbations* (see Chapter 14). A perturbation is an interruption in functioning—like if a player in the orchestra missed a section in the music, got completely lost, then found their way again. A dynamic system will adjust to this misstep by reacting flexibly and then reestablishing the order following the same simple, local rules that created the pattern in the first place. The fumbling player would pay attention to her neighbors (who would, in turn, pay attention to her), find the thread of the song, and all of them—as a unit—would resynchronize their efforts. Order would be reestablished by a collective effort.

We could imagine a static system—say, each "player" in the orchestra was a recording being played on a CD player (or MP3 player, or computer, or a phone, or whatever recording device is currently hip to play music on) without reference to its neighbors. In that case, if one of the recordings got off for a moment (it got paused and then unpaused, for example), it would not (could not) recover. It would continue playing, out of sync, for the rest of the song. Static systems are not capable of adjusting for perturbations.

Self-Organized Systems Have Multistable States

Dynamic systems tend to have attractor states (see Chapter 14). That is, there are certain patterns of behavior that are considered "stable" or are able to be maintained over time. In the convection cells of heated oil, for example, the cells form in a particular size. They also alternate their movement (one roll will move clockwise, the next counterclockwise, the next clockwise, and so on, see Figure 16.1). This is a stable coordination, and it will be maintained as long as ΔT remains in the critical zone.

The emergence of alternating cells at a critical ΔT is a given, but the *actual pattern of the alternation is not.* There are actually two different possible organizations, both equally possible (see Figure 16.1). Both of these are stable attractors, and which one the system ends up in is essentially a coin toss. This is the idea of *multistability*—the presence of more than one stable emergent state. Self-organized systems are frequently multistable.

Another example you can try at home (if you have a bathtub and a little time on your hands). After a bath, watch the behavior of the water when you remove the drain plug. Before the plug is removed, there is no pattern to the movement of the water. Individual water molecules are just bouncing around. Gravity is pulling the water downwards, but the tub is exerting an equal force against gravity, so nothing much is happening. When the plug is removed, the

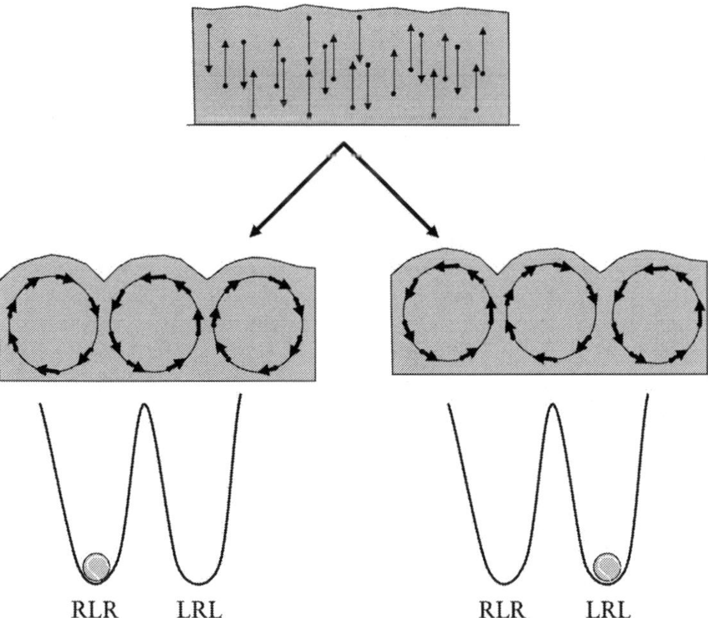

Figure 16.1 The rolls of the Rayleigh-Bénard convection cells will always spontaneously appear at the critical ΔT and will always alternate, but which pattern (RLR vs. LRL) emerges is random. Both are stable attractors for the system.

water will respond to the available downward pathway toward the pull of gravity by moving in that direction.

Eventually, the water will organize into a swirl (a vortex), which allows the water to drain faster. That vortex could be clockwise or counterclockwise; both are stable forms. By the way, if you have heard that Northern Hemisphere bathtubs will swirl counterclockwise and Southern Hemisphere bathtubs will swirl clockwise (due to the movement of the Earth), it's true! But it's true *only if there are no other influences.*[2] The reality is, there are always other influences, like the movement of your feet in the tub, that changes the direction of the swirl. But just like with the convection cells, there are two possible stable states, and one will always spontaneously appear. The system is multistable.

Multistability has the benefit of *multirealizability*. What this means is that the individual pieces can rearrange themselves in more than one way and achieve multiple different goals. So your leg muscles can be involved in jumping, but they can also twist, skip, whirl, arabesque, kick, skate, walk, and so on and on and on! This makes self-organized systems an excellent candidate for theories of action (see Chapter 9) that have frequently run into problems when trying more traditional, hierarchical (read: other-organized) explanations for movement.

Self-Organized Systems Show Parameter Tuning

Self-organized systems often have a variable that, as it is changed, changes the behavior of the system as a whole. For example, ΔT is this variable in a Rayleigh-Bénard convection system. Rayleigh-Bénard convection cells only appear once ΔT reaches a critical value. It will stay in that stable state (with the two possible organizations) until ΔT reaches a second (higher) critical value. At that point, the oil will start to boil.

In the bathtub example, the size of the drainpipe plays a similar role in changing the behavior of the water: *Below* a critical value, the water will drip too slowly to create the vortex; *above* a different critical value, a swirl won't form, and the water will be turbulent (i.e., disordered or irregular) instead. Drainpipe sizes *in-between* those two critical values will create a stable vortex.

Changing the parameter will change how the oil molecules or water flows are organized. In this way, they control the behavior of the system and so are often called *control parameters*. Another example is speed in the finger tapping paradigm of the Haken-Kelso-Bunz equation (see Chapter 14); as speed is increased, the stability of the various coordination patterns between the fingers is changed.

Understanding the rules of the system, including the control parameters, is a big part of the work in studying self-organized systems. In addition to satisfying academic curiosity, understanding control parameters would allow us to control systems that might have become stable in forms that are unhealthy—a fibrillating heart, for example (more on this in the next section; see McCabe, 2014).

In Search of Examples

Inspired by Claudia's insistence that many other self-organized systems existed, Fred decided to ask around to learn more about them. He happens to be friends with a *lot* of scientists of various flavors, so he figures that if he asks them, they might have some good examples to share. In order to visit the first person on his list, he travels to the local university. While walking across the campus grounds, he notices that all over the campus, the groundskeeping crews have torn up many of the roads, sidewalks, and pathways and have replaced them with brand new grass. Fred remembers that one of the university's recent initiatives was to covert the campus into a "walking campus"—one that easily affords walking from place to place but not so much driving from place to place.

Even though the grass was relatively new, he could see that some trails had started to form in the grass where people had been walking from one place to another. Not wanting to ruin the new grass any further, he chose the path that was pointing more or less in the direction he wanted to go and followed it. On his way, he came across a groundskeeper named Dagmar, and he asked her about the lack of designed pathways. Dagmar explained it was a new method of choosing path locations that relied on self-organization. (Fred was so excited!)

The plan was to allow walkers the freedom to walk wherever it made sense to them. At first, there would be a lot of individual pathways, but over time (as some of the grass started to wear down), walkers would follow previously trodden paths (just as Fred had), and eventually, all (or at least most) walkers would end up following the chosen paths. The groundskeeping crew would then put concrete sidewalks wherever those paths were, confident that they would be in places that people wanted to walk. Dagmar further explained that the method was partly based on the way ants self-organize into paths when hunting for food. This reminded Fred that he was on his way to meet someone really important (his crush, Carol!), so he thanked Dagmar and hurried off.

Ants and Fireflies

Carol happened to be a famous entomologist, so Fred had decided to start by visiting her (partly because he thought he had heard something about bugs being self-organizing and partly because this looked like an *excellent* opportunity to start a conversation). He told her the story about the convection cells and the walking paths on campus and asked if she knew any examples of insects exhibiting self-organizing behavior. Carol *lit up*. This is her favorite topic! As it turns out, there are a *lot* of examples of self-organizing behavior in insects; she asked him to meet her at a local hill at twilight so she could show him her two favorite examples. Fred is excited—how romantic!

When Fred arrived at the hill that evening, he saw that Carol had set up a blanket under a tree and had brought a kind of picnic. The "food" consisted of petri dishes of some kind of liquid. Carol explained that ant colonies (and here she pointed nearby where a few wandering ants could be seen) were a great example of self-organizing systems. She put down two dishes of the liquid a few meters apart and told Fred that one of them was a good food source (it had more nutrients in it) and one was a poor food source (it had fewer nutrients in it). They sat down to watch the behaviors of the ants. How . . . romantic?

At first, the ants just wandered around. Fred could see that sometimes they would wander out in search of food and, having found none, return to their nearby nest. While most of the time, the ants would return via the same path, that was not always the case. Sometimes they would take an entirely different (usually more direct) route back. Fred was amazed they could do that, considering that this was like Fred walking from one end of a strange city to the other and then finding his way back again by a completely different (and shorter!) route. Carol explained that ants had good orienting sense—like homing pigeons, they were aware of which direction their nest was in. They did not need to retrace their steps to find their way home.

Eventually, the ants found the food sources. At first, ants were taking multiple pathways to both food sources. Over time, however, they stopped taking the longer paths to the good food source (and only took the shortest, most direct route). And they stopped visiting the poor food source altogether (see Figure 16.2). As Fred and Carol watched, she explained how the ants accomplished this. First, the ants that found food (and *only* those ants that found food) would use a gland in their rear end to lay a pheromone trail—a chemical that the other ants could smell—on the way back to the nest. Other ants looking for food will then follow pheromone trails (which lead them to the food).

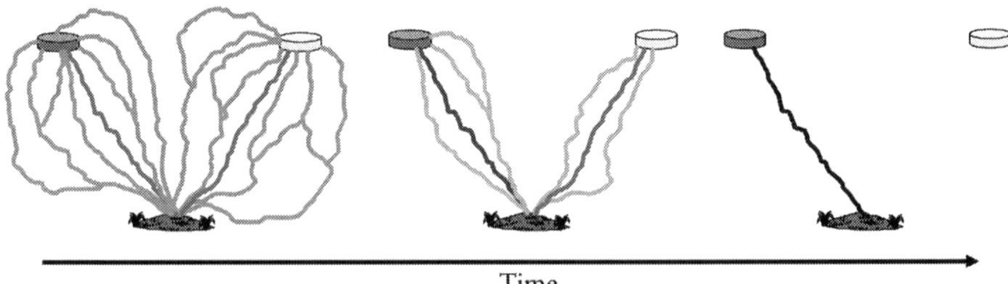

Figure 16.2 Pathing behavior of ants. Paths with higher pheromone concentrations have darker lines, and paths with lower concentration have lighter lines. At first (*left*), there are multiple paths being used to get to and from both sources of food. After a while, the number of paths decreases (*middle*) mostly by eliminating any paths that require detours (i.e., turns *away* from the nest). By the end (*right*), only direct paths remain, and the more nutritious food (darker dish) is more frequently visited than the less nutritious food (lighter dish).

Given that there are a *lot* of ants and a *lot* of them will find food, at first the ants will follow *lots* of paths. But here's where that orienting sense comes in! On the way back to the nest, they will follow the pheromone paths *so long as it doesn't cause them to turn away from the nest.* If it does, they will either turn back to the nest (cutting off the detour) or go all the way back to the food to find a more pheromone-heavy trail home.

The forager ants will also leave a higher concentration of pheromone for more nutritious food. This is why the ants will eventually stop visiting the poorer food source and instead visit the better food source (see Figure 16.2).

All told, the pathing behavior boils down to a few basic rules (1) put down a pheromone trail after finding food (more pheromone for more exciting food) and (2) follow the path of the highest pheromone concentration (both to and from the food), provided it does not cause you to turn away from home on the way back. That's it! With just those rules, ants can find the shortest path to the best food and bring it all efficiently back to the nest.

As the darkness fell, and the ants started to get harder and harder to see, Fred and Carol lay back on the blanket and looked up at the tree and the rapidly appearing stars. How romantic! Fred was just about to break the awkward silence when he noticed that the hundreds of fireflies in the tree above his head were flashing in sync. On-off, on-off, on-off. He sat up, amazed, and realized that it wasn't just their tree—there were trees all over the area, and *all of them* were full of fireflies flashing collectively in sync! He turned to Carol to point out this incredible sight and saw that she was watching him, amused. This was the second example that Carol had planned for Fred!

The synchronization of fireflies has been a source of amazement and study for some time (e.g., Blair, 1915; Richmond, 1930) since it is both obvious and seemingly inexplicable. There have been many other-organized mechanisms proposed for the phenomena, but all proved to be impossible or did not match the data. For example, some suggested that there is some kind of external "go signal" for the flashing, such as lightning or a particular smell that, although it is completely unnoticed by the humans watching, acts as a stimulus to start the flashing. Once they start, the fireflies just continue to flash in a predictable and steady rhythm.

But this "go signal" idea doesn't match the data. It's true that each species of firefly has a particular average rate of flashing,[3] but there is variability. A given firefly may flash, say, about once per second on average, but any given flash will be one second *plus or minus 200 ms*. Or in other words, the flashes of a single insect are not steady enough to maintain the rhythm after a collectively noticed "go signal". Similarly, their line of sight is too obstructed by the branches and leaves of the trees for one "conductor" to be visible to all of the fireflies and thus driving the whole flock across the valley. On top of that, their reaction times (about 55–80 ms) are much slower than the flash itself (about 30 ms), which means that any follow-the-leader mechanism will leave most of the fireflies hopelessly behind (Hanson et al., 1971)

Carol explained that careful studies using a fake lantern (the part of the firefly that lights up is called their "lantern") to stimulate flashing in a captive firefly revealed that the synchronized flashing was entirely due to local forces (Buck et al., 1981). When a firefly flashes, it takes about 800 ms to "recharge" the lantern, but they don't always flash right away—there's often a small delay between when they *can* flash and when they *do* flash. In the absence of any other stimulus, the firefly will flash as described previously, about once a second, with a variability of 200 ms. But when they can see a flash from the fake lantern just *before* they flash, their *next* flash will happen a little sooner. And when they can see a flash from the fake lantern just *after* they flash, their *next* flash will happen a little later. Statistical modeling has shown that this is all that is needed to create large-scale synchronization. Or in other words, the *entire hillside* can flash in sync just by individual fireflies synching with their neighbors.

Box 16.1 Synchronized Flashing—an Evolutionary Perspective

There are a few theories for why some fireflies might adapt to synchronize their flashes. After all, not all fireflies do so! Flashing is part of mating: the male fireflies are the ones that flash brightly (if you see a firefly flashing, chances are you are seeing the male). After a specific delay, the females flash in response to let the males know they are interested in mating. The female response is far dimmer.

In a situation where the fireflies congregate in large groups (like Fred and Carol's trees), synchronization is useful for a handful of reasons. For one, it allows for periods of sustained darkness, during which the female's dimmer return flash is more visible (if the male cannot see the female's flash, he can't find her and do the firefly equivalent of exchanging phone numbers). For another, the brightness of the male flash is attractive to the female; by flashing together, the males can amplify each other's signals to look more attractive.[4] In the same way, they can keep from drowning each other out by distracting the female with overlapping unsynchronized flashes that would divert her attention.

Scientists (Buck & Buck, 1976; Strogatz & Stewart, 1993) have made statistical models to figure out what the control parameters are of the self-organizing firefly system. It turns out there are two control parameters that determine whether or not a particular species will synchronize its flashing when congregating in large groups. The first is the *variability of flashing*. If there is a large variability in the average length of time in-between flashing, then the collective (the group) will never settle on a common flashing rhythm—they will not flash in-sync. The second is how interested the fireflies are in following their neighbors (in the model, this is a measure called "coupling"). If they are only loosely coupled, they will not synchronize.

Measurements on actual firefly behavior have supported these findings—firefly species that have low variability and change their behavior more when presented with a false lantern flash (which indicates that they are tightly coupled to a nearby flashing stimulus) will synchronize. Firefly species that have higher variability and/or are less susceptible to the false lantern flashes (that is, they are loosely coupled) will not synchronize.

What is interesting about this is that evolution is likely *not* selecting for synchronization behavior *itself*, but rather it seems to be adjusting those two control parameters.

Over time, if synchronous flashing is useful, a species will become less variable and more tightly coupled. If it's not useful, other parameters are selected for. Put it another way, there is no gene that codes for synchronization; synchronization is a by-product of *other* behaviors—it is a gift with purchase (see Chapter 15). This is the evolutionary equivalent of changing the orientation of the soup cans in order to affect the synchronization of metronomes (see Chapter 4).

As their "date" was coming to an end (Fred thought it had gone quite well), Carol urged him to look into the skyscraper building behavior of termites (Brossard et al., 2007), the nectar source selection of bees (Camazine & Sneyd, 1991), or the nest building of wasps (Karsai & Pénzes, 1993). Fred got the sense she could go on listing examples, but he asked her for a follow-up date instead. Maybe this time at a restaurant, with candles and a tablecloth—and no bugs!

Metal Beads

Delighted by his success with Carol (both romantically and scientifically), he called up his friend Bob (the ice-cube-melting physicist we met in Chapter 3) to talk about it. Bob was happy for Fred's romantic endeavors but immediately shifted focus to Fred's interest in self-organizing systems. He knew about some of these too! In fact, physics is *full* of such systems. After all, in nonliving systems, the components (like grains of sand or balls rolling downhill) are naturally minimally intelligent and driven entirely by local forces (like gravity and friction). Bob invited Fred to his lab to observe an experiment using metal beads—yes, metal beads (Kondepudi, Kay, & Dixon, 2015).

In this paradigm (see Figure 16.3), small metal beads are put into a petri dish. Around the outside of the dish is a grounding ring, and on one side of the dish is a source of electricity. Electricity, Bob explained, wants to get to the ground. Or in other words, the electricity is going to find the shortest path from the source to the grounding ring in order to dissipate the energy as quickly as possible (see Chapter 15)—just like lightning does during an electrical

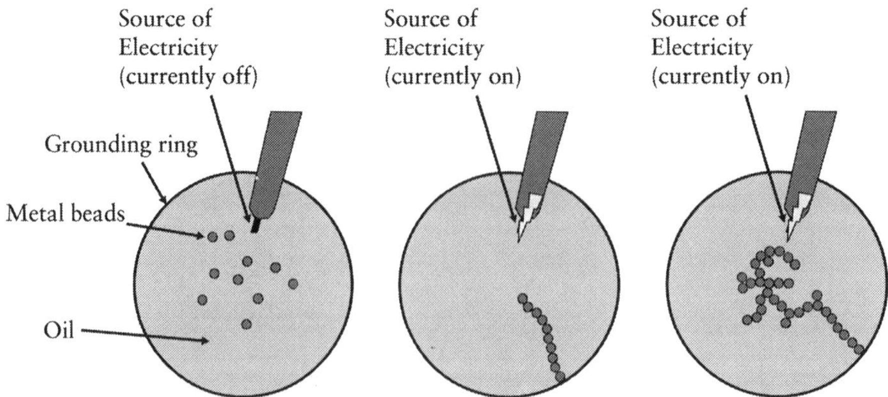

Figure 16.3 Metal beads in a petri dish filled with oil (an insulating material) with a metal grounding ring and a source of electricity. *Left:* before the electricity is turned on, the beads have no particular organization. *Middle and right:* after the electricity is turned on, the beads self-organize into a line or "tree" structure and dramatically increase the dissipation of the electrical energy.

storm. The dish is filled with oil (the oil does not conduct electricity well and also acts as a lubricant for the beads).

Bob turned on the electricity, and after a few seconds of wandering around, the beads snapped into a line! One end of the line connected to the grounding ring, and the other looked like it was reaching for the source of the electricity. Bob turned the electricity off, added more beads, and turned it on again. This time, the beads snapped into a complex branching tree-like structure.

And that's not all! Bob had a way of measuring how much energy was being dissipated by the system (how much entropy was being produced), and the moment the beads snapped into a pattern (whether a line or a tree), entropy production jumped *way* up. It's just like the convection cells!

Fred was struck by how much the beads looked like they were alive[5]—he knew they couldn't possibly be sentient or *trying* to follow any rules (like the fireflies or the people walking across campus could be), but they still created patterns and performed behaviors that were remarkably lifelike *just by following the rules of physics*.

Belousov-Zhabotinsky Reaction

Fred's next stop was his friend Agnes, who is a chemist. After he explained what he was looking for, Agnes immediately started pulling chemicals out of the storage closet and mixing them in a petri dish. She explained that she was putting two categories of chemicals into the dish: those that were going to run a particular chemical reaction and those that would react to products of the chemical reaction by changing color (so Agnes and Fred could more easily see what was happening as the chemical reaction occurred).

At first, the combination of the chemicals in the petri dish just looked like a purple liquid. Then, little by little, spots appeared and grew. Eventually, there were obvious patterns of alternating blue and red colors (see Figure 16.4, *left*). Agnes explained that they were watching what is called an autocatalytic reaction. "Auto" means "self", as in "automatic." "Catalytic" refers to the activity of a catalyst—a substance that increases the rate of a chemical reaction. So an autocatalytic reaction is one that creates its own catalyst and therefore increases its own rate of chemical reaction.

In this case, the first set of chemical reactions produced a new chemical, and the new chemical was fuel for a second chemical reaction. The second chemical reaction, in turn, produced a chemical that was fuel for the first chemical reaction (see Figure 16.4, *right*).

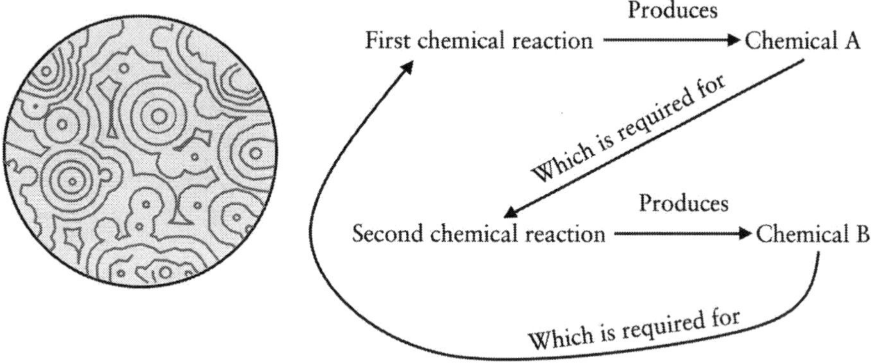

Figure 16.4 *Left:* Belousov-Zhabotinsky reaction in a petri dish (in real life, it's red and blue; here, the blue is indicated by the lines and the red by the wider spaces). *Right:* a (simplified) schematic of the reaction—each stage creates the chemical needed for the next stage.

When these chemicals were put into a petri dish, the chemical reactions went back and forth, making the chemicals necessary for the other reaction to happen. Once the first reaction finished in a location, all of the surrounding areas now had the chemical they needed to do the *next* reaction. Once those areas were finished, they made the chemicals available to the next surrounding areas and so on. This was why the bull's-eye patterns appeared.

Fred was fascinated! And also confused—he swore he had seen this exact pattern before in a picture on his friend Alan's living room wall. But Alan wasn't a chemist; he's a mycologist (a person who studies fungi). Why would he have a chemical reaction on his wall? Fred resolved to ask him.

Cellular Slime Molds

Once Fred got a chance to visit his friend Alan, he found out that the picture he remembered was *not* the Belousov-Zhabotinsky reaction after all! Alan explained that it was the patterns formed by an organism called a cellular slime mold. The cellular slime mold is a fascinating creature that isn't easily categorized into one type of life-form or another because it acts differently at different times in its life cycle (see Figure 16.5, *left*). These patterns (see Figure 16.5, *right*) are formed during the *aggregation* stage of its development. The similarity to the Belousov-Zhabotinsky patterns is not entirely coincidental, however, as this system *also* self-organizes and produces autocatalytic reactions that move outward from a center location.

Much like Carol, Alan was talking about his *favorite topic*. The cellular slime mold is *just so neat*—it starts as a single-celled organism, feeding on bacteria (usually in damp areas like decaying wood or leaf piles) and multiplies by reproducing asexually (each cell just splits into multiple cells). At this point, the distribution of the cells in the area is fairly uniform.

Once a slime mold cell runs out of food in a particular area, it starts the aggregation stage. The hungry cell sends out a chemical signal indicating that they are out of food and it's time to form a larger group. When a nearby slime mold cell senses that signal, they (1) repeat the distress signal and (2) move toward the source of the signal they detected. There is a five- to eight-minute refractory period, during which the cell (1) cannot send out the signal again *and* (2) releases a second chemical, which "clears the air" of the first signal. These two factors

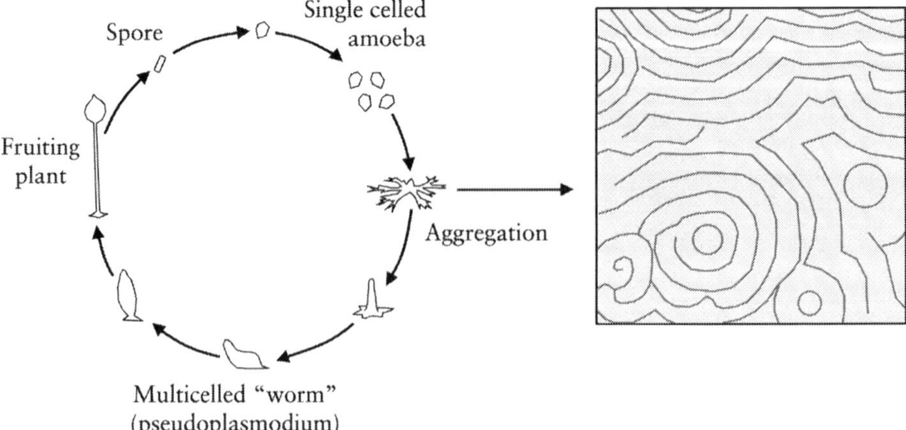

Figure 16.5 *Left*: the life cycle of the cellular slime mold (see text for details). *Right*: patterns formed by the aggregation phase of the cellular slime mold.

keep the aggregation signal from moving randomly and instead keep it moving away from the original hungry cell (and toward other cells).

Once all the cells clump together, *these same rules* result in the cells combining into a multicellular organism. You read that right—they go from a bunch of single-celled organisms to a *single multicellular organism*. It's a little complicated as to how this happens (because it's now a three-dimensional problem instead of a two-dimensional one), but the short version is that the aggregation signal and movement of the cells eventually results in the formation of a worm-like structure. Moreover, following *the same rules* outlined previously results in the tail end of the worm turning into a twisting spiral that moves the worm forward like a boat propellor.

Being a larger organism allows the cellular slime mold to move more easily; this worm-like creature can move across larger distances than a single cell could. It will travel as a unit until it senses a new (sufficiently rich) source of food, and then the cells that were on the *front* of the worm (that were not involved in the back propellor part) will *turn into a plant*. The plant will grow, then produce and release spores into the nearby area. The spores grow into single-celled organisms, and the whole process starts again.

You see, Alan explained, at various parts of its life cycle, the cellular slime mold is a single-celled organism, a multicellular worm, a fruiting plant, and a spore (see Figure 16.5, *right*). It's unclassifiable! Its mutirealizable! And each part of this cycle is governed by self-organizing factors, not some kind of blueprint.

Temperature Regulation

Fred's investigations had introduced him to a whole range of phenomena that he had never encountered before, but he also wanted to know if there were more examples from things that he was more familiar with than metal beads and slime molds. He asked his friend Smitsman, a biologist, if he had any examples of self-organization from human biology. Smitsman assured him that there were *plenty*. He first explained that the body is better thought of as a system than as a machine (see Chapter 4), but that most explanations of the body treat it more like a machine.

Take, for example, temperature regulation. The typical explanation of how humans maintain a body temperature[6] of 97.9°F (36.62°C) is that they have a kind of thermostat in their brain. The thermostat has a set point, and whenever the body temperature deviates from that set point, the body acts to restore it (e.g., by sweating if the body is too hot or shivering if the body is too cold).

But this doesn't match the data! For one thing, average body temperatures vary from person to person *and* vary over the course of the day for a particular person. As we discussed in Chapter 14, dynamical systems are rarely static, and using summary statistics (like an average) to describe them just doesn't work. The body's temperature fluctuates across the day—increasing after eating, decreasing while sleeping, increasing when doing exercise, decreasing while reading, etc.

Fevers also present an interesting problem. If the set point hypothesis is right, then a fever would represent a set point change—like turning up the thermostat in your house. In that case, the body temperature should rise gradually, then level off and maintain the higher temperature. *But that's not what happens*. During a fever, body temperature fluctuates wildly, spiking high, then returning to normal, staying slightly elevated before spiking again. Either the central executive is playing around with the thermostat, or something else is going on.

Another possibility is that the body's temperature is an *emergent property*. There are a lot of different systems in our bodies, all trying to do their job. There's the respiratory system, the endocrine system, the digestive system, the circulatory system, the nervous system, and so on and on and on. Each of these systems has a temperature at which it is most efficient.

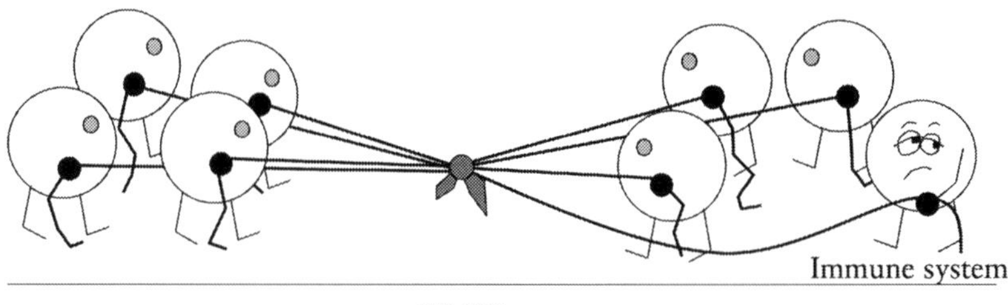

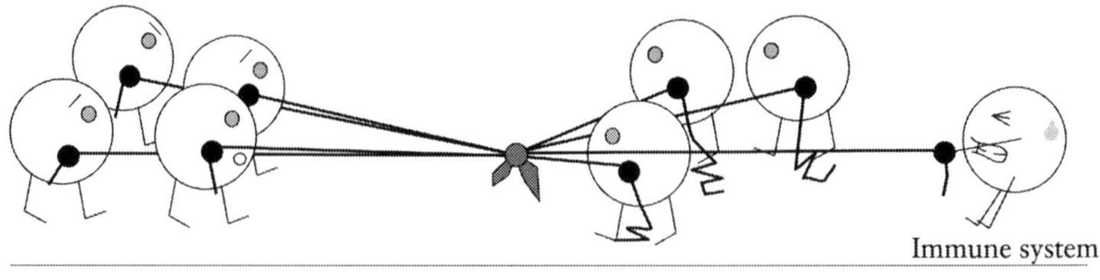

Figure 16.6 Self-organization of temperature regulation. *Top*: With no current infection, the immune system is not working as hard. Emergent temperature is 97.9°F (36.62°C). *Bottom*: with active infection, the immune system is working hard to raise the body temperature to help it fight off the infection. Cold systems are reacting to the sudden change. Emergent temperature is 101.2°F (38.44°C).

The digestive system, for example, works better at slightly higher temperatures; the nervous system (the brain and nerves) works better at slightly lower temperatures.

Imagine that each of these systems is playing a tug of war with the body's temperature in order to move it toward their particular optimal level (see Figure 16.6). Sometimes, they wouldn't tug that hard (for example, when there's no food to digest, the digestive system might not be pulling at all), and sometimes they might tug very hard (right after that huge plate of Thanksgiving dinner, the digestive system is working overtime). This would explain the fluctuations across the day, as well as between people.

And so, what of fevers? A fever is what happens when the immune system starts taking a more active role. It is most efficient at higher temperatures, so when the body is fighting an infection, it starts pulling *hard* to get the temperature up. But the other parts of the body are going to be actively fighting it (the nervous system, in particular, cannot function at very high temperatures, and above a certain point, the heat will start causing neurological damage), which is why fevers are not a steady state—several systems of the body are in active tug of war over the temperature (see Mitchell, Snellen, & Atkins, 1970, for a more technical treatment of this concept).

Hearts: Building and Beating

At Smitsman's suggestion, Fred contacted his friend Rebecca, who is a cardiologist. Apparently, hearts exhibit self-organization in a number of different ways while still following a central signal. Like the ditch-diggers described at the beginning of the chapter, the heart could be considered a *partially* self-organized system.

Rebecca showed Fred some petri dishes in which she had prepared some heart cells. In one, the heart cells were not touching each other; in the other, they were crowded together in a thin sheet. In the first petri dish, Fred could see that the individual cells were beating! Apparently, heart cells will beat (i.e., *contract*) independent of being part of a heart. But they weren't all beating at the same time, some were beating faster, some slower. In the second dish (where they were touching each other), the heart cells were beating synchronously. Rebecca explained that this dish had *started* like the first dish, with all the cells beating at different rhythms, but after a few days they had synchronized. Much like the fireflies on the tree, individual heart cells will attempt to coordinate with the cells around them, creating a steady synchronized beat.

The second dish, Rebecca explained, is comparable to an embryonic heart (the heart of a developing human, about six weeks into gestation). The gestation process first builds two tubes (a lot of stuff in our bodies starts as tubes, they are easy to build) of heart cells. Those tubes then fuse together (see Figure 16.7, *top*) and start beating in sync because of self-organization. Interestingly, this beating (and subsequent moving around of fluid) is what *causes* those tubes to loop around each other and form the adult four-chambered heart (Bartman & Hove, 2005). Or in other words, by following the simple rules of (1) beat, and (2) try to synchronize your beating with your neighbors, the heart cells will both synchronize *and* form the complex mature heart structure.

The adult four-chambered heart still uses those same rules to keep the heart beating in such a way that it pumps blood through the body. It's not *fully* self-organized, as there is a "pacemaker" signal that comes from a part of the heart called the *sinoatrial node* (SAN). The SAN is like the hungry cell in the cellular slime molds. It is the first cell to send out the "squeeze" signal, but the "squeeze" signal isn't sent to *all* the heart cells—just the nearby ones. Those cells send it to their neighbors, and those neighboring cells send it to their neighbors and so on until the entire heart squeezes (see Figure 16.7, *bottom*). The only difference between the slime mold's hungry cell and the SAN is that the SAN can receive signals from the brain telling it to increase

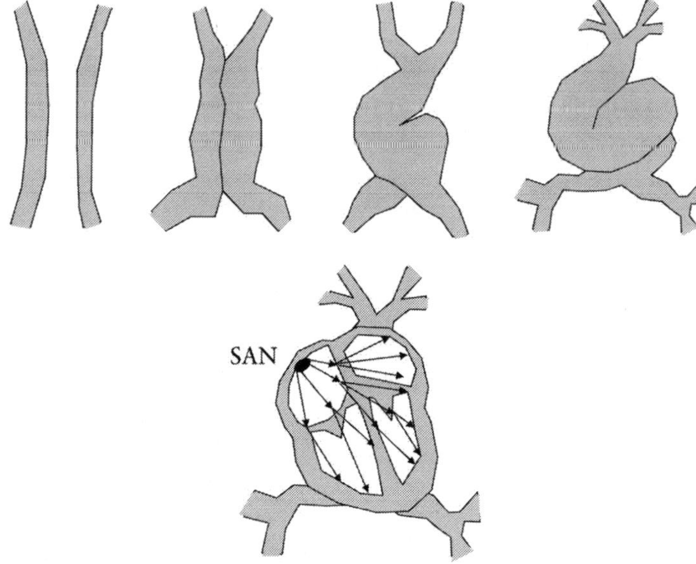

Figure 16.7 *Top*: The developing embryonic heart starts as two separate tubes. They fuse together, and the beating of the cells causes them to loop around each other to form the adult heart. *Bottom*: The adult heart. One area of the heart called the sinoatrial node (SAN) sends out a "squeeze" signal, which spreads through the heart. There are two dynamically stable patterns, one healthy and one deadly.

or decrease the rate of beating in order to adjust to external circumstances (like beating faster during exercise or during an encounter with your crush).

It turns out that this self-organized rhythm is *bistable*, just like the bathtub or the convection cells. There are *two* dynamically stable patterns even in perfectly healthy hearts. The first is our usual "thump *thump*, thump *thump*, thump *thump*", which results in blood being pumped through the body at a steady rate, bringing oxygen and other nutrients to our tissues. The second is what is called *fibrillation*—a kind of feedback beat where the top chambers and the bottom chambers are beating independently of each other. A fibrillating heart does not pump blood. A *defibrillator* (the paddle-shocking thing you see on medical TV shows all the time) essentially detects this irregularity and will *stop the heart* (temporarily!) in an attempt to get the heart back into the healthy, dynamic mode when it restarts itself. (On TV, they will sometimes use a defibrillator to *restart* the heart, but that isn't possible. All it can do is stop it, and hope it restarts with a healthy rhythm.)

Why Self-Organized Systems?

So what have we learned (apart from the fact that Fred has a *lot* of scientist friends)? For one thing, self-organized systems seem to be everywhere! We've given a few examples here, but we had *so many more* that we didn't have space for. In fact, as we said at the beginning of this chapter, the ecological perspective is that *most* systems are self-organized.

Given that, it is worth asking *why*. Why is it that self-organized systems are common where other-organized (with explicit instructions from an organizer or by using a template, for example) are rare? Our argument at the beginning of this chapter was that to allow other-organization was in violation of ecological principles—and that's true! But it's also not the whole argument.

Imagine that you are a god. Go you! You are creating the universe, and you can make it any way you want. You have *choices*. You could make organisms that build themselves via a template. You could organize everything *yourself*. You could create demigods that organize everything on your behalf. Why might you choose self-organizing systems over something else? Apart from the fact that organizing everything yourself seems like a *lot of work* (we're also assuming you're a lazy god, apparently), it might also be in the best interests of the thing you are creating if you *let it organize itself*.

Mixing metaphors a bit, think about your godlike self as an architect trying to help a fleet of contractors build a bunch of houses. You're going to want the houses to be roughly similar (so you don't have to come up with something new each time), but if you try to make them *identical*, you're going to run into problems. If you give the contractors a single blueprint, they will quickly run into difficulty when the plot of land is a funny shape, or there are a lot of earthquakes in this area, or more people need to fit into the house, or *any number* of other local constraints. There's no way to draw a single blueprint that will work in all of those circumstances (and all *future* circumstances).

If, instead, you give the contractors a few rules to follow—for example, a list of things each house needs to have—kitchen, bedroom, bathroom, power sockets every 12 feet, etc.—and then allow them to make choices based on the context, the houses will be far more adapted to their circumstances. The contractors will have much more *flexibility*, and you (the divine architect) will have to do a lot less work.

The suggestion here (and in Box 16.1) is that evolution is not the process of changing a *blueprint*. This is yet another reason why DNA cannot be thought of as a blueprint. After all, the amount of information needed to describe the adult human is much *much* larger than the amount of data that is able to be stored in DNA. Instead, the DNA sets up the rules (like telling heart cells to beat and to synchronize with their neighbors), and the dynamic structure of the body and its behaviors self-organizes from there.

Box 16.2 Self-Organizing Robots

The amazing utility of self-organizing systems is starting to make its way into the engineering world. There are a number of attempts to make robots that can work on the principles of self-organization and do a wide variety of complex tasks. At Harvard University, for example, the Wyss Institute for Biologically Inspired Engineering has developed a robot (or rather, a swarm of little robots) that, following very simple rules, can *build whole houses* (Goldfield, 2018). They were inspired by termites (Carol was right, you really should go look them up) who can build skyscrapers (if termites were human-sized, their nests would be up to a mile high and five miles in diameter!) just by following very simple, local rules.

The Wyss Institute robots are programmed to follow rules like the following: (1) Find a place where there is a block in front of you and a block to the left and place a block there. (2) If there are no places that match that description, climb up one level. (3) Once you place your block, go get another block. From those rules, they can build impressive structures on varying terrain and respond in real time if there is a destruction of part of the structure. In the lab, that destruction is the experimenter stealing blocks, but the goal is to make robots that could build whole buildings on other planets and react adaptively if one of the structures was destroyed by something like an asteroid or a wind storm.

And they aren't the only ones! Bristol University's robotics lab has made coin-sized robots that build, well, big blobs at the moment. In this case, they aren't trying to make a predetermined shape; they are fiddling with the rules they give the robots and seeing what shapes they make in response, with the ultimate goal of creating robots that can exhibit the kind of multirealizability that natural systems show all the time.

Notes

1. In a rigid hierarchy (as opposed to a flexible hierarchy) the orders go from top to bottom. The operators at the bottom have no ability to influence *upward*, and an operator's position in the hierarchy is fixed. In a flexible hierarchy, positions might change and upward influence is possible, but the top operators are still in charge. Self-organization is neither of these—no one is in charge, and yet everyone is.
2. There's a great video about this on Veritasium's (as well as Smarter Every Day's) YouTube channel: www.youtube.com/watch?v=mXaad0rsV38.
3. That varies by temperature—they are cold-blooded, so the metabolic rate that powers the flashing changes based on the temperature.
4. Brings new meaning to the term "wing man"!
5. It's worth watching these beads in action, check out the supplemental materials from that study: https://journals.aps.org/pre/abstract/10.1103/PhysRevE.91.050902#supplemental.
6. You've probably heard the average human body temperature is 98.6°F (37°C)—but it turns out that this number is wrong! Or at least, it's out of date. The actual average temperature has been getting lower for generations, likely due to a decrease in chronic infections (Protsiv et al., 2020).

17 Intelligent Life

One afternoon, Fred is at Uncle Jimmy's house for a movie marathon. Uncle Jimmy is a fan of movies where aliens come to Earth, particularly *really old* movies with laughable special effects and awfully human-looking aliens. After finishing *The Attack of the Killer Chemeros*, Fred asks his uncle if he thinks there really could be intelligent life on other planets. Uncle Jimmy pauses for a long moment and asks Fred, "Well, what counts as intelligent? What counts as life?"

Uncle Jimmy's questions are *not* easy ones. Fred certainly couldn't come up with any answers right away. Try it yourself! Put down this book (or whatever device you are using to read the book) for a few minutes and try to come up with a definition for life that *includes* everything you think is alive and *excludes* everything you think is not. Or a definition for intelligence that *includes* everything you think is intelligent and *excludes* everything that you think is not. In the latter case, your definition should probably not include the ability to perform well on standardized cognitive tests (because the chances that an alien could take our Earth-based IQ tests and/or list Earth facts are slim). It's remarkably difficult to come up with definitions that are sufficiently *inclusive* without being insufficiently *exclusive*. It is no wonder that many have thrown up their hands and channeled US Supreme Court Justice Potter Stewart—who, in declining to even *attempt* to define pornography, wrote, "I know it when I see it" (Jacobellis v. Ohio, US, 1964).

Why Definitions Matter

The Stewart cop-out is certainly attractive (and will likely become even *more* attractive once we start wading into the candidate definitions for life and intelligence and the ways in which they fall short). After all, in a daily-life kind of way it's usually sufficient to say, "I know that thing is alive and that thing isn't", but for scientists, it's not a great option.

This book began with an argument that we need to be thoughtful and explicit about our assumptions. We argued that in order to have a coherent science, we must acknowledge and inventory our assumptions carefully and make arguments for why we make the ones we make (see Chapters 1–4). Here in the last chapter, we are suggesting that the same is also true for our definitions. Two scientists can't be expected to have a reasonable debate on the nature of intelligence without first agreeing on what they are talking about!

And sometimes, definitions of terms are essential to defining how a particular science progresses. "Life", for example, is the purview of biology. It might get further subdivided into different areas of biology focusing on different *types* of life (marine biology focuses on aquatic life, for example). But either way, the biologist will study those things that are *included* in the definition of life and *not* study those things that are *excluded* from such a definition. The marine biologist will study plankton but not the sand on the ocean floor. And the evolutionary biologist *won't* study viruses if they are excluded from the definition of life (Rosen, 1991; but see Box 17.2).

DOI: 10.4324/9781003145691-20

In every science, there are terms that get used with some frequency despite some degree of confusion, disagreement, and imprecision in the definitions of those terms. Some words might have different definitions when used in general conversation than they do when used in scientific conversation, or they may have different definitions when used in psychology than they do in biology. Even different *areas* of psychology might have different definitions and uses for terms, such as cognition, consciousness, perception, action, life, intelligence, and so on.

And as we have seen, the ecological perspective has its own way of defining the relevant terms and concepts, consistent with its assumptions and guidelines (see Chapters 3 and 4). It's worth mentioning, here at the beginning of this chapter, that even *within ecological psychology*, there is some debate about what the right terms are and what they mean. But teasing out shades of meaning by (sometimes heated) discussion is often informative about the subject matter. Or in other words, as we debate the topic, we may come to better understand it. This chapter isn't going to attempt to provide a definitive definition of either life or intelligence but rather to introduce you to the debate.

How to Make a Definition

It turns out that there is more than one way for Fred to go about developing a definition (in this case, definitions of "life" and "intelligence"). We're not going to talk about all of them here but instead focus on three possibilities: *a posteriori, a priori*, and iterative.

To make a definition *a posteriori* (Latin for "from what comes after"), Fred would first make lists of everything that he thinks should be *included* in the definition and everything that should be *excluded* from the definition. So for example, if he's looking for a definition for "life", he might put humans, grass, bunnies, and fish on the list of things that need to be included, and he might put sand, rocks, fire, and automobiles on the list of things that need to be excluded.

After that, he will examine the lists and use inductive reasoning to figure out how the items on the first list differ from the items on the second list. (Inductive reasoning is when you take a list of examples and try to figure out what principles unite them; deductive reasoning is the reverse—using a definition or set of principles to figure out what would or would not fit, see Figure 17.1.)

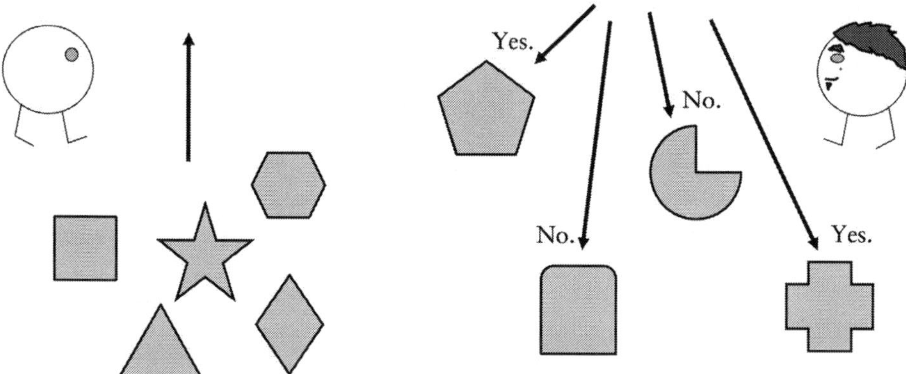

Figure 17.1 Fred (on the left) is doing inductive reasoning, recognizing that all the shapes are ones with only straight edges and angles. Tetsushi (on the right) is doing deductive reasoning, recognizing that some of the shapes match the definition of "straight edges and angles" and some don't.

This is not always an easy process! Figuring out what unites all of the items on the first list but does not apply to anything on the second list can be tricky. Fred notices, for example, that most of the things on his "things to be included" list consume oxygen, but then he realizes that one of the things on his "things to be excluded" list also consumes oxygen (fire). And actually, grass doesn't consume oxygen so much as *produce* it. Hmmm . . . He tries again—all the things on his "to be included" list use energy! But then, so does the automobile (which, of course, is on his "to be excluded" list). And so on.

And this highlights the problem with *a posteriori* definitions—they are very sensitive to what appears on the particular lists that Fred makes to start. That is, once Fred has come up with principles that accurately discriminate between his two lists, it is almost guaranteed that someone else (or even Fred himself) will come along and point out that there is some living thing that is being improperly *excluded* or some nonliving thing that is being improperly *included*, and he will have to start all over. An *a posteriori* definition often does a great job for the items that are included on the initial lists but not necessarily for making generalizations that apply *beyond* these particular items. An *a posteriori* definition, for example, may not easily apply to newly discovered life (like the hundreds of species that live off the energy produced by geothermal vents deep in the ocean) or life on other planets.

To make a definition *a priori* (Latin for "from what is before"), Fred would need to pretend that he doesn't know the specifics of the thing he is defining (or at least, he will try to ignore those specifics for a little bit). Instead, he will focus on creating a definition that works in *principle* rather than one that is based on specific examples. He might imagine what he would accept as *alive* if he saw it on another planet, for example. Or he might ask himself what an artificially created system would need to have or would need to be able to *do* for him to think that it was *alive*. Or in other words, what would constitute *artificial life?*

This is a *lot* harder. For one thing, it's not really possible for Fred to pretend he doesn't know what is considered to be alive and what isn't. For another, it's hard to imagine types of life that we have not yet encountered (evolution has a much better imagination than we do). So extrapolating from *life here* to *life elsewhere* is a difficult problem at best.

Having said that, *a priori* definitions have the advantage of being more generalizable to new cases. Any definition of life that we develop ought to apply to new life-forms that we might encounter (such as alien life). Of course, that only holds true if the definition was well-written in the first place!

Our last option—an iterative definition—is a kind of combination of the two. Here, a combination of Fred's *a posteriori* observations are combined with *a priori* intuitions to create a working definition. He then applies that working definition to many systems (via deductive reasoning). If he finds that some things are being excluded that should be included (or vice versa), he adjusts the definition to fit (rather than starting over).

The question here is when to stop the iterative process: do we, at some point, allow for the possibility that our carefully crafted definition might be smarter than our "I know it when I see it" intuitions? Or in other words, if Fred creates what he sees as a solid definition for life and then suddenly discovers that there are some things he previously thought were not alive that nevertheless meet the definition, does he change the definition or change his intuition?

What Is Life?

Given the choice between the definition of life and the definition of intelligence, Fred decides to start with the definition of life because he is sure it will be easier. He is, after all, able to generate lists of things that are alive and things that are not with some ease. He decides to enlist the help of his friend Tetsushi. He's the friend Fred goes to whenever he needs a reality check because Tetsushi sees things in ways Fred doesn't (and isn't afraid to tell Fred when he's being silly). He figures that if the two of them can come up with a coherent definition for life, then Uncle Jimmy will be sure to accept it.

The vast majority of definitions of life are essentially a checklist of properties, *all* of which an organism must have in order to be considered alive. This illustrates the difference between a *necessary* condition and a *sufficient* condition. A necessary condition is a description of (one of) the things that *must occur* for a given situation to occur. In other words, the situation will *not* occur when that condition is not met. For example, the presence of hydrogen is a necessary condition for the formation of water. Hydrogen *must be present* for water to form, and water cannot be formed in the *absence* of hydrogen.

With respect to living systems, a necessary condition describes a property that all living systems *must exhibit* in order for them to be considered alive. Moreover, a system cannot be considered alive if it does not exhibit this property (regardless of any other properties that it might exhibit). Importantly, to reject a given condition as necessary for being alive, we only have to show a single counterexample of something that is alive that does not exhibit that property.

A sufficient condition is a description of something that *guarantees that* a situation will occur. In other words, the situation will *always* occur when that condition is met *but can also occur when that condition is not met.* For example, being a dog is a sufficient condition for being an animal, but it is possible to be an animal without being a dog—just ask Fred's cat!

With respect to living systems, a sufficient condition describes a property that is enough (*on its own*) for us to consider that system to be alive. However, it is possible for a system to be alive and not exhibit this property so long as it exhibits *some other* property that is enough (on its own) for the system to be considered alive. In order to reject a condition as sufficient for being alive, we only have to show a single counterexample of something that *exhibits* that property but is *not alive.*

We're telling you all this because, for better or worse, almost all definitions of life are lists of necessary (but not sufficient) traits.

A List of Necessary (but Not Sufficient) Traits of Life

Fred and Tetsushi decide to start by listing candidate traits that living things seem to have and trying to see if there are living things that do not exhibit that particular property (or nonliving things that do). If so, then that property will be eliminated as either a necessary or sufficient condition for being alive.

Consume Energy

As before, Fred suggests that all living things (must) consume energy. Tetsushi agrees, but (like Fred) he points out that there are a number of nonliving things that *also* consume energy (automobiles but also fire, computers, refrigerators, and battery-powered flashlights). Given these examples, they decide that consuming energy is a necessary condition, even if it is not a sufficient one. In other words, being alive requires consuming energy, but consuming energy is not enough (on its own) for something to be alive.

And consuming energy seems like a sensible necessary condition given Fred's knowledge of thermodynamics (see Chapter 15). According to that theory, life *probably* began because there was clumped-up energy that needed to be dissipated (or dissipated faster). And just like the convection cells and the metal beads (see Figures 15.9 and 16.3), organized matter is faster at dissipating energy than disorganized matter. So if there were a *lot* of clumped-up energy, it is sensible that something *very* organized (like a living system) spontaneously emerged to dissipate the energy as quickly as possible.

And given what we know of the universe, we would expect the same thing to occur on planets that orbit stars like our sun, where there is energy (from the sun) pouring down on the planet. Therefore, it's likely that life would emerge on other planets in the same way that it emerged here. Given all of that, if we were to find life on another planet, it's hard to *imagine* that it would be possible for it to live without consuming energy.

Another way of putting this condition is that it is likely that all living systems are *dissipative systems* (systems that dissipate energy). But of course, we know that there are dissipative systems that are not alive! Convection cells are not alive. Neither are the vortices formed in a bath as it drains. And neither are automobile engines. What we *don't* have are any examples of living systems that are *not* dissipative systems. Sounds like a pretty reasonable necessary (but not sufficient) condition!

The process of a living system consuming energy is called metabolizing energy. It involves converting food (which differs from organism to organism—for the plant, light is food; for Fred, plants are food) into energy that can be used to run the organism's various systems and eliminating waste. This is part of the reason why some people suggest that most battery-powered items can be safely ignored as being examples of living things—they consume energy, but they do not *metabolize* it. The power stored in the battery is already in a useable form, and there is no metabolic waste. Having said that, an automobile certainly converts the energy in the gasoline into movement, and there is certainly metabolic waste—exhaust fumes and heat. (Although see Box 17.2 for more on this, particularly how it relates to viruses.)

Ability to Replicate

Perhaps the most common principle proposed for the definition of life is the ability to make more of itself. Fred is sure this will need to be included—he spent a lot of time talking about evolution with his Grandpa Tom (see Chapter 15), and he's certain that the organisms will need to be able to make more of themselves in order for their respective species to change over generations. He also knows it won't necessarily eliminate robots from the definition because he recently heard about robots that can replicate (Kriegman et al., 2021).

Tetsushi is not so sure. First, he's not sure that the ability to change over generations (that is, the ability to *evolve*) is a necessary part of being alive. Would this mean a species isn't considered alive until after it has been altered through evolution? Fred suggests that maybe they could just say that being alive means having the *capacity* (or potential) to evolve. But Tetsushi counters that this requires foreseeing the future—what if a species *is* capable of replicating but is not capable of changing anything about its species (not capable of evolving) when it does so? How would we (as scientists) know that ahead of time?

Second, and perhaps more importantly, the ability to replicate is not inherent in all members of a species. Humans (or other animals) that are born sterile are not able to replicate and yet are most assuredly alive. Mules (the offspring of a male donkey and a female horse) are, as a species, mostly unable to replicate. Yet obviously, they are alive.

And what of members of a species that have the *potential* (or once had the potential) to replicate but currently cannot do so? A human woman past menopause or a male finch isolated on an island with no female of the species, for example? Do they cease to be alive once the potential for reproduction is eliminated?

It might be possible to get around these counterexamples by talking about the *potential* to replicate as being different from the *actual ability* to replicate (Ruiz-Mirazo, Peretó, & Moreno, 2004). The suggestion here is that the structures necessary for reproduction are available in *some* members of the species, so even if a *particular member* of that species is unable to replicate due to specific circumstances, the entire species is alive by default. Part of this argument relies on the fact that living systems have DNA (or at least RNA) that carries instructions for how to build that system in the next generation. Maybe the *instructions* for replication are as good as replication. Maybe? Alas, as we've mentioned several times in this book, DNA doesn't really provide instructions or blueprints (see Box 15.1) for a fully realized offspring.

Tetsushi also points out that the condition also doesn't help us much with the alien life problem—if we encountered an alien species that was communicating with us and showing us their fancy alien gadgets, we wouldn't stop to ask about their replication process (or sequence their DNA) before categorizing them as alive.

Cellular

Fred moves on to a new idea. He suggests that all living things have (or are) cells (Klyce, 2017). This would allow for the inclusion of single-celled organisms but would exclude things like automobiles or fire, which consume energy but are not cellular. Bonus! Tetsushi thinks that sounds pretty good, but it does seem to run into a couple of problems. For one, is each of the individual cells that comprise (the parts of) organisms alive? Is a heart cell alive independent of the human it is in?

Tetsushi also points out that in order for this to work, they would need a definition of what a *cell is*. Fred thinks for a bit and suggests that a cell is a membrane-enclosed structure that can live on its own (because it metabolizes energy). Tetsushi thinks that this definition has potential but that it might run into problems with *mitochondria*—one of the structures inside some kinds of cells (see Box 17.1).

Box 17.1 Eukaryotic Cells and Prokaryotic Cells

To explain what Tetsushi's concern is, we have to understand a bit about cells and cellular life. Bear with us because this gets a bit technical! In general, there are two different types of cells: eukaryotes and prokaryotes (see Figure 17.2). Eukaryotes are the type of cells that make up plants and animals (and sometimes single-celled organisms). These cells have a nucleus (a smaller walled-off section in the center usually containing the DNA of the cell, among other things), have more complicated DNA, and have the structures within them that are called mitochondria (more on this in the next paragraph). Prokaryotes, on the other hand, are very simple cells. They don't have a

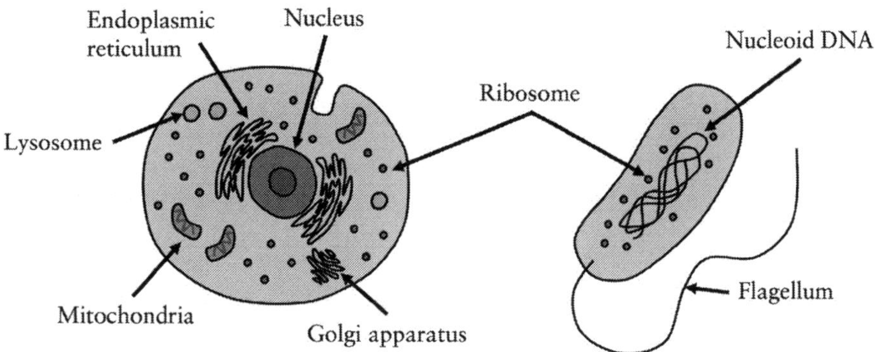

Figure 17.2 Eukaryotic cells (*left*) have (among other things) *mitochondria*; prokaryotic cells (*right*) do not.

nucleus, they replicate quickly because their DNA is simpler, they don't combine into multicellular organisms, and they don't have mitochondria. The most common form of this type of cell is bacteria.

Mitochondria are sometimes referred to as the powerhouse of the cell because they are responsible for processing energy into a form the cell can use. Mitochondria are membrane-enclosed structures that metabolize energy. So are they cells (within other cells)? And they even have their own DNA.[1] So are they alive? If we make the argument that mitochondria are *not* cells or are *not* alive, then we cannot really make the argument that prokaryotes (like bacteria) are alive because they have basically the same structure and perform the same activities (e.g., metabolizing) as mitochondria. We either have to conclude that prokaryotic cells (like bacteria) are *not* alive or that eukaryotic cells (which are alive) have other cells inside them (which are *also* alive). It sounds like the plot of one of those bad science fiction movies that Uncle Jimmy likes. But one that is based on a true story!

Semipermeable Boundary

Another frequently suggested item on the checklist of a living system is that it has some kind of surface that surrounds it and keeps it separate from its environment. Essentially, a boundary is necessary in order to keep bad stuff out and good stuff in (Koshland, 2002).

At first glance, this makes sense. After all, animals have skin, and cells have walls. But after thinking about it for a bit, both Fred and Tetsushi become skeptical of this condition. After all, many things have to go into and out of an organism in order for it to stay alive. Energy in the form of food has to enter the organism, and waste products have to leave. Think about eating a sandwich (or even breathing)—at what point does the sandwich (or the inhaled air) go from being part of the environment and become part of *you*? At what point does your waste (or exhaled air) go from being part of you to being part of the environment? And when an animal uses a tool like a stick to extend their reach or probe a surface, is the stick temporarily part of them or part of the environment (see Chapter 8)? What about someone who uses a prosthetic limb or a wheelchair or a video game controller (see Chapters 12 and 13)? Or two (or more) people who perform a task like a three-legged race together (see Chapter 11)? At best, it's a fuzzy line.

And that's not all! Humans need sunlight to produce vital vitamin D; some ocean-based animals need the salt in the water surrounding them, or their bodies would wither due to osmosis, and so on. Whether, where, and how a boundary exists between organism and environment *just isn't that simple*. Which is (yet another) reason why in ecological psychology we do not separate the two (see Chapter 4). While we agree that organisms need some way to keep good stuff in and bad stuff out, it does not follow that all living organisms need a fixed boundary that separates them from the environment. Rather, organism and environment are part of a reciprocal *system*.

Self-Organizing and Self-Maintaining

Given his recent experience with self-organization and how it seemed to be everywhere in living systems, Fred suggests that living systems would need to be self-organizing, and additionally, they would need to be able to "fix" themselves if they "broke". They would have to be able to heal themselves.

Much like the suggestion that living systems need to consume energy, this one seems to rest directly on our understanding of the beginnings of life. After all, in order for life to *start*, it would have *had to create itself*. It would have had to self-organize! Scientifically speaking, there was simply nothing else around at the time to create it (or organize it)!

Additionally, being alive is a dangerous business filled with small and large injuries. In order to *stay* alive, organisms must have some way of repairing harm (Koshland, 2002). Both Fred and Tetsushi agree that self-organization and self-maintenance seem necessary for any kind of life.

Growth

Tetsushi suggests that all living things *grow*. That is, they take in matter and/or energy from their surroundings and become larger or change shape. Even single-celled organisms will change shape and grow as they prepare for asexual reproduction. But Fred points out that crystals also grow, and they do it by taking on matter from their surroundings. In fact, plenty of nonliving things will change shape—rivers cut paths through solid rock and fire "grows" into spaces with more fuel. They agree that growth could be another necessary but not sufficient condition.

Movement as Response to the Environment

Thinking for a bit about the need to consume energy and the fact that a local energy source will (eventually) be used up, Tetsushi suggests that a living organism would need to be able to *move*. That is, it would need to be able to leave a current source of energy and go find another source if necessary. Fred likes that idea, and reasons that it further implies an ability to understand (or know about) the environment—it does no good to be able to move without the ability to first realize that the current food source is running low and the ability to recognize a new food source once it is found. In other words, they need a continuous relationship between perceiving and acting (and perhaps knowing) (see Chapters 5–9, 12, Figure 12.1).

As Churchland (1994) put it, living things need to engage in the four Fs: feeding, fleeing, fighting, and . . . reproduction. *All* of those processes are going to require movement. Movement for the purpose of achieving a goal (like finding a food source) is different from other kinds of movement. An animal walking up a hill to fetch a pail of water is alive. A ball rolling down a hill *moves* but is not alive. Movement as a criterion for being alive has to be movement that is self-generated and overcomes local physical forces rather than movement that is involuntary and is completely subject to local physical forces. By this definition, a tree "moves" when it grows its roots in a particular direction, pushing through soil and seeking out water and nutrients deep underground.

Of course, there already exist robots that can move from one place to another in order to perform a given task because of an "understanding" of the environment. Robots patrol the aisles of supermarkets looking for spills and either alert the staff or clean it up themselves! Automated vacuums and lawn mowers map out the space and clean living rooms and mow lawns, respectively, all over the world. You can make the argument that these robots are programmed (and living systems are self-organized and not programmed). But that argument leads us back to the concern about encountering alien life—if it moved and acted *as if* it were alive, would it matter if it turned out to be a race of robots?

Box 17.2 Are Viruses Alive?

As we have pointed out, people attempting to define life do so (regardless of the method of defining) by eventually comparing their definition to a consensus list. Mules are alive; fire is not. Bacteria are alive; robots are not. But that overstates the nature of the consensus—there are a handful of cases that are especially controversial. For example, there is a considerable amount (more than you might think) of debate about the status of *viruses*.

Viruses are, well, odd. They are, for all intents and purposes, just DNA in a protein coat. The coat is designed to break into living cells (like yours) and deposit the DNA inside (for example, you might have heard of the "spike protein" associated with the COVID-19 virus, which is a description of the protein coat). Once inside, the host cell (yours) doesn't recognize the foreign DNA as different from the native DNA, and so it helps the invading virus replicate, metabolize, and perform its tasks (see Box 15.1 for the activity of DNA). Without a host cell, the virus cannot make more of itself or metabolize energy. Many see that as damning evidence against the idea that viruses are alive (Ruiz-Mirazo et al., 2004; Brown of Brown & Bhella, 2016).

However, you could also make the argument that requiring another living organism for survival is characteristic of almost *all* living organisms (Bhella of Brown & Bhella, 2016). An obvious example are parasitic organisms like climbing vines which depend on the host organism to survive. But even humans require plants to metabolize sunlight for us—we eat that energy when we eat plants or when we eat animals that (in turn) ate the plants. Without those organisms to metabolize the sun's energy,[2] we would die just as surely as the virus would. Also, the host cell doesn't need to be alive! Viruses can move into a "dead" cell and use the cell's machinery for replication and metabolism (Villarreal, 2004).

It may not *matter* whether we classify viruses as alive or not (and it's possible that they occupy a kind of gray area in-between) because the point is that they are *important* to the study of life and its evolution. An increasing number of scientists (e.g., Bell, 2001; Suzan-Monti, La Scola, & Raoult, 2006) think that the nucleus in eukaryotic cells began as a trapped virus, still in its protein coat. If that's the case, they are of vital interest to anyone studying the evolution and activity of any multicellular organism.

I Know It When I See It

Fred and Tetsushi are getting a little frustrated with coming up with a list of necessary and/or sufficient criteria for life. Not all of them seem to work, and they have a growing concern that an alien life-form (or even undiscovered life right here on Earth) could exist that did not have some of the criteria they listed. They also feel like they keep coming up with examples of nonliving things that meet the criteria that they have come up with. They decide to try to limit the list to those qualities that likely define life from first principles. First principles are those fundamental concepts that cannot be derived from other concepts. For example, it isn't necessary to include the quality of "growing or changing" if we have already included the idea of "consuming energy" (which will, because of the nature of entropy, require change).

After much debate, they decide that the principles which seem the most fundamental are consumption of energy, self-organization and repair, and perceiving-acting. They decide that although these are necessary, they are still not *sufficient* because they could imagine a self-organized system (like Bob's beads!) that still meets this definition. But it's the best they could do.

And this is, more or less, the state of the debate. There are a number of lists similar to the one that Fred and Tetsushi developed, each with its own complications and gray areas. Each ends up including or excluding things it shouldn't, and no one can agree on the "best" definition. Which raises the question: does it matter? We made the argument at the beginning that it *does*—largely because it clarifies the boundaries of science. But if it turns out that those boundaries are fuzzy, does it matter? Shouldn't scientists merely expand their study to the boundary cases as well? Won't we "know it when we see it" if we come across it on an alien planet?

What Is Intelligence?

Fred's experience with defining life led him to believe (probably correctly) that defining intelligence was going to be just as difficult (perhaps even more so). This time, he enlisted the help of his friend Nia because she's the kind of friend who thinks deeply about stuff other people take for granted.

"Classical" Definitions of Intelligence

Scientists and philosophers have been trying to define intelligence for a very long time. Unfortunately, much like definitions of life, progress has been slow and consensus is a very long way off. The general intuition (the kind of answer you might get from asking a friend what they think intelligence means) is that it's about knowing stuff (e.g., Taine, 1872) or the ability to make new discoveries through investigation and reasoning (e.g., Bühler, 1918/2013) or more generally the ability to adapt to new situations (e.g., Claparède, 1917). The well-known developmental psychologist Piaget (1947/2003) argued that a fundamental aspect of intelligence was the ability to make plans that included situations not immediately present. Or in other words, you had to be able to *remember* and *imagine*. Dennett (1984)[3] suggested that intelligence is about the ability to be *surprised*. In order to be surprised, you had to have had *expectations* and understand that those expectations are being violated. Or in other words, the hallmarks of intelligence are planning and being able to understand the consequences of your plan.

Fred went into this adventure assuming that the "outside the box" answer to intelligence might have something to do with multiple intelligences—like the work by Gardner (1993) that suggested that the typical "cognitive" intelligence (the ability to solve puzzles and word problems) was only a tiny fraction of what human intelligence is. Gardner proposed other types of intelligence (eight in all), like kinesthetic, musical, and interpersonal. However, while Nia thought that Gardner might be right that intelligence was more than just mental abilities, she pointed out that this was still a very human-centric view of intelligence. Consequently, it wouldn't really help with the problem raised by Uncle Jimmy: what would we recognize as intelligence if we saw it in a new species? Surely, we wouldn't wait for them to make music before we could see that they were something we would categorize as intelligent?

The problem with all such definitions is that they are not terribly specific, nor are they terribly generalizable to a possible alien species. You cannot take any one of those criteria and create a test that would (in an unbiased way) delineate intelligent aliens from nonintelligent ones. And partially, that's because these criteria were not developed to be used in that fashion!

Most of the efforts at creating a definition for intelligence are explicit attempts to *quantify* intelligence in (and among) *humans*. That is, intelligence tests based on these criteria are intended to tell the difference between geniuses and fools; they are not intended to tell the difference between something that has *no* intelligence (like a rock) and something that might have *some* intelligence (like Fred or even a single-celled organism; more on this in the next section), which means that *all* such definitions will necessarily be very human-centric.

If we want a definition that will apply to our possible alien friends, we need one that can identify the difference between something that is merely mechanical and one that has true intentionality. That is, we need to be able to tell the difference between something just responding to local forces (like a rock rolling down a hill) and one that is going *against* local forces in order to reach some goal (like a person walking up a hill to fetch a pail of water). Note that this overlaps, to some degree, with the first-principles criteria that Fred and Tetushi developed for being alive.

The Turing Test and the Chinese Room Problem

It turns out that this is an *old* question. It is most often asked in the context of attempting to create *artificial* intelligence (see Churchland & Churchland, 1990). Can we *make* a system that we would consider intelligent? Turing proposed a way to identify an artificial system as intelligent: can it impersonate a human well enough to fool an average person? Or in other words, if an average person has a conversation with it, will they be able to realize that the thing they are talking to is *not a person*? Turing proposed this well before the modern computer era made textual communication (like chat rooms and texting) a possibility, but the idea is one a modern internet user will recognize: can you tell if you're talking to a chatbot? If the bot is good enough to fool you, then Turing suggested it should be considered intelligent.

Many computer programs have passed the Turing test as originally proposed. In all likelihood, you have chatted with just such a bot when trying to get help on a website or when debating politics on a social media page. But people are still wary of calling this "intelligence". As Bruineberg, Chemero, and Rietveld put it, "the field of artificial intelligence: where a particular behavior . . . is a sign of genuine intelligent behavior until a computer can actually do it, after which it is understood as merely a case of pattern recognition" (2019).

Nia's take on the Turing test is that it feels like the wrong question to her, or at least a question badly posed. She invites Fred to consider the situation in Figure 17.3. In it, Fred is in a room. There is a slot on one of the walls. Nia is standing outside and can write whatever she wants on a piece of paper and slide it into the slot to him. He can then write on a piece of paper and send it back out to Nia (passing notes more or less like this is what we did before there was texting).

Fred has in the room a stack of binders that have rules. One such rule reads as follows: if you see the symbols "你好吗", you should reply back with these symbols "我很好". Fred (in the room) does not know what any of those symbols mean, but it turns out that the rule gives

Figure 17.3 The Chinese Room Problem: Fred (inside the room) has binders that tell him simple rules for replying to comments made in Chinese. Nia (outside the room) can pass notes written in Chinese into the room. Fred can follow the instructions and respond sensibly to Nia's notes. Does Fred speak Chinese?

him the ability to have a quick exchange in Chinese ("你好吗" means "How are you?" and "我很好" means "I am good"). A person on the outside could send in the first set of symbols and get a sensible (if not terribly interesting) response.

Now let's say that Fred has a *lot* of these binders (all based on similar exchanges of Chinese characters), and leaving aside the time it takes to search the binders for the right response, he could carry on a reasonable conversation with Nia (who happens to be fluent in Chinese). So here is Nia's question: in this scenario, *does Fred speak Chinese*? What does it mean to speak Chinese? If the meaning of that phrase is just the ability to reasonably fool the other person, then sure! Fred speaks Chinese. But if it's actually *understanding* what you are trying to communicate and being able to decide for yourself *what* to communicate, then no, Fred does not speak Chinese.

As Nia points out, Fred has to agree to one of two things: either (1) that speaking Chinese includes something outside of the ability to combine rules (which means that computers as we currently understand them will *never* be able to do this) or (2) that the *room itself* (which includes Fred and the binders and the papers for communicating on) understands Chinese even if Fred himself doesn't.

Nia's example is known as the Chinese Room Problem (Searle, 1980) and is used to highlight the difference between syntax and semantics. Syntax is a set of rules—like grammar or the binders in the room with Fred. Semantics is meaning—like what it *means* to say "I am good" in response to the question "How are you?"—it could mean you're fine, or it could mean you are not great, or it could mean you are angry at the person asking the question!

Fred's ability to communicate with Nia in Chinese is based entirely on syntax. But Nia argues that if we are going to understand intelligence broadly enough to include potential aliens, we are going to need to include semantics. Fred counters that we cannot reasonably know whether an alien race actually *has* a semantic understanding. After all, Nia would have been sufficiently fooled by Fred in the Chinese room. How would she know what *Fred's* experience was? (And by extension, how would we know what the experience of the alien was?) Nia's experience was the same either way—she had a pleasant conversation in Chinese. So how would Nia infer what *Fred* felt?

A Different Approach

Fred suggests that they should create a definition of intelligence that does not require inferring the experience of the organism in question (as the semantics argument of the Chinese Room Problem cautions against) and does not rely on the ability to solve problems (as the classical, cognitivist definitions would have it) and isn't human-centric. He also thinks (based on his discussions with Tetsushi) that the fundamentals of intelligence are going to have something to do with the ability to navigate in and manipulate parts of the environment, possibly in service of finding and dissipating energy.

Importantly, he wants to preserve the possibility of artificial intelligence. He is *really invested* in the idea of someday having a true artificial intelligence (those are *his* favorite kinds of movies), but he also cannot see why something artificial *couldn't* be intelligent. If it met all the definitions, it would be quite human-centric to think otherwise.

After some discussion, Nia and Fred decide that their definition of intelligence really has two parts: foraging and the ability to perceive and behave with respect to affordances (see Chapter 5).

Foraging

Fred and Nia start with the idea that any system we would consider intelligent is going to exhibit *behavior* of some kind. Behavior implies movement; movement implies the use of energy. Even a ball rolling down a hill is using energy! The difference between a ball rolling down a hill and an intelligent system is that the latter is using energy *to maintain itself* (the way we eat food to stay alive).

Systems that maintain themselves through the dissipation of energy are called *autocatakinetic* (ACK) systems (Stepp & Srinivasa, 2012). There are many nonliving, non-intelligent systems that are considered ACK (the convection cells, for example, require a constant source of energy to maintain their shape). However, an *intelligent* system (whether biological or artificial) should be capable of finding *new* energy to consume in order to maintain itself (the way a lion hunts a gazelle or when Fred goes to the store to buy more food when his cupboards get empty). In other words, it should be able to *forage*.

Foraging cannot just be about first exhausting a local source of food and then moving to the next, nearest source. In a sense, that is what fire does. It consumes the local tinder (say, crumpled up newspaper) and moves to the next burnable object (say, a log). The fire cannot leave the fireplace and seek out something more exciting and bigger to burn (say, your house) unless it has some very local pathway (say, a blanket put too close to the fire). It is entirely tied to *local* energy potentials.

Here is the problem with being completely tied to local energy potentials: they might run out before you can find and/or move to a new source of energy. And if the source runs out, you might not have *enough* energy to get to another source. Look at Figure 17.4: Fred is on a road trip. Sure, he can stay in his car with the car running sitting next to the gas station and keep filling up, but eventually that station will run out of gas. If Fred stays there until his car runs out of gas, his road trip is over. If, instead, he fills up at the first station and then *leaves* (even though there is gas left at the station), he can use that onboard energy potential to move to another gas station farther away.

Fred and Nia, therefore, decide that a minimum requirement for intelligence is the ability to *leave* a local energy potential and *go find a better one* or at least a *different one* (Swenson, 2009; Swenson & Turvey, 1991). Fred compares it to the time that he realized all he had left in the house was mustard—sure, it technically has calories, so it *technically* was food, but it doesn't make a great meal. He left that food source to go buy a sandwich at the deli, then used *that* energy to go buy groceries.

Use of Affordances

Inherent in the idea of foraging is the ability to use some kind of perceptual ability to go find more food. While the perceptual system(s) of a given organism may not be immediately

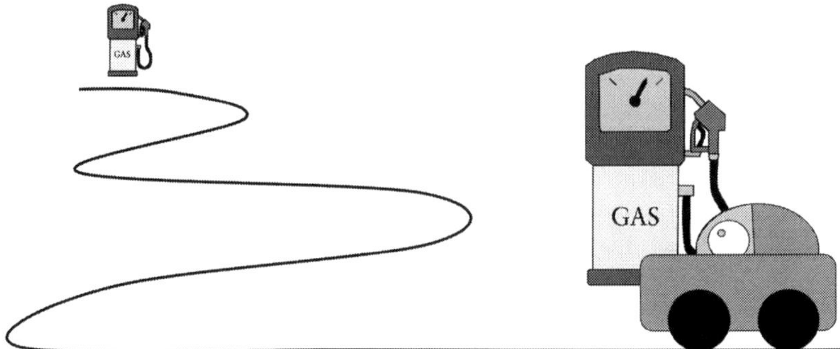

Figure 17.4 If Fred remains at the gas station until the gas station runs out of gas, he may not have enough fuel to make it to the next station. If, however, he fills up at the first station, he can use that onboard energy to travel to the next station.

obvious to us (human) observers, an intelligent agent must be able to navigate within the world based on their own abilities. Because of this, Fred and Nia decide the ability to perceive and behave with respect to affordances (see Chapter 5) would be an indication of intelligence (Turvey & Carello, 2012).

What is interesting about the notion of affordance use is that it neatly sidesteps the issue of whether we need to infer the subjective experience of the organism with regards to syntax and semantics. As Turvey and Carello (2012, p. 5) said, "affordances are the semantics of ecology". Affordances are organism-specific opportunities for action. Affordances *are* meaning. Or in other words, evidence that an organism was using affordances to guide behavior would *by definition* mean that they had an appreciation of semantics and not just syntax.

Perceiving and behaving with respect to affordances also demonstrates certain characteristics of an intelligent system—*flexibility*, *prospectivity*, and *retrospectivity* (E. Gibson, 1994; Turvey & Carello, 2012). *Flexibility* is the ability to use multiple methods to bring about a specific goal—Fred could drive to the grocery store, he could walk to the corner mart, or he could order food online and have it delivered. No matter the means, Fred still achieves the same end. *Prospectivity* is the ability to organize your behavior with respect to current *and future* contexts—if on the way to the grocery store Fred sees that there is bad traffic ahead, he can turn around *before he gets to it* and go to the corner mart instead. *Restrospectivity* is the ability to organize your behavior with respect to *previous* contexts—if Fred has previously tried to go to the grocery store on Saturday mornings and found it impossibly crowded, he can try going on Monday afternoons instead.

What Fred and Nia decide is that if an organism exhibits those three characteristics while perceiving and behaving with respect to affordances, they are exhibiting intelligence. And (importantly to Fred because of his desire for true artificial intelligence) the size, shape, or composition of the organism would not matter. An artificial organism that can recognize and behave with respect to affordances should be certified as intelligent, just like a biological system with the same ability might.

Ecological psychologists call this idea *physical intelligence*. This is to separate it from the *cognitive intelligences* listed at the beginning of this section and to deliberately leave open the possibility that intelligence is not just inherent in biological organisms, so we are not just interested in *biological intelligence* (Shaw & Kinsella-Shaw, 2012). The label of physical intelligence encourages us as scientists to revisit our own biases when it comes to deciding what is and what is not intelligent.

Surprising Intelligence

After his conversations with Nia, Fred realizes that he is fighting his *own* biases when it comes to intelligence. He is used to thinking of it as something that only humans and maybe a few other animals possess (his friend Keonho has a dog named Larry that can do some pretty amazing tricks), but these discussions have made him reconsider this idea. He decides to go to the library and ask for information on intelligent behavior in surprising places.

Barrier 1: Humans Versus Animals

After listening to Fred's story, the librarian, Audrey, tells him about the history of definitions of intelligence. Historically, she says, scientists and philosophers refused to accept the possibility of intelligence in anything other than humans. They would dismiss the intelligent behaviors of other animals as mere "instinct" or "reflex" and not reflecting actual thought. This began to change (in large part) because of Darwin's (1881/2004) work. His insistence that all organisms were descendants of much simpler organisms opened the field to the idea that *animals*, at least, could be intelligent. Audrey helps Fred find several examples.

Worms. Darwin (1881/2004) described the behavior of worms as intelligent, remarking that they "act in the same manner as would a man [*sic*] under similar circumstances" (pp. 37–38). He observed that worms would first dig a burrow to live in that was the right size and shape to keep the worm comfortable and properly moist and then would line that burrow with leaves. To do the latter, the worm would forage for appropriately sized and shaped leaves, circle around them until it found the most graspable bit (prospectivity!), pull the leaf toward the burrow, and pull it down into the burrow *in a very particular way* so that the leaf would curl on itself into a tube shape and line the burrow against the elements. If the curling wasn't working properly, the worm would back out of the burrow, find a different graspable part of the leaf, and try again (retrospectivity!). More than this, worms will be choosy about where to grasp asymmetric leaves and less choosy about where to grasp symmetric leaves. And when leaves are not present, they will use other materials that serve the same purpose, such as paper strips (flexibility!).

Crows. A quick search of the internet will bring up dozens of videos of crows acting intelligently—using a lid of a cup as a sled and sledding down the snow on a roof repeatedly, for example. There are also videos of them dropping nuts on crosswalks so that cars can run over them and crack the shells—and the crows eventually learn from experience to wait until the "walk" sign is displayed to go out into the road and eat the nut (retrospectivity!). One study set out to investigate whether and how captive crows used a hooked piece of wire to pull a basket of food out of a tube (see Figure 17.5). The crows accomplished this task with ease (prospectivity!). But the *remarkable* part happened when the researchers gave one of the wires to the crow without bending it into a hook first. The crow examined the situation and, after realizing that the unbent wire could not be used to retrieve the basket, used the tube as a brace and *bent the wire into a hook* (flexibility!) (Weir, Chappell, & Kacelnik, 2002).

Spiders. The most visible intelligent behavior of spiders is in their ability to construct their webs in a wide variety of circumstances and arrangements of anchor points—and even modify the tension of the strands of the web based on its energetic needs (flexibility!) (Watanabe, 2000). But some of their most interesting behavior is far less visible to the untrained eye. Take, for example, the tiny spider *Portia labiate* (McCrone, 2006). It can plan hours-long attack strategies in order to capture its prey—often other spiders (prospectivity!). It will attack in one fashion if the prey is carrying its own offspring, and so is unlikely to drop it in the course of defending itself, and in a different fashion if the prey is carrying its own meal, and so is likely to drop it and in the course of defending itself (flexibility!). The attack plan often requires tracking around the prey and jumping on it from behind—a move that puts the prey out of sight for long periods of time (retrospectivity!). It will even pluck the web of spiders in

Figure 17.5 Crows will use bent wires to pull an otherwise unreachable basket of food out of a tube. When the wire was given to one crow unbent, the crow created its own hook by bending the wire itself.

particular patterns to mimic the struggles of a trapped insect in order to lure the spider out of hiding. And it does all of this with an estimated 600,000 neurons (for reference, a human has roughly 100 billion brain cells).

Barrier 2: Animals Versus Plants

Fred is pretty easily convinced that non-human animals are intelligent. Even if he hadn't seen Keonho's dog, Larry, ride a skateboard, he would have been quite ready to believe that animals use affordances to guide behavior. But Audrey next suggests something he *isn't* so ready to believe,—that *plants* exhibit intelligent behavior all the time! (For these and other examples, see Carello et al., 2012). What is so surprising about this revelation is that plants might exhibit *any* behavior at all. After all, he asks Audrey, "Don't they just . . . sit there?" Audrey points out that while a lot of the behavior of plants is *very* slow in comparison to animals (growing in a particular direction, for example, rather than moving a limb), it is still *behavior*. And, she reminds him, the goal here is to show that the behavior of the candidate system exhibits the three characteristics of intelligence that Fred and Nia have settled on.

Poplar tree. The natural enemy of the poplar tree is the caterpillar. When the caterpillar starts eating the leaves, the tree will emit a gas that will attract predators of the caterpillar. But that's not all! The gas alerts the nearby poplar trees (who, in turn, emit the gas as well), which also attracts predators of the caterpillar—it's essentially a chemical call for help (prospectivity)! Interestingly, if an experimenter cuts the leaves of the tree with scissors (mimicking the caterpillars' bites), the tree will, at first, release the chemical call for help but will cease doing so after repeated cuts. Instead, it will release a different chemical that helps soothe and heal the cuts made by the scissors. If a caterpillar then starts to eat the leaf, the tree will once again release the chemical help signal (Dicke, van Loon, & Soler, 2009). Or in other words, the tree learns from past experience (retrospectivity!) to discriminate between caterpillar and human damage and exhibit appropriate behavior in response to each scenario.

Dodder plant. The dodder is a parasitic plant that grows over other ground plants, tapping into them and feeding off the nutrients they provide. If you place a dodder plant in the middle of a platform with no host plants available, it will grow, but not in any particular direction. If you put a less nutritious host (like a wheat plant) on one side, the dodder will grow in the direction of the wheat plant. However, if you put a wheat plant on one side and a more nutritious host (like a tomato plant) on the other, the dodder will grow toward the tomato plant (see Figure 17.6, Runyon, Mescher, & De Moraes, 2006). In fact, if a dodder plant is tethered to a very poor host (one that has been leached of almost all nutrients, so is a poor meal, like Fred's mustard), it will not even bother trying to eat it. It will, instead, grow *away* from the host in search of a better meal (Kelly, 1992). It does what Fred did when he left the mustard and went to the grocery store. Or in other words, the dodder plant can *plan ahead* (prospectivity!) and choose the best host available—*all without touching any of the hosts*.

Venus flytrap. Not all plants rely on just sunlight and nutrients from the soil or another plant. The Venus flytrap is a carnivore—it attracts bugs to its jaw-like leaves (see Figure 17.7), which have hair-like sensors on them. When the hair-like sensors indicate the presence of a potential prey item, the leaves snap closed, trapping the bug. The leaves then seal around the bug and flood it with a digestive enzyme. After closing, the jaws might not be able to open again for another week, so making a mistake and closing around, say, a raindrop could be quite costly. To avoid this, the Venus flytrap does not close until it receives *two* signals from the hairs. And then, it waits until it receives *several more* before it floods the chamber with digestive enzymes (Böhm et al., 2016). Or in other words, the Venus flytrap can *count* the number of stimulations in order to ensure it has captured a bug rather than a raindrop (restrospectivity!).

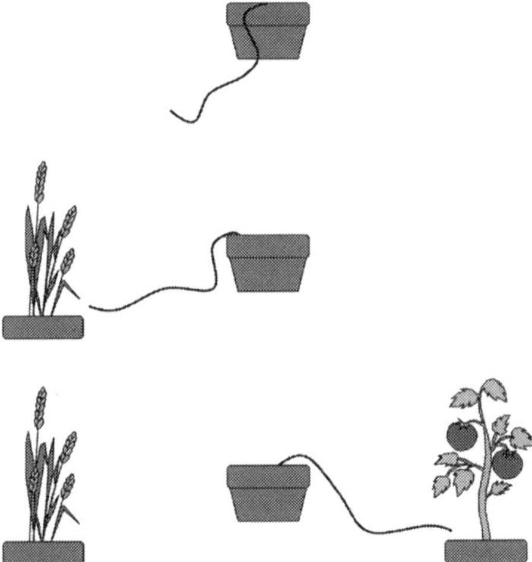

Figure 17.6 *Top:* when there is no source of food, the dodder plant will grow in every direction with equal probability. *Middle*: when there is a source of food, even a poor one like a wheat plant, the dodder will grow toward it. *Bottom:* when there are two sources of food, and one is poor (wheat plant) and one is rich (tomato plant), the dodder will grow toward the rich food.

Figure 17.7 The Venus flytrap has tiny hairs that sense the movements of a fly. Once the hairs are stimulated several times in a row (which a fly would do, but not a drop of rain), the flytrap closes, trapping the fly within.

Barrier 3: Multicellular Versus Single-Celled Organisms

Fred is, frankly, blown away by the examples Audrey is showing him. He ultimately concedes that plants seems to be showing flexibility, prospectivity, and retrospectivity. But Audrey isn't done! We are used to thinking about the behavior of large, multicellular organisms. It might be a stretch to think of a dodder plant *planning ahead*, but not an impossible leap given what complex (read: multicellular) organisms they are. But Audrey points out, such multicellular complexity may not be necessary for adaptive, intelligent behavior. In fact, there are examples of intelligent behavior in unicellular organisms. Fred's jaw dropped. *Gasp!* Is Audrey suggesting that microscopic single-celled organisms (can) exhibit intelligent behavior? Yes. Yes, she is.

Difflugia. Take a drop of water from a marsh and put it under a microscope, and you might find a single-celled organism from the genus *Difflugia.* Though tiny and seemingly unremarkable, they exhibit behavior you might expect to see only in far more complex organisms. For example, if you "catch" them by erecting a kind of semicircular wall to impede their progress, they will stop and turn around before leaving (suggesting it has a "head" and a "tail" and prefers to travel head-first). It forages for food (bacteria) and will slow down its reproduction if there is a food shortage (flexibility!) (Ford, 2006).

And if the environment becomes inhospitable, it will *build itself a home* to protect itself (prospectivity!). That's right. *Difflugia* will gather materials from the silt in the marsh and use what amounts to their own spit to glue it together to build a protective shell around itself. Even more interestingly, it will sort through the silt to find its *preferred building materials.* Some prefer silica sand; others select centric diatoms (an even smaller single-celled organism). The shells are made of hundreds of small pieces, expertly arranged (Turvey, 2015). Some species will even create "teeth" around the opening and use their shell as a weapon for hunting food (prospectivity *and* flexibility!) (Han et al., 2008). They may be small, but they are mighty—showing the exact same kinds of behaviors as their multicellular cousins. They forage for food, plan ahead, and flexibly respond to their environments.

Cellular slime molds. Elsewhere in this book, we have discussed the remarkable organism that is the cellular slime mold (see Chapter 16). We recognize it's a bit of a cheat to put slime molds in this section because for at least part of their life cycle, they are most accurately described as multicellular organisms. That said, for *part* of their life cycle they are single-celled, and they show remarkable behavior during that phase. For example, they can make decisions about risk and reward (prospectivity!) that show sensitivity to context (flexibility!). As a basic ability, they are able to tell the difference between a high-nutrient food and a low-nutrient food and selectively prefer the high-nutrient food. But their choice behavior is more complex than this. Light is a danger to cellular slime molds (which is why they generally grow under leaves or other dark places), so if you present them with the choice between a low-nutrient food in the shade and a high-nutrient food in the light, they will only choose the higher-nutrient food if it's *much better* than the low-nutrient food (Latty & Beekman, 2010). Or in other words, they are only willing to risk exposure to the light if it means getting a *great meal* (prospectivity!).

Barrier 4: Biological Organisms Versus Nonbiological Systems

Fred finally asks the question he had been wanting to ask for a while—is it possible for a *nonliving* system (and here he really means a robot, like those in his movies) to exhibit the kind of intelligence that he, Audrey, Nia, and Tetsushi have been talking about? Audrey points out that robots as we typically think of them—programmed to perform a given set of behaviors or achieve a given set of goals—are going to be prone to the syntax-versus-semantics problem that Fred and Nia encountered earlier when they were talking about the Chinese Room Problem. Does the robot vacuum know what it is doing and why it is doing it?

Audrey suggests that Fred look for nonliving systems that are *not* programmed but nonetheless exhibit remarkable behavior. She assures him we are a long way off from robots that will rise up and take over the world, but there are efforts at creating nonprogrammed—or at least *minimally* programmed—robots that can do surprising things (see Box 16.2, Kriegman et al., 2021).

Moreover, we're starting to understand how intelligence could *evolve* from non-intelligence. Audrey tells Fred of a few examples of behavior that could be considered *almost intelligent*. They exhibit some (but not all) of the traits that Fred and Nia discussed.

Beads. The self-organizing abilities of metal beads were introduced in Chapter 16, but we did not fully cover all the behaviors they are capable of performing. As discussed, the beads will self-organize into a tree structure when there is a source of electricity and a nearby grounding ring (Figure 16.3). We argued that this was to maintain the fastest rate of entropy production. What we did not talk about at the time was that these structures can "heal" if they are damaged! That is, if the experimenter breaks apart the tree, the beads will rearrange themselves and reform a tree—not the exact *same structure* but one that dissipates the *same amount of energy* (Kondepudi et al., 2015). Or in other words, they exhibit *flexibility* when it comes to reaching their goal (of maximizing the rate of entropy production). The bead structures will also move around in order to soak up as much electrical charge as possible (De Bari et al., 2019)—a behavior not unlike biological foraging.

Droplets. Small drops of different fluids can exhibit a wide variety of interesting behaviors under the right circumstances. One example you can try at home: food coloring droplets. Start by getting a glass microscope slide very, very clean (to get it clean enough, you'll probably have to hold it in a Bunsen burner flame or put it in the oven). Next, create several different samples of distilled water mixed with different amounts of food coloring. Place two of these drops of different food coloring concentration next to each other, and one will chase the other around the slide (see Figure 17.8, *top*)! Researchers have managed to observe elaborate movement of the droplets under such circumstances. For example, by also taking advantage of the fact that the droplets won't cross a line drawn in marker, they can make a dozen randomly placed

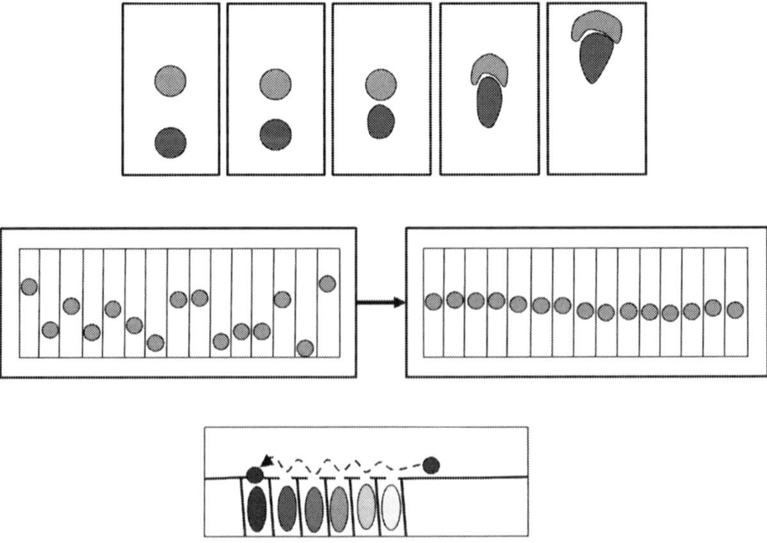

Figure 17.8 Under the right conditions, food coloring droplets will chase each other (*top*), align with each other (*middle*), and "look" for the same concentration and join it (*bottom*).

droplets align with each other (see Figure 17.8, *middle*). In another experiment, they presented the droplet with different "bins" containing different concentrations of food coloring, and the droplet moved bin by bin until it "found" the bin containing the same concentration as itself and then joined it (see Figure 17.8, *bottom*; Cira, Benusiglio, & Prakash, 2015)! Again, while we'd be hard-pressed to call it awareness, the droplets were able to avoid local bins in favor of bins farther away (prospectivity!).

Benzoquinone flakes. Small, irregularly shaped flakes of a chemical substance called benzoquinone (BQ) will float on top of water. While floating, the flakes start to dissolve. The process of dissolving makes the water around saturated with dissolved BQ and makes it harder for the remaining flakes to dissolve. So they go looking farther away for places to dissolve (places with more pure water). This is like when Fred and Claudia go to the movies, and all the good seats are taken, so they have to walk farther and sit in the back. What is interesting about this is that if you put several such flakes in a petri dish, they will begin to form a *flock* (like a whole *group* of people moving to the back of the theater together). You would think this would be the opposite of what they would *want* to do since being near another dissolving flake increases the amount of dissolved BQ surrounding them—but they flock together anyway! The flocks will move around the dish *together* (like a social synergy, see Chapter 11), even going so far as to move together through gates (not unlike biological organisms using affordances to guide behavior!) and respond to temperature differences and to magnetic fields (Satterwhite-Warden et al., 2019). We know why a group in a theater would do this (it's more fun to watch a movie with friends), but it's not entirely clear why the BQ flakes do this. Perhaps their capabilities are increased by working together (like the social affordances in Chapter 11), or perhaps they are competing less when they work together (like the fireflies in Chapter 16). Regardless, they are showing context-sensitive behavior that seems to ignore local gradients.

Intelligent Life on Other Planets

And so, after all this, what is the answer to Fred's initial question? Does intelligent life exist on other planets? We obviously do not know the answer for sure (unless scientists are hiding some pretty *big news*), but we've come a long way to understanding our own *question*, at least. And given the nature of the question, it is hard to imagine that life would not exist somewhere else. The conditions that seem to create it are likely to exist in many other places. We just might have to be prepared for it to look very different from intelligent life here on Earth.

Notes

1. It's true—mitochondria have their own DNA that is different from the rest of the cell's DNA. In humans, at least, the mitochondrial DNA is inherited from the mother and is slower to mutate than the rest of the DNA. This is the subject of the easy-to-read book *The Seven Daughters of Eve* (2001) by Bryan Sykes.
2. Not to mention the complex biome that is the bacteria that live in our digestive tract and are required for proper digestion!
3. Dennett makes this argument in the context of talking about artificial intelligence and what is called the frame problem; we don't have room for it here, but it's an amusing and informative read and we recommend it highly.

References

Abbs, J. H., & Connor, N. P. (1989). Motor coordination for functional human behavior: Perspectives from a speech motor data base. In S. Wallace (Ed.), *Perspectives on the coordination of movement* (pp. 157–183). Amsterdam: North-Holland.

Adolph, K. E. (2019). An ecological approach to learning in (not and) development. *Human Development, 63*, 180–201.

Adolph, K. E., Cole, W. G., Komati, M., Garciaguirre, J. S., Badaly, D., Lingeman, J. M., . . . & Sotsky, R. B. (2012). How do you learn to walk? Thousands of steps and dozens of falls per day. *Psychological Science, 23*, 1387–1394.

Adolph, K. E., & Franchak, J. M. (2017). The development of motor behavior. *Wiley Interdisciplinary Reviews. Cognitive Science, 8*(1–2). https://doi.org/10.1002/wcs.1430

Adolph, K. E., & Hoch, J. E. (2019). Motor development: Embodied, embedded, enculturated, and enabling. *Annual Review of Psychology, 70*, 141–164. https://doi.org/10.1146/annurev-psych-010418-102836

Adolph, K. E., Kaplan, B. E., & Kretch, K. S. (2021). Infants on the edge: Beyond the visual cliff. In A. Slater & P. Quinn (Eds.), *Developmental psychology: Revisiting the classic studies, 2nd ed.* (pp. 51–72). London: Sage.

Adolph, K. E., Kretch, K. S., & LoBue, V. (2014). Fear of heights in infants? *Current Directions in Psychological Science, 23*, 60–66.

Adolph, K. E., Vereijken, B., & Shrout, P. E. (2003). What changes in infant walking and why. *Child Development, 74*(2), 475–497. https://doi.org/10.1111/1467-8624.7402011

Agyei, S. B., Holth, M., van der Weel, F. R., & van der Meer, A. L. (2015). Longitudinal study of perception of structured optic flow and random visual motion in infants using high-density EEG. *Developmental Science, 18*(3), 436–451. https://doi.org/10.1111/desc.12221

Alexander, R. M. (1992). *The human machine: How the body works*. New York: Columbia University Press.

Alhazen, I. (1983). *Book of optics* (Sabra, A. I., Trans.). The Optics of Ibn al-Haytham two volumes. London: Warburg Institute, 1989 (Original work published c. 1000).

Allen, L. K., Perret, C., Likens, A., & McNamara, D. S. (2017). What'd you say again? Recurrence quantification analysis as a method for analyzing the dynamics of discourse in a reading strategy tutor. In *Proceedings of the seventh international learning analytics and knowledge conference* (pp. 373–382). Vancouver, BC: ACM.

Altenhoff, B. M., Pagano, C. C., Kil, I., & Burg, T. C. (2017). Learning to perceive haptic distance-to-break in the presence of friction. *Journal of Experimental Psychology: Human Perception and Performance, 43*(2), 231–244. https://doi.org/10.1037/xhp0000298

Amazeen, E. L., & Turvey, M. T. (1996). Weight perception and the haptic size—weight illusion are functions of the inertia tensor. *Journal of Experimental Psychology: Human Perception and Performance, 22*(1), 213–232. https://doi.org/10.1037/0096-1523.22.1.213

Amazeen, P. G., Amazeen, E. L., & Turvey, M. T. (1998). Dynamics of human intersegmental coordination: Theory and research. In D. A. Rosenbaum & C. E. Collyer (Eds.), *Timing of behavior: Neural, psychological, and computational perspectives* (pp. 237–259). Cambridge, MA: The MIT Press.

American Psychological Association. (n.d.). Depression. *APA Dictionary of Psychology*. Retrieved June 2021, from https://dictionary.apa.org/depression.

Anderson, M. L. (2014). *After phrenology: Neural reuse and the interactive brain*. Cambridge, MA: The MIT Press.

Anderson, M. L., Richardson, M. J., & Chemero, A. (2012). Eroding the boundaries of cognition. Implications of embodiment. *Topics in Cognitive Science, 4*(4), 717–730. https://doi.org/10.1111/j.1756-8765.2012.01211.x

Aristotle (c. 350 BCE). *Metaphysics.*

Arzamarski, R., Isenhower, R. W., Kay, B. A., Turvey, M. T., & Michaels, C. F. (2010). Effects of intention and learning on attention to information in dynamic touch. *Attention, Perception & Psychophysics, 72*(3), 721–735. https://doi.org/10.3758/APP.72.3.721

Avelar, B. S., Mancini, M. C., Fonseca, S. T., Kelty-Stephen, D. G., de Miranda, D. M., . . . & Silva, P. L. (2019). Fractal fluctuations in exploratory movements predict differences in dynamic touch capabilities between children with Attention-Deficit Hyperactivity Disorder and typical development. *PLoS ONE, 14*(5), e0217200.

Baillargeon, R. (1993). The object concept revisited: New directions in the investigation of infants' physical knowledge. In C. E. Ganrud (Ed.), *Visual perception and cognition in infancy* (pp. 265–315). Hillsdale, NJ: Erlbaum.

Balasubramaniam, R., Riley, M. A., & Turvey, M. T. (2000). Specificity of postural sway to the demands of a precision task. *Gait & Posture, 11*(1), 12–24. https://doi.org/10.1016/s0966-6362(99)00051-x

Bardy, B. G., Oullier, O., Bootsma, R. J., & Stoffregen, T. A. (2002). Dynamics of human postural transitions. *Journal of Experimental Psychology: Human Perception and Performance, 28*(3), 499–514. https://doi.org/10.1037/0096-1523.28.3.499

Bargh, J. (2017). *Before you know it: The unconscious reasons we do what we do.* New York: Simon & Schuster.

Bartman, T., & Hove, J. (2005). Mechanics and function in heart morphogenesis. *Developmental Dynamics: An Official Publication of the American Association of Anatomists, 233*(2), 373–381.

Beek, P. J., & Santvoord, A. V. (1992). Learning the cascade juggle: A dynamical systems analysis. *Journal of Motor Behavior, 24*(1), 85–94.

Belen'kii, V. Y., Gurfinkel, V. S., & Pal'tsev, Y. I. (1967). Elements of control of voluntary movements. *Biofizika, 12*(1), 135–141.

Bell, P. J. L. (2001). Viral eukaryogenesis: Was the ancestor of the nucleus a complex DNA virus? *Journal of Molecular Evolution, 53*(3), 251.

Belnap, S. C., Currea, J. P., & Lickliter, R. (2019). Prenatal incubation temperature affects neonatal precocial birds' locomotor behavior. *Physiology & Behavior, 206,* 51–58.

Bénard, H. (1900). "Les tourbillons cellulaires dans une nappe liquide" [Cellular vortices in a sheet of liquid]. *Revue Générale des Sciences Pures et Appliquées* (in French), *11,* 1261–1271, 1309–1328.

Bennett, K. B., & Flach, J. M. (2011). *Display and interface design: Subtle science, exact art.* Boca Raton, FL: CRC Press.

Bentley, A. F. (1954/1975). The fiction of the "retinal image". In A. F. Bentley & S. Ratner (Eds.), *Inquiry into inquires: Essays in social theory* (pp. 268–285). Boston, MA: Beacon Press.

Berkeley, G. (1709). *An essay towards a new theory of vision.* Dublin: Aaron Rhames.

Bernstein, L. E., Auer, E. T., Jr., & Takayanagi, S. (2004). Auditory speech detection in noise enhanced by lipreading. *Speech Communication, 44*(1), 5–18. https://doi.org/10.1016/j.specom.2004.10.011

Bernstein, N. (1967). *The coordination and regulation of movements.* Oxford: Pergamon Press.

Bertenthal, B. I., & Bai, D. L. (1989). Infants' sensitivity to optical flow for controlling posture. *Developmental Psychology, 25,* 936–945.

Biswas, A., Oh, P. I., Faulkner, G. E., Bajaj, R. R., Silver, M. A., Mitchell, M. S., & Alter, D. A. (2015). Sedentary time and its association with risk for disease incidence, mortality, and hospitalization in adults: A systematic review and meta-analysis. *Annals of Internal Medicine, 162*(2), 123–132.

Bjorklund, D. F., & Casey, K. B. (2017). *Children's thinking: Cognitive development and individual differences.* Thousand Oaks, CA: Sage.

Blaesing, B., & Cruse, H. (2004). Stick insect locomotion in a complex environment: Climbing over large gaps. *The Journal of Experimental Biology, 207*(Pt 8), 1273–1286. https://doi.org/10.1242/jeb.00888

Blair, K. G. (1915). Luminous insects. *Nature, 96,* 411–415.

Böhm, J., Scherzer, S., Krol, E., Kreuzer, I., von Meyer, K., Lorey, C., . . . & Hedrich, R. (2016). The Venus flytrap Dionaea muscipula counts prey-induced action potentials to induce sodium uptake. *Current Biology, 26*(3), 286–295.

Bongers, R. M., Smitsman, A. W., & Michaels, C. F. (2003). Geometrics and dynamics of a rod determine how it is used for reaching. *Journal of Motor Behavior, 35*(1), 4–22. https://doi.org/10.1080/00222890309602117

Boring, E. G. (1950). *A history of experimental psychology.* New York: Appleton-Century-Crofts.

Boschker, M. S., Bakker, F. C., & Michaels, C. F. (2002). Memory for the functional characteristics of climbing walls: Perceiving affordances. *Journal of Motor Behavior, 34*(1), 25–36. https://doi.org/10.1080/00222890209601928

Box, G. E. P. (1976). Science and statistics. *Journal of the American Statistical Association*, *71*(356), 791–799.

Bril, B., & Brenière, Y. (1993). Posture and independent locomotion in early childhood: Learning to walk or learning dynamic postural control? In G. J. P. Savelsbergh (Ed.), *The development of coordination in infancy* (pp. 337–358). Amsterdam: North-Holland/Elsevier Science Publishers. https://doi.org/10.1016/S0166-4115(08)60959-0

Bril, B., Dupuy, L., Dietrich, G., & Corbetta, D. (2015). Learning to tune the antero-posterior propulsive forces during walking: A necessary skill for mastering upright locomotion in toddlers. *Experimental Brain Research*, *233*(10), 2903–2912. https://doi.org/10.1007/s00221-015-4378-6

Brossard, M., López-Hernández, D., Lepage, M., & Leprun, J. C. (2007). Nutrient storage in soils and nests of mound-building Trinervitermes termites in Central Burkina Faso: Consequences for soil fertility. *Biology and Fertility of Soils*, *43*(4), 437–447.

Brown, N., & Bhella, D. (2016, November). Are viruses alive? *Microbiology Today*. Retrieved from https://microbiologysociety.org/publication/past-issues/what-is-life/article/are-viruses-alive-what-is-life.html

Bruggeman, H., & Warren, W. H. (2010). The direction of walking—but not throwing or kicking—is adapted by optic flow. *Psychological Science*, *21*(7), 1006–1013. https://doi.org/10.1177/0956797610372635

Bruggeman, H., Zosh, W., & Warren, W. H. (2007). Optic flow drives human visuo-locomotor adaptation. *Current Biology*, *17*, 2035–2040. https://doi.org/10.1016/j.cub.2007.10.059

Bruineberg, J., Chemero, A., & Rietveld, E. (2019). General ecological information supports engagement with affordances for 'higher' cognition. *Synthese*, *196*(12), 5231–5251.

Buck, J., & Buck, E. (1976). Synchronous fireflies. *Scientific American*, *234*(5), 74–85.

Buck, J., Buck, E., Case, J. F., & Hanson, F. E. (1981). Control of flashing in fireflies. *Journal of Comparative Physiology*, *144*(3), 287–298.

Bühler, K. (1918/2013). *The mental development of the child: A summary of modern psychological theory*. New York: Routledge.

Bunge, M. (1979). *Ontology II: A world of systems*. Dortrecht, Netherlands: D. Reidel.

Burnay, C., & Cordovil, R. (2016). Crawling experience predicts avoidance of real cliffs and water cliffs: Insights from a new paradigm. *Infancy*, *21*(5), 677–684. https://doi.org/10.1111/infa.12134

Burton, G. (1992). Nonvisual judgment of the crossability of path gaps. *Journal of Experimental Psychology: Human Perception and Performance*, *18*(3), 698–713. https://doi.org/10.1037/0096-1523.18.3.698

Burton, G. (1993). Non-neural extensions of haptic sensitivity. *Ecological Psychology*, *5*(2), 105–124. https://doi.org/10.1207/s15326969eco0502_1

Burton, G., & Cyr, J. (2004). Gap crossing decisions in the sighted and visually impaired. *Ecological Psychology*, *16*(4), 303–317.

Burton, G., Turvey, M. T., & Solomon, H. Y. (1990). Can shape be perceived by dynamic touch? *Perception & Psychophysics*, *48*(5), 477–487. https://doi.org/10.3758/BF03211592

Cabe, P. A., & Pittenger, J. B. (2000). Human sensitivity to acoustic information from vessel filling. *Journal of Experimental Psychology: Human Perception and Performance*, *26*(1), 313–324. https://doi.org/10.1037/0096-1523.26.1.313

Cabrera, F., Sanabria, F., Jiménez, Á. A., & Covarrubias, P. (2013). An affordance analysis of unconditioned lever pressing in rats and hamsters. *Behavioural Processes*, *92*, 36–46. https://doi.org/10.1016/j.beproc.2012.10.003

Caldeira, P., Fonseca, S. T., Paulo, A., Infante, J., & Araújo, D. (2020). Linking tensegrity to sports team collective behaviors: Towards the group-tensegrity hypothesis. *Sports Medicine—Open*, *6*(1), 24. https://doi.org/10.1186/s40798-020-00253-y

Camazine, S., Deneubourg, J. L., Franks, N. R., Sneyd, J., Bonabeau, E., & Theraula, G. (2001). *Self-organization in biological systems*. Princeton, NJ: Princeton University Press.

Camazine, S., & Sneyd, J. (1991). A model of collective nectar source selection by honey bees: Self-organization through simple rules. *Journal of Theoretical Biology*, *149*(4), 547–571.

Campos, J. J., Anderson, D. I., Barbu-Roth, M. A., Hubbard, E. M., Hertenstein, M. J., & Witherington, D. (2000). Travel broadens the mind. *Infancy: The Official Journal of the International Society on Infant Studies*, *1*(2), 149–219. https://doi.org/10.1207/S15327078IN0102_1

Carello, C., Anderson, K. L., & Kunkler-Peck, A. J. (1998). Perception of object length by sound. *Psychological Science*, *9*(3), 211–214. https://doi.org/10.1111/1467-9280.00040

Carello, C., Grosofsky, A., Reichel, F. D., Solomon, H. Y., & Turvey, M. T. (1989). Visually perceiving what is reachable. *Ecological Psychology*, *1*(1), 27–54. https://doi.org/10.1207/s15326969eco0101_3

Carello, C., & Moreno, M. (2005). Why nonlinear methods. In *Tutorials in contemporary nonlinear methods for the behavioral sciences* (pp. 1–25). Retrieved from www.nsf.gov/pubs/2005/nsf05057/nmbs/nmbs.pdf

Carello, C., Thuot, S., Anderson, K. L., & Turvey, M. T. (1999). Perceiving the sweet spot. *Perception, 28*(3), 307–320. https://doi.org/10.1068/p2716

Carello, C., & Turvey, M. T. (2015). Dynamic (effortful) touch. *Scholarpedia, 10*(4), 8242.

Carello, C., & Turvey, M. T. (2017). Useful dimensions of haptic perception: 50 years after the senses considered as perceptual systems. *Ecological Psychology, 29*(2), 95–121. https://doi.org/10.1080/10407413.2017.1297188

Carello, C., & Turvey, M. T. (2020). Challenging the axioms of perception: The retinal image and the visibility of light. In J. B. Wagman & J. J. Blau (Eds.), *Perception as information detection: Reflections on Gibson's ecological approach to visual perception* (pp. 51–70). New York: Routledge.

Carello, C., Vaz, D., Blau, J. J. C., & Petrusz, S. (2012). Unnerving intelligence. *Ecological Psychology, 24*(3), 241–264.

Carello, C., & Wagman, J. B. (2009). Mutuality in the perception of affordances and the control of movement. In D. Sternad (Ed.), *Progress in motor control: A multidisciplinary perspective* (pp. 273–289). New York: Springer. http://doi.org/10.1007/978-0-387-77064-2_14

Carello, C., Wagman, J. B., & Turvey, M. T. (2005). Acoustic specification of object properties. In J. Anderson & B. Anderson (Eds.), *Moving image theory: Ecological considerations* (pp. 79–104). Carbondale, IL: Southern Illinois Press.

Carroll, S. B. (2005). *Endless forms most beautiful: The new science of evo devo and the making of the animal kingdom*. New York: WW Norton & Company.

Casey, M. B., & Martino, C. M. (2000). Asymmetrical hatching behaviors influence the development of postnatal laterality in domestic chicks (Gallus gallus). *Developmental Psychobiology: The Journal of the International Society for Developmental Psychobiology, 37*(1), 13–24.

Cesari, P., & Newell, K. M. (1999). The scaling of human grip configurations. *Journal of Experimental Psychology: Human Perception and Performance, 25*(4), 927–935. https://doi.org/10.1037/0096-1523.25.4.927

Cesari, P., & Newell, K. M. (2000). Body-scaled transitions in human grip configurations. *Journal of Experimental Psychology: Human Perception and Performance, 26*(5), 1657–1668. https://doi.org/10.1037/0096-1523.26.5.1657

Chang, C. H., Wade, M. G., & Stoffregen, T. A. (2009). Perceiving affordances for aperture passage in an environment-person-person system. *Journal of Motor Behavior, 41*(6), 495–500. https://doi.org/10.3200/35-08-095

Chemero, A. (2003). An outline of a theory of affordances. *Ecological Psychology, 15*(2), 181–195. https://doi.org/10.1207/S15326969ECO1502_5

Chemero, A. (2009). *Radical embodied cognitive science*. Cambridge, MA: The MIT Press.

Chen, F. C., & Stoffregen, T. A. (2012). Specificity of postural sway to the demands of a precision task at sea. *Journal of Experimental Psychology. Applied, 18*(2), 203–212. https://doi.org/10.1037/a0026661

Chiovaro, M., & Paxton, A. (2020). Ecological psychology meets Ecology: Apis mellifera as a model for perception-action, social dynamics, and human factors. *Ecological Psychology, 32*(4), 192–213. https://doi.org/10.1080/10407413.2020.1836966

Chomsky, N. (1980). Rules and representations. *Behavioral and Brain Sciences, 3*(1), 1–15.

Churchland, P. M., & Churchland, P. S. (1990). Could a machine think? *Scientific American, 262*(1), 32–37.

Churchland, P. S. (1994). Can neurobiology teach us anything about consciousness? *Proceedings and Addresses of the American Philosophical Association, 67*, 23–40.

Cira, N. J., Benusiglio, A., & Prakash, M. (2015). Vapour-mediated sensing and motility in two-component droplets. *Nature, 519*(7544), 446–450.

Claparède, E. (1917). La psychologie de l'intelligence. *Scientia, 11*(22).

Cole, W. G., Chan, G. L. Y., Vereijken, B., & Adolph, K. E. (2013). Perceiving affordances for different motor skills. *Experimental Brain Research, 225*(3), 309–319. https://doi.org/10.1007/s00221-012-3328-9

Colinvaux, C. (1979). *Why big fierce animals are rare*. Princeton, NJ: Princeton University Press.

Comalli, D., Franchak, J., Char, A., & Adolph, K. (2013). Ledge and wedge: Younger and older adults' perception of action possibilities. *Experimental Brain Research, 228*, 183–192.

Cook, R., Bird, G., Catmur, C., Press, C., & Heyes, C. (2014). Mirror neurons: From origin to function. *The Behavioral and Brain Sciences, 37*(2), 177–192. https://doi.org/10.1017/S0140525X13000903

Correia, V., Araújo, D., Cummins, A., & Craig, C. M. (2012). Perceiving and acting upon spaces in a VR rugby task: Expertise effects in affordance detection and task achievement. *Journal of Sport & Exercise Psychology, 34*(3), 305–321. https://doi.org/10.1123/jsep.34.3.305

Covarrubias, P., Cabrera, F., & Jiménez, Á. A. (2017). Invariants and information pickup in the senses considered as perceptual systems: Implications for the experimental analysis of behavior. *Ecological Psychology, 29*(3), 231–242. https://doi.org/10.1080/10407413.2017.1332460

Croker, S. (2012). *The development of cognition*. Andover, UK: Cengage.

Cuijpers, L. S., Den Hartigh, R. J., Zaal, F. T., & de Poel, H. J. (2019). Rowing together: Interpersonal coordination dynamics with and without mechanical coupling. *Human Movement Science, 64*, 38–46.

Curry, C., Peterson, N., Li, R., & Stoffregen, T. A. (2020). Postural precursors of motion sickness in head-mounted displays: Drivers and passengers, women and men. *Ergonomics, 63*(12), 1502–1511. https://doi.org/10.1080/00140139.2020.1808713

Dahl, A., Campos, J. J., Anderson, D. I., Uchiyama, I., Witherington, D. C., Ueno, M., . . . & Barbu-Roth, M. (2013). The epigenesis of wariness of heights. *Psychological Science, 24*(7), 1361–1367. https://doi.org/10.1177/0956797613476047

Darwin, C. (1881/2004). *The formation of vegetable mould, through the action of worms*. Whitefish, MT: Kessinger Publishing.

Davis, T. J., Riley, M. A., Shockley, K., & Cummins-Sebree, S. (2010). Perceiving affordances for joint actions. *Perception, 39*(12), 1624–1644. https://doi.org/10.1068/p6712

Dawkins, R. (1982). *The extended phenotype: The long reach of the gene*. Oxford: Oxford University Press.

Day, B., Wagman, J. B., & Smith, P. J. (2015). Perception of maximum stepping and leaping distance: Stepping affordances as a special case of leaping affordances. *Acta Psychologica, 158*, 26–35. https://doi.org/10.1016/j.actpsy.2015.03.010

De Bari, B., Dixon, J. A., Kay, B. A., & Kondepudi, D. (2019). Oscillatory dynamics of an electrically driven dissipative structure. *PLoS ONE, 14*(5), e0217305.

de Haan, S., Rietveld, E., Stokhof, M., & Denys, D. (2013). The phenomenology of deep brain stimulation-induced changes in OCD: An enactive affordance-based model. *Frontiers in Human Neuroscience, 7*, 653. https://doi.org/10.3389/fnhum.2013.00653

Dennett, D. C. (1984). Cognitive wheels: The frame problem in AI. In C. Hookway (Ed.), *Minds, machines, and evolution* (pp. 129–150). Cambridge: Cambridge University Press.

Dennett, D. C. (2010). *Content and consciousness*. New York: Routledge.

Dent-Read, C., & Zukow-Goldring, P. (Eds.). (1997). *Evolving explanations of development: Ecological approaches to organism-environment systems*. Washington, DC: American Psychological Association.

Descartes, R. (1637). *Discourse on the method of rightly conducting one's reason and of seeking truth in the sciences*.

Dicke, M., van Loon, J. J. A., & Soler, R. (2009). Chemical complexity of volatiles from plants induced by multiple attack. *Nature Chemical Biology, 5*, 317–324.

Dotov, D. G., Nie, L., & Chemero, A. (2010). A demonstration of the transition from ready-to-hand to unready-to-hand. *PLoS ONE, 5*, e9433.

Eggers, J. (2020). A closer look at the compensating polar planimeter. *The College Mathematics Journal, 51*(2), 105–116.

Empedocles. (1966). *On Nature* (Long, A. A., Trans.) Thinking and sense-perception in Empedocles: Mysticism or materialism? *The Classical Quarterly, 16*(2), 256–276. (Original work published ca. 495–435 B. C. E.).

Esch, H. E., Zhang, S., Srinivasan, M. V., & Tautz, J. (2001). Honeybee dances communicate distances measured by optic flow. *Nature, 411*(6837), 581–583. https://doi.org/10.1038/35079072

Evans, D. C. (2017). *Bottlenecks: Aligning UX design with user psychology*. New York: Apress.

Fajen, B. R. (2005a). Calibration, information, and control strategies for braking to avoid a collision. *Journal of Experimental Psychology: Human Perception and Performance, 31*(3), 480–501. https://doi.org/10.1037/0096-1523.31.3.480

Fajen, B. R. (2005b). Perceiving possibilities for action: On the necessity of calibration and perceptual learning for the visual guidance of action. *Perception, 34*(6), 717–740. https://doi.org/10.1068/p5405

Fajen, B. R. (2007). Affordance-based control of visually guided action. *Ecological Psychology, 19*(4), 383–410. https://doi.org/10.1080/10407410701557877

Fajen, B. R. (2013). Affordance perception and the visual control of locomotion. In F. Steinicke, Y. Visell, J. Campos, & A. Lécuyer (Eds.), *Human walking in virtual environments* (pp. 79–98). New York: Springer. https://doi.org/10.1007/978-1-4419-8432-6_4

Fajen, B. R., & Devaney, M. C. (2006). Learning to control collisions: The role of perceptual attunement and action boundaries. *Journal of Experimental Psychology: Human Perception and Performance, 32*(2), 300–313. https://doi.org/10.1037/0096-1523.32.2.300

Fajen, B. R., & Matthis, J. S. (2011). Direct perception of action-scaled affordances: The shrinking gap problem. *Journal of Experimental Psychology: Human Perception and Performance, 37*(5), 1442–1457. https://doi.org/10.1037/a0023510

Favela, L. H., Amon, M. J., Lobo, L., & Chemero, A. (2021). Empirical evidence for extended cognitive systems. *Cognitive Science, 45*. https://doi.org/10.1111/cogs.13060

Favela, L. H., Riley, M. A., Shockley, K., & Chemero, A. (2018). Perceptually equivalent judgments made visually and via haptic sensory-substitution devices. *Ecological Psychology, 30*(4), 326–345. https://doi.org/10.1080/10407413.2018.1473712

Fink, P. W., Foo, P. S., & Warren, W. H. (2009). Catching fly balls in virtual reality: A critical test of the outfielder problem. *Journal of Vision, 9*(14), 1–8. https://doi.org/10.1167/9.13.14

Fitch, H. L., Tuller, B., & Turvey, M. T. (1982). The Bernstein perspective: III. Tuning of coordinative structures with special reference to perception. In J. A. S. Kelso (Ed.), *Human motor behavior: An introduction* (pp. 271–281). Hillsdale, NJ: Lawrence Erlbaum Associates.

Fitzpatrick, P., & Flynn, N. (2010). Dynamic touch perception in preschool children. *Ecological Psychology, 22*(2), 89–118.

Flach, J., & Voorhorst, F. (2019). *A meaning processing approach to cognition. What matters?* New York: Routledge.

Fodor, J. A. (1980). Methodological solipsism considered as a research strategy in cognitive psychology. *Behavioral and Brain Sciences, 3*(1), 63–73. https://doi.org/10.1017/S0140525X00001771

Ford, B. J. (2006). Revealing the ingenuity of the living cell. *Biologist, 53*(4), 221–224.

Fowler, C. A. (1986). An event approach to the study of speech perception from a direct-realist perspective. *Journal of Phonetics, 14*(1), 3–28. https://doi.org/10.1016/S0095-4470(19)30607-2

Fowler, C. A. (2018). Direct perception of speech. In *Oxford research encyclopedia of linguistics*. Oxford: Oxford University Press. https://doi.org/10.1093/acrefore/9780199384655.013.407

Franchak, J. M. (2020). Looking with the head and the eyes. In J. B. Wagman & J. J. C. Blau (Eds.), *Perception as information detection: Reflections on Gibson's ecological approach to visual perception* (pp. 205–221). New York: Routledge.

Franchak, J. M., & Adolph, K. E. (2012). What infants know and what they do: Perceiving possibilities for walking through openings. *Developmental Psychology, 48*, 1254–1261.

Franchak, J. M., & Adolph, K. E. (2014). Gut estimates: Pregnant women adapt to changing possibilities for squeezing through doorways. *Attention, Perception, & Psychophysics, 76*(2), 460–472. https://doi.org/10.3758/s13414-013-0578-y

Franchak, J. M., Celano, E. C., & Adolph, K. E. (2012). Perception of passage through openings depends on the size of the body in motion. *Experimental Brain Research, 223*, 301–310. https://doi.org/10.1007/s00221-012-3261-y

Franchak, J. M., Kretch, K. S., & Adolph, K. E. (2018). See and be seen: Infant-caregiver social looking during locomotor free play. *Developmental Science, 21*, e12626.

Franchak, J. M., Kretch, K. S., Soska, K. C., & Adolph, K. E. (2011). Head-mounted eye tracking: A new method to describe infant looking. *Child Development, 82*, 1738–1750.

Franchak, J. M., van der Zalm, D. J., & Adolph, K. E. (2010). Learning by doing: Action performance facilitates affordance perception. *Vision Research, 50*(24), 2758–2765. https://doi.org/10.1016/j.visres.2010.09.019

Frank, T. D., Blau, J. J. C., & Turvey, M. T. (2009). Nonlinear attractor dynamics in the fundamental and extended prism adaptation paradigm. *Physics Letters A, 373*, 1022–1030.

Galantucci, B. (2005). An experimental study of the emergence of human communication systems. *Cognitive Science, 29*(5), 737–767.

Gardner, H. (1993). *Multiple intelligences: The theory in practice*. New York: Basic Books.

Garrett, S. R., Pagano, C., Austin, G., & Turvey, M. T. (1998). Spatial and physical frames of reference in positioning a limb. *Perception & Psychophysics, 60*(7), 1206–1215. https://doi.org/10.3758/BF03206170

Gaver, W. W. (1993a). What in the world do we hear? *Ecological Psychology, 5*(1), 1–29. https://doi.org/10.1207/s15326969eco0501_1

Gaver, W. W. (1993b). How in the world do we hear? Explorations in ecological acoustics. *Ecological Psychology, 5*(4), 285–313. https://doi.org/10.1207/s15326969eco0504_2

Gibson, E. J. (1994). Has psychology a future? *Psychological Science, 5*(2), 69–76.

Gibson, E. J. (2003). What psychology is about: Ruminations of an opinionated aged psychologist. *Ecological Psychology, 15*(4), 289–295. https://doi.org/10.1207/s15326969eco1504_4

Gibson, E. J., & Pick, A. D. (2000). *An ecological approach to perceptual learning and development*. New York: Oxford University Press.

Gibson, E. J., Riccio, G., Schmuckler, M. A., Stoffregen, T. A., Rosenberg, D., & Taormina, J. (1987). Detection of the traversability of surfaces by crawling and walking infants. *Journal of Experimental Psychology: Human Perception and Performance, 13*, 533–544.

Gibson, E. J., & Walk, R. D. (1960). The "visual cliff". *Scientific American, 202*(4), 64–71. https://doi.org/10.1038/scientificamerican0460-64

Gibson, J. J. (1966). *The senses considered as perceptual systems*. Boston: Houghton Mifflin.

Gibson, J. J. (1979/2015). *The ecological approach to visual perception: Classic edition*. New York: Psychology Press.

Gibson, J. J., & Waddell, D. (1952). Homogeneous retinal stimulation and visual perception. *American Journal of Psychology, 65*, 263–270.

Gilden, D. L. (2001). Cognitive emissions of 1/f noise. *Psychological Review, 108*(1), 33–56. https://doi.org/10.1037/0033-295X.108.1.33

Goldfield, E. (2018). *Bioinspired devices: Emulating nature's assembly and repair process*. Cambridge, MA: Harvard University Press.

Goldin-Meadow, S. (2005). *The resilience of language: What gesture creation in deaf children can tell us about how all children learn language*. Hove, East Sussex, UK: Psychology Press.

Goldstein, E. B. (2018). *Cognitive psychology: Connecting mind, research, and everyday experience*. Boston: Cengage.

Goodwin, B. C. (1994). *How the leopard changed its spots: The evolution of complexity*. Princeton, NJ: Princeton University Press.

Gordon, C., & Webb, D. (1996). You can't hear the shape of a drum. *American Scientist, 84*(1), 46–55. Retrieved from www.jstor.org/stable/29775597

Gordon, M. S., & Rosenblum, L. D. (2004). Perception of sound-obstructing surfaces using body-scaled judgments. *Ecological Psychology, 16*(2), 87–113. https://doi.org/10.1207/s15326969eco1602_1

Gottlieb, G. (1992). *Individual development and evolution: The genesis of novel behavior*. New York: Oxford University Press.

Gottlieb, G. (1997). *Synthesizing nature—nurture: Prenatal roots of instinctive behavior*. Mahwah, NJ: Erlbaum.

Gottlieb, G. (1999). *Probabilistic epigenesis and evolution*. Worcester, MA: Clark University Press.

Gottlieb, G. (2000). Environmental and behavioral influences on gene activity. *Current Directions in Psychological Science, 9*(3), 93–97.

Gregory, R. L. (2009). *Seeing through illusions*. Oxford: Oxford University Press.

Griffin, D. R. (1958). *Listening in the dark: The acoustic orientation of bats and men*. New Haven, CT: Yale University Press.

Guski, R. (1992). Acoustic tau: An easy analog to visual tau? *Ecological Psychology, 4*, 189–197. https://doi.org/10.1207/s15326969eco0403_4

Gutta, S., & Philomin, V. (2004). *U.S. Patent No. 6,812,846*. Washington, DC: U.S. Patent and Trademark Office.

Haddad, J. M., Rietdyk, S., Claxton, L. J., & Huber, J. E. (2013). Task-dependent postural control throughout the lifespan. *Exercise and Sport Sciences Reviews, 41*(2), 123–132. https://doi.org/10.1097/JES.0b013e3182877cc8

Haken, H., Kelso, J. A. S., & Bunz, H. (1985). A theoretical model of phase transitions in human hand movements. *Biological Cybernetics, 51*, 347–356.

Hamlin, A. J. (1897). An attempt at a psychology of instinct. *Mind, 6*(21), 59–70.

Han, B. P., Wang, T., Lin, Q. Q., & Dumont, H. J. (2008). Carnivory and active hunting by the planktonic testate amoeba Difflugia tuberspinifera. *Hydrobiologia, 596*(1), 197–201.

Hanson, F. E., Case, J. F., Buck, E., & Buck, J. (1971). Synchrony and flash entrainment in a New Guinea firefly. *Science, 174*(4005), 161–164.

Harrison, S. J., & Richardson, M. J. (2009). Horsing around: Spontaneous four-legged coordination. *Journal of Motor Behavior, 41*(6), 519–524. https://doi.org/10.3200/35-08-014

Hartman, L. S., Kil, I., Pagano, C. C., & Burg, T. (2016). Investigating haptic distance-to-break using linear and nonlinear materials in a simulated minimally invasive surgery task. *Ergonomics, 59*(9), 1171–1181.

Heft, H. (2020). Revisiting "The discovery of the occluding edge and its implications for perception" 40 years on. In J. B. Wagman & J. J. C. Blau (Eds.), *Perception as the detection of information: Reflections on Gibson's ecological approach to visual perception* (pp. 188–204). New York: Routledge.

Helmholtz, H. (1910/2000). *Handbuch der physiologischen Optik, Dritter Brand* (J. P. C. Southall as Helmholtz's Treatise on Physiological Optics, Transl. Vol. III). Bristol: Thoemmes.

Heras-Escribano, M. (2019). *The philosophy of affordances*. London: Palgrave Macmillan.

Hickok, G. (2014). *The myth of mirror neurons: The real neuroscience of communication and cognition*. New York: WW Norton & Company.

Higuchi, T., Cinelli, M. E., Greig, M. A., & Patla, A. E. (2006). Locomotion through apertures when wider space for locomotion is necessary: Adaptation to artificially altered bodily states. *Experimental Brain Research, 175*(1), 50–59. https://doi.org/10.1007/s00221-006-0525-4

Higuchi, T., Murai, G., Kijima, A., Seya, Y., Wagman, J. B., & Imanaka, K. (2011). Athletic experience influences shoulder rotations when running through apertures. *Human Movement Science, 30*(3), 534–549. https://doi.org/10.1016/j.humov.2010.08.003

Higuchi, T., Takada, H., Matsuura, Y., & Imanaka, K. (2004). Visual estimation of spatial requirements for locomotion in novice wheelchair users. *Journal of Experimental Psychology: Applied, 10*(1), 55–66. https://doi.org/10.1037/1076-898X.10.1.55

Higueras-Herbada, A., de Paz, C., Jacobs, D. M., Travieso, D., & Ibáñez-Gijón, J. (2019). The direct learning theory: A naturalistic approach to learning for the post-cognitivist era. *Adaptive Behavior, 27*(6), 389–403. https://doi.org/10.1177/1059712319847136

Holmes, N. P., Spence, C., & Giard, M.-H., & Wallace, M. (Eds.). (2004). The body schema and multisensory representation(s) of peripersonal space. *Cognitive Processing, 5*(2), 94–105. https://doi.org/10.1007/s10339-004-0013-3

Hubel, D. H., & Wiesel, T. N. (1962). Receptive fields, binocular interaction and functional architecture in the cat's visual cortex. *The Journal of Physiology, 160*(1), 106.

Hume, D. (1739/2000). *A treatise of human nature* (D. F. Norton & J. Norton, Eds.). Oxford: Oxford University Press.

Iacoboni, M. (2009). *Mirroring people: The new science of how we connect with others*. New York: Farrar, Straus and Giroux.

Ingle, D. (1973). Spontaneous shape discrimination by frogs during unconditioned escape behaviour. *Physiological Psychology, 1*, 71–73. https://doi.org/10.3758/BF03326870

Iram, D., Riaz, R., & Iqbal, R. K. (2019). Usage of potential micro-organisms for degradation of plastics. *Open Journal of Environmental Biology, 4*(1), 007–015.

Isenhower, R. W., Richardson, M. J., Carello, C., Baron, R. M., & Marsh, K. L. (2010). Affording cooperation: Embodied constraints, dynamics, and action-scaled invariance in joint lifting. *Psychonomic Bulletin & Review, 17*(3), 342–347. https://doi.org/10.3758/PBR.17.3.342

Jacobellis v. Ohio, 378, U. S. 184 (U. S. Supreme Court, 1964). Retrieved from https://supreme.justia.com/cases/federal/us/378/184/

Jacobs, D. M., & Michaels, C. F. (2007). Direct learning. *Ecological Psychology, 19*, 321–349.

Jancer, M. (2018, December). How road designers are manipulating us into being more careful drivers. *Car and Driver*.

Jayne, B. C., & Riley, M. A. (2007). Scaling of the axial morphology and gap-bridging ability of the brown tree snake, *Boiga irregularis*. *Journal of Experimental Biology, 210*, 1148–1160. https://doi.org/10.1242/jeb.002493

Jiménez, Á. A., Ochoa, D. A., Amazeen, P. G., Amazeen, E. L., & Cabrera, F. (2019). Affordances guide choice behavior between equal schedules of reinforcement in rats. *Ecological Psychology, 31*(4), 316–331. https://doi.org/10.1080/10407413.2019.1599686

Jiménez, Á. A., Sanabria, F., & Cabrera, F. (2017). The effect of lever height on the microstructure of operant behavior. *Behavioural Processes, 140*, 181–189. https://doi.org/10.1016/j.beproc.2017.05.002

Johnson, D. (2012). Stair safety: Bottom of flight illusion. *Work (Reading, Mass.), 41*(Suppl 1), 3358–3362. https://doi.org/10.3233/WOR-2012-0607-3358

Jones, K. S., & Garcia, N. A. (2021). How do people perceive other people's affordances, and how might that help us design robots that can do so? *Ecological Psychology, 33*(3–4), 147–172. https://doi.org/10.1080/10407413.2021.1965478

Juarrero, A. (2013). Downward causation: Polanyi and Prigogine. *Tradition and Discovery: The Polanyi Society Periodical*, *40*(3), 4–15.

Jung, C. G. (1916). The structure of the unconscious. *Collected Works*, 7.

Kac, M. (1966). Can one hear the shape of a drum? *Mathematics Monthly*, *73*(4), 21–23. Retrieved from www.jstor.org/stable/2313748

Karasik, L. B., Tamis-LeMonda, C. S., & Adolph, K. E. (2011). Transition from crawling to walking and infants' actions with objects and people. *Child Development*, *82*, 1199–1209.

Karsai, I., & Pénzes, Z. (1993). Comb building in social wasps: Self-organization and stigmergic script. *Journal of Theoretical Biology*, *161*(4), 505–525.

Kayed, N. S., Farstad, H., & van der Meer, A. L. (2008). Preterm infants' timing strategies to optical collisions. *Early Human Development*, *84*(6), 381–388. https://doi.org/10.1016/j.earlhumdev.2007.10.006

Kayed, N. S., & van der Meer, A. L. H. (2000). Timing strategies used in defensive blinking to optical collisions in 5- to 7-month-old infants. *Infant Behavior & Development*, *23*, 253–270.

Kayed, N. S., & van der Meer, A. L. H. (2007). Infants' timing strategies to optical collisions: A longitudinal study. *Infant Behavior & Development*, *30*, 50–59.

Keizer, A., Smeets, M. A., Dijkerman, H. C., Uzunbajakau, S. A., van Elburg, A., & Postma, A. (2013). Too fat to fit through the door: First evidence for disturbed body-scaled action in anorexia nervosa during locomotion. *PLoS ONE*, *8*(5), e64602. https://doi.org/10.1371/journal.pone.0064602

Kello, C. T., & Van Orden, G. C. (2009). Soft-assembly of sensorimotor function. *Nonlinear Dynamics Psychology Life Sciences*, *13*(1), 57–78.

Kelly, C. K. (1992). Resource choice in Cuscuta europaea. *Proceedings of the National Academy of Science*, *89*, 12194–12197.

Kelso, J. A. S. (1995). *Dynamic patterns: The self-organization of brain and behavior*. Cambridge, MA: The MIT Press.

Kelso, J. A. S., Tuller, B., Vatikiotis-Bateson, E., & Fowler, C. A. (1984). Functionally specific articulatory cooperation following jaw perturbations during speech: Evidence for coordinative structures. *Journal of Experimental Psychology. Human Perception and Performance*, *10*(6), 812–832. https://doi.org/10.1037//0096-1523.10.6.812

Kilner, J. M., Neal, A., Weiskopf, N., Friston, K. J., & Frith, C. D. (2009). Evidence of mirror neurons in human inferior frontal gyrus. *The Journal of Neuroscience: The Official Journal of the Society for Neuroscience*, *29*(32), 10153–10159. https://doi.org/10.1523/JNEUROSCI.2668-09.2009

Kilner, J. M., Paulignan, Y., & Blakemore, S. J. (2003). An interference effect of observed biological movement on action. *Current Biology: CB*, *13*(6), 522–525. https://doi.org/10.1016/s0960-9822(03)00165-9

Kim, N. G., & Kim, H. (2017). Schizophrenia: An impairment in the capacity to perceive affordances. *Frontiers in Psychology*, *8*, 1052. https://doi.org/10.3389/fpsyg.2017.01052

Klyce, B. (2017). *What is life*? Retrieved from www.panspermia.org/whatis2.htm

Kolarik, A. J., Cirstea, S., Pardhan, S., & Moore, B. C. (2014). A summary of research investigating echolocation abilities of blind and sighted humans. *Hearing Research*, *310*, 60–68. https://doi.org/10.1016/j.heares.2014.01.010

Konczak, J., Meeuwsen, H. J., & Cress, M. E. (1992). Changing affordances in stair climbing: The perception of maximum climbability in young and older adults. *Journal of Experimental Psychology. Human Perception and Performance*, *18*(3), 691–697. https://doi.org/10.1037//0096-1523.18.3.691

Kondepudi, D., Kay, B., & Dixon, J. (2015). End-directed evolution and the emergence of energy-seeking behavior in a complex system. *Physical Review E*, *91*(5), 050902.

Koshland, D. E. (2002). The seven pillars of life. *Science*, *295*(5563), 2215–2216.

Koslucher, F. C., Haaland, E., & Stoffregen, T. A. (2016). Sex differences in visual performance and postural sway precede sex differences in visually induced motion sickness. *Experimental Brain Research*, *234*, 313–322. https://doi.org/10.1007/s00221-015-4462-y

Kretch, K. S., & Adolph, K. E. (2013). Cliff or step? Posture-specific learning at the edge of a drop-off. *Child Development*, *84*, 226–240.

Kretch, K. S., Franchak, J. M., & Adolph, K. E. (2014). Crawling and walking infants see the world differently. *Child Development*, *85*, 1503–1518.

Kriegman, S., Blackiston, D., Levin, M., & Bongard, J. (2021). Kinematic self-replication in reconfigurable organisms. *Proceedings of the National Academy of Sciences*, *118*(49).

Kugler, P. N., & Turvey, M. T. (1987). *Information, natural law, and the self-assembly of rhythmic movement*. Hillsdale, NJ: Lawrence Erlbaum Associates.

Kunkler-Peck, A., & Turvey, M. T. (2000). Hearing shape. *Journal of Experimental Psychology: Human Perception and Performance, 26*(1), 279–294. https://doi.org/10.1037/0096-1523.26.1.279

Laland, K. N., Odling-Smee, J., & Feldman, M. W. (2000). Niche construction, biological evolution, and cultural change. *Behavioral and Brain Sciences, 23*(1), 131–146.

Latash, M. L. (2012). The bliss (not the problem) of motor abundance (not redundancy). *Experimental Brain Research, 217*(1), 1–5. https://doi.org/10.1007/s00221-012-3000-4

Latash, M. L., & Turvey, M. (Eds.). (1996). *On dexterity and its development*. Mahwah, NJ: Lawrence Erlbaum Associates.

Latty, T., & Beekman, M. (2010). Food quality and the risk of light exposure affect patch-choice decisions in the slime mold Physarum polycephalum. *Ecology, 91*(1), 22–27.

Lee, D. N. (1976). A theory of visual control of braking based on information about time-to-collision. *Perception, 5*(4), 437–459. https://doi.org/10.1068/p050437

Lee, D. N. (2009). General Tau Theory: Evolution to date. *Perception, 38*(6), 837–850. https://doi.org/10.1068/pmklee

Lee, D. N., & Aronson, E. (1974). Visual proprioceptive control of standing in human infants. *Perception & Psychophysics, 15*(3), 529–532.

Lee, D. N., & Lishman, J. R. (1975). Visual proprioceptive control of stance. *Journal of Human Movement Studies, 1*, 87–95.

Lee, D. N., & Reddish, P. E. (1981). Plummeting gannets: A paradigm of ecological optics. *Nature, 293*(5830), 293–294. https://doi.org/10.1038/293293a0

Lee, D. N., van der Weel, F. R., Hitchcock, T., Matejowsky, E., & Pettigrew, J. D. (1992). Common principle of guidance by echolocation and vision. *Journal of Comparative Physiology A, 171*, 563–571. https://doi.org/10.1007/BF00194105

Lewontin, R. C. (1978). Adaptation. *Scientific American, 239*, 156–169.

Lewontin, R. C. (2001). *The triple helix: Gene, organism, and environment*. Cambridge, MA: Harvard University Press.

Lightfoot, D. (1991). *How to set parameters: Arguments from language change*. Cambridge, MA: The MIT Press.

Lishman, J. R., & Lee, D. N. (1973). The autonomy of visual kinaesthesis. *Perception, 2*(3), 287–294.

Lobo, L., Nordbeck, P. C., Raja, V., Chemero, A., Riley, M. A., Jacobs, D. M., & Travieso, D. (2019). Route selection and obstacle avoidance with a short-range haptic sensory substitution device. *International Journal of Human-Computer Studies, 132*, 25–33.

Lock, A., & Collett, T. (1979). A toad's devious approach to its prey: A study of some complex uses of depth vision. *Journal of Comparative Physiology, 131*, 179–189. https://doi.org/10.1007/BF00619078

Locke, J. (1690). *An essay concerning humane understanding* (1st ed., 1 Vols.). London: Thomas Basset.

Loehr, J. D., Sebanz, N., & Knoblich, G. (2013). Joint action: From perception-action links to shared representations. In W. Prinz, M. Beisert, & A. Herwig (Eds.), *Action science: Foundations of an emerging discipline* (pp. 333–356). Cambridge, MA: The MIT Press.

Lombardo, T. J. (1987). *The reciprocity of perceiver and environment*. Hillsdale, NJ: Lawrence Erlbaum Associates.

Long, L. O., Pagano, C. C., Singapogu, R. B., & Burg, T. C. (2016, September). Surgeon's perception of soft tissue constraints and distance-to-break in a simulated minimally invasive surgery task. In *Proceedings of the human factors and ergonomics society annual meeting* (Vol. 60, No. 1, pp. 1600–1604). Los Angeles, CA: SAGE Publications.

Mace, W. M. (2020). Getting into the ambient optic array and what we might get out of it. In J. B. Wagman & J. J. C. Blau (Eds.), *Perception as the detection of information: Reflections on Gibson's ecological approach to visual perception* (pp. 73–89). New York: Routledge.

Malebranche, N. (1678/1997). Elucidation on optics. In T. M. Lennon & P. J. Olscam (Eds.), *Search after truth: With elucidations of the search after truth* (pp. 687–719). Cambridge: Cambridge University Press.

Mamassian, P., Landy, M., & Maloney, L. T. (2002). Bayesian modelling of visual perception. In R. P. N. Rao, B. A. Olshausen, & M. S. Lewicki (Eds.), *Probabilistic models of the brain: Perception and neural function* (pp. 13–36). Cambridge, MA: The MIT Press.

Mangalam, M., Chen, R., McHugh, T. R., Singh, T., & Kelty-Stephen, D. G. (2020). Bodywide fluctuations support manual exploration: Fractal fluctuations in posture predict perception of heaviness and length via effortful touch by the hand. *Human Movement Science, 69*, 102543. https://doi.org/10.1016/j.humov.2019.102543

Mangalam, M., Wagman, J. B., & Newell, K. M. (2018). Temperature influences perception of the length of a wielded object via effortful touch. *Experimental Brain Research, 236*(2), 505–516. https://doi.org/10.1007/s00221-017-5148-4

Mark, L. S. (1987). Eyeheight-scaled information about affordances: A study of sitting and stair climbing. *Journal of Experimental Psychology: Human Perception and Performance, 13*(3), 361–370. https://doi.org/10.1037/0096-1523.13.3.361

Mark, L. S., Nemeth, K., Gardner, D., Dainoff, M. J., Paasche, J., Duffy, M., & Grandt, K. (1997). Postural dynamics and the preferred critical boundary for visually guided reaching. *Journal of Experimental Psychology: Human Perception and Performance, 23*(5), 1365–1379. https://doi.org/10.1037/0096-1523.23.5.1365

Marsh, K. L., Isenhower, R. W., Richardson, M. J., Helt, M., Verbalis, A. D., Schmidt, R. C., & Fein, D. (2013). Autism and social disconnection in interpersonal rocking. *Frontiers in Integrative Neuroscience*, 7, 4. https://doi.org/10.3389/fnint.2013.00004

Marsh, K. L., Johnston, L., Richardson, M. J., & Schmidt, R. C. (2009). Toward a radically embodied, embedded social psychology. *European Journal of Social Psychology, 39*(7), 1217–1225. https://doi.org/10.1002/ejsp.666

Marsh, K. L., Richardson, M. J., Baron, R. M., & Schmidt, R. C. (2006). Contrasting approaches to perceiving and acting with others. *Ecological Psychology, 18*(1), 1–38. https://doi.org/10.1207/s15326969eco1801_1

Masataka, N. (1994). Effects of experience with live insects on the development of fear of snakes in squirrel monkeys, Saimiri sciureus. *Animal Behavior, 46*, 741–746.

Mauerberg-deCastro, E., Moraes, R., & Campbell, D. F. (2012). Short-term effects of the use of non-rigid tools for postural control by adults with intellectual disabilities. *Motor Control, 16*(2), 131–143. https://doi.org/10.1123/mcj.16.2.131

McBeath, M. K., Shaffer, D. M., & Kaiser, M. K. (1995). How baseball outfielders determine where to run to catch fly balls. *Science, 268*, 569–573. https://doi.org/10.1126/science.7725104

McBride, D. M., & Cutting, J. C. (2019). *Cognitive psychology: Theory, process, and methodology* (2nd ed.). Thousand Oaks, CA: Sage.

McCabe, V. (2014). *Coming to our senses: Perceiving complexity to avoid catastrophe*. New York: Oxford University Press.

McCrone, J. (2006). Smarter than the average bug. *New Scientist, 190*(2553), 37–39.

McGraw, M. B. (1935). *Growth: A study of Johnny and Jimmy*. New York: Appleton-Century Crofts.

McGraw, M. B. (1945). *The neuromuscular maturation of the human infant*. New York: Columbia University Press.

Metzger, W. (1930). Optische Untersuchungen im Ganzfeld II [Optical investigations in the whole field]. *Psychologizche Forschung, 13*, 6–29.

Michaels, C. F., & Palatinus, Z. (2014). A ten commandments for ecological psychology. In R. Shapiro (Ed.) *The Routledge handbook of embodied cognition* (pp. 19–28). New York: Routledge.

Michaels, C. F., & Zaal, F. T. J. M. (2002). Catching fly balls. In K. Davids, G. J. P. Savelsbergh, S. J. Bennett, & J. van der Kamp (Eds.), *Interceptive actions in sport: Information and movement* (pp. 172–183). London: Routledge.

Miller, D. B. (1997). The effects of nonobvious forms of experience on the development of instinctive behavior. In C. Dent-Reed & P. Zukow-Goldring (Eds.), *Evolving explanations of development* (pp. 457–507). Washington, DC: American Psychological Association.

Mitchell, D., Snellen, J. W., & Atkins, A. R. (1970). Thermoregulation during fever: Change of set-point or change of gain. *Pflügers Archiv, 321*(4), 293–302.

Molyneux, W. (1688). *Letter to John Locke*.

Moreno, M. A., Stepp, N., & Turvey, M. T. (2011). Whole body lexical decision. *Neuroscience Letters, 490*(2), 126–129. https://doi.org/10.1016/j.neulet.2010.12.041

Müller-Frommeyer, L. C., Kauffeld, S., & Paxton, A. (2020). Beyond consistency: Contextual dependency of language style in monolog and conversation. *Cognitive science, 44*(4), e12834.

Munafo, J., Diedrick, M., & Stoffregen, T. A. (2017). The virtual reality head-mounted display Oculus Rift induces motion sickness and is sexist in its effects. *Experimental Brain Research, 235*(3), 889–901. https://doi.org/10.1007/s00221-016-4846-7

Muroi, D., Hiroi, Y., Koshiba, T., Suzuki, Y., Kawaki, M., & Higuchi, T. (2017). Walking through apertures in individuals with stroke. *PLoS ONE, 12*(1), e0170119. https://doi.org/10.1371/journal.pone.0170119

Muroi, D., Ohtera, S., Kataoka, Y., Banno, M., Tsujimoto, Y., Tsujimoto, H., & Higuchi, T. (2019). Obstacle avoidance training for individuals with stroke: A systematic review and meta-analysis. *BMJ Open*, *9*(12), e028873. https://doi.org/10.1136/bmjopen-2018-028873

Muybridge, E. (1957). *Animals in motion*. Mineola, NY: Dover Publications.

Neuhoff, J. G. (2018). Adaptive biases in visual and auditory looming perception. In T. L. Hubbard (Ed.), *Spatial biases in perception and cognition*. Cambridge: Cambridge University Press. https://doi.org/10.1017/9781316651247

Newman, M. E. J. (2005). Power laws, Pareto distributions and Zipf's law. *Contemporary Physics*, *46*(5), 323–351. https://doi.org/10.1080/00107510500052444

Nikolas, M. A., Elmore, A. L., Franzen, L., O'Neal, E., Kearney, J. K., & Plumert, J. M. (2016). Risky bicycling behavior among youth with and without attention-deficit hyperactivity disorder. *Journal of Child Psychology and Psychiatry, and Allied Disciplines*, *57*(2), 141–148.

Nonaka, T. (2013). Motor variability but functional specificity: The case of a C4 tetraplegic mouth calligrapher. *Ecological Psychology*, *25*(2), 131–154.

Nonaka, T. (2020). The triad of medium, substance, and surfaces for the theory of further scrutiny. In J. B. Wagman & J. J. C. Blau (Eds.), *Perception as information detection: Reflections on Gibson's ecological approach to visual perception* (pp. 21–36). New York: Routledge.

Norman, D. (2013). *The design of everyday things: Revised and expanded edition*. New York: Basic Books.

Okumura, M., Kijima, A., Kadota, K., Yokoyama, K., Suzuki, H., & Yamamoto, Y. (2012). A critical interpersonal distance switches between two coordination modes in kendo matches. *PLoS ONE*, 7(12), e51877. https://doi.org/10.1371/journal.pone.0051877

Okumura, M., Kijima, A., & Yamamoto, Y. (2017). Perception of affordances for striking regulates interpersonal distance maneuvers of intermediate and expert players in kendo matches. *Ecological Psychology*, *29*(1), 1–22. https://doi.org/10.1080/10407413.2017.1270147

O'Neill, S. M., & Russell, M. K. (2017). Impact of postural stability and modality on the perception of passage and surface climbing. *Ecological Psychology*, *29*(1), 54–68. https://doi.org/10.1080/10407413.2017.1270153

Ossmy, O., Hoch, J. E., MacAlpine, P., Hasan, S., Stone, P., & Adolph, K. E. (2018). Variety Wins: Soccer-playing Robots and infant walking. *Frontiers in Neurorobotics*, *12*, 19. https://doi.org/10.3389/fnbot.2018.00019

Pagano, C. C., & Day, B. (2019). Ecological interface design inspired by "the meaningful environment". In J. B. Wagman & J. J. C. Blau (Eds.), *Perception as information detection: Reflections on Gibson's ecological approach to visual perception* (pp. 37–50). New York: Routledge.

Pagano, C. C., Day, B., & Hartman, L. S. (2021). An argument framework for ecological psychology and architecture design. *Technology | Architecture | Design*, *5*(1), 31–36.

Pagano, C. C., & Turvey, M. T. (1992). Eigenvectors of the inertia tensor and perceiving the orientation of a hand-held object by dynamic touch. *Perception & Psychophysics*, *52*(6), 617–624. https://doi.org/10.3758/bf03211699

Pagano, C. C., & Turvey, M. T. (1995). The inertia tensor as a basis for the perception of limb orientation. *Journal of Experimental Psychology: Human Perception and Performance*, *21*(5), 1070–1087. https://doi.org/10.1037/0096-1523.21.5.1070

Pagano, C. C., & Turvey, M. T. (1998). Eigenvectors of the inertia tensor and perceiving the orientations of limbs and objects. *Journal of Applied Biomechanics*, *14*(4), 331–359.

Palatinus, Z., Kelty-Stephen, D. G., Kinsella-Shaw, J., Carello, C., & Turvey, M. T. (2014). Haptic perceptual intent in quiet standing affects multifractal scaling of postural fluctuations. *Journal of Experimental Psychology: Human Perception and Performance*, *40*(5), 1808–1818.

Parnas, J., & Henriksen, M. G. (2018). Selfhood and its disorders. In G. Stanhgellini, M. Broome, A. Reballo, A. V. Fernandez, P. Fusar-Poli, & R. Rsofort (Eds.), *The Oxford handbook of phenomenological psychopathology*. Oxford: Handbooks Online. https://doi.org/10.1093/oxfordhb/9780198803157.013.52

Passos, P., Araújo, D., & Volossovitch, A. (2016). *Performance analysis in team sports*. New York: Routledge.

Passos, P., Cordovil, R., Fernandes, O., & Barreiros, J. (2012). Perceiving affordances in rugby union. *Journal of Sports Sciences*, *30*(11), 1175–1182. https://doi.org/10.1080/02640414.2012.695082

Patrick, S. K., Noah, J. A., & Yang, J. F. (2009). Interlimb coordination in human crawling reveals similarities in development and neural control with quadrupeds. *Journal of Neurophysiology*, *101*(2), 603–613. https://doi.org/10.1152/jn.91125.2008

Pereira, T., van Emmerik, R., Misuta, M. S., Barros, R., & Moura, F. A. (2018). Interpersonal coordination analysis of tennis players from different levels during official matches. *Journal of Biomechanics, 67*, 106–113. https://doi.org/10.1016/j.jbiomech.2017.11.036

Petersson, P., Waldenström, A., Fåhraeus, C., & Schouenborg, J. (2003). Spontaneous muscle twitches during sleep guide spinal self-organization. *Nature, 424*(6944), 72–75.

Piaget, J. (1947/2003). *The psychology of intelligence*. New York: Routledge.

Piaget, J. (1952). *Origins of intelligence*. New York: International Universities Press.

Piaget, J. (1954). *The construction of reality in the child*. New York: Basic Books.

Plato. (c. 375 BC) *The Republic*.

Profeta, V., & Turvey, M. T. (2018). Bernstein's levels of movement construction: A contemporary perspective. *Human Movement Science, 57*, 111–133. https://doi.org/10.1016/j.humov.2017.11.013

Protsiv, M., Ley, C., Lankester, J., Hastie, T., & Parsonnet, J. (2020). Decreasing human body temperature in the United States since the industrial revolution. *Elife, 9*, e49555.

Raja, V. (2018). A theory of resonance: Toward an ecological cognitive architecture. *Minds & Machines, 28*, 29–51. https://doi.org/10.1007/s11023-017-9431-8

Raja, V., & Anderson, M. L. (2019). Radical embodied cognitive neuroscience. *Ecological Psychology, 31*(3), 166–181. https://doi.org/10.1080/10407413.2019.1615213

Ramenzoni, V. C., Davis, T. J., Riley, M. A., & Shockley, K. (2010). Perceiving action boundaries: Learning effects in perceiving maximum jumping-reach affordances. *Attention, Perception & Psychophysics*, 72(4), 1110–1119. https://doi.org/10.3758/APP.72.4.1110

Ramenzoni, V. C., Riley, M. A., Davis, T., Shockley, K., & Armstrong, R. (2008). Tuning in to another person's action capabilities: Perceiving maximal jumping-reach height from walking kinematics. *Journal of Experimental Psychology. Human Perception and Performance, 34*(4), 919–928. https://doi.org/10.1037/0096-1523.34.4.919

Ranganathan, R., Lee, M. H., & Newell, K. M. (2020). Repetition without repetition: Challenges in understanding behavioral flexibility in motor skill. *Frontiers in Psychology, 11*, 2018. https://doi.org/10.3389/fpsyg.2020.02018

Rayleigh, L. (1916). On the convective currents in a horizontal layer of fluid when the higher temperature is on the under side. *Philosophical Magazine*, 6th series, *32*(192), 529–546.

Reed, C. M., Rabinowitz, W. M., Durlach, N. I., Braida, L. D., Conway-Fithian, S., & Schultz, M. C. (1985). Research on the Tadoma method of speech communication. *The Journal of the Acoustical Society of America*, 77(1), 247–257. https://doi.org/10.1121/1.392266

Reed, E. S. (1982). An outline of a theory of action systems. *Journal of Motor Behavior, 14*(2), 98–134. https://doi.org/10.1080/00222895.1982.10735267

Reed, E. S. (1988). *James J. Gibson and the psychology of perception*. New Haven, CT: Yale University Press.

Reed, E. S. (1996). *Encountering the world: Toward an ecological psychology*. Oxford and New York: Oxford University Press.

Richardson, M. J., Marsh, K. L., & Baron, R. M. (2007a). Judging and actualizing intrapersonal and interpersonal affordances. *Journal of Experimental Psychology. Human Perception and Performance, 33*(4), 845–859. https://doi.org/10.1037/0096-1523.33.4.845

Richardson, M. J., Marsh, K. L., Isenhower, R. W., Goodman, J. R., & Schmidt, R. C. (2007b). Rocking together: Dynamics of intentional and unintentional interpersonal coordination. *Human Movement Science, 26*(6), 867–891. https://doi.org/10.1016/j.humov.2007.07.002

Richardson, M. J., Marsh, K. L., & Schmidt, R. C. (2010). Challenging egocentric notions of perceiving, acting, and knowing. In L. F. Barrett, B. Mesquita, & E. Smith (Eds.), *The mind in context* (pp. 307–333). New York: Guilford.

Richmond, C. A. (1930). Fireflies flashing in unison. *Science, 71*, 537–538.

Riehl, C. (2013). Evolutionary routes to non-kin cooperative breeding in birds. *Proceedings of the Royal Society B: Biological Sciences, 280*(1772), 20132245.

Riehm, C., Chemero, A., Silva, P. L., & Shockley, K. (2019). Virtual auditory aperture passability. *Experimental Brain Research, 237*, 191–200. https://doi.org/10.1007/s00221-018-5407-z

Rieser, J. J., Pick, H. L., Jr, Ashmead, D. H., & Garing, A. E. (1995). Calibration of human locomotion and models of perceptual-motor organization. *Journal of Experimental Psychology: Human Perception and Performance, 21*(3), 480–497. https://doi.org/10.1037//0096-1523.21.3.480

Rietveld, E. (2016). Situating the embodied mind in a landscape of standing affordances for living without chairs: Materializing a philosophical worldview. *Sports Medicine, 46*(7), 927–932. https://doi.org/10.1007/s40279-016-0520-2

Rietveld, E., & Kiverstein, J. (2014). A rich landscape of affordances. *Ecological Psychology, 26*(4), 325–352. https://doi.org/10.1080/10407413.2014.958035

Riley, M. A., Richardson, M. J., Shockley, K., & Ramenzoni, V. C. (2011). Interpersonal synergies. *Frontiers in Psychology, 2*, 38. https://doi.org/10.3389/fpsyg.2011.00038

Riley, M. A., & Van Orden, G. C. (2005). Tutorials in contemporary nonlinear methods. *National Science Foundation*. Retrieved from https://www.researchgate.net/profile/Joseph-Hamill-2/publication/51404288_Developmental_changes_in_the_dynamical_structure_of_postural_sway_during_a_precision_fitting_task/links/56eff9eb08ae52f8ad7f86e7/Developmental-changes-in-the-dynamical-structure-of-postural-sway-during-a-precision-fitting-task.pdf

Rizzolatti, G., & Fabbri-Destro, M. (2010). Mirror neurons: From discovery to autism. *Experimental Brain Research, 200*(3–4), 223–237. https://doi.org/10.1007/s00221-009-2002-3

Rizzolatti, G., & Sinigaglia, C. (2008). *Mirrors in the brain: How our minds share actions and emotions*. Oxford: Oxford University Press.

Robart, R. L., & Rosenblum, L. D. (2009). Are hybrid cars too quiet? *Journal of the Acoustical Society of America, 124*(4), 2744. https://doi.org/10.1121/1.4784573

Rodkey, E. N. (2015). The visual cliff's forgotten menagerie: Rats, goats, babies, and myth-making in the history of psychology. *Journal of the History of the Behavioral Sciences, 51*(2), 113–140. https://doi.org/10.1002/jhbs.21712

Rosen, R. (1991). *Life itself: A comprehensive inquiry into the nature, origin, and fabrication of life*. New York: Columbia University Press.

Rosenbaum, D. A. (2017). *Knowing hands: The cognitive psychology of motor control*. Cambridge: Cambridge University Press.

Rosenblum, L. D. (2005). The primacy of multimodal speech perception. In D. Pisoni & R. Remez (Eds.), *Handbook of speech perception* (pp. 51–78). Malden, MA: Blackwell.

Rosenblum, L. D. (2011). *See what I'm saying: The extraordinary power of our five senses*. New York: W. W. Norton.

Rosenblum, L. D., Carello, C., & Pastore, R. E. (1987). Relative effectiveness of three stimulus variables for locating a moving sound source. *Perception, 16*(2), 175–186. https://doi.org/10.1068/p160175

Rosenblum, L. D., Gordon, M. S., & Jarquin, L. (2010). Echolocating distance by moving and stationary observers. *Ecological Psychology, 12*(3), 181–206. https://doi.org/10.1207/S15326969ECO1203_1

Rosenblum, L. D., Johnson, J. A., & Saldaña, H. M. (1996). Point-light facial displays enhance comprehension of speech in noise. *Journal of Speech Language and Hearing Research, 39*(6), 1159 1170. https://doi.org/10.1044/jshr.3906.1159

Rosenblum, L. D., & Robart, R. L. (2007). Hearing silent shapes: Identifying the shape of a sound-obstructing surface. *Ecological Psychology, 19*(4), 351–366. https://doi.org/10.1080/10407410701557844

Rosenblum, L. D., Wuestefeld, A. P., & Anderson, K. L. (1996). Auditory reachability: An affordance approach to the perception of sound source distance. *Ecological Psychology, 8*(1), 1–24. https://doi.org/10.1207/s15326969eco0801_1

Rosenblum, L. D., Wuestefeld, A. P., & Saldaña, H. (1993). Auditory looming perception: Influences on anticipator judgments. *Perception, 22*, 1467–1482.

Rossen, R. (Director). (1961). *The Hustler* [film]. 20th Century Studios.

Ruiz-Mirazo, K., Peretó, J., & Moreno, A. (2004). A universal definition of life: Autonomy and open-ended evolution. *Origins of Life and Evolution of the Biosphere, 34*(3), 323–346.

Runeson, S. (1977). On the possibility of "smart" perceptual mechanisms. *Scandinavian Journal of Psychology, 18*(1), 172–179.

Runeson, S. (1988). The distorted room illusion, equivalent configurations, and the specificity of static optic arrays. *Journal of Experimental Psychology: Human Perception and Performance, 14*(2), 295.

Runyon, J. B., Mescher, M. C., & De Moraes, C. M. (2006). Volatile chemical cues guide host location and host selection by parasitic plants. *Science, 313*, 1964–1967.

Russell, J. R., Huang, J., Anand, P., Kucera, K., Sandoval, A. G., Dantzler, K. W., . . . & Strobel, S. A. (2011). Biodegradation of polyester polyurethane by endophytic fungi. *Applied and Environmental Microbiology*, 77(17), 6076–6084.

Russell, M. K. (1999). Auditory perception of unimpeded passage. *Ecological Psychology, 11*(2), 175–188. https://doi.org/10.1207/s15326969eco1102_3

Russell, M. K., & Brown, S. (2020). Using sound to create and detect occlusion of an unseen sound source. *Auditory Perception & Cognition, 2*(4), 207–229. https://doi.org/10.1080/25742442.2020.1773731

Saarni, C., Campos, J. J., Camras, L. A., & Witherington, D. (2006). Emotional development: Action, communication, and understanding. In N. Einsenberg (Ed.), *Handbook of child psychology. Vol. 3. Social, emotional, and personality development* (pp. 226–299). New York: John Wiley & Sons.

Saeedpour-Parizi, M. R., Hassan, S. E., Baniasadi, T., Baute, K. J., & Shea, J. B. (2020). Hierarchical goal effects on center of mass velocity and eye fixations during gait. *Experimental Brain Research, 238*(11), 2433–2443. https://doi.org/10.1007/s00221-020-05900-0

Satterwhite-Warden, J. E., Kondepudi, D. K., Dixon, J. A., & Rusling, J. F. (2019). Thermal- and magnetic-sensitive particle flocking motion at the air-water interface. *The Journal of Physical Chemistry B, 123*(17), 3832–3840. https://doi.org/10.1021/acs.jpcb.9b00414

Scarr, G. (2014). *Biotensegrity: The structural basis of life.* Pencaitland: Handspring Publishing.

Schellingerhout, R., Bongers, R. M., Van Grinsven, R., Smitsman, A. W., & Van Galen, G. P. (2001). Improving obstacle detection by redesign of walking canes for blind persons. *Ergonomics, 44*(5), 513–526.

Schellingerhout, R., Smitsman, A. W., & Cox, R. F. (2005). Evolving patterns of haptic exploration in visually impaired infants. *Infant Behavior and Development, 28*(3), 360–388.

Schiff, W., & Oldak, R. (1990). Accuracy of judging time to arrival: Effects of modality, trajectory, and gender. *Journal of Experimental Psychology: Human Perception and Performance, 16*(2), 303–316. https://doi.org/10.1037/0096-1523.16.2.303

Schmidt, R. A., Lee, T. D., Winstein, C. J., Wulf, G., & Zelaznik, H. N. (2020). *Motor control and learning: A Behavioral emphasis.* Champaign, IL: Human Kinetics.

Schmidt, R. C., Carello, C., & Turvey, M. T. (1990). Phase transitions and critical fluctuations in the visual coordination of rhythmic movements between people. *Journal of Experimental Psychology. Human Perception and Performance, 16*(2), 227–247. https://doi.org/10.1037//0096-1523.16.2.227

Schmidt, R. C., Nie, L., Franco, A., & Richardson, M. J. (2014). Bodily synchronization underlying joke telling. *Frontiers in Human Neuroscience, 8*, 633. https://doi.org/10.3389/fnhum.2014.00633

Schmidt, R. C., & Richardson, M. J. (2008). Dynamics of interpersonal coordination. In *Coordination: Neural, behavioral and social dynamics* (pp. 281–308). Berlin & Heidelberg: Springer.

Schmidt, R. C., & Turvey, M. T. (1994). Phase-entrainment dynamics of visually coupled rhythmic movements. *Biological Cybernetics, 70*(4), 369–376. https://doi.org/10.1007/BF00200334

Schouenborg, J. (2008). Action-based sensory encoding in spinal sensorimotor circuits. *Brain Research Reviews, 57*(1), 111–117.

Scorsese, M. (Director). (1986). *The Color of Money* [film]. Touchstone Pictures, Silver Screen Partners.

Searle, J. R. (1980). Minds, brains, and programs. *Behavioral and Brain Sciences, 3*(3), 417–424.

Sebanz, N., Bekkering, H., & Knoblich, G. (2006). Joint action: Bodies and minds moving together. *Trends in Cognitive Sciences, 10*(2), 70–76. https://doi.org/10.1016/j.tics.2005.12.009

Serres, J. R., & Ruffier, F. (2017). Optic flow-based collision-free strategies: From insects to robots. *Arthropod Structure & Development, 46*(5), 703–717. https://doi.org/10.1016/j.asd.2017.06.003

Shaffer, D. M., Krauchunas, S. M., Eddy, M., & McBeath, M. K. (2004). How dogs navigate to catch Frisbees. *Psychological Science, 15*(7), 437–441. https://doi.org/10.1111/j.0956-7976.2004.00698.x

Shapiro, A., & Todorović, D. (Eds.). (2017). *The Oxford companion of visual illusions.* New York: Oxford University Press.

Shaw, R. E., & Kinsella-Shaw, J. M. (2012). Hints of intelligence from first principles. *Ecological Psychology, 24*, 60–93.

Shaw, R. E., & Kinsella-Shaw, J. M. (2020). The challenge of an ecological approach to event perception: How to obtain forceful control from forceless information. In J. B. Wagman & J. J. C. Blau (Eds.), *Perception as information detection: Reflections on Gibson's ecological approach to visual perception* (pp. 90–109). New York: Routledge.

Shockley, K., Carello, C., & Turvey, M. T. (2004). Metamers in the haptic perception of heaviness and moveableness. *Perception & Psychophysics, 66*(5), 731–742. https://doi.org/10.3758/bf03194968

Shockley, K., Grocki, M., Carello, C., & Turvey, M. T. (2001). Somatosensory attunement to the rigid body laws. *Experimental Brain Research, 136*(1), 133–137. https://doi.org/10.1007/s002210000589

Shockley, K., Richardson, D. C., & Dale, R. (2009). Conversation and coordinative structures. *Topics in Cognitive Science, 1*(2), 305–319. https://doi.org/10.1111/j.1756-8765.2009.01021.x

Shultz, T. R. (2003). *Computational developmental psychology*. Cambridge, MA: The MIT Press.

Silva, P. L., Garganta, J., Araújo, D., Davids, K., & Aguiar, P. (2013). Shared knowledge or shared affordances? Insights from an ecological dynamics approach to team coordination in sports. *Sports Medicine, 43*(9), 765–772. https://doi.org/10.1007/s40279-013-0070-9

Silva, P. L., Harrison, S., Kinsella-Shaw, J., Turvey, M. T., & Carello, C. (2009). Lessons for dynamic touch from a case of stroke-induced motor impairment. *Ecological Psychology, 21*(4), 291–307.

Smart, L. J., Hassebrook, J. A., & Teaford, M. A. (2020). Acting is perceiving. Experiments on perception of motion in the world and movements of the self, an update. In J. B. Wagman & J. J. C. Blau (Eds.), *Perception as information detection: Reflections on Gibson's ecological approach to visual perception* (pp. 174–187). New York: Routledge.

Solomon, H. Y., & Turvey, M. T. (1988). Haptically perceiving the distances reachable with hand-held objects. *Journal of Experimental Psychology. Human Perception and Performance, 14*(3), 404–427. https://doi.org/10.1037//0096-1523.14.3.404

Sonoda, K., Asakura, A., Mioura, M., Elwood, R. W., & Gunji, Y.-P. (2012). Hermit crabs perceive the extent of their virtual bodies. *Biology Letters, 8*, 495–497. https://doi.org/10.1098/rsbl.2012.0085

Sonoda, K., Moriyama, T., Asakura, A., Furuyama, N., & Gunji, Y. P. (2013). Can hermit crabs perceive affordance for aperture crossing? In T. Gilbert, M. Kirkilionis, & G. Nicolis (Eds.), *Proceedings of the European conference on complex systems 2012* (pp. 553–557). Springer Proceedings in Complexity. Cham: Springer.

Spivey, M. (2008). *The continuity of mind*. Oxford: Oxford University Press.

Srinivasan, M. V., Zhang, S., Altwein, M., & Tautz, J. (2000). Honeybee navigation: Nature and calibration of the" odometer". *Science, 287*(5454), 851–853. https://doi.org/10.1126/science.287.5454.851

Steinmetz, S. T., Layton, O. W., Powell, N. V., & Fajen, B. R. (2020). Affordance-based versus current-future accounts of choosing whether to pursue or abandon the chase of a moving target. *Journal of Vision, 20*(3), 8–8. https://doi.org/10.1167/jov.20.3.8

Stephen, D. G., Dixon, J. A., & Isenhower, R. W. (2009). Dynamics of representational change: Entropy, action, and cognition. *Journal of Experimental Psychology. Human Perception and Performance, 35*(6), 1811–1832. https://doi.org/10.1037/a0014510

Stepp, N., & Srinivasa, N. (2012). A formal model for autocatakinetic systems. *Ecological Psychology, 24*(3), 204–219.

Stoffregen, T. A. (2003). Affordances as properties of the animal-environment system. *Ecological Psychology, 15*(2), 115–134. https://doi.org/10.1207/S15326969ECO1502_2

Stoffregen, T. A. (2011). Motion sickness considered as a movement disorder. *Science & Motricité, 74*, 19–30. https://doi.org/10.3917/sm.074.0019

Stoffregen, T. A. (2016). Functional control of stance in older adults. *Kinesiology Review, 5*(1), 23–29. https://doi.org/10.1123/kr.2015-0049

Stoffregen, T. A., Chen, F. C., Varlet, M., Alcantara, C., & Bardy, B. G. (2013). Getting your sea legs. *PLoS ONE, 8*(6), e66949. https://doi.org/10.1371/journal.pone.0066949

Stoffregen, T. A., Mantel, B., & Bardy, B. G. (2017). The senses considered as one perceptual system. *Ecological Psychology, 29*(3), 165–197.

Stoffregen, T. A., Pagulayan, R. J., Bardy, B. G., & Hettinger, L. J. (2000). Modulating postural control to facilitate visual performance. *Human Movement Science, 19*(2), 203–220.

Stoffregen, T. A., & Pittenger, J. B. (1995). Human echolocation as a basic form of perception and action. *Ecological Psychology, 7*(3), 181–216. https://doi.org/10.1207/s15326969eco0703_2

Stoffregen, T. A., Yang, C. M., Giveans, M. R., Flanagan, M., & Bardy, B. G. (2009). Movement in the perception of an affordance for wheelchair locomotion. *Ecological Psychology, 21*(1), 1–36. https://doi.org/10.1080/10407410802626001

Strogatz, S. H., & Stewart, I. (1993). Coupled oscillators and biological synchronization. *Scientific American, 269*(6), 102–109.

Suzan-Monti, M., La Scola, B., & Raoult, D. (2006). Genomic and evolutionary aspects of Mimivirus. *Virus Research, 117*(1), 145–155.

Swanson, L. W. (2015). *Neuroanatomical terminology: A lexicon of classical origins and historical foundations*. New York: Oxford University Press.

Swenson, R. (1997). Autocatakinetics, evolution, and the law of maximum entropy production: A principled foundation towards the study of human ecology. *Advances in Human Ecology, 6*, 1–48.

Swenson, R. (2009). The fourth law of thermodynamics: The law of maximum entropy production (LMEP). *Chemistry, 18*, 333–339.

Swenson, R., & Turvey, M. T. (1991). Thermodynamic reasons for perception-action cycles. *Ecological Psychology, 3*(4), 317–348.

Sykes, B., & Ricketts, T. (2001). The seven daughters of Eve. *Nature, 413*(6853), 254–254.

Taine, H. (1872). *On intelligence* (Vol. 1). New York: Holt & Williams.

Tanaka, M. (1973). The anisotropic structure of personal space. *Japanese Journal of Educational Psychology, 21*, 223–232. https://doi.org/10.5926/jjep1953.21.4_223

Thaler, L., & Goodale, M. A. (2016). Echolocation in humans: An overview. *WIREs Cognitive Science*, 7(6). https://doi.org/10.1002/wcs.1408

Thaler, R. H., & Sunstein, C. R. (2006). *Nudge: Improving decisions about health, wealth, and happiness*. London: Penguin Books.

Thelen, E. (1989). The (re) discovery of motor development: Learning new things from an old field. *Developmental Psychology, 25*(6), 946.

Thelen, E., Schöner, G., Scheier, C., & Smith, L. B. (2001). The dynamics of embodiment: A field theory of infant perseverative reaching. *Behavioral and Brain Sciences, 24*(1), 1–34.

Thielman, G. T., Dean, C. M., & Gentile, A. M. (2004). Rehabilitation of reaching after stroke: Task-related training versus progressive resistive exercise. *Archives of Physical Medicine and Rehabilitation, 85*(10), 1613–1618. https://doi.org/10.1016/j.apmr.2004.01.028

Thomas, B. J., Hawkins, M. M., & Nalepka, P. (2017). Perceiver as polar planimeter: Direct perception of jumping, reaching, and jump-reaching affordances for the self and others. *Psychological Research, 82*, 665–674. https://doi.org/10.1007/s00426-017-0858-6

Thomas, B. J., & Riley, M. A. (2015). The selection and usage of information for perceiving and remembering intended and unintended object properties. *Journal of Experimental Psychology: Human Perception and Performance, 41*(3), 807–815. https://doi.org/10.1037/xhp0000050

Thomas, B. J., Riley, M. A., & Wagman, J. B. (2020). Information and its detection: The consequences of Gibson's theory of information pick up. In J. B. Wagman & J. J. C. Blau (Eds.), *Perception as the detection of information: Reflections on Gibson's ecological approach to visual perception*. New York: Routledge.

Tomono, T., Makino, R., Furuyama, N., & Mishima, H. (2019). How does a Walker Pass between two people standing in different configurations? Influence of personal space on aperture passing methods. *Frontiers in Psychology, 10*, 2651. https://doi.org/10.3389/fpsyg.2019.02651

Tuller, B., Turvey, M. T., & Fitch, H. L. (1982). The Bernstein perspective: II. The concept of muscle linkage or synergy. In J. A. S. Kelso (Ed.), *Human motor behavior: An introduction* (pp. 253–270). Hillsdale, NJ: Lawrence Erlbaum Associates.

Turvey, M. T. (1977). Preliminaries to a theory of action with reference to vision. In R. E. Shaw & J. Bransford (Eds.), *Perceiving, acting, and knowing: Toward an ecological psychology* (pp. 211–263). Hillsdale, NJ: Erlbaum.

Turvey, M. T. (1990). Coordination. *American Psychologist, 45*, 938–953.

Turvey, M. T. (1992). Affordances and prospective control: An outline of the ontology. *Ecological Psychology, 4*(3), 173–187. https://doi.org/10.1207/s15326969eco0403_3

Turvey, M. T. (2004). Space (and its perception): The first and final frontier. *Ecological Psychology, 16*(1), 25–29. https://doi.org/10.1207/s15326969eco1601_3

Turvey, M. T. (2007). Action and perception at the level of synergies. *Human Movement Science, 26*(4), 657–697. https://doi.org/10.1016/j.humov.2007.04.002

Turvey, M. T. (2013). Ecological perspective on perception-action: What kind of science does it entail? In W. Prinz, M. Beisert, & A. Herwig (Eds.), *Action science: Foundations of an emerging discipline* (pp. 139–170). Cambridge, MA: The MIT Press.

Turvey, M. T. (2015). Quantum-like issues at nature's ecological scale (the scale of organisms and their environments). *Mind and Matter, 13*(1), 7–44.

Turvey, M. T. (2019). *Lectures on perception: An ecological perspective*. New York: Routledge.

Turvey, M. T., Burton, G., Amazeen, E. L., Butwill, M., & Carello, C. (1998). Perceiving the width and height of a hand-held object by dynamic touch. *Journal of Experimental Psychology Human Perception and Performance, 24*(1), 35–48. https://doi.org/10.1037//0096-1523.24.1.35

Turvey, M. T., Burton, G., Pagano, C. C., Solomon, H. Y., & Runeson, S. (1992). Role of the inertia tensor in perceiving object orientation by dynamic touch. *Journal of Experimental Psychology. Human Perception and Performance, 18*(3), 714–727. https://doi.org/10.1037//0096-1523.18.3.714

Turvey, M. T., & Carello, C. (2012). On intelligence from first principles: Guidelines for inquiry into the hypothesis of physical intelligence (PI). *Ecological Psychology, 24*(1), 3–32.

Turvey, M. T., Fitch, H. L., & Tuller, B. (1982). The Bernstein perspective: 1. The problems of degrees of freedom and context conditioned variability. In J. A. S. Kelso (Ed.), *Human motor behavior: An introduction* (pp. 239–252). Hillsdale, NJ: Lawrence Erlbaum Associates.

Turvey, M. T., & Fitzpatrick, P. (1993). Commentary: Development of perception-action systems and general principles of pattern formation. *Child Development, 64*(4), 1175–1190.

Turvey, M. T., & Fonseca, S. T. (2009). Nature of motor control: Perspectives and issues. *Advances in Experimental Medicine and Biology, 629*, 93–123. https://doi.org/10.1007/978-0-387-77064-2_6

Turvey, M. T., & Fonseca, S. T. (2014). The medium of haptic perception: A tensegrity hypothesis. *Journal of Motor Behavior, 46*(3), 143–187. https://doi.org/10.1080/00222895.2013.798252

Turvey, M. T., & Sheya, A. (2017). Non-obvious influences on perception-action abilities. *Psychonomic Bulletin & Review, 24*(5), 1597–1603.

Turvey, M. T., Shockley, K., & Carello, C. (1999). Affordance, proper function, and the physical basis of perceived heaviness. *Cognition, 73*(2), B17–B26. https://doi.org/10.1016/s0010-0277(99)00050-5

Uchiyama, I., Anderson, D. I., Campos, J. J., Witherington, D., Frankel, C. B., Lejeune, L., & Barbu-Roth, M. (2008). Locomotor experience affects self and emotion. *Developmental Psychology, 44*, 1225–1231.

Vallacher, R. R., Coleman, P. T., Nowak, A., & Bui-Wrzosinska, L. (2010). Rethinking intractable conflict: The perspective of dynamical systems. *American Psychologist, 65*, 262–278.

Vallacher, R. R., Read, S. J., & Nowak, A. (2002). The dynamical perspective in personality and social psychology. *Personality and Social Psychology Review, 6*(4), 264–273.

van de Langenberg, R., Kingma, I., & Beek, P. J. (2007). Perception of limb orientation in the vertical plane depends on center of mass rather than inertial eigenvectors. *Experimental Brain Research, 180*(4), 595–607. https://doi.org/10.1007/s00221-007-0891-6

van der Meer, A. L. H. (1997). Visual guidance of passing under a barrier. *Early Development & Parenting, 6*(3–4), 149–157. https://doi.org/10.1002/(SICI)1099-0917(199709/12)6:3/4<149::AID-EDP154>3.0.CO;2-2

van der Meer, A. L. H., Ramstad, M., & van der Weel, F. R. (2008). Choosing the shortest way to mum: Auditory guided rotation in 6- to 9-month-old infants. *Infant Behavior and Development, 31*, 207–216.

van der Meer, A. L. H., & van der Weel, F. R. (2011). Auditory guided arm and whole body movements in young infants. In P. Strumello (Ed.), *Advances in sound localization* (pp. 297–314). Vienna: InTech.

van der Meer, A. L. H., & van der Weel, F. R. (2020). The optical information for self-perception in development. In J. B. Wagman & J. J. C. Blau (Eds.), *Perception as information detection: Reflections on Gibson's ecological approach to visual perception* (pp. 110–129). New York: Routledge.

van der Meer, A. L. H., van der Weel, F. R., & Lee, D. N. (1994). Prospective control in catching by infants. *Perception, 23*, 287–302.

van der Meer, A. L. H., van der Weel, F. R., Lee, D. N., Laing, I. A., & Lin, J.-P. (1995). Development of prospective control of catching moving objects in preterm at-risk infants. *Developmental Medicine and Child Neurology, 37*, 145–158.

van Dijk, L., van der Sluis, C. K., & Bongers, R. M. (2017). Reductive and emergent views on motor learning in rehabilitation practice. *Journal of motor behavior, 49*(3), 244–254. https://doi.org/10.1080/00222895.2016.1191418

van Dijk, L., van der Sluis, C. K., van Dijk, H. W., & Bongers, R. M. (2016a). Learning an EMG controlled game: Task-specific adaptations and transfer. *PLoS ONE, 11*(8), e0160817. https://doi.org/10.1371/journal.pone.0160817

van Dijk, L., van der Sluis, C. K., van Dijk, H. W., & Bongers, R. M. (2016b). Task-oriented gaming for transfer to prosthesis use. *IEEE Transactions on Neural Systems and Rehabilitation Engineering: A Publication of the IEEE Engineering in Medicine and Biology Society, 24*(12), 1384–1394. https://doi.org/10.1109/TNSRE.2015.2502424

Van Orden, G. C., Holden, J. G., & Turvey, M. T. (2003). Self-organization of cognitive performance. *Journal of Experimental Psychology: General, 132*(3), 331–350. https://doi.org/10.1037/0096-3445.132.3.331

Van Orden, G. C., Hollis, G., & Wallot, S. (2012). The blue-collar brain. *Frontiers in Physiology*, *3*, 207. https://doi.org/10.3389/fphys.2012.00207

Van Valen, L. A. (1973). A new evolutionary law. *Evolutionary Theory*, *1*, 1–130.

Van Valen, L. A. (1977). The red queen. *The American Naturalist*, *111*(980), 809–810.

Vaz, D. V., Silva, P. L., Mancini, M. C., Carello, C., & Kinsella-Shaw, J. (2017). Towards an ecologically grounded functional practice in rehabilitation. *Human Movement Science*, *52*, 117–132.

Velasco, C., Jones, R., King, S., & Spence, C. (2013). The sound of temperature: What information do pouring sounds convey concerning the temperature of a beverage. *Journal of Sensory Studies*, *28*, 335–345. https://doi.org/10.1111/joss.12052

Vicente, K. J. (2004). *The human factor: Revolutionizing the way people live with technology*. New York: Routledge.

Vicente, K. J., & Rasmussen, J. (1990). The ecology of human-machine systems II: Mediating "direct perception" in complex work domains. *Ecological Psychology*, *2*(3), 207–249.

Vilhelmsen, K., Agyei, S. B., van der Weel, F., & van der Meer, A. (2019). A high-density EEG study of differentiation between two speeds and directions of simulated optic flow in adults and infants. *Psychophysiology*, *56*(1), e13281. https://doi.org/10.1111/psyp.13281

Vilhelmsen, K., van der Weel, F. R., & van der Meer, A. L. (2015). A high-density EEG study of differences between three high speeds of simulated forward motion from optic flow in adult participants. *Frontiers in Systems Neuroscience*, *9*, 146. https://doi.org/10.3389/fnsys.2015.00146

Villarreal, L. P. (2004, December). Are viruses alive? *Scientific American*. Retrieved from www.scientificamerican.com/article/are-viruses-alive-2004/

Von Frisch, K. (2014). *Bees: Their vision, chemical senses, and language*. Ithaca, NY: Cornell University Press.

Wade, M. G., & Kazeck, M. (2018). Developmental coordination disorder and its cause: The road less travelled. *Human Movement Science*, *57*, 489–500.

Wagman, J. B. (2010). What is responsible for the emergence of order and pattern in psychological systems? *Journal of Theoretical and Philosophical Psychology*, *30*(1), 32–50. https://doi.org/10.1037/a0018292

Wagman, J. B. (2020). A guided tour of Gibson's Theory of Affordances. In J. B. Wagman & J. J. C. Blau (Eds.), *Perception as the detection of information: Reflections on Gibson's ecological approach to visual perception* (pp. 130–148). New York: Routledge.

Wagman, J. B., & Abney, D. H. (2012). Transfer of recalibration from audition to touch: Modality independence as a special case of anatomical independence. *Journal of Experimental Psychology: Human Perception and Performance*, *38*(3), 589–602. https://doi.org/10.1037/a0025427

Wagman, J. B., Caputo, S. E., & Stoffregen, T. A. (2016). Hierarchical nesting of affordances in a tool use task. *Journal of Experimental Psychology. Human Perception and Performance*, *42*(10), 1627–1642. https://doi.org/10.1037/xhp0000251

Wagman, J. B., & Carello, C. (2001). Affordances and inertial constraints on tool use. *Ecological Psychology*, *13*(3), 173–195. https://doi.org/10.1207/S15326969ECO1303_1

Wagman, J. B., & Carello, C. (2003). Haptically creating affordances: The user-tool interface. *Journal of Experimental Psychology. Applied*, *9*(3), 175–186. https://doi.org/10.1037/1076-898X.9.3.175

Wagman, J. B., & Hajnal, A. (2014a). Task specificity and anatomical independence in perception of properties by means of a wielded object. *Journal of Experimental Psychology. Human Perception and Performance*, *40*(6), 2372–2391. https://doi.org/10.1037/xhp0000014

Wagman, J. B., & Hajnal, A. (2014b). Getting off on the right (or left) foot: Perceiving by means of a rod attached to the preferred or non-preferred foot. *Experimental Brain Research*, *232*(11), 3591–3599. https://doi.org/10.1007/s00221-014-4047-1

Wagman, J. B., & Hajnal, A. (2016). Use your head! Perception of action possibilities by means of an object attached to the head. *Experimental Brain Research*, *234*(3), 829–836. https://doi.org/10.1007/s00221-015-4509-0

Wagman, J. B., Langley, M. D., & Farmer-Dougan, V. (2017). Doggone affordances: Canine perception of affordances for reaching. *Psychonomic Bulletin & Review*, *24*, 1097–1103. https://doi.org/10.3758/s13423-016-1183-6

Wagman, J. B., Langley, M. D., & Farmer-Dougan, V. (2018). Carrying their own weight: Dogs perceive changing affordances for reaching. *Quarterly Journal of Experimental Psychology*, *71*(5), 1040–1044. https://doi.org/10.1080/17470218.2017.1322990

Wagman, J. B., Lozano, S., Jiménez, A., Covarrubias, P., & Cabrera, F. (2019). Perception of affordances in the animal kingdom and beyond. In I. Zepeda, J. Camacho, & E. Camacho (Eds.), *Aproximaciones al estudio del comportamiento y sus aplicaciones* (Vol. II, pp. 70–108). Ocotlátan, Mexico: Universidad de Guadalajara.

Wagman, J. B., & Miller, D. B. (2003). Nested reciprocities: The organism—environment system in perception—action and development. *Developmental Psychobiology, 42*(4), 317–334.

Wagman, J. B., Shockley, K., Riley, M. A., & Turvey, M. T. (2001). Attunement, calibration, and exploration in fast haptic perceptual learning. *Journal of Motor Behavior, 33*(4), 323–327. https://doi.org/10.1080/00222890109601917

Wagman, J. B., & Stoffregen, T. A. (2020). It doesn't add up: Nested affordances for reaching are perceived as a complex particular. *Attention, Perception, & Psychophysics, 82*, 3832–3841. https://doi.org/10.3758/s13414-020-02108-w

Wagman, J. B., & Taylor, K. R. (2004). Chosen striking location and the user-tool-environment system. *Journal of Experimental Psychology. Applied, 10*(4), 267–280. https://doi.org/10.1037/1076-898X.10.4.267

Wagman, J. B., & Taylor, K. R. (2005). Perceiving affordances for aperture crossing for the person-plus-object system. *Ecological Psychology, 17*(2), 105–130. https://doi.org/10.1207/s15326969eco1702_3

Wagman, J. B., Thomas, B. J., & McBride, D. M. (2018). Perceiving and remembering affordances for others are continuous processes. *Experimental Psychology, 65*(6), 385–392. https://doi.org/10.1027/1618-3169/a000424

Wagman, J. B., Thomas, B. J., McBride, D. M., & Day, B. M. (2013). Perception of maximum reaching height when the means of reaching are no longer in view. *Ecological Psychology, 25*, 63–80.

Wallman, J. (1979). A minimal visual restriction experiment: Preventing chicks from seeing their feet affects later responses to mealworms. *Developmental Psychobiology: The Journal of the International Society for Developmental Psychobiology, 12*(4), 391–397.

Warren, W. H. (1984). Perceiving affordances: Visual guidance of stair climbing. *Journal of Experimental Psychology: Human Perception and Performance, 10*(5), 683–703. https://doi.org/10.1037/0096-1523.10.5.683

Warren, W. H., & Verbrugge, R. R. (1984). Auditory perception of breaking and bouncing events: A case study in ecological acoustics. *Journal of Experimental Psychology: Human Perception and Performance, 10*(5), 704–712. https://doi.org/10.1037/0096-1523.10.5.704

Warren, W. H., & Whang, S. (1987). Visual guidance of walking through apertures: Body-scaled information for affordances. *Journal of Experimental Psychology: Human Perception and Performance, 13*(3), 371–383. https://doi.org/10.1037/0096-1523.13.3.371

Watanabe, T. (2000). Web tuning of an orb-web spider, Octonoba sybotides, regulates prey-catching behaviour. *Proceedings of the Royal Society of London. Series B: Biological Sciences, 267*(1443), 565–569.

Weast, J. A., Shockley, K., & Riley, M. A. (2011). The influence of athletic experience and kinematic information on skill-relevant affordance perception. *Quarterly Journal of Experimental Psychology, 64*(4), 689–706. https://doi.org/10.1080/17470218.2010.523471

Weast, J. A., Shockley, K., Riley, M. A., Cummins-Sebree, S., Richardson, M. J., Wirth, T. D., & Haibach, P. C. (2019). Perception of another person's maximum reach-with-jump height from walking kinematics. *Quarterly Journal of Experimental Psychology, 72*(8), 2018–2031.

Weast, J. A., Walton, A., Chandler, B. C., Shockley, K., & Riley, M. A. (2014). Essential kinematic information, athletic experience, and affordance perception for others. *Psychonomic Bulletin & Review, 21*(3), 823–829. https://doi.org/10.3758/s13423-013-0539-4

Weber, E. H. (1834). *De Pulsu, resorptione, auditu et tactu: Annotationes anatomicae et physiologicae . . .* Leipzig: CF Koehler.

Weinberg, S. (1983). Why the renormalization group is a good thing. In A. Guth, K. Huang, & R. Jaffe (Eds.), *Asymptotic realms of physics*. Cambridge, MA: The MIT Press.

Weir, A. A., Chappell, J., & Kacelnik, A. (2002). Shaping of hooks in New Caledonian crows. *Science, 297*(5583), 981.

Wernecke, H. (2018). *Lorenz system: An interactive simulation of a chaotic attractor*. Retrieved June 3, 2021, from https://itp.uni-frankfurt.de/~gros/StudentProjects/Example_2018_LorenzSystem/

Withagen, R., & Caljouw, S. R. (2016). "The end of sitting": An empirical study on working in an office of the future. *Sports Medicine, 46*(7), 1019–1027.

Withagen, R., & van Wermeskerken, M. (2010). The role of affordances in the evolutionary process reconsidered: A niche construction perspective. *Theory & Psychology, 20*(4), 489–510.

Witherington, D. C., Campos, J. J., Anderson, D. I., Lejeune, L., & Seah, E. (2005). Avoidance of heights on the visual cliff in newly walking infants, *Infancy*, 7, 285–298.

Woollacott, M., & Shumway-Cook, A. (2002). Attention and the control of posture and gait: A review of an emerging area of research. *Gait & Posture*, *16*(1), 1–14. https://doi.org/10.1016/s0966-6362(01)00156-4

Wundt, W. (1897). *Outlines of psychology* (C. H. Judd, Trans.). Leipzig: Wilhelm Engelmann (Reprinted Bristol:Thoemmes, 1999); first published in German as Wundt, W. (1896). *Grundriss der Psychologie*. Leipzig: Wilhelm Engelmann.

Yang, J., Yang, Y., Wu, W. M., Zhao, J., & Jiang, L. (2014). Evidence of polyethylene biodegradation by bacterial strains from the guts of plastic-eating waxworms. *Environmental Science & Technology*, *48*(23), 13776–13784.

Yasuda, M., Wagman, J. B., & Higuchi, T. (2014). Can perception of aperture passability be improved immediately after practice in actual passage? Dissociation between walking and wheelchair use. *Experimental Brain Research*, *232*, 753–764. https://doi.org/10.1007/s00221-013-3785-9

Ye, L., Cardwell, W., & Mark, L. S. (2009). Perceiving multiple affordances for objects. *Ecological Psychology*, *21*(3), 185–217.

Yu, C., & Smith, L. B. (2013). Joint attention without gaze following: Human infants and their parents coordinate visual attention to objects through eye-hand coordination. *PLoS ONE*, *8*, e79659. https://doi.org/10.1371/journal.pone.0079659

Zaff, B. (1995). Designing with affordances in mind. In J. Flach, P. Hancock, J. Caird, & K. Vincente (Eds.), *Global perspectives on the ecology of human machine systems* (Vol. 1, pp. 238–272). Hillsdale, NJ: Lawrence Erlbaum Associates.

Zajonc, A. (1993). *Catching the light: The entwined history of light and mind*. New York: Bantam Books.

Index

Made in the USA
Columbia, SC
11 January 2025

51591431R10187